Using the *Texas Wri...*

Your *Texas Write Source* book is loaded with information to help you learn about writing. One section that will be especially helpful is the "Proofreader's Guide" at the back of the book. This section covers all of the rules for language and grammar.

The book also includes units covering the types of writing that you may have to complete on district or state writing tests. At the end of each unit, there are samples and tips for writing in science, social studies, and math.

Texas Write Source will help you with other learning skills, too—test taking, note taking, and speaking. This help makes *Texas Write Source* a valuable writing and learning guide in all of your classes.

Your *Texas Write Source* guides . . .

With practice, you will be able to use the guides explained below to quickly find information in this book.

The **CONTENTS** lists the major sections of the book and the chapters found in each section.

The **INDEX** (starting on page 808) lists the topics covered in the book in alphabetical order. Use the index when you are interested in a specific topic.

The **COLOR CODING** used for "Basic Grammar and Writing," "A Writer's Resource," and the "Proofreader's Guide" make these important sections easy to find.

The **SPECIAL PAGE REFERENCES** in the book tell you where to turn for additional information about a specific topic.

If at first you're not sure how to find something in *Texas Write Source*, ask your teacher for help. With a little practice, you will find everything quickly and easily.

TEXAS WRITE SOURCE

Authors
Dave Kemper, Patrick Sebranek, and Verne Meyer

Consulting Author
Gretchen Bernabei

Illustrator
Chris Krenzke

GREAT SOURCE®

HOUGHTON MIFFLIN HARCOURT

TEXAS
WRITE
SOURCE
Online
www.hmheducation.com/tx/writesource

Copyright © 2012 by Houghton Mifflin Harcourt Publishing Company

Printed in the U.S.A.

ISBN-13   978-0-547-39488-6

3 4 5 6 7 8 9 10 0914 19 18 17 16 15 14 13 12 11

4500305883   B C D E F G

Quick Guide

contents

Texas Write Source

The Forms of Writing

DESCRIPTIVE WRITING

NARRATIVE WRITING

PERSUASIVE WRITING

RESPONDING TO TEXTS

CREATIVE WRITING

RESEARCH WRITING

The Tools of Language

Basic Grammar and Writing

WORKING WITH WORDS

BUILDING EFFECTIVE SENTENCES

process SPEAK resource
focus proofreader's guide
Contents

xv

CONSTRUCTING STRONG PARAGRAPHS

A Writer's Resource

Proofreader's Guide

Why Write?

The following story by Mr. James Pearson, a high school basketball coach, will help answer this question.

When I was in eighth grade, basketball was my life. But I couldn't try out for the team unless I improved my grades.

I started with language arts and asked Ms. Libby what I could do. She told me to spend more time on my writing, and she gave me this advice: *Write down what you are thinking. Then read your writing. Write some more and then read it again. Do some more writing, and so on. Back and forth.* I followed her advice and found out that I could write.

That advice helped me through middle school, high school, *and* college. It also helped me get the grades to play basketball. If I hadn't listened to Ms. Libby back then, I might not be a coach today.

Writing can do many things if you give it a chance. For one thing, it can help you reach your goals, just like it helped Coach Pearson reach his. Read on to find out more about the value of writing.

What's Ahead

- Reasons to Write
- Creating a Writing "SourceBank"

ELPS 3G

Reasons to Write

Writing makes you a better thinker because it helps you explore your experiences. Writing also makes you a better learner because it helps you understand the subjects you are studying. And finally, the writing you do now will make you a better writer next month, next year, and forever.

Writing for All the Right Reasons

Explore Your Personal Thoughts

Writing in a personal journal helps you learn important things about yourself and feel more confident in your ability to write.

Better Understand New Ideas

Writing in a classroom journal or a learning log helps you make sense of what you are learning, and it helps you remember things better.

Show Learning

Writing essays, developing reports, and answering essay-test questions can show teachers what you have learned. These forms of writing can also help you assess your own understanding of classroom material.

Share Your Ideas

Writing stories and poems to share brings out the best in you as a writer because you are writing for an interested audience, such as your classmates.

 Think of your writing as a special opportunity to learn and to grow, and you will soon understand its value—in school and in life. So what should you do? Just start writing for all the right reasons!

 Write to learn. Write for 5 minutes about the following quotation: "Writing is one of the best learning tools for all students in all subjects." In your writing, explain one or more ways that writing has helped you learn about something in school or in your personal life. Share your thoughts with a partner.

Creating a Writing "SourceBank"

To think like a writer, you should act like one. You can do this by creating your own "SourceBank" of possible writing ideas. The activities listed below will get you started. (Also see pages 606–609.)

Look around you for ideas. Be on the lookout for writing inspiration anywhere, anytime. For example, while walking along, you and a friend might see a well-cared-for, healthy plant perched in front of a rundown building. A "flower in the rough" scene like this could give you an idea for a story, a poem, or an essay.

 Carry a small pocket notebook to record ideas. (It's hard to remember everything!) You might also want to write about some of the "found" ideas in your personal journal.

Get involved in your community. Visit museums, historical sites, businesses, and churches. Volunteer your services to a local day care or the park district. Each new experience will give you fresh ideas for writing.

Explore available resources. Surf the Internet and prowl around your library for writing ideas. Make a list of Web sites, articles, and books that you would like to explore. Also become a regular reader of your local newspaper.

Create a personal almanac. Take a close look at your life up to now and list people, places, and things that have mattered the most to you. Here's what you might include:

- Personal skills and interests (singing)
- Memorable firsts (learning to ski)
- Memorable lasts (breaking my ankle)
- School memories (joining the track team)
- Unforgettable people (my great-aunt)
- Unforgettable places (McKinley Hill)
- Favorite books and movies (The Giver)
- Things to change (homework routine)

 Develop an almanac. Copy the headings above into your writing notebook. Leave plenty of space after each. Then list personal ideas under the headings and continue to add ideas throughout the school year. Use some of these ideas as starting points for your writing.

4

publish EDIT

draft

ELPS 2C, 2G, 2H, 2I, 3D, 3E, 4G

The Writing Process

Writing Focus

Grammar Focus

- **Parallel Structures**
- **Verb Tenses**

Learning Language

Work with a partner. Read the meanings and share answers to the questions.

1. An experience is one or more events that happen to you.
   What is an interesting experience you have had?

2. Writing that is narrative tells a story.
   Have you ever written a narrative? What was it about?

3. You can't forget something that is unforgettable.
   What is an unforgettable experience you've had?

4. Transition words help you change from one idea to another.
   Think of some examples of transition words.

prewrite.

revise

Understanding the Writing Process

Most people simply look up at the night sky and say, "Ahh!" Serious stargazers, however, follow a process. They memorize star charts, check weather reports for best viewing times, set up their equipment, and gaze at the right corner of the sky at the right time. The process they follow allows them to see things that most people would miss.

Serious writers also follow a process. There is nothing instant about developing effective writing. It results from prewriting, drafting, revising, and editing. This chapter will help you learn more about the writing process and build some valuable writing habits.

What's Ahead

- **Building Good Writing Habits**
- **The Writing Process**
- **The Process in Action**
- **Getting the Big Picture**

ELPS 3G, 3H

Building Good Writing Habits

Professional writers have had to do a lot of practicing to develop their skills. Follow the tips below and you will begin to improve your own writing skills.

Keep a writer's notebook or folder.

Reserve a part of a folder or notebook for your personal writing. Underline any ideas you might want to use in a writing assignment.

> Keep a diary [or writer's notebook]. It's a place to write about things that happen, and also to write about the feelings you're having.   —William Zinsser

Write every day, preferably at a set time.

Get into a regular writing routine, and stick to it. You set aside time to practice other skills. Do the same with your writing.

> The idea is to get the pencil moving quickly.
>   —Bernard Malamud

Write with feeling.

How do you truly feel about your subject? Relax and let those emotions hit the page. (You can always tone them down later if you need to.)

> Every time I sit down and write, I know it's going well when it sort of takes over and I get out of the picture.
>   —Sandra Bolton

 Write about a quotation. Write nonstop for 5-8 minutes about one of the quotations and what it means to you. Discuss your thoughts with a partner.

TEKS 8.14A, 8.14C

PROCESS

The Writing Process

Good writing almost always goes through a series of changes before it is ready to share. That is why writing is called a *process*. The steps in this process are described below.

The Steps in the Writing Process

Prewriting

At the start, you think about the purpose and audience to decide on an appropriate genre for conveying the intended meaning. Then you select a topic, collect details, and plan how to use them.

Drafting

In this step, you complete the first draft, using the prewriting plan as a guide. This draft is your *first* chance to get everything down on paper while thinking about the purpose, audience, and genre.

Revising

Now you review your first draft with the purpose, audience, and genre in mind. Then you change the parts of your writing that may be confusing or incomplete and ask someone to review it.

Editing

You then check your revised writing for correctness before preparing a neat final copy. You proofread the final copy for errors before sharing or publishing it.

Publishing

This is the final step in the writing process. Publishing is to a writer what an exhibit is to an artist—an opportunity to share your work with others.

Analyze your process. How would you classify yourself as a writer? Are you carefree, creative, dramatic, private, public, detailed, and so on? Or are you a combination of some of these? Explain.

 TEKS 8.14A, 8.14B

The Process in Action

The next two pages show you the writing process in action. The graphic below reminds you that you can move back and forth between the steps in the writing process.

Prewriting Selecting a Topic

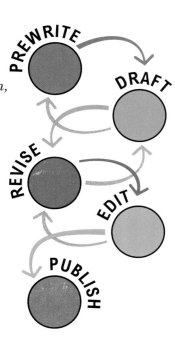

- Think about your writing assignment: *What do you want to do in your writing (share, inform, persuade, entertain, be creative)? Who is your audience? What form or genre are you using?* These are your questions of purpose, audience, and form or genre.
- Select a specific topic that really appeals to you.

Gathering and Organizing Details

- Learn as much as you can about the topic before you start your first draft.
- Consider the purpose of the assignment and what to emphasize in the writing—either an interesting part of the topic or your personal feelings about it. This will be the focus, or thesis, of your writing.
- Decide which details you want to include in your writing. Also decide on the best way to organize the details and form a plan.

Drafting Developing the First Draft

- When you write your first draft, concentrate on getting your ideas on paper. Don't try to produce a perfect piece of writing.
- Use the details you collected and your prewriting plan as general guides, but feel free to add new ideas as you go along.
- Make sure your writing has a beginning, a middle, and an ending.
- Think about your purpose, audience, and genre as you write.

⭐ **TEKS** 8.14C

Revising **Improving Your Writing**

■ Review your first draft, but only after setting it aside for a while.

■ Think about how well you addressed questions of purpose, audience, and genre.

■ Use these questions as a general revising guide:

- **Is my writing focused on one main idea?**
- **Do all the details relate to that idea?**
- **Is my writing well organized and easy to follow?**
- **Are my ideas clear and developed enough to help my reader understand and appreciate them?**
- **Do I explain my ideas with unique and thoughtful details?**
- **Does my writing sound like me?**
- **Do I sound interested in my topic?**

■ Try to have at least one other person review your work.

■ Make as many changes as necessary to improve your first draft.

Editing **Checking for Conventions**

■ Edit for correctness by checking for grammar, mechanics, and spelling errors. Also ask someone else to check your writing for errors.

■ Then prepare a neat final copy of your writing. (See pages 24–26 for tips and an example.) Proofread this copy for errors before sharing it.

Publishing **Sharing Your Writing**

■ Share your finished work with your classmates, teacher, friends, and family members.

■ Consider including the writing in your portfolio.

■ Think about submitting your writing to your school newspaper or some other publication.

Consider the process. The graphic on page 8 reminds you that you sometimes have to go back and repeat a step before you can move forward in your writing. In a brief paragraph, describe a writing assignment in which you had to move back and forth between the steps in the writing process.

Getting the Big Picture

Coaches know what it takes to build a successful basketball team: strong rebounders, tough defenders, and good shooters. Experienced writers also know what it takes to produce successful writing: clear *focus and coherence*, good *organization*, strong *development of ideas*, effective use of *voice*, and correct *conventions* (grammar, mechanics, and spelling).

Of course, these same traits are important in your own writing as well. You should deal with them as they become important at different points in the writing process. Remember that the writing process helps you slow down and give each trait or part of writing the proper attention.

☐ **Focus and Coherence**
  ☐ **Organization**
    ☐ **Development of Ideas**
      ☐ **Voice**
        ☐ **Conventions**

Use the writing process. Imagine that you are doing a writing assignment. On your own paper, match each activity on the left to its proper place in the writing process on the right.

___ **1.** Check the first draft for voice and personality.   **A.** Prewriting

___ **2.** Organize your details for writing.   **B.** Drafting

___ **3.** Display the final copy on your Web site.   **C.** Revising

___ **4.** Double-check the punctuation of dialogue.   **D.** Editing

___ **5.** Develop an ending that gets the reader thinking.   **E.** Publishing

One Writer's Process

Writers need the freedom to choose and to experiment when they write. Without this freedom, writing has little meaning or importance to them. For this reason, you must think of writing as a process. You will do your best work when you select topics that truly interest you and decide how you want to write about them.

This chapter shows the process used by student writer Isabel Santos as she wrote about her visit to *Freedom Schooner Amistad*. As you will see, this writing had special meaning to Isabel because she was writing about people who were fighting for their freedom.

What's Ahead

- Previewing the Goals
- Prewriting
- Drafting
- Revising
- Editing
- Publishing
- Assessing the Final Copy
- Reflecting on Your Writing

ELPS 2G, 2I, 3G, 4C, 4I, 4K

Previewing the Goals

Before Isabel began writing, she looked at the goals for her personal narrative assignment, which are shown below. These goals helped her get started.

Focus and Coherence

Make sure the main idea is clear and then use specific details that support the main idea.

Organization

Make sure that the details are organized so that each sentence is logically linked to the next sentence.

Development of Ideas

Make sure that the ideas are fully developed with original thoughts and opinions.

Voice

Make sure the writing expresses your personality and personal viewpoint.

Conventions

Be sure your grammar, punctuation, capitalization, and spelling are correct.

 To understand the important goals for Isabel's assignment, discuss the following questions with a partner:

1. What type of topic should Isabel select? Why?
2. Why is logical organization important in a narrative?
3. What's one way Isabel can add personality to her story?

Prewriting Selecting a Topic

Isabel was given the following assignment: Write a personal narrative about an eye-opening or learning experience. To select a topic, she listed experiences and starred the one that interested her the most.

Eye-Opening Experiences

neighborhood carnival

Freedom Schooner Amistad ✶

Texas State Aquarium

Botanical gardens in Austin

 List three or four eye-opening experiences in your own life. Put a star next to the one that would make the best topic. Write a brief paragraph (four or five sentences) explaining why you would write about this topic.

Gathering and Organizing Details

Isabel wanted to focus on the story of the African captives aboard *La Amistad*. She used the 5 W's and H to gather information about their story.

5 W's and H Chart

Who?	49 African captives
What?	the captives took control of the ship
When?	in 1839
Where?	aboard La Amistad in the Atlantic Ocean
Why?	because they had been kidnapped from their homes
How?	broke free from their captors

Isabel also wanted to connect her visit to the *Freedom Schooner* with the story of the African captives. She created a time line. Notes above the line describe her feelings. Notes below the line tell what happened to the captives.

Time Line

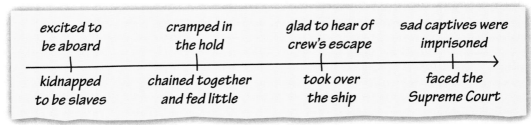

Drafting **Developing Your First Draft**

Isabel wrote her first draft using her 5 W's and H chart and her time line as a guide. She didn't try to get everything right in this draft. Her only goal was to get all her ideas on paper. (**There are some errors in Isabel's first draft.**)

The beginning introduces the experience.

Last summer, the Freedom Schooner Amistad sailed to Chicago. I couldn't wait to get aboard. My excitement at seeing this beautiful ship was soon forgoten when I heard the terrible story.

I've always loved stories about the high seas. I've always wanted to climb up a ship's pole and shout, Land ho"!

Dialogue helps move the story along.

"The ceiling in here would have been three ft. lower" said the Captain. He lowered his hand from just over his head to the middle of his waist. In this room, the captives sat in chains.

The wooden ceiling and walls seemed to close on me. The ship moved a little, even docked here. I could only imagine how much it tossed on the high seas.

A personal viewpoint is shared.

All these people had been kidnaped from there homes in Africa and were being sold into slavery. I moved to steady myself, and my ankles and wrists tingled.

One night, a captive broke free from his chains and freed the other prisoners. He opened the hatch and attacked. In the fight, three people were killed. The

Historical details add interest.

rest of the crew were captured and tied up. The next morning, the captive told the crew to sail toward the rising sun, toward Africa.

The word Africa sounded like "freedom." I felt better. The story wasn't over.

Every night, the crew secretly turned the ship around, heading west. They wasted two months at sea, and without food and water, it killed ten more captives. Then la Amistad was found by an American ship, which brought it to shore.

"That's when they were set free, right?" I asked.

The captain turned toward me and said "that's when they were charged with mutiny and murder."

I couldn't stand up now so I sit down on the floor and listen. The Africans were captive again. The question was are they legal slaves or not? A whole bunch of trials followed after that. The last one was in front of the Supereme Court, which finally said it would be right for the captives to get set free and be able to go back home.

The ending ties everything together and gives a final viewpoint.

I felt better after that. When we came back up on deck, I felt like shouting Freedom Ho!

 On page 13, you can see how Isabel gathered details for her narrative. Does her first draft include all of these details? Does she add any new details? Explain your answers to a partner.

ELPS 2C, 2G, 2H, 2I, 3D, 3G, 4C, 4G, 4K

Revising **Improving Your Writing**

Once Isabel finished her first draft, she looked again at the goals on page 12 and used them as a revising guide. Her thoughts tell you what changes she planned to make.

Focus and Coherence

Make sure there is only one main idea and that all the details support that idea.

"My focus is on one main idea, but some details aren't related to it."

Organization

Make sure that the details are in a logical order and each idea is connected to the one that comes before it.

"The sentences in the second paragraph are not in the correct order."

Voice

Make the writing sound like you, and use dialogue to show each speaker's personality.

"I should add more personal feelings to show that I really care about this experience."

Team up with a partner to review Isabel's first draft. Discuss at least two things that you like about the draft and one or two things that could be improved. Write down your responses.

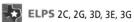
Reviewing Isabel's First Revision

After Isabel reviewed her first draft, she made the following revisions to the *focus and coherence* and *organization* of her essay.

A key idea is moved.

Last summer, the Freedom Schooner Amistad sailed to Chicago. I couldn't wait to get aboard. My excitement at seeing this beautiful ship was soon forgotten when I heard the terrible story.

I've always loved stories about the high seas. I've always wanted to climb up a ship's pole and shout, Land ho"!

New details make the ideas clearer.

"The ceiling in here would have been three ft. *as we stood in the small cargo bay of the boat* lower" said the Captain. He lowered his hand from just over his head to the middle of his waist. He told us *for three days in the heat of the tropics* that in this room, the captives sat in chains.

The wooden ceiling and walls seemed to close on me. The ship moved a little, even docked here. I could only imagine how much it tossed on the high seas.

A personal feeling is added.

The heat, the room, the fact that All these people had been kidnaped from there homes in Africa *—it all made me feel sick* and were being sold into slavery. I moved to steady myself, and my ankles and wrists tingled.

One night, a captive broke free from his chains and freed the other prisoners. He opened . . .

Review Isabel's revisions. Identify two of the changes that seem the most effective. Explain your choices to a partner.

ELPS 4C, 4I, 4K

Revising **Using a Peer Response Sheet**

One of Isabel's classmates read her essay. He used a rubric like the one on pages **50–51** and spotted more places that could use improvements. Isabel's classmate wrote his comments on a "Peer Response Sheet"

Peer Response Sheet

Writer: *Isabel Santos*   Responder: *David Rivera*

Title: *Freedom Ho!*

What I liked about your writing:

 * *You got my attention right away.*

 * *You mix the captain's words and your own thoughts.*

 * *You sound really interested in the experience.*

Changes I would suggest:

 * *In the beginning, could you tell why you like sea stories?*

 * *What "terrible story" do you mean?*

 * *How many captives were there?*

 * *Where is the ship docked?*

 Try IT Review the classmate's suggestions for improvements listed above. Which one do you think is the most important? Explain. Also think of one suggestion of your own. Pay special attention to the focus and coherence and organization in the writing.

Revising with a Peer Response Sheet

Using the comments made by her classmate, Isabel revised her story again. She added some important details.

What do you love about sea stories?

What terrible story?

What kind of captives? How many were there?

Where is the ship docked?

with their sailors, cannons, and pirates
I've always loved stories about the high seas.

I've always wanted to climb up a ship's pole and

shout, Land ho"! Last summer, the Freedom Schooner

Amistad sailed to Chicago. I couldn't wait to get aboard.

My excitement at seeing this beautiful ship was soon
of the original Amistad
forgotten when I heard the terrible story.

"The ceiling in here would have been three ft.

lower" said the Captain as we stood in the small

cargo bay of the boat. He lowered his hand from just

over his head to the middle of his waist. He told us
forty-nine african
that in this room, the captives sat in chains for three

days in the heat of the tropics.

The wooden ceiling and walls seemed to close on me.
at navy pier
The ship moved a little, even docked here, I could only

imagine how much it tossed on the high seas.
49
The heat, the room, the fact that all these people had

been kidnaped from there homes in Africa and were

being sold into slavery—it all made me feel sick. I

moved to steady myself, and my ankles and . . .

 Discuss with your classmates the changes the writer makes (shown on pages 17 and 19). Which additions seem the most effective? What other types of changes does Isabel make? How effective are the changes?

 ELPS 2C, 2I, 3D, 3E, 3G, 4C, 4G, 4I, 4K

Revising **Focusing on Ideas and Originality**

Once Isabel was done revising for focus and coherence and organization, she went back to the rubric again, checking her work for *development of ideas* and *voice*. Her comments tell how she planned to revise her writing for style.

Development of Ideas

Make sure each sentence adds meaning to the ones before it and that your ideas are original.

"I can see that some of my ideas need to be fleshed out a bit more."

Voice

Make sure the writing sounds like you and expresses your personal viewpoint.

"I should add more personal feelings to show that I really care about this experience."

Try IT Team up with a partner to review Isabel's revised writing on page 19 for style. Identify two sentences that could be developed more fully. Then identify a place where Isabel could express her personal viewpoint more clearly.

Checking Isabel's Improvements in Style

Next, Isabel concentrated on the style of her writing. She paid special attention to the development of her ideas and expressing her viewpoint.

Nautical terms improve the level of language.

I've always loved stories about the high seas, with their ~~sailors~~ [swashbucklers], cannons, and pirates. I've always wanted to climb up a ship's ~~pole~~ [mast] and shout, Land ho"! [So] Last summer, [when] the Freedom Schooner Amistad sailed to Chicago, I couldn't wait to get aboard. My excitement at seeing this beautiful ship was soon forgotten [though,] when I heard the terrible story of the original Amistad.

Combined sentences and transitions improve fluency.

"The ceiling in here would have been three ft. lower" said the Captain as we stood in the small cargo bay of the ~~boat~~ [schooner]. He lowered his hand from just over his head to the middle of his waist. ~~He told us~~ [and added] that in this [tiny] room, the forty-nine african captives ~~sat~~ [crouched] in chains for three days in the [blistering] heat of the tropics.

Stronger words are chosen.

The wooden ceiling and walls seemed to close on me. The ship ~~moved~~ [rolled] a little, even docked here at navy pier. I could only imagine how much it [must have] tossed on the high seas. The heat, the [cramped quarters] ~~room~~, the fact that all these 49 people had been kidnaped from . . .

 Try It Compare your ideas for changing Isabel's writing (page 20) with the changes she has made. How are her changes alike or different from your recommendations?

ELPS 2C, 2I, 3G

Editing Checking for Conventions

At last it was time for Isabel to edit her story for *conventions*. If she had worried about grammar, punctuation, capitalization, and spelling too soon, she may have forgotten to make the other changes that dramatically improved her work. Her comment tells how she planned to edit her writing for one of the conventions.

Conventions

Be sure that your grammar, mechanics, and spelling are correct.

> *"I'll carefully check my narrative for punctuation."*

For help with conventions, Isabel turned to the "Proofreader's Guide" in the back of her *Texas Write Source* book. She also used the editing checklist shown below.

Editing Checklist

GRAMMAR

_____ **1.** Do I use correct forms of verbs (*had gone*, not *had went*)?

_____ **2.** Do my subjects and verbs agree in number? (*Each* of them *has* a chance to win.)

_____ **3.** Do I use the right word (*to, too, two*)?

MECHANICS

_____ **4.** Do I use end punctuation after all my sentences?

_____ **5.** Do I use commas correctly?

_____ **6.** Do I punctuate dialogue correctly?

_____ **7.** Do I start all my sentences with capital letters?

_____ **8.** Do I capitalize all proper nouns?

SPELLING

_____ **9.** Have I spelled all my words correctly?

_____ **10.** Have I double-checked words my spell-checker might miss?

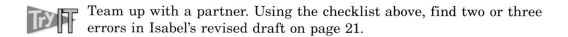 Team up with a partner. Using the checklist above, find two or three errors in Isabel's revised draft on page 21.

Checking Isabel's Editing for Conventions

Isabel edited her narrative for grammar, mechanics, and spelling. (See inside the back cover of this text for the common editing and proofreading marks.)

Spelling errors are corrected.

I've always loved stories about the high seas, with
their ~~swashbuckelers,~~ *swashbucklers* cannons, and pirates. I've always
wanted to climb up a ship's mast and shout, "Land ho"!

So last summer, when the Freedom Schooner Amistad sailed
to Chicago, I couldn't wait to get aboard. My excitement at
seeing this beautiful ship, though, was soon ~~forgoten~~ *forgotten* when I

Punctuation mistakes are fixed.

heard the terrible story of the original Amistad.

    "The ceiling in here would have been three ~~ft.~~ *feet* lower,"
said the Captain as we stood in the small cargo bay of the
schooner. He lowered his hand from just over his head to
the middle of his waist and added that in this tiny room, the

Treatment of measurements and numbers is corrected.

~~forty-nine~~ *49* african captives crouched in chains for three days
in the blistering heat of the tropics.

    The wooden ceiling and walls seemed to close *in* on me. The

Capitalization errors are corrected.

ship rolled a little, even docked here at navy pier. I could only
imagine how much it must have tossed on the high seas. The
heat, the cramped . . .

 Review Isabel's editing for conventions in the paragraphs above. Did you find some of the same errors when you edited her earlier draft on page 21?

Publishing Sharing Your Writing

Isabel used the tips below to help her write the final copy of her story. (See pages **25–26**.)

Focus on Presentation

Tips for Handwritten Copies

■ Use blue or black ink and write neatly.

■ Write your name according to your teacher's instructions.

■ Skip a line and center your title; skip another line and start your writing.

■ Indent every paragraph and leave a one-inch margin on all four sides.

■ Write your last name and page number on every page after page 1.

Isabel Santos

Freedom Ho!

I've always loved stories about the high seas, with their swashbucklers, cannons, and pirates. I've always wanted to climb up a ship's mast and shout, "Land ho!" So last summer, when the *Freedom Schooner Amistad* sailed to Chicago, I couldn't wait to get aboard. My excitement at seeing this beautiful ship, though, was soon forgotten when I heard the terrible story of the original *Amistad*.

"The ceiling in here would have been three feet lower," said the captain as we stood in the small cargo bay of the schooner. He lowered his hand from just over his head to the middle of his waist and added that in this tiny room, 49 African captives crouched in chains for three days in the blistering heat of the tropics.

The wooden ceiling and walls seemed to close in on me. The ship rolled a little, even docked here at Navy Pier. I could only imagine how much it must have tossed on the high seas. The heat, the cramped quarters, the fact that all these 49 people had been kidnapped from their homes in Africa and were being sold into slavery—it all made me feel sick. I crouched to steady myself, and my ankles and wrists tingled as if I wore invisible shackles.

One moonless night, though, a captive named Sengbe Pieh broke free from his chains and freed the other prisoners. He opened the hatch and crept onto the deck, where the crew slept. Only the man at the helm was awake. Sengbe and the captives attacked. In the fight, one African was killed, as well

Santos 2

and the
he had said
ory wasn't
heading
ck of food
ad was
g Island

ked old
n they

ough
ives
Cuba or
finally to

to the
ted to

Santos 2

One moonless night, though, a captive named Sengbe Pieh broke

Isabel Santos

Freedom Ho!

I've always loved stories about the high seas, with their swashbucklers, cannons, and pirates. I've always wanted to climb up a ship's mast and shout, "Land ho!" So last summer, when the *Freedom Schooner Amistad* sailed to Chicago, I couldn't wait to get aboard. My excitement at seeing this beautiful ship, though, was soon forgotten when I heard the terrible story of the original *Amistad*.

"The ceiling in here would have been three feet lower," said the captain as we stood in the small cargo bay of the schooner. He lowered his hand from just over his head to the middle of his waist and added that in this tiny room, 49 African captives crouched in chains for three days in the blistering heat of the tropics.

The wooden ceiling and walls seemed to close in on me. The ship rolled a little, even docked here at Navy Pier. I could only imagine how much it must have tossed on the high seas. The heat, the cramped quarters, the fact that all these 49 people had been kidnapped from their homes in Africa and were being sold into slavery—it all made me feel sick. I crouched to steady myself, and my ankles and wrists tingled as if I wore invisible shackles.

Tips for Computer Copies

■ Use an easy-to-read font and a 12-point type size.

■ Double-space and leave a one-inch margin around each page.

Isabel's Final Copy

Isabel was proud of her finished story. Presenting it to the class allowed her friends to share the eye-opening experience of being aboard the *Freedom Schooner Amistad*.

Isabel Santos

Freedom Ho!

I've always loved stories about the high seas, with their swashbucklers, cannons, and pirates. I've always wanted to climb up a ship's mast and shout, "Land ho!" So last summer, when the *Freedom Schooner Amistad* sailed to Chicago, I couldn't wait to get aboard. My excitement at seeing this beautiful ship, though, was soon forgotten when I heard the terrible story of the original *Amistad*.

"The ceiling in here would have been three feet lower," said the captain as we stood in the small cargo bay of the schooner. He lowered his hand from just over his head to the middle of his waist and added that in this tiny room, 49 African captives crouched in chains for three days in the blistering heat of the tropics.

The wooden ceiling and walls seemed to close in on me. The ship rolled a little, even docked here at Navy Pier. I could only imagine how much it must have tossed on the high seas. The heat, the cramped quarters, the fact that all these 49 people had been kidnapped from their homes in Africa and were being sold into slavery—it all made me feel sick. I crouched to steady myself, and my ankles and wrists tingled as if I wore invisible shackles.

One moonless night, though, a captive named Sengbe Pieh broke free from his chains and freed the other prisoners. He opened the hatch and crept onto the deck, where the crew slept. Only the man at the helm was awake. Sengbe and the captives attacked. In the fight, one African was killed, as well as two crew members. The rest of the crew were captured and tied up. The next morning, Sengbe told the crew to "sail toward the rising sun, toward Africa."

When the captain said the name "Africa," it was as if he had said the word "freedom." For a moment, I felt better. But the story wasn't over. Every night, the crew secretly turned the ship around, heading west. That way, they wasted two months at sea, and the lack of food and water killed 10 more of the captives. At last, *La Amistad* was found by an American ship, which brought it to shore at Long Island Sound.

"That's when they were set free, right?" I asked.

The captain turned toward me, and his brown eyes looked old and sad, as if he'd seen all these things himself. "That's when they were charged with mutiny and murder."

I couldn't stand up anymore and sat down on those rough boards to listen to the story. The Africans had become captives again. The question was whether they were legal slaves in Cuba or were illegal slaves taken from Africa. Numerous trials led finally to the Supreme Court, where John Quincy Adams argued their case. He helped the captives win their freedom.

When we came up out of that cramped and hot hold into the cool winds off Lake Michigan, I felt like I had been freed. I wanted to climb the mast and shout, "Freedom ho!"

Evaluating and Reflecting on the Final Copy

Isabel's teacher used a rubric like the one that appears on pages 50–51 to assess Isabel's final copy. The teacher also included comments about Isabel's writing.

4 Score

You have selected an excellent experience to share. All the details you included focus on your experience on the Amistad and give a complete picture of the story. I also have a good understanding of what the experience meant to you. Your ideas are logically organized and flow smoothly. Your progression from sentence to sentence and paragraph to paragraph is good and controlled. There is depth of thought in your narrative. I can hear your personality come through. I was engaged in your story. Your word choice, sentence structure, and proper use of grammar all enhance the effectiveness of your story.

Review the assessment. Do you agree with the comments and score made by Isabel's teacher? Why or why not? Explain your feelings in a brief paragraph.

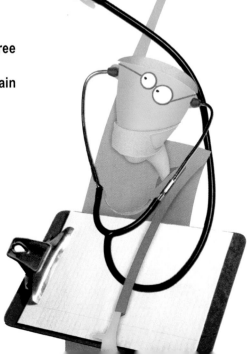

ELPS 4K

Evaluating and Reflecting on Your Writing

After the whole process was finished, Isabel filled out a reflection sheet. This helped her think about the assignment and plan for future essays.

Isabel Santos

My Personal Narrative

1. **The best score for my personal narrative is...**
   4.

2. **It's the best score because...**
   I think I was able to effectively connect my own experience with a tragic historical event.

3. **The best part of my narrative is...**
   how I was able to describe what I was thinking and feeling while I heard the story of the Amistad.

4. **The part that still needs work is...**
   the amount of detail I included. I could have made the Africans' experiences easier for the reader to follow.

5. **The main thing I learned about writing a personal narrative is...**
   that it must build in suspense and drama to hold the reader's interest.

respect cooperate **SHARE**
comment react

Peer Responding

Sharing a piece of writing with your classmates can be a nerve-racking experience. Even professional writers like Mem Fox sometimes get nervous when reading their own work aloud to others: "In those sessions in which each of us reads our writing to the class, we shake with nerves."

The truth is, though, that you—and all writers—need an audience. You need someone to let you know what makes sense and what is unclear. You get the best feedback from your peers in response sessions.

This chapter is all about sharing your writing and making the best possible use of the responses you get from your fellow writers.

Learning Language

Work with a partner. Read the meanings and share answers to the questions.

1. A peer is a person the same age as you or the same rank as you.
   Who are your peers in your school?

2. A response is an answer to a question.
   What would be your response to the question, "Where were you born?"

3. A comment is an opinion you give about something.
   What is one comment that you would make about your favorite book?

4. When something makes sense, it is understandable.
   What is one way to make sure your writing makes sense to your reader?

What's Ahead

- Peer-Responding Guidelines
- Sample Peer Response Sheet

Peer Resp

Writer: ....Lana

Title: ....Changing Faces

What I liked about your writing:
* The general comments in t
  the essay.
* Your description of each fam
* I learned a lot about Albert E
  paragraph.

Changes I would suggest:
* Could you include more details
  did you include her as one of th

Peer-Responding Guidelines

At first, you may work with only one person: a teacher or a classmate. This person does not expect your writing to be perfect. He or she knows that you are still working on your paper.

Later, you may have a chance to work with a small group. After a while, you will find that responding to someone's writing is much easier than you thought it would be.

The Author's Role

Select a piece of writing to share and make a copy of it for each group member.

Guidelines	Sample Responses
● **Introduce your piece of writing.** But don't say too much about it.	This paper is about our dependence on the automobile. I decided on this topic after watching a TV show.
● **Read your writing out loud.** Or ask group members to read it silently.	Automobiles are a primary cause of pollution. They are very dangerous. They present many problems. . . .
● **Invite your group members to comment.** Listen carefully.	Okay, everyone, now it's your turn to talk. I'm listening.
● **Take notes** so you will remember what was said.	So, which statistics should I add?
● **Answer all questions** the best you can. Be open and polite.	Yes, the automobile is one of the major causes of global warming.
● **Ask for help from your group** with any writing problems you are having.	In my ending, is it clear what I want the reader to do?

The Responder's Role

Responders should show an interest in the author's writing and treat it with respect.

Guidelines	Sample Responses
● **Listen carefully.** Take notes so that you can make helpful comments.	Notes: What is the problem with sport utility vehicles?
● **Look for what is good** about the writing. Give some positive comments. Be sincere.	Most of your statistics are convincing.
● **Tell what you think could be improved.** Be polite when you make suggestions.	Could you discuss alternatives to car travel?
● **Ask questions** if you need more information.	Where did you get your statistics about the number of roads in our cities?
● **Make other suggestions.** Help the writer improve his or her work.	Could you include a stronger call to action?

Helpful Comments

In all your comments, be as specific as you can be. This will help the writer make the best changes.

Instead of . . .	Try something like . . .
Your beginning doesn't work.	**Your focus statement sounds a little too wordy.**
Your writing is boring.	**Most of your sentences begin with "It is" or "It may."**
I can't understand one part.	**The part about road rage needs more explanation.**

 Suppose you are the responder to one of the essays on pages 140–141, 208–209, or 278–279. Carefully read the essay. Then write responses to it using the samples at the top of this page as a guide.

TEKS 8.14E
ELPS 5F

Sample Peer Response Sheet

Your teacher may want you and a classmate to react to each other's writing by completing a response sheet like the one below. (Sample comments are included.)

Peer Response Sheet

Writer: *Lana*   Responder: *Jesse*

Title: *Changing Faces*

What I liked about your writing:

* *The general comments in the beginning drew me into the essay.*

* *Your description of each famous person is very clear.*

* *I learned a lot about Albert Einstein in the fifth paragraph.*

Changes I would suggest:

* *Could you include more details about Helen Keller? Why did you*

  include her as one of the changing faces?

* *Your essay would be even better if it contained a little bit more of*

  your personality. Could you let people know that you really care

  about these people?

Practice. Use the feedback from your classmate to revise your final draft.

1 Read the peer response sheet.

2 Identify the places in your writing that the peer response sheet refers to.

3 Use the comments to revise your final draft.

Understanding the Traits of Writing

What are your favorite foods? Popcorn? Pancakes? Watermelon? Whatever they are, you wouldn't dump them all into a taco shell and take a bite. That wouldn't make sense.

In the same way, there's more to writing than putting a bunch of words on the page. Effective writing maintains a *focus* on one main idea, has clear *organization*, and appropriate *voice*. Effective writers develop their *ideas* using thoughtful details and pay attention to *conventions*. This chapter will teach you how to use these five traits of writing. Before you know it, you'll be using words in ways that clearly express your best thoughts and feelings.

What's Ahead

- **Introducing the Traits**
- **Understanding Focus and Coherence**
- **Understanding Organization**
- **Understanding Development of Ideas**
- **Understanding Voice**
- **Understanding Conventions**

ELPS 2C, 4C

Introducing the Texas Traits

The traits listed below identify the main features found in good writing. If you write with these traits in mind, you'll be pleased with the results.

Focus and Coherence

Effective writing is focused on one main idea, and all the details relate to that main idea.

Organization

Strong writing is logically organized and easy to follow from beginning to end.

Development of Ideas

Good writing describes ideas with unique and specific details.

Voice

The best writing reveals the writer's voice and lets the reader know the writer is interested in the topic.

Conventions

Good writing is carefully edited to make sure it is easy to understand. The writing follows the rules for grammar, mechanics, and spelling.

One additional trait to consider is the presentation of your writing. The best writing looks neat and follows guidelines for margins, indenting, spacing, and so on. The way the writing looks on the page attracts the reader and makes him or her *want* to read on.

TEKS 8.14A
ELPS 2C , 4C, 5G

Understanding Focus and Coherence

All writing begins with a topic. Your job as a writer is to choose a topic and one main idea related to that topic. Then you have to make sure your writing as a whole is focused around that main idea.

PROCESS

How can I select the best topic for writing?

Selecting a topic is different for each genre of writing. Use the information below as a guide for selecting the best topics.

Descriptive Writing

Purpose: To present clear pictures of people, places, and objects
Key reminder: Select topics that you know well or that you can observe or research.
Example topics: Describing a neighbor, the bus stop, a special outfit

Narrative Writing

Purpose: To share memorable experiences
Key reminder: Select experiences that you can recall in great detail.
Example topics: Remembering meeting a relative, experiencing stage fright, getting lost

Expository Writing

Purpose: To share information, to explain
Key reminder: Select topics that you can research.
Example topics: Sharing information about tornadoes, peer pressure

Persuasive Writing

Purpose: To convince the reader to agree with your opinion
Key reminder: Select topics that you have strong feelings about and that you can research to find supporting facts and details.
Example topics: Arguing for or against study halls, final exams, curfews

Write "Topics for Writing" at the top of a piece of paper. Down the left-hand margin list the following headings (leave five to seven lines after each heading): *Personal Narrative Writing, Descriptive Writing, Expository Writing,* and *Persuasive Writing.* Under each heading, list possible writing topics for each type of writing. Add to the list throughout the school year.

TEKS 8.14A
ELPS 4C

How should I write about a topic?

Writer William Zinsser says, "Clutter is the disease of American writing." You can avoid this disease by making sure you focus on one main idea about your topic. Then you won't clutter your writing with unnecessary details that don't relate to the main idea. Writing a thesis statement can help keep your writing on track.

> The peregrine falcon, a lightning-quick bird of prey *(topic)*,
> is an endangered species. *(main idea)*

What should I do first to gather details?

The first thing you should do is find out what you already know about a topic. Here are three ways to collect your thoughts about a writing topic:

Freewriting Write freely for at least 5 to 10 minutes, exploring your topic from a number of different angles. The key is to keep your fingers or your pen moving to see what thoughts come to mind.

Listing Jot down things that you already know about your topic and any questions you have about it. Keep your list going as long as you can.

Clustering Create a cluster with your specific topic as the nucleus word. (See page 97.)

How can I gather additional details?

Collecting additional details may be a problem unless you have a variety of gathering strategies to use. Here are four of them to choose from.

Ask questions. List questions that come to mind and then find answers to them. You can also ask the 5 W's—*Who? What? When? Where?* and *Why?*—about your topic. Add *How?* for even better coverage.

"Talk" about your topic. Write a dialogue between two people who talk about your topic. (You may or may not want to be one of the speakers.) The two speakers should build on each other's comments as they go along. Keep the conversation going as long as you can.

Focus on a specific audience. Write about your topic to a specific group or audience. You could write to a classroom of preschoolers, a live television audience, the local school board, or the readers of a popular teen magazine. This focus will help you see your topic in new ways.

Read about your topic. Refer to the Internet, nonfiction books, magazines, and newspapers for information. Take notes as you read.

 **TEKS** 8.14B
ELPS 4C

conventions   development of ideas
VOICE   organization   focus & coherence   37
Traits of Writing

PROCESS

How can I choose the right details?

After you develop a strong, focused main idea, you have to choose the right kinds of details to support it. All the details in a piece of writing should contribute to the reader's understanding of that main idea.

Thesis statement: Playing on the baseball team was a great experience because I learned many important lessons.

Details that support the main idea: I learned how to work together with others. I learned not to get angry when teammates made mistakes.

Details that do not support the main idea: I also liked math class. Sports help you to be healthy.

How can I connect my ideas?

Every paragraph in a composition must relate to the main idea. Each paragraph or idea should also connect to the one that comes before it, so your writing flows smoothly from one idea to the next.

Main idea of composition: Everyone should join a club at school.

Main idea of first paragraph: Joining a club is a great way to learn a new hobby or skill.

Main idea of second paragraph: You're more likely to make new friends in a club because you have something in common with the other members.

Main idea of third paragraph: It's a lot of fun doing something you enjoy with others who share your interest.

How can I make my writing more coherent?

Good writers have a strong introduction and conclusion in their writing. Often the introduction will tell the reader what the piece of writing is about, and the conclusion effectively sums up the writer's ideas. This adds depth to a piece of writing and makes it feel more coherent.

Introduction: I used to not like dogs. In fact, I was afraid of them and couldn't understand why some people treat them like a part of the family. However, I recently learned why they are called "man's best friend."

Conclusion: After I saw a stray dog save my neighbor's life, I understood why so many people love a dog as part of the family.

 Choose a topic and write a thesis statement. Then quickly write as many details as you can. Next, look at each detail and ask, "Does this relate to the main idea?" Cross out the ones that don't. Keep your thesis statement and list of supporting details for use later.

 **TEKS** 8.14B
ELPS 4C, 4K

Understanding Organization

> Strong writing is well organized from start to finish. Writer Stephen Tchudi (pronounced "Judy") calls organizing a paper the "framing" process: "Just as a carpenter puts up a frame of a house before tacking on the outside walls, a writer needs to build a frame for a paper."

How can transitions help me organize my writing?

Linking words and phrases (transitions) can help you organize the details in each mode of writing. (Also see pages 634–635.)

Descriptive: You can use the following transitions, which show location, to arrange details in your descriptions.

above	across	below	beneath	on top of	to the right	in back of

On top of **the track our car groaned to a halt. Then the rain suddenly rushed down.** . . . . Below **us a huge pool of water waited**. . . .

Narrative: You can use the following transitions, which show time, to arrange details in your narratives.

after	before	during	first	second	today	next	then

I squeezed my grandmother's hand, holding on with all my strength. First, **when we entered the classroom, I let go and walked around.** Then **I headed back toward my grandmother—only she wasn't there.**

Expository: You can use the following transitions to organize comparisons and contrasts.

(when comparing)	like	also	both	in the same way	similarly
(when contrasting)	but	still	yet	on the other hand	unlike

Both **fossil fuels and sunlight can produce energy to run cars and heat homes.** . . . But **solar energy has some distinct advantages**. . . .

Persuasive: You can use the following transitions to organize the details in your persuasive essays.

in fact	in addition	equally important	all in all

In fact, **more cars and more roads lead to more congestion in busy areas.** . . . All in all, **the automobile is the leading cause of air pollution**. . . .

conventions development of ideas
VOICE organization focus & coherence
Traits of Writing

39

PROCESS

TEKS 8.14A
ELPS 3D, 4K

How else can I organize my writing?

Many of the essays that you will be asked to write require two different types of thinking about a topic. There's the comparison-contrast essay, the problem-solution essay, and so on. To organize these types of essays, you have to consider the two parts of the topic.

Creating a Two-Part Focus Statement

To help you organize a two-part essay, you need to develop an effective focus statement, but only after you have gathered enough facts and details. If you can't think of a focus statement for your two-part essay, complete one of the patterns below. (See pages 610–611 for two-part graphic organizers.)

For problem-solution essays:

. . . could be fixed if . . .
. . . won't change until . . .
   The lack of open gym time for basketball (part 1) could be fixed if **the community center extended its hours** (part 2).

For cause-effect essays:

Because of . . . we now . . .
When . . . happened, I *(we, they)* . . .
   Because of **the stricter grade requirements** (part 1), we now **have fewer students going out for sports** (part 2).

For comparison-contrast essays:

_____ and _____ are both . . . but they differ in . . .
While _____ and _____ have . . . in common, they also . . .
   Sharks and **dolphins** are both **fascinating sea creatures** (part 1), but they differ in **many significant ways** (part 2).

For before-after essays:

Once I *(we, they, it)* . . . , but now . . .
I *(we, they, it)* . . . until . . .
   Once I **had trouble understanding American culture** (part 1), but now **it makes much better sense to me** (part 2).

Write a focus statement for each two-part essay shown above. Think of topics that you know well or have strong feelings about. Share your statements with your classmates for discussion.

ELPS 4C, 4K

Texas Traits Understanding Development of Ideas

> Once you know what ideas you want to include in your writing, develop them in depth. There's a relationship between good thinking and good writing. Good writing is not based on how much you say, but on how well you say it.

How can I help my reader appreciate my ideas?

Use specific examples to develop your idea. Don't be too general or vague. You don't have to give many examples—just include the ones that are the most meaningful to you:

Main idea: My grandmother is my hero.

Specific examples: She successfully ran a 300-acre farm by herself after my grandfather died suddenly. She was the first woman president of our state's Farm Association. She started the first homeless shelter in our area. Even though she was always so busy, she learned how to play the guitar and became very good at it!

General examples: She worked hard. She was kind. She was always very busy.

How should I present my ideas?

Good writers use their own unique, personal experiences to write about their ideas. They also make interesting connections between ideas, or present their ideas from an unusual perspective.

Main idea: We should preserve the small park on Main St. and not build a new apartment building there.

Personal experience: I have been going to that park since I was a baby. It's the only park within walking distance to my house. Many of my friends and family don't have backyards, and we meet in the park to do many things.

Connect ideas: If we take away that park, what will stop other companies from taking over other green spaces in our community? People need a connection to nature, and these small parks provide the only opportunity for many of us to have some "green" in our lives.

Unusual perspective: I am a rare yellow-throated warbler, and my home is a tree in the park on Main St.

 Write a focus statement about your personal hero. Then write three important details about why that person is your hero. Be as specific as possible so a reader understands why you feel the way you do.

How can I make my writing unique?

Adding style to your writing helps make it unique. Taking some risks with your composition, such as using figures of speech or anecdotes when appropriate, enhances the quality of your writing and makes it your own.

Figures of Speech are creative comparisons that help you explain something or create a special effect. They help the reader see the world through your eyes. Two common figures of speech are similes and metaphors.

Simile

■ A **simile** compares two unlike things using the word *like* or *as*.

The fire leaped like an attacking panther onto the helpless van in the driveway.

Metaphor

■ A **metaphor** compares two unlike things without using *like* or *as*.

In most high schools across the country, football is king during the fall season.

Anecdote

■ **Anecdotes** are brief "slices of life," or mini-stories, that help you make a point about your topic. They allow you to *show* your readers something rather than tell them matter-of-factly. Anecdotes are a great way for you to express what you think is the most important part of your idea.

Joe and Ki, two elderly Koreans, shake hands and formally bow to each other. Samantha and Susan, two Americanized teenagers, give each other a kiss on the cheek and then hug.

(These brief anecdotes, or slices or life, come from an expository essay comparing Korean and American culture. They provide the reader with a vivid image of how the two cultures differ.)

 Look at the list of details that you created (page 37). Try to make some of the details more specific. Then choose one and write a simile, a metaphor, and an anecdote about it.

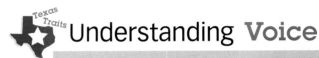

Understanding Voice

Author Sandra Belton says, "I write for myself because that's who I have to please first." When someone writes for her- or himself, the person's writing voice shines through.

How can I sound confident in my writing?

You will sound confident in your writing if you . . .

- show genuine interest in your topic,
- know a great deal about it, and
- share your honest thoughts and feelings.

Writing without Confidence

For my history project, I thought I might build a model castle and then write about it.

To build the castle, I will need to learn a lot about castles and figure out how to build one. Maybe I could use some plywood, clay, and stuff like that.

My project should give the class some idea about medieval castles. If you think I might be on the right track, please let me know.

Writing with Confidence

For my history project on medieval life, I plan to build a scale model (2' x 2') of an English castle and write an essay on the construction of castles for protection.

To complete this project, I will need books on medieval castles, a 3' x 3' plywood board for the base, modeling clay for the walls, toilet paper rolls for the frame of the towers, toothpicks and glue for . . .

My project will help the class understand how a castle was built and how it was used. I would appreciate any suggestions before I get started.

Should I sound enthusiastic in my writing?

Yes, your readers will appreciate it if you sound enthusiastic because it means that you truly care about your topic. However, be careful not to sound too enthusiastic. Too much excitement in your voice will sound phony.

 Write a brief note to a coach, a director, an advisor, or a parent displaying a confident voice.

conventions development of ideas
VOICE organization *focus & coherence*

PROCESS

How can I engage the reader in my writing?

You will engage your readers if …

- you make sure that your personal viewpoint comes through in your writing.
- your composition has a "face." This means that your readers should feel as if you're talking to them person to person.
- you include vivid details that help readers visualize what you describe.

Writing with Personality

When I was five, I wanted to run away from home. My new squawking, smelly, drooling baby sister got all the attention, and there was not a crumb left for me. I put all my most important things in a brown paper bag: my teddy bear, my favorite DVD, my princess tiara, and, of course, a pair of clean socks. Ready to go, I clutched the bag to my chest, looked both ways, and tip-toed to the back door. Just as I opened the door, there was a huge crash of thunder and a mile-long bolt of lightening. All of a sudden, I realized my sister wasn't so bad. I walked to my room with my head held high, put on my tiara, and watched my DVD.

Writing without Personality

When I was five I wanted to run away from home. I had a new baby sister. She got a lot of attention. I put some things in a bag and walked to the back door. Unfortunately, there was thunder and lightening. I went back up to my room and watched a DVD.

Notice how the first paragraph helps you picture the writer more clearly. Adjectives like "squawking, smelly, drooling" tell you how she feels about her baby sister. The specific items she packs help you picture how old she is and what she enjoys doing. Details like these show the writer's personal viewpoint and bring her voice alive.

 Think of something funny that happened to you recently. Tell the story out loud to yourself or to a friend. Now write the story using the same words and expressions. Read your story. Does it sound like you?

Understanding Conventions

Good writing follows the conventions, or basic rules, of the language. These rules cover grammar, mechanics, and spelling. When you follow these rules, the reader will find your writing much easier to understand and enjoy.

How can I make sure my writing follows the rules?

A checklist like the one below can guide you as you look over your writing for errors. When you are not sure about a certain rule, refer to the "Proofreader's Guide" (pages 640–797).

Conventions

GRAMMAR

_____ **1.** Do I use correct forms of verbs *(had gone,* not *had went)*?

_____ **2.** Do my subjects and verbs agree in number *(the boy eats* and *the boys eat)*?

_____ **3.** Do I use the correct word *(to, too,* or *two)*?

MECHANICS

_____ **4.** Do I use end punctuation after all my sentences?

_____ **5.** Do I use commas correctly in compound sentences?

_____ **6.** Do I use commas correctly in a series?

_____ **7.** Do I use apostrophes correctly to show possession *(that girl's purse* and *those girls' purses)*?

_____ **8.** Do I start every sentence with a capital letter?

_____ **9.** Do I capitalize the proper names of people and places?

SPELLING

_____ **10.** Have I checked my spelling using a spell-checker?

_____ **11.** Have I also checked the spelling by myself?

 Have at least one other person check your writing. Professional writers have trained editors to help them with this step in the process. You should ask your classmates, teachers, and family members for help.

How can I make my writing interesting to read?

Each sentence in a composition is important. How each sentence flows into the next is also very important. Varying your sentences can help make your writing clearer and more interesting to the reader. Here are some things to keep in mind when writing longer, more complex sentences.

Parallel structure means using the same pattern of words to show that two or more ideas are related and have the same importance.

Incorrect Alonso is a good baseball player, he works hard in school, and a skillful cook.

Correct Alonso is a good baseball player, a hard-working student, and a skillful cook.

Consistent tense means using the correct tense throughout your writing.

Incorrect I went to Austin with my family last summer. My father wants to "get a feel" for the city, so we were walking everywhere. My feet are sore!

Correct I went to Austin with my family last summer. My father wanted to "get a feel" for the city, so we walked everywhere. My feet were sore!

It is important to **clearly identify what is being modified.**

Incorrect Maria cooked dinner for her family, but he didn't like it.

Correct Maria cooked dinner for her family, but her brother didn't like it.

 Write sentences describing a friend, a family member, and your favorite place. Use parallel structure in each of your sentences. Also make sure that your tense is consistent and that you've clearly identified who or what you're describing. Read your sentences aloud to a classmate and have him or her identify any errors.

How do I know if my sentences have enough variety?

Use these strategies to test your sentences for variety.

■ When you edit your writing, list the opening words in each of your sentences. Decide if you need to vary some of your beginnings.

■ Identify the number of words in each sentence. Consider changing the length of some of your sentences if too many of them have the same number of words.

■ Check the transitions in your sentences—*first of all*, *in addition*, *however*, and so on. When you revise your writing, add transitions as needed to make the connections between your sentences easier to follow.

Why are correct punctuation and capitalization important?

Good writers use punctuation to make their writing easy to read. You want your readers to concentrate on your ideas and not have difficulty understanding what you are trying to say.

Incorrect Every time aunt anna comes to visit she eats a lot plays games with us and tells jokes. she's really fun?

Correct Every time Aunt Anna comes to visit, she eats a lot, plays games with us, and tells jokes. She's really fun!

Incorrect A person, Who lives in a cold climate, must love snow.

Correct A person who lives in a cold climate must love snow.

 Write a paragraph about a family vacation, using sentences of varying lengths. Now write it again, leaving out the punctuation and capitalization. Exchange papers with a partner and try to correct the punctuation and capitalization in each other's paragraph.

Evaluating Your Writing

How can a writer be measured? A tape measure can tell the writer's hat size, but it can't even begin to measure the person's *development of ideas,* unique writing *voice,* and use of *conventions.* A rubric can measure these things.

Rubrics have other uses as well. They can help to prepare a writer at the beginning of a project. They can also guide a writer through the development of a first draft and aid in the revising and editing process. By using the rubric throughout the writing process, a writer can also make sure that his or her final work is ready for assessment. In this chapter, you will learn about all these uses of a rubric—and more!

What's Ahead

- **Understanding Holistic Scoring**
- **The *Write Source* Scoring Rubric**
- **Model Essays**
- **Evaluating an Essay**

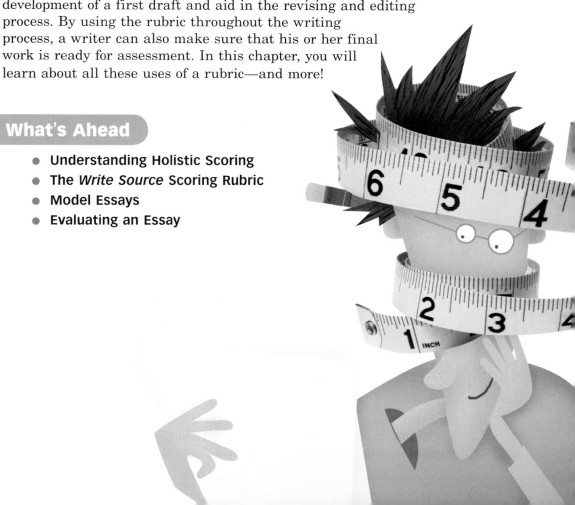

Understanding Holistic Scoring

A piece of writing can be divided into different parts: *focus and coherence, development of ideas, voice, organization,* and *conventions.*

Sometimes a writer can get a different score for each part of their essay, and then those scores are totaled to get a final score. Holistic scoring is a different way to score a piece of writing.

Someone using holistic scoring looks at the *whole* piece of writing and gives a score based on its overall quality. For example, some people can write thoughtfully and develop their ideas very clearly, but they are bad at spelling. Does that mean their writing is bad? Not at all. In holistic scoring, essays are not given low scores just because they have some mechanical errors. They aren't given high scores just because they are well organized. The reader gets an overall impression of the piece of writing and gives a score based on that impression.

The *Write Source* Holistic Scoring Rubric uses a scale of 1-4:

 A **4** means **highly effective** presentation of the writer's ideas.

 A **3** means **generally effective** presentation of the writer's ideas.

 A **2** means **somewhat effective** presentation of the writer's ideas.

 A **1** means **ineffective** presentation of the writer's ideas.

When you use a holistic rubric, follow these steps to evaluate the piece of writing as a whole:

- Think about how well the writing addresses the five traits.
- Ask: What is the total impression the writing makes on the reader?
- Assign a score of 1, 2, 3, or 4 that stands for the overall quality of the writing.

 Select a piece of writing that you have completed. Consider it as a whole and decide whether it should receive a score of 1, 2, 3, or 4. Be ready to explain why you think it deserves that score.

Reading a Rubric

For the rubrics in this book, the four score points are color coded. There is a description for each rating to help you evaluate your writing.

The *Write Source* Scoring Rubric

Score Points	Descriptions of Traits	
4 Writing that fits this score is very strong.	**Focus and Coherence** Maintains focus throughout the writing. All ideas clearly connect to each other and to the main idea. Meaningful introduction and conclusion add depth to the composition.	**Organization** Uses an effective organizational pattern for the purpose and audience. Has a smooth and logical flow, with meaningful transitions that help the reader move from one idea to the next.
3 Writing that fits this score is strong in most ways.	**Focus and Coherence** For the most part, maintains focus. Most ideas are clearly connected to each other and to the main idea. Introduction and conclusion add some depth to the composition.	**Organization** Organizational pattern is mostly effective for the purpose and audience. Generally flows but could use a few more transitions. Minor wordiness or repetition.

Guiding Your Writing

A rubric helps you . . .

- plot your course—knowing what is expected,
- create a strong first draft—focusing on *focus and coherence, organization,* and *voice,*
- revise and edit your work—considering each trait, and
- assess your final writing—rating the traits and the whole assignment.

 Reflect on your work with rubrics. On your own paper, explain your experience with rubrics. When have you used them? How well did they work for you? What have they taught you about writing? If you've never used a rubric, explain how you have generally evaluated your writing. Share your thoughts with your class.

ELPS 4C, 4K

 Texas Traits

The *Write Source* Scoring Rubric

Use the descriptions for each score to holistically evaluate your writing or that of your peers.

Writing at this score point is very strong.

Focus and Coherence
Maintains focus throughout the writing. All ideas clearly connect to each other and to the main idea. Meaningful introduction and conclusion add depth to the composition.

Organization Uses an effective organizational pattern for the purpose and audience. Has a smooth and logical flow, with meaningful transitions that help the reader move from one idea to the next.

Writing at this score point is strong in most ways.

Focus and Coherence For the most part, maintains focus. Most ideas are clearly connected to each other and to the main idea. Introduction and conclusion add some depth to the composition.

Organization
Organizational pattern is mostly effective for the purpose and audience. Generally flows but could use a few more transitions. Minor wordiness or repetition.

Writing at this score point is strong in a few ways.

Focus and Coherence Is somewhat focused. May suddenly shift from one idea to another, but the ideas are related. Some ideas do not add to the writing. Introduction and conclusion do not add depth.

Organization
Organizational pattern may not suit the purpose and audience. Thoughts do not always flow clearly or logically. Wordiness or repetition may interfere with ideas.

Writing at this score point is weak.

Focus and Coherence
Lacks focus. Includes a large amount of information not connected to the main idea. Is missing an introduction and/or conclusion.

Organization Has no clear organizational pattern or logical flow of ideas. Has no transitions or uses ones that do not make sense. Wordiness and repetition interfere with ideas.

Development of Ideas
Supports all ideas
thoroughly and with
specific detail. Shows
deep or creative thinking
that adds to the overall
quality of the writing.

Voice Engages the
reader throughout
the writing. Sounds
authentic and original;
expresses the writer's
personality or unique
viewpoint.

Conventions Shows
a strong command of
grammar, sentence
structure, mechanics,
and spelling.

Development of Ideas
Supports all ideas,
but some need to
be developed more
thoroughly. Development
may be thoughtful but
may not show creative
thinking.

Voice Engages the
reader for most of
the writing. Sounds
authentic and original
and expresses
the writer's unique
viewpoint.

Conventions Includes
only minor errors in
grammar, sentence
structure, capitalization,
punctuation, and
spelling.

Development of Ideas
Support is general or
shows little depth of
thinking. Support may be
only a list. Information
may be missing. The
message may be
unclear.

Voice Engages the
reader in some parts
of the writing. Sounds
authentic and original in
only a few places. Does
not express a unique
viewpoint.

Conventions Several
errors in grammar,
sentence structure,
mechanics, and spelling.
Errors may interfere
with the reader's
understanding.

Development of Ideas
Does not support ideas
or provides only general
and unclear support.
Important information
may be left out. The
message is unclear.

Voice Does not
engage the reader.
Does not sound
authentic and original.
Does not express a
unique viewpoint.

Conventions Major
errors in grammar,
sentence structure,
mechanics, and spelling.
These problems interfere
with the reader's
understanding.

Model Essays

To learn how to evaluate a narrative, you'll use the scoring rubric on pages 50–51 and the narratives that follow. These narratives are examples of writing for each score on the rubric.

Notice that this first personal narrative received a score of 4. Read the description for a score of 4 on pages 50–51. Then read the narrative. Use the same steps to study the other examples. Always remember to think about the overall quality of the writing.

Writing that fits a score of 4 is very strong.

Focuses on one experience— trying out for the school musical

Few errors in conventions

Not Shy Anymore

I was always the shy girl. Meeting people for the first time was difficult for me. In school, my hands started to shake if the teacher called on me—even if I knew the right answer! People usually described me as "quiet." However, all that changed when I tried out for the school musical.

One day, I was walking down the hall between classes, singing to myself. I made sure my voice was very low so no one could hear me. As it turned out, I wasn't quiet enough. My favorite teacher, Ms. Montero, suddenly came up behind me and exclaimed, "Carmen! What a beautiful voice!" I jumped ten feet in the air. I looked up at her and whispered, "You mean me?" Ms. Montero said, "Of course I mean you. You are trying out for the school musical next week. I know you are shy, but it will be a good experience for you. Now get to class."

My heart was beating out of my chest. My hands tingled. I felt like there wasn't enough air in the whole school. I went to class, but all I could think about was trying out for the musical. Me? A beautiful voice? I had always loved to sing, but only when I was alone.

ELPS 4I, 4K

ASSESS
rate *evaluate* improve
measure
Evaluating Your Writing

53

PROCESS

Inner dialogue helps add voice.

Strong details add to development.

Ending expresses writer's feelings about the experience.

After school I told my best friend Lisa what happened. "You DO have a beautiful voice!" she said. So I thought, "If Ms. Montero and Lisa think I can sing, maybe I can at least try it." Their confidence in me made me believe in myself.

The day of the tryouts came. I heard Ms. Montero call my name. It was my turn. Somehow, I made my legs walk up the stairs. Somehow, I stood on the stage, opened my mouth, and music came out. I lost myself in the song, and then suddenly, it was over. Ms. Montero smiled and Lisa clapped and cheered. I did it! I sang in front of other people! And I was good!

Well, I got a small part in the musical. We practiced after school every day, and I loved it. I made friends, I learned more about singing, and most of all, I found out that believing in yourself is important. I'm not the shy girl anymore.

Writing that fits a score of 3 is strong in most ways.

Focuses on one experience— getting inspired to help at the animal shelter

Good use of voice

Good control of conventions

An Inspiration

Last year in class, we read about Dr. Jane Goodall, the famous scientist. She studies chimpanzees and other animals. She helps people to understand that we must all protect animals and their environment so that they don't become extinct. The more I read about Jane Goodall and her work, the more inspired I was. I thought, "What can I do to help animals?" Thinking about that question changed my life in an important way.

Jane Goodall works with wild animals. We don't have any wild animals in my town. But we have lots of dogs and cats. A lot of them don't have homes. When I see stray dogs and cats around I ask, "How can I help them?"

I asked my mother to take me to our local animal shelter. So she did. We pet some of the cats and played with some of the dogs. I asked one of the volunteers in the shelter what they needed. She said that the shelter always needed pet food. That gave me an idea.

The next day, I made an announcement at school. I asked everyone to bring in dog or cat food. They could bring it to my science teacher's class, Mr. Farrell. He loves dogs. I didn't know if the other students would be interested in helping

Good use of transitions

Ending wraps up ideas

animals. But the next day, I was really surprised. Almost all the students brought in some food. And not only the students, but the teachers and staff, too!

My mother and I took all of the food to the shelter. They were very happy. The animals were happy, too. Now I go to the shelter once a week with my mom and play with the dogs and cats. I bring food sometimes. Maybe someday, I can do even more to help animals—just like Jane Goodall.

ELPS 4I, 4K

Writing that fits a score of 2 is strong in some ways.

Focuses on one experience— trying out for the track team

Dialogue and personality create voice.

Not all details focus on the main idea

Several errors in conventions

I'm Fast!

My school has a track team. All my friends are on it. But not me. I was never good at sports. My dad played football in high school. I tried baseball, basketball, soccer. I just wasn't good. So, I never tried out for track. One day, my friends said to me, "Why don't you just try it. Maybe you can run." I didn't believe them, but they wouldn't leave me alone. They said, "C'mon! Try it!" So I did. Boy, was I surprised.

I went to the tryouts. I was really nervous. I thought I would be the slowest person in the hole world. Mr. Engel is the track coach. He also teaches math. Everyone likes him. He called me up to the starting line. I thought, I'm gonna do my best. All of a sudden, he yelled Go! My legs started moving faster and faster. I felt like flying. It was great!

After I crossed the finish line, Mr. Engel told me, "Your the second fastest runner today. Your on the team." I couldn't believe it. My friends slapped me on the back. Now we are on the team together. I'm glad I tried something new. Now I know I'm fast.

ELPS 4I, 4K

ASSESS
rate evaluate improve
measure
Evaluating Your Writing

57

PROCESS

Writing that fits a score of 1 is weak.

Focus is not clear.

Few specific details

Ideas are repeated again and again.

Many errors in conventions

Texas state aqarum

My clas went to texas state aquarum. It was fun. There are many fish and animals. I saw many fish. Also, I saw see tertels. They are endangerd. We learned alot.

The aquarum was fun. I lerned a lot . The person at the aquarum told us about the see tertles. We must protect them. Sometimes they get sick from polushun. Or they get caut in a fishermans net. I want to help them.

At home I red about tertles. They are intresting. They need our help. We should not pollut the ocean. I like see turtles. The aqarum was fun. I want to go there again. I want to see the tertles again.

ELPS 4G, 4I, 4K

Evaluating an Essay

Read the essay that follows and focus on the strengths and weaknesses in it. Then follow the directions at the bottom of the page. (**The essay contains errors.**)

Our Turn to Shine

Jonesburg Jr. High doesn't have a drama program, so junior high students have to try out for senior high plays. Upper-class actors get all the good parts, and younger students end up in the chorus or as extras. It's time for Jonesburg Jr. High to start its own drama club.

First of all, a junior high drama club would give students a chance at the lead roles. Instead of always standing in the background, they could learn lines, sing solos, and be the stars. As it is, junior high students don't get to feel much pride in senior high plays.

A drama club in the junior high would also help students learn about drama. It doesn't take much acting skill to sit in the background and pretend to make conversation or to stand and hold a spear. Also, junior high students often feel like they are "trespassing" when they participate in senior high plays. Instead of learning about drama, many younger students are learning that they don't want to be involved in drama.

Some people object that a junior high drama club would compete against the senior high program. However, a junior high program would actually support drama at the upper levels. It would train students in acting, singing, and dancing and would help set up drama supporters for the years to come.

Jonesburg Jr. High needs to start its own drama club. It would teach students about drama and help the senior high program. If someone asks about junior high drama, say, "It's long overdue!"

Use the scoring rubric. Assess the persuasive essay you have just read using the rubric on pages 50–51 as a guide. Record your rating and comments on a separate piece of paper.

ELPS 2C, 3E

Publishing Your Writing

To build a kite, you begin with simple things: paper, a frame, and plenty of string. Still, when these elements are put together well, the kite will leap and soar in the sky. Everyone for miles around will be able to marvel at it.

Writing is the same way. An essay begins with paper, a framework of ideas, and a string of thought. Put the pieces together well, and you'll create something that will soar. After you finish your work, you'll naturally want everyone to see it. For that, you will need to know your publishing options.

This chapter will help you get your writing ready to publish and give you a variety of publishing ideas. (Also see "Creating a Portfolio" on pages 67–71.)

Learning Language

Work with a partner. Read the meanings and share answers to the questions.

1. To publish means to present your writing publicly so that other people can read it.
   What is one way to publish your writing?

2. The way your writing looks to your reader is the design.
   What are some tools you could use to design your writing?

3. Something that is online can be found on the Internet.
   What is one thing that you like to do online?

4. When you carry out something, you have completed it.
   What is one task that you will carry out today?

What's Ahead

- Sharing Your Writing
- Preparing to Publish
- Designing Your Writing
- Making Your Own Web Site
- Publishing Online

Sharing Your Writing

Some publishing ideas are easy to carry out, like sharing your writing with your classmates. Other publishing ideas take more time and effort, like entering a writing contest. Try a number of these publishing ideas during the school year. All of them will help you grow as a writer.

Performing

- Sharing with Classmates
- Reading to Various Audiences
- Giving a Multimedia Presentation
- Videotaping for Special Audiences
- Performing Onstage

In School

- School Newspapers
- Classroom Collections
- School Literary Magazines
- Writing Portfolios

Posting

- Classroom Bulletin Boards
- School or Public Libraries
- School Display Cases
- Business Windows
- Clinic Waiting Rooms
- Literary/Art Fairs

Self-Publishing

- Family Newsletters
- Greeting Cards
- Bound Writings
- Online Publications

Sending It Out

- Local Newspapers
- Area Historical Society
- Young Writers' Conferences
- Magazines and Contests
- Various Web Sites

 Plan your publishing. Select three or four pieces of writing that you feel are your best work. Using the lists above, decide which specific type of publishing (performing onstage, business windows, and so on) would be the best for each of your selected works. Then make specific proposals for publishing each one.

PROCESS

Preparing to Publish

Your writing is ready to publish when it is clear, complete, and correct. Getting your writing to this point requires careful revising and editing. Follow the tips below to help you prepare your writing for publication.

Publishing Tips

- **Ask for advice during the writing process.**
  Be sure that your writing answers any questions your readers may have about your topic.

- **Check the focus and coherence, organization, development of ideas, voice, and conventions in your writing.**
  Every part of your writing should be clear and complete.

- **Work with your writing.**
  Continue working until you feel good about your writing from beginning to end.

- **Check your writing for conventions.**
  In addition, ask at least one classmate to check your work for correctness. Another person may catch errors that you miss.

- **Prepare a neat finished copy.**
  Use a pen (blue or black ink) and write on one side of the paper if you are writing by hand. If you are writing with a computer, use a font that is easy to read. Double-space your writing.

- **Know your options.**
  Explore different ways to publish your writing. (See page 60.) Start small; then venture into more demanding—and creative—options.

- **Follow all publication guidelines.**
  Just as your teacher wants assignments presented in a certain way, so do the newspapers, magazines, or Web sites. Check for submission guidelines.

> Save all drafts for each writing project. If you are preparing a portfolio (see pages 67–71), you may be required to include early drafts as well as finished pieces.

Designing Your Writing

Whenever you write, always focus on *what you say* before worrying about *how it looks*. Only when you're satisfied with content and style should you concentrate on design. For handwritten papers, write the final copy neatly in blue or black ink on clean paper. When using a computer, follow the guidelines below.

Typography

- Use an easy-to-read font. Generally, a serif font is best for the body, and a sans serif style is used for contrast in headings.

  The letters of serif fonts have "tails"—as in this sentence.

  The letters of sans serif styles are plain—as in this sentence.

- Use a title and headings. Headings break writing into smaller parts, making the writing easier to follow.

Spacing and Margins

- Use one-inch margins on all sides of your paper.
- Indent the first line of every paragraph.
- Use one space after every period and comma.
- Avoid awkward breaks between pages. Don't leave a heading or the first line of a paragraph at the bottom of a page or a column. Never split a hyphenated word between pages or columns.

Graphic Devices

- If appropriate, use bulleted lists in your writing. Often, a series of items works best as a bulleted list (like the ones on this page).
- Consider including graphics. A table, a chart, or an illustration can help make a point clearer. But keep each graphic small enough so that it doesn't dominate the page. A larger graphic can be displayed by itself on a separate page.

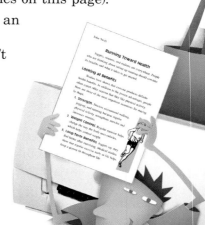

Analyze effective design. Working with a partner, compare the design features of articles from two different magazines. How are the design features of the two articles the same? How are they different? Decide which one is the most effective based on its audience and purpose.

PROCESS

Computer Design in Action

The following two pages show a well-designed student report. The side notes explain the design features.

The title is 18-point type.

The main text is 12-point type and double-spaced throughout.

Headings are 14-point type.

A graphic is inserted for visual interest.

Numbered lists identify main points.

John Swift

Running Toward Health

Joggers, runners, and walkers are everywhere. People who are thinking about taking up running should consider its benefits and what it takes to get started.

Looking at Benefits

Studies have shown that exercise produces definite health benefits. In addition to the proven advantages, people often report other reasons that they like physical activity. Here are three of the most important incentives for staying in shape.

1. **Strength.** Doctors recommend walking, jogging, and running because regular physical activity strengthens muscles and increases stamina.

2. **Weight Control.** Regular exercise helps change the way the body uses calories, which helps control weight.

3. **Long-Term Benefits.** Joggers say they feel better after exercising. Medical studies show that regular exercise early in life helps keep a person fit throughout life.

The writer's name and page number appear on every page starting with page 2.

A bulleted list helps organize the essay.

Margins are at least one inch all around.

Getting Started

Getting started is simple. Compared to many forms of exercise, jogging is easy and inexpensive because a fancy gym or costly equipment is not needed. The following suggestions can help someone start off "on the right foot."

- **Finding the right clothes.** Wear good quality, comfortable running shoes; they are really the only special equipment required. Light, roomy jogging clothes are best. More thin layers can be added in cold weather.
- **Setting aside time.** Block out 30 to 60 minutes for exercise every day. Make jogging a regular part of your schedule.
- **Running regularly.** Gradually increase time and distance. Don't try to run 10 miles the first day.

After a few weeks of regular jogging, the initial aches and pains will disappear. Then more options open up such as jogging for longer periods of time and for longer distances. There are also long-distance races, which can be very rewarding. Joggers who keep running are becoming healthier and stronger all the time.

Design a page. Create an effective design for an essay or a report you've already written. Share your design with a classmate to get some feedback: Does your design make the writing appealing to the reader? Is it clear and easy to follow? Does your design distract the reader in any way?

Making Your Own Web Site

You can make your own Web site if your family has an Internet account. Be sure you get the permission of your parents or guardians. Then ask your provider how to get started. If you are using a school account, ask your teacher for help. Use the questions and answers below as a starting point.

How do I plan my site?

Think about the purpose of your Web site and how many pages you need. Do you want a single page, or would several linked pages work better? Check out other sites for ideas. Then make sketches to plan your pages.

How do I make the pages?

Start each page as a text file by using your computer. Many new word processing programs let you save a file as a Web page. If yours doesn't, you will have to add HTML (Hypertext Markup Language) codes to format the text and make links to graphics and other pages. You can find instructions for HTML on the Net or at the library.

How do I know whether my pages work?

You should always test your pages. Using your browser, open your first page. Then follow any links to make sure they work correctly. Also make sure that all the graphics appear and that the pages look perfect.

How do I get my pages on the Net?

You must upload your finished pages to the Internet. Ask your Internet provider how to do this. After the upload, visit your site to make sure it still works. Also, check it from other computers if possible.

How do I let people know about my site?

Once your site is up, e-mail your friends and tell them to visit it!

 Plan your own Web site. You might consider a site about your family or one of your special interests. Answer the following questions to help you get organized: What will be the title of the site? What would be a good picture or illustration for the opening page? Where will the links on the opening page lead your visitors?

Publishing Online

The Internet offers many publishing opportunities, including online magazines and writing contests. The information below will help you submit your writing for publication on the Net. (At home, always get a parent's approval first. In school, follow all guidelines for computer use.)

How should I get started?

Check with your teacher to see if your school has its own Web site where you can post your work. Also ask your teacher about other Web sites. There are a number of online magazines that accept student writing. Visit some of these magazines to learn about the types of writing they usually publish.

How do I search for possible sites?

Use a search engine to find places to publish. Some search engines offer their own student links.

How do I submit my work?

Before you do anything, make sure that you understand the publishing guidelines for each site. Be sure to share this information with your teacher and your parents. Then follow these steps:

- **Send your writing in the correct form.**
  Some sites have online forms. Others will ask you to send your writing by mail or e-mail. Always explain why you are sending your writing.
- **Give the publisher information for contacting you.**
  However, don't give your home address or any other personal information unless your parents approve.
- **Be patient.**
  A site may contact you within a week to confirm that your work has arrived. Be patient, though; it may be several weeks before you hear whether your writing will be used or not.

 Search for Web sites. Search the Internet for sites that publish student work. Find out what forms of writing each site accepts. Make a list of these sites, including the URL address, and the type of writing each site publishes. Share your list with your class to create a comprehensive list of sites. When you complete writing assignments for school or write on your own, consider submitting your work for publication.

Creating a Portfolio

A person who has spent the day fishing may get his or her picture taken while holding up a stringer of fish. Of course, that stringer won't hold the small fish, only the big, beautiful ones—the "keepers."

Writers do the same thing with their writing. Instead of hanging their "keepers" on a string, though, they put them in a portfolio. A portfolio allows a writer to show off his or her best work.

This chapter will help you to assemble a writing portfolio. The following pages explain the types and parts of portfolios, as well as planning ideas.

Learning Language

Work with a partner. Read the meanings and share answers to the questions.

1. A portfolio is a case (or computer folder) where you keep your best work.
   What is one piece of schoolwork that you'd like to put in your portfolio?

2. An evaluation is the grade and/or comments that your teacher, or someone else, gives about your work.
   Do you like to read evaluations of your work?

3. A goal is something you want to achieve or be successful at in the future.
   What is one goal that you have for next week?

4. When you show off something, you want others to see it because you're proud of it.
   What is something you'd like to show off to your classmates?

What's Ahead

- **Types of Portfolios**
- **Parts of a Portfolio**
- **Planning Ideas**
- **Sample Portfolio Reflections**

Types of Portfolios

There are four basic types of portfolios you should know about: a showcase portfolio, a growth portfolio, a personal portfolio, and an electronic portfolio.

Showcase Portfolio

A showcase portfolio presents the best writing you have done in school. A showcase is the most common type of portfolio and is usually put together for evaluation at the end of a grading period.

Growth Portfolio

A growth portfolio shows your progress as a writer. It contains writing assignments that show how your writing skills are developing:

- writing beginnings and endings,
- writing with voice,
- using specific details, and
- using transitions.

Personal Portfolio

A personal portfolio contains writing you want to keep and share with others. Many professional people—including writers, artists, and musicians—keep personal portfolios. You can arrange this type of portfolio according to different types of writing, different themes, and so on.

Electronic Portfolio

An electronic portfolio is any type of portfolio (showcase, growth, or personal) available on a CD or a Web site. Besides your writing, you can include graphics, video, and sound with this type of portfolio. This makes your writing available to friends and family members no matter where they are!

 Showcase your strengths. Review your writing from the most recent grading period and then select the pieces that you consider your best efforts. Write a paragraph that summarizes the strengths of your work. Also mention one skill that you still need to develop.

Parts of a Portfolio

A showcase portfolio is one of the most common types of portfolios used in schools. It may contain the parts listed below, but always check with your teacher to be sure.

- A **table of contents** lists the writing samples you have included in your portfolio.

- A **brief essay** or **letter** introduces your portfolio—telling how you put it together, how you feel about it, and what it means to you.

- A **collection of writing samples** presents your best work. Your teacher may require that you include all of your planning, drafting, and revising for one or more of your writings.

- A **cover sheet for each sample** explains why you selected it.

- **Evaluations, reflections,** or **checklists** identify the basic skills you have mastered, as well as those skills that you still need to work on.

Gathering Tips

- **Keep track of all your work.** Include your prewriting notes, first drafts, and revisions for each writing assignment. Then, when you put together a portfolio, you will have everything that you need.

- **Store all of your writing in a pocket folder or computer file.** This will help you keep track of your writing as you build your portfolio.

- **Set a schedule for working on your portfolio.** You can't put together a good portfolio by waiting until the last minute.

- **Take pride in your work.** Make sure that your portfolio shows you at your best.

Write your cover sheets. For each piece of writing that you include in your portfolio, write a cover sheet. Explain why the writing is a good example of your work. Tell what makes it stand out from other writing you have done. Finally, tell why you included it in your portfolio.

Planning Ideas

The following tips will help you choose your best pieces of writing to include in your portfolio.

1 Be patient.

Don't make quick decisions about which pieces of writing to include in your portfolio. Just keep gathering everything—including all of your drafts—until you are ready to review all of your writing assignments.

2 Make good decisions.

When it's time to choose writing for your portfolio, review each piece. Remember the feelings that you had during each assignment. Which piece makes you feel the best? Which one did your readers like the best? Which one taught you the most?

3 Reflect on your choices.

Read the sample reflections on page 71. Then answer these questions about your writing:

- Why did I choose this piece?
- Why did I write this piece? (What was my purpose?)
- How did I write it? (What was my process?)
- What does it show about my writing ability?
- How did my peers react to this writing?
- What would I do differently next time?
- What have I learned since writing it?

4 Set future writing goals.

After putting your portfolio together, set some goals for the future. Here are some goals that other students have set:

I will write about topics that really interest me.

I will spend more time on my beginnings and endings.

I will make sure that my sentences read smoothly.

I will support my main points with convincing details.

Set your goals. After you finish putting together a portfolio, set some goals for your future writing. Review the student goals listed above and then identify three goals that would improve your writing.

Sample Portfolio Reflections

When you take time to reflect on your writing assignments, think about the process that you used to develop each one. Also think about what you might do differently next time. The following samples will help you with your own reflections.

Student Reflections

Of all the writing in my portfolio, I am proudest of my persuasive essay about volunteering at the Humane Society. It was a challenge. To write persuasively, I had to understand my topic, my feelings about it, and my reader's feelings. Every word mattered. I worked hard on that essay, but in the end, it helped convince two of my friends to volunteer.

—Melissa Breen

My expository essay turned out really well because I was interested in my topic. It was easy to break the subject down into its parts because I understood it. I seem to have trouble whenever I have to summarize information from other sources, because it's hard to organize the information in a way that is different from the original. The strongest part of my expository essay is the way I used comparisons with everyday things to help explain difficult ideas.

—Thad Molumba

Professional Reflections

As you continue writing and rewriting, you begin to see possibilities you hadn't seen before.

—Robert Hayden

The only way, I think, to learn to write short stories is to write them, and then try to discover what you have done.

—Flannery O'Connor

SPECIFY

picture

ELPS 2C, 2G, 2H, 2I, 3G, 3H, 4C, 4G

TEXAS
WRITE
SOURCE
Online
www.hmheducation.com/tx/writesource

Descriptive Writing

Writing Focus
- **Descriptive Paragraph**
- **Descriptive Essay**

Grammar Focus
- **Verbs and Adjectives**

Learning Language

Learning these words and expressions will help you understand this unit.

1. Words that give you a picture in your head are descriptive.
   Name a descriptive word for the color of the sky.

2. A person's physical appearance is what they look like.
   Describe your physical appearance.

3. Concrete details are things that you can see or touch.
   What are some concrete details that tell about your classroom?

4. Someone who is up for an adventure is willing to try something new or dangerous.
   What kind of sport might be interesting to someone who is up for an adventure?

express
describe
portray

Descriptive Writing

Descriptive Paragraph

By skillfully brushing paint onto a canvas, an artist can create a vision of a distant landscape or an image of an amazing person. When you write descriptively, you can do the same thing. By carefully arranging words on a piece of paper, you can create a vision of a faraway place or a wonderful likeness of a person.

In this unit, you will write a paragraph that paints a picture of a person. Your goal is to write a description that makes the person come alive for the reader.

Writing Guidelines

Subject: A favorite person

Purpose: To describe what a person looks like

Form: Descriptive paragraph

Audience: Classmates

ELPS 4C, 4G, 4I, 4K

Descriptive Paragraph

A descriptive paragraph offers a detailed picture of a person, a place, a thing, or an event. It begins with a **topic sentence** that tells what the paragraph is about. The sentences in the **body** include descriptive details about the topic, and the **closing sentence** wraps up the paragraph. In the paragraph below, the writer used specific details to describe a painter.

Topic Sentence

Body

Closing Sentence

A "Painting" of Rosa

Standing more than six feet tall, Rosa is someone I look up to. Other than her height, the first thing I notice about her is her curly, red hair. It's like sparks of fire peeking out from underneath the paint-speckled cap that she wears backward on her head. When Rosa smiles, her perfect row of white teeth flashes against her tan face. Whenever I see her heading off to work, she is constantly moving. Zipping back and forth with boxes of rollers, lots of paint buckets, bulky old drop cloths, and new rolls of tape, she loads all her gear into her van. Rosa and her once-white jumpsuit look like the paint-chip aisle at the hardware store—splattered with color from the top of her head to the toes of her now rainbow-colored canvas shoes. If I spot her at the end of the day, I always see a fresh set of speckles from that day's job.

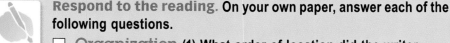

Respond to the reading. On your own paper, answer each of the following questions.

- ☐ **Organization** **(1)** What order of location did the writer generally follow *(top to bottom, left to right)*? Explain.
- ☐ **Development of Ideas** **(2)** In the first sentence, what detail gets the reader's attention?
- ☐ **Voice & Conventions** **(3)** What adjectives are used to create a clear picture of the person? List three of them.

Prewriting **Selecting a Topic**

First, you must choose a person to write about. Listing is a good way to get started. The writer of the paragraph on page 74 made lists of people whose physical appearances were interesting to him.

People I Know	People I See Often
* Dr. Willard, the eye doctor	* The old man who feeds the ducks
* My great-grandpa Salvatore	* The little kid who hangs out near my grandma's
* Ron, the junk guy	* Rosa the painter
* My oldest sister, the chef	

Select a topic. Make lists of interesting people you know or often see during your daily activities. Then circle one to describe in a paragraph.

Gathering Details

Your descriptive paragraph should show instead of tell. Before you write your paragraph, jot down concrete details that show what your person looks like from head to toe.

Collect your details. To get started, answer the following questions about your person.

1 Is there any feature that is immediately noticeable (height, color of hair, smile, freckles, posture, and so on)?

2 How can I describe the person's hair, face, and posture?

3 What type of clothes does this person wear?

4 Do the clothes have anything to do with a particular job?

5 Does the person move in a special way or wear unusual shoes?

6 What one word comes to mind when I see this person?

DESCRIPTIVE

TEKS 8.14B, 8.14C, 8.14D
ELPS 5D, 5G

Drafting Creating Your First Draft

The goal of a first draft is to get all your ideas down on paper and build on those ideas to create a focused piece of writing. Follow these guidelines.

- Start with a topic sentence that catches your reader's attention. Include a noticeable feature of the person you're describing.

- Use order of location (head to toe) to organize the details in the body. Be sure to stay focused on the topic. Include details from your chart on page 75.

- End with a sentence that keeps the reader thinking about the person.

Write your first draft. Build on your ideas or details to create a focused draft, thoroughly describing your topic from head to toe. Give your paragraph a title when you are finished.

Revising Improving Your Writing

Now that you have finished your first draft, you need to review it and make revisions. Add, delete, or move parts to ensure vivid images that are clear and interesting to your reader.

Revise your paragraph. Use the following questions as a guide.

1 Does my topic sentence introduce the person and mention a noticeable feature?

2 Have I included details that create a clear, vivid image of the person?

3 Have I organized the details from head to toe?

4 Do I sound interested in the description?

5 Do I use specific nouns, verbs, and adjectives?

Editing Checking for Conventions

Carefully edit your revised paragraph, making sure to check for spelling errors. Then write a neat final copy.

Edit and proofread your work. Use the checklist on page 44 to check your writing for errors, especially spelling errors. Then write a neat final copy of your paragraph.

Descriptive Writing

Describing a Person

Every person is unique. Think of people you know and admire. What do they look like? What are their personality traits? What makes them interesting or special? Answering these questions will give you a variety of details to include in a descriptive essay about a person.

In this unit, you will read an essay describing a person who loved to snowmobile. Then you will write an essay that describes a person who has influenced you in a positive way.

Writing Guidelines

Subject: A person who has positively influenced you

Purpose: To describe a person

Form: Descriptive essay

Audience: Classmates

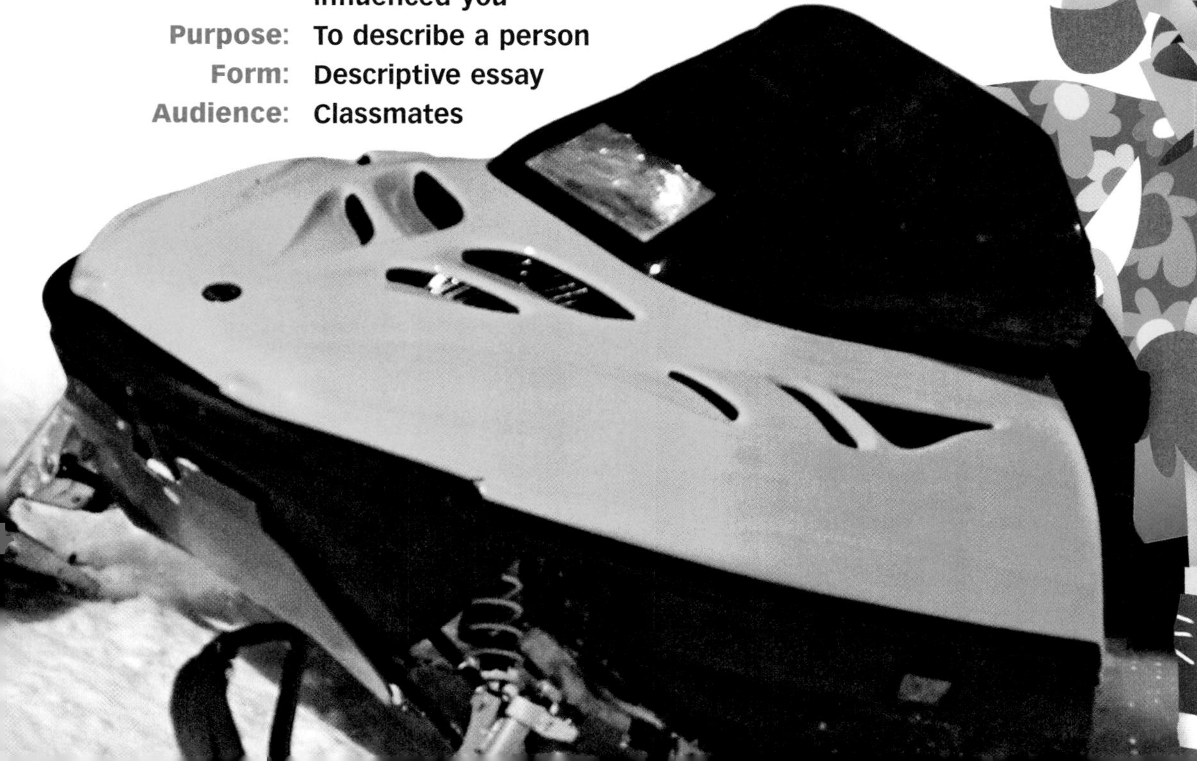

ELPS 4I

Descriptive Essay

In this sample essay, the writer describes his cousin Charlie. As you read the description, look at the notes in the left margin. They explain the important parts of the essay.

The Price of Danger

Beginning

The beginning introduces the person.

My older cousin Charlie was always up for an adventure, especially if it was dangerous. Charlie took lots of risks. Then, one day, he had a snowmobile accident that changed his life. The doctors said that he might never walk again. Charlie said they were wrong.

Middle

The first middle paragraph describes the physical appearance (from head to toe).

Charlie is a big guy who is more than six feet tall and weighs 260 pounds. His size, along with his long, black hair, makes him look strong, like a fullback or a wrestler. Because he works out with weights, his arm muscles are like iron. He likes to wear tight T-shirts to show off his biceps and abs. These days, Charlie is wearing baggy sweatpants to cover up the scars on his legs, which are banged up and twisted from the accident. His feet sometimes drag along the ground when he walks with his forearm crutches. The doctors aren't sure when or if Charlie will ever fully recover.

The next middle paragraph describes the personality.

For me, the best thing about Charlie is that he's not a quitter. If someone tells him he can't do something, he will prove that he can. In the beginning, when Charlie was in rehab, he got tough with himself. At every session, he pushed himself hard to walk again. When the physical therapist told Charlie to take a break, my cousin would say, "No way, man! I want to do this now." Charlie kept

ELPS 2G, 2H, 2I, 3D, 3E,
3G, 3H, 4C, 4I, 4J, 4K

DESCRIPTIVE

Middle
The third middle paragraph shares an anecdote.

Ending
The ending tells how the person influenced the writer.

pushing himself. Before long he was getting around pretty well without any help. However, I know Charlie. He's not going to be satisfied until he can walk without his crutches.

Before the accident, Charlie liked riding his snowmobile and his motorcycle and jogging with his black Lab, Tex. These days he's finding other ways to keep active. When the whole family got together at Thanksgiving, Charlie couldn't play on our pickup football team. That didn't stop him. He did a super job of coaching us from the sidelines.

My cousin Charlie has taught me two important lessons. First, I realize I should check out all the safety rules before I try something risky. Second, the best way to get through bad times is to have the right attitude. Charlie's attitude is just as strong as he is. I believe that someday Charlie will walk the way he did before, just like he says he will.

Respond to the reading. Discuss the following questions about the essay with a partner.

☐ **Development of Ideas** **(1) What special challenge does the subject of the essay face? (2) What physical features does the writer describe to create a picture for the reader? (3) What details give the reader an insight into the subject's personality?**

☐ **Organization** **(4) How does the writer organize the middle paragraphs?**

☐ **Voice & Conventions** **(5) What words or phrases show that Charlie has had a positive influence on the writer? List two. What specific verbs and adjectives help show the writer's voice?**

 TEKS 8.14A
ELPS 5G

Prewriting Selecting a Topic

Your essay should describe a person's appearance and personality. It should also tell how the person inspired you in a positive way. A chart, like the one below, can help you choose a person to write about and identify the ways in which he or she has influenced you.

Topic Chart

Person	Positive Influence
Dr. Julie, the veterinarian	– caring person – honest person – generous with her time
Mr. Hayes, the chorus director	– patient teacher – explores different types of music – teaches foreign language songs
Adamay, my neighbor	– loves adventure

Create a topic chart. In the first column, list at least three people who interest you. In the second column, tell how each person has influenced you in a positive way. Choose one of the people as the subject of your essay.

Gathering Details

Next, analyze your subject as you gather details. Think carefully about the person's appearance, personality, special skills, talents, and interests.

Collect details. Answer the following questions to help you find information to include in your essay.

1 What does the person look like? (Describe him or her from head to toe.)

2 What personality traits does the person have? (Think about feelings and emotions. Is this person quiet? Funny? Outgoing? Kind?)

3 Which of the personality traits is most clear to you? (Think of an experience or event during which this personality trait was evident.)

4 How has this person positively influenced you?

Organizing Your Details

A chart can help you build on ideas and details to create an organized piece of writing. Jot down descriptions of the person's physical appearance (from head to toe) and personality. Also include a short story (anecdote) to illustrate your subject's key personality trait.

Organizing List

Subject	Dr. Julie, the veterinarian
Physical Appearance	short, big smile, white lab coat, blue jeans, red sneakers
Key Personality Trait	kind
Anecdote	caring for Snoops

Prewrite

Organize your details. Make a chart like the one above. List details about the person's physical appearance, in the order you plan to describe them. Also list a key personality trait and an anecdote to illustrate that trait.

Using Verbs and Adjectives

Interesting and specific words help create a strong voice and add personality to your writing. Keep the following tips about word choice in mind as you write:

- Use specific verbs to show action.

  attacked   wandered   examined

- Use adjectives to help readers "see" the scene.

  tiny woman   straight, blond hair   five feet tall

Make a list of specific verbs and adjectives to describe your person's actions and appearance. Use the best ones in your essay.

 **TEKS** 8.14A
ELPS 5G

Drafting **Starting Your Essay**

The beginning paragraph should catch your reader's interest and introduce your topic—a person who has positively influenced you. Here are two approaches.

Beginning Paragraph

■ **Briefly explain how you know the person.** Is he or she a family member? Friend? Teacher? Include some interesting details to draw the reader into your essay.

> The writer makes a personal connection.
>
> *Dr. Julie is the veterinarian for our family's pets. She gives shots to our dogs and cats every year, and she took care of our parakeet, Squeeker, when he broke his wing last fall. The most important thing she ever did for us was to save our spaniel, Snoops, when he was attacked by a coyote that wandered into our yard.*

■ **Begin with an important fact.** Share one important reason why you admire the person; tell something interesting that the person did or something unusual that happened to him or her.

> The writer shares an interesting detail.
>
> *If it weren't for Dr. Julie, our veterinarian, Snoops would be dead. She saved our spaniel's life after he was attacked by a coyote that had wandered into our yard last fall.*

Using an Engaging Voice

Voice is the special way that a writer expresses ideas and emotions. It shows that the writer really cares about the subject and the audience. When you write, keep the following tips about voice in mind:

● Write as if you were telling a friend about this person.

● Show enthusiasm for your subject and express your true feelings.

● Make sure you use a consistent point of view.

Write your beginning paragraph. Choose one of the approaches above to get started. If you don't like how your first attempt turns out, try another one.

TEKS 8.14B
ELPS 5G

Developing the Middle Part

The middle part of your essay will include three paragraphs. The first describes the person's appearance, and the second focuses on personality. The third should include an anecdote that demonstrates a key personality trait.

Middle Paragraphs

The first paragraph describes Dr. Julie with specific physical details.

Dr. Julie is a tiny woman, about five feet tall, who always greets everyone with a big smile. Her blond hair is pulled up into a twist. Seeing her in her white lab coat, blue jeans, and red tennis shoes, a person would never guess that she would be strong enough to handle large animals. But the day Snoops was attacked, she hoisted him up onto the examining table just as if she were lifting a cat.

The second paragraph describes Dr. Julie's personality.

Dr. Julie is hardworking and caring. Whenever she examines a pet, she talks quietly the whole time to calm the animal. She also carefully explains what she's doing as her strong hands gently feel for a trouble spot. Everyone is thankful that Dr. Julie takes emergency calls both day and night.

Finally, the writer shares an anecdote about Dr. Julie.

The day that Dr. Julie examined Snoops, she was honest with her diagnosis. "He has some very bad bites, and he's lost a lot of blood," she said. "However, I'm not going to give up on him." Dr. Julie stated that Snoops needed surgery to save his life. It was hard to leave him at the clinic, but Dr. Julie was very reassuring. That's another great thing about her. She cares about animals, and she also cares about people. When the surgery was over, I could hear the happiness in her voice, and I knew that Snoops was going to be fine.

DESCRIPTIVE

Draft **Write your middle paragraphs.** Use the details you gathered (page 80) and your organizing list (page 81). Describe your person's appearance and personality. Include an anecdote to illustrate a key personality trait.

84

Drafting **Ending Your Essay**

The ending clearly signals that your description is complete. In your last sentence or two, leave the reader with a final idea or image—something that will keep him or her thinking about your topic.

Ending Paragraph

The writer makes a final personal connection.

From watching Dr. Julie, I've learned that sincerely caring about people and animals is so important. Every time Snoops comes and lays his head in my lap, I think of Dr. Julie and smile.

 Write your ending paragraph. Wrap things up by explaining how the person has had a positive influence on you.

Revising **and** Editing

A first draft can always be improved. By adding, deleting, or reorganizing some details, you can make your description better.

 Revise your first draft. Revise your first draft using the questions below as a guide. Then add a title.

☐ Focus and Coherence Do I have a clear and focused topic? Do my details and anecdotes relate to the main topic in a coherent way? Did I include all the necessary elements for this form of writing?

☐ Development of Ideas Have I included enough specific details about the person's appearance and personality? Did I include an anecdote?

☐ Organization Do I have a clear beginning, middle, and ending? Did I ensure coherence within my essay by using transitions such as *however, then, next, first,* or *on the other hand?*

☐ Voice Do I sound interested in the person and in my audience?

 Edit your description. Once you have completed your revising, use the checklist on page 44 to edit your essay for errors. Then write a clean final copy to share.

Descriptive Writing
Across the Curriculum

Since its creation in 1876, the telephone has been used to carry descriptions of people, places, and things across the land. A clear phone description lets the listener feel as if he or she is "right there" with the speaker. A clear written description can do the same thing for readers.

You will use descriptive writing in almost all of your classes. In social studies, you may be asked to write an eyewitness report about a famous historical person. In math, your teacher may require you to describe an object using geometric terms. In science class, you may need to describe a place you visited on a field trip. Your description will be successful if your readers can clearly imagine the topic in their minds.

What's Ahead

- **Social Studies**: Writing a Project Proposal
- **Math**: Describing an Object
- **Science**: Writing a Field-Trip Report
- **Practical Writing**: Writing a Friendly Letter

Social Studies:
Writing a Project Proposal

Descriptive writing comes in many different forms. The following proposal, written by a student team, describes a tutoring project they plan to do for their social studies class.

The **heading** identifies the writers and their proposed project.

The **beginning** describes the project.

The **middle** part gives details about the project.

The **ending** asks for approval of the project.

Date: January 12, 2009
To: Mrs. Munn, Room 210
From: The Titan Group: Todd Davis, LaToya Wilson, Jacque Trevino, Becky Jackson
Subject: Volunteer Tutoring

Project Description: An article in our school paper stated that Lincoln Elementary School needed eighth-grade students to tutor third graders in reading. We would like to volunteer our services starting February 3.

What We Need: We need written permission from you, our parents, and our principal. We also need written approval from the principal and the third-grade teachers of Lincoln Elementary School.

What We Will Do: On Tuesdays and Thursdays, during our fourth-period study hall, we will walk across the playground to Lincoln Elementary School to our assigned classrooms. We will help third-grade students by listening to them read, helping them with their reading assignments, and reading to them.

Outcome: At the end of this project, we will report on the students' progress and show a videotape of our students reading during one of our last sessions. It will show how the tutoring helped.

We hope you will approve our proposal. If you have any suggestions or changes, please let us know.

TEKS 8.14C
ELPS 5D, 5G

DESCRIPTIVE

Writing Tips

Before you write . . .

● **Choose a project that interests you.**
Working alone or with a team of classmates, choose
a project you will enjoy doing.

● **Do your research.**
Decide specifically what you will do and what you will
need to complete your project.

● **Plan your proposal.**
Collect details in order to describe the project to your teacher.
Your goal is to present a clear description of your work plan.

During your writing . . .

● **Write a clear beginning, middle, and ending.**
In the *heading* give the date, your teacher's name and room
number, the names of your team members, and the subject of
your project. Next, clearly describe the project. For the other
parts of your proposal, follow the model on page 86.

● **Order your ideas.**
Make sure you've included all the information in the
correct order.

● **Use precise words.**
Make your description clear and easy to follow. Use specific
nouns and verbs.

After you've written a first draft . . .

● **Check for completeness.**
Make sure that you have included all the details that your
teacher needs to understand the project.

● **Check for correctness.**
Proofread your proposal for grammar, punctuation,
capitalization, and spelling errors.

Select a project that you or your team would like to do. Write a project
proposal using the tips above.

Math: Describing an Object with Geometric Terms

Sometimes an object can be described with geometric terms. The writer of this essay describes a quartz crystal as a hexagonal prism.

A Crystal Clear Hexagon

The **beginning** introduces the object.

The **middle** describes the top, bottom, and side views of the object.

The **ending** makes a final comment.

In the world, both natural and man-made objects have geometric shapes. Triangles, rectangles, squares, circles, cubes, cones, and pyramids can be seen in nature and in the world every day. Another common hexagon in nature is the glasslike quartz crystal.

A hexagonal prism crystal is a shape with six sides. The base of a quartz crystal is a hexagon with equal sides and equal angles. A perpendicular rectangle rises from each side from the base. The six rectangles of equal size rising from the base form a six-sided or hexagonal box. The top of the crystal is the same shape as the base.

When looking at the bottom or the top of the crystal, the viewer will see a perfect hexagon. A side view will reveal three long rectangles. From this view, the top and the bottom rectangles are each attached to the middle rectangle at an angle of 60 degrees.

Focusing on geometric shapes to describe an object can help someone else visualize it. Describing something in geometric terms may also make it easier to remember facts and information about the object.

express SPECIFY portray
picture describe
89

Writing in Math

TEKS 8.14C
ELPS 5F, 5G

DESCRIPTIVE

Writing Tips

Before you write . . .

- **List some geometric terms that could be used to describe a flat or three-dimensional object.**
  Make notes or sketches on the list. Review any terms you are unsure of.

- **Choose an object that can be described with geometric terms.**
  Study the object and look at it from all different angles.

- **Make notes as you observe the object.**
  Jot down specific geometric terms you could use to enable a reader to visualize the object.

During your writing . . .

- **Write a clear beginning, middle, and ending.**
  Introduce the object and then describe it using geometric terms. End with a final comment about your topic or about using geometric terms to describe everyday objects.

- **Organize your description.**
  Describe your object using a spatial method of organization (top to bottom, left to right, and so on).

- **Use varied sentence structures.**
  Include simple, compound, and complex sentences to make your description flow smoothly.

After you've written a first draft . . .

- **Check for completeness.**
  Have you included enough details to clearly describe your object? Did you use a variety of sentence types including simple, compound, and complex sentences?

- **Check for correctness.**
  Proofread your writing for grammar, punctuation, capitalization, and spelling errors.

Write a short essay, using geometric terms to describe an object. Include a variety of sentence types. Share your essay with your classmates.

Science: Writing a Field-Trip Report

In science class, you may be asked to describe your observations on a recent field trip. This student writer describes a field trip to an observatory.

The beginning introduces the topic.

The middle clearly describes important parts of the observatory.

The ending makes a final observation.

McDonald Observatory

On March 3, our class visited the McDonald Observatory. The observatory is located at the summit of Mt. Locke in the Davis Mountains. It really feels like being in the middle of nowhere. You see nothing but mountains in the distance. Being 7,000 feet above sea level in the dry mountain air makes the observatory a great location for astronomy.

The observatory is home to the Hobby Eberly Telescope (HET). It is the third largest single structure optical telescope in the world. It looks like an enormous cannon peeking from the observatory dome. Another famous telescope located there is called the Harlan Smith Telescope. NASA used this telescope to prepare to fly the Viking missions to Mars and the Voyager missions to planets in the far reaches of our solar system.

A theater in the observatory allows visitors to get a first-hand look at the stars. Reclining chairs give you a full view of the domed ceiling movie screen. A man's voice narrates as the Milky Way, planets, and meteorites zoom across the sky. Among the stars are constellations like Ursa Major and Orion. A sunrise in the eastern sky signals the end of the show.

The McDonald Observatory is filled with interesting telescopes and equipment. There are many fun and exciting programs to help children and adults learn about astronomy.

TEKS 8.14C
ELPS 5D, 5G

DESCRIPTIVE

Writing Tips

Before you write . . .

- **Choose a topic that interests you.** Select a recent field trip related to your class.

- **List main ideas you want to include.** You can't tell everything about the field trip, so choose one or two impressive things to write about.

- **Gather specific details.** Think about your destination. Use sensory details to describe the sights and sounds of the place.

Sensory Chart

Subject:				
Sights	Sounds	Smells	Tastes	Feelings

During your writing . . .

- **Write a clear beginning, middle, and ending.** Introduce the topic in the beginning part. In the middle, describe the place by including specific details. Close by sharing a final thought about the experience.

- **Organize your details.** You may organize your details by order of location (*left to right, top to bottom, near to far*) or time order (*first, second, next, last*). Choose the pattern that works best for your description.

- **Use strong words.** A strong description creates vivid images by using specific nouns, action verbs, and well-chosen adjectives.

After you've written a first draft . . .

- **Check for completeness.** Make sure that you include vivid images and details that help the reader see the place in his or her mind.

- **Check for correctness.** Proofread your report for punctuation, capitalization, spelling, and grammar errors.

Select a recent or past field trip and describe what you saw. Follow the tips above as you write. Be sure to include vivid images.

TEKS 8.17B

Practical Writing:
Writing a Friendly Letter

A friendly letter often includes descriptive writing. The writer of the following letter uses descriptions to express his opinion and a complaint and to request information.

The **heading** includes your address and the date.

The **salutation** identifies the person you're writing to.

The **beginning** introduces the writer.

The **middle** describes a complaint and requests information.

The **ending** makes plans for future contact.

The **closing** and **signature** complete the letter.

100 Windwater Drive
Odessa, TX 79763
August 26, 2012

Dear Mr. Alberts,

My name is Joaquin, and I will be a new student at Windwater Middle School next year. I just moved to Texas from Washington. Music is very important to me. I feel that every student should learn to play an instrument.

I happen to play an unusual instrument. I have taken harp lessons for the past several years. My family owns a beautiful harp made of maple. It even has gold touches on the finishes. My hope is to continue with my lessons so that I will one day be able to perform.

Unfortunately, I notice that Windwater Middle School does not offer lessons for the harp. I have not been able to locate any private teachers in the area either. A clerk at the local music shop suggested I contact you for information about a program for the harp that you teach at the local community college. Could you please send me information about the times and locations of the class? I would also like to know the cost.

Thank you for the information. I look forward to having you as a teacher and talking more about the harp.

Sincerely,
Joaquin Fernandez

TEKS 8.14D, 8.17B
ELPS 5D, 5G

Writing Tips

Before you write . . .

- **Choose a subject.** Select a person to write to.
- **Select a topic for your letter.** Pick a topic that you want to discuss with this person. Think of an opinion you would like to express and a complaint you have that is related to the topic. Then decide what information you might need to solve the problem.
- **Gather details.** List important facts or information that will help you explain your complaint.
- **List the information you're asking for.** Figure out the specific information that you will request. Make a list. You might want to includes dates, times, locations, or costs.

During your writing . . .

- **Include all the important information.** Be sure to correctly write your address and the date. Double check the spelling of the person's name to whom you are sending the letter.
- **Order your ideas.** Make sure you have included all the important information in an order that makes sense.
- **Use precise words.** Only ask for what you need. Explain your complaint with clear, concise words. Don't include information that your reader doesn't need to know.

After you've written a first draft . . .

- **Check for completeness.** Make sure that you've included enough information to give the reader a clear understanding of your opinion, complaint, and request.
- **Check for correctness.** Proofread your letter to make sure there are no mistakes in grammar, punctuation, capitalization, and spelling.

DESCRIPTIVE

Write a personal letter to someone. In your letter, share an opinion, express a complaint, and request information. Use the tips above.

relate *tell*

ELPS 2C, 2G, 2H, 2I, 3G, 3H, 4C

Narrative Writing

Writing Focus

- **Narrative Paragraph**
- **Personal Narrative**
- **Biographical Narrative**

Grammar Focus

- **Subject-Verb Agreement**

Learning Language

Work with a partner. Read the meanings and share answers to the questions.

1. A personal narrative is a story about an experience you have had.
   Have you ever written a personal narrative? What did you write about?

2. A moment of discovery is an experience in which you learn something that affects your life in some important way.
   Describe a moment of discovery that you have had. How did it affect your life?

narrate remember share

Narrative Writing
Narrative Paragraph

Has anyone ever offered you a "penny for your thoughts"? Has anyone ever pulled a quarter out of your ear?

Actually, your thoughts are worth much more than pennies and quarters. By the end of eighth grade, a typical public school system has spent more than $60,000 to educate *each student*. To you, your thoughts are even more valuable. Your mind is a treasure trove of discoveries and "aha!" moments.

One way to count up the treasures in your head is to write about them. A narrative paragraph gives you a chance to record a moment of discovery and share it with others. It's a trick as neat as pulling a quarter out of your ear!

Writing Guidelines

Subject: **A moment of discovery**

Purpose: **To entertain**

Form: **Narrative paragraph**

Audience: **Classmates**

ELPS 4C, 4G, 4I, 4K

Narrative Paragraph

A "moment of discovery" is a perfect subject for a narrative paragraph. In the student model below, Eric describes a special moment when he figured out his first magic trick. The **topic sentence** introduces the topic, the **body** explains what happened, and the **closing sentence** wraps things up with a final thought.

Topic Sentence
· · · · · · · · · · · · ·

Body

Closing Sentence
· · · · · · · · · · · · ·

A Handy Trick

Grandpa grinned and held out his hand in front of me. He snapped his fingers, and a quarter appeared in his palm. Rapidly, he rolled his fingers, and the quarter vanished. I'd seen this trick a hundred times, but today I was determined to figure it out. The quarter appeared again, and vanished again. I stared carefully at Grandpa's hands. He held his left hand out to his side, palm open. His right hand was in front of him and open underneath, with the back facing me. He turned his right hand over, and I glimpsed the quarter in his clenched fist. I snatched the quarter from his hand and held it just as he had shown me. Then, with a grin of my own, I snapped my fingers, and the quarter appeared. Grandpa still had many tricks up his sleeve, but that was one trick I had learned.

Respond to the reading. **Answer the following questions on your own paper.**

☐ **Development of Ideas** **(1) What moment of discovery is the story about?**

☐ **Organization** **(2) Are the details of the paragraph organized by importance, time, or some other pattern of organization?**

☐ **Voice & Conventions** **(3) What vivid verbs help re-create the moment of discovery?**

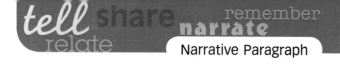
TEKS 8.14A, 8.14B
ELPS 5G

Prewriting **Selecting a Topic**

Whenever you learn something new, you have a moment of discovery. To find a topic for his narrative paragraph, Eric made a cluster of these moments.

Topic Cluster

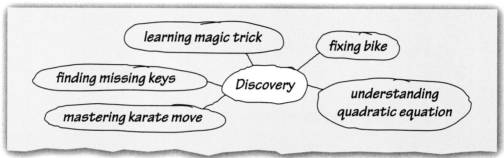

Create a cluster. On your own paper, write "Discovery" and circle it. Make a cluster of four or five of your own moments of discovery. Choose one of these moments to write a paragraph about.

Gathering Details

One way to gather details about the moment of discovery is to use a before-after chart. Eric created the following chart about his "aha!" moment.

Before-After Chart

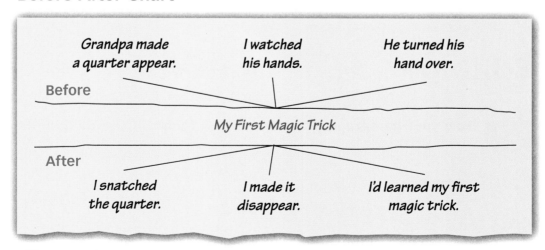

Create a before-after chart. Make a chart like the one above. Write what happened before and after your moment of discovery.

NARRATIVE

 **TEKS** 8.14B
ELPS 3H, 5D, 5G

Drafting **Creating Your First Draft**

A well-written narrative paragraph should focus on a main idea and maintain that focus throughout the entire paragraph.

- To establish a focus, begin the paragraph with a thesis statement, the main idea of the writing.
- In the body of the paragraph, write sentences that build on and contribute to the reader's understanding of that idea. Any sentence that does not relate to the main idea does not belong.
- End with a sentence that brings your thoughts about the idea to a satisfying close.

 Write your first draft. Write about your moment of discovery as you would tell it to a friend. Use your before-after chart to guide you.

Revising **Improving Your Paragraph**

Here are a few tips to guide the revision of your paragraph.

- **Show, don't tell.** Instead of telling the reader that "Jenna was excited," show it: "Jenna clapped wildly and screamed, "Go team!""
- **Build to the high point.** Lead up to the moment of discovery.
- **Rewrite sentences if needed.** Check for sentences that are awkward or unclear. Rewrite them so that they flow nicely.

 Revise your paragraph. Focus on ideas, organization, voice, word choice, and sentence fluency as you revise your narrative paragraph.

Editing **Checking for Conventions**

After you finish revising, check your paragraph for conventions.

 Edit your paragraph. Carefully read your paragraph. Use the following questions as you check for errors.

1 Have I spelled all my words correctly?

2 Did I use punctuation marks correctly?

3 Are there any grammatical mistakes?

Proofread your narrative. Make a clean final copy of your paragraph and check it for any remaining errors. Then share your moment of discovery with your classmates.

Narrative Writing

Writing a Personal Narrative

At one time or another, most students have had to write a narrative entitled "What I Did Last Summer." Many of those essays could be summed up this way: "I mowed the lawn—over and over and over. . . ." A more thoughtful narrative, though, would focus on a few related experiences the writer had and would show how those experiences changed him or her in some way.

A personal narrative is a piece of writing that describes an experience you have had. An effective personal narrative does not just describe the experience, but instead shows how it changed you or taught you an important lesson. The key to this form of writing is to maintain the focus on how you changed or what lesson you learned, by describing actions and events that led to this change. Everything you write should contribute to the reader's understanding of how the experience changed you. By the time you are done writing, you will become wiser about life—and what it has to offer.

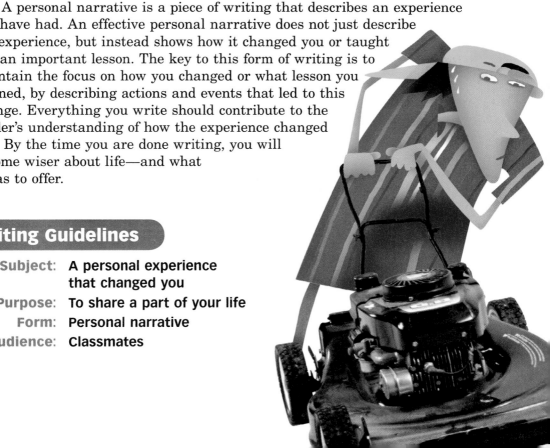

Writing Guidelines

Subject:	**A personal experience that changed you**
Purpose:	**To share a part of your life**
Form:	**Personal narrative**
Audience:	**Classmates**

ELPS 2C

Understanding Your Goals

Your assignment in this chapter is to write about a time in your life when you changed. The following goals will help you plan and write your personal narrative. On pages 50–51, you will find a rubric that will guide you through your writing.

Focus and Coherence

Select an experience in your life that changed you. Focus on the idea of that change and include events and details of how the experience led to that change.

Organization

Present ideas so that each sentence links to the next in a way that makes sense. Each sentence should move your idea forward and deepen the reader's understanding of that idea. Each paragraph should build on the one before it.

Development of Ideas

Develop ideas in depth. Flesh out ideas so that each sentence adds meaning to the sentences that come before it. Make your writing your own; develop original ideas and present them in unique ways.

Voice

Use a unique, individual voice that expresses your personality or personal viewpoint. Make a connection with and engage the reader.

Conventions

Be sure that your punctuation, capitalization, spelling, and grammar are correct.

 Literature Connection. You can find a personal narrative in *Caught by the Sea: My Life on Boats*, by Gary Paulsen.

Personal Narrative

In this sample narrative, the student author focuses on how he changed after getting to know his elderly neighbor. The key parts of the personal narrative are described in the left margin.

Focus and Coherence

In the beginning, the writer establishes his thesis statement, the focus of his personal narrative.

Organization

Each sentence moves the idea forward, deepening the reader's understanding.

Getting to Know Joe

Last summer, I learned that helping people is what life is all about. The person who taught me this lesson was someone who I would have least likely expected to teach me anything. He is my neighbor, Joe Perez.

I live in an old two-story home in Newark. My neighbors are mostly retired people with perfect front yards. Joe Perez lives on the corner. Joe and I did not get along. He's very picky about his yard. Every morning he does something to make the lawn look better. If we goof around and step on his grass, Joe yells at us. I figured he's just a cranky old man with no life. I didn't understand why he had to be so grumpy, or why keeping a nice lawn was so important to him.

Through mid-July Joe's lawn was perfect, but then I noticed some changes. I didn't see Joe outside as much. We didn't miss him, though. Over time, his grass grew brown and shaggy, and weeds took over his flower beds. It wasn't like him to let things go like that. Although I didn't care that much about Joe or his lawn, I wondered why he wasn't taking care of his yard anymore.

Then one day I was sitting on the curb waiting for one of my buddies when Joe came out on his porch. "Oh great," I thought to myself. "Here it comes." He didn't yell at me, though. Instead he started swaying back and forth. Then he fell down! Nothing like this had ever happened to me, but I

NARRATIVE

⭐ ELPS 2G, 2H, 2I, 3D, 3E, 3G, 3H, 4C, 4G, 4I, 4K

Development of Ideas

Ideas are developed in depth. The idea has fleshed-out details so that each sentence adds meaning to those before it.

Voice

The writer's voice expresses his personality. He makes a connection with the reader.

knew what to do. I pulled out my cell phone and called 911. "My neighbor, Mr. Perez, just passed out! He lives on the corner of Garden and Mills," I blurted. Joe was awake, but he was as white as a ghost. He stared blankly at me. I know he was scared. At that moment, I saw Joe as a person, just like me. But he needed my help.

The paramedics took Joe to the hospital. He was going to be all right. I have to admit, I was surprised at how happy I was to hear that. Yes, Joe could be a grumpy old man, but I guess I cared about him more than I realized.

Later Joe thanked me. Then I asked, "Is there anything I can do for you, Mr. Perez?" Little did I know that one question would change everything between us.

Joe found lots of things I could do in his yard. I started to appreciate the pride Joe felt in his well-kept lawn. Before long, I was the one yelling at kids to stay off the grass!

A year has passed, and each week I help Joe. I also help some of the other older neighbors. My friendship with Joe has really changed me. It has taught me that I can make a difference in people's lives, and when I do, it makes a difference in my life, too.

Respond to the reading. Why is "Getting to Know Joe" a good piece of writing? To find out, answer these questions.

☐ **Focus and Coherence** (1) What is the writer's thesis statement, or focus for his essay?

☐ **Organization and Development of Ideas** (2) How does the writer develop his ideas to keep the narrative moving forward?

☐ **Voice** (3) What words and phrases does the writer use to establish a unique voice and express his personality?

ELPS 5G

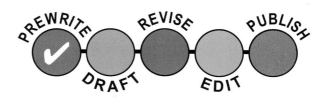

PREWRITE · REVISE · PUBLISH · DRAFT · EDIT

Go Online!

Prewriting

Before you can begin writing your personal narrative, you need to choose an event in your life to write about. In your prewriting, you will choose a topic, gather details, and organize your thoughts.

Keys to Effective Prewriting

1. Think about several important events in your life that had a significant effect on you and/or changed you in some way.

2. Choose one event to share with your readers.

3. Identify key details related to this event.

4. Organize your ideas so they maintain focus on your thesis statement.

5. Gather specific details and feelings that show how this event changed you or taught you something.

6. Work on establishing a unique individual voice that will express your personality or personal viewpoint.

PROD. NO. · SCENE · TAKE · ROLL · SOUND · DATE

NARRATIVE

ELPS 5G

Prewriting **Selecting a Topic**

A personal narrative is a form of narrative writing that tells about an event or experience. It should focus on why the event or experience is important and how it changed you. It should include descriptive details, as well as your thoughts, feelings, and reactions to the event.

One way to find a topic is to list meaningful events and experiences you have had that changed you. They should be events that you remember well because of the impact they had on you.

Important Events List

> *Was hospitalized with an appendicitis attack*
>
> *Took a train trip with my grandmother*
>
> *Went canoeing with the youth group*
>
> *Participated in the school's spelling bee*
>
> *Joined the Junior Drum and Bugle Corp*
>
> *Volunteered at the local nursing home*
>
> *Transferred to a new school*
>
> *Helped my neighbor take care of her dog*
>
> *Reason: I chose this topic because it changed me in so many ways.*

Make an "Important Events List." List a number of important experiences in your life. Circle the experience you want to use as the topic of your personal narrative. Then write your reason for choosing this topic.

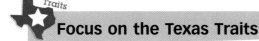

Focus on the Texas Traits

Focus and Coherence As you choose a topic, keep in mind that you will want to maintain a focus on how the event or experience changed you.

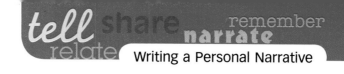
Focusing Your Topic

After you have chosen a period of time in your life that has changed you in some important way, you should write a sentence or two that will give your personal narrative a focus. You should mention both the event or experience and the way in which it changed you. The examples below will help you understand how the two parts work together.

Weak Focus

One Saturday night a year ago, I learned that my friends are not always right.
("One Saturday night" is not an extended period of time.)

The last month of track meets really taught me something.
("Really taught me something" should be more specific.)

Strong Focus

The last month of track meets taught me that champions are made from discipline, determination, and sweat.

 First, carefully read the following sentences. Then identify the ones you feel would make a good focus for a personal narrative.

1. Felicia and I had played in tennis tournaments all summer, but we learned more about friendship than about tennis.
2. I met my grandfather for the first time at my cousin's wedding.
3. I surprised my mother by making supper.
4. I lived with my grandparents for a semester while my parents were busy starting a new business.
5. When my little sister was born, my life changed completely.

 Focus your topic. Using the topic you selected (page 104), write a sentence or two that will give your narrative a good focus. Be sure you state both the event or experience and the important way in which your life changed.

NARRATIVE

ELPS 3H, 5G

Prewriting **Freewriting**

Now that you've chosen an event to write about, you need to search your memory for information. Freewriting is an excellent way to recall details without worrying about organization or correctness.

The example of freewriting below was done by the writer of the essay on pages 111–114. Notice that after she finished her writing, she located and underlined the key events. These key events eventually became part of the topic sentences in the middle paragraphs.

Freewriting

The drum and bugle flyer I brought home from school really got Dad talking about his days in the drum corps. His stories convinced me to sign up for summer band camp. I felt excited and nervous on that first day of camp. I heard Mr. D, the director, was very strict. He was! <u>My first day of practice</u> *was unbelievable.* <u>All of our practices</u> *were tough. We marched like soldiers. My friend, Marcia, quit during the first week. I didn't have that choice. (Our family has this rule: Whatever you start, you finish.) I have to admit that I really liked being in the* <u>parades</u>*.* <u>Field competitions</u> *were the best. We always placed somewhere in the top three. In August we traveled to Canada for a competition. I thought the name of it—a* <u>tattoo</u>*—was weird. We came in first and won an international trophy. . . .*

Prewrite

Freewrite. Write nonstop for 5 to 10 minutes about your topic. Write down all your thoughts and don't stop to revise or correct your writing. Then read through your paper and underline the key events that took place.

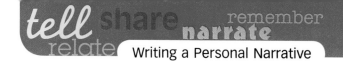
Gathering Details

Now it's time to recall more about the events and choose how you want to organize your writing. Our writer thought about each event and made a chart to record her details. She decided to describe the events chronologically, as this is how the change came about. She used the chart to organize her essay.

Specific Details Chart

Key Events	Details	Change
First day of practice	hot summer day sore feet Mr. D.—very strict	doing new things can be uncomfortable
Daily practices	intense practices kept bumping into people quickly improved	wanted to quit, but was determined to get better
Parades and competitions	teamwork performed in all kinds of weather	could face difficult challenges even though overwhelmed
The tattoo	packed stadium competed with the best marching bands	feels good to accomplish something that I thought I couldn't

NARRATIVE

Create a details chart. Record your key events in a chart like the one above. Then jot down details for each event and any change that resulted.

Focus on the Texas Traits

Organization Narrative writing is usually organized chronologically to help the story flow smoothly from beginning to end. For other patterns of organization, see page 613.

ELPS 5G

Prewriting **Understanding Tone**

When you write about an important event in your life and how it changed you, you tell about an experience that is all your own. To help engage your reader, you must express an individual voice that sounds like you. You want your personality or personal viewpoint to come through. The attitude you communicate to your reader is called *tone*.

There are several ways to enhance the tone of your writing. One is to choose words that convey strong feeling, or *connotation*. Another is to create the atmosphere, or *mood*, of the setting. You can do this using *imagery*, or words that engage the senses. All of these strategies engage the reader and help express your unique voice.

In the examples below, note how the writer replaces neutral words with words that communicate an attitude, or tone.

Neutral: **Mr. D. was a man with short hair.**
Strong: Mr. D. was a drill sergeant with a crew cut.

Neutral: **Mr. D. walked before us and spoke loudly.**
Strong: Mr. D. paced before us and barked loudly.

 Read the following sentences. For each, indicate which of the words in parentheses helps enhance the tone of the sentence.

1. The tough schedule *(affected, shook)* my confidence.
2. Mr. D. told me my playing added *(spark, something)* to the trumpet section.
3. Before the competition, Mr. D. *(huddled, met)* with us like a *(leader, football coach)*.
4. As we took the field, we marched like a *(conquering army, big group)*.
5. The *(hard, grueling)* practices paid off when we *(won, dominated)* the competition.

 Enhance tone. Review the "Specific Details Chart" you created (page 107). For each event or detail you recorded, write one word or phrase that would clearly express your tone or attitude. Use these words and phrases as you write your first draft.

TEKS 8.14C
ELPS 5G

Go Online!

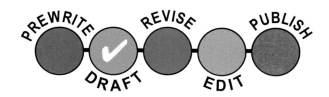

PREWRITE ✓ REVISE PUBLISH
DRAFT EDIT

Drafting

Now that you have gathered and organized your details, you can begin writing the first draft of your personal narrative.

Keys to Effective Drafting

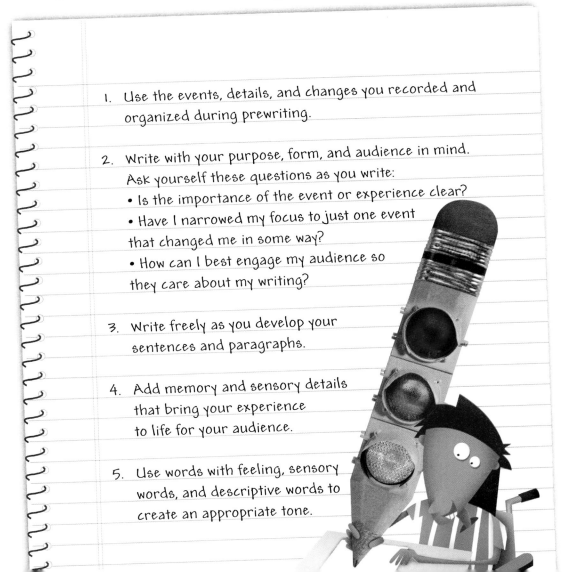

NARRATIVE

1. Use the events, details, and changes you recorded and organized during prewriting.

2. Write with your purpose, form, and audience in mind. Ask yourself these questions as you write:
   • Is the importance of the event or experience clear?
   • Have I narrowed my focus to just one event that changed me in some way?
   • How can I best engage my audience so they care about my writing?

3. Write freely as you develop your sentences and paragraphs.

4. Add memory and sensory details that bring your experience to life for your audience.

5. Use words with feeling, sensory words, and descriptive words to create an appropriate tone.

TEKS 8.16
ELPS 5G

Drafting **Getting the Big Picture**

The chart below shows how the parts of a personal narrative fit together. (The examples are from the essay on pages 111–114.) You're ready to write once you've . . .

- collected plenty of details about the experience and
- organized the details chronologically.

Beginning

The **beginning** gives background information and focuses on what led up to the event.

Opening Sentences

I was never interested in joining any group or sport during the summer. . . . so I decided to give it a try. It was the best decision I've ever made.

Middle

The **middle** part uses a variety of details to show how the writer felt about the event.

I will never forget my first day of practice . . .

. . . when his voice exploded through the bullhorn, I shivered.

The best part of that summer was our tattoo in Windsor, Canada.

Ending

The **ending** explains how the event changed the writer's life.

Closing Sentences

After last summer, I am not the same Julie Patterson anymore. . . . I actually enjoy performing in front of people now.

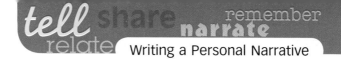
Starting Your Personal Narrative

Now that you've selected a topic and gathered details, you are ready to begin writing. In the opening, you need to accomplish three things:

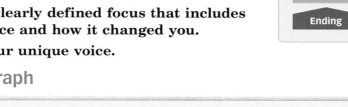

- Engage your reader right away.
- Establish a clearly defined focus that includes the experience and how it changed you.
- Establish your unique voice.

Beginning Paragraph

> The writer sets the scene and introduces the focus, or thesis, of her writing.

I was never interested in joining any group or sport during the summer. I liked hanging out with my friends and doing odd jobs to make extra cash. But then last summer I decided to do something different. I joined the Warrentown Junior Drum and Bugle Corps. It was the best decision I've ever made, because it helped make me a confident and outgoing person who enjoys working with others.

NARRATIVE

Using Transitions

A personal narrative should be coherent—every sentence and paragraph should contribute to your thesis. Using effective transitions can help you move your reader smoothly from one sentence to the next and one paragraph to the next, so that your narrative feels coherent. Look at the transition words below.

Transition Words and Phrases

about	but	now	this time	usually
as soon as	during	recently	today	when
before	later	so far	until	whenever
besides	next	then	until now	while

Write your beginning. On your own paper, write the beginning of your personal narrative. Use transitions to create a coherent piece of writing.

TEKS 8.16
ELPS 5G

Drafting **Developing the Middle Part**

Now that you have your reader's attention and have established a clear focus, it's time to add details. Throughout your piece, support your thesis with the most important and interesting details. Everything you write should contribute to your reader's understanding of your experience and how it changed you. Use the tips below to maintain that focus:

- **Use sensory details to support your thesis.**
- **Choose words that maintain your voice and create an appropriate tone. (See page 108.)**
- **Use dialogue to help engage the reader.**

Middle Paragraphs

The writer tells about key events related to the experience.

Dialogue is used to show the personality of an important person.

I will never forget my first day of practice with the drum and bugle corps. The director, Mr. DeRusha, stepped onto the football field and ordered us all to sit along the 50-yard line. I nervously tapped the keys of my trumpet. I'd heard that Mr. D. had a reputation for being tough. He looked like one of those army drill sergeants on TV. He was tall and had a fresh crew cut, and when his voice exploded through the bullhorn, I shivered, even though it was almost 70 degrees outside.

"Listen up, people!" he barked. "Welcome to the Warrentown Junior Drum and Bugle Corps. Being in a drum and bugle corps means you are alert and prepared at all times. Is that understood?"

He paced back and forth in front of us. "By the end of the summer, you will learn to respect this organization, yourselves, and each other." Then his shadow stopped over me. He must have read my name tag.

I couldn't even look up when I heard him call my name and tell me to polish my horn.

 **TEKS** 8.16
ELPS 5F, 5G

tell share remember
relate narrate

113

Writing a Personal Narrative

NARRATIVE

The writer supports her clearly defined focus, or thesis. Each sentence adds meaning to the sentences that come before it.

Strong sensory details keep the reader engaged. The writer reflects on the consequences of her own and others' actions.

"Yes, sir, "I answered, almost choking on the words.

Many times during those first weeks, when the demands of practice were shaking my confidence, I thought about quitting. That's when Mr. D. came along and announced, "Miss Patterson, you add a spark to this trumpet section. Good job." Sometimes I wondered if Mr. D. could read minds. He always seemed to know just who needed to hear encouraging words.

The best part of that summer was our tattoo in Windsor, Canada. A tattoo is a type of nighttime marching competition. We were competing for an international trophy. Just before our performance, Mr. D. huddled with us like a football coach.

"You are the finest band here tonight," he said. "You know it. I know it. Now go out there and make sure everyone else knows it!"

"Yes, sir!" we shouted.

Marching in a strong, straight line, we were a band with a mission. The explosions of applause we heard during our performance propelled us to hit clearer notes and create sharper steps. We had never sounded so good. At the end, the audience went crazy and rewarded us with a standing ovation. We did it. We dominated the competition and came home with a trophy.

Draft

Write your middle paragraphs. Review the drafting tips on page 112, and use your "Specific Details Chart" (page 107). Focus on your thesis and consider the consequences of your own and others' decisions and actions.

 TEKS 8.14C, 8.16
ELPS 5G

Drafting Ending Your Personal Narrative

The ending builds on the paragraphs that came before it to make a final point about the thesis. You should reflect on decisions or actions you made and the significance of the event or experience. Your ending should be thoughtful and give the reader a satisfying sense of closure.

■ **Coming Full Circle**

You can "come full circle" if you reflect on decisions or actions in both the beginning and the ending. This approach could have been used in this personal narrative:

Reflection in the Beginning

I snapped to attention when the band director hurried onto the marching field, barking orders.

Reflection in the Ending

Now, three months later, I still snap to attention whenever Mr. D. barks orders, but I do it because I respect him, not because I'm afraid of him.

■ **Explaining Your Change**

The writer chose to reflect on how her decision to join the marching band led to a change in her. (See the model below.)

Ending Paragraph

I still get goose bumps when I think about the band. Mr. DeRusha is a great director who taught me about discipline and respect. After last summer I am not the same Julie Patterson anymore. Today I feel good about my ability to play the trumpet, and I actually enjoy performing in front of people. When I look back on my decision to join the band, I realize it was one smart move!

The writer reflects on her decision.

Draft

Write your ending. Complete your narrative by writing the final paragraph. You may want to use one of the above ways to end your narrative.

Get ready to revise. Read over your narrative in its entirety. Before you begin to revise, think about how well you addressed questions of form, purpose, and audience.

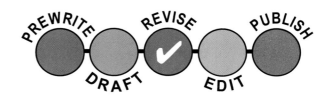

PREWRITE REVISE ✓ PUBLISH
DRAFT EDIT

Revising

You've worked hard while writing your first draft. During the next step in the writing process, you'll have the chance to go back and improve it. By adding, deleting, or moving parts, you will make your writing even better.

Keys to Effective Revising

1. Set your writing aside for a while so you'll have a fresh perspective as you begin to revise.

2. Read your writing out loud to see if you've presented your ideas in a logical way and in the proper form.

3. Mark any spots that don't seem to move your thesis forward.

4. Review your word choices to be sure you've used the best possible words to express your ideas and create vivid images.

5. Mark any spots where you haven't maintained a consistent point of view.

6. Check to see that you've used a variety of strategies to enhance the tone as a way to engage your reader.

NARRATIVE

TEKS 8.14C, 8.16
ELPS 5G

Revising for Focus and Coherence

When you revise for focus and coherence, check specifically for internal coherence. Make sure you have presented your details in a logical manner so that your reader can easily follow the progression of your ideas.

Do I use internal coherence?

To accomplish internal coherence, state a clear thesis in your opening paragraph. Then, as you write, every paragraph should logically lead to the next, supporting your thesis and deepening your reader's understanding of your ideas. Each sentence should offer details that are essential to the support of your thesis. Any details that don't belong weaken the focus and coherence of your essay. As you read your draft, ask yourself these questions:

- Have I clearly stated my thesis?
- Does each paragraph have a clear focus and contribute to my reader's understanding of my thesis?
- Does each sentence build on the one before it so that readers can easily follow my ideas?

To maintain focus and coherence, each paragraph should begin with a topic sentence. A topic sentence is like a mini-thesis; it states the main idea of the paragraph. The sentences that follow offer necessary details to support the main idea. If a sentence does not support the topic sentence, it needs to be rewritten or taken out.

 Identify each of the following as a topic sentence or a detail sentence.

1. Volunteering in the nursing home made me a compassionate person.
2. Mr. Simpson seemed sad when his visitors left.
3. Not making the soccer team was the best thing that ever happened to me.
4. There were many reasons why I did not want to volunteer.
5. Volunteers worked Saturdays, my day to sleep in.

 Read through your first draft. Check for internal coherence by making sure each paragraph has a topic sentence and includes only essential details to support it. Revise or add topic sentences as needed and cross out sentences that don't belong. Make sure you progress from one idea to the next in a logical way.

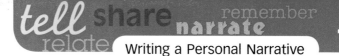

TEKS 8.14C, 8.14E, 8.16
ELPS 3E

Do I use external coherence?

While internal coherence has to do with presenting your ideas in a logical way, *external coherence* has to do with presenting your ideas in the proper form. For example, when you are writing a letter, you need to use proper letter format, including a salutation or greeting, a body, and a closing and signature to end the letter. You also need to include particular details within the body of the letter, such as a clear reason for why you are writing. In this case, the form is the personal narrative.

As you revise your draft, be sure you have met all the criteria for a personal narrative.

- Is your essay about just one event or experience?
- Do you clearly state your thesis—how that event or experience changed you?
- Do all the details you include relate to or support your thesis?
- Does your personality and personal viewpoint come through?
- Do you present your ideas in chronological order, or the most logical order possible?

One way to find out if your personal narrative has external coherence is to share your first draft with classmates. They may notice a lack of external coherence that you cannot. The following tips can help you organize a small group to discuss your work:

Discussion Tips

1. Provide a copy of your work to two to five classmates.
2. Allow them to read your work before you meet.
3. Ask them to evaluate your use of external coherence. Did you present your ideas in the proper form?
4. If the answer to 3 is no, ask group members to elaborate. What would they suggest you do to improve your external coherence?
5. Ask them what you could do to improve your piece overall. What could you add or cut?

Meet with peers. Share your work with a small group of classmates. Follow the tips above. Make changes to improve the external coherence of your writing.

NARRATIVE

Revising **for** Organization

When you revise for *organization*, consider using dialogue to develop your narrative. Also check that you have a clear beginning, middle, and ending to your story.

How can dialogue help me develop my narrative?

You have most likely heard the expression "show don't tell" in reference to writing. Dialogue lets you show what people in your story say. This allows readers to see for themselves what the people think and how they respond to events and other characters. It's amazing how much you can show about someone not only through what they say but how they say it. There are two ways to write dialogue.

- **Direct Dialogue**

  Direct dialogue lets you show the exact words of a person. Use direct dialogue when the things a person says reveal an idea very clearly or show something about the person. Also include active verbs and adjectives to show *how* the person speaks.

  > My little brother Jake looked up at me with his face all scrunched up. "When I'm 14, I'll boss you around."
  > "When you're 14," I said, "I'll be 22."
  > He shook his head sadly. "All right, I'll wait till I'm 23."

- **Summarized Dialogue**

  Summarized dialogue allows you to *tell* what the speaker says. Use summarized dialogue when you want to keep the action moving, rather than show the speaker's actual words.

  > I corrected Jake again, telling him I would be 30 when he was 23. He was persistent, upping the age to 31, then 39, and on until I was 111 years old. I told him I probably wouldn't last that long.

Check your quotations. Find places where dialogue could help you develop your narrative. (See page 618 for tips on punctuating dialogue.) Include dialogue where you want to highlight important details about characters, but don't overdo it.

TEKS 8.14B

Do my beginning, middle, and ending work well?

You will know if your personal narrative is organized well after you answer the following questions.

1. Does my beginning introduce an event in my life and grab my reader's attention?

2. Have I presented the middle in chronological order?

3. What time transitions have I used? (See page 111.)

4. In the ending, do I tell the reader how my life changed because of this event?

Check the parts of your personal narrative. Read through each part of your essay, while answering the questions above. Make needed changes.

Organization
Direct and summarized dialogue improve the narrative.

NARRATIVE

when I heard him call my name and tell
I couldn't even look up. ~~"Miss Patterson. It is~~
me to polish my horn.
~~an important rule here at the Warrentown Junior~~

~~Drum and Bugle Corps for everyone to clean his~~

~~or her trumpet!"~~

"Yes, sir," I answered, almost choking on the words.
~~I mumbled that I understood what he said.~~

Many times during those first weeks, when

the demands of practice were shaking my

confidence, I thought about quitting. . . .

TEKS 8.14C
ELPS 5D, 5G

Revising for Development of Ideas

When you revise, you want to make sure you have developed your ideas in depth so they are clear to your reader. To help you do this, look for and replace any general, weak words with stronger, more precise words. They will help engage your reader so that he or she can follow your ideas and remember your overall message.

Have I used precise words to develop my ideas?

Precise words present vivid images and clear details for your reader. The more precise your words are, the easier it will be for readers to visualize what you describe and understand how you felt about it. The chart below shows how you can make general nouns, verbs, and adjectives more vivid and precise.

Nouns		Verbs		Adjectives	
General	*Precise*	*General*	*Precise*	*General*	*Precise*
teacher	instructor coach professor	**tell**	narrate report relate	**good**	well-behaved obedient mannerly
park	square woods commons	**walk**	march stroll plod	**different**	distinct unique unusual

Do this activity with a partner:

1. Choose another important event from your past and write two sentences: a topic sentence and a supporting sentence. Be sure to include several nouns, verbs, or adjectives and give the paper to your partner.

2. Ask your partner to choose one to three general nouns, verbs, or adjectives in your sentences. Make them more precise so that they better develop your idea.

3. Try to make another round of changes on the same words; choose the best words to develop your idea.

4. Repeat the process, using sentences your partner wrote.

5. Discuss how precise words improved the sentences.

Check for precise words. Look at your nouns, verbs, and adjectives. Have you chosen the most precise words to develop your ideas and make them clear? If not, replace your general words with more precise ones.

TEKS 8.14C
ELPS 5G

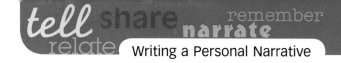
tell share remember
relate **narrate**
Writing a Personal Narrative

121

How can word choice help me create vivid images?

Words that appeal to your reader's senses can help create vivid images, which in turn can influence the development of your ideas. For example, if you're writing about a scary event in your life, the words you choose can put your readers right there in the action, helping them "see" what you saw and feel your fear. When your readers can feel what you felt, smell what you smelled, and so on, they will have no problem grasping your ideas.

Development of Ideas
Precise words create vivid images and influence the development of ideas.

> *Marching* a band with a mission.
> *~~Walking~~ in a strong, straight line, we were ~~a big~~*
> *explosions*
> *~~group of people.~~ The ~~sound~~ of applause we heard*
> *propelled to clearer*
> *during our performance ~~made~~ us hit ~~right~~ notes and*
> *create sharper*
> *~~make better~~ steps. We had never sounded so good.*
>
> *At the end, the audience went crazy and rewarded*
>
> *us with a standing ovation. We did it.*

NARRATIVE

Try It

Read the following sentences. In each, replace the neutral underlined word or words to create a more vivid image as described in parenthesis.

1. I <u>listened</u> for the results of the tryouts. *(nervous)*
2. After my name was not called, I <u>walked</u> away. *(disappointed)*
3. I <u>watched</u> as my friend celebrated making the team. *(jealousy)*
4. After I talked to the coach, I felt <u>better</u>. *(hopeful)*
5. I will work <u>hard</u> to make it next year. *(determination)*

Revise

Check word choice. Read through the first draft of your personal narrative, noting words that could be replaced to create more vivid images. Use a thesaurus to find more precise synonyms to replace these words. (For tips on using a thesaurus, see page 529.) Make sure the synonyms you choose accurately convey the emotion or mood you are trying to get across.

 **TEKS** 8.14C

 *Texas Traits* **Revising for Voice**

Personal narratives can be told from the first-person (*I, me*) or third-person (*he, she*) point of view. Whichever point of view you decide to use, when you revise for voice, you need to ensure a consistent point of view throughout your writing.

Is my point of view consistent?

If you write in the first person, you describe things and events subjectively, which means you express your feelings toward the subject. Subjective writing tends to include more vivid word choice because you might include figures of speech or words with strong connotations to express your opinions and feelings. Third person is a good point of view to use if you want to describe things more objectively, which means you leave out your feelings about the subject.

First Person

My stomach burned with fire as I waited for the results of the test.
(The writer expresses how her stomach felt as she waited.)

Third Person

Julio and Ivan paced as they waited for the results of the test.
(The writer describes the boys, but you don't hear their thoughts.)

 Try It   These sentences are written in third person. Imagine you are the person mentioned in each sentence and rewrite it using first person. Use more vivid words to describe the actions and your feelings.

   1. Matt walked into Mr. Smith's classroom for the test.
   2. Marissa looked at the stairs of the tall dark house.
   3. Dylan's face turned red when he saw what had happened.
   4. Jasmyne returned to her house after the fire.
   5. Pedro saw his mother holding a puppy in her arms.
   6. Anita sat on the edge of her seat, waiting to hear if her name would be called.

 Revise   **Check for point of view.** Check your narrative to ensure you have used a consistent point of view throughout it. Rewrite any sentences as needed.

Do I use a range of literary strategies to enhance my tone?

The tone of your writing affects how your readers feel about your topic. You can use a variety of literary strategies to enhance the tone of your writing and help your readers better understand your feelings. Here are just a few strategies you can use to enhance tone, along with examples:

■ **Metaphor:** A figure of speech that describes something by comparing it to something else, without using *like* or *as*. Metaphors help your reader create a vivid mental image.

> Bart was a hog and ate all the pizza.

■ **Simile:** A figure of speech that compares two unlike things using *like* or *as*. Like metaphors, similes allow your reader to create a strong mental image.

> I felt like a thief, stealing her limelight.

■ **Repetition:** When a specific word or phrase is repeated several times, usually in close proximity, to emphasize tone.

> What if I don't make the team? What if I make the team and then fail? What if I make the team, but my best friend doesn't?

The use of "What if" more than once sets a tone of nervousness.

■ **Dialogue:** A conversation between two or more persons. Dialogue allows you to tell your reader exactly what was said and how.

■ **Hyperbole:** A description that exaggerates, usually using extremes or superlatives, to convey a positive or negative attribute.

> I was by far the worst player who had ever tried out.

This hyperbole tells your reader how you feel about your ability to play.

 Imagine you are trying out for a team sport. Your attitude about trying out may range from absolute dread to real excitement. Use the literary strategies explained above to write a sentence that conveys each of the attitudes below.

1. fear **4.** confidence

2. sadness **5.** pride

3. excitement

 Enhance your tone. **As you read through your writing, think of the attitude you want to reveal. Be sure to use a range of strategies to enhance the tone of your writing.**

NARRATIVE

ELPS 2C, 5G

Revising Using a Checklist

Revise

Check your revising. **On a piece of paper, write the numbers 1 to 10. If you can answer "yes" to a question, put a check mark after that number. If not, continue to work with that part of your personal narrative.**

Focus and Coherence

_____ **1.** Do I present my ideas in a logical way?

_____ **2.** Do I present my ideas in the proper form?

Organization

_____ **3.** Do I use dialogue effectively?

_____ **4.** Are my beginning, middle, and ending effective?

Development of Ideas

_____ **5.** Do I use precise words?

_____ **6.** Do I use words that create vivid images?

Voice

_____ **7.** Is my point of view consistent throughout?

_____ **8.** Have I used a variety of literary strategies to enhance the tone?

Conventions

_____ **9.** Have I corrected any punctuation and/or grammar errors?

_____ **10.** Have I checked to be sure all words are spelled correctly?

Revise

Make a clean copy. When you've finished revising your essay, make a clean copy before you begin to edit.

Go Online!

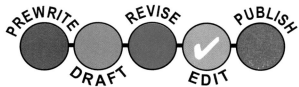

PREWRITE REVISE PUBLISH

DRAFT EDIT

Editing

After you have finished revising your writing, it's time to edit your work for conventions: grammar, mechanics (punctuation, capitalization), and spelling.

Keys to Effective Editing

1. Use a dictionary, a thesaurus, and the "Proofreader's Guide" in the back of this book.

2. Be sure you use a variety of sentences, including simple, compound, and complex sentences.

3. Check your writing for correctness of punctuation, capitalization, spelling, and grammar.

4. Edit on a printed computer copy and then enter your changes on the computer.

5. Use the editing and proofreading marks inside the back cover of this book.

NARRATIVE

Grammar

How can I check for subject-verb agreement?

As you check for subject-verb agreement, you need to remember that subjects and verbs must always agree in number. That means if the subject is singular, the verb must be singular; if the subject is plural, the verb must be plural. (See pages 570–571.)

> Don't forget that most nouns ending in *s* or *es* are plural, and most verbs ending in *s* are singular."

Singular Subject-Verb Agreement

Beth volunteers **at the city's food pantry.**

Plural Subject-Verb Agreement

Her friends volunteer **at the city's park department**.

 Choose a verb for each subject, making sure the two agree in number. Then write a complete sentence for each subject-verb pair. Finally, label each subject-verb pair as singular or plural.

	Subjects	*Verbs*	
1.	The semi driver	take	arranges
2.	Voters	draws	read
3.	They	collect	is
4.	Maurice	receive	blinks
5.	Lights	glows	fade
6.	The student	plays	understand

 Check your subject-verb agreement. Make sure that your subjects agree with the verbs in each of the sentences in your narrative. Make any necessary corrections.

tell share remember
narrate
relate   Writing a Personal Narrative

127

TEKS 8.14D
ELPS 5D

Do my verbs agree with their compound subjects?

To check your subject-verb agreement with compound subjects, you need to remember the following rules:

■ If the compound subject uses *and* as a connector, the verb applies to both subjects and should be plural.

Lia and Ramon carry **the school's banner in the Memorial Day Parade**.

■ If the compound subject uses *or* or *nor* as a connector, the verb must agree with the subject closest to it.

Either band members or Mr. Kurz needs **to collect the flags**.

Read each of the following sentences. Write "A" if the subject and verb agree in number. If they don't agree, rewrite the sentence.

1. Terry and José wants to study German.

2. Neither Colby nor Ramon sings in the chorus.

3. Every weekend, Jason and Leela volunteer at the animal shelter.

4. Their older brother and sister works at the grocery store.

5. After the race, Jodie or Chantell congratulate the winner.

6. Neither the flowers nor the cats triggers Alex's allergies.

7. The music and video games echo through the halls.

8. Every Sunday, Ling and Jules meets at the bowling alley.

9. Either Juan or his brothers is coming to the game tonight.

10. Will Tiana and Julio makes the cookies for the party?

Check your compound subjects. Make sure your compound subjects agree in number with their verbs.

Learning Language

If you have difficulty deciding whether the verb should be singular or plural, try these tips: When two subjects are joined by "and," replace the subjects with "They" to figure out which form of the verb to use. For example, if you don't know whether to say "Lia and Ramon carry," or "Lia and Ramon carries," replace "Lia and Ramon" with "They": *They carry the banner.* When two subjects are joined by "or" or "nor," say the sentence using only the second subject. For example, if you were trying to decide whether to write "Lia or Ramon *has*" or "Lia or Ramon *have* the banner," just say "Ramon": *Ramon has the banner.* Try this with a partner, using the sentences from the Try It.

NARRATIVE

 **TEKS** 8.14C
ELPS 5D, 5F

Sentence Structure

How can I vary my sentences?

When you write, you want to vary the types of sentences you use. This makes your writing more interesting for your reader. You can vary your writing by using a combination of simple, compound, and complex sentences. To understand how these sentences differ, see below.

- A **simple sentence** is an independent clause that has a subject and a predicate.
  Anya likes dogs.

- A **compound sentence** has at least two independent clauses joined by a conjunction.
  Anya likes dogs, so she got a job at the animal shelter.

- A **complex sentence** has an independent clause and one or more dependent clauses.
  As long as Anya keeps her grades up, she plans on working at the shelter two days a week.

 Rewrite the following simple sentences to make them the type of sentence shown in parenthesis.

1. Ms. Phram contacts the radio station. (complex)
2. Tomorrow José will speak to our class. (compound)
3. Maria was waiting for us at the bus stop. (compound)
4. Manuel watches the eagle soar. (complex)
5. Rosa is on the soccer team and gets good grades. (complex)
6. Jennifer wants to be a doctor and studies hard. (complex)
7. Liu plays the flute. (compound)
8. Cameron scored 20 points in the basketball game. (complex)
9. Principal Jenkins will announce the winners. (compound)
10. Lourdes wants to ask Jaime to the dance. (complex)

 Check your sentence types. Skim your writing to ensure you have used a variety of sentence types. Rewrite as necessary to make your writing interesting. Be sure you have included some of each type of sentence described above.

Mechanics: Capitalization

Do I use proper capitalization?

To check that you have used proper capitalization, you need to remember that certain types of words are always capitalized. The most common types of words that need to be capitalized in a personal narrative include the following:

■ the first and last words and all other words in titles except articles (*a, an, the*) and short prepositions (*in, of, for . . .*)

■ the first word of a sentence

■ proper nouns and adjectives formed from proper nouns (*China, Chinese*)

■ the pronoun *I*

■ the first word in a quotation (*Mom said, "Clean your room."*)

■ a person's title when it precedes his or her name (*General Fuller, Judge Vaquera, Mrs. James*)

 Read the following paragraph. Correct any errors in capitalization.

NARRATIVE

Cleaning Cages And Changing lives

I have always loved animals. But we live with uncle Jack—Who's allergic to almost everything—so i cannot have pets. That's why I almost jumped out of my shoes when julie asked, "do you want to volunteer at the smith county Animal Shelter with me?" I asked my Mom right away, and she said, "of course!" That was two weeks ago, and my work there has made my love for animals grow. The Shelter's vet, dr. smith, says i will make a great vet some day. For now, all I do is clean the cages. But I feel like I am making a big difference for both the animals and the people who adopt them.

 Check your capitalization. Make sure you use proper capitalization throughout your essay.

TEKS 8.14D

Editing **Using a Checklist**

Check your editing. On a piece of paper, write the numbers 1 to 12. If you can answer "yes" to a question, put a check mark after that number. If not, continue to edit for that convention.

Conventions

GRAMMAR

_____ **1.** Do I use correct forms of verbs (*had gone*, not *had went*)?

_____ **2.** Do my subjects and verbs agree in number?
(She and I *were* going, not She and I *was* going.)

MECHANICS

_____ **3.** Do I use a mix of simple, compound, and complex sentences?

_____ **4.** Do I start all my sentences with capital letters?

_____ **5.** Do I capitalize all proper nouns?

_____ **6.** Do I use end punctuation after all my sentences?

_____ **7.** Do I use commas after introductory word groups and transitions?

_____ **8.** Do I use commas between equal adjectives?

_____ **9.** Do I punctuate dialogue correctly?

_____ **10.** Do I use apostrophes to show possession? (a *boy's bike*, not a *boys bike*)

SPELLING

_____ **11.** Have I spelled all my words correctly?

_____ **12.** Have I double-checked the words my spell-checker may have missed?

Creating a Title

- Use strong, colorful words: **Marching to Confidence**
- Give the words rhythm: **Step High, Work Hard**
- Be imaginative: **About-Face for Julie**

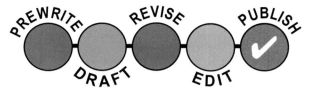

TEKS 8.14E

Go Online!

Publishing

Sharing Your Personal Narrative

After you have worked so hard to improve your writing, make a neat, final copy to share. You may also decide to present your story in the form of a class magazine, a reading, or a recording. (See the suggestions below.)

Publish

Make a final copy to hand in to your teacher. When you write your final copy, follow your teacher's instructions or use the guidelines below to format your story. Create a clean copy of your personal narrative and carefully proofread it.

Focus on Presentation

- Use blue or black ink and write neatly.
- Write your name in the upper left corner of page 1.
- Skip a line and center your title; skip another line and start your writing.
- Double-space your essay.
- Indent every paragraph and leave a one-inch margin on all four sides.
- Write your last name and the page number in the upper right corner of every page after the first one.

NARRATIVE

Share with a Group
Share your writing with a group of peers. Adjust your presentation to your audience's needs. You may need to read slowly or explain terms.

Make a Recording
Record your personal narrative. Give the recording as a gift. Speak clearly and at a slower pace if the gift is for an older adult.

Create a Class Magazine
Make a class magazine. As you design it, keep your audience in mind, and add colorful artwork to make the magazine lively. Staple everything together.

Evaluating a Narrative

To learn how to evaluate a narrative, you'll use the scoring rubric on pages 50–51 and the narratives that follow. These narratives are examples of writing for each score on the rubric.

Notice that this first personal narrative received a score of 4. Read the description for a score of 4 on pages 50–51. Then read the narrative. Use the same steps to study the other examples. Always remember to think about the overall quality of the writing.

Writing that fits a score of 4 is very strong.

Me, a Musician?

The narrative has a clearly defined focus from the beginning.

Who, me? I wasn't the musician in the family. My sister Daneesha was. She's a junior in high school and she's been playing guitar since she was eight. In contrast, I was just Dee. That isn't even my full first name. People liked me but they didn't expect too much of me. My grades were good, but hers were better than anyone's. My teachers all asked whether I was as smart as her. I didn't know what to answer.

I think I started wanting to play the guitar because Daneesha started going out more to babysit or go out with

The narrator's voice is lively and likeable.

some boy. As a result, the guitar was laying around the house with no one to play it. It looked lonely.

One Saturday afternoon, when I had already finished reading my book for the day, I snuck into Daneesha's room. I sat on her bed, unlatched the guitar case, and strummed a really ugly chord. I almost ran out without ever touching it

Vivid details make the reader wonder what's going to happen next.

again! Then I noticed the instruction book on her desk. It had charts showing all the chords and lessons teaching you how to do different things like fingerpicking, which I didn't know anything about then.

Dialogue brings characters to life.

When Daneesha came home for dinner, I already knew E, E minor, and A.

"What are you saying?" she exclaimed when she heard me play my chords. "Who taught you that?"

"I did," I replied humbly.

"And what are you going to do next?" she asked.

"What do you think I should do next?"

She led me by the hand into her room and said in a serious voice, "Girl, we are going to teach you to play this thing."

Transitions show time order and connect ideas.

Daneesha began giving me guitar lessons every Saturday morning. It quickly became my favorite two hours of the entire week. I learned that she's a great teacher. She was always patient with me, because I learned some things better than others. For example, I learned chords quickly, but I had a lot of trouble getting the right wrist position because my hands are small. Similarly, I got to do bar chords early but I couldn't press hard at first.

I practiced and practiced every day after school and all weekend. Suddenly, playing guitar was all I wanted to do. Every so often I would pick my head up from looking at the fingerboard and notice how much better I was than the time before. Daneesha said it was scary.

Ending is coherent with what went before and makes the reader look ahead.

Then it happened: my parents bought me my own guitar! Now Daneesha and I play together. She's still my teacher, but I learn better now that I can copy her at the same time. Sometimes she lets me play lead. I haven't told her yet, but when we grow up we're going to have a band.

NARRATIVE

ELPS 4I, 4K

Writing that fits a score of 3 is strong in most ways.

One Person, Two Languages

I do not remember coming to this country because I was only three then. But my parents have told me about it often. One of the hardest things for them and for me was the language barrier. When I was learning to read and write, I complained alot about having to learn two languages, but then I realized there are many advantages to being bilingual.

Before i started school, life didn't seem that much different to me in America. My parents chose to come to Houston because my father had a brother here, and also it is a city with many Vietnamese people. My father worked on a dirty, old shrimp boat for a while but then he got a better job in a car repair shop. My mother's first job was cleaning up in a nail salon in a rundown mall. Then she borrowed money to open a bakery where she bakes delicious banh mi. They are Vietnamese sub sandwiches. They have light golden crusts and savory meats, pickles, and homemade mayo.

At first we were poor, but I did not mind because I was just a kid. I was too busy having fun. We lived in a tiny apartment, but we hade a TV and there were nice nieghbors in our building. I was the youngest so I was like everybodys' baby.

Everybody in our neighborhood spoke Vietnamese. I can still speak good Vietnamese. But I had a problem at first because the adults around me did not speak good English. My parents did not speak any English at all when they came here. Also I did not have big brothers or sisters to teach me. I am the only child. So I did not get enough practice speaking English when I was that age.

There is clearly defined focus on a phase of life when he changed.

Strategy of using connotations enhances tone.

Narrator's voice expresses genuine feelings.

Sentences should be combined for fluency.

I still had a thick accent when I entered first grade. That was a hard year for me. I had to learn two alphabets at the same time. In school I learned the English alphabet and at home I was starting to read the Vietnamese alphabet. They are similar but the Vietnamese one has 29 letters plus some special characters called digraphs plus accent marks. So it can get confusing. But once you know both, it is a great feeling.

My best friend in first grade was Karen. She was Vietnamese-American but her family came here in the 1980's so she had perfect English. Karen always talked to me at lunch. I think she was not very popular because she had aloud, screechy voice and she cried in class, and I was nice to her so she talked to me every day. It was good for my English, plus she made a friend.

Now that I am in eigth grade, I still have more of an accent than most of my Vietnamese-American friends, but I have no problem in English. It is weird, because a lot of the time I have to translate for my parents. For instance when we have a parent-teacher conference. I think it has helped me grow up faster. I am lucky because I can use two languages. I did not always think I was lucky, but now I do.

> There are some spelling errors, but they do not interfere with readability.

> The writer reflects on decisions and actions.

Writing that fits a score of 2 is strong in some ways.

Beginning does not grab reader's attention.

The writer is telling, not showing and few details are used.

Frequent errors in spelling are distracting.

The narrative keeps a clearly defined focus.

Narrator's voice expresses sincere feelings.

Pet Sitting

I do pet sitting. It has made me more responsible. I started six months ago when this naybor of ours asked me if I wanted to. I said yes. I liked the idea right away. She was going away for a weekend, I think she was going on a trip and asked me if I wanted to pet sit for Ray. Ray is a black lab. I said yes.

She wrote a list of things for me to do like, fill his bowl with water, pour his food and walk him. Ray is a smart dog. He knew where he wanted to walk. He knows all he other dogs in the aria and when they see each other they sniff each other, bark, and run around barking. Its hilairious.

Word got around and people started asking me to pet sit for their pets to. Prety soon I was the most popular pet sitter in the nayborhood. I have three pets now that I sit for a lot, well every one or two weeks. There's Archabald, hes a irish setter. It was hard for me to control him at first but now he knows me and lets me. Mr. Snuff who is a cat. He is an old cat who is black and white. I like him but I hardly ever see him because he hides. Basically I leave his food and water and that's all.

I like pet sitting because I have always liked animals. Now that I am around animals so much I want to have a job with them, maybe a Vet. Pet sitting changed me. It made me think about my goals. I am a more responsable person now. I like having my own spending money and I'm better at saving because I worked hard for it.

Writing that fits a score of 1 is weak.

Fosil Hunting

When we went fosil hunting first we went to glen rose where dinosaur valley state pk is. They have some of the bigest dinosaur foot prints in the world. It's a real small town thogh. You can go up to them and put your hand in them to see how much biger the dinosaur foot print is. That was very cool I was impresed.

We liked that so much we disided to go fosil hunting on our own. Next weekend we did. We broght two hamers a brush, gogles for all of us and plastic bags. Then we went to work. We parked by side of the road and walked in til we came to a clif. You could see the layers of rock where the prehistoric animals had lived. 113 milion years ago! This area was under the sea and when sea animals died they sank to the botom and got covered up. They turned into rock. When the land rose the fosils were in the rocks.

We al took turns with the hamers. Some of us found a fosil and some didnt. But we still wanted to find more fossils so the next week we went on a feild trip at McKinney Falls. The gide showed us fosils along Onion Creek. They were sea creatchurs with coiled shells. Some were small and some were large the ones he showed us were small.

The event changed me because before I was not interested in fosils but now I am.

Lack of clearly defined, coherent focus

Many errors in spelling, grammar, and mechanics

Lack of vivid detail

NARRATIVE

Evaluating and Reflecting on Your Writing

You've put a lot of time and effort into your personal narrative. Now take some time to score and think about your writing. On your own paper, finish each sentence starter below. To score your writing, refer to the scoring rubric on pages 50–51 and the examples you just read.

My Personal Narrative

1. The best score for my personal narrative is...

2. It's the best score because...

3. The best part of my narrative is...

4. The part that still needs work is...

5. The main thing I learned about writing a personal narrative is...

Narrative Writing

Biographical Narrative

What would it be like to live another person's life? Imagine being your brother on his first day at army boot camp or your grandmother as she decided to leave Peru and travel to the United States.

Writing a biographical narrative gives you the chance to take a walk in someone else's shoes. By learning about another person's life experiences and writing about them, you can feel as if you are experiencing the events yourself.

In this chapter, you will read a biographical narrative about a young girl's decision to leave her homeland. Then you will write your own biographical narrative.

Writing Guidelines

Subject:	**An experience of someone you know**
Purpose:	**To tell a story**
Form:	**Biographical narrative**
Audience:	**Classmates**

Biographical Narrative

A biographical narrative tells a true story from someone else's life. Alayna wrote about her grandmother Maria's decision to come to the United States as a student from Peru.

Beginning

The beginning introduces the main character and the choice she faces.

Middle

The middle describes the setting and uses action and dialogue to develop the narrative.

A Life-Changing Decision

"So, Maria," asked her father, paging nervously through his newspaper, "have you decided yet?"

"No, Papa," Maria answered.

It was the spring of 1965, and Maria had a life-changing decision to make. Would she stay with her family and friends in Lima, Peru, or accept the scholarship she was being offered at a university in the United States? She knew the choice would change her life forever.

Maria gazed out at the plaza in front of her home and heard the crystal-toned chimes of the beautiful cathedral in the distance. Her eyes wandered then to her father's bookstore, where she worked, just walking distance away. She could almost smell the familiar musty odor of the old books that lined the dusty shelves. Maria sighed. Lima was home, but the United States would let her fulfill her dream.

Maria had always wanted to be a nurse, but when she had been a little girl, polio had withered her right leg. The disease had left her with a permanent limp. In Peru, a person like Maria could not easily become a nurse, but in the United States she knew she could follow her dream.

"We need to notify the university by tomorrow," her father said softly, his newspaper crinkling.

NARRATIVE

Middle

The tension builds to a high point.

Maria's heart started pounding, and her mind raced. The future was so uncertain, but part of her loved that fact! Did she have the courage to go to America? Could she bear to stay in Peru?

"Papa, I want to go to America!"

Maria's father jumped up and came to her, hugging her tightly. His eyes looked sad, but he smiled and said, "You will be able to do so much in the United States. They have a modern way of thinking, and if you work hard, they'll give you a chance to live your dreams."

A few months later, Maria's family and friends took her to the airport. They held hands in a circle while they sang "La Flor de la Canela," a Peruvian folk song about love and family. Maria waved one last good-bye before disappearing down the long hallway. With each step, she knew she was growing up.

Ending

The ending shows how the experience changed the person.

As the plane lifted off the ground, Maria felt in her heart that she would never come back to Peru to live. Through tear-filled eyes, she watched the cities, villages, and lush, green mountains of her home get smaller and smaller. She closed her eyes and took a deep breath. Her new life had begun.

Responding to the reading. Answer the following questions about the biographical narrative.

☐ **Development of Ideas** **(1) What details help flesh out the ideas for the reader?**

☐ **Organization (2) How does the writer organize the details to move the story forward?**

☐ **Voice (3) What words or phrases engage the reader's interest? Which ones show how the characters felt?**

 **TEKS** 8.14A, 8.16
ELPS 4G, 5G

Prewriting **Selecting a Topic**

To find an appropriate topic for her biographical narrative, Alayna considered a range of strategies. She decided a line diagram would best fit her needs. She began by writing down on the diagram people she knew well. Under each name, she wrote interesting stories they had told her.

Line Diagram

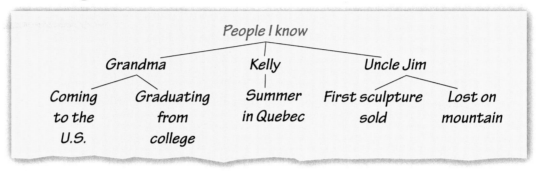

 Choose your topic. Create your own line diagram. Think of people you know and interesting stories they have told you. Choose a story that you would like to learn about and share with others.

Gathering Details

Consider the consequences of characters' actions. Alayna used the 5 W's and H to gather details from Grandma about her decision to come to the U.S.

5 W's Chart

1. _Who_ was involved? Maria, Papa, and her family and friends
2. _What_ happened? Maria decided to leave Peru for the U.S.
3. _When_ did the event happen? Spring of 1965
4. _Where_ did the event happen? Lima, Peru
5. _Why_ did it happen? Maria's dream to be a nurse
6. _How_ did she feel about the event? Scared, sad, and excited

 Gather details. Write down questions based on the 5 W's and H. Then ask your subject to tell his or her story and reflect on the consequences of the actions he or she took. Write down the answers to your questions.

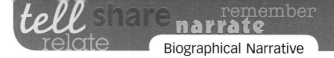

TEKS 8.14B
ELPS 5G

Organizing Details

Choosing the appropriate organizational strategy is important in any writing. Since most biographical narratives are organized chronologically, Alayna used a time line to organize what she had gathered about her grandmother's story. Above the line, she wrote the events. Below it, she wrote details.

Time Line

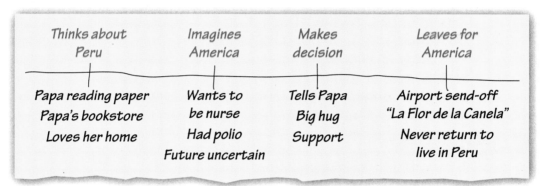

Thinks about Peru	Imagines America	Makes decision	Leaves for America
Papa reading paper	Wants to be nurse	Tells Papa	Airport send-off
Papa's bookstore	Had polio	Big hug	"La Flor de la Canela"
Loves her home	Future uncertain	Support	Never return to live in Peru

Prewrite

Create a time line. Use the model above to help you organize your details into a time line. Above the line, list key events. Below it, list details you would like to include in your biographical narrative.

NARRATIVE

Texas Traits

★ Focus on the Texas Traits

Organization

Narratives follow a plot line that sustains reader interest. The **beginning** sets up an engaging storyline that grabs the reader's attention. The **rising action** builds suspense. The **high point** brings the person and the conflict face-to-face, and the **ending** tells how the person changed. Create a similar plot line for your story.

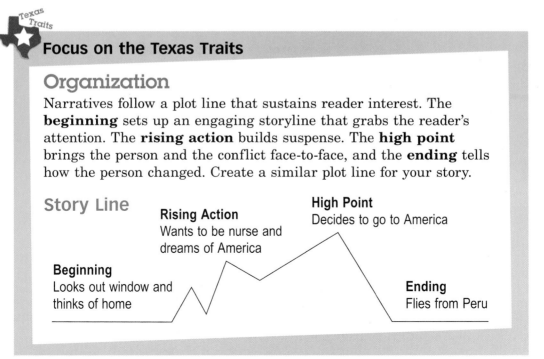

Story Line

High Point
Decides to go to America

Rising Action
Wants to be nurse and dreams of America

Beginning
Looks out window and thinks of home

Ending
Flies from Peru

144

 ELPS 5G

Drafting **Creating Your First Draft**

As you write your first draft, be sure to follow your time line. Use the tips below as a guide.

Beginning

Grab the reader's attention and set the stage for your story.

- **Set the time and place.** *It was the spring of 1965 . . . in Lima, Peru.*
- **Use sensory details to make the setting believable.** *Heard the crystal-toned chimes... smelled the musty odor of the old books.*
- **Start in the middle of the action.** *"So, Maria," asked her father, "have you decided yet?"*

Rising Action

Pull the reader into the story and build suspense.

- **Include thoughts and feelings.** *Lima was so comfortable and familiar, but the United States would let her fulfill her dream.*
- **Use action.** *Maria's heart started pounding, and her mind raced.*
- **Use sensory details.** *Maria's father jumped up and came to her, hugging her tightly. His eyes looked sad, but he smiled and said, . . .*

High Point

Use a range of literary strategies to enhance the tone of the conflict.

- **Use questions to define the high point.** *Did she have the courage to go to America? Could she bear to stay in Peru?*
- **Use dialogue to heighten the moment.** *"I want to go to America!"*

Ending

Describe how the person changed.

- **Describe the final scene.** *Through tear-filled eyes, she watched the cities, villages, and lush, green mountains of her home get smaller and smaller.*
- **Show how the event changed the person.** *She closed her eyes and took a deep breath. Her new life had begun.*

Write the first draft. Use your time line (page 143) and follow the tips above. Focus on getting all your ideas on paper.

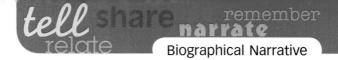
Revising Improving Your Writing

Once you finish your first draft, take a break. When you come back to your story, it will be easier for you to see the parts that need improvement. Check your work for the following traits of writing.

☐ **Focus and Coherence** Remain focused on the main idea throughout.

> *In Peru, a person like Maria could not easily become a nurse, but in the United States she knew she could follow her dream.*

☐ **Organization** Logically link each sentence to the next.

> *Maria waved one last good-bye before disappearing down the long hallway. With each step, she knew she was growing up.*

☐ **Voice** Make sure that the voice fits the person and the event.

> *The future was so uncertain, but part of her loved that fact!*

☐ **Development of Ideas** Be original in your writing and "flesh out" ideas with fresh images and strong writing.

> *Through tear-filled eyes, she watched the cities, villages, and lush, green mountains of her home get smaller and smaller.*

☐ **Conventions** Vary your sentences, using compound and complex sentences.

> *Maria's heart started pounding, and her mind raced . . . . Maria's father jumped up and came to her, hugging her tightly.*

> **Choppy**
>
> *They held hands in a circle. They sang "La Flor de la Canela." It was a Peruvian folk song about love . . .*
>
> **Combined**
>
> *They held hands in a circle while they sang "La Flor de la Canela," a Peruvian folk song about love . . .*

Revise your narrative. Use the guidelines above as you review your story and make changes.

 **TEKS** 8.14D, 8.14E
ELPS 5D

Editing Checking for Conventions

When you're finished revising, it's time to edit your biographical narrative for conventions.

Conventions

Review your grammar, mechanics, and spelling. The following checklist can help you.

GRAMMAR

_____ **1.** Do I use correct forms of verbs (*had wanted* not *did wanted*)?

_____ **2.** Do my subjects and verbs agree in number? (We *were* going . . . not We *was* going . . .)

_____ **3.** Do I use the right words? (*new, knew*)

MECHANICS

_____ **4.** Do I use commas correctly?

_____ **5.** Do I include the correct punctuation at the end of every sentence? (*Could she bear to stay in Peru?*)

_____ **6.** Do I put quotation marks and punctuation in the right place?

_____ **7.** Do I use apostrophes to show possession? (*Maria's family*)

_____ **8.** Do I capitalize all proper nouns? (*Lima, Peru*)

_____ **9.** Do I begin every sentence with a capital letter?

SPELLING

_____ **10.** Have I checked my spelling?

Edit your biographical narrative. After you edit, let someone else look over your work for anything you missed. Then create a final copy and proofread it.

Publishing Sharing Your Writing

A biographical narrative can bring you closer to friends and family. Share your story with the person who lived it.

Share your biographical narrative. Read your story to the person who experienced it and give him or her a copy to keep.

Narrative Writing
Across the Curriculum

Narratives set a course for adventure. In history class, you could write a historical narrative about being the barrel maker aboard the *Mayflower*. In math, you might write about your adventures learning new math concepts. For science class, you might even write a narrative about being a gigantic thunderhead!

This chapter contains samples of narratives like these. It also helps you create e-mails and respond to prompts on writing tests. No matter what the class or assignment, narrative writing can bring any subject to life.

What's Ahead

- **Social Studies:** Recalling a Historical Moment
- **Math:** Writing a Math Autobiography
- **Science:** Writing About a Natural Formation
- **Practical Writing:** Creating an E-Mail Message
- **Writing for Assessment**

Social Studies:
Recalling a Historical Moment

American history is filled with important events. In the letter below, a student writes about a historical moment as if he had experienced it firsthand.

The **beginning** contains an opinion.

The **middle** expresses a complaint.

The **ending** contains a request from the letter writer.

Dear John,

It has been several months since the *Mayflower* landed and we arrived in this New World. The winter was cruel and cold, but somehow we survived it. Now the weather is changing, and spring will soon be here. We are beginning to carve a new settlement out of this land of dark forests. This New World, despite its challenges, is a fine place and I know we will make it our home for many years to come.

While we will soon be able to grow food, we have a desperate need for clothing and other comforts. We have no materials to make new clothes and those we have are worn and old. Many of us are dressed in tatters and suffer terribly from the cold. It is a serious problem.

I know you intend to join our settlement on the next ship coming from England. Could you talk to the expedition's leaders and tell them of our dire need of clothing? We could use food supplies, too, although I imagine the ship will be well stocked with them. The clothing, however, is a need they may have overlooked. I will be deeply grateful for whatever you can do. I look forward to seeing your smiling face among us soon.

Your faithful friend,

Brian

TEKS 8.16, 8.17B
ELPS 3H, 5G

NARRATIVE

Writing Tips

Before you write . . .

- **Select a topic.**
  Choose a historic moment to write a letter about, such as Paul Revere's ride, crossing the prairies, or the day Teddy Roosevelt refused to shoot a bear cub. Page through your history textbook for other ideas. Select a single important moment so that you can write a well-focused narrative letter about it to a friend.
- **Research your topic.**
  Read about the event and gather details about the place and time.

During your writing . . .

- **Write as if you experienced or witnessed the event.**
  Use the "I" voice. Imagine yourself to be part of this event in order to get a feel for the experience. Then record what you would see, hear, and so forth. Include feelings and reflections.
- **Show how the event affected you.**
  Put yourself in the center of the action and imagine a complaint, an opinion, or a request you might have had.
- **Ask for a response from the other person.**
  Make a request of the other person to do something that will address your complaint, fulfill a need, or answer a question.

After you've written a first draft . . .

- **Revise your first draft.**
  Check your letter's format and organization to be sure it is correct and easy to follow.
- **Check for accuracy.**
  Double-check your historical facts—dates, names, and so on.
- **Edit for correctness.**
  Check for errors in punctuation, spelling, and grammar.

 Select a moment from American history. Research the event and place yourself in the middle of it. Write a letter to a friend or family member that is historically accurate and engages your reader.

Math: Writing a Math Autobiography

A math autobiography lets students reflect on their experiences with math. In the following autobiography, a student writes about how she has used math in the past and in the present, and how she expects to use it in the future.

Math Matters

The **beginning** reflects on the student's first experiences with math.

I remember the first day I stopped using my fingers to add and subtract. It felt so good to finally "get it." I've come a long way since then, but I still feel just as good every time I learn a new math skill.

The **middle** gives details about the way the student currently uses math.

I use math a lot in my daily life. When I was younger, I used math to do simple things like make change. Now I can solve more difficult problems. For example, my dad and I put a wood floor in our game room. We took measurements and used equations to find the square footage. That was especially tough because the game room has two small closets. Afterward, Dad and I were able to decide how much wood to buy.

I've come so far in math that now I'm a math tutor. I helped one boy, Chris, understand how to isolate variables. Suddenly, all those equations didn't scare him anymore. He finished his assignment and got an A on it.

The **ending** suggests how she will use math in the future.

I feel great that I can do so many things with math. It's even better now that I can help other kids. I know I'll find many new ways to use my math skills in the future for school, work, and everyday life.

Writing Tips

Before you write . . .

- **Focus on thoughts and feelings about math.**
  Think of math experiences that made you proud, nervous, excited, or confused. Remember the first time you learned to multiply and the times you've used math in everyday life.

- **Select specific examples to mention.**
  Include only those examples that will appeal to your reader and make an interesting personal narrative.

During your writing . . .

- **Focus on examples.**
  Describe specific times when math has been helpful —or difficult—for you.

- **Shape your narrative.**
  Give your story about math a beginning, middle, and end. Let your reader know how you feel about math—whether you like it or struggle with it, and why.

After you've written a first draft . . .

- **Revise your first draft.**
  Add any examples that would clarify your focus and bring more coherence to your narrative; remove examples that don't.

- **Check your organization.**
  Make sure the sentences and details they contain are linked to one another in a logical way.

- **Edit for correctness.**
  Check for errors in punctuation, capitalization, spelling, and grammar.

NARRATIVE

 Write your own math autobiography. Share specific examples that tell the reader about your overall experience with math.

Science:
Writing About a Natural Formation

When you use "personification" in your writing, you give human qualities or characteristics to a nonhuman thing. In science, you can use personification to imagine being a natural formation. In the narrative below, a student personified a thunderhead.

The **beginning** introduces the natural formation.

The **middle** provides details from the point of view of the formation.

The **ending** completes the narrative.

Big Fellow in the Sky

People sometimes call me a cumulonimbus. That's right, I'm a cloud. My body is made of tiny water droplets that attach to dust, sea salt, and even pollution. (Yuck!)

The first half of my name, cumulus, means "heap." That describes how I begin my life, like a heap of puffy cotton balls. I fly low and constantly change shape to look like different animals. It's a fun way to pass the time on warm, sunny days.

The second half of my name, nimbus, means "precipitation." As the sun warms the air close to the ground, I grow from a modest cumulus cloud to a monster cumulonimbus – a thunderhead. The warm air rises rapidly, pushing the tiny water droplets inside me higher and higher. They bump into each other and form raindrops.

My negatively charged electrons get attracted to the positively charged protons in the ground. Then the positive and negative charges crash into a bolt of electricity making me a shocking fellow. I immediately hear a rolling round of applause, er, thunder. It's great to be a cumulonimbus!

Writing Tips

Before you write . . .

- **Select a topic that interests you.**
  Check your science book for natural formations to write about. Consider formations such as waterspouts, hurricanes, glaciers, fault lines, craters, or canyons.

- **Research the topic.**
  Check your textbook, an encyclopedia, or a Web site to learn about the formation you have chosen.

During your writing . . .

- **Write from the point of view of the formation.**
  Use the "I" voice and imagine yourself as the formation. Tell about where you come from, what you do, and how you change.

- **Include thoughts and feelings.**
  Indicate what your formation does and thinks, likes and dislikes.

- **Include reflections.**
  Make sure you include reflections on your actions (or the actions that shaped you) and their consequences.

After you've written a first draft . . .

- **Revise your narrative.**
  Make sure your essay is organized logically. Check to see that it is informative and easy to follow.

- **Check for accuracy.**
  Double-check the facts in your story.

- **Edit for correctness.**
  Review your work, looking for errors in punctuation, spelling, capitalization, and grammar.

NARRATIVE

 Select a natural formation that you'd enjoy writing a narrative about. Research your topic and write a story from the point of view of the formation. Share your narrative with your classmates.

Practical Writing:
Creating an E-Mail Message

E-mail has become an important link between teachers and students. In the following narrative e-mail, a student tells a teacher about a tour she went on for extra credit.

The **heading** includes sending information and a subject line.

Send Mail or Discussion Group Message

Send   Quote   Address   Attach   Spelling   Save   Security   Stop

To ▾ ▸ Skimbell@groverclevelandjrhigh.edu

Subject: Extra-credit trip to the recycling plant   **Priority:** Normal ▾

Normal ▾   12 ▾

Dear Mrs. Kimbell:

The **beginning** tells the reason for the e-mail.

Thanks for your suggestions about interesting places to visit. I decided to go on the recycling plant tour and was glad I did. I took Jesse along, and we learned a lot. I didn't know our city recycles a hundred tons of bottles, cans, and paper each day.

The **middle** describes the events of the day.

When we walked into the plant, we saw a giant vacuum that sucks up paper from mixed recyclables. Then we watched strong magnets lift cans off a conveyor belt and drop them into holding bins. Finally, we saw the baled recyclables ready to be shipped off to reuse. I couldn't believe how much stuff there was.

I'm now more aware of recycling around me. After our tour, I pointed out that almost every container our lunches came in is made of recyclable materials, including plastic containers and paper bags.

The **ending** closes with the writer reflecting on her decision.

On the way home, we talked about what we can do to get our school more involved in recycling. Visiting the recycling plant has made me a different person. I realize how important recycling is and how it's saving our planet. Maybe we could discuss some of our ideas after class sometime.

Sincerely,

Angie Howard
ahoward@groverclevelandjrhigh.edu

Writing Tips

Before you write . . .

- **List the details you want to report.**
  Write down your experience, putting events in time order.

During your writing . . .

- **Complete the e-mail heading.**
  Fill in the address line and make sure each character is correct. Then write a subject line that clearly indicates the reason for the e-mail.

- **Greet the reader and give your reason for writing.**
  Start with a polite greeting. Follow by telling why you are sending the e-mail.

- **Be conversational but proper.**
  Make sure your sentences are clear and complete. You may use an informal voice, but your grammar should be correct.

- **Describe what happened and what was said.**
  Describe your experience and include any important conversations you had.

- **End politely.**
  Close with "Sincerely," or another closing you might use in a letter. Type your name below.

After you've written a first draft . . .

- **Reread your e-mail.**
  Don't simply press "Send." Make sure your e-mail is clear and complete.

- **Check for correctness.**
  Check for errors in grammar, mechanics (punctuation, capitalization), and spelling.

NARRATIVE

 Think of a school-related event that you enjoyed and select a teacher or mentor who was involved with the event. Write an e-mail message to the person, sharing your experience. (You can send the e-mail or merely treat it as a class assignment.)

Narrative Writing
Writing for Assessment

Many state and school writing tests include a prompt that asks you to recall a personal experience or respond to a "what if" question. Study the following sample prompt.

Prompt

Life is one long string of learning experiences. From the time that you were a newborn to your eighth-grade year, you have learned many lessons. Think back to an experience that taught you an important lesson. Describe the experience and what you learned.

Analyzing the Prompt

Whenever you respond to a writing prompt, the first step is to make sure you understand exactly what the prompt is asking to do. As you read a prompt, ask yourself the following questions:

- What genre or form is the prompt asking me to write?
- What topic does the prompt ask me to write about?
- What purpose does the prompt give for the piece of writing?
- Does the prompt identify an audience?
- What specific information does the prompt tell me to include?

Some prompts will not provide the answers to all these questions. For example, many prompts do not specify an audience, in which case your audience is the person who will be scoring the assessment. Any questions that the prompt does not answer, you will need to decide for yourself.

As with any writing that you do, it's important to make sure you know your purpose. Look for key words in the prompt that tell what your purpose will be. In this case, the prompt says "describe the experience and what you learned." *Describe* is a key word that tells your purpose. The specific information you need to include is details about your experience and your thoughts about what you learned.

TEKS 8.14A
ELPS 4I, 4J, 4K, 5G

Prewriting **Selecting a Form**

The prompt doesn't tell you what form of writing to use. How can you decide which one would be most appropriate? Think about which form or genre the prompt seems to call for.

Is the prompt asking you to:
- describe a person or place?
- offer a solution to a problem?
- explain how to do something?
- share a personal experience?
- give information?
- persuade your audience to do something?

Answering the questions above will help you decide on a genre.

Carl could see that the prompt was asking him to share a personal experience. He decided the best form was a narrative because it allowed him to tell a story of a time when he learned an important lesson.

NARRATIVE

Planning the Writing

Carl recalled the lesson he learned from rope climbing at summer camp. He decided to write about that experience. To plan his draft, Carl used a time line. It helped him choose events and organize them.

Time Line

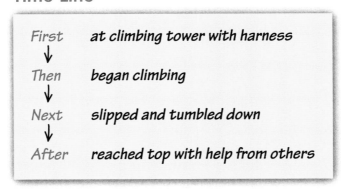

First → at climbing tower with harness

Then → began climbing

Next → slipped and tumbled down

After → reached top with help from others

Response to a Narrative Prompt

Next, Carl used his time line to write his personal narrative. Read Carl's narrative and think about how well he addressed his purpose and form.

The **beginning** sets up the experience.

Each **middle** paragraph describes events that took place.

A Hard Lesson to Learn

Whenever I face a challenging situation, I tell myself, "This will make a good story—if I ever get through it!" Challenges may not be fun, but they often teach important lessons. Just last summer at camp, I faced a rope course that taught me to believe in myself and other people as well.

I stood in front of a 50-foot-tall climbing tower built out of telephone poles. Handholds were bolted to the sides of the poles, and I wore a special harness with belaying ropes. Still, the climb to the top would take all the arm and leg strength I had, as well as faith in two people I hardly knew.

The rope attached to my harness went up over the top of the tower and back down into a locking device held by my cabin mate, Eric. Another boy named Taylor backed him up, but I wasn't sure I could trust either of them. It was too late to turn back, though. I didn't want Eric, Taylor, or other campers to see me lose my nerve.

Numbly, I stepped to the base of the tower. I grabbed a pair of handholds. The rope on my harness drew tight as Eric pulled on it. Swallowing my fear, I lifted myself up onto the pole. As I rose, Eric and Taylor drew in the slack of my belaying rope. Soon I was 10 feet off the ground, then 20, and then 30. I paused, smiling as I caught my breath. I should have believed in myself.

 **ELPS** 2G, 2H, 2I, 3D, 3E, 3G, 3H, 4C, 4G, 4I, 4K

NARRATIVE

The **ending** paragraph reflects on the experience.

Suddenly I slipped, tumbling away from the tower. My belaying line snapped tight, and I hung there, 25 feet up.

"I got you," Eric called out. "Swing back over and grab on."

I did, and realized I should have believed in Eric and Taylor, too. Panting a little, I continued to climb until I reached the platform at the top. When I got there, I cheered, and so did Eric, Taylor, and everyone down below.

That day, I learned that it took two things for me to climb that tower. First, I had to believe in myself. Second, I had to believe in others. That's a lesson I'll be able to use throughout my life.

 Respond to the reading. Answer the following questions to see how the traits were used in Carl's response.

☐ **Focus and Coherence** (1) What is the focus of this narrative? (2) What did the writer learn?

☐ **Organization** (3) How did the writer organize the paragraphs in the narrative?

☐ **Voice** (4) What words and phrases express how the writer's mood changed within the narrative?

 Literature Connection: An example of a narrative is "Harriet Tubman: Conductor on the Underground Railroad" by Anne Petry.

 ELPS 3H, 4I, 4J 5G

Writing Tips

Use the following tips as a guide when responding to a narrative writing prompt.

Before you write . . .

- **Understand the prompt.**
  Remember that a narrative prompt asks you to tell a story. Decide on a form for your writing.

- **Plan your time wisely.**
  Take several minutes to plan your writing. Use a graphic organizer like a time line to help with planning your writing.

Time Line

Subject:	_____
First:	_____
	_____
	_____
Finally:	_____

During your drafting . . .

- **Decide on a focus for your narrative.**
  Use key words from the prompt as you write your focus statement.

- **Be selective.**
  Tell only the main events in your experience.

- **End in a meaningful way.**
  Reflect on the importance of the narrative.

After you've written a first draft . . .

- **Check for completeness and correctness.**
  Present events in order. Delete any unnecessary details and neatly correct any errors.

 Plan and write a response. Respond to the prompt on page 156. Complete your writing within the period of time your teacher gives you. Remember to select a form and use the tips above.

Narrative Writing in Review

Purpose: In narrative writing, you *tell a story* about something that has happened.

Topics: Narrate . . . an experience that taught you something,
an experience that changed you,
a story about another person's life,
a time of personal change, or
a memorable event.

Prewriting

Select a topic from your own (or another's) life. List important times in your life to use as possible topics. (See page 104.)

Organize key events. Do some freewriting to arrange key events in chronological order. (See page 106.)

Remember the details by creating a chart of details and feelings. (See page 107.)

Drafting

In the beginning, grab the reader's attention and use transitions to smoothly move the reader through your opening paragraph. (See page 111.)

In the middle, use dialogue, sensory details, and personal feelings. "Show, don't tell," to help the reader understand the experience. (See pages 112–113.)

In the ending, tie the beginning to the ending or explain the importance of the event or experience. (See page 114.)

Revising

Review the focus and coherence, organization, and development of ideas first. Then check **voice** and **conventions.** Combine and expand sentences to eliminate choppy writing. (See pages 116–124.)

Editing

Check your writing for conventions. Check your writing for subject-verb agreement, and ask a friend to check the writing, too. (See pages 126–130.)

Make a final copy and proofread it for errors before sharing it with other people. (See page 131.)

Assessing

Use the rubric to assess your finished writing. (See pages 50–51.)

NARRATIVE

describe
define

TEXAS
WRITE
SOURCE
Online
www.hmheducation.com/tx/writesource

Expository Writing

Writing Focus

- **Expository Paragraph**
- **Classification Essay**
- **Comparison-Contrast Essay**

Grammar Focus

- **Showing Possession**
- **Punctuating Dependent Clauses**

Learning Language

Read the meanings and share answers to the questions.

1. An expository essay is one that explains something.
   What can you write an expository essay about?
2. A category is a group of similar things.
   Oranges, apples, and bananas can be put into what category?
3. To compare is to say how two or more things are alike.
   Compare your two favorite books.
4. To contrast is to say how two or more things are different.
   Contrast your two favorite books.

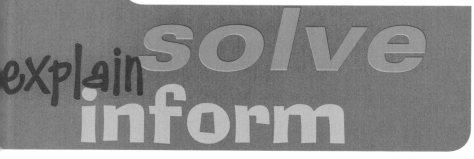

explain solve
inform

Expository Writing

Expository Paragraph

Astronomers estimate that the universe contains ten thousand billion billion stars. That's a 1 with 22 zeroes after it! Even so, those innumerable stars fall into just seven main types. Seven is a much more manageable number than ten thousand billion billion!

Whenever you separate something into types or parts, you are classifying it. In this chapter, you will write a classification paragraph that will break a topic into categories. When you are finished, you can share with your reader a part of your universe.

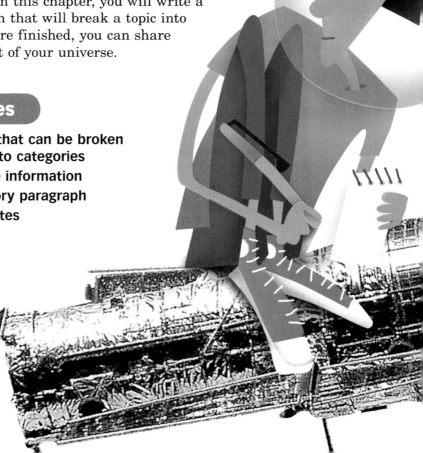

Writing Guidelines

Subject: A topic that can be broken down into categories

Purpose: To share information

Form: Expository paragraph

Audience: Classmates

⭐ ELPS 5B, 5G

Expository Paragraph

The classification paragraph is a simple way to present the parts of a topic. It begins with a **topic sentence** that tells what the paragraph will be about. The **body** sentences that follow present the categories along with specific details about each. Finally, the **closing sentence** wraps up the paragraph. The following paragraph classifies the types of "planets" in our solar system.

Topic Sentence

Body

Closing Sentence

Three Types of Planets

People often think all planets are alike, but there are actually three types of planets in the solar system. The terrestrial planets are made of rock and metal and are closest to the sun. These include the midsize planets Mercury, Venus, Earth, and Mars. They rotate slowly and don't have many moons. Farther from the sun are the planets called gas giants, Jupiter, Saturn, Uranus, and Neptune. They are called gas giants because they are formed from gases such as hydrogen and helium. Gas giants rotate fast and have many moons. Finally, planetoids are objects made up of rock and ice and are too small to be true "planets." Planetoids sometimes even get pulled into a planet's gravitational field and become moons themselves. Whether they are terrestrials, gas giants, or planetoids, the planets in the solar system are fascinating.

Respond to the reading. On your own paper, answer each of the following questions.

☐ **Development of Ideas** **(1) What three categories does the writer give?**

☐ **Organization** **(2) How does the writer organize the specific categories (order of location, order of importance, time order)?**

☐ **Voice** **(3) What words or phrases show that the writer is knowledgeable about the topic?**

TEKS 8.14A

Prewriting Selecting a Topic

To select a topic, make a diagram. Select two things you know about and write them at the top. Then list the different categories that can be found in each topic. The writer of the paragraph on page 164 created the following diagram and put a star next to the topic she wanted to write about.

Line Diagram

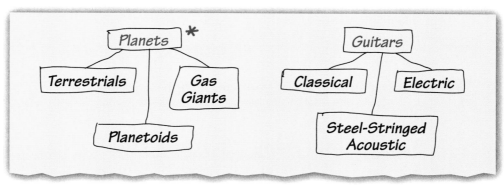

Create a diagram and select a topic. Using the diagram above as a guide, create your own, listing two or three topics that interest you along with their categories. Put a star next to the topic you would like to write about.

Writing a Topic Sentence

Many subjects are too broad for a single paragraph. You can't sum up the universe, for example, in one paragraph. However, you can explain the types of planets in our solar system. Your topic sentence should (1) name the topic, and (2) mention its categories. A simple formula follows.

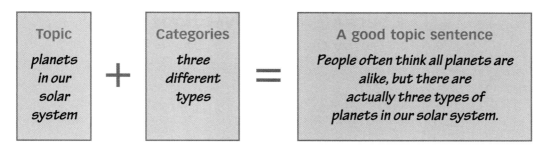

Topic		Categories		A good topic sentence
planets in our solar system	**+**	three different types	**=**	*People often think all planets are alike, but there are actually three types of planets in our solar system.*

Write your topic sentence. Use the basic formula above to write a topic sentence for your paragraph. You may need to try a few different versions to make this sentence say exactly what you want it to say.

EXPOSITORY

TEKS 8.14B, 8.20A, 8.21

Drafting Developing Your First Draft

A classification paragraph consists of a topic sentence, a body with supporting details, and a closing sentence. These steps allow you to create a focused piece of writing.

- Include your topic sentence at the beginning of the paragraph.
- Write body sentences that build on the ideas in the topic sentence and explain your topic's categories. Arrange the details in the best possible order: order of importance, chronological (time) order, or order of location. (See page 613.)
- Sum up the topic with a thoughtful closing sentence.

 Write the first draft of your paragraph. Write freely and don't worry about making mistakes. Just get all your ideas on paper.

Revising Improving Your Paragraph

After you finish your paragraph, check it for *focus and coherence, organization, development of ideas*, and *voice*.

 Review your paragraph. Think about the following questions as you revise your writing.

1 Is my writing focused on one controlling idea? Does everything relate to that idea?

2 Are my categories and details organized in the best way?

3 Are my ideas developed enough to help my reader understand them?

4 Do I sound knowledgeable about and interested in my topic?

Editing Checking for Conventions

After you revise your paragraph, check it for *conventions*.

 Edit your work. Answer the questions below.

1 Is my capitalization correct?

2 Have I used punctuation correctly?

3 Have I spelled all the words correctly?

4 Have I showed possession correctly?

 Proofread your paragraph. After making a neat copy of your paragraph, check it one more time for errors.

Expository Writing
Classification Essay

Medieval soldiers came in three varieties: foot soldiers, archers, and knights. Foot soldiers dressed in mismatched armor and carried simple weapons such as poleaxes or flails. Archers often wore no armor, but stood behind other troops to shoot their long bows. Knights wore suits of armor, fought from horseback, and used swords, lances, and shields.

When you identify the types or categories of something, you are using classification. In this chapter, you will write a classification essay. The key is to select a topic that you know well and can separate into categories.

Writing Guidelines

Subject: A topic that can be broken down into categories
Purpose: To share information
Form: Classification essay
Audience: Classmates

Understanding Your Goals

When you plan your expository essay, keep the following goals in mind. Understanding how these goals relate to the traits of writing will help you write an excellent expository essay. The scoring rubric on pages 50–51 will also help you.

Focus and Coherence

Write about only one topic. To help your readers understand your topic, clearly state your controlling idea at the beginning, and choose categories that directly relate to that topic. Then write a conclusion that sums up what you are trying to explain in your essay.

Organization

Develop a precise pattern of organization for each category and clearly connect the details.

Development of Ideas

Choose a topic that can be broken down into at least three classes or categories. Then support each with a variety of interesting details.

Voice

Use words and details that fit your purpose and connect with the reader.

Conventions

Use grammar, mechanics (punctuation, capitalization), and spelling correctly.

 Literature Connection. You can find expository paragraphs under the headings "Three Sets of Legs" and "Man or Machine?" in the article "Robo-Legs."

Classification Essay

In the expository essay below, the writer identifies and explains three types of armor that have been developed over thousands of years of history. The key parts of the expository essay are listed in the left margin.

Centuries of Protection

Beginning

The beginning introduces the topic and presents the controlling idea. (**underlined**).

Officer T. J. Cosford, a guest speaker at Cooper School, showed students a bulletproof vest. This type of body armor once saved his partner's life. While armor has been used throughout the ages, the materials used to make it have changed a great deal over time. From chain mail to steel suits to Kevlar vests, armor has protected people for centuries.

Middle

The first middle paragraph describes the first category and explains its drawbacks.

Even though armor had been around for more than 2,500 years, the first important change in armor took place around 1000 C.E. That was when soldiers began wearing chain mail. Chain mail was made of thousands of little metal rings hooked together. The thin rings formed a kind of metal cloth that could be draped around a soldier's body. It was lighter than a metal plate and could cover large areas of a soldier's body. However, chain mail was not perfect. It did very little to stop the impact of a blow from a sword. The chain mail wearer still could be injured or killed.

The second category is explained.

The next type of armor, the steel suits worn by knights in the 1400s, was a step up from chain mail. A complete suit had the following parts: a breastplate, a back plate, flexible arm and leg covers, gloves, shoes, and a helmet with a hinged door that protected the face. Besides being extremely heavy, the armored suits were expensive to make. Only the rich could afford to wear them. A knight needed people to help him get dressed and mount his horse for battle. Although these steel

EXPOSITORY

suits offered excellent protection from weapons, they made movement very awkward. If he was knocked from his horse, a soldier in a suit of armor was as good as dead.

Middle
The third middle paragraph describes the third category and explains its advantages.

Today, the newest armor is made of plastics and man-made fabrics. One of these is Kevlar, invented in the 1970s. Kevlar is a lightweight fiber that is stronger than steel and more flexible than chain mail. With enough layers, Kevlar can stop a speeding bullet. The protective clothing items—helmets, jackets, vests, and boots—worn by today's soldiers contain Kevlar.

Ending
• • • • • • • • • • • • • •
The ending considers the overall importance of the topic.

People have always needed to protect themselves in battle, and through the years, they found newer and better ways to do it. Types of protection have evolved from chain mail and metal suits to man-made materials. Battle armor will continue to evolve as long as it is needed. Science fiction suggests that someday people may be protected by invisible force fields. In the meantime, people like Mr. Cosford will continue to rely on the latest forms of armor.

Respond to the reading. Answer the following questions about the essay you just read.

☐ **Development of Ideas** **(1) What is the writer's topic? (2) What three main categories does the writer cover?**

☐ **Organization** **(3) Can you find the pattern that is used to organize each middle paragraph? Explain it. (4) How does the writer tie the ending to the beginning?**

☐ **Voice** **(5) How does the writer show personal interest in and knowledge of the topic? Give an example of each.**

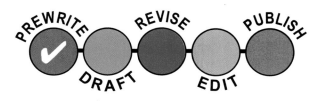

Prewriting

Prewriting is the first step in the writing process. It involves selecting a topic, gathering specific details, and organizing your ideas.

Keys to Effective Prewriting

1. Select a topic that you know well or one you would like to know more about.

2. Write a controlling idea that clearly states the topic and mentions its main types or categories.

3. Gather details that will make your essay clear and interesting.

4. Organize your details into three or four main categories.

5. Plan your essay using an organized list or an outline.

 **TEKS** 8.14A

Prewriting Selecting a Topic

The writer of the model essay on protective armor chose a topic that could be broken down into at least three main categories. Choose from the following general subjects for the brainstorming activity below.

clothing	education	health	occupation
exercise	friends	machines	recreation
food	goals	art/music	science

Prewrite

Brainstorm for topics. To brainstorm for topics, you think freely about all the possibilities. You don't stop to think about any one idea. Just keep listing.

1 Select four general subjects that appeal to you from the list above.

2 On your own paper, draw a gathering chart like the one shown below. Write your four subjects on the top line.

3 List possible writing topics under each general subject.

4 Star the two topics that interest you the most. (You will use these topics in the next exercise.)

Gathering Chart

RECREATION	GOALS	ART/MUSIC	SCIENCE
biking *	climbing a	photography	animal
canoeing	mountain	popular	defenses *
skateboarding		music	storms

Texas Traits

Focus on the Texas Traits

Development of Ideas The writer of the sample essay on pages 169–170 wrote about a topic that interested both him and his classmates. The topic worked well because it could be divided into three main categories that could be supported with specific details.

TEKS 8.17A(ii)

Sizing Up Your Topic

Once you have selected two possible topics, you should test them to see if they can be broken down into three or four categories. Use the guidelines below to test your topics:

Too Broad . . . Topics that are too broad have too many categories to explore. For example, "animals" has so many categories that you couldn't possibly cover them all in one essay.

Too Narrow . . . If a topic can't be easily broken down into categories, it is too narrow. For example, "octopus ink" would be too narrow.

Just Right . . . "Animal defenses" could include three or four natural methods that animals use to protect themselves. It is just right.

Prewrite

Choose your topic. On your own paper, write the two topics you starred in the exercise on page 172. Beneath each one, list at least three main categories of the topic. When you are finished, ask yourself the following questions about each topic. Then choose the better topic.

1 Does this topic have three or four main categories?

2 Could I find enough details to support each main category?

3 Is this topic *too broad, too narrow,* or *just right*?

Focusing Your Topic

Once you have selected a topic, it's time to write a *controlling idea* (also called a *thesis* or *focus statement*). An effective controlling idea identifies the topic you will write about and how it can be broken down. (Sometimes you may want to actually name the specific categories in your controlling idea.)

The following formula was used to write a controlling idea for an essay about animal defenses.

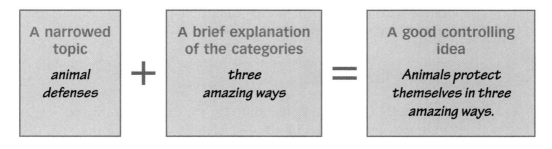

A narrowed topic		A brief explanation of the categories		A good controlling idea
animal defenses	**+**	*three amazing ways*	**=**	*Animals protect themselves in three amazing ways.*

Prewrite

Write your controlling idea. Using the formula shown above, write a controlling idea for your classification essay.

EXPOSITORY

Prewriting **Gathering and Sorting Details**

Now that you have selected your topic and written your controlling idea, you can begin gathering and sorting details. Sorting helps you see how many details you have for each category. Study the sorting chart below from the student essay about how animals protect themselves.

 If you think of something you would like to add to your list, but you don't know enough about it, write it down as a question and circle it. Do whatever reading or researching is necessary to answer your questions.

Sorting Chart

Changing Colors	Using Chemicals	Releasing Body Parts
- Snowshoe rabbits turn white in winter.	- Skunks spray a stinky liquid.	- Starfish drop arms.
- Cuttlefish turn colors.	- Some frogs taste bad.	*(Do they regrow their lost parts?)*
(Is there a color that cuttlefish can't change to?)	- Octopuses shoot dark, cloudy ink.	- Salamanders can regrow a leg or tail.

 Create your sorting chart. On your own paper, draw a sorting chart like the one above. At the top, write the three or four main categories you've chosen to write about. Then, in each column, list specific details for each category and add any questions you may have.

Focus on the Texas Traits

Organization If you are able to divide your topic into three or four main categories, you will also be able to easily divide your essay into clear paragraphs. Remember that each paragraph should address one main category of the topic.

TEKS 8.14B, 8.17A(iii)

Writing Topic Sentences

The topic sentence of each middle paragraph should clearly identify one of the categories. Each topic sentence should also include a transition that moves the reader smoothly from one category to the next. The writer of the essay on animal defenses used the topic sentences below to rate the defenses from least to most unusual. (For more information on topic sentences, see pages **614–615**.)

Topic Sentences

Topic sentence 1: *One common way animals protect themselves is by changing color to blend in with their environment.*

Topic sentence 2: *A more unusual way animals avoid attack is by giving off a chemical that smells bad or clouds the surroundings.*

Topic sentence 3: *Perhaps the most amazing way animals protect themselves is by releasing a tail or another body part to get away when captured.*

Prewrite

Write your topic sentences. Use the above models to help you write your topic sentences.

1 Keep your controlling idea in mind as you write each topic sentence.

2 Be sure each topic sentence addresses one of the main categories mentioned in the controlling idea.

3 Include a transition to introduce or say something important about the category. (For more information on transitions, see pages **634–635**.)

EXPOSITORY

Texas Traits

Focus on the Texas Traits

Voice In a classification essay, you want to sound both interested and knowledgeable. Search for fascinating details and amazing facts to include in your writing.

176

Prewriting Organizing Your Ideas

The controlling idea identifies the overall topic and main categories of the classification essay. Each category becomes a topic sentence in the actual essay.

Directions

Write your controlling idea (thesis).

Write the first category.

List your first example.

List your second example.

Write the second category.

List your first example.

List your second example.

Write the third category.

List your first example.

List your second example.

Organized List

Animals protect themselves in three amazing ways.

1. Changing color to blend in with surroundings
   - Rabbit turns brown in summer, white in winter
   - Cuttlefish changes to color of surroundings

2. Using chemicals
   - Skunk repels attackers with foul-smelling liquid
   - Octopus squirts dark, inky fluid

3. Releasing body parts
   - Salamander and starfish drop a limb
   - Gecko drops its tail to get away

Make sure you have approximately the same number and kinds of details for each main category in your essay. When you revise, you will check for a balance of information from one paragraph to the next.

Make an organized list. To create your list, follow the "Directions" in the sample above. You will use this list as you write your essay.

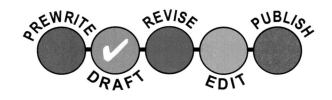

Drafting

Once you've finished your prewriting, it's time to write your first draft. You're ready to write a first draft when you know enough about your topic and have written a clear controlling idea.

Keys to Effective Drafting

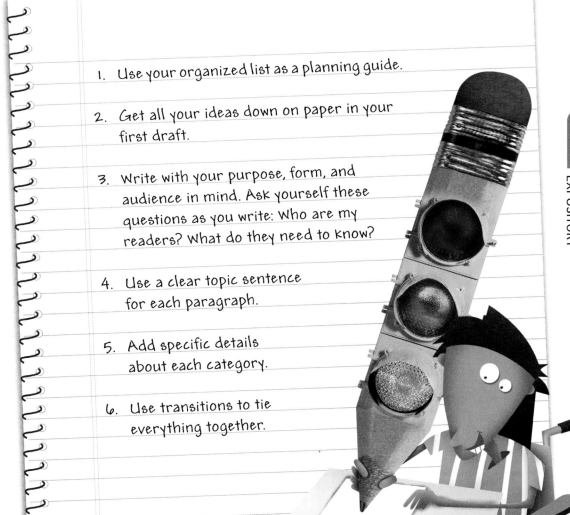

1. Use your organized list as a planning guide.

2. Get all your ideas down on paper in your first draft.

3. Write with your purpose, form, and audience in mind. Ask yourself these questions as you write: Who are my readers? What do they need to know?

4. Use a clear topic sentence for each paragraph.

5. Add specific details about each category.

6. Use transitions to tie everything together.

EXPOSITORY

 TEKS 8.14B, 8.17A(i), 8.17A(ii), 8.17A(iii)

Drafting Getting the Big Picture

Now that you have organized your categories into a logical order, you can begin writing your first draft. The graphic below shows how a classification essay is put together.

The opening paragraph contains a clear controlling idea. The middle contains several supporting paragraphs, each one covering one main category of the topic. The closing paragraph sums up the essay. (The examples used below are from the sample essay shown on pages 179–182.)

Beginning

The **beginning** captures the reader's interest, introduces your topic, and gives your controlling idea.

Middle

The **middle** presents each category of your topic. Each middle paragraph includes one category and strong supporting details.

Controlling Idea
Animals protect themselves in three amazing ways.

Three Topic Sentences
One common way animals protect themselves is by changing color to blend in with their environment.

A more unusual way animals avoid attack is by giving off a chemical that smells bad or clouds the surroundings.

Perhaps the most amazing way animals protect themselves is by releasing a tail or another body part to get away when captured.

Ending

The **ending** reminds the reader of the essay's focus and suggests the importance of the topic.

Closing Sentence
However, without their amazing defenses, some animals would not survive.

 Look at the three middle paragraphs of the model essay on pages 169–170. On your own paper, list the details that support the topic sentence in each paragraph.

TEKS 8.14B, 8.17A(ii)
ELPS 3G, 3H

Starting Your Essay

Begin by writing your opening paragraph as freely as you can. This paragraph should make the reader want to read your entire paper. It should also introduce the controlling idea.

Several ways to begin a classification essay are shown below. Each of these examples is written in a different voice, but any would offer an interesting beginning. You might use one or more of these to start your essay.

- **Share interesting or surprising details about the subject.** *They sting! They stink! They taste bad! What could "they" possibly be? They are animals that protect themselves in amazing ways.*
- **Ask a question.** *What if you could suddenly change colors and blend into the background?*
- **Give interesting background information.** *For years, people have found many ways to protect themselves. Today, they wear camouflage uniforms and shoot pepper spray.*

Beginning Paragraph

In the beginning paragraph below, the writer combines interesting details with a question to introduce the controlling idea.

> The writer provides interesting background information and asks a question.
>
> The writer includes a controlling idea (underlined).

For years, people have found many ways to protect themselves. Today, they wear camouflage uniforms and shoot pepper spray. Where did people get the ideas for these forms of protection? They may have come from the unusual ways animals defend themselves. Animals protect themselves in three amazing ways.

EXPOSITORY

Write an opening. Write two beginning paragraphs, using one or more of the techniques given above. Read your paragraphs to a partner and ask which opening will better capture the reader's attention and which one has a stronger voice.

⭐ **TEKS** 8.14B, 8.17A(iii), 8.17A(v)

Drafting **Developing the Middle Part**

After writing your beginning paragraph, you are ready to develop the middle of your essay. Each middle paragraph should focus on one main category of your topic and include the specific details from your organized list (page 176). A well-organized paragraph uses a variety of details.

1. The **topic sentence** introduces the topic of the paragraph. (See the underlined sentence in the paragraph below.)

2. The **specific details** in each paragraph support the topic sentence. Here are several different ways to add details to your writing:

   - **Include facts and examples.**
   - **Explain a term.**
   - **Make a comparison.**
   - **Ask thought-provoking questions.**
   - **Include imagery and figurative language to help readers picture what you describe.**
   - **Include an anecdote about a personal experience.**

3. The **closing sentence** ends the paragraph and provides a final thought.

Middle Paragraphs

Topic Sentence	<u>*One common way animals protect themselves is by changing color to blend in with their environment.*</u> *A good example of this is the snowshoe rabbit. This rabbit turns from brown in summer to white in winter. In summer, its brown fur blends in with golden summer grasses; in winter its fur turns white and it disappears in the snowy landscape. Cuttlefish also change color to blend with their surroundings. Without the ability to change color, some species of animals would probably be extinct*
Specific Details	
Closing Sentence	*by now.* **Humans have borrowed this idea to make camouflage clothing.**

TEKS 8.14B, 8.17A(iii), 8.17A(v)

Topic Sentence

> A more unusual way animals avoid attack is by giving off a chemical that smells bad or clouds the surroundings. The skunk defends itself by releasing a foul-smelling chemical from glands found beneath its tail.

Specific Details

> Because the chemical can severely sting eyes, and the smell is enough to send predators hurrying away, any animal that tangles with a skunk surely won't do it twice! An octopus squirts a dark, inky fluid in front of its attackers. The ink clouds the water and lets the octopus escape.

Closing Sentence

> Did these protective methods give someone the idea for pepper spray?

Topic Sentence

> Perhaps the most amazing way animals protect themselves is by releasing a tail or another body part to get away when captured. When a limb is trapped, these animals simply release it and go.

Specific Details

> A salamander's tail will fall off to allow escape, and a starfish's detached arm will grow into a new starfish! The gecko, a tropical lizard, can drop its tail, which then keeps moving to distract the attacker. After the animal escapes, the lost body part will grow back.

Closing Sentence

> Wouldn't it be amazing if humans possessed the ability to regrow parts?

EXPOSITORY

Write your middle paragraphs. Use your organized list (page 176) to help you write your middle paragraphs. Also consider the drafting tips listed below.

Drafting Tips

Using a variety of rhetorical devices makes writing interesting.

- **Use imagery to help readers visualize details.**
- **Ask questions to help readers connect to your ideas.**

TEKS 8.17A(i)

Drafting **Ending Your Essay**

In your ending paragraph, you need to restate your controlling idea and make a final statement. Below are two different ending paragraphs for the essay on animal defenses.

Beginning

Middle

Ending

Ending Paragraphs

The writer asks the reader to think about the topic and then offers a final thought.

Imagine that an individual's skin turned color when he or she went from a red carpet to green grass. What if someone simply dropped a leg if he or she got hurt in an accident, only to have a new leg grow back? Some ways animals use to protect themselves may seem like science fiction. However, without their amazing defenses, some animals would not survive.

Your final paragraph could also

- summarize all your main points, and
- emphasize the special importance of the overall topic.

The writer suggests the importance of the essay and its information.

Nature has provided animals with many different ways to protect themselves. They blend in with their surroundings, give off bad-tasting or bad-smelling chemicals, or even drop a captured limb. Over the years, humans have observed and copied many of these defenses. Human beings may be more intelligent, but they can still learn a lot from animals.

Write your ending paragraph. Write a final paragraph for your essay using the suggestions above.

Write your complete first draft. Bring all the parts of your first draft together to form a complete essay.

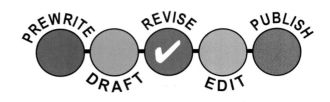

Revising

A first draft never turns out quite right. One part may need more details. Another part may not be clear enough. Another part may be too dull. To fix or improve these parts, you need to carefully revise your first draft.

Keys to Effective Revising

1. Read through your entire draft to get a feeling for how well your essay works.

2. Make sure your controlling idea states your topic clearly.

3. Check your paragraphs to make sure the details relate to the topic sentence and are in logical order.

4. Be sure you've used a knowledgeable, interested voice, and have incorporated a variety of rhetorical devices.

5. Check your writing for precise words and a variety of sentences.

6. Use the editing and proofreading marks inside the back cover of this book.

Revising for Focus and Coherence

When you revise for *focus and coherence*, you make sure you have written about only one topic. All your categories and supporting details should directly relate to your controlling idea. This will ensure that your essay has internal coherence. Your essay should have a beginning that states your topic clearly and an ending that sums up the supporting details about the topic. These help readers understand the importance of the overall topic.

Have I focused on one topic?

You know you have focused on one topic if all the ideas and details in your essay are about that topic. Do not include any information that does not relate to the topic.

 Read the paragraph and identify the topic. Then tell which ideas do not belong.

> Ants protect themselves in very interesting ways. One way they protect themselves is by living in large groups and having different jobs. Some ants guard the door to the colony's nest and keep enemies out. The queen ant is in the nest. Ants protect each other. They give warnings to other ants when there is danger. Chimpanzees love to eat ants. Some ants have venom to protect themselves from enemies. It's amazing that such a small animal has so many ways to protect itself!

 Check your essay. Read through your first draft or have your partner read it. Be sure all ideas are connected to your topic.

Focus and Coherence
An off-topic sentence was deleted.

The boll weevil is a small beetle that feeds on cotton buds and flowers. It is believed to have migrated from Mexico, across the Rio Grande near Brownsville, Texas, in the late 1800s. ~~In Mexico, the Rio Grande is called the Rio Bravo.~~ By the early 1920s, the boll weevil had devastated cotton crops throughout the American South.

TEKS 8.14C, 8.14E
ELPS 3E

How do I know if my beginning works well?

For your essay to have external coherence, you need to have a strong beginning. Your beginning works well if it interests the reader, introduces the topic, and has a clear controlling idea. In a classification essay, your beginning should make it clear to the reader that you plan to break a topic down into categories and describe those categories. When reviewing your beginning, ask these questions:

1. What grabs my interest?
2. What makes me want to keep reading?
3. Which sentence states the controlling idea of the essay?
4. Does the controlling idea give a clear idea what the essay will be about?
5. What specific information will I find out about the topic?

Review your beginning. Reread your beginning. Have a partner review it, too. Discuss the answers to the questions above with your partner. Does your beginning catch a reader's interest? Does it clearly state the topic? If not, ask your partner for suggestions about how to improve it. Revise your beginning as needed.

How do I know if my ending is strong?

A strong ending is also important for external coherence. An effective ending restates the focus and makes a final statement. It expresses your final thoughts on the topic and provides a satisfying close to the essay. You know your ending is strong if it . . .

- summarizes all your main points,
- emphasizes the special importance of the overall topic, or
- asks the reader to think about the topic.

Check your ending. Did you end your essay in one of the ways listed above? Invite a partner to read it and tell whether it is strong. If not, try writing another ending.

EXPOSITORY

 TEKS 8.14C, 8.17A(iii), 8.17A(v)

Revising for Organization

When you revise for *organization*, you need to check your details carefully. In a classification essay, the details should be clearly connected. They should also be arranged in the same pattern in each paragraph. Effective transitions should be used to link sentence to sentence and paragraph to paragraph. (For additional information on organization, see pages 612–613.)

Are my details clearly connected?

Your details are clearly connected when they build from one idea to the next. Here is a strategy to help you tie your ideas together.

- **Repeating a key word.**

  The hermit crab's shell does not cover its soft abdomen. **To protect its** abdomen, **the crab backs into an abandoned shell and adopts it as its own.** (The key word *abdomen* connects the details.)

Am I using effective transitions?

One way to help readers see the connection between details and ideas is to use transition words and phrases. They are the "glue" that holds your essay together. The following words are often used to make transitions:

In addition to	For this reason	For example	Like
Because of	Therefore	For instance	Also
As	Another [reason, way, kind of]		

 Read the following paragraph and then list four key words and two transition words or phrases that help to connect the sentences.

1   Seals, sea lions, and walruses are members of the same family,
2 but each has its unique characteristics. The walrus, for example,
3 has unique tusks that make it easy to pick out in a crowd. The tusks
4 are actually huge canine teeth that the walrus uses to establish
5 dominance and secure the best basking spots. To get to these
6 prime spots, the walrus uses its tusks to help pull itself onto rocky
7 or icy shores. Once on shore, the walrus is able to keep other sea-
8 going mammals away by simply displaying its super-sized teeth.

 Check your details. Read through your essay to check for clearly connected details. If you need to, add key words or transitions to create a link between your ideas.

TEKS 8.14B, 8.17A(iii)

Do I follow a precise pattern in my essay?

You have followed a precise pattern if each main category is covered in the same way, with about the same number and types of details. You can establish this pattern in your organized list or outline. (See page 176.)

 Read the following paragraph. Then number your paper from 1 to 4 and arrange the four sentences below so they follow the same pattern used in the paragraph.

> The folk guitar neck is designed for playing popular music. The neck is tightly glued or bolted to the body to hold up to the tension of the steel strings. The strings are close together on the slender neck, making it easier to use a pick. Because the neck joins the body at the 14th fret, the musician can reach very high notes.

1. Because nylon strings cause less pressure, the wide neck can be carved together with the body.
2. The neck joins the body at the 12th fret to keep the tones low.
3. If you enjoy playing "art" music, the classical guitar is for you.
4. The wide neck keeps the strings spaced for easy finger picking.

 Check for paragraph pattern. Review each middle paragraph of your essay to see if you have followed the same pattern for each category. If sentences seem out of place or could be arranged in a more logical order, circle and move them, as shown in the example below.

Organization
A sentence was moved for a more precise pattern.

A good example of this is the snowshoe rabbit. Its change in color makes it hard for predators to see the rabbit in dry summer grass and winter snow. This rabbit turns from brown in summer to white in winter.

EXPOSITORY

Revising for Development of Ideas

As you revise for *development of ideas*, check to see if you used different kinds of details. In a classification essay, you should also be offering information that is new and interesting to your reader.

How can I use different kinds of details?

You can use details to define, explain, or compare ideas in your essay.

- **Definitions** usually answer the question "What is it?"

  Octopus ink makes it hard for predators—the animals attacking the octopus—to see where the octopus is going.

- **Explanations** answer the question "What does it do?" or "Why or how does it do it?"

  An octopus squirts ink to cloud the water and let the octopus escape.

- **Comparisons** answer the question "What is it like?"

  The ink the octopus squirts is like the dust that hides a car on a dirt road.

 Below are six sentences from a classification essay on types of clocks. For each, tell whether the detail used is an explanation, a definition, or a comparison. Use the above questions to help you.

1. Ancient people often used the sun to tell time with an obelisk, a tall, tapered structure with a pyramid-like top.
2. Like obelisks, sundials also use the sun to tell time.
3. Modern watches are more accurate than nature's clocks.
4. Quartz crystals keep accurate time by using an electric field.
5. Quartz watches use an LCD, or liquid crystal display, to show time.
6. Atomic clocks are accurate to one-millionth of a second per year.

 Review your writing. Look for ideas that may need more explanation and for terms that need defining. Also consider making a comparison if it would make your ideas clearer.

Use precise words and phrases to give your writing clarity. Also avoid the trap of overusing modifiers.

How can I find precise words?

One way to find just the right word for your essay is to use a thesaurus. A thesaurus is a book that lists synonyms and antonyms. If your thesaurus is arranged alphabetically, look up your word as you would in a dictionary. If you are using a traditional thesaurus, look up your word in the index.

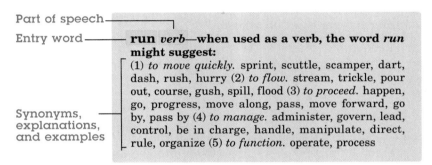

Part of speech

Entry word ——— **run** *verb*—**when used as a verb, the word** *run* **might suggest:**

(1) *to move quickly.* sprint, scuttle, scamper, dart, dash, rush, hurry (2) *to flow.* stream, trickle, pour out, course, gush, spill, flood (3) *to proceed.* happen, go, progress, move along, pass, move forward, go by, pass by (4) *to manage.* administer, govern, lead, control, be in charge, handle, manipulate, direct, rule, organize (5) *to function.* operate, process

Synonyms, explanations, and examples

Not every synonym for a word has the same meaning. Note how the above thesaurus entry is numbered to show the different meanings of the word. When you use a synonym, be sure it fits your meaning.

 Using the thesaurus entry above, find two synonyms to replace the word "run" in each of the following sentences. Make certain your choice fits the meaning of each sentence.

1. Once the skunk has stopped the attack, it can run to safety.
2. Li was selected to run the school garage sale.
3. Whenever it rains, the water runs over the dam.

 Check your essay for precise word choice. Go through your essay and circle two or three plain words. Use a thesaurus to replace them with more interesting words. Be sure each new word has the precise meaning you need.

EXPOSITORY

 Revising for Voice

When revising for *voice* in a classification essay, you must be certain that your voice fits your purpose and reaches the audience.

How can I tell if my voice fits my purpose?

You can tell if your voice fits your purpose in a classification essay if your writing presents interesting information without sounding too informal.

 Below are four passages from classification essays. Decide which of the passages present the facts in a clear and interesting way without sounding too personal or informal.

1 The saguaro cactus survives in the desert by storing water in its stem. The stem tissue can swell up to three times its size as it absorbs the rain.

2 Pitcher plants are really cute. Their leaves are kind of like water pitchers filled with a gross nectar that attracts insects. The bugs then slip on the slimy sides, plop into the liquid, and become plant food.

3 I was bowled over when I learned that the giant redwood tree actually needs a forest fire to reproduce! It's true—the heat of the fire forces the pine cones to open and drop their seeds. Cool!

4 Prairie grasses have adapted to the many fires common to their habitat. The growing structure of the plant is actually located under the ground. This way, when the top of the plant is burned away, new growth can spring up within a few days.

 Check your voice. Answer the following questions. If your voice is not quite right for the purpose of your essay, change some words or sentences.

1 Do I state the facts in a clear and interesting way?

2 Do I avoid words that sound too informal or personal?

TEKS 8.14C, 8.14E,
8.17A(v)
ELPS 3H

Does my voice connect with my audience?

Your voice will connect with your audience if your essay is informational and engaging. You can make this connection with your audience in several ways.

- **Use specific examples.** Specific examples can make your thoughts clearer and more interesting to the reader.
  General detail: Giant redwood trees are tough.
  Specific examples: Giant redwood trees can have bark two feet thick. The bark helps the trees survive droughts, insect attacks, and even forest fires.

- **Share an anecdote.** A brief anecdote or story can make your information easier to understand.
  People who are sprayed by a skunk try everything from bathing in tomato juice to covering themselves in baking soda.

- **Relate your topic to the reader.** Allow your audience to see how the topic affects their lives.
  If prairie grasses hadn't adapted to survive fires, the prairies would have eventually dried up and blown away. The loss of prairies would have changed the ecology of the entire country.

Check reader reaction. Ask a classmate to read your essay and suggest ways you could create a stronger connection. Use the strategies above as you revise.

EXPOSITORY

Voice
A sentence was added to connect the topic with the reader's life.

After the animal escapes, the lost body part will grow

back. *Wouldn't it be amazing if humans possessed the*
      ∧ *ability to regrow parts?*

      Imagine that an individual's skin turned color when he

or she went from a red carpet to green grass. . . .

Revising Using a Checklist

Check your revising. On a piece of paper, write the numbers 1 to 14. If you can answer "yes" to a question, put a check mark after that number. If not, continue to revise that part of your essay.

Focus and Coherence

_____ **1.** Have I focused on one controlling idea?

_____ **2.** Do my categories relate to my controlling idea?

_____ **3.** Does my beginning clearly state my controlling idea?

_____ **4.** Does my ending restate my controlling idea in a way that makes the reader think?

Organization

_____ **5.** Does my beginning grab the reader's attention?

_____ **6.** Do the details in each paragraph support the topic sentence?

_____ **7.** Are my ideas and details clearly connected?

_____ **8.** Do I use effective transitions between sentences and paragraphs?

_____ **9.** Do I follow a precise pattern?

Development of Ideas

_____ **10.** Do I cover at least three specific categories of my topic?

_____ **11.** Do I include different kinds of interesting details?

_____ **12.** Do I have a clear controlling idea?

Voice

_____ **13.** Does my voice fit my purpose?

_____ **14.** Have I used different ways to connect with my audience?

When you've finished revising, make a clean copy before you edit. This makes checking for conventions easier.

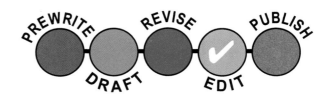

Editing

After you've finished revising your essay, it's time to edit your work for conventions: grammar, mechanics (punctuation, capitalization), and spelling.

Keys to Effective Editing

1. Use a dictionary, a thesaurus, and the "Proofreader's Guide" in the back of this book.

2. Check your writing for correctness of grammar, punctuation, capitalization, and spelling.

3. If you're using a computer, edit on a printed computer copy. Then enter your changes on the computer.

4. Use the editing and proofreading marks located inside the back cover of this book.

TEKS 8.17A(v), 8.19C

 Editing **for Conventions**

Grammar

When you revise for conventions, make sure that you use a variety of sentence types. Also make sure that you use parallel structure.

Do I use sentences with parallel structure?

Parallel structure means using the same pattern of words to show that two or more ideas have the same importance. You can connect these ideas with conjunctions such as *and* and *or*.

Marcos likes fishing, camping, **and** swimming.
Rosa doesn't like to cook **or** to wash dishes.
Dora finished the test, closed her notebook, **and** walked out of the class.
Diego will either go to see a movie **or** go to his friend's house.

 To make sure your sentences have parallel structure, put words or phrases that appear on either side of connecting words in a column and see if they have the same pattern.

 These sentences do not have parallel structure. Rewrite them so they do have parallel structure.

1. On Saturdays, I like to read, shopping, and walk my dog.
2. Next week Clara will fly to Mexico and visiting her grandmother.
3. After school, I practice piano or playing soccer is fun.
4. For dinner, I'll have a hamburger, some pizza, or I'll make pasta.
5. My favorite activities are playing basketball, listening to music, and I draw cartoons.
6. When my grandmother makes tortillas, she mixes the flour and baking soda, adds water and shortening, and kneading the dough.

 Find sentences in your essay that have *and* or *or*. Look at the words and phrases on each side and see if they use the same pattern. Correct any sentences that do not have parallel structure.

TEKS 8.19A(iv), 8.19A(v), 8.19B
ELPS 2C

How can I differentiate between main and subordinate clauses?

A main clause has a subject and a verb and is a complete idea. A subordinate clause begins with a subordinating conjunction or a relative pronoun and has a subject and a verb. However, it is not a complete thought.

Examples of subordinating conjunctions:

after	although	as	because	before
even though	since	that	until	when

Examples of relative pronouns:

that	which	who	whose

Because it rained, **we couldn't go to the beach.**
subordinate clause   *main clause*

I liked the book that I finished yesterday.
main clause   *subordinate clause*

Circle the main clauses and underline the subordinate clauses.

Alex went to school even though he felt sick. After he got to school, he felt worse. He went to the nurse. "You have a fever, which is not good. Wait here until I call your mother, " she said.

A subordinate clause cannot stand alone. To figure out if a clause is subordinate, ask yourself, "Do I need more information to understand what is happening?"

Check for clauses. Review your sentences. Add subordinate clauses to give more information. Make sure subordinate clauses are not standing alone.

Learning Language

Read the meanings and share answers to the questions with a partner.

1. A subordinate clause gives more information about the main clause. **What subordinate clause can you add to this main clause: I like dogs?**

2. Two things that follow the same direction or pattern are parallel. **Give an example of a sentence with parallel structure.**

EXPOSITORY

⭐ TEKS 8.14C, 8.14D

Sentence Structure

How can I combine sentences using subordinating conjunctions?

You can combine two closely related sentences into one complex sentence by using a subordinating conjunction. (See pages **579** and **792** for a list of conjunctions.)

> Cats get frightened by loud noises. They arch their backs and hiss.

By adding the subordinating conjunction "when," you create a subordinate clause and turn the two short sentences into one complex sentence.

> When cats get frightened by loud noises, they arch their backs and hiss.
>
> (or) Cats arch their backs and hiss when they get frightened by loud noises.

 When the subordinate clause (also called a *dependent clause*) begins a sentence, it is followed by a comma. Usually, when the subordinate clause comes at the end of a sentence, no comma is used.

 Combine the following sentence pairs by using the subordinating conjunction given in parentheses.

1. Porcupine fish are usually left alone by predators. Their bodies are covered with sharp spines. *(because)*
2. Puffer fish gulp water to expand their size. Larger fish can't get puffer fish into their mouths. *(when)*
3. The red panda has an extra thumb like the giant panda. It is more closely related to the raccoon. *(although)*
4. The koala is often called a "bear." It is not a bear at all but a marsupial. *(even though)*
5. The biggest bird in the world is the ostrich. It can grow up to nine feet tall. *(which)*

 Combine short sentences. Underline any closely related sentences in your essay. Try to combine some of them using subordinating conjunctions.

 **TEKS** 8.14D, 8.19A(v),
8.19B, 8.20B(i)

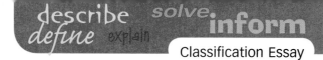

Mechanics: Punctuation

How should I use commas with subordinating conjunctions?

When the dependent clause is at the beginning of the sentence, place a comma after it. Generally, do not use a comma when the dependent clause comes after the main clause. (See page **565** and **794.1**.)

> Because the viceroy butterfly looks like the bad-tasting monarch, **many predators leave it alone**.

> **The stonefish is often ignored by predators** because it looks just like a rock on the ocean floor.

 Write the following complex sentences on your paper, placing commas where necessary.

1. Because some birds can puff up their feathers to appear larger than they are predators leave them alone.
2. The turtle's shell is a fortress when the animal is under attack.
3. Unless it moves a fawn can hide in the brush from a predator.
4. Hedgehogs can avoid being eaten when they roll into a tight ball.
5. Though the lowland gorilla seems aggressive it is passive.
6. Because their leg bones are so thin bats cannot walk.

 Edit your essay. Check to be sure that you correctly punctuated any dependent clauses.

EXPOSITORY

Conventions
Errors with commas are corrected.

When a limb is trapped ⁁, these animals simply

release it and go. To allow escape ⁁, a salamander's tail will

fall off and a starfish's arm will detach . . .

⬥ **TEKS** 8.14D, 8.20A, 8.21

Editing **Using a Checklist**

Check your editing. On a piece of paper, write the numbers 1 to 10. If you can answer "yes" to a question, put a check mark after that number. Continue editing until you can answer all the questions with a "yes."

Conventions

GRAMMAR

_____ **1.** Can I differentiate between a main clause and a subordinate clause?

_____ **2.** Do I use main and subordinate clauses correctly?

_____ **3.** Do I use parallel structure in my sentences?

MECHANICS

_____ **4.** Do I correctly punctuate subordinate clauses?

_____ **5.** Do I correctly punctuate sentences with parallel structure?

_____ **6.** Do I capitalize proper nouns?

_____ **7.** Do I begin each sentence with a capital letter?

SPELLING

_____ **8.** Have I spelled all my words correctly?

_____ **9.** Have I used the spell-checker on my computer?

_____ **10.** Have I double-checked the words my spell-checker may have missed?

Creating a Title

For a classification essay, the title should do one of the following:

■ Name the topic: **Ways Animals Defend Themselves**

■ Catch the reader's imagination: **Animal Armor**

■ Establish the tone: **Staying Alive: Animal Adaptations**

TEKS 8.14E

Go Online!

Publishing

PREWRITE · REVISE · PUBLISH
DRAFT · EDIT

Sharing Your Essay

After you have worked so hard writing your essay, you'll want to proofread it and make a neat copy to publish. You might want to use one of the suggestions below. Choose the suggestion that is appropriate for your audience.

Publish

Make a final copy. Follow your teacher's instructions or use the guidelines below to format your essay. Create a clean final copy of your essay and carefully proofread it.

Focus on Presentation

- Use blue or black ink and write neatly.
- Write your name in the upper left corner of page 1.
- Skip a line and center your title; skip another line and start your writing.
- Indent every paragraph and leave a one-inch margin on all four sides.
- Write your last name and the page number in the upper right corner of every page after the first one.

EXPOSITORY

Produce a Book

Turn your essay into a picture book by adding pictures with captions. Make a cover out of cardboard and include your title and name. Punch holes along the left side and fasten the pages together with yarn or secure with brads.

Display Your Essay in School

Ask your teacher if there is a special section or showcase for student papers.

Create a Poster

Attach your essay pages to a large piece of tagboard and add illustrations and informative side notes for each section. Include Web-site addresses for further information on each main idea.

Evaluating a Classification Essay

To learn how to evaluate a classification essay, you'll use the scoring rubric on pages **50–51** and the essays that follow. These essays are examples of writing for each score on the rubric.

Notice that this first essay received a score of 4. Read the description for a score of 4 on pages **50–51**. Then read the essay. Use the same steps to study the other examples. Always remember to think about the overall quality of the writing.

Writing that fits a score of 4 is very strong.

Strong controlling idea creates coherence.

Specific details support the main idea.

Martial Arts: Not Only for Fighting

If you listen to middle school students talking, you could easily get the impression that all of them are experts in martial arts. Kids my age love to boast about how great they are at karate and what belts they have earned. However, martial arts isn't about hitting people and hurting people. Martial arts masters who have studied for many years often teach their students that the goal is not to fight. There are many different kinds of martial arts, and many of them mix fighting skill with a way of life that seeks peace.

Karate is a famous Japanese martial art that looks violent because of its hard kicks, punches, and sparring. Karate students train hard and get an excellent workout, building their strength and stamina and learning how to move their bodies. They practice complicated forms that take a long time to learn perfectly. One of the first things you learn in a good karate school, though, is that you should use your skills only in the school and not in the street. (I go to a good karate school, so I know.) Really you're studying karate in order to overcome your inner enemy, such as a lack of confidence. That is the goal of many martial arts.

For example, aikido, which is also Japanese, is all about peace and not hurting people. Aikido hardly ever uses punches or kicks. It is just defensive, and it mainly uses rolls and throws that don't cause injury. The idea is that if someone attacks you, you should do just enough so that you can get away safely. Rolling is important because it takes you away from an attacker, out of reach. When aikido students throw somebody, they use the attacker's own force against him rather than attacking back. One of the main skills in aikido is just learning to step away from the attacker! For people who want to learn to protect themselves and hate fighting, aikido is a great choice.

Another nonviolent martial art is capoeira, a Brazilian art that is also a kind of dance and a game! Capoeira is done to music, and it's more like a show than a fight. The fighters stand inside a circle of people, who include musicians and singers. You'll see twirling kicks and leg sweeps, often back-kicks with the player's hands on the ground. Players use fakes to try to trick their opponents into making a bad move. Capoeira is about having fun as part of a group, and it teaches you to be aware of danger and know how to get out of it.

Each kind of martial art offers a different kind of exercise, and each one teaches people to improve themselves as much as they can. If you train in a martial art, you may become much stronger and quicker, and you may learn how to move away from trouble—you may even learn to dance!

Paragraphs have topic sentences and closing sentences.

Vivid nouns and action verbs paint a picture.

Sentences are varied and fluent.

EXPOSITORY

Writing that fits a score of 3 is strong in most ways.

Clouds, Clouds, Clouds

Describing clouds is a very enjoyable activity that most people have done. Many people describe clouds by comparing them to other things, such as animals. "That cloud looks like a rabbit," someone will say. Then another person will say, "That cloud looks like a lion." Scientists also describe clouds, but they don't do it by comparing clouds to animals. They have a system that puts clouds into groups by height and shape. The names of the different types of clouds refer to their height and their shape.

The highest-level clouds often have "cirr" or "cirro" or "cirrus" in their names. Cirrus clouds look thin and wispy. They are formed at high altitudes where the temperature is very cold, and so cirrus clouds are made of ice crystals. Cirrus clouds usually occur in fair weather with blue skies however, if high clouds form a thick sheet, it probably means rain and they are called cirrostratus. Cirrus clouds are among the most beutiful types but people who love clouds think there all beutiful.

Middle-level clouds usually have "alto" in their names. Altostratus clouds are thick and gray or blue-gray and cause overcast skies without much sunlight.

Low-level clouds look entirely different from cirrus clouds. They often have "strat" in their names. "Strat" comes from a Latin word that means "layer." Stratus clouds are low and thick. They cover the sky like a blanket. Most stratus clouds are made of water droplets, because they are close to the ground, but in cold winter weather stratus clouds may

The essay starts with a strong focus.

Errors in usage, spelling, and mechanics

One paragraph is not fully developed.

sometimes also contain ice. When stratus clouds are very dark and bring rain, they are called nimbostratus, because the prefix "nimbo" means rain.

The writer's voice conveys interesting details.

Then there's a kind of very popular cloud that is built up vertically rather than horizontally. This is the cumulus cloud. They have flat bottoms and they are big, white, and fluffy above that. These are the clouds that people often compare to cotton balls or rabbits. Cumulus clouds often go along with beautiful weather. However, they can build up to become thunder clouds, which are known as cumulonimbus. Summer lightning storms often go along with cumulonimbus.

Closing paragraph of a coherent, organized piece of writing

Clouds are beautiful, but they are important too. If you know something about clouds, you can often predict the weather. Next time you see a thick layer of altostratus clouds moving slowly across the sky, you will be able to predict that they will bring light to moderate rain. And you will be able to share with people that the high, thin clouds are made of ice crystals. There are more type of clouds, but the main categories are high, middle, low, and vertical. Keep watching clouds and reading about them, and you will learn more all the time.

Writing that fits a score of 2 is strong in some ways.

Beginning states the topic but is not interesting.

Sentences are awkward and there are many errors.

Ideas are not well developed or coherent.

The voice is interested, but the ending is not informative.

Three Great Types of Music

All music is good if its the kind of music you like to listen to but diffrent people like diffrent kinds, so I'm going to discuss three of them. One is rock, the other is country, and the other is blues.

Blues started out as an old form of music that was often made by African-Americans who lived Down South and worked on farms. They created the blues to express their feelings such as sadness. But the blues doesn't make you sad if you listen to it it makes you happy! That's the secret of the blues. The first blues players had instruments like acustick guitars and harmonicas and later the blues went electric! People were playing the blues in cities like Chicago so more people got to hear the blues and like it. Today everyone knows about the blues.

Country is another type of music it was first made by people in places in TN and KY. They were also poor people and many of them lived in the mountains and hills. They played guitars, fiddles, banjoes, etc. They often had high voices and sang harmony. Also country started out with acustick and then went electric. Many of the old country musisians actually loved the blues too. They learned from it.

Then you have rock which everybody listens to now. Rock is electric almost all the time. The interesting thing is that rock is partly blues and partly country in addition to being itself. Rock is the perfect music because it has all those eliments and also a great beat and great electric sounds.

Writing that fits a score of 1 is weak.

No strong focus statement

Some details, but many, many errors

Details not focused or informative, Show little depth of thinking

Friendly voice, but no coherent conclusion

EXPOSITORY

3 meals a day

They say you got to eat 3 meals a day and I believe it. All the meals are important and give you nutrishion. Each one of them has its own speshial place in your day.

The first meal of the day of course is breakfast and people sometimes say its the most important meal. You shud always eat a good breakfast. One of the best is eggs. You can eat eggs any way you want like fried or scrambeled and you can also have bacin with it or other kinds of breakfast meat. I like orange juice and milk for breakfast too. You start off your day that way and you wont get tired in the morning like some people do.

Lunch. Its more of a fun meal you can have a sandwich usally and maybe some chips on the side. This meal is to keep you going through a long day but it doesn't have to be big. If you eat to big a lunch youll get sleepy in the afternoon which is not good. Eat a lite lunch and then thats helthy.

Diner is my faverite because you sit down with your family and talk. It's a hot meal and you might have meat potatos and a veggie or a salad. It's a family time and also for nutrishion. It got to last you till breakfast. Then it starts all over again. I hope you always enjoy your meals.

Evaluating and Reflecting on Your Writing

You've put a lot of time and effort into your classification essay. Now take some time to score and think about your writing. On your own paper, finish each sentence starter below. To score your writing, refer to the scoring rubric on pages **50–51** and the examples you just read.

My Classification Essay

1. The best score for my classification essay is . . .

2. It's the best score because . . .

3. The best part of my classification essay is . . .

4. The part that still needs work is . . .

5. The main thing I learned about writing a classification essay is . . .

Expository Writing
Comparison-Contrast Essay

"Day One: I was about to begin my dive in the Amazon when I noticed a strange school of fish below my canoe. They look like harmless pacus, but they may be their close cousins, piranhas. I wish I could decide which they were. . . . "

Whenever you are trying to decide between two things, you are comparing and contrasting them. You look at how they are similar, and how they are different. Then you make a decision based on that information.

On the following pages, you'll read an expository essay comparing and contrasting two American cities. The guidelines that follow will help you write your own comparison-contrast essay.

Writing Guidelines

Subject:	**Two similar topics that interest you**
Purpose:	**To explain**
Form:	**Comparison-contrast essay**
Audience:	**Classmates**

Comparison-Contrast Essay

Making comparisons can result in new insights about a topic: two American cities, two types of sports, two admirable people. For the following essay, the writer compares two cities.

Beginning
The topics are introduced, and the controlling idea (underlined) sets up the comparison.

Middle
The first middle paragraph addresses differences point by point.

Cities Between the Waters

Brad Janty lives in Madison, Wisconsin, and loves it. When his cousin Jim from Seattle visits, Brad shows him the sights. They shop for music on State Street, visit the farmer's market on the capitol square, and end the day listening to jazz on the Union Terrace overlooking Lake Mendota. When Brad visits Jim in Seattle, Jim shows him the sights there. They go to the shops in Pike Place Market, explore Underground Seattle, and eat lunch in the Space Needle. Madison and Seattle may seem different, but they have much in common.

Of course, there are plenty of differences between the cities. At 540,000 people, Seattle is more than twice the size of Madison, which has 205,000 people. Seattle is the largest city in its state, and though Madison is not Wisconsin's largest city, it is the state capital. The Madison area's main products are milk and cheese. Seattle, on the other hand, is known for its cutting-edge technology. Seattle is surrounded by majestic natural wonders, such as mountains, rain forests, and the ocean. Madison's surroundings are a little more humble. It has hills instead of mountains, oak groves instead of rain forests, and lakes instead of the ocean. Madison, in the Midwest, has hot summers and cold winters, while Seattle, on the West Coast, has a temperate climate.

TEKS 8.20B(ii)
ELPS 5G

The second middle paragraph addresses similarities point by point.

Parentheses are used to add an interesting but less important detail.

Ending

The ending adds a final reflection about the comparison.

        Despite their differences, Madison and Seattle have many similarities. Both cities sit on narrow strips of land between two bodies of water. In Madison, we have Lake Mendota and Lake Monona. Seattle lies between Lake Washington and Puget Sound. Both cities are in the northern part of the country. Madison's latitude is 43 degrees, and Seattle's is 47. Each has a huge state university, the University of Wisconsin and the University of Washington (both are UW's). Madison and Seattle even lie on the same Interstate, I-90, although they're 2,000 miles apart. Either is worth a trip, though, because both are exciting and fun places to visit.

        In some ways, none of these features define the two cities. Madison and Seattle have the same soul. Both places are full of tie-dyed clothes, well-worn jeans, and leather sandals. Both have an exciting music scene. It's the atmosphere in each city that most makes them similar. Whether Jim is visiting Brad or Brad is visiting Jim, they always feel at home.

EXPOSITORY

Respond to the reading. On your own paper, write answers to the following questions about the sample essay.

☐ **Development of ideas** **(1) What two things does the writer compare? (2) What two similarities and two differences interest you?**

☐ **Organization** **(3) How do the two middle paragraphs support the controlling idea?**

☐ **Voice** **(4) What words and phrases reveal how the writer feels about the two cities? (5) How does the writer show knowledge about the two cities?**

TEKS 8.14A, 8.17A(iv)
ELPS 4C

Prewriting Selecting a Topic

Your teacher may assign a general subject for your essay. For the subject "American Cities," the writer used freewriting to find two cities to write about.

Freewriting

> Well, let's see. American cities. There's the big three, of course: New York, Chicago, and L.A. But I've never visited any of these cities. The only city I know something about is Madison from visiting my good friend there. Mad Town's cool. I've also heard from my friend that Seattle is cool. I think I'll compare these two cities, if I can find enough about both of them. . . .

Prewrite

Select your topic. Do a freewriting to find two topics you know enough about to compare and contrast.

Gathering Details

After you've finished your freewriting and found two topics, gather details from several sources. Make a gathering chart with two columns, as below. In each column, list all the details you have gathered for the topics. If you think of additional details, add them as you go.

Gathering Chart

Madison, WI	Seattle, WA
Lakes Mendota and Monona, Farm products, Latitude 43°, UW, 205,000 people, State capital, Snowy–31", Babcock Hill ice cream, Historical museums, Hills, Near Wisconsin Dells . . .	Largest city in state, 540,000 people, Rainy–34", I-90, Mountains, Space Needle, Puget Sound, West Coast, Known for technology, Latitude 47°, UW, Pike Place Market . . .

Prewrite

Create a gathering chart. Fill in a gathering chart like the one above. If you can't find many details, you may want to choose another topic.

TEKS 8.14A, 8.14B

Organizing Details

The writer used the following Venn diagram to organize ideas for his essay. In the center, he wrote the similarities between the cities. In the outer circles, he listed the contrasting ideas from his gathering chart, matching a point about one city to a corresponding point about the other city. If a fact for one city did not have a matching idea for the other, he did not use it in the essay.

Venn Diagram

Madison, WI
Midwest
Hills, trees
Population 205,000
Milk and cheese
State capital
Snowy

Both Cities
I-90
UW
Lots to see
Latitude (43°/47°)
Precipitation
(31"/34")

Seattle, WA
West Coast
Mountains, rain forest
Population 540,000
Computers, technology
Largest city in state
Rainy

Create a Venn diagram. Make a Venn diagram like the one above to organize the similarities and differences of your topics.

Forming a Thesis Statement

A good controlling idea, expressed in a thesis statement, gives the topics to be compared and introduces a general comparison.

Sample Thesis Statements

> Madison and Seattle may seem different, but they have much in common.

> Many people confuse viruses and bacteria, but if you examine them closely, you'll find they are totally different organisms.

> Although the sequoia and giant redwood seem similar, they are in fact very different.

Write a thesis statement. Using the samples given above, write a thesis statement for your comparison-contrast essay.

EXPOSITORY

 TEKS 8.14B, 8.17A(i), 8.17A(iii), 8.20A, 8.20B(ii), 8.21

Drafting Creating Your First Draft

When you write your comparison, pay close attention to each of the main parts: beginning, middle, and ending. Leave out extraneous information as you write, and make sure there are no inconsistencies within and between parts.

- **Beginning** Grab your reader's attention by starting strong. Then provide details that lead up to your thesis, or controlling idea.
- **Middle** Organize your middle paragraphs by discussing each topic point by point, as the writer did on pages **208–209**. Make sure your details all support the thesis; do not include unrelated details. Put interesting but less important details in parentheses.
- **Ending** Bring the writing to an effective close. One way is to sum up the comparison. Another way is to reflect or comment on it.

 Write your first draft. Refer to your Venn diagram and controlling idea to help you write the first draft of your comparison-contrast essay.

Revising Improving Your Writing

After you finish your draft, review your work for the following traits:

- ☐ **Focus and Coherence** Does the controlling idea name my two topics and state my focus? Any inconsistencies or extraneous ideas?
- ☐ **Organization** Does the essay have a clear beginning, middle, and ending? Does each paragraph focus on one part of the comparison-contrast theme?
- ☐ **Development of Ideas** Will the details grab readers' attention?
- ☐ **Voice** Is my voice appropriate for the topic?
- ☐ **Conventions** Do I use strong nouns, verbs, and modifiers? Do my sentences vary in length?

 Revise your writing. Ask yourself the questions listed above. Decide how you will revise. Make whatever changes are needed.

Editing Checking for Conventions

Find and correct any errors in grammar, sentence structure, capitalization, punctuation, and spelling.

 Edit your work: Ask: Have I used the correct past tense verbs? Is my capitalization correct? Have I ended each sentence with a punctuation mark? Have I spelled everything correctly?

Expository Writing

Across the Curriculum

Explanations are handy in all sorts of places. For example, imagine that you and six hungry friends need to share one pizza. Can you explain a way to cut the pizza so everyone gets a fair share? Perhaps you could divide 360° by 7 to discover that each piece should be 51.42°. The rest is a matter of working with the protractor and the pizza cutter. On the other hand, you could simply let each person cut a piece of the pizza, and afterward, in reverse order, choose the piece he or she will eat!

This section includes many amazing explanations. You will read a news report about the death of Julius Caesar, an explanation of a mathematical operation, a summary of a science experiment, a business letter, and a friendly letter. You'll even learn how to respond to an expository writing prompt. So turn to these pages anytime you've got some explaining to do.

What's Ahead

- **Social Studies**: Writing a News Report
- **Math**: Explaining a Mathematical Operation
- **Science**: Writing an Observation Report
- **Practical Writing**: Drafting a Business Letter, Drafting a Friendly Letter
- **Writing for Assessment**

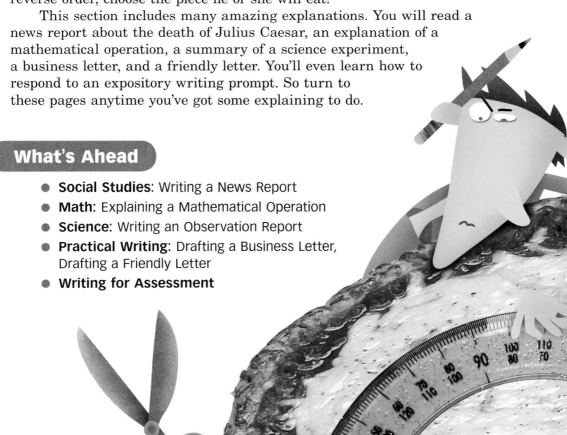

Social Studies: Writing a News Report

One way to understand a historical event is to write a news story about it. The following news story was written for a history class. Notice how the student reports the story as if it were a current event.

The **beginning** includes a strong headline that grabs the reader's attention. The most important details come first.

Caesar Slain on Senate Floor

MARCH 15, ROME: Julius Caesar is dead. Caesar had just arrived in the senate when a mob of senators with knives leapt up and attacked him. Caesar's own friend, Brutus, was allegedly among the attackers. He reportedly stabbed Caesar, too.

Caesar's autopsy recorded 23 stab wounds, though witnesses estimate the number of attackers to have been much higher. One senator, who did not want his name given, stated, "The conspiracy included at least 60 senators, but Brutus and Cassius were the ringleaders."

The **middle** includes facts reported in an interesting way.

Brutus and Cassius did little to hide their guilt. Following the attack, they and other conspirators paraded through the streets. Crowds picked up the shouts, "Tyranny ends" and "The Republic returns!"

This latest shock comes just five years into Caesar's reign. Though always popular with the people, Caesar had many enemies in the senate.

"I warned him," a soothsayer outside the senate building claimed. Asked how he knew about the plot ahead of time, the soothsayer denied any involvement in the conspiracy.

The **ending** avoids editorializing (giving an opinion).

Hope for the empire now rests with a new group: Gaius Octavius, Marcus Anthony, and Marcus Lepidus. Though hiding in undisclosed locations, the three have made pledges to raise armies and battle Brutus and Cassius across the whole empire.

TEKS 8.17A(iv)
ELPS 2C, 5B

Writing Tips

Before you write . . .

- **Select a topic.**
  Your teacher may assign a topic, or you may choose an event you are familiar with or are studying about.
- **Gather details.**
  Use the 5 W's and H to help you gather key information.
- **Consider the participants.**
  Consider the event and the people involved.
- **Think of your audience.**
  What information would be most important to them?

During your writing . . .

- **Organize your report.**
  Use the inverted pyramid style of organization. First synthesize the ideas you've gathered from several sources. Place the most important information in the very first sentence. Then answer as many of the 5 W's and H questions as you can. Add less important information later.

Most Important

Least

- **Focus on voice.**
  As you write, use active verbs, strong sentences, and brief paragraphs. Avoid editorializing (giving your opinion).

After you've written a first draft . . .

- **Write a strong headline.**
  Make sure your headline grabs the reader's attention and has a subject and a verb.
- **Check for completeness and correctness.**
  Make sure you've included the information your reader needs to understand the story. Check your use of conventions.

EXPOSITORY

 Choose an interesting historical event from the time period you are studying. Write it up as a news story. Get your facts right, but make it interesting, too.

Math: Explaining a Mathematical Operation

In math class, you may be asked to explain a mathematical operation. The writer of this essay was asked to show how percentages are used to calculate discounts and sales tax.

The **beginning** tells why the operation is important.

The **middle** uses specific details to explain the operation.

The **ending** makes a final observation.

Using Percentages

Discount and sale signs are posted everywhere on shops. Before shoppers get to the checkout line, they may want to know how much they're going to save on a sale item, and how much they need to pay. To do this, shoppers need to understand how to work with percentages.

Suppose someone finds a really cool pair of sandals on sale for 20% off the original price of $19. To find out the discount, a shopper should multiply $19 by 20%. The product, $3.80, is the discount. Next, he or she should subtract $3.80 from the original price of $19. The sale price is $15.20. Figuring out the cost of sale items requires two simple steps: (1) multiply the price by the percentage, and (2) subtract the product from the original price.

To figure the sales tax, a shopper should follow almost the same process. He or she should multiply the price of the item by the sales tax percentage (5%, 6%, 7% . . .), and then, instead of subtracting the product from the cost, add it. A shopper must remember that if there's a sales tax, he or she will need more money at checkout time.

Understanding how to work with percentages will help shoppers in many ways. They'll especially need to know all about them when they visit their favorite stores in the mall.

TEKS 8.17A(ii)
ELPS 5B

Writing Tips

Before you write . . .

- **Choose a familiar mathematical operation.**
  If your teacher has not assigned a particular mathematical operation, search for one in your notes or math textbook.
- **Study the operation.**
  Make sure you thoroughly understand the process needed to perform the operation. Think of how the operation can be applied to everyday life.
- **Plan the steps.**
  Break your operation into manageable steps. List them in the correct order and check them by working through the process.

During your writing . . .

- **Write a clear beginning, middle, and ending.**
  Begin by introducing the operation and clearly stating your purpose: to explain how to perform the operation. Next, explain the process (or steps) in a clear manner. Provide an example of how the operation can be applied to everyday life. End with a thought that leaves the reader thinking about the operation.
- **Organize your explanation.**
  Decide on the order of organization that would clearly present the operation to your reader (time order, numbered steps, and so on).
- **Use specific terms.**
  Include words that are associated with the specific math operation.

After you've written a first draft . . .

- **Check for completeness.**
  Make sure that you have included all the information a reader needs to understand the process you are explaining.
- **Check for correctness.**
  Edit and proofread your work to eliminate errors in spelling, punctuation, and other conventions.

EXPOSITORY

Write directions for a mathematical operation that you are learning in math class. Use specific examples and clear steps.

Science: Writing an Observation Report

Experiments are at the heart of science. A good way to review and analyze an experiment is to write an observation report. The following report is based on a student's experiment involving root growth.

The **beginning** identifies the focus of the experiment.

The **middle** identifies the process.

The **ending** explains what the writer has learned.

Do Bean Roots Always Grow Downward?

Scientific question: Do bean roots always grow downward?

Hypothesis: The roots of beans placed in different growing positions will always grow downward toward the center of the earth.

Procedure: Four lima beans were glued onto a sponge with the concave sides facing different directions: down, up, left, and right. The sponge was moistened and placed in a zippered plastic bag. Several small slits were cut in the bag and the bag was tacked to a bulletin board. The bag was watered daily through the slits.

Observations:

Day 3: Small sprouts have appeared from each bean.

Day 5: The roots from the beans facing left and right are growing horizontally, the bean facing down has roots growing downward, and the bean facing up has roots growing upward.

Day 7: The roots from the left- and right-facing beans have bent downward. The bean facing down grew its roots straight down. The roots from the bean facing up have curved to the right and now go over the bean.

Day 9: The roots from all of the beans are growing downward.

Conclusion: Lima bean roots may initially sprout upward or horizontally but will always bend to finally grow downward.

TEKS 8.17A(iii)
ELPS 5B

Writing Tips

Before you write . . .

- **Take notes during the experiment.**
  Take careful notes so that you will have enough information to write an effective summary.
- **Follow the correct form.**
  Use the form your teacher requests or the one used for the sample on page 218. Remember that observation reports usually follow the scientific method and include these five parts: *scientific question, hypothesis, procedure, observations,* and *conclusion.*

During your writing . . .

- **Explain the focus of the experiment.**
  Identify the scientific question and the hypothesis that you explored.
- **List the steps in the procedure.**
  Make sure each step is clear and logically organized. Leave out extraneous information.
- **Include all of your observations.**
  List your personal observations chronologically.
- **Base your conclusions on what you observed.**
  Make careful observations so that your conclusions are accurate.

After you've written a first draft . . .

- **Use accurate terminology.**
  Find out the correct scientific terms for things you observe and use those terms in your report.
- **Check for completeness and correctness.**
  Go over your report to make sure that there are no mistakes. Answer any questions that the reader might have about the experiment. Then check your writing for errors.

EXPOSITORY

 Write an observation report for an experiment your teacher assigns. Make sure your report is logically organized and consistent with what you observe.

 TEKS 8.17B

Practical Writing:
Drafting a Business Letter

Sometimes the best way to make a change in your school or community is to write a letter. In the following letter to his principal, Alejandro Alvarez asks for lights on a soccer field.

The letter follows the correct format. (See pages 222–223.)

1080 Burns Road
Orange Park, FL 32000
May 5, 2011

Principal Jorge Rodriguez
Cardosa Middle School
116 Shelton Street
Orange Park, FL 32000

Dear Mr. Rodriguez:

The **beginning** introduces the student and his complaint.

As a soccer team member at Cardosa Middle School, I have a request. We need lights for nighttime games. When school starts in the fall, it gets darker earlier and earlier. It's hard for our teams to finish games safely. It really isn't fair to the coaches and teams.

The **body** provides details to explain the situation. It also contains the writer's opinion and complaint, as well as a request.

I realize that lighting is expensive. However, a lighted field could be used by the whole community, so the community could help pay for it. The soccer team could even run a citywide fund-raiser.

Adding lights to our soccer field would make a huge difference for our team. We would appreciate you making the request at the next school board meeting.

The **closing** includes a polite request.

Sincerely,

Alejandro Alvarez
Alejandro Alvarez

TEKS 8.14A, 8.17A(ii), 8.17B

ELPS 5G

Writing Tips

Use the following tips as a guide when you are asked to write a letter. (Also see pages **222–223**.)

Before you write . . .

- **Choose a topic that you care about.**
  Make a list of problems in your school or community and think of possible solutions. Choose a problem that is important to you.

- **Gather information.**
  Learn as much as you can about the problem. Find facts to support your solution.

- **Consider your reader.**
  Determine what the person you are writing to needs to know.

During your writing . . .

- **Keep it short.**
  Make your point quickly and stay focused on the main idea. Your letter should not be longer than one page.

- **State the problem and your solution.**
  Make sure your purpose for writing is clearly stated. Explain why the situation exists and how it can be fixed.

- **Be polite.**
  Use a courteous voice to the reader.

After you've written a first draft . . .

- **Check for completeness.**
  Make sure you did not leave out any important facts or reasons.

- **Check for correctness.**
  Read your letter several times. Double-check the address and spelling of all names. Correct any errors in punctuation, capitalization, spelling, and grammar.

EXPOSITORY

 Think of something you would like to write a letter about to an official in your community. Then write the letter, making sure to explain the problem as you see it. Express your opinion about the issue, and include a request for information or for something to be done.

TEKS 8.17B

Parts of a Business Letter

1 The heading includes your address and the date. Write the heading at least one inch from the top of the page at the left-hand margin.

2 The inside address includes the name and address of the person or organization you are writing to.

- If the person has a title, be sure to include it. (If the title is short, write it on the same line as the name. If the title is long, write it on the next line.)

- If you are writing to an organization or a business—but not to a specific person—begin the inside address with the name of the organization or business.

3 The salutation is the greeting. Always put a colon after the salutation.

- If you know the person's name, use it in your greeting.

  Dear Mr. Carranza:

- If you don't know the name of the person who will read your letter, use a salutation like one of these:

  Dear Store Owner:
  Dear Sir or Madam:
  Dear Madison Soccer Club:

4 The body is the main part of the letter. Do not indent the paragraphs; instead, skip a line after each one. This is where you include your complaint/opinion, and your request for information.

5 The closing comes after the body. Use **Yours truly** or **Sincerely** to close a business letter. Capitalize only the first word of the closing and put a comma after the closing.

6 The signature ends the letter. If you are using a computer, leave four spaces after the closing; then type your name. Write your signature in the space between the closing and the typed name.

Try IT Find a letter at home or in a book and bring it to school. Label each part of the letter using the words in blue above.

Business-Letter Format

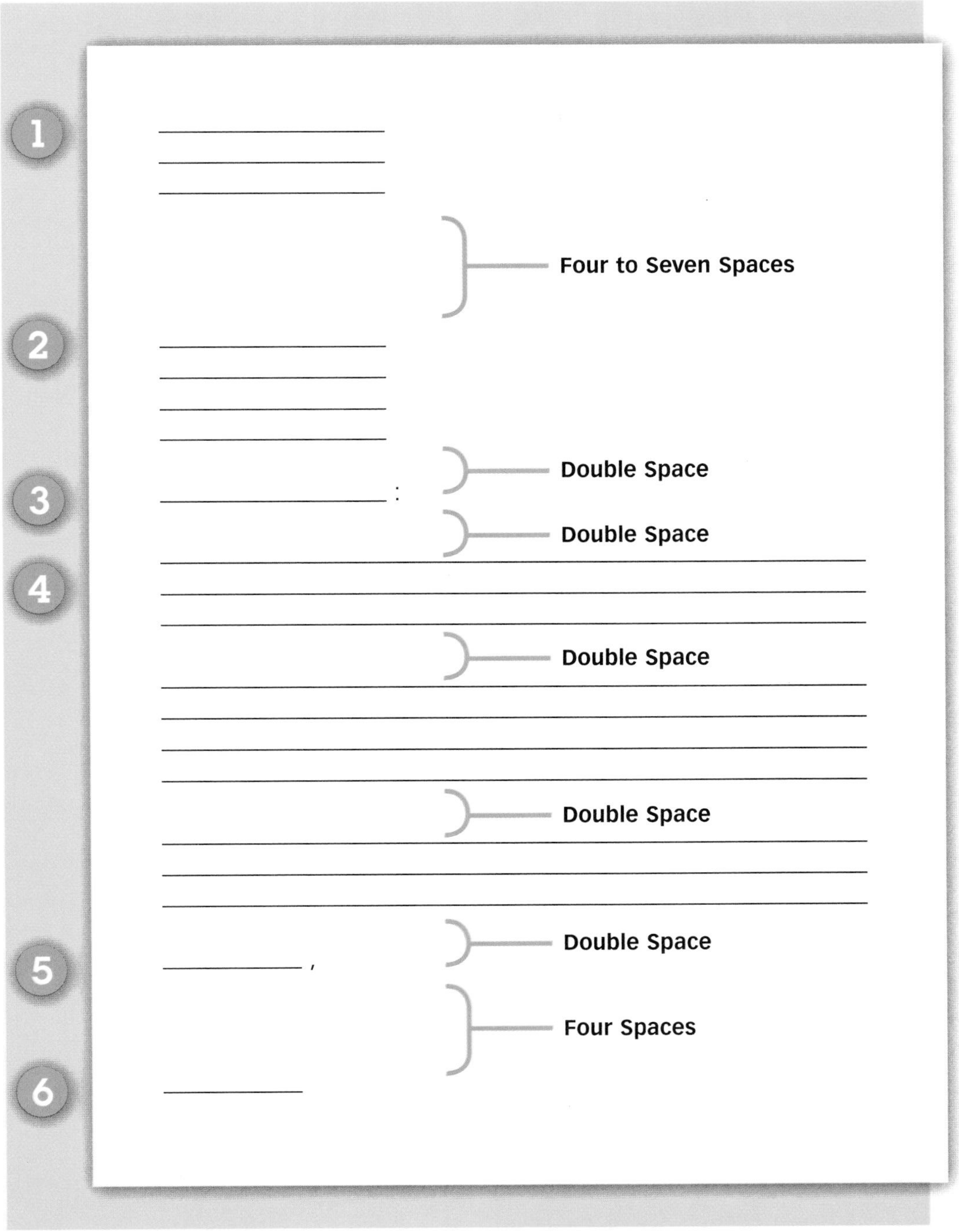

1

2

Four to Seven Spaces

3

Double Space

:

Double Space

4

Double Space

Double Space

5

Double Space

,

Four Spaces

6

 TEKS 8.17B

Practical Writing:
Drafting a Friendly Letter

You can write a friendly letter to give your opinion, make a complaint, or request information. A friendly letter is usually written to a friend, family member, or someone you know well.

The **heading** includes the date.

The **salutation** usually begins with Dear and is followed by the name of the person you are writing to.

The **body** includes your opinion, request, or complaint.

The **closing** is followed by a comma.

Your **signature**

February 3, 2011

Dear Carlos,

How are you? I hope your school year is going well. I'm doing just OK in math this year, but I'm doing great in science class. We're learning about cells and stuff and it's really interesting! My science teacher, Mr. Garcia, is funny and he uses songs to help us remember everything.

Anyway, I'm writing to ask you about the soccer camp you went to last summer. I want to go this summer, too. I need some information about it. How many days was it? Did you like the coaches? How many other kids were there? Do we have to bring our own snacks?

My mom says I can go, as long as I keep my grades up. So hurry and write me back! I really want to go!

Say "hi" to your family for me.

Your friend,

Eduardo

Tips for Writing a Friendly Letter

1 The heading includes the date and your address if you do not know the recipient well. Write it in the upper right-hand margin.

2 The salutation is the greeting. It is informal and can start with *Dear _____, Hi _____,* or *Hello _____.* Always use a comma after the person's name.

3 The body is the main part of the letter. The tone should be friendly, even if making a complaint or giving a strong opinion about something.

4 Like in any writing, the ideas should be well organized. Each paragraph should have one controlling idea.

5 The last sentence or two of the body can have a friendly request or comment.

6 The closing is informal. Some examples: *Your friend _____, Miss you, Best wishes, See you soon.* The closing is aligned with the heading and should be followed by a comma and your signature.

After you've written your first draft . . .

- **Check for completeness.**
  Did you say what you wanted to say? Are your ideas clearly stated? Is your tone friendly?

- **Check for correctness.**
  Read your letter several times. Double-check your sentence structure. Correct any errors in mechanics, spelling, and grammar.

EXPOSITORY

Think of something that you want information about, have an opinion about, or want to make a complaint about. Write to a friend or family member about it. (You may send the letter or simply treat it as a school assignment.)

Expository Writing
Writing for Assessment

Many state and school writing tests ask you to respond to an expository prompt. An expository prompt will ask you to explain something or share information. Study the sample prompt below.

Prompt

There are many inventions that have made life easier. Think of one invention that has had a significant impact on modern life. Then write an essay explaining several ways this invention has changed the way people live.

Analyzing the Prompt

When you respond to a writing prompt, the first step is to make sure you understand exactly what the prompt is asking you to do. As you read a prompt, ask yourself the following questions:

- What genre, or form, is the prompt asking me to write?
- What topic does the prompt ask me to write about?
- What purpose does the prompt give for the piece of writing?
- Does the prompt identify an audience?
- What specific information does the prompt tell me to include?

Most prompts will not provide the answers to all of these questions. You will need to decide some things for yourself. For example, the prompt may give a general topic, but you have to narrow it down to something more specific.

Some prompts do tell you the genre, such as narrative or expository, but others do not. You may have to figure out the genre from clues in the prompt. Look for key words that tell you the genre and the purpose for the piece of writing. The prompt above says, "write an essay explaining . . . ." An essay that explains something is expository, so that is the genre. Your purpose is to explain how a particular invention has changed the way people live.

TEKS 8.14A

Prewriting Selecting a Specific Topic

The prompt doesn't say which invention to write about. There have been many, many important inventions. How can you decide which one to write about? First you need to brainstorm possibilities. You probably don't have unlimited time, so you need to make a quick decision. Give yourself a time limit, such as one to two minutes, to list as many options as possible. Then think about the following as you consider which option to choose:

- Will you be able to look up any facts or details? If not, how much information do you know about the topic?
- Are you interested in the topic? Will others find it interesting?
- Do you have enough to say about the topic to meet the requirements of the prompt?

Mateo came up with a list of five possible topics: cell phones, computers, cars, trains, and airplanes. Mateo loves cars and thinks they are the most interesting of the five topics he listed. He also knew that there would be plenty to say about how the car changed the modern world, so he chose cars as his specific topic.

Planning the Writing

To plan his draft, Mateo used a topic cluster. It helped him choose his details and organize them.

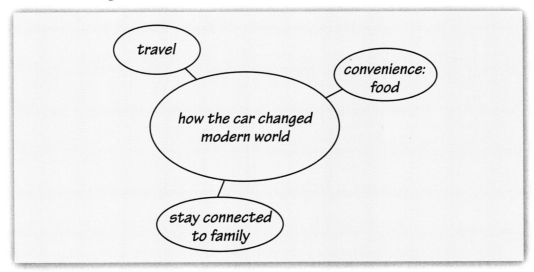

EXPOSITORY

Drafting Writing the Expository Essay

Study the sample student response below.

Response to an Expository Prompt

The **beginning** paragraph states the thesis statement (underlined).

Each **middle** paragraph covers one main point.

The writer's clear organization makes the essay easy to follow.

Cars Changed the World

It's hard to imagine life without cars. They take us to the supermarket, to work, and to visit family that live far away. <u>By making it easier for the average person to get from point A to point B, the invention of the car changed the modern world forever.</u>

Think about the simple act of getting important supplies, like food. Before the car, most people had to grow their own food, or live very close to someone who did. Now, food goes from the grower to the store. You can live almost anywhere because food will be brought to a supermarket near you.

What about work? Before the car, the world was a very big place. It was extremely difficult for people to travel outside of the town or area where they lived to work. If there were no job opportunities close enough to someone's home that they could walk or ride a horse to work, they would have to move somewhere else. They might have to leave behind their family and friends, and traveling back home for visits was often very difficult. Car travel has greatly expanded people's job options by allowing them to travel to jobs that are farther from home.

Well-developed ideas and good examples show thoughtfulness.

Let's not forget how the invention of the car affected the family. Before the car, family members had to live and work in the same place if they wanted to see each other. Now, families can live and work in different cities and towns and still celebrate family events together. Taking a family vacation––something most families do these days––was a luxury that was much too expensive for a lot of working families before the invention of the car.

The **ending** gives the reader something to think about.

Even if you only like cars for the way they look, you can't deny that they make our modern world easier to get around! How would your life be different without them?

Respond to the reading. Answer the following questions about the sample essay.

☐ **Focus and Coherence** (1) What is the controlling idea? (2) Do all paragraphs relate to the controlling idea?

☐ **Organization** (3) Is the essay easy to follow?

☐ **Development of Ideas** (4) Are the ideas explained using thoughtful details?

☐ **Voice** (5) How do you know the writer cares about the subject?

Literature Connection: You can find an example of expository writing in "Over the Top: The True Adventures of a Volcano Chaser" by Renee Skelton.

EXPOSITORY

Writing Tips

Before you write . . .

- **Understand the prompt.**
  Remember that an expository prompt asks you to explain. Decide on a specific topic for your writing.
- **Plan your time wisely.**
  Take several minutes to plan your writing. Use a graphic organizer like a cluster to help with planning your writing.

Cluster

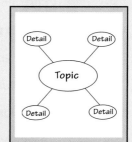

During your drafting . . .

- **Decide on a focus for your essay.**
  Keep your main idea or purpose in mind as you write.
- **Be selective.**
  Use examples and explanations to directly support your focus.
- **End in a meaningful way.**
  Remind the reader about the importance of the topic.

After you've written a first draft . . .

- **Check for completeness and correctness.**
  Present your details in a logical order and correct errors in capitalization, punctuation, spelling, and grammar.

Plan and write a response. Respond to the prompt on page 226. Complete your writing within the period of time your teacher gives you. Remember to select a specific topic and use the tips above.

Expository Writing in Review

Purpose: In expository writing, you *explain something* to readers.

Topics: Explain . . . the kinds of something,
how things are similar or different,
how to do or make something,
the causes of something, or
the definition of something.

Prewriting

Select a topic that you know something about or one you want to learn more about. (See pages 172–173.)

Gather and sort details and organize them chronologically, point by point, or in order of importance. (See pages 174 and 176.)

Write a thesis statement, telling exactly what topic you plan to write about. (See page 173.)

Drafting

In the beginning, introduce your topic, say something interesting about it, and state your focus. (See page 179.)

In the middle, use clear topic sentences and specific details to support the thesis statement. (See pages 180–181.)

In the ending, summarize your writing and make a final comment about the topic. (See page 182.)

Revising

Review the focus and coherence, development of ideas, organization, and **voice.** (See pages 184–192.)

Editing

Check your writing for conventions. Also have a trusted classmate edit your writing. (See pages 194–198.)

Make a final copy and proofread it for errors before sharing it. (See page 199.)

Assessing

Use the rubric to assess your finished writing. (See pages 50–51.)

EXPOSITORY

persuade

argue

Persuasive Writing

Writing Focus

- Persuasive Letter
- Friendly Letter
- Personal Commentary

Grammar Focus

- Avoiding Double Subjects
- Subject-Verb Agreement
- Pronoun Agreement

Learning Language

Learning these words and expressions will help you understand this unit.

1. A **controversy** is something that people disagree about.
   Name something at school that there is a controversy over. What is your opinion about it?

2. You are **persuasive** when you try to get others to think the way you do.
   When have you been persuasive?

convince

reason   support

Persuasive Writing

Persuasive Paragraph

Where do you stand on the new weekend curfew? What's your position on the cancellation of school dances? When you "take a stand" or "defend a position," you state what you think about an important issue.

What positions have you, or could you, defend? One way to defend a position is to write a persuasive paragraph in which you state your position and provide reasons to support it. In this chapter, you will read a sample persuasive paragraph defending the position that winning in sports is about more than trophies. Afterward, you'll write a "position" paragraph of your own.

Writing Guidelines

Subject: **An important issue**

Purpose: **To support your position**

Form: **Persuasive paragraph**

Audience: **Classmates, parents, guardians**

Persuasive Paragraph

In a persuasive paragraph, you state your position in the **topic sentence**. The **body** of the paragraph supports the position, and the **closing sentence** restates it. The following paragraph was written by Elena, a student who argued that participating in sports makes for healthy living.

Topic Sentence

Body

Closing Sentence

Join a Winning Team

Sports tone up students' bodies and also their minds. To start with, sports are a fun way to stay healthy and physically fit. Growing kids need physical activity to build strong bones and improve hand-eye coordination. Sports also improve muscle strength, flexibility, and the cardiovascular system. In addition, sports teach students to work well with others and have a good attitude. The challenge of the game helps players learn to keep going and never give up. Because they learn determination, students who play sports often do better in school. Playing sports is good for the body and mind, so no matter who scores the most points, everybody wins!

Respond to the reading. After reading the paragraph above, write answers to the following questions.

- ☐ **Development of Ideas** (1) What is the writer's position? (2) What reasons support the position?
- ☐ **Organization** (3) What transitions does the writer use in the body sentences of the paragraph?
- ☐ **Voice** (4) What specific words or phrases make this paragraph persuasive? Find two.

TEKS 8.14A

Prewriting Selecting a Topic

Think about a debate you recently had with another person. Elena charted recent debates to find a position she wanted to write about.

Topics Chart

Debates	
I said...	The other person said...
School lunch is too expensive.	It's cheaper than fast food.
I need more allowance.	Then do more chores.
✱ Sports are good for students.	Sports make students too competitive.
School starts too early.	It's better than getting out too late.

Select a position. Create a chart like the one above. List debates you have had with other people. Write down what you said and what the other person said. Then select a position you would like to write about in a paragraph.

Gathering Reasons

Next you need to gather reasons to support your position. Elena gathered supporting reasons by turning her position into a question that started with "Why?" Then she answered the question in as many ways as she could.

Supporting Reasons

Why are sports good for students?
- ~~Lots of people enjoy them.~~
- Participating in sports improves flexibility.
- Sports activities help build strong bones and muscles.
- ~~Athletes are more popular than other kids.~~
- Sports teach kids to keep trying and never give up.
- Kids who play sports often do well in school.

List your reasons. Turn your position into a question that starts with "Why?" Then answer the question in as many ways as possible. Review your list and cross out any reasons that are not very persuasive.

PERSUASIVE

TEKS 8.14B

Drafting Creating Your First Draft

As you write the first draft of your paragraph, follow these tips.

- Write a **topic sentence** that clearly states your position. Try different versions until you feel satisfied with the sentence.
- Create **body sentences** that provide your supporting reasons. Use transitions to help connect the ideas in your sentences.
- Write a **closing sentence** that restates your position in a fresh, different way.

 Write your first draft. Use the tips above and your prewriting to guide you. The purpose of your first draft is to get your ideas on paper.

Revising Improving Your Writing

Once your first draft is finished, it's time to revise it. Check your *focus and coherence, organization, development of ideas, voice,* and *conventions.*

 Revise your paragraph. Let the questions below guide the revision of your paragraph.

1 Does the topic sentence clearly state my position?

2 Do the reasons support my position?

3 Do my reasons appear in an effective order? Do I use transitions to tie my ideas together?

4 Does my word choice make my paragraph sound persuasive?

5 Do my sentences flow smoothly?

Editing Checking for Conventions

After you revise your paragraph, check it for *conventions.*

 Edit your paragraph. Ask yourself the following questions.

1 Have I used the correct spelling, punctuation, and capitalization?

2 Have I checked for errors in grammar?

 Proofread your paragraph. Make a final copy of your paragraph and check it one more time before sharing it with your audience.

Persuasive Writing

Writing a Persuasive Letter

Hubbub, tussle, scrap, ruckus, hoo-hah, squabble, tiff—English has hundreds of words that describe differences of opinion. Anytime you get a large group of people together, whether in a school or in a community, differences of opinion are bound to come up.

Perhaps people in your school disagree about creating an open study hall. Maybe school board members are debating a change in the school mascot. It might even be that your city is squabbling over a new housing development.

One form of persuasive writing helps you deal with differences of opinion. By stating a position and defending it, you can convince others to agree with you. In this chapter, you will write a persuasive letter about a controversy in your school or community.

Writing Guidelines

Subject: A controversy in your school or community

Purpose: To defend a position

Form: Persuasive letter

Audience: Classmates and community members

Understanding Your Goals

Your assignment in this chapter is to write a well-organized persuasive letter that reflects an opinion, registers a complaint, and requests information. The goals listed below will help you plan your letter. The scoring rubric on pages 50–51 will also help you. Refer to it often to improve your writing.

Focus and Coherence

Write about a topic that you have an opinion on. Include a complaint, and request some kind of information. Be sure to stay on point and include only details that help you express your thoughts and clearly explain what you need. Include a way for the person to reach you with the information or items you request.

Organization

Introduce yourself and your opinion at the beginning of your letter. Then express your complaint and request information. Make sure you don't repeat information or add unnecessary details.

Development of Ideas

Use precise details when telling about your complaint to help the reader understand your issue. Be very specific about the information or items you are requesting.

Voice

Use persuasive words that balance facts with feelings.

Conventions

Check your writing for errors in grammar, mechanics (punctuation, capitalization), and spelling.

Literature Connection. An example of a persuasive letter is "The First Americans" by The Grand Council Fire of American Indians.

TEKS 8.17B

Persuasive Letter

In a persuasive letter, you share your position about an issue and try to convince your reader to feel the same way. In the letter that follows, the student writer expresses an opinion on allowing students more options during study hall.

7689 Coldstone Drive
Fairbanks, AK 99701
October 23, 2011

Opening

The opening introduces the topic and states an opinion (underlined).

Dear Mr. Rivera,

Study hall is very important for most students here at Carona Middle School. Many really count on this time to finish homework and study for tests. <u>That is why it is time to make study hall more effective by making it more open.</u>

Middle

In the middle paragraphs, the writer makes a complaint and then presents reasons to support it.

I was upset to read the article in last week's newsletter supporting only closed study hall. The newsletter should have also shared information about open study hall. Then faculty and students can make an informed choice.

Open study hall is one way of letting hardworking students go where they need to go to get more work done. The library, computer lab, or art room might sometimes be better places for students to do their work. An open study hall plan would allow them to accomplish more.

An open study hall would also motivate students to take study hall more seriously. When hardworking students earn the privilege of leaving the room, other students would want to do the same. The only way would be to study more.

PERSUASIVE

TEKS 8.17B, 8.18B
ELPS 5G

Most importantly, an open study hall teaches responsibility. It would be a great way to prepare students for high school where nobody will hold their hands. They need to learn how to manage their time now. An open study hall would help.

Understandably, Principal Ramos and some teachers are worried about students wandering the halls, but just because study hall would be open doesn't mean students could wander. They would still have to use hall passes and arrange with specific teachers to come to their rooms. If students are caught abusing this privilege, then it could be taken away from them.

Study hall would be more effective if it were open. I hope you will consider publishing an article to support an open study hall. Could you please give me the deadline for submitting an article to the next newsletter? I can be reached in Mr. Blanco's study hall during 8th period.

Yours truly,
Ramona Heinz

This writer considers alternative positions and answers possible concerns and counter-arguments.

Closing
. . . .
The closing paragraph restates the writer's position and requests information.

Respond to the reading. Answer the following questions about the sample essay.

☐ **Development of Ideas** **(1) What three reasons does the writer use to support her position?**

☐ **Organization** **(2) Which paragraph expresses a complaint? (3) Which paragraph answers a concern and a counterargument?**

☐ **Voice** **(4) Does the writer sound knowledgeable and persuasive? Explain.**

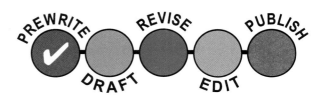

Prewriting

In prewriting, you will select a controversial issue, gather reasons and details, and organize your ideas. Solid prewriting makes persuasive writing much easier.

Keys to Effective Prewriting

1. Select a controversial issue in your school or community, decide what your opinion is, and figure out who you could write a letter to about it.

2. Gather reasons and details that support your opinion. Keep your reader in mind and think about the details or reasons that would be most likely to persuade him or her.

3. Select an important objection or concern that you can address.

4. Write a clear position statement to guide you.

5. Create a list or an outline as a planning guide.

PROD. NO.
SCENE
TAKE
ROLI
SOUND

PERSUASIVE

 **TEKS** 8.14A

Prewriting **Selecting a Controversy**

A controversy happens when there are differing opinions concerning an important issue. A student named Beatriz used sentence starters to brainstorm about controversies in her school and community.

Sentence Starters

People at my school disagree about . . .
    – whether we should go to block scheduling.
    – 45-minute bus rides.
    – all the fund-raisers.
    – whether graduation should be a bigger deal.

People in my neighborhood disagree about . . .
    – what should happen to that empty lot.
    – all the "no skateboarding" signs.
    – the woods for sale next to the school. ✳
    – the 10:00 p.m. curfew.
    – the Labrador that barks all night.

Prewrite

List controversies. On your own paper, complete the two sentence starters above. Try to come up with at least three endings for each sentence. Choose a controversy that you feel strongly about and write a sentence that states your position.

    I think Belmer Woods should be
    turned into a park.

Texas Traits

★ Focus on the Texas Traits

Development of Ideas Choose an issue that you feel strongly about. You'll have an easier time finding support and defending a position that you really believe in.

TEKS 8.14B, 8.18C

Gathering Reasons to Support Your Position

Once you have stated your position, you need to gather reasons to support it. A table diagram can help. The tabletop presents your position. The table legs support that position by answering the question "Why?" The following table diagram helped Beatriz gather reasons for her position.

Table Diagram

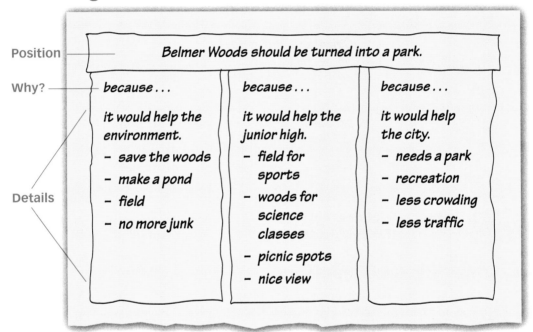

Position — Belmer Woods should be turned into a park.

Why? —

because...

it would help the environment.
- save the woods
- make a pond
- field
- no more junk

because...

it would help the junior high.
- field for sports
- woods for science classes
- picnic spots
- nice view

because...

it would help the city.
- needs a park
- recreation
- less crowding
- less traffic

Details

Prewrite

Create a table diagram. Use the sample as a guide to create your own table diagram. In the top box, write your position. In three or four boxes beneath it, write reasons that answer the question "Why?" Then add details about each reason.

PERSUASIVE

Texas Traits

Focus on the Texas Traits

Organization A table needs at least three legs to keep from wobbling and falling over. In the same way, your position essay needs at least three supporting reasons. In your essay, you will organize these reasons by building toward the most important one.

Prewriting **Consider Objections**

Answering the question "Why?" helped you gather support for your position. Next, answering the question "Why not?" will help you gather support to answer possible objections or concerns. If you understand objections the reader might have, you can defend against them and make your position stronger. One way to think of objections is to imagine arrows the reader might shoot at your position. Beatriz wrote her objections inside arrows.

Position   Objections—Why not?

I think Belmer   because . . . we need more houses.
Woods should
be turned into a   because . . . a park would be too expensive. ✱
park.
                          because . . . we need a new mall instead.

Prewrite **Gather objections.** Write your position. Then draw arrows that list objections to your position (answer "Why not?"). Star your strongest objection.

Countering an Objection

When you counter an objection, you argue against it. Then think about possible counterarguments the reader might make in response and answer those, too. Beatriz countered the following objection with the reasons below.

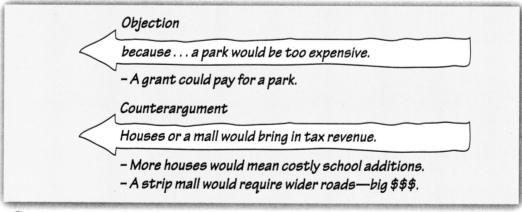

Objection

because . . . a park would be too expensive.

– A grant could pay for a park.

Counterargument

Houses or a mall would bring in tax revenue.

– More houses would mean costly school additions.
– A strip mall would require wider roads—big $$$.

Prewrite **Counter an important objection.** List reasons that counter the strongest objection to your argument and answer possible counterarguments.

TEKS 8.14A, 8.18A, 8.18B

Writing a Position Statement

Your position statement should clearly tell what you think about the controversy. Beatriz wrote down her position. Then she tried two other ways to state it. She put a star next to the statement that worked best.

Position Statements

> Belmer Woods should be turned into a park.
>
> The best way to develop Belmer Woods would be to make it a park. ★
>
> Instead of more houses or stores, the land should become a park.

Write your position statement. Write three different versions. Then choose the statement you feel works best.

Writing Topic Sentences

Next, you need to write topic sentences for your middle paragraphs. Beatriz used a chart. She wrote her reasons in the left column and corresponding topic sentences in the right column.

Outline Chart

Reasons	Topic Sentences
It would help the environment.	First of all, a park would be the right choice for the environment.
It would help the junior high.	Turning Belmer Woods into a park would also help the junior high.
It would help the city.	The most important reason to create a new park is that the whole city would benefit.
Objection: A park would be too expensive.	Some people say the city doesn't have enough money to create a park.

Write topic sentences. Make an outline chart like the one above. In the left column, list the reasons from your table diagram (page 243) and the objection you chose (page 244). In the right column, create topic sentences.

PERSUASIVE

TEKS 8.14B, 8.18B, 8.18C

Prewriting Organizing Your Letter

The following directions can help you create an organized list for your letter. The organized list brings together all the ideas of your prewriting and prepares you to write your first draft.

Directions

Organized List

Write your position statement.

The best way to develop Belmer Woods would be to make it a park.

Write your first topic sentence.

1. *First of all, a park would be the right choice for the environment.*

List facts and details.

   - *save part of forest*
   - *make pond and field*
   - *stop pollution and graffiti*

Write your second topic sentence.

2. *Turning Belmer Woods into a park would also help the junior high.*

List facts and details.

   - *field for sports teams*
   - *forest for science classes*
   - *picnic areas for clubs*

Write your third topic sentence.

3. *The most important reason to create a new park is that the whole city would benefit.*

List facts and details.

   - *no parks on west side*
   - *west side already crowded*
   - *houses/strip mall not needed*

Write your fourth topic sentence.

4. *Some people say the city doesn't have enough money to create a park.*

List facts and details.

   - *new houses = school additions*
   - *new strip mall = road work*
   - *cheaper to make park*

Prewrite

Create an organized list. Use the "Directions" above to organize your position statement, topic sentences, and details. This list will guide you as you write your first draft.

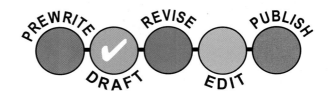

TEKS 8.14B

Go Online!

PREWRITE • DRAFT ✓ • REVISE • EDIT • PUBLISH

Drafting

After you create a plan for your essay, you are ready to get all of your ideas on paper.

Keys to Effective Drafting

1. Use your organized list or outline as a planning guide.

2. Write with your purpose, form, and audience in mind. Ask yourself these questions as you write:
   - Am I staying on topic throughout the letter?
   - Do I follow the format for a business letter?
   - Do I speak directly and clearly to my audience?

3. Be sure to include all the parts of a business letter.

4. State your position in the first paragraph.

5. Use specific details to support your position.

6. Address an important objection and possible counterarguments.

PERSUASIVE

Drafting Getting the Big Picture

Now that you have finished prewriting, you are ready to create a first draft of your letter. The graphic that follows shows how the parts of your letter will fit together. (The examples are from the student letter on pages 249–252.)

Beginning

The **beginning** introduces the controversial issue and states the writer's position.

Position Statement

The best way to develop Belmer Woods would be to make it a park.

Middle

The **middle** paragraphs support the writer's position.

The **last middle** paragraph answers an important objection.

Topic Sentences

First of all, a park would be the right choice for the environment.

Turning Belmer Woods into a park would also help the junior high.

The most important reason to create a new park is that the whole city would benefit.

Some people say the city doesn't have enough money to create a park.

Ending

The **ending** revisits the position.

Closing Sentence

Many people have ideas about developing Belmer Woods, but only a park would be best for the community.

Starting Your Letter

The beginning of your letter needs to introduce the topic and state your opinion as clearly as possible. Remember that your readers should quickly be able to understand why you are writing. Here are some ways to begin.

> Beginning
>
> Middle
>
> Ending

- **Identify yourself.**
  As students at Belmer Junior High, we are used to looking out the windows and seeing Belmer Woods.

- **Dramatize the controversy.**
  Bulldozers and chain saws are about to destroy Belmer Woods.

- **State the facts.**
  Developers are planning to cut down the trees in Belmer Woods.

- **Be creative.**
  When developers look at Belmer Woods, they don't see green leaves, but green stacks of cash.

Beginning Paragraph

Beatriz begins her letter by making a connection with the reader. Then she introduces the topic and states her opinion about it.

> 1002 Belmer Woods Drive
> Belmer, WI 53998
> September 23, 2012
>
> Dear Editor,
>   As students at Belmer Junior High, we are used to looking out the windows and seeing Belmer Woods. Now we see a sign: "For Sale, 20 acres, Zoned Residential/Commercial." There are many ideas about how Belmer Woods should change. However, the best way to develop Belmer Woods would be to make it a park.

The controversy is introduced.

The position is stated (underlined).

Write an opening. Write the beginning paragraph of your letter. Use one of the strategies above to get your reader's attention. Then introduce the topic and state your position.

TEKS 8.14B, 8.14C,
8.17A(v), 8.18B

Drafting **Developing the Middle**

Now it's time to write the middle of your letter. Start each paragraph with a topic sentence and add details that support it. Your last middle paragraph should address an objection and answer possible counterarguments.

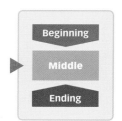

Using Transitions

Transitions will help you show the order of importance in your paragraphs. The following sets of transitions would work well with your first three middle paragraphs.

First of all, **Also,** **Most importantly,**	**To begin,** **Also,** **Finally,**	**To start with,** **In addition,** **Most significantly,**

Middle Paragraphs

The topic sentence introduces the topic (underlined).

The body supports the topic sentence.

Use transitions to show the order of importance of your arguments.

First of all, a park would be the right choice for the environment. Part of the forest could be saved, and earthmovers could dig out a pond. The grassy part on the north could remain as a field for soccer or baseball. Making the land into a park would also help protect the environment. Nobody would be able to dump junk or car tires there anymore or carve graffiti into the trees. A park would both preserve and protect the environment.

Turning Belmer Woods into a park would help the junior high, **as well.** Gym classes and sports teams could use the field on the north side. Science classes could study the plants, trees, and insects in the wooded spots. **In addition,** any clubs in the school would be able to hold

TEKS 8.14B, 8.17A(v),
8.18B, 8.18C

events the wooded spots and in the picnic areas. So,
Belmer Junior High would be a better place if students
had a park next door.

   The most important reason to create a new
park is that the whole city would benefit. Currently,
there are no parks on the west side of town, but there
are plenty of houses. A park would give all those people
somewhere to go for recreation. A new subdivision or
a new strip mall would just make the west side overcrowded and create traffic problems.

   *While some people say the city doesn't have enough
money to create a park, a subdivision or a strip mall would
cost even more.* For example, if a hundred new families
moved in, the city would have to add on to the schools.
Likewise, if a strip mall were built, the city would have to
widen the roads. Those projects would cost a lot more
than creating a park, and we could apply for grants to help
fund the park.

> **The middle paragraphs build to the most important reason.**
>
> **A variety of transitions are used to link paragraphs and sentences within the paragraphs.**
>
> **The last middle paragraph counters an objection.**

Write your middle paragraphs. Use the table diagram that you created
in prewriting to help you draft middle paragraphs that support your opinion.
Make sure your ideas are logically organized to support your viewpoint.

Drafting Tips

- **Follow the plan** in your organized list.
- **Use transitions** to show order of importance.
- **Include clear reasons** and avoid sounding emotional.
- **Respond to an objection** and counterarguments.

Drafting **Ending Your Letter**

The hard work is done. You have stated your position, supported it with reasons, and responded to an objection. Now you are ready to write your ending paragraph. If you aren't sure what to write in your ending paragraph, follow these guidelines.

> Beginning
>
> Middle
>
> ▶ Ending

Sentence 1: Revisit your position.

Sentence 2: Sum up the main support for your position.

Sentence 3: Sum up the objection and your response to it.

Sentence 4: Leave the reader with a strong final thought.

Ending Paragraph

The position is restated.

The paragraph sums up support for the position.

> In conclusion, the best way to improve Belmer Woods is to make it into Belmer Park. The park would help the environment, the junior high, and the city. Many people have ideas about developing Belmer Woods, but only a park would be best for the majority of the community.
>
> Sincerely,
> Beatriz Alvarez

Write your ending. Write the final paragraph of your letter. Restate your position and sum up the reasons for it. Leave the reader with something to think about.

Form a complete first draft. Write a complete copy of your letter. Skip every other line if you write by hand, or double-space if you use a computer. This will give you room for revising.

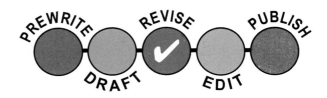

Revising

When you revise, you add or remove details, shift parts of the letter, and work on creating a more persuasive voice. You also check your word choice and refine your sentences.

Keys to Effective Revising

1. Read your letter aloud to get a feeling for how well it works.

2. Make sure you clearly state your position.

3. Make sure your reasons are accurate and logical and fit your purpose and audience.

4. Be sure you consider and respond to readers' objections and counterarguments.

5. Check that you have used a variety of transitions to link paragraphs.

6. Make sure you include both facts and opinions.

7. Use the editing and proofreading marks inside the back cover of this book.

PERSUASIVE

Revising for Focus and Coherence

When you revise for *focus and coherence*, consider your audience. Make sure you have used logical reasons that are likely to persuade them. Avoid "fuzzy thinking" that may make them question the strength of your argument. Also look for ways to strengthen your response to any objections your reader(s) may have.

How can I avoid "fuzzy thinking" in my essay?

You can avoid "fuzzy thinking" by making sure the reasons you use are accurate and logical. If even one of your supporting reasons is not logical, your position will be shaky, like a table with a bad leg. Here are three common types of "fuzzy thinking" errors to check for.

- **Half-truths:** Avoid telling only half of the story.
  Building a dam would help animals by giving them new habitats.
  This is a half-truth because dams also destroy habitats.

- **Exaggerations:** Avoid stretching the truth.
  Next the school board will force students to clean the highway!
  This exaggeration merely makes the writer sound unrealistic.

- **All-or-nothing statements:** Avoid oversimplifying complex issues.
  If the school bans fund-raisers, we'll never have new uniforms.
  Few people would believe that these are the only options.

How can I persuade my audience?

As you look over your reasons, be sure to think not only about your biggest concerns but also what your audience will be most concerned about. In her letter, Beatriz pointed out that a shopping mall would create more traffic because she knew that city officials would be concerned about that. She also responded to what would probably be their greatest concern: cost.

 Read the following sentences and identify the fuzzy thinking in each.
  1. The mayor wants to put every curfew breaker into prison.
  2. The school food is what is making eighth graders gain weight.
  3. If the state doesn't change the tests, no one will graduate.
  4. Television is the reason kids are getting bad grades.

 Check for fuzzy thinking. Read the body of your essay and look for half-truths, exaggerations, and all-or-nothing statements. Revise your essay to eliminate any fuzzy thinking and to address your audience's concerns.

How can I check my response to an objection?

When you are defending a position, you should answer a key objection your reader may have and argue against it. As you think about how to write your argument, be sure to consider the main reason for the objection. Also consider what counterarguments your reader might make in response to your argument and answer those, as well.

For example, Beatriz knew town officials would probably object to the cost of the park, so she pointed out that the town could apply for a grant. She also anticipated their counterargument that other options could create tax dollars, so she pointed out that those alternatives would also create expenses. To check your response to an objection and counterarguments ask yourself the following questions:

1. What is the *main point* of the objection?

2. What *argument* can I make to deal with the main point?

3. How can I respond to *counterarguments* readers might make?

 Read the following objection paragraph. Use the three questions above to decide what changes could improve the paragraph.

> 1   Some teachers object to cell phones because they are
> 2   too disruptive in class. That's a serious concern, but why can't
> 3   teachers just start class saying, "Please turn off all cell phones"?
> 4   For that matter, students with cell phones can talk quietly so that
> 5   everyone else can still hear the lecture. Finally, students could
> 6   just use cell phones for sending text messages. They are silent.

 Review your objection paragraph. Ask yourself the three questions above and revise as needed to make the paragraph more effective.

Focus and Coherence
Weak reasons are replaced with more effective ones.

Some people ~~are against creating~~ a park. However, *say the city doesn't have enough money to create*

a subdivision or a strip mall ~~isn't any good, either~~. If *would cost even more.*

a hundred new families moved in, the city would have *to add on to the schools*

~~all kinds of problems~~. If a strip mall were built, the city

would have ~~even more trouble~~. . . . *to widen the roads*

PERSUASIVE

 **TEKS** 8.14B, 8.14C, 8.18C
ELPS 4G

Revising for Organization

When you revise your writing for *organization*, check the overall structure of your letter. Also be sure you have placed your reasons in the most convincing order. Often, in persuasive writing, it is best to end with your strongest argument, so that you can build up to it. Readers are most likely to remember the last thing they read.

How can I check the arrangement of my reasons?

The best way to check the arrangement of your reasons is to follow the three guidelines below.

- Save your most important reason until last.
- Use words such as "first of all," "in addition," and "most importantly" to help the reader understand the organization of your reasons.
- Use the final middle paragraph to answer an objection and counterarguments.

 Read the following topic sentences from a letter about junior high graduation. Put them in the most effective order. Transition words and phrases will help you.

1. Junior high graduation also marks a big change for students.
2. The most important reason to treat junior high graduation more seriously is that it tells students their work is important.
3. It is true that the school board is concerned about the cost of a more elaborate graduation.
4. For one thing, parents want to make the junior high graduation a bigger event.

 Check the order of your reasons. Do you build to the most important reason? Do you respond to an objection? Do you tie your paragraphs together with transitions? Revise until you can answer each of these question with a "yes."

 Vary the transitions you use. Do not use the same transition over and over again. Too many "In additions," will bore the reader and make your writing appear uncreative.

TEKS 8.14B, 8.14C, 8.17A(v), 8.18C

How can I improve the overall organization of my letter?

You can improve your letter's organization by making sure you have used transitions to link paragraphs. Notice the following transitions and how they are used.

To show time or sequence:

after, before, until, meanwhile, first, later, as soon as

To add information:

again, for instance, next, in addition, also, along with

To conclude or summarize:

in conclusion, in summary, finally, lastly

Revise

Check your overall organization. Review your letter, checking to see if you have used transitions to link paragraphs. If so, make sure you have used a variety of transition words. If not, add transitions from the list above.

Organization
The writer added transition words to improve the overall organization of the letter.

While
⋀ Some people say the city doesn't have enough money

to create a park, a subdivision or a strip mall would cost

For example,
even more. ⋀ If a hundred new families moved in, the city

Likewise,
would have to add on to the schools. ⋀ If a strip mall were

built, the city would have to widen the roads. Those

projects would cost a lot more than creating a park.
In conclusion,
⋀ The best way to improve Belmer Woods is to make it

into Belmer Park.

PERSUASIVE

Texas Traits Revising for Development of Ideas

When you check your letter for *development of ideas*, make sure you have included both facts and opinions.

Do I use both facts and opinions in my letter?

Remember to differentiate between facts and opinions as you review your evidence and be sure to include both in your letter.

Facts...	**Opinions...**
• tell about the way things are.	• tell how a person thinks or feels.
• can be checked or proven.	• are often stated with feeling words (think, believe, feel).

Opinion: Belmer Woods is too beautiful to be turned into a strip mall.
(This statement expresses a feeling that cannot be proven true.)

Fact: Belmer Woods covers 20 acres of land.
(This statement can be proven true.)

 Number a piece of paper from 1 to 6. Read the statements below and decide if they are facts or opinions. Write "O" for opinion and "F" for fact.

  1. A park is the best option for this community.
  2. The woods are the largest in the county.
  3. The woods are the most inviting in the county.
  4. The park commissioner says that Belmer Woods should become a park.
  5. We believe a housing development would be bad for the community.
  6. Belmer Woods is one of only four forested areas in the town.

 Check for facts and opinions. Read your letter. Look for evidence to differentiate facts and opinions in your writing. Make sure that you have written your sentences clearly enough that your reader will be able to tell opinions from facts.

TEKS 8.14C

How can qualifiers make my writing more persuasive?

Qualifiers can make your writing more persuasive because they limit or "qualify" a statement. Few statements are *always* true for *everyone*. Sometimes, adding a qualifier to a sentence can help make your point or claim more believable for your audience and better address your purpose.

Qualifiers				
some	others	many	often	frequently
few	most	several	occasionally	usually

 Read the following sentences. Rewrite each sentence and add a qualifier to help achieve your purpose and make your claim more believable for your audience.

1. Students don't take responsibility for their own education.
2. Drivers are careless on the road behind the school.
3. Teachers never attend the school productions.
4. Students don't care about the student council elections.
5. Parents ignore the parking rules.
6. Students have no manners in the lunch room.

 Check your use of qualifiers. Review your letter. Rethink ways you can add qualifiers to address your purpose and make it easier for your audience to believe your claims.

Development of Ideas
A statement was qualified to make a claim more believable.

In addition, the park would cost the city less than a new subdivision or strip mall. ~~Everyone has~~ *Many people have* ideas about developing Belmer Woods, but only a park would be best for the community.

PERSUASIVE

Revising **for** Voice

To revise for *voice*, make sure your writing voice is persuasive, consistent, and balanced. If you get too emotional, people are likely to think you are not being reasonable and may ignore your arguments. If you are too dry, people may not be swayed by your points. Aim for just the right balance of logical reasoning with some emotional appeal.

Do I balance facts and feelings?

You use a balanced voice if you focus on facts first and back them up with feelings. If your letter focuses on feelings first, it will sound emotional and unconvincing.

Too Emotional

The Qwik-E-Stop is a bad place. The manager seems distrustful of kids. The whole time you feel just awful. You feel as if you need to get out of there as soon as possible.

On the other hand, if your letter focuses solely on facts, it will sound too dull. Feelings give meaning to facts.

Too Dry

The Qwik-E-Stop is on Main Street. It allows only two students in at a time. The manager enforces this rule. If two kids are inside, other kids wait outside.

A persuasive voice balances facts and feelings.

A Balanced Voice

The Quik-E-Stop on Main Street allows only two students in at a time, and the manager closely watches any students who enter the store. This policy and the attitude of the manager make kids feel unwelcome.

Check your voice for balance. Read through your letter. Do you include both facts and feelings? If your voice sounds too emotional, add facts. If it sounds too dull, add feelings. Revise until you reach a balance.

TEKS 8.14C

Do I use a consistent point of view?

You can check for a consistent point of view by looking at the pronouns in your letter. A persuasive essay should use mostly third-person pronouns: *he, she, it, they.* Your teacher may also allow you to use some first-person pronouns: *I, me, we, us.* However, you should avoid second-person pronouns: *you, your.* They can make your writing seem too personal, as if you are focused only on your own concerns. They can also make your readers feel as if you are aiming criticisms or complaints directly at them.

 Read the following paragraph. Find five places where the voice shifts from third person to second person. Then suggest what changes would make the voice consistent.

1   Whenever students go into Quick-E-Stop, the manager
2 watches your hands and your pockets. He asks the students if
3 you plan to buy something. Even if the students pull out their
4 money, the manager still scowls as if he doesn't want you there.
5 He doesn't thank them or tell them to have a nice day, but just
6 stares at you until you leave.

 Check consistency of voice. Read your letter, paying special attention to pronouns. Revise any spot where the voice shifts.

Voice
An inconsistent point of view is corrected.

Students at Belmer Junior High are used to

looking out the windows of the school and seeing

Belmer Woods. Now when you̶ look out, you̶ see a sign: (they) (they)

"For Sale, 20 acres, Zoned Residential/Commercial."

Belmer Woods is about to . . .

PERSUASIVE

Revising **Using a Checklist**

Check your revising. On a piece of paper, write the numbers 1 to 10. If you can answer "yes" to a question, put a check mark after that number. If not, continue to work on that part of your letter.

Focus and Coherence

_____ **1.** Do I state my position clearly?

_____ **2.** Have I included accurate and logical reasons to address my purpose and persuade my audience?

_____ **3.** Did I think about the views of my readers and answer their concerns with appropriate counterarguments?

Organization

_____ **4.** Are my reasons in the most persuasive order?

_____ **5.** Have I used a variety of transitions to effectively link paragraphs?

Development of Ideas

_____ **6.** Do I differentiate between facts and opinions in my letter?

_____ **7.** Have I included qualifiers to make my claims more believable for my audience and to better address my purpose?

Voice

_____ **8.** Do I balance facts and opinions?

_____ **9.** Do I use a consistent point of view?

_____ **10.** Does my voice sound natural and confident?

Make a clean copy. When you've finished revising, make a clean copy before you edit. This makes checking for conventions easier.

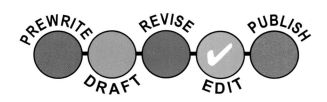

Go Online!

Editing

PREWRITE REVISE PUBLISH DRAFT EDIT ✓

After you finish revising your letter, you are ready to edit for *conventions*: grammar, mechanics (punctuation, capitalization), and spelling.

Keys to Effective Editing

1. Use a dictionary, a thesaurus, and the "Proofreader's Guide" in the back of this book.

2. Check that pronouns agree with their antecedents in your writing.

3. Be sure you don't have double-subjects in your sentences.

4. Make sure you have used complete sentences.

5. Check that your sentences begin in a variety of ways.

6. Check your writing for correctness of punctuation, capitalization, and spelling.

7. Use the editing and proofreading marks inside the back cover of this book.

PERSUASIVE

 **TEKS** 8.14D, 8.19C

Editing for Conventions

Grammar

Do my pronouns agree with their antecedents?

Every pronoun has an antecedent. An antecedent is the noun (or pronoun) that a pronoun refers to or replaces. Pronouns and their antecedents must agree—both should be singular or plural. (See pages 537–538.)

Pronoun agreement is especially tough with singular nouns that refer to people. It is incorrect to use a plural pronoun (they, them, their) after a singular noun (student, teacher, parent).

Incorrect   Every student should make sure they vote today.
singular   *plural*

Correct   Every student should make sure he or she votes today.
singular   *singular singular*

(or)   Students should make sure they vote today.
        plural   *plural*

(or)   Every student should make sure to vote today. (No pronoun)

 Rewrite each sentence to correct pronoun-antecedent agreement.

1. No one should leave their litter in the empty lot.
2. Everyone should pick up their own trash.
3. Each student should be responsible for their own garbage.
4. A person who eats candy should put the wrapper in their pocket.
5. Every student should take pride in their school.

 Check your pronouns and antecedents. Read your letter and make sure that your pronouns agree with their antecedents.

 persuade convince support
argue reason
Persuasive Letter
265
TEKS 8.14D
ELPS 2C, 3C

How can I avoid creating a double subject?

You can avoid creating a double subject by making sure that you do not place a pronoun immediately after the subject of a sentence. (See page 572.)

Incorrect

Principal Jenson he **should support the mentoring program.**

Correct

Principal Jenson **should support the mentoring program.**

(or) He **should support the mentoring program.**

 Rewrite each sentence to correct the double subject.

1. Students and teachers they need this mentoring program.
2. Ms. Dorn she will be the sponsor.
3. Students with special skills they will be the mentors.
4. Principal Alvarez he should provide a work space.
5. Parents and students they should support this plan.

 Check for double subjects. Read your letter and look for pronouns that immediately follow the subject. Correct any double subjects.

Conventions
A pronoun-antecedent error was removed and a double subject was corrected.

Nobody would be able to dump junk or car tires there

anymore, ~~and they wouldn't be allowed to~~ or carve graffiti

into the trees. A park ~~it~~ would both preserve and protect

the environment.

PERSUASIVE

Learning Language

Subject pronouns are used in the subject of a sentence. Working with a partner, read aloud each of the subject pronouns below—both singular and plural. Then take turns using each pronoun in a sentence. Be sure to not use double subjects. **Singular:** I, you, he, she, it **Plural:** we, you, they

Sentence Structure

When you edit for sentence structure, check to see whether all your sentences are complete and whether you varied the way your sentences begin.

How do I know if my sentences are complete?

Your sentences are complete if each one includes at least one subject and one predicate and expresses a complete thought. If a group of words is missing a subject, a predicate, or is not a complete thought, it is a fragment. (See pages 562–564.)

 Number your paper from 1 to 10. Read the following groups of words. If a group is a complete sentence, write an "S" after its number. If a group is a fragment, write an "F" after it. Rewrite any fragments to make them complete sentences.

1. The city should tear out the old railroad tracks and convert them into a bike path.
2. An exceptional idea.
3. Bike riders and joggers could reach the downtown with ease.
4. Would be a great way to stay in shape.
5. If the city wants to give citizens a new way to get around.
6. The trains currently go under all the major thoroughfares, so the route wouldn't stop traffic.
7. Giving people an alternative way to get to work or school.
8. Because gas prices continue to rise, bike riding and jogging are becoming more popular.
9. Although some people say that the old rail lines are too dirty for foot traffic.
10. Wish the city council would consider the proposal.

 Review your sentences. Check the sentences in your letter and make sure that each contains at least one subject and one predicate. Revise any incomplete sentences.

persuade **convince** support
argue reason

267

Persuasive Letter

TEKS 8.14C, 8.17A(v)
ELPS 5F

How can I vary my sentence beginnings?

If most of the sentences in a paragraph begin with a subject followed by a verb, you need to vary the structure. You can create a variety of sentence structures by adding a word, a phrase, or a clause to the beginning of some sentences. Note the difference between the following paragraphs.

Similar Beginnings

> **The school auditorium should be torn down and rebuilt. The roof leaks. The chairs are uncomfortable. People don't enjoy coming to our concerts. They might come if the auditorium were fixed.**

Varied Beginnings

> **The school auditorium should be torn down and rebuilt.** When it rains, **the roof leaks.** To make matters worse, **the chairs are uncomfortable. People don't enjoy coming to our concerts.** However, **they might come if the auditorium were fixed.**

Check your sentence beginnings. Read your letter, looking for places where your sentences all begin with a subject followed by a verb. In such places, use a variety of sentence structures by adding words, phrases, or clauses to some of the sentences. Trade papers with a partner and read each other's revised versions to see if they flow better. Discuss whether other sentences could be improved.

Conventions
The writer changed the beginnings of two sentences to vary the sentence structure.

Part of the forest could be saved, and
Earthmovers could dig out a pond. The grassy part on

the north could remain. As a field for soccer or baseball.

Making the land into a park would also help. To protect

the environment. Nobody would be able to dump junk or

car tires there anymore...

PERSUASIVE

⬤ **TEKS** 8.14D, 8.20A, 8.21

Editing Using a Checklist

Check your editing. On a piece of paper, write the numbers 1 to 10. If you can answer "yes" to a question, put a check mark after that number. If not, continue to edit for that convention.

Conventions

GRAMMAR

_____ **1.** Do my pronouns agree with their antecedents?

_____ **2.** Have I avoided double subjects?

_____ **3.** Do my subjects and verbs agree in number? (She and I *are* going, not She and I *is* going.)

_____ **4.** Have I varied my sentence structure with different beginnings?

MECHANICS

_____ **5.** Do I use end punctuation after all my sentences?

_____ **6.** Do I use a comma when beginning a sentence with a phrase or clause?

_____ **7.** Do I start all my sentences with capital letters?

_____ **8.** Do I capitalize all proper nouns and proper adjectives?

SPELLING

_____ **9.** Have I spelled all words correctly?

_____ **10.** Have I checked the words my spell-checker may have missed?

Creating a Title

■ Sum up the controversy: Where Will the Woods Go?

■ Write a slogan: Support the Woods, Support the Community!

■ Be creative: Belmer Park, the Classroom of the Future!

TEKS 8.14E

Publishing

PREWRITE • DRAFT • REVISE • EDIT • PUBLISH ✓

Sharing Your Letter

After writing, revising, and editing your position letter, you'll want to make a neat, final copy to share. You may also want to stage a debate, publish it in a newspaper, or turn it into a speech.

Make a final copy. Follow your teacher's instructions or use the guidelines below to format your letter. (If you are using a computer, see page 62.) Create a clean final copy of your letter and carefully proofread it.

Focus on Presentation

- Use blue or black ink and write neatly.
- Include your full address and the date at the top of the letter.
- Write the name and address of the person you are sending it to. Then include a greeting, or salutation, to the person.
- Leave a blank line between paragraphs, and start each at the left margin.
- Include a closing and a signature.

Stage a Debate
Gather a group of classmates who have opposite opinions about the same issue. Stage a debate. Present your position, allow others to present theirs, and defend each position.

Create a Speech
Make your letter into a persuasive speech. Create visual aids that will help you get your point across. Then present your position to an audience that you want to persuade.

Publish in a Newspaper
Submit your letter to the editor of your school or community newspaper. Check submission guidelines. Then send your work in.

PERSUASIVE

Evaluating a Persuasive Letter

To learn how to evaluate a persuasive letter, you'll use the scoring rubric on pages **50–51** and the letters that follow. These letters are examples of writing for each score on the rubric.

Notice that this first persuasive letter received a score of 4. Read the description for a score of 4 on pages **50–51**. Then read the letter. Use the same steps to study the other examples. Always remember to think about the overall quality of the writing.

Writing that fits a score of 4 is very strong.

Vivid beginning shows writer's voice.

Reasons are in a persuasive order.

Dear Editor,

"Hurray, school's over! No more pencils, no more books, no more teacher's dirty looks!" Have you ever heard these sounds around a schoolyard in late May or June? Everyone has. These are the exclamations students make at the end of the school year. But is a long summer vacation the best thing for education, or for students' futures?

Some educators, parents, and even students don't think so. They think a long summer break is out of date and hurts students' performance. They feel it is time to join the 21st century and have a longer school calendar. When I first heard this idea, I was against it, but now that I have read about the reasons for and against year-round school, I have come to the conclusion that it makes a lot of sense.

One argument in favor of longer school years is that the old system was invented for a society where more people were farmers and kids had to work in the fields in summer. But most people are no longer farmers. Instead of working in the fields next to their parents, too many students just hang around.

Qualifiers make it more persuasive.

Varied sentence structures

Facts balanced with feelings

Today, many educators feel that a long summer break actually harms students. During the summer, most students are not reading much, and they are not moving forward in their work. In fact, during the summer many students forget a lot of what they learned. When school starts again in the fall, the first weeks have to be spent reviewing. If students go to school all year, that lag does not occur. Students have not had time to forget their courses, and they are always ready to learn new material.

The plan I favor is to have a shorter summer vacation, about a month long, with more breaks during the year. Throughout the year, there would be one week off after every four weeks of school. Some people object to this plan. They say that cutting the summer vacation would keep teens from getting summer jobs. They also point out that if a school district was on a different schedule from the ones around it, then its teams would not be able to play the other teams. I think those objections have a point, but they are much less important than teaching young people more successfully. Our nation needs to keep up with other nations.

Some American schools have tried year-round education with good results, for instance in Oxnard, California. In Texas, many districts tried it in the 1990s, but most switched back because the change was not popular. But it is the 21st century now. It's a new world out there. Let's keep up with it by learning as much as we can!

Sincerely,
Julia Gomez

Writing that fits a score of 3 is strong in most ways.

Our Town Needs a Helmet Law

Dear Editor,

I'm proud to live in this town. It's just about the friendliest, safest, cleanest, most fun place I can imagine. It's a great place for bicycle riding, too. We have good bike lanes on city streets, and we have bike paths that go into the country. But there's one thing we don't have, and that's a bicycle helmet law.

Consistent point of view and voice

When I go bike riding, I notice that only about two-thirds of the other riders are wearing helmets. It's surprising in a place like this. I really started noticing it last month when I saw a bicyclist sitting on the curb holding her head. She wasn't wearing a helmet and had fallen and hit her head. She told my dad that she was okay, but I wondered, what if she hadn't been okay? She could have died. That's when I decided that we need a helmet law.

There's one huge reason to believe in helmet laws, and that's because they work. There's a lot of statisticks about it. One study in 2005 found that in 86% of fatal bicycle crashes in the United States, the rider wasn't wearing a helmet. There have also been studies in individual states like New York, New Jersey, Florida, California, and provences of Canada. All of them found that bicycle injuries fell a lot after there were helmet laws. In my opinion, that reason is more important than any reason on the other side could be. Just think of all the people in this community who go bike riding without helmets, including many children. If even one of their lives could be saved, the law would be a good one.

Balances facts and feelings

A few spelling errors

Avoids unfair words and uses qualifiers

Some people say that a helmet law would decrease their freedom. However, there are many laws that force people to act safely in other areas. For example, there are seat belt laws in cars. They help reduce deaths from car accidents. They are effective, and people do not protest against them. There are smoke detector laws. They help reduce deaths from fire. Of course there are laws against smoking in many public places, and that cuts down some people's freedom but it also saves many lives each year. And there are motorcycle helmet laws. Most people accept such laws. They should accept bicycle helmet laws too. Additionally, helmet laws are only for children in many places, so adults would not have to worry about a decrease in their freedom.

Some people also say that if helmets are required, less people would ride bicycles, so that would be a bad effect of the law. However, that has not been proved.

The best thing would be if the town could pass a helmet law, but if that doesn't happen, then at least the town should help raise awareness that people should wear a helmet. They could wear one voluntarilly. That could avoid some injuries and deaths too. So whether there's a law or not, wear a helmet!

Sincerely,
Tony Romano

PERSUASIVE

Writing that fits a score of 2 is strong in some ways.

Stop Watering

Dear Mayor Alonso,

Are you tired of the drout yet? I am. That's all people talk about around here anymore, how hot it is and how it never rains. We need some rain or the lawns and people's gardens will die and the water level in the lake will go down.

That's why I'm writing you this letter. I'm writing to ask you to put in lawn watering restricksions for when people water their lawns. I know you have the power to do this and I just want you to do it soon not waiting too late. We need to save water now.

Here is my suggession. As of immediately, Tell people that they can only water once a week. If you live in a odd-numbered house you get to water on Saturday and if you live in a even-numbered house you get to water on Sunday. I think this is fair. It gives everyone a chance to water one day a week. That isn't much, but it will keep everything from dyeing.

Also you should say that people can only water their lawns in the morning or the evening. They should not water in the middle of the day when the sun is so bright it evaporates all the water.

It is true that a few idiots will protest but they are selfish. All they care about is their lawns, not whether the city has enough water. Thank you for reading this letter, and I hope you have a good day.

Sincerely,
Jenny Zamoyski

Many errors in spelling, grammar, usage, and mechanics

Presents a strong position

Uses unfair words

Writing that fits a score of 1 is weak.

Incorrect format— should be a letter

Shows lack of interest

Many errors in conventions

Not coherent or focused

To Much home work

We get to much home work, we shudnt' have so much. Thats my position and I dont' have much more to say about it but since you want me to write a whole letter I will.

Why do we get so much home work? I dont' kno the answer, if you kno tell me.

May be teacher's want to make sure we are home at night instead of on the street. I can under stand that.

I think teacher probably wants us to learn. But more home work is not the way. More home work makes us not like it.

If you wanted some one to like some thing would you give them so much they were sick of it. Thats what I think.

Some home work is okay. I wud do it then. If for example we had 10 math q's not 25.

If you no what 6 X 9 is (54) you dont' have to say it five times. You can just say it onse.

Some people think I dont' want to lern that is not always true. I want to lern. I am writeing & reading more. I like the last book I read. There is just to much Home Work.

Evaluating and Reflecting on Your Writing

You've put a lot of time and effort into your persuasive letter. Now take some time to score and think about your writing. On your own paper, finish each sentence starter below. To score your writing, refer to the scoring rubric on page **50–51** and the examples you just read.

My Persuasive Letter

1. The best score for my persuasive letter is . . .

2. It's the best score because . . .

3. The best part of my letter is . . .

4. The part that still needs work is . . .

5. The main thing I learned about writing a persuasive letter is . . .

Persuasive Writing

Creating a Personal Commentary

Everyone is unique. Each person has a one-of-a-kind personality and a special way of looking at life. Even identical twins have their own viewpoints to share with the world.

In a personal commentary, a writer can express his or her personal views. News programs often provide commentaries about politics, the economy, or current events, but a commentary can deal with just about any aspect of life.

On the next few pages, you'll read a student's personal commentary about what she has learned from playing violin. Then you will learn to write a commentary of your own.

Writing Guidelines

Subject: A reflective look at life
Purpose: To state your personal view
Form: Personal commentary
Audience: Classmates

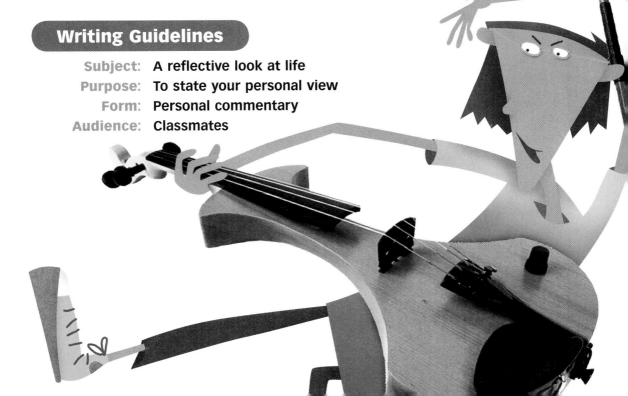

Personal Commentary

A personal commentary expresses your unique view of some aspect of life. In the commentary that follows, Sarita tells how music has taught her some important lessons about life, lessons that the whole world should learn.

Beginning

The topic is introduced, and the personal view is given (underlined).

Middle

The middle paragraphs support the writer's viewpoint.

Music Teaches Harmony

Some people think music is just a hobby that doesn't have any value in real life. After all, how often does a person need to know how to read notes? To me, though, music teaches some of the most important lessons of life. Music teaches me how to work hard while staying in harmony with others.

My experience with music began with hard work. When I was eight years old, I took my first violin lesson. It was frustrating because I didn't even get to use a real violin! Sometimes I wanted to give up, but my mom kept telling me, "Someday you'll be able to play any kind of music you want on your violin. But to reach that day, you have to keep practicing." I did keep practicing, and hard work has rewarded me. Now, whenever I have to learn something hard, I know I have to stick with it until the job is done.

Performing music brings me together with people. I'll never forget the day I joined the middle school orchestra. The sound of everyone tuning up was music to my ears! As I played the notes in front of me, I looked around at all the other people playing along. Our bows and fingers moved together to create a sound I could never have made by myself. Even though I knew only a couple other kids in the group, suddenly, I belonged.

Playing with others teaches me about harmony. Every instrument has its own voice, but all the instruments together make a bigger, more wonderful sound. When I play alone, my violin sounds sweet and sad. But when a viola plays along, there's a new dimension to the music. A cello adds its deep harmony, and clarinets and flutes seem to dance. Then come drums and trumpets, and the music comes alive.

Ending
· · · · · · · · · · · ·
The writer's viewpoint is summed up in a thoughtful way.

I've met a lot of people who aren't exactly like me, but music reminds me that differences are important. Without differences, there's no harmony. On the other hand, harmony doesn't just happen. It takes practice, hard work, and dedication. I wish everybody in the world could learn the lessons music has taught me.

Respond to the reading. On your own paper, answer each of the following questions about the personal commentary.

☐ **Organization** **(1) What reasons support Sarita's viewpoint?**

☐ **Development of Ideas** **(2) What is the main point of Sarita's commentary?**

☐ **Voice** **(3) What words or phrases show Sarita's passion about the topic?**

PERSUASIVE

 **TEKS** 8.14A

Prewriting **Selecting a Topic**

Everyone has a different idea of what is important in life. Whatever is most important to you can teach you a great deal about life in general.

Sarita used freewriting to think about what was most important in her own life. She wrote until she found a topic for her personal commentary.

Freewriting

> *What's most important in my life? Definitely music. I want to be a great violinist. It's not just that, though. When I joined the school orchestra, I realized music was a group thing. A whole bunch of people get together to make something beautiful. You have to cooperate. You have to work hard but stay in harmony. It's kind of like life. . . .*

Choose your topic. Freewrite about the things that are most important to you. Continue to write until you discover a topic you would like to write about in a personal commentary.

Connecting Your Topic to Life

Now that you've chosen a topic, it is time to connect your topic to life. Sarita used a cluster to think about the lessons that music teaches her.

Cluster

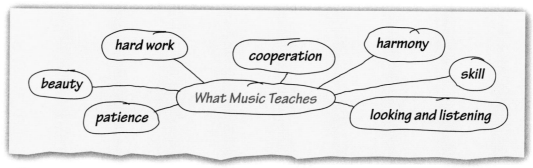

Create a cluster. Write "What _____ Teaches" in the center of a piece of paper and circle it. Around this circle, add more circles and write the lessons that your topic teaches in each. Choose three or four lessons you want to focus on.

TEKS 8.14A, 8.18C

Gathering Details

Each lesson you chose from your cluster (page 280) will become a paragraph in your commentary. Now you need to gather details about each lesson. Sarita made a chart, listing the lessons at the top and the details underneath.

Gathering Chart

hard work	cooperation	harmony
– tough to start	– joined orchestra	– different sounds
– kept practicing	– listened to others	– different rhythms
– practice rewarded	– suddenly belonged	– new dimension

Gather details. **Create a chart like the one above. List details about three or four lessons your topic teaches about life.**

Developing Your Viewpoint

Before you write your essay, you need to state your basic viewpoint and write topic sentences. Remember that a commentary is your opinion about the state of the world around you. Use the following tips to guide you in your planning.

■ Personal viewpoint

Write a sentence that expresses what the activity has taught you. This will be your own opinion. Try three versions and choose the best one. This sentence will appear in your first paragraph and will guide your writing.

> Music teaches me how to work hard while staying in
> harmony with others.

■ Topic sentences

Write a topic sentence that sums up each lesson. Each of these sentences will begin a middle paragraph. While your topic sentences will express your opinions, include some facts in the paragraphs to support your viewpoint.

> My experience with music began with hard work.
> Playing with others teaches me about harmony.

Develop your viewpoint. Use your chart and the tips above to write your personal viewpoint and topic sentences. Remember, these express your beliefs or feelings and will be opinions.

PERSUASIVE

TEKS 8.14B, 8.19C,
8.20A, 8.20B(i), 8.21

Drafting Developing Your First Draft

Use the following tips as you write your first draft.

- **Opening paragraph:** Get your reader's attention, introduce your topic, and provide your basic viewpoint.
- **Middle paragraphs:** Begin each middle paragraph with a topic sentence. After it, include details that support the sentence. Use transitions to link ideas.
- **Closing paragraph:** Thoughtfully summarize your topic and the lesson it teaches about life.

Create your first draft. Follow the tips above and focus on getting your ideas on paper.

Revising Improving Your Writing

The following questions will help you revise your commentary.

- ☐ **Organization** Does each middle paragraph begin with a topic sentence? Does each include supporting details?
- ☐ **Development of Ideas** Did I include information from my gathering chart? Did I clearly state my personal viewpoint? Did I include my opinions and facts to support them?
- ☐ **Voice** Does my voice sound clear and natural? Did I avoid sounding too emotional or too dry?

Revise your writing. Ask yourself the questions above and revise your commentary to improve these traits of writing.

Editing Checking for Conventions

Find and correct any errors in grammar, sentence structure, mechanics (capitalization, punctuation), and spelling.

Edit and proofread your work. Use the following questions to check and correct your personal commentary.

1 Do my pronouns agree with my antecedents?

2 Did I use a variety of structures at the beginning of my sentences?

3 Is my capitalization and spelling correct?

4 Have I correctly punctuated clauses and phrases?

Persuasive Writing
Across the Curriculum

Persuasive writing can help you present a convincing case in any class. In social studies, you may be asked to write a newspaper editorial about a community issue in which you call readers to action. Your math teacher may ask you to gather statistics and use them in an argument. In science, you may have to use a graph to make a point about pollution. A persuasive letter can also bring about changes in your school or community—such as lights for a popular soccer field.

The following pages will teach you about all these forms of persuasion and will also prepare you for responding to a persuasive prompt on a timed writing test.

What's Ahead

- **Social Studies:** Writing an Editorial
- **Math:** Developing a Statistical Argument
- **Science:** Creating a Persuasive Graph
- **Practical Writing:**
  Drafting a Business Letter
- **Writing for Assessment**

 TEKS 8.17A(v)

Social Studies: Writing an Editorial

An editorial or a letter to the editor expresses a writer's opinion about a current issue or problem. The following editorial was written in a social studies class and focuses on a downtown library.

The **beginning** introduces the topic and gives an opinion.

The **middle** provides supporting reasons for the opinion.

The writer uses a variety of sentence structures, making the editorial more interesting to read.

The **ending** gives a call to action.

Protect the Future of Our History

Springfield has grown in the past 10 years, but the center of the city is dying. People would rather build on the outskirts than fix up the downtown. As a result, the city is losing its heart and its history. Now the mayor proposes that the city tear down Springfield Public Library in the old courthouse and build a new library at the city limits. This can't happen.

The library building was built in 1893 as the first county courthouse. It became the library in 1982, when the new courthouse was built. The building has been the center of town for more than 100 years and should be saved, not destroyed.

This historic building is a symbol of the city. It's on the postcards and afghans sold at the Historical Society Museum. The library building even appears on the city's official stationery—the same paper used to propose tearing it down.

Citizens of Springfield should save the public library and save the downtown! If Springfield is willing to spend $6 million on a new library, why not spend the same money fixing up the old one? Even if the renovation costs more, the city shouldn't care only about money. The city's history is important as well. On November 15th, citizens of Springfield should vote "no" for the new library.

TEKS 8.17A(v), 8.18C
ELPS 5B

Writing Tips

Before you write . . .

- **Select an issue that you care about.**
  Think about problems or issues in your school or community.
  Choose a topic that you feel strongly about.

- **Do your research.**
  Gather facts and details
  that will help you explain
  the topic to readers. Use
  the information to come
  up with a realistic solution.

During your writing . . .

- **State your opinion.**
  Explain the problem and why you are concerned about it.

- **Support your opinion.**
  Back up your argument with facts from your research that help
  support your opinion. Address opposing points of view. Then
  offer a solution.

- **Restate your opinion and call for action.**
  Ask readers to get involved.

After you've written a first draft . . .

- **Review your argument.**
  Make sure that your opinion is clear and supported by facts.

- **Check your facts.**
  Double-check your facts to make sure they are correct.

- **Review your sentences.**
  Use a variety of sentence structures. Vary sentences by adding
  phrases and clauses.

- **Check for conventions.**
  Correct errors in grammar, mechanics (punctuation,
  capitalization), and spelling.

PERSUASIVE

Create your own editorial on an issue by using the tips above. Then
submit your editorial to your school paper or a local newspaper.

Math: Developing a Statistical Argument

A statistical argument uses numbers to prove the value of something. For the following assignment, a student used statistics to decide which pack of blended fruit drinks provides a better value.

The beginning sets up the problem.

The middle provides statistics and equations.

The ending gives the solution.

Get the Best Value

Which pack of blended fruit drinks gives a better value for the money?
* a 12-pack of 12-ounce cans that costs $3.95
* a 6-pack of 16.9-ounce bottles that costs $2.50

First, one must find out how many ounces are in each pack. To do this, a person should multiply the ounces per can or bottle by the number of cans or bottles in a pack.

Ounces per can/bottle	x	Number of cans/bottles	=	Total ounces
12	x	12 cans	=	144
16.9	x	6 bottles	=	101.4

Then a person should find the price per ounce by taking the total price for each pack and dividing it by the total number of ounces.

Total price	÷	Total ounces	=	Price per ounce
$3.95	÷	144	=	.027
$2.50	÷	101.4	=	.025

So, on an ounce-by-ounce basis, the 6-pack of larger bottles is cheaper. The 12-pack costs a little more per ounce, but if the juice is for school lunches, the smaller cans may avoid waste and allow individual servings. So value depends partly on use.

Writing Tips

Before you write . . .

- **Begin by asking a "value" question.**
  Ask a question about the value of something. For example, which package of dog food gives the best value, or which amusement park provides the best value for the entertainment dollar.
- **Plan your steps.**
  Make a list of steps and equations that you need to follow to answer the value question. Check your equations and answers for accuracy.

During your writing . . .

- **Introduce the question.**
  Begin your paper by indicating what question your argument will address.
- **Provide statistics.**
  Let readers know the facts and figures you will be using to argue your point.
- **Show the process step-by-step.**
  Write the equations you use to make your statistical argument. Lead readers through each step.
- **Interpret the statistics.**
  End by telling readers what the statistics mean.

After you've written a first draft . . .

- **Check for completeness.**
  Make sure you haven't left out important variables and steps.
- **Check for correctness.**
  Fix any errors in math, punctuation, capitalization, spelling, or grammar.

 Write your own statistical argument. Choose a question of value that you can argue using statistics. Then lead your readers through the equations needed to argue your point.

Science: Creating a Persuasive Graph

A graph can quickly persuade readers about a problem. The following graph shows the increase in automobile pollution since 1998.

The **beginning** introduces the graph.

The **middle** presents the figures visually.

The **ending** provides the student's call to action.

Absolutely Exhausted

Although the United States produces more carbon dioxide (the greenhouse gas CO_2) than any other country, China will soon produce more according to the Environmental Protection Agency. In the United States, total gasoline CO_2 emissions have risen by 9% since 1998.

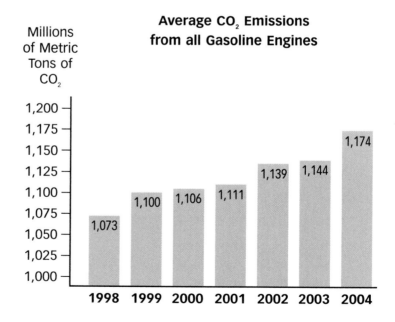

Millions of Metric Tons of CO_2

Average CO_2 Emissions from all Gasoline Engines

Year	Value
1998	1,073
1999	1,100
2000	1,106
2001	1,111
2002	1,139
2003	1,144
2004	1,174

This bar graph shows the increase in carbon dioxide gases per year from all gasoline engines since 1998. Carpooling, using less air conditioning, and walking are some simple ways to reduce emissions.

Writing Tips

Before you write . . .

- **Select a topic.**
  Think about a science issue that involves numbers: water quality, food production, or weather patterns, for example. Select a topic you care about and state your position about it.
- **Research your topic.**
  Find out the facts and figures behind the issue. Decide which facts would make the most persuasive graph.
- **Choose a type of graph.**
  Select a type that works best to present your argument. (See page 637 for different types of graphs.) Make sure you have all the facts you need.

During your writing . . .

- **Introduce your topic and your argument.**
  Write one or two brief paragraphs that put the facts in perspective.
- **Draw your graph.**
  Lay out your graph so that the information is clear.
- **Provide your viewpoint.**
  Sum up the figures in a persuasive way.

After you've written a first draft . . .

- **Check for completeness.**
  Make sure that you included all the necessary details and facts to support your argument. Ask another student to look at your graph to see if it is easy to understand.
- **Check for conventions.**
  Correct any errors in punctuation, capitalization, spelling, and grammar.

PERSUASIVE

 Pick a science issue that you care about and that includes statistics (numbers). Gather information about it and create a persuasive graph that demonstrates your position. Present your graph in class.

 8.17B

Practical Writing: Writing a Business Letter

In real-world situations, one of the best ways to get something done is to write a persuasive letter. A student wrote the letter below to convince a sports arena manager to replace tickets purchased for a school event.

The letter follows the correct format.

5500 Miarka Ln.
Moore, Texas 78057
May 12, 2011

Daria Marcus, Manager
Triple Star Stadium
9009 West Homerun Dr.
San Antonio, Texas 78201

Dear Ms. Marcus:

The beginning paragraph introduces the issue and makes a request.

The River Middle School student council looks forward to attending a Triple Star baseball game every year. However, this year we have a problem with our ticket order. We asked to sit together, but the tickets have us seated in different spots. We would like to return the tickets and get new ones that are together.

The body includes details and reasons for the request.

Sitting together is important because it helps our teachers supervise us. Also, we come to celebrate the end of the year together. Since we have purchased so many tickets, we hope you will be able to help us.

The closing requests information.

Please call me at 555-1999 to let me know if this is possible. Also let me know what I need to do to change our tickets. Thank you for your time.

Sincerely,
Xavier Rivera

TEKS 8.17A(ii), 8.17B

Writing Tips

Before you write . . .

- **Use the correct format.**
  Be sure to start with the correct heading. Then include a salutation. After the body of your letter, end with the proper closing.
- **Select a topic.**
  Think of something you would like to ask someone to do—send you information, correct a problem, explain an issue.
- **Gather information.**
  Collect all the facts and details your reader will need.

During your writing . . .

- **Get right to the point.**
  Identify yourself and tell the person why you are writing. Include only the important details.
- **Be businesslike.**
  Write in a clear, businesslike voice. Be reasonable in your request. Also be sure to thank the person for his or her help.
- **Provide information for a response.**
  Include all contact information that the person will need in order to respond to your request.

After you've written a first draft . . .

- **Check for completeness.**
  Make sure you have given the reader all the information he or she needs.
- **Check for correctness.**
  Double-check names and addresses and all facts. Proofread your letter for correctness in grammar, punctuation, capitalization, and spelling.

PERSUASIVE

Think of a problem in your school or community and who could help you solve it. Write a persuasive letter stating an opinion, registering your complaint, and requesting information to solve the problem.

Persuasive Writing
Writing for Assessment

Many writing tests contain a prompt that asks you to state an opinion and support it with convincing reasons. Study the following sample prompt and student response.

Prompt

The principal at your school is developing a school improvement plan and is asking students for suggestions of ways to improve the school. Write about an improvement you would like to see made at your school. Try to convince the principal and the rest of the school that your idea could work and would benefit everyone.

Analyzing the Prompt

The first step, when responding to a prompt, is to make sure you understand exactly what it is asking you to do. As you read the prompt, ask yourself the following questions:

■ What genre or form is the prompt asking me to write?
■ What topic does the prompt ask me to write about?
■ What purpose does the prompt give for the piece of writing?
■ Does the prompt identify an audience?
■ What specific information does the prompt tell me to include?

Most prompts will not provide the answers to all these questions. You will need to decide some things for yourself.

The prompt doesn't specifically say that the genre is persuasive, but you can tell from the key words "Try to convince . . ." that you are being asked to write a persuasive piece. The prompt also tells you your purpose and your audience. You must think of a suggestion and convince the principal and the rest of the school that it can be done and will benefit everyone. That means you will have to think of reasons that will be convincing to that group of people. The only thing left for you to decide is what your specific topic will be.

Prewriting **Selecting a Topic**

Take a minute or two to brainstorm a list of possible topics. Then review them and consider which one would be the best choice to write about. When choosing a persuasive topic, it is important to consider the following:

- Can you think of at least three or four good reasons in support of your idea or opinion?
- Can you offer responses for any likely objections and counterarguments to your idea or opinion?
- Does your idea or opinion meet all the requirements stated in the prompt?

Answering the questions above will help you decide on a topic.

Anna came up with three ideas: renovate the gym, add French to the curriculum, and plant a garden in front of the school. She decided the best topic was planting a garden because it would benefit everyone, and she could support it with good reasons and respond to possible objections.

Planning the Writing

Anna decided to use a table diagram to plan her writing. The diagram helped her to form her opinion statement and choose the reasons that best supported it.

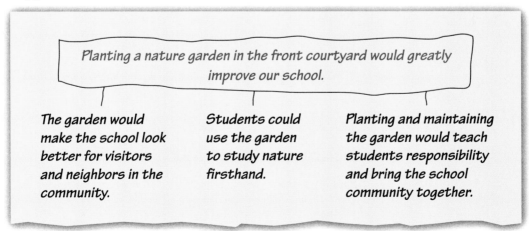

Planting a nature garden in the front courtyard would greatly improve our school.

| The garden would make the school look better for visitors and neighbors in the community. | Students could use the garden to study nature firsthand. | Planting and maintaining the garden would teach students responsibility and bring the school community together. |

PERSUASIVE

Drafting Writing the essay

Anna used her table diagram to write her persuasive essay.

Response to a Persuasive Prompt

The **beginning** includes the opinion statement (underlined).

Imagine entering school to the sound of birds singing, the smell of flowers, and the view of colorful butterflies. This dream could be a reality at Spring Grove Middle School. <u>Planting a nature garden in the front courtyard would greatly improve our school.</u>

The garden would make the school look better for visitors and neighbors in the community. Currently, our entrance is rocky and bare. This is not welcoming and does not match the green lawns of neighbors who live nearby. By planting a nature garden we would brighten our front door and make our school blend in better with the neighborhood.

Each **middle** paragraph gives facts to support the opinion statement.

Students would also benefit from the garden because they could use it to study nature firsthand. Several science classes study plants, butterfly life cycles, and insects. All of these topics could be viewed right outside our front door. In fact, teachers could even plan lessons that involve mini field trips to the garden.

Finally, planting and maintaining the garden would teach students responsibility and bring the school community together. Parents, students, and teachers

persuade convince support
argue reason

Writing for Assessment

295

TEKS 8.18B
ELPS 5G

could work together to plan and plant the garden. Then different classes could be assigned throughout the year to weed it and keep it clean. Everyone could have a job, so everyone would feel involved.

A nature garden would be a great improvement to our school. It may seem like a lot of work, but the hard work will help to build our school community. We can also try to get local garden stores to donate flowers and supplies to keep the costs low. In the end, the effort will be well worth it. A nature garden will improve our school both inside and out!

The **ending** paragraph considers the views of others and anticipates and responds to possible concerns or objections.

Respond to the reading. Answer the following questions to see how the traits were used in Anna's response.

☐ **Focus and Coherence** (1) What is the opinion in the essay? (2) What words from the prompt also appear in Anna's essay?

☐ **Development of Ideas** (3) What reasons does Anna give to support her opinion?

☐ **Organization** (4) Where does Anna anticipate reader concerns and answer possible concerns?

Literature Connection: Read another example of persuasive writing in the essay "The Sanctuary of School" by Lynda Barry.

PERSUASIVE

 **TEKS** 8.18A, 8.18B, 8.18C

Writing Tips

Before you write . . .

● **Understand the prompt.**
Remember that a persuasive prompt asks you to state and support an opinion. Be sure you know your purpose and your audience.

● **Plan your response.**
Spend a few minutes planning before you start to write. Use a graphic organizer (table diagram) as a guide.

During your drafting . . .

● **Share an opinion statement.**
Think of an opinion that you can clearly support.

● **Build your argument.**
Think of reasons that support your opinion.

● **End effectively.**
Explain what you would like to see done.

After you've written a first draft . . .

● **Check for clear ideas.**
Rewrite any ideas that sound confusing.

● **Check for conventions.**
Correct errors in punctuation, capitalization, spelling, and grammar.

Table Diagram

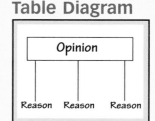

 Plan and write a response. Respond to the prompt on page 292. Complete your writing within the period of time your teacher gives you. Remember to use the tips above.

Persuasive Writing in Review

Purpose: In persuasive writing, you work to *convince people* to think the way you do about something.

Topics: Persuade readers . . . to agree with your opinion or position,
to take an action,
to support a cause, or
to solve a problem.

Prewriting

Select a topic that you care about, one that you can present confidently and that is appropriate for your audience. (See page **242**.)

Gather ideas about your topic. (See pages **243–244**.)

Write a position statement that identifies your opinion. (See page **245**.)

Organize your ideas in a list or an outline with your position statement at the top, followed by sentences with supporting facts or details beneath each. (See page **246**.)

Drafting

In the beginning, grab the reader's attention and clearly state your position. (See page **249**.)

In the middle part, devote a paragraph to each reason; include supporting facts and examples. Address an objection to your position. (See pages **250–251** and **254–255**.)

In the ending, restate your position and sum up your reasons for it. (See page **252**.)

Revising

Review for focus and coherence, development of ideas, organization, and voice. Avoid fuzzy thinking. Check your responses to objections, review your overall organization, and be sure to balance facts and opinions. (See pages **254–262**.)

Editing

Check your writing for conventions. Look for use of complete sentences and a variety of sentence structures. Ask a friend to edit the writing, too. (See pages **264–268**.)

Make a final copy and proofread it for errors before sharing it with your audience. (See page **269**.)

Assessing

Use the scoring rubric as a guide to assess your finished writing. (See pages **270–271**.)

PERSUASIVE

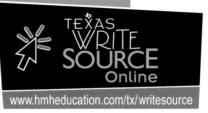

Responding to Texts

Writing Focus
- Paragraph Response
- Analyzing a Theme
- Respond to an Article

Grammar Focus
- Nouns in Apposition
- Participles
- Writing Complex Sentences

Learning Language

Learning these words and expressions will help you understand this unit.

1. A present participle is a verb that ends in *-ing* and acts as an adjective in a sentence.

   Which word is the present participle in this sentence? The crying baby was hungry.

Responding to Texts

Paragraph Response

Just as the ABC's are the building blocks of words, paragraphs are the building blocks of essays. Once you can write solid paragraphs about literature, you'll be better prepared to write whole essays about the poems, stories, and novels that you read.

On the next page, you will read a sample paragraph that responds to Langston Hughes's poem, "The Kids in School with Me." It deals with learning the fundamentals of life—not just the ABC's. Then you will write a paragraph response about a short story or poem you have read recently.

Writing Guidelines

Subject: A short story or poem
Purpose: To respond to the theme
Form: Paragraph
Audience: Classmates

Paragraph Response

When you write a paragraph about a short story or poem you've read, you may be asked to focus on a theme. The **topic sentence** identifies the story, the author, and the theme. The **body sentences** explain the theme, and the **closing sentence** tells something important about it. In the following response, Marco writes about the theme of diversity in "The Kids in School with Me," a poem by Langston Hughes.

Topic Sentence

Body

Closing Sentence

"The Kids in School with Me"

In the poem "The Kids in School with Me," Langston Hughes dreams about a school where diversity would be appreciated. The poet describes kids in a classroom. The students have dark skin, freckles, black hair, or other features. Some kids are from different countries around the world, including Russia, China, Poland, Spain, and Greece. Although every student is unique in some way, they are all in the classroom together. Together they study reading and math. All of them work toward graduation, and their motto is "One for All and All for One!" This poem says that if people could only look past color and race, all children would just be kids in school.

Respond to the reading. On your own paper, answer each of the following questions.

☐ **Development of Ideas (1)** What theme in the poem does the writer think is most important?

☐ **Organization (2)** How does the topic sentence introduce the theme? **(3)** How does the closing sentence sum up the theme?

☐ **Voice (4)** Does the writer sound knowledgeable about the poem? Explain.

TEKS 8.14A

Prewriting Selecting a Topic

Your first step in writing a response to literature is choosing a short story or poem to write about. Marco began by listing some of his favorites.

Topic List

"Raymond's Run" by Toni Cade Bambara

"The Kids in School with Me" by Langston Hughes *

"Mr. Misenheimer's Garden" by Charles Kuralt

 Choose a short story or poem. Make a list of your favorite short stories or poems. Place a star (*) next to the one that interests you most.

Finding a Theme

A theme is the lesson about life in a piece of literature. The details in a story or poem are clues to the themes. Marco began his search for a theme by listing details from the poem. Then he reviewed the details and listed some possible themes.

Theme Chart

Details	Themes
– America	
– students from around the world	getting along
– different hair, eyes, smiles, skin colors	
– studying together	learning together
– "One for All and All for One!"	
– public school	appreciating *
– Polish, Greek, Russian, Chinese	diversity

 List details and themes. Create a list of details from the short story or poem you have chosen. Beside it, list themes that relate to those details. Finally, choose one theme to write about.

RESPONSE

TEKS 8.14A, 8.20A, 8.21

Drafting Creating Your First Draft

A paragraph has three main parts: a topic sentence, the body, and a closing sentence. The following tips will help you create each part.

- **Topic sentence:** Write a sentence that names the short story or poem, its author, and the theme you will focus on.
- **Body:** Write sentences that explain the theme using examples from the piece of literature.
- **Closing sentence:** End with a sentence that sums up the theme.

Write the first draft of your paragraph. Use the tips above as you write your response paragraph.

Revising Improving Your Paragraph

After you've written your first draft, you need to revise your paragraph to improve on your *focus and coherence, organization, development of ideas, voice,* and *conventions.*

Review your paragraph. Use the following questions as a guide to your revision.

1. Have I written about one important theme?
2. Do my sentences appear in the best order?
3. Does my interest in the story or poem show in my voice?
4. Have I used some of the same words the author used?
5. Do my sentences flow smoothly?

Editing Checking for Conventions

Next, check your paragraph for *conventions.*

Edit your work. Use the following questions to guide your editing.

1. Have I checked my punctuation, capitalization, and spelling?
2. Have I used the right words (*to, two, too*)?

Proofread your paragraph. After you make a neat copy of your final paragraph, check it one more time for errors.

Responding to Texts
Analyzing a Theme

A great work of art is more than just paint on canvas. A masterpiece gives viewers a reason to stop and stare and get lost in the painting. It has depth and meaning.

When people talk about the depth and meaning of a piece of literature, they are referring to the literature's theme. Theme is the lesson that a book or story teaches the reader about life. In this chapter, you will write an essay that examines how the theme develops through the characters and events in a piece of literature.

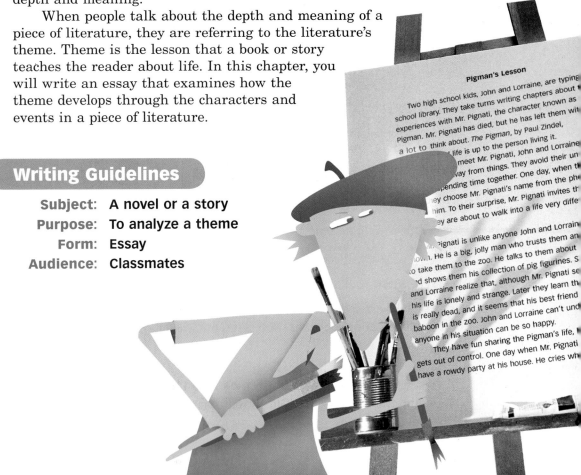

Pigman's Lesson

Two high school kids, John and Lorraine, are typing school library. They take turns writing chapters about experiences with Mr. Pignati, the character known as Pigman. Mr. Pignati has died, but he has left them wit a lot to think about. *The Pigman*, by Paul Zindel,

life is up to the person living it. meet Mr. Pignati, John and Lorraine way from things. They avoid their un pending time together. One day, when th ey choose Mr. Pignati's name from the ph him. To their surprise, Mr. Pignati invites th ey are about to walk into a life very diffe

Mr. Pignati is unlike anyone John and Lorrain own. He is a big, jolly man who trusts them an to take them to the zoo. He talks to them about d shows them his collection of pig figurines. S and Lorraine realize that, although Mr. Pignati se his life is lonely and strange. Later they learn th is really dead, and it seems that his best friend baboon in the zoo. John and Lorraine can't und anyone in his situation can be so happy.

They have fun sharing the Pigman's life, gets out of control. One day when Mr. Pignati have a rowdy party at his house. He cries wh

Writing Guidelines

Subject:	**A novel or a story**
Purpose:	**To analyze a theme**
Form:	**Essay**
Audience:	**Classmates**

Understanding Your Goals

Texas Traits

Your assignment in this chapter is to write an essay that explains the theme, or main idea of a story. A theme can usually be expressed as a statement about life. The goals listed below will help you. The scoring rubric on pages 50–51 will also help you. Refer to it often to improve your writing.

Focus and Coherence

Explain your interpretation of the theme in a clear thesis statement that expresses your controlling idea. Make sure all your ideas are connected to each other and the controlling idea.

Organization

Be sure to state the book's title, author, and theme in the introduction. Present evidence from the story in a coherent, logical order.

Development of Ideas

Use specific details from the story to build on ideas that support your controlling idea. Include only the events and details that are relevant to your thesis.

Voice

Make your writing sound natural and maintain a consistent point of view.

Conventions

Be sure your grammar is correct. Use complete sentences. Check for correct punctuation, capitalization, sentence structure, and spelling.

Literature Connection. You will be able to respond to a literary text by reading the folktale "The Old Grandfather and His Little Grandson," as retold by Leo Tolstoy.

Response Essay

The novel *The Pigman* tells about two high school students who meet an unusual man named Mr. Pignati. A student who read the book wrote this essay about the theme of the story.

Beginning

The beginning introduces the book and focuses on the theme (underlined).

Middle

Each middle paragraph explains a different stage in the development of the theme.

Pigman's Lesson

Two high school kids, John and Lorraine, are typing in the school library. They take turns writing chapters about their experiences with Mr. Pignati, the character known as the Pigman. Mr. Pignati has died, but he has left them with a lot to think about. *The Pigman,* by Paul Zindel, shows that people make their own happiness.

Before they meet Mr. Pignati, John and Lorraine seem to be running away from things. They avoid their unhappy homes by spending time together. One day, when they are bored, they choose Mr. Pignati's name from the phone book and call him. To their surprise, Mr. Pignati invites them to his house. They are about to walk into a life very different from their own.

Mr. Pignati is unlike anyone John and Lorraine have ever known. He is a big, jolly man who trusts them and offers to take them to the zoo. He talks to them about his wife and shows them his collection of pig figurines. Slowly, John and Lorraine realize that, although Mr. Pignati seems happy, his life is lonely and strange. Later they learn that his wife is really dead, and it seems that his best friend is Bobo, a baboon in the zoo. John and Lorraine can't understand how anyone in his situation can be so happy.

They have fun sharing the Pigman's life, but then the fun gets out of control. One day when Mr. Pignati is gone, they have a rowdy party at his house. He cries when he sees the damage and calls the police. John and Lorraine are ashamed that they have been disloyal to him, and they offer to pay for the damages. They also arrange to meet Mr. Pignati at the zoo. The two kids want to get back the happiness that they have lost.

Middle
The last middle paragraph covers the final stage in the development of the theme.

The trip to the zoo is a disaster. First of all, they discover that Bobo has died. The shock causes Mr. Pignati to collapse on the floor of the monkey house. Lorraine backs away, unable to handle what has happened. John stays with Mr. Pignati, who dies of a heart attack. John is deeply moved by Mr. Pignati's death. He is bothered by the thought that "it's possible to end your life with only a baboon to talk to."

Ending
The ending paragraph revisits the theme.

Lorraine feels extremely guilty about the way they took advantage of Mr. Pignati. John feels bad, too, but he has learned a valuable lesson. Before, he had spent too much time getting back at people. But because of Mr. Pignati's kindness, John realizes that leading a better life is completely up to him. As he states at the end of the story, "Our life would be what we made of it—nothing more, nothing less."

Respond to the reading. Answer the following questions about the sample response to literature.

☐ Organization (1) Are the steps in the theme's development in time order or order of importance?

☐ Development of Ideas (2) Which quotation means the same thing as the underlined theme in the first paragraph? (3) Which character seems to understand this theme?

☐ Voice (4) Does the writer sound knowledgeable about the book? Explain.

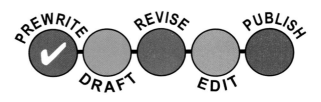

Prewriting

Prewriting is the first step in the writing process. It involves selecting a book or short story to write about, listing important ideas and events that support your central focus, and planning the organization of your paragraphs.

Keys to Effective Prewriting

1. Select an interesting book or story you've read recently.

2. Identify the main theme of the story.

3. Jot down the key events and details in the development of the theme.

4. Write a beginning that introduces the book or story and includes a thesis statement giving your opinion about the theme.

5. In the middle paragraphs, include only those details that provide evidence of your understanding of the theme.

6. Think of an ending that will recap the most important message of the story.

PROD. NO.

SCENE   TAKE   ROLL

SOUND

RESPONSE

TEKS 8.14A, 8.17C

Prewriting Selecting a Topic

A theme is the lesson or main idea that an author expresses to the reader. Sometimes the theme is openly stated in the story, but more often it is not. Here are some places to look for clues about the theme:

- The title of the story ("Among the Brave")
- Statements about life ("Maybe we are too busy being flowers . . . instead of something worthy of respect . . . like being real people.")
- The lessons that the characters learn (John realizes that leading a better life is completely up to him.)

 Think about the lessons or main ideas in the stories you have read recently. List the titles and themes of the ones that hold the most meaning for you.

Topics Chart

1. <u>The Call of the Wild</u> teaches you that only the strong survive.

★ 2. "Raymond's Run" is about a runner who finds out what is really important in life.

3. The three children in <u>To Kill a Mockingbird</u> learn that prejudging people is wrong.

   Reason:
   ★ I will write about "Raymond's Run" because we sometimes focus too much on the things in life that shouldn't really matter.

 Choose your topic. Put a star next to the story that you would like to write about. Under the list, explain the reason for your choice.

Focus on the Texas Traits

Development of Ideas Thinking about the characters and what they do can help you understand the theme. Pay attention to the main characters for clues about how the author feels about life.

TEKS 8.17C

Gathering Details

Now that you have selected a story and a theme, you should think about how the theme develops. By reviewing the key thoughts, feelings, and actions of the main character, you can chart important stages in the development of the theme. The sample chart below is for the essay on pages 313–316.

Theme Chart

Title: *"Raymond's Run"*

Theme: *Winning isn't the most important thing in life.*

First Stage: The theme in the early part of the story

Squeaky thinks that winning the May Day race again will make her important, but she doesn't think that taking care of her brother Raymond is anything special.

Middle Stages: Important developments that follow the first stage

As the race day approaches, Squeaky concentrates so hard on training that she thinks the only way she can be successful is to win.

On the day of the race, Squeaky loses her concentration because she suddenly realizes that Raymond is kneeling down and getting ready to run, too.

Final Stage: The last stage of the theme's development

Squeaky is confused as she crosses the finish line because she realizes that something has become more important to her than winning.

Prewrite

Chart your theme. Write the theme at the top of a chart like the one above. Then identify three or more stages in the story that help develop or show the theme. Under each stage, list some of the main character's thoughts, feelings, and actions at that time.

RESPONSE

TEKS 8.14A, 8.14B, 8.17C

Prewriting **Writing a Controlling Idea**

Now that you have identified the main character and the stages in the development of the theme, you are ready to write your controlling idea.

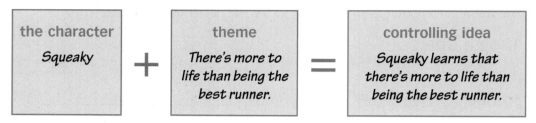

the character		theme		controlling idea
Squeaky	**+**	*There's more to life than being the best runner.*	**=**	*Squeaky learns that there's more to life than being the best runner.*

Form a focus. Write a controlling idea for your analysis of a theme using the formula above.

Organizing the Middle Paragraphs of Your Essay

After you write a controlling idea, plan the middle paragraphs of your essay. Each middle paragraph should cover a different stage in the development of the theme.

Below, the writer of the sample essay on pages 313–316 planned the order of the middle paragraphs. She wrote a topic sentence for each stage.

Topic Sentences

Topic Sentence 1

Along with being a great runner, Squeaky does another thing well, too, although she doesn't take credit for it.

Topic Sentence 2

Competition is important to Squeaky, so she concentrates more and more on winning as the race day approaches.

Topic Sentence 3

The day of the race is a special day for Squeaky.

Topic Sentence 4

Squeaky can't believe what she's seeing, but she knows that something very important is about to happen.

Plan your middle paragraphs. Review your "Theme Chart." Add any stages you feel may be necessary. Then write a topic sentence for each of your middle paragraphs and decide the best order for the paragraphs.

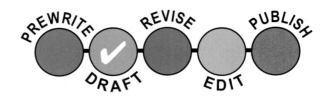

Drafting

After you've done your prewriting, you can begin writing your essay. Use your controlling idea, theme chart, and topic sentences as a guide.

Keys to Effective Drafting

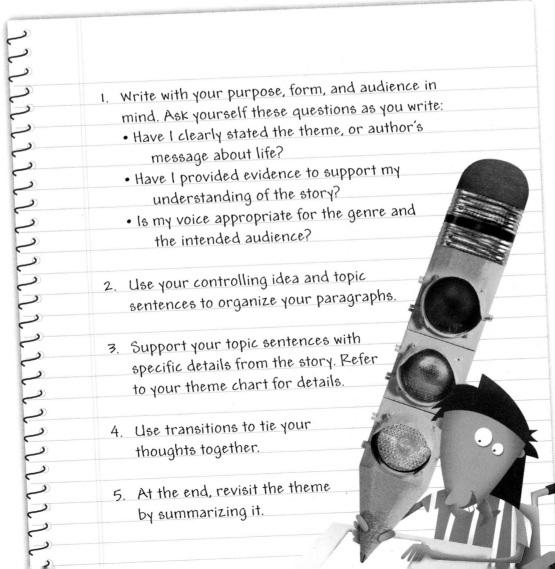

1. Write with your purpose, form, and audience in mind. Ask yourself these questions as you write:
   - Have I clearly stated the theme, or author's message about life?
   - Have I provided evidence to support my understanding of the story?
   - Is my voice appropriate for the genre and the intended audience?

2. Use your controlling idea and topic sentences to organize your paragraphs.

3. Support your topic sentences with specific details from the story. Refer to your theme chart for details.

4. Use transitions to tie your thoughts together.

5. At the end, revisit the theme by summarizing it.

TEKS 8.14B

Drafting **Getting the Big Picture**

The following chart shows how the three parts of a response to literature fit together. (The examples are from the essay on pages 313–316.) You're ready to write your response if you have . . .

- discovered the theme,
- written a clear thesis statement that expresses your controlling idea about the theme and other information, and
- planned your paragraphs.

Beginning

The **beginning** paragraph introduces the character and states the theme.

Controlling Idea
Eventually, Squeaky learns that there's more to life than being the best runner.

Middle

The four **middle** paragraphs show four stages in the development of the theme.

Four Topic Sentences
Along with being a great runner, Squeaky does another thing well, too, although she doesn't take credit for it.

Competition is important to Squeaky, so she concentrates more and more on winning as the race day approaches.

The day of the race is a special day for Squeaky.

Squeaky can't believe what she's seeing, but she knows that something very important is about to happen.

Ending

The **ending** paragraph revisits the theme and summarizes it.

Closing Sentence
The theme of the story is clear: Winning isn't the most important thing in life.

TEKS 8.14B, 8.17C

Starting Your Essay

The opening of your essay should include . . .

- ■ background about the events and characters that help develop the theme,
- ■ the title and author of the work, and
- ■ your thesis statement about the theme of the story.

> Beginning
>
> Middle
>
> Ending

Beginning Paragraph

The beginning paragraph below starts with background information about the main character and ends with the thesis statement about the theme.

The first part gives background. **The last sentence is the thesis statement** (underlined).	*The main character in Toni Cade Bambara's story "Raymond's Run" is Squeaky, an aspiring runner. Squeaky is the reigning champion for her age group in the 50-yard dash at the Harlem May Day celebration. She practices running and thinks about it almost constantly as she prepares to defend her title. Eventually, Squeaky learns that there's more to life than being the best runner.*

Draft

Write your beginning. Write the beginning paragraph of your essay. Include background information, the title and author, and your thesis statement.

Drafting Tips

- ● **Talk about the story with a classmate** before you start writing.
- ● **Write freely,** letting your ideas flow without worrying about neatness.
- ● **Be sure that you have included enough details** to help your reader understand the point you're making.

RESPONSE

TEKS 8.14B, 8.17C

Drafting Developing the Middle

Each middle paragraph tells about one of the stages in the development of the theme. These paragraphs focus on the thoughts, feelings, and actions of important characters during each stage. Every middle paragraph should contain a topic sentence.

Beginning

Middle

Ending

Middle Paragraphs

These paragraphs show the theme's development.

The first sentence forms a transition from the previous paragraph to this one.

Each topic sentence covers a stage of the theme (underlined).

Along with being a great runner, Squeaky does another thing well, too, although she doesn't take credit for it. Taking care of her older brother Raymond is a major responsibility in her life. Squeaky says, "He needs looking after 'cause he's not quite right." She does her duty without really thinking about it.

Competition is important to Squeaky, so she concentrates more and more on winning as the race day approaches. Her main worry is a new girl named Gretchen, who everybody says is very fast. Squeaky psychs up by picturing herself running, almost flying, to the finish line far ahead of Gretchen and the other competitors. She thinks that winning this race is the only way that she can be successful.

The day of the race is a special day for Squeaky. She has to take care of Raymond, so she sits him down on the playground swings and goes to the starting line. However, just before the race, she looks to the side, and there's Raymond on the other side of the fence, kneeling down like he's in the race, too.

evaluate · PREVIEW · experience
react · answer

315

Analyzing a Theme

TEKS 8.14B, 8.14C,
8.17C

> *Squeaky can't believe what she's seeing, but she* *knows that something very important is about to* *happen.* When the gun starts the race, she sprints off, still watching Raymond. He keeps up with the leaders, and people start cheering for him. Raymond is running faster than anyone thought he could, and that makes his sister proud of him. When Squeaky crosses the finish line, she is confused and doesn't think that she has won.

The last stage in the theme's development is described in the last paragraph.

Draft **Write your middle paragraphs.** Write the middle paragraphs of your essay, using your topic sentences and theme chart as a guide. Fill in details as they are needed. Use transitions to connect your ideas.

Using Key Words for Transitions

To create a smooth flow of ideas in your middle paragraphs, tie them together with transitions. Repeating key words is a good way to connect a paragraph to the one before it. The key words below (colored) create a transition between the second and third middle paragraphs shown on page 314.

... She thinks that winning this race is the only

way that she can be successful.

The day of the race is a special day for

Squeaky....

Drafting **Ending Your Essay**

Your essay starts with a statement about the theme. It then goes on to show how the theme develops in stages through the characters and events. Here are some suggestions to help you make your final comments about the theme.

- Show how a character has changed.
- Quote significant lines from the story.
- Predict how the theme might affect a character in the future.
- State the theme as a basic rule of life.

| Beginning |
| Middle |
| Ending |

 Quoting lines directly from the book or story can lend support to your ideas and make them stronger in the eyes of the reader.

Ending Paragraph

The ending paragraph below tells about Squeaky's realization of what is really important in life.

> **The last sentence restates the theme (underlined).**
>
> Finally, when things calm down, the announcer says that Squeaky came in first, and Gretchen was second. Squeaky suddenly realizes that Raymond's happiness is what is really important to her. In the past, she and Gretchen had focused on competing against each other. Now she smiles at Gretchen and thinks that maybe Gretchen would like to help her coach Raymond. Squeaky has a new reason to feel pride in her accomplishments. <u>The theme of the story is clear: Winning isn't the most important thing in life.</u>

 Write your ending. Write the last paragraph of your essay. Be sure to end by revisiting the theme. (Use one of the four suggestions at the top of this page.)

 Form a complete first draft. Make a complete copy of your essay. Double-space or write on every other line so that you have room for revising.

Go Online!

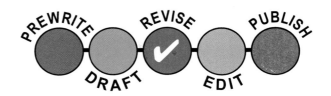

PREWRITE   REVISE ✓   PUBLISH
   DRAFT   EDIT

Revising

Now that you've finished your first draft, you're ready to begin revising. Focus on ideas, organization, and other traits to make changes that will improve your writing.

Keys to Effective Revising

1. Read your essay to yourself to get a feeling of how well it works. Then ask a classmate to read it and give you feedback.

2. Check your introduction and controlling idea to see how well it introduces the story's theme.

3. Be sure that each event and detail you've included supports an understanding of the story's theme.

4. Check your choice of words and your voice to see if it sounds natural and convincing.

5. Check to be sure you use transitions as you present evidence.

6. Use the editing and proofreading marks inside the back cover of this book.

RESPONSE

 **TEKS** 8.17A(i), 8.17C

Revising **for** Focus and Coherence

Focus and Coherence are key elements of an effective essay. Use the information below as a guide to revising your essay for focus and coherence.

Does my controlling idea introduce the story's theme?

You know your controlling idea is effective when it states a specific theme and relates it to the story through the author, the title, or the character.

Poorly Developed Focus

People don't understand each other.
(The theme is too general, and it is not related to a story.)

Well-Developed Focus

In *To Kill a Mockingbird*, the three children learn that it sometimes takes a crisis before people can see the good in others.
(The theme is specific, and it is clearly related to the story.)

 The following controlling ideas are poorly developed. What kind of information should be added to make each one better?

1. *The Call of the Wild* is about wildness.
2. The story's main character, Vicki, realizes something about hope.
3. "The Gift of the Magi" has an interesting ending.
4. In Mark Twain's book, a boy learns that freedom carries responsibilities.
5. The story is about a boy who recovers from his injuries when he stops feeling sorry for himself.
6. In the book *Roll of Thunder, Hear my Cry,* a lot of bad things happen to the Logan family.

 Check your opening. Review your opening paragraph. Pay close attention to the theme in your controlling idea and how it relates to the story.

TEKS 8.17A(i), 8.17C

Did I present an effective introduction?

The introduction to your essay should include the name of the book or story you've read, the author, and an introduction to the book's theme, or the central message of the book. It might also introduce the name of a main character who was affected by the events of the story.

 Read the introduction below, which is the beginning of a student essay. Then answer the questions that follow.

1 The novel To Kill a Mockingbird by Harper Lee takes place
2 in Alabama during the Depression. The book is about the Finch
3 family—Atticus Finch, an upstanding lawyer and extremely
4 moral man, and his two young children—and something they
5 experience one summer in the 1930s. The book is narrated by the
6 main character, Jean Louise Finch, whom everyone calls "Scout."
7 Scout, her brother Jem, and their friend Dill are curious about a
8 mysterious neighbor, Boo Radley. The book unfolds into a coming-
9 of-age novel as Scout is changed forever when she learns about
10 justice and prejudice, and about the goodness of people as well
11 as their dark sides.

● What specific information does the writer give about the book?
● Why do you think this is important in understanding the theme?
● What themes are presented? What do you think Scout learns?

 Revise for introduction. Check to see whether you named the title and author correctly. Check to see how effectively you introduced the theme and the main character(s).

Focus and Coherence
An important character in the development of the theme is added to the introduction.

In the story "Raymond's Run" by Toni Cade Bambara,

Squeaky, the main character, is very focused on running

*   until her brother, who she cares for, proves*
and winning races ~~but learns~~ that there are more
*   ^*

important things in life.

RESPONSE

Revising for Organization

Organization is the way that you arrange your ideas within the essay. Use the following information to review and revise the organization of your essay.

Do my topic sentences relate to the controlling idea?

The topic sentences in your middle paragraphs will relate to the focus if they sound like they flow from the controlling idea expressed in the thesis statement in the first paragraph.

 Read the thesis statement and the topic sentences below. On your own paper, write the words in each topic sentence that relate to the focus.

Thesis Statement

Eventually, Squeaky learns that there's more to life than being the best runner.

Topic Sentences

Along with being a great runner, Squeaky does another thing well, too, although she doesn't take credit for it.

Competition is important to Squeaky, so she concentrates more and more on winning as the race day approaches.

The day of the race is a special day for Squeaky.

Squeaky can't believe what she's seeing, but she knows that something very important is about to happen.

 Check your topic sentences. At the top of a sheet of paper, write a thesis statement that expresses your controlling idea. Then write the topic sentences from your middle paragraphs under that. Rewrite any topic sentences that do not relate to the controlling idea.

TEKS 8.17A(i), 8.17C

What's the best way to end my essay?

Your ending should revisit the theme and leave the reader with something to think about. A good way to emphasize the theme is to use one of the following suggestions.

- Show how a character has changed.
- Quote an important line from the story.
- Predict how the theme might affect a character in the future.
- State the theme as a basic rule of life: *Winning isn't the most important thing in life.*

 For each of the following endings, identify the suggestion (listed above) that the writer used.

1. John now realizes that how he lives his life is completely up to him.
2. The author sees José, the "born worker," as a boy with a fine future.
3. Through the chain of events in the story, the author seems to be saying that revenge doesn't pay.
4. The title of the book is a clue to its theme if you think about the line that it comes from: "Mockingbirds don't do one thing but make music for us to enjoy. That's why it's a sin to kill a mockingbird."

 Review your essay for organization. Be sure that the theme is explained clearly in the beginning and restated effectively in the ending.

Organization	
A restatement of the theme is added.	*Now she smiles at Gretchen and thinks that*
	maybe Gretchen would like to help her coach Raymond.
	Squeaky has a new reason to feel pride in her
	The theme of the story is clear: Winning isn't the
	accomplishments.∧ *most important thing in life.*

RESPONSE

 TEKS 8.17C, 8.20B(ii)

Revising for Development of Ideas

Did I use quotations to emphasize certain ideas?

Quoting directly from a book or story can be an effective way to emphasize important ideas in your essay. Quotations also lend credibility to your writing, showing that you read the text carefully and identified direct evidence to support your points. A quotation could be used to . . .

- highlight an important statement by the author,
- reflect something about the character being quoted, or
- express the theme.

 Read the sentences below, which come from the closing paragraph of a student essay. Why did the writer include the direct quotation? Refer to the list above to help you decide.

1   Atticus Finch's earliest lesson to Scout is simple: "You never
2   really understand a person until you consider things from his
3   point of view . . . until you climb into his skin and walk around in it."
4   Throughout the novel, Scout is learning to understand people.

tip If you need to change a quote slightly, to replace a pronoun with a name or capitalize a letter, use brackets around the changed part, as in "[Mrs. Dubose] was the bravest person I ever knew."

 Review your first draft for ideas. Check to see whether you have used quotations effectively. Also check to make sure they fit naturally within the flow of your writing and that you have punctuated them correctly.

Development of Ideas
A direct quotation is inserted to emphasize a point.

Taking care of her older brother Raymond is a
     Squeaky says, "He needs looking after 'cause
major responsibility in her life. She does her   he's not
                                                  quite right."
duty without really thinking about it.

TEKS 8.14C

Are my words appropriate for the audience?

Your voice should be clear, confident, and knowledgeable. It should be natural, but not too casual. Avoid street talk and slang, as well as words that sound too showy or formal. Be sure your words are appropriate for the form (an essay) and for your audience. Take out anything that does not contribute to a focused, organized piece of writing.

- Lorraine thought that John was acting dumb.
  (This use of *dumb* is slang.)
- Lorraine thought that John was acting nonsensically.
  (*Nonsensically* is too showy in this context.)
- Lorraine thought that John was acting foolishly.
  (*Foolishly* is an appropriate word.)

 Read the paragraph below and decide whether the underlined words are slang or too showy. Choose more appropriate words.

1   They have fun sharing the Pigman's life, but then everything
2   <u>gets nuts</u>. One day when he is gone, they have a <u>happening</u>
3   <u>party</u>. He cries when he sees the damage and calls the <u>law</u>
4   <u>enforcement authorities</u>. John and Lorraine are <u>disconsolate</u>
     when they realize how much they have hurt Mr. Pignati.

 Revise for word choice. Look back at the way you used words in your essay. Look for any words that are slang or sound too showy. Replace words that are not appropriate for this genre or your audience.

Development of Ideas
Slang and showy words are replaced with more appropriate language.

Competition
~~Domination in athletics~~ is important to Squeaky, so
concentrates more and more on
she ~~freaks out about~~ winning as the race day approaches.

Her main worry is about a new girl named Gretchen, who

everybody says is very fast.

RESPONSE

Revising **for** Voice

Voice is the "sound" of your writing. The information below will help you revise your essay so that it sounds natural and creates an appropriate mood.

How do I know whether my writing has a natural voice?

Your writing has a natural voice if it sounds like you and is neither too formal nor too informal. Writers sometimes create language that is too formal because they think that it sounds impressive. Others use language that is too casual or informal. Neither one will sound natural.

Too Formal

The consequence of the experience was that the adolescent female came to a new realization of what was right and what was wrong.

Too Informal

That girl sure did learn her lesson all right.

The voice in the revised sentence below sounds more natural.

Natural

Because of the experience, the girl learned a lesson about how to tell right from wrong.

The best way to hear how your essay sounds is to read it aloud. If you think it sounds unnatural, so will the reader. You may also want to read your essay aloud to friends or family members to see if they think it sounds natural.

Check for natural voice. Reread your essay, marking any sections that sound too formal or too informal. Rewrite those parts so that they sound more natural.

Is my point of view consistent?

Your point of view reflects how you feel about the book and its message. As you write, make sure that the way you describe the events and details helps your readers understand your opinions about the book's meaning and message. Your thesis, or controlling idea, should be consistent throughout your essay, and the details you include should clearly support the points you want to make.

 Read the following paragraphs. Discuss them with a partner and decide which convey a consistent point of view.

1. Scout makes some important discoveries about life. She learns a valuable lesson from Boo that, despite differences among people, they are basically good.

2. Scout is actually the one who teaches others some important lessons. She learns a lot from Atticus, who is a very wise and caring father.

3. The experiences Scout has are central to understanding the book's themes. Scout stands for all of us when she learns to ask: *What is fair and just in judging people and circumstances?*

 Be sure that your point of view is consistent. Think about what you want to say in your essay. What point or points do you want to convey to help your audience understand the book? Review your writing and make necessary changes.

Voice
Words that are not consistent with the point of view are eliminated.

Finally, when things calm down, the announcer says that Squeaky came in first. Squeaky ~~is happy that~~ ~~Gretchen was second but she~~ suddenly realizes that Raymond's happiness is what really matters to her.

RESPONSE

Revising Using a Checklist

Check your revising. On a piece of paper, write the numbers 1 to 12. If you can answer "yes" to a question, put a check mark after that number. If not, continue to work with that part of your essay.

Focus and Coherence

_____ **1.** Have I developed a thesis, or controlling idea, for my essay?

_____ **2.** Do I show an understanding of the book and its message?

_____ **3.** Have I created an effective beginning that introduces the book's theme?

Organization

_____ **4.** Have I created an organized piece of writing?

_____ **5.** Do I use transitions to connect my thoughts?

_____ **6.** Have I reordered parts that are out of place

_____ **7.** Does my essay end with a restatement of the book's theme?

Development of Ideas

_____ **8.** Have I considered how well I've addressed my purpose and audience?

_____ **9.** Have I cut unnecessary details that do not support my controlling idea?

_____ **10.** Do I include examples of events that support my thinking?

Voice

_____ **11.** Is my voice knowledgeable and natural to suit the assignment?

_____ **12.** Have I maintained a consistent point of view?

Make a clean copy. When you've finished revising your essay, ask a classmate to read it and offer feedback. Make any needed revisions. Then create a clean copy for editing.

Editing

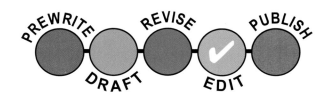

PREWRITE REVISE PUBLISH

DRAFT EDIT ✓

After you've finished revising your essay, it's time to edit for the following conventions: punctuation, capitalization, spelling, and grammar.

Keys to Effective Editing

1. Use a dictionary, a thesaurus, and the "Proofreader's Guide" in the back of this book.

2. Check for any words or phrases that are slang or "too showy" for your readers.

3. Check to be sure that your voice is natural and your point of view is consistent.

4. Check your writing for correctness of grammar, mechanics (punctuation and capitalization), sentence structure, and spelling. Use the editing and proofreading marks on the inside back cover of this book.

5. If you are using a computer, edit on a printed computer copy. Then enter your changes on the computer.

RESPONSE

 **Editing** for **Conventions**

Grammar

When you edit for *grammar*, you make sure you use nouns, verbs, and other parts of speech correctly.

How can I use appositive phrases in my writing?

You can make your writing more interesting when you use a variety of sentence types. One way to vary your sentences is to add appositive phrases. An appositive phrase adds new information about a noun in the sentence. When the information in an appositive phrase is optional, or not necessary to understand the point of the sentence, the phrase should be set off by commas.

> **My favorite book, *To Kill a Mockingbird,* is on most middle school reading lists.**

> **The book *Huckleberry Finn* is banned in some schools.**

In the first example, the information in the appositive phrase is not essential, so it is set off with commas. The reader doesn't need to know which book it is to understand that your favorite book is on the reading lists. In the second example, the reader needs to know which book is banned, so the appositive is not set off with commas.

 Rewrite the following sentences. Circle the noun to which the phrase refers, and add commas where needed.

1. Picasso's painting "Three Musicians" was done in 1921.
2. The team's most valuable player Pepe Sanchez got a trophy in recognition of his efforts.
3. I made copies of my favorite recipe Guacamole Dip and Pita Pieces to give to friends.
4. We invited Ms. Santini the school principal to see our class presentations.
5. Sitha's experiment Creating a Volcano won third-prize at the Science Fair.

 You can use appositive phrases to combine short simple sentences:

> **Tabby got stuck in a tree. Tabby is my cat.**

> **Tabby, my cat, got stuck in a tree.**

TEKS 8.19A(i), 8.19A(iii)
ELPS 5F

How do I combine sentences for greater variety?

A *participial phrase* is a group of words that begins with a participle. A *participle* is a verb that functions as an adjective. Present particles always end in *-ing*. You can combine two short sentences using a participial phrase. In the sentence below, the word *having* is a participle.

Two Short Sentences

Eagles have excellent eyesight.
Eagles can spot prey from high up in the sky.

Combined Sentence

Having excellent eyesight, eagles can spot prey from high up in the sky.

participial phrase

GRAMMAR
Try IT

Rewrite the sentences below using participial phrases. Underline the present participle in each sentence.

   Juan hoped to win the race. Juan ran as fast as he could.
   The twins shared a cookie. They skipped down the street.

Edit

Revise for sentence variety. Check your essay for short sentences that can be combined.

Conventions
Short sentences are combined using participial phrases.

Keeping an eye on Raymond,
∧*Squeaky gets ready for the race with Gretchen.*
                    ∽ *Still watching Raymond,*
~~She keeps an eye on Raymond.~~ *Squeaky starts to run when*

the gun goes off. ~~She still watches Raymond.~~ *Raymond is*

running incredibly fast.

Learning Language

Words that end in *-ing* can act as nouns, verbs, or adjectives. Read these three sentences and tell what part of speech the *-ing* word is in each one.

   Swimming is my favorite sport. The rotting broccoli smelled terrible.
   I am running in a race today.

RESPONSE

Sentence Structure

To revise for *sentence structure*, check the clarity, flow, and smoothness of your sentences. The information below will help you.

How can I make my sentences flow more smoothly?

You can make your sentences flow more smoothly by using a relative pronoun (*who, that, which*) to join short sentences. The following example shows two short sentences and a combined sentence with a relative pronoun.

> **Two Short Sentences**
>
> **José works harder than his cousin Arnie. Arnie avoids physical labor whenever possible.**
>
> **Combined Sentences with a Relative Pronoun**
>
> **José works harder than his cousin Arnie,** who **avoids physical labor whenever possible.**

 Rewrite the following sentences, using relative pronouns to combine each pair of short sentences into a longer one.

1. José is a boy with a fine future. José comes from a hardworking family.
2. José and Arnie get a job cleaning a swimming pool. The pool is owned by a friend of Arnie's father.
3. José is annoyed that he has to scrub the pool. Scrubbing the pool is supposed to be Arnie's job.

 Use commas to set off a clause beginning with a relative pronoun if the clause is *not necessary* to the basic meaning of the sentence. (See 758.3 and 740.6.)

> **Soccer,** which is a favorite sport in many other countries, **is becoming popular in the United States.**

Commas should not set off a clause that is necessary to understand the meaning of the sentence.

> **Soccer** that is played indoors **is a very high-scoring game.**

 Edit for conventions. Reread your essay and look for places where the writing seems choppy. Use relative pronouns to create complex sentences.

Mechanics: Punctuation

How do I punctuate direct quotations?

Use quotation marks to enclose direct quotations. An indirect or reworded quotation needs no quotation marks. Read the following paragraph and note the way the blue quotations are punctuated.

Colonel Sanders said, "Mr. Leghorn won't be with us tonight." **The Colonel also told us that** Leghorn had been detained in the kitchen. **Everyone in the audience was upset by the news, and one of the dancers asked,** "Can it be true?" **Others wondered** who could possibly call the square dance as well as the trusty Mr. L. **Finally, a voice from the back of the room suggested that** Mr. Terpsichore would make a good substitute. **At that, Mr. Terpsichore stepped forward, looked at the band, and said,** "Hit it, boys!"

Copy the following paragraph, inserting any punctuation needed for quotations. (See 658.1 and 660.1.)

1   José's father sometimes exclaims, Life is hard! But José is not
2   discouraged. He feels that his muscles need to work hard, and
3   he tells his cousin Arnie that he will not rest until he finds a job.
4   Arnie then asks, Do you want to work together?

Edit for conventions. Check your essay for punctuation, especially punctuation used in direct and indirect quotations.

Conventions	
Commas are added and quotation marks are removed.	Finally when things calm down the announcer says that, "Squeaky came in first, and Gretchen was second." Squeaky suddenly realizes that . . .

TEKS 8.14D, 8.21

Editing **Using a Checklist**

Check your editing. On a piece of paper, write the numbers 1 to 13. If you can answer "yes" to a question, put a check mark after that number. If not, continue to edit for that convention.

Conventions

GRAMMAR

_____ **1.** Do my subjects and verbs agree in number?

_____ **2.** Have I used the correct forms of verbs?

_____ **3.** Have I distinguished between verbs and participles?

_____ **4.** Do I use participles and appositive phrases correctly?

_____ **5.** Do I use different sentence structures for variety?

MECHANICS

_____ **6.** Do I use commas after introductory word groups?

_____ **7.** Do I use commas with my appositive phrases?

_____ **8.** Do I use commas to set off participial phrases?

_____ **9.** Do I use quotation marks to indicate direct quotes?

_____ **10.** Have I correctly punctuated my quotations?

SPELLING

_____ **11.** Have I spelled all my words correctly?

_____ **12.** Have I used the right words (example: *to, too, two*)?

_____ **13.** Have I double-checked the words my spell-checker may have missed?

Creating a Title

- Use the title of the book or story: **"Raymond's Run"**
- Refer to the character: **Squeaky's Victory**
- Be creative: **Crossing the Line**

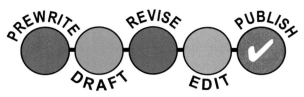

Publishing
Sharing Your Essay

Now that you've finished writing, revising, and editing your essay, it's time to make it look good. You may also want to present your essay in some other form: illustrations, sharing with your classmates, or a submission to a literary magazine. (See the suggestions in the boxes below.)

 Make a final copy. Follow your teacher's instructions or use the guidelines below to format your paper. (If you are using a computer, see pages 62–64.) Write a final copy of your essay and proofread it for errors.

Focus on Presentation

- Use blue or black ink and write neatly.
- Write your name in the upper left corner of page 1.
- Skip a line and center your title; skip another line and start your writing.
- Indent every paragraph and leave a one-inch margin on all four sides.
- Write your last name and the page number in the upper right corner of every page after the first one.

Make Illustrations

Draw one or more illustrations of key scenes in the development of the theme. Write a caption at the bottom of each illustration and post them in your classroom.

Submit Your Essay to a Literary Magazine

If your school has a literary magazine, submit your essay for publication. Write a cover letter explaining why classmates might be interested in your essay.

Share It with Your Classmates

Give a short introduction to the book or short story you wrote about and then read your essay to the class.

RESPONSE

Evaluating a Response to Literature

To learn how to evaluate a response to literature, you'll use the scoring rubric on pages **50–51** and the responses that follow. These responses are examples of writing for each score on the rubric.

Notice that this first response received a score of 4. Read the description for a score of 4 on pages **50–51**. Then read the response. Use the same steps to study the other examples. Always remember to think about the overall quality of the writing.

Writing that fits a score of 4 is very strong.

Blackwing Kiln

In *Blackwing Kiln*, a novel by Mary Bao, a family of Vietnamese immigrants, the Pham family, comes to the small town of Blackwing, Minnesota after the end of the Vietnam War. At first they feel lost there, because not only are they in a new country, but the weather is completely different from what it was in their beloved homeland. In addition, the people of the small town in the big, northern woods don't exactly make them feel welcome at first. In spite of these hardships, however, the Phams succeed and become a welcomed part of the community. Josephine Pham, the narrator who is also the protagonist, becomes a popular girl at school. Along the way, Josephine learns not to judge people by first impressions, and to be patient with herself and others.

To develop this theme, the novel follows the experiences of the Pham family, showing how the people of Blackwing are prejudiced against them at the start. The Phams similarly judge the Americans by first impressions. The Phams don't try to socialize with the Americans at first. They just build their pottery kiln in the middle of the woods and don't see anyone. As a result, Josephine becomes unhappy and lonely.

Appropriate literary terms

Effective controlling idea

Appropriate words—not slangy, not showy

Writer uses quotations as evidence.

As the summer goes on, the Phams realize they need more contact with the outside in order to sell their pottery. They rent a store in Blackwing, but they mostly avoid people and people avoid them. Mr. Pham tells Josephine, "We don't need anyone but ourselves." In the same chapter, a man from the town, Mr. Henry, says about the Phams, "We don't need them here." That shows the theme that both sides are judging each other without knowing each other.

Then, someone breaks a window of the Pham's shop. You might think this would draw people further apart, but when the towns-people see the Phams quietly fixing their window, they are ashamed that there is hatred in their community, and they help out, including painting a new sign for the shop and beginning to buy the pottery.

Writer uses key words as transitions.

All this time, Josephine has been feeling impatient. She is impatient with prejudice and wants to move, and she is impatient with her parents for not moving. She thinks the kids in the town are against her—but really they just don't know her and she doesn't know them. When they get to know each other, Josephine and the other kids accept each other. If she had remained impatient, she would not have made friends with them.

Shows stages of theme development

Theme's importance

This book shows that in order to conquer prejudice you have to be patient with other people, because you have to wait till you find out who they are for themselves, not just as a stereotype. If you learn to be patient with people, you learn to be patient with yourself. This is a lesson many people need to learn, and I'm glad I learned it from Blackwing Kiln.

RESPONSE

Writing that fits a score of 3 is strong in most ways.

Cut-Ear's Pack

I read a book called Cut-Ear's Pack, by Frederick Joplin, which is about a pack of Arctic white wolves in the future who have to deal with changes in the environment. It's about the year 2060. Cut-Ear has that name because he once had part of his ear cut off in a fight with another wolf, although Cut-Ear won and remained as the alpha male. As the novel opens, the pack is faced with warming temperature in their Artic territory, which they like because it means the musk oxen and caribou which are there prey are traveling farther north. However, it also brings trouble, because it brings compitition from other wolves and it brings humans. The pack survives because Cut-Ear leads them to be adaptable, and the theme is we all need to adapt to a changing world.

The competition from other wolves is what happens first, and the gray wolves from farther south have larger packs so they have an advantage. But Cut-Ear's pack has an advantage too because they are on their home teritory. Also they are skilled at hunting musk oxen. In the spring, Cut-Ear's mate has a litter of four pups instead of two or three, and this shows the pack is adapting because Arctic wolves didn't usually (I mean in our era) have as big litters as other wolves. In addition, Cut-Ear wins a fight with the alpha of a gray wolf pack and drives them off.

So far so good, but worse is to come when human hunters pop onto the scene. Arctic wolves have very little contact with humans compared to most wolves, and they don't fear humans. At first the wolves just stand there and

Unimportant details

Voice sounds natural

Appropriate words for audience

look at the humans. This could be a disastre for Cut-Ear's pack. In a tragic scene, one of Cut-Ear's offspring, Slim, is shot and killed by a hunter. This makes Cut-Ear realize (in a wolf way) that they have to avoid humans from now on. Which isn't easy, especially because the Artic wolve's white fur stands out. But they learn how by hiding amid rocks and caves.

They become even more adaptable when Cut-Ear's oldest son, Thick Fur, goes out on his own to start his own pack. He doesn't mate with another Arctic wolf female. He mates with a gray wolf. (The two kinds of wolf are the same species just slightly different. They can create offspring.) In other words his decendant's packs will not be as bright white so they won't be as easy to hunt. This is science fiction and it happens in the future, so it doesn't have to be true, but it could happen.

Cut-Ear's Pack is a very exciting book that people who are interested in nature, animals, or the future will all enjoy. Cut-Ear is an excellent character even though he is an animal. He is brave, cunning, and strong, and he takes care of his pack to the best of his ability. Most of all, he shows that if you adapt, you can survive. That is something everyone needs to understand.

Some errors

Ending restates theme and explains its importance.

Writing that fits a score of 2 is strong in some ways.

I, Tabitha Justice

Did you ever hear of Tabitha Justice, the slave who became a famous poet in the 1800s? Probably not, because she wasn't a real person. But she's the hero of this novel by Paulette Welles and it's a good book which I liked very much.

The theme is that people can overcome being opresed. Tabitha is a character who has to do whatever her Master tells her and no questions asked. She is a made who waits in the dining room and is not allowed to speak there. Also she is not allowed to learn to read and right. That is true of all the slaves on the Plantation. However, some of them learn to read and right anyway. Because they are so thirsty for Knowledge. That is the first example of how they overcome.

For the second example, Tabitha begins writing poems at night. She doesn't tell anyone. She is afraid to. One day, the poems are gone. They have vanished!! Lucky she has them memarized. The Overseer found them. He does not turn her in, but starts treating her worse. It does not stop Tabitha from writing poems.

She starts being treated so bad that her brother and her escape on the underground Railroad. Then she met a woman who helps her get her poems pubblished. She is famous, but some people don't even believe she could write the poems. She convinces hem. She writes a poem while they are waching. She still has things to overcome, but she knows she can do it.

No title or clear thesis

Many errors in capitalization and spelling

Shows stages of development of theme

Closing does not discuss theme's importance.

Writing that fits a score of 1 is weak.

No identification of title or author

Many errors in spelling and grammar

Writer describes development of plot, not theme.

Writer sounds uninterested.

Rescuing Mr. Mulberry

Mr. Mulbery is a cat in this story. Him and his human family go on vacyshun. Driving. Mr. M has to stay in the carier most of the time so they let him out for brakes. One time he ecscapes. That could rune the whole trip. But his family theyre name is Blount loves him they wont leave him. They look all over and evenshuly find him. This shows that people in a family shoud love each other. Inculding animals.

Theyres lot of places in the story where it shows that people in a family shoud love each other. First the oldest kid wants to leave but the youngest crys because he realy loves the cat. The whole family sides w/ him. They have adventures when they are looking for the cat. They look in a farm and the farmer tries to chace them but they become frends. The farmer starts lookin for the cat to. Then this whole town is lookin for the same cat. Sure enuff they find him.

Turns out they had as much fun looking for this cat than they would of on a whole vacyshion. And they still get to go on the trip. The cats happy too, he gets back to his human family. They all tryd together. So it was a better vacayshun because they had to look for him. If you believ that then this book tells you its important.

Evaluating and Reflecting on Your Writing

You've put a lot of time and effort into your essay. Now take some time to score and think about your writing. On your own paper, finish each sentence starter below. To score your writing, refer to the scoring rubric on pages 50–51.

My Theme Analysis

1. The best score for my essay is . . .

2. It's the best score because . . .

3. The strength of my essay is . . .

4. The part that still needs work is . . .

5. The main thing I learned about writing an analysis of a theme is . . .

6. Here is one question I still have about writing an analysis of a theme . . .

7. Right now I would describe my writing ability as (excellent, good, fair, poor) . . .

Responding to Texts

Writing a Response to an Expository Text

Did you know that it takes 43 separate muscles to frown, but only 17 to smile! Do you enjoy reading facts about the human body? Perhaps you like to read about animals or sports or outer space.

Expository writing is writing that explains facts or ideas. You find this kind of writing in articles and magazines. A response to expository writing is different from a response to a story. This type of response usually highlights important facts or information contained in the article.

On the next page, you will read a sample paragraph that responds to an article. Then you will write a response paragraph of your own.

Writing Guidelines

Subject: A book or article
Purpose: To show understanding
Form: Essay
Audience: Classmates

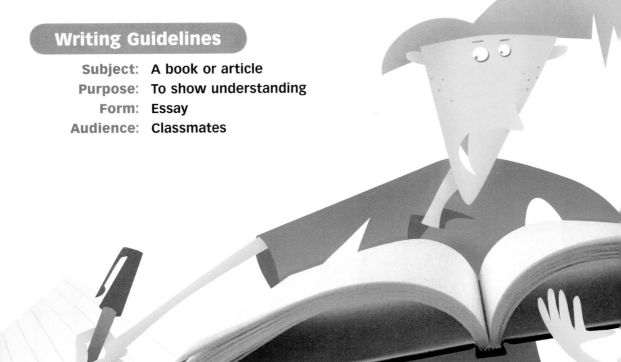

 **TEKS** 8.17C

Respond to a Magazine Article

When responding to a magazine article, you provide evidence from the text that shows you understand the material. The following student sample is a response to an article about a brave soldier from the American Revolution.

Beginning

The introduction sets the tone for a most unusual story.

Middle

The middle gives details about Samson's life and service in the army.

Deborah Samson

The American Revolution and the years surrounding it are an important time in our nation's history, which is why *Our History* magazine devoted an entire issue to it this past July. Of all the articles, the remarkable story of one brave soldier caught and sustained my attention.

Robert Shurtleff enlisted in the Continental Army in 1782 to fight in the American Revolutionary War. He was tall and as strong as the rest of the men, but Robert Shurtleff had a secret: He was really a 21-year-old woman named Deborah Samson!

Deborah Samson was five foot seven, taller than the average men of her time. She was strong, too, from working on a farm. When war broke out, Deborah wanted to help, but girls were not allowed to enlist, so she decided to disguise herself as a man. The article includes an illustration of a soldier, which helped me picture Deborah in uniform.

As part of the Light Infantry Company of the Fourth Massachusetts Regiment, Deborah was a brave soldier who displayed much courage. In one battle, she was hit in the leg with a musket ball. Afraid of her secret being revealed, Deborah hid her injury and tried to cut out the musket ball herself with a penknife! To me, that shows as much courage and strength as facing a British soldier in battle.

TEKS 8.17C
ELPS 5G

Later on, Deborah was admitted to a hospital with a high fever. The doctor discovered her secret, but he told no one. He took Deborah to his own home to recuperate until "Robert" was well enough to earn an Honorable Discharge in 1783. Deborah returned home, married in 1785, and had three children.

In 1792, she petitioned the Massachusetts State Legislature for back pay. According to the article, "the army had withheld her pay after discovering that she was a woman." She was awarded the back pay based on her exceptional record; however she did not get a pension like the rest of the soldiers, even though she had been honorably discharged. Why? Because she was a woman!

Paul Revere wrote a letter on her behalf and the military finally awarded her a pension in 1805. It came to $4 a month. A second petition, approved by Congress, finally awarded her the $76 per month pension that her fellow soldiers received.

The article does an excellent job of explaining the challenges Deborah faced. I agree with the writer that she is a model to all women, not only for her brave fighting during the war, but also for her fight for equality after the war had ended.

A quotation from the article provides an important detail.

Ending
• • • • • • • • • • • •
The ending reflects on the important role Samson played during the American Revolution.

Respond to the reading. Answer the following questions about the sample essay.

☐ **Development of Ideas** **(1) What person is the article about? What is unusual about her story? (2) How does the writer introduce the person and her unique story?**

☐ **Organization** **(3) How does the order of events help build a focused, coherent piece of writing?**

☐ **Voice** **(4) How does the writer personally connect with the article? Does the writer convey interest and excitement about what she has learned?**

Prewriting Selecting an Expository Text

To get started, select a nonfiction book or article you would like to write about. Lupita began by listing all the nonfiction she had recently read.

Topics List

Nonfiction text	Author
Space Shuttle article	NASA online
book about nutrition	Amy Caldera
article about chimps	Tom Dominic*

Select an expository text. List nonfiction books and articles you've read. Put a star (*) next to the one that you would like to write about. Have your teacher approve your choice.

Respond to a Magazine Article

When you respond to a magazine article, you provide evidence from the text to demonstrate your understanding of the material. In the following student sample, the writer has just read an article about chimpanzees. The side notes will help you understand how to respond to expository writing.

Beginning
The beginning tells what the article is about.

Middle
The middle gives facts and includes a quotation.

> Did you know that chimps and humans share 99% of the same genetic materials? Scientists have been studying chimps since the 1960s. One of the first scientists to work with chimps was Jane Goodall. She realized that chimps were intelligent and emotional creatures. Goodall once wrote, "What I have learned from them has shaped my understanding of human behavior, of our place in nature."

TEKS 8.17A(iii)

Drafting Creating Your First Draft

Now that you've selected a nonfiction book or article, begin gathering details to write your first draft. Sentence starters provide one way to gather information for a response to expository text. On your own paper, complete each of the sentence starters to help you think about what you've learned.

Sentence Starters

The first thing I noticed about the article/book was . . .

The most interesting thing about the article/book is . . .

A few quotes that help show what the article/book is about are . . .

A few interesting facts about the topic are . . .

The article/book is important to me because . . .

Write the first draft. Use your notes from the sentence starters to help plan and write the first draft of your response.

Eliminate Extraneous Information

Your draft should be logically organized with facts and details that support the controlling idea of your writing. Reread your draft and eliminate facts and details that don't belong.

Focus and Coherence
A sentence with extraneous information was cut.

Everyone loves a race. In this race, the best-trained athletes are dogs! The race is called the Iditarod. Every year in Alaska teams of sled dogs compete in this week-long race that covers more than 1,000 miles.

The dogs aren't alone, however. A person called a "musher" is along for the ride. The mushers stand on the back of their sleds for hours guiding their teams. Mushers care for and feed their dogs, which they raise from puppies. A special bond develops between dogs and mushers. ~~It's probably like the bond between a pet and its owners.~~

RESPONSE

 TEKS 8.14E, 8.17C, 8.20A, 8.20B(i), 8.21

Revising Improving Your Writing

After you finish your first draft, revise it for the following traits.

☐ **Focus and Coherence** Does my response revolve around a central, controlling idea? Is my writing focused and logical?

☐ **Organization** Does my writing build on ideas that support my controlling idea?

☐ **Development of Ideas** Have I used transitions to tie the ideas together? Have I included facts that the audience will find interesting?

☐ **Voice** Is my voice natural? Have I avoided slang, and "showy" words?

☐ **Conventions** Is my grammar correct? Have I used complete sentences? Have I checked for punctuation, capitalization, and spelling?

Revise your response. Ask yourself the questions above. Revise your response to improve these traits of writing.

Editing Checking for Conventions

When you edit your writing, check to be sure you've used a variety of sentence structures.

☐ **Conventions** Have I checked punctuation and capitalization? Have I checked spelling and grammar? Have I added commas after introductory phrases? Have I punctuated sentences correctly?

Edit your work. Ask yourself the questions above as you edit your work. Make a clean final copy and proofread it.

Publishing Sharing Your Writing

Once you've finished writing, share your work.

■ Read the essay to your class.

■ Submit your essay to a school publication or online site that publishes student work.

Share your ideas. Choose one of the publishing ideas above or come up with your own.

Responding to Texts
Across the Curriculum

An old saying goes, "A picture is worth a thousand words." That's because a picture can show something that happened a thousand miles away or a hundred years ago. By responding to pictures, articles, and Web sites, you can learn about the world around you. In social studies, you can study photos from another time or place. In science, you can read articles that push the frontiers of technology. And by exploring the Web, you can see things on the other side of the world—or the universe!

After working with the different forms of response writing on the following pages, you will get a chance to practice responding to a timed test prompt.

What's Ahead

- **Social Studies:** Responding to a Historical Photo
- **Science:** Summarizing a Science Article
- **Practical Writing:** Evaluating a Web Site
- **Writing for Assessment**

Social Studies:
Responding to a Historical Photo

Social studies explores the way people have lived in different places and at different times. A picture tells a story without any words. You can use your observational skills and information from social studies class to write a response to a historical photograph.

In her social studies textbook, Selena saw a picture of kids working at midnight in a glass factory in the early 1900s. It showed her what life must have been like for kids who had to work to help their families make enough money.

No Time to Play

The beginning introduces the photo.

In the past, kids worked long hours in factories with terrible working conditions. This picture from 1908 shows child laborers at midnight in a glass factory. The dark room is crowded with pipes, tables, glass bottles, and a brick oven. Everything is smoky and covered with dirt. One of the boys wears a shirt with a big hole on the shoulder. His pants are ripped, too. A few of the boys look up toward the camera, very tired and a little surprised. Maybe they are wondering why someone would take a picture of them. Pictures like this made people want to outlaw child labor. Today, kids spend their time at school or at home with family and friends. Even though a picture may be sad to look at, it can teach valuable lessons about the country's past.

The middle describes the photo.

The ending reflects on the photo's value.

TEKS 8.23A, 8.25A
ELPS 5B

Writing Tips

Before you write . . .

- **Choose a picture.**
  Search through your history book or the Internet to find a historical picture to write about.

- **Imagine being a person in this picture.**
  Think about what it must have been like to live in another time and place.

- **Think about why this picture is important.**
  Ask yourself what this picture shows about the society of the time. Ask yourself how pictures such as this one may have brought about the changes evident in today's society.

During your writing . . .

- **Focus on the main features of the picture.**
  Start with the first thing you notice. Describe it and then shift to other details in a logical fashion.

- **Share interesting details.**
  Let the images in the photograph suggest sounds, smells, textures, and other details.

After you've written a first draft . . .

- **Revise your response.**
  Make sure you have connected the picture's historical setting to the present day. Check to see that your details appear in the best possible order.

- **Double-check important facts.**
  Make sure the names and dates in your paragraph are correct.

- **Check for correctness.**
  Check the conventions in your response. Then make a final copy of your work and proofread it for errors.

 Search your textbook, the library, or the Internet for a historical photograph that interests you. Look for information that can help you understand the historical significance of the picture. Write a paragraph that responds to the photo. Use the information above as a guide.

RESPONSE

Science: Summarizing a Science Article

Every day, magazines, newspapers, and Web sites report the fascinating discoveries of science. Summarizing an article can help you understand it. The following article, "Batteries Driving the Future," explains the technology of hybrid cars. The paragraph "Battery Included" summarizes the article.

Batteries Driving the Future

As the world's population swells, the demand for cars increases. More cars mean more pollution, but scientists and the automotive industry have found a way to reduce this problem: the hybrid car.

Hybrid cars use an electric motor and a gasoline engine. The electric motor is powered by a long-lasting battery, which is charged by a generator built into the car. This combination of devices provides an extremely efficient use of gasoline. Here's how hybrid cars work:

- When a hybrid car is starting and going slowly, the electric motor powers the car.
- At higher speeds, the gasoline engine takes over. The engine sends power to a generator, which charges the battery.
- If the car is going uphill or speeding up, the electric motor and gasoline engine work together.
- During slowing down and braking, the generator charges the battery.

Hybrid cars are becoming increasingly popular as consumers seek vehicles that lessen environmental impact. Their sleek designs make them visually appealing and aerodynamic. The fuel efficiency of hybrid cars reduces reliance on gasoline. As hybrids grow in popularity, there's no doubt that batteries will drive the future of the automotive industry.

Battery Included

Topic Sentence

The article "Batteries Driving the Future" explains how hybrid cars use an electric motor and a gasoline engine. The electric motor, which works at low speeds, gets its power from a battery. The battery doesn't need to be plugged in, since it is charged by a generator in the car. Hybrid cars have a smooth shape for both style and aerodynamics, and they use less fuel, making them better for the environment. *The world and its people are beginning to benefit from hybrid cars.*

Body

Closing Sentence

TEKS 8.23A, 8.25A
ELPS 5B

Writing Tips

Before you write . . .

● **Gather science magazines.**
Check your school library for magazines such as *National Geographic* or *Current Science.* Also check the Internet for scientific articles from sources such as www.nasa.gov. Your teacher may know of other sources.

● **Read the article and take notes.**
Read your selection once to get the overall idea of the article. Then reread the material and take notes about important information.

● **Organize your paragraph.**
Identify the main idea of the article. Gather only the details needed to support the main idea.

During your writing . . .

● **Focus on the main idea.**
Use your topic sentence to identify the main idea in the article. In the body, include key details to support it. End with a clear closing sentence.

● **Be brief.**
Make sure your summary is only about a third of the length of the original article.

After you've written a first draft . . .

● **Check your facts.**
Make sure that you have accurately recorded key facts from the article.

● **Check for conventions.**
Correct any errors in spelling, punctuation, capitalization, and grammar.

Find an interesting science article in a magazine or on the Internet. Read the article and write a summary of it using the tips above as a guide. Make sure to double-check the facts in your response.

Practical Writing:
Evaluating a Web Site

Web sites combine words and graphics to inform, persuade, or entertain. One student filled out the following form to evaluate a Web site about origami.

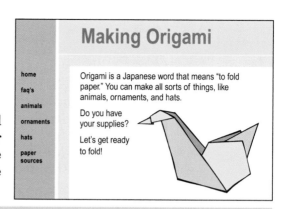

Making Origami

home
faq's
animals
ornaments
hats
paper sources

Origami is a Japanese word that means "to fold paper." You can make all sorts of things, like animals, ornaments, and hats.

Do you have your supplies?

Let's get ready to fold!

Web Site Evaluation

Complete this form by filling in the subject of the Web site, circling its purpose, and rating its parts. Then add your overall comments at the bottom.

Web-site subject and address: *Origami, www.origami.hby.net*

Purpose:	inform		persuade		(entertain)
Information					
incomplete	1	2	(3)	4	5	thorough
Navigation					
confusing	1	2	(3)	4	5	simple
Layout					
distracting	1	2	3	(4)	5	helpful
Text (words)					
muddled	1	2	3	4	(5)	legible
Graphics (pictures)					
dull	1	2	3	(4)	5	engaging
Colors					
boring	1	2	3	(4)	5	appealing

The strong points: *The green and gold colors grabbed my attention. The different letter style for the title makes it stand out.*

Possible improvements: *Information about what supplies are needed and what to click next should be included.*

Writing Tips

If you are asked to evaluate a Web site, use the following tips to guide you through the process.

Before you write . . .

- **Study the form you will be using.**
  If you are given a form, review it so that you know which details to judge.
- **Review the Web site.**
  Look carefully at the site's information, navigation method, layout, and so forth. Use the form to guide you.

During your writing . . .

- **Follow all of the directions.**
  Complete the whole form.
- **Make your comments clear.**
  Give criticism that could improve the site.

After you've written a first draft . . .

- **Double-check your answers.**
  Make sure your responses are clear and complete.

Review the evaluation form on page 352. Then study the Web page below. On your own paper, write at least two "strong points" and two "possible improvements" for the Web page.

 Lawrence Middle School

home   calendar   clubs   courses   schedule   library   sports   staff   contact

The field trip to Chicago is coming up. We'll visit the Museum of Natural History. They have full-size dinosaur skeletons on display. Be sure to get your permission slip in soon.

RESPONSE

TEKS 8.17C

Responding to Texts
Writing for Assessment

On some tests, you may be asked to read a story and write a response to it. The next two pages give you an example of such a test. Read the directions, the story, and the student's comments (in blue). Then read the student's response on pages 356–357.

Response to Literature Prompt

DIRECTIONS:

- Read the following story.
- As you read, make notes. (Your notes will not be graded.)
- After reading the story, write an essay about it. You have 45 minutes to read, plan, write, and proofread your work.

When you write, focus on the author's message in the story and show your insight into the characters and ideas. Use clear organization and support your focus with examples from the text.

It Wasn't About Fish

Juan sat on his front porch and watched the road. "Any time now." Under his left elbow was a bag stuffed with a week's worth of clothes and a pair of hip waders. Under his right elbow was a five-gallon bucket loaded with a tackle box and three rods, broken down to fit in Dad's hatchback.

"Where is he?" Juan muttered, checking his watch.

"Maybe he decided to cancel."

Juan glanced irritably over his shoulder to see his little sister grinning at him through the living room window. Her brown hair stuck out in ponytails on the sides of her face. He shook his head. "Yeah, right. Not two years in a row." ← *Canceled before*

Berta vanished from the window and opened the front door, dragging her own pack.

"You're not going, Berta. Mom said you couldn't."

"It's not up to Mom," she replied, sitting down beside the fishing gear. "Dad gets to decide."

TEKS 8.17C

Just what I need, Juan thought, *a 10-year-old sister trying to muscle in on my spring-break trip.* "You're not going. You'll get to go when you're 11. I have one more year, just me and Dad." Since the separation, Juan and Berta had had to fight over chances like these. "Besides, you don't even like fishing."

"Maybe I do," she said. "I just need somebody to show me how."

Juan leaned back, smiling cruelly. "All right, Sis—first I'll teach you how to put worms on a hook. Then I'll teach you how to gut a fish and skin it and cut off its head."

Not nice

"Gross!" Berta said, retreating into the house.

Laughing, Juan sighed and settled in. The fact was, he wasn't crazy about any of that stuff, either. Fishing was more about sitting in a boat with Dad and just talking, just being together on a still lake. It wasn't about fish.

"Where is he?"

He knows.

The phone rang. Juan felt his breath leave in a great gush. He knew what this call was about, even before Mom answered it. His teeth creaked against each other as he waited for the inevitable.

"Honey," Mom said, cracking the door open behind him. "Sorry. That was your dad. He's stuck at work again. He's going to have to cancel the trip. I'm sorry, Juanito."

"Don't call me that," he snapped, crouching forward as if he'd just been punched in the gut. He caught his head in his hands. *Instead of fishing, I'll be stuck at home all week with Little Miss—*

The door creaked open again, and soft footsteps came on the porch behind Juan. Berta sank down beside the fishing gear. She picked at her pack of clothes. "I wanted him to change his mind."

Juan's face flushed with anger. "You wanted him to cancel?"

Berta stared at him, her eyes wide between her ponytails. "No, way, Juan. I wanted him to take me along, too."

The red in Juan's face dissolved. *Berta wants this trip as much as I do.* Juan suddenly felt rotten. "You really want to learn to fish?"

Berta's eyes were brimming as she nodded.

"Well, I can teach you. I know everything Dad knows."

"Honest?" — *Thinks about someone else*

"Sure." Juan stood up, lifting Berta's pack and his own in one hand. His other hand hoisted the fishing gear. "Mom, fire up the minivan. I'm going to teach you two how to fish!"

Student Response

The following essay shows a student response to the story "It Wasn't About Fish." Note how the student uses details from the story to support the focus.

Beginning

The first paragraph names the story and gives a thesis statement (**underlined**).

"It Wasn't About Fish" is a coming-of-age story in which a big disappointment tests the main character. Juan's father, who is separated from Juan's mother, had promised to take the boy on a fishing trip. Juan is eager to be with his dad and away from his 10-year-old sister. Then Juan's dad calls to cancel the trip for the second year in a row. <u>The way that Juan handles this disappointment shows that he is growing up.</u>

At first, Juan is only thinking about himself. He has packed all his things and is waiting impatiently for his dad to drive up. When Juan's sister, Berta, says she wants to go on the trip, too, he tells her she can't. He isn't paying any attention to her feelings. Berta doesn't give up, so Juan even scares her off by telling her, "I'll teach you how to gut a fish and skin it and cut off its head." Juan wants the fishing trip all to himself.

Middle

The middle paragraphs include examples and details from the story to explain characters and themes.

When Juan's dad calls to cancel the trip, Juan starts thinking in a different way. First, he is crushed. He feels abandoned. Afterward, when Berta comes out, Juan gets angry. He thinks she wanted their dad to cancel. Really, she wanted to go along. Once Juan sees that Berta feels as left out as he does, he starts to act more mature. Instead of just thinking about himself,

Juan actually thinks about spending more time with his mom and his little sister.

I think the title tells a lot about the theme of this story. Juan realized that the trip "wasn't about fish," but about spending time with his dad. When the trip is canceled, Juan realizes he can go fishing anyway with the rest of his family. Instead of counting on his dad to teach him, Juan becomes the teacher.

Ending

The ending sums up the character's change and the theme.

At the beginning, Juan thinks only about himself and is pretty unhappy. By the end, he is thinking about others, and he is happy. Juan has learned that the trip is about being with family.

Respond to the reading. Answer the following questions about the student response.

☐ Development of Ideas **(1) What is the focus of the student's response? (2) What feelings does this student describe?**

☐ Organization **(3) How did the notes on pages 354–355 help the student organize the response?**

☐ Voice **(4) What words or phrases from the story does the writer quote? (5) Were these examples effective?**

RESPONSE

Practice Writing Prompt

Response to a literature prompt. Carefully read the directions below. Use 10 minutes at the beginning to read the story, make notes, and plan your writing. Also leave time at the end to proofread your work.

DIRECTIONS:

- Read the following story.
- As you read, make notes *on your own paper.*
- After reading the story, write an essay about it. You have 45 minutes to read, plan, write, and proofread your work.

When you write, focus on the author's message in the story and show your insight into the characters and ideas. Use clear organization and support your focus with examples from the text.

Mountain Encounter

Elena leaned against a large boulder and gasped for breath. She stared at the clear blue sky overhead. A small bird flew along, disappearing into the trees. Elena sighed and wished that she could fly like that bird. Instead, she was stuck here, slogging along on the trail. She looked ahead at the dirt path that switched back and forth up the steep mountainside. Her parents and little brother, Diego, were already at the next bend.

"C'mon, Elena!" shouted Diego. He smirked back at her as he skipped along the path.

Taking a deep breath, Elena pushed herself away from the coolness of the boulder. Her feet ached with each step. Her back was hot and sweaty under a backpack that held snacks, a bottle of water, sunscreen, and her camera. "Why did I have to come along?" Elena grumbled as she stumbled over a tree root. She just couldn't keep up with her family on these hikes. They set one pace, and Elena set another.

The voices of her family echoed from the trail ahead, and her mother's laughter floated down through the trees. Elena glared at her own feet. Puffs of dust rolled up around the boots with each arduous step. If only she could catch up . . .

Thirty agonizing minutes later, Elena slouched on a rock. "I'm taking another break!"

A faint response came from the trail ahead: "We're at the next lookout point. We'll wait for you here."

At the next lookout point . . . What beautiful things were they seeing while Elena was stuck in the dust of the trail? She slid her backpack off and grabbed her water bottle. The water was warm and tasted like plastic. Yuck. She spit it onto the ground and watched the water slowly seep into the dirt.

Maybe next year, I won't come on the family vacation. Elena reached for her backpack. Then her mouth dropped open in shock.

Just a few feet ahead on the trail stood a doe and two fawns. The deer stared at Elena with their soft brown eyes. The doe waited as her fawns skipped across the trail. They were so close, Elena wanted to reach out and touch their velvety reddish-brown coats. Instead, she held her breath and watched in quiet wonder. The fawns were so tiny and delicate. She couldn't believe how fragile they looked, and yet they playfully hopped and bounced about. All too soon, the fawns wandered off with the doe patiently following behind. As suddenly as they had appeared, the deer faded away into the woods.

Elena stared in amazement at the empty trail.

"C'mon, Elena!" Diego called from ahead. "You're missing the view."

Nope, she thought, *I have my own view.* But out loud she replied, "I'm coming!" Elena smiled and started back up the trail, walking at her own pace.

RESPONSE

Response to Expository Text

You may be asked to read an article and write a response to it on a school or state test. Use the information below to help you write your essay. Then read one student's response and evaluate it.

Tips for Writing a Response to Expository Texts

- Take 10 minutes at the beginning to read the article and plan your writing. Also leave time at the end to proofread your work.
- Paraphrase when retelling details from the article.
- Include specific details and quotations that show you understand the text.

Response to Expository Text Prompt

DIRECTIONS:

- Read the following article.
- As you read, you may make notes or underline parts. (Your notes will not be graded.)
- After reading the story, write an essay about it. You have 45 minutes to read, plan, write, and proofread your work.

When you write, focus on the author's main point and show your insight into the facts and information presented. Use clear organization and support your focus with examples from the text.

Up and Running

Today, there are many kinds of athletic shoes to fit everyone's taste, budget, and sport. There are shoes for everything from dancing and karate, to soccer and running. Athletic shoes are not only for sports, either. They are high fashion. We take for granted the choices that are out there. But the invention of athletic shoes didn't happen overnight. It was a "feat" that happened one step at a time.

Hundreds of years ago, people wore shoes made from fur, leather, wood—even leaves! The Indians of Central and South America covered their feet with the sap that came from the bark of certain trees. When the warm gummy sap dried, they'd put on another layer. The result was a pair of shoes that fit like a glove!

In the late 1700s, a British traveler visited Brazil and saw these soft shoes. He took home a sample to show a chemist friend named Joseph Priestley. Priestley named the substance rubber. Many people experimented with rubber so it wouldn't melt or crack from the cold. In 1839, Charles Goodyear succeeded.

By the late 1800s, people were wearing cloth shoes with rubber soles. The shoes were comfortable and became popular for playing tennis. In one advertisement, the shoes were called "sneakers" because they were so quiet. The name stuck.

In the 1900s, sports sneakers hit the market. These shoes now had features to improve players' games on different types of courts and fields. Nike, Inc. was the first sneaker company to serve this market, starting in the 1960s. It didn't take long for others to catch up.

The demand for comfortable, fashionable, and functional footwear seems to keep growing, and new technologies continue to change the playing field. When it comes to fashion and fitness, people never seem to run out of good ideas.

TEKS 8.17C
ELPS 5G

Student Response

Here is one student's response to the prompt on page 360.

Feet First!

My mother always says, "If your feet hurt, you can't do anything right!" That's probably why so many people wear sneakers. It hasn't always been that way, though. Like many things we take for granted, the invention of good, comfortable sneakers didn't just happen overnight.

According to the article "Up and Running," the idea for rubber-soled sneakers dates back hundreds of years. Indians in the jungles of Central America put rubbery sap on their feet. An English visitor to the jungle named the sap "rubber."

It took more than a hundred years for someone to perfect that rubber so that it was suitable for shoes. That man was Charles Goodyear. To prove his success, the article states: "By the late 1800s, people were wearing cloth shoes with rubber soles."

Sneakers were first used for playing tennis. Then, when Nike came on the scene in the 1960s, their use exploded into other sports. More companies started making sneakers. More features were introduced. Today, thankfully, there are sneakers for everyone—from babies to older adults—in colors and styles to suit everyone's tastes. Who would've thought something as common as sneakers had such a long and interesting history?

Respond to the reading. Answer the questions to see how the student used the writing traits.

☐ Organization **(1) How did the writer share information from the article?**

☐ Focus and Coherence **(2) What was the overall controlling idea of the response? (3) What evidence from the article did the writer use to support points made?**

☐ Voice **(4) How well did the writer retell the information in his or her own words?**

TEKS 8.17C

Responding to Texts in Review

How to Analyze a Theme in Literary Texts

When you respond to literature, you respond in three parts. Each part has a purpose.

Beginning
Middle
Ending

Beginning
What is the book's message? Your opening paragraph introduces the book and closes with your controlling idea, or thesis statement, about the book's theme.

Middle
How is the theme developed? The middle paragraphs retell significant events and details that support your point of view.

End
How has the character changed? Your ending restates the theme and shows its affect on the main character.

How to Respond to Expository Texts

When you respond to expository text, you demonstrate your understanding of what you've read and tell why you find the topic interesting.

Beginning
What is this article about? Your beginning gets the readers' attention by telling what the book or article is about and why you find the topic interesting.

Middle
What are some interesting facts about the subject? Your middle paragraphs share information about the topic so your readers will become knowledgeable about it.

End
What have I learned? Your ending sums up the main points and gives reasons why you think they are important.

Prewrite Gather details. Decide on a form to write the response.

Draft Develop your beginning, middle, and end.

Revise Review your focus and coherence, organization, and development of ideas. Check your voice.

Edit Check for conventions. Look for punctuation, capitalization, spelling and grammar errors. Make a clean copy of your essay to hand in.

RESPONSE

imagine
entertain

✪ **ELPS** 2C, 3C, 3G, 3H, 4C

Creative Writing

Writing Focus
- Stories
- Poems

Learning Language

Work with a partner. Read the meanings and share answers to the questions.

1. A story is a work of fiction, or writing about people or events that aren't real or didn't really happen.
   What are some examples of fiction that you have read?

2. The plot of a story is the events that happen.
   Describe the plot of your favorite story.

3. Narrative poems tell a story.
   How are narrative poems different than other poems?

4. Cooperative learning takes place when students work together to understand ideas.
   Why is this activity an example of cooperative learning?

show
create
discover

Creative Writing
Writing Stories

"I'm not a kid anymore!" At some time, you may have said these words to the adults in your life. But when you cross over from adolescence to adulthood, it's a gradual process. You may not even feel it happening. Even so, at some point you suddenly realize that you have grown up.

Stories about growing up are called "coming of age" stories. The main character has a significant experience, whether big or small, that makes him or her more mature. In this chapter, you will read a "coming of age" story and then develop a story of your own to share.

Writing Guidelines

Subject:	**Growing up**
Purpose:	**To entertain**
Form:	**Short story**
Audience:	**Classmates**

 **TEKS** 8.15A(ii)

Short Story

The following story is about how a young man learns to be more sensitive to others in his family.

Shifting Gears

Beginning

The beginning introduces the characters, the setting, and the conflict.

Felipe pressed his nose against the store window that stood between him and a metallic-blue 21-speed racer. "Look at that bike, Emilia! I WANT that bike!"

"Get away from there before Mr. Huan makes you clean the drool from his store window!" His friend Emilia laughed and pulled Felipe away.

"Well, my birthday's tomorrow, and I've been dropping a lot of hints at home, like ads and pictures of the bike. I've just got to have it so I can go anywhere I want!"

"Your dad's out of work," Emilia said quietly, "and I bet that bike's awfully expensive."

Felipe didn't answer. *Yeah*, he thought, *but you only turn 13 once. Mom and Dad always promised me something special when I became a teenager.* He jumped on a hydrant and balanced a moment before jumping down again. "He'll find a job soon."

Rising Action

The rising action builds the suspense.

When he got home, his parents were in the kitchen talking. Felipe waved to them on his way to the living room. Flopping down on the couch, he dug between the cushions for the remote. As he flipped through TV stations, he caught snatches of his parents' conversation. There were words like "overqualified" and "mortgage" and something about unemployment checks. Felipe turned the volume higher.

The next morning, Felipe's father woke him. "Hey, Champ, Mom had to go to work early, so I'll be making your birthday breakfast. Anything special? Maybe something with wheels?"

Felipe was suddenly wide awake. He threw back the covers and bounded into the kitchen. There, wrapped in old newspaper

TEKS 8.15A(ii)
ELPS 5G

CREATIVE

and tied with a crooked bow, was a bicycle-shaped package.

"Dad!" Felipe tore through the newspaper, and then suddenly stopped and stared. There stood not the shiny racing bike but a secondhand 10-speed. The chrome had been shined up, and the frame was freshly painted, but it was not new—and it was not what he had hoped for. There was an awkward silence as he stared at the gift shining hopefully amidst the crumpled newspaper.

He looked away, swallowing down a lump. *Dad knows I wanted a new bike,* he thought, *not an old used one.*

"I know it's not exactly what you wanted, but . . . " his dad's words trailed off. Felipe looked up at him and saw his own disappointment mirrored in his father's eyes. He thought of the hours his father must have spent sanding and painting, shining and oiling, to give his son something special. Suddenly, he was ashamed of himself.

"Are you kidding, Dad?" Felipe hugged his father. "Hey, now I can get a paper route and help out around here." It had been a long time since they had hugged, and Felipe was surprised to find he was nearly as tall as his father. "Thank you, Dad!"

The phone rang, and Felipe ran to answer it.

"Hi, Emilia! Come on over and see my new bike! We can go for a ride down to the river." Felipe looked over at his father, who smiled back as he picked up the crumpled paper.

High Point

The high point is when the main character has a moment of realization and moves toward adulthood.

Ending

The ending shows how the character has matured.

Respond to the reading. Review the story and answer the following questions.

☐ **Development of Ideas** **(1) What does Felipe want? (2) What could keep him from getting it?**

☐ **Organization** **(3) What events make up the rising action? Name three.**

☐ **Voice** **(4) What words or phrases suggest the bike was disappointing? List at least two. (5) What statements suggest Felipe has changed? List at least two.**

 TEKS 8.15A(ii), 8.15A(iv)

Prewriting **Finding a Character**

When writing a story, you should first select an interesting main character. Make a quick list of qualities that person might have.

The writer of "Shifting Gears" chose a teenage boy as the main character and made the following list. Note that the qualities he underlined and decided to use for the character are in sharp contrast to each other. This should make for an interesting character that the reader will want to know more about.

Quick List

> Character: a boy turning 13, Felipe
>
> Qualities: <u>active</u>, heroic, <u>selfish</u>, <u>unrealistic</u>, <u>enthusiastic</u>,
> helpful, nasty, cheerful

Make a quick list. Start with any type of person and list qualities that person might have. Underline the interesting ones you might want to use.

Selecting a Conflict

Every story needs an engaging story line that includes a conflict. A conflict is created when a character wants something and has to overcome an obstacle to get it. The writer of the story used a "What If?" chart to develop the conflict for his story.

"What If?" Chart

Character's Want	What If? (Conflict)
Character wants a new bicycle.	Parents feel it's not safe.
	✱ The father is unemployed (no money).
	The character has a physical handicap.

Create a "What If?" chart. Imagine what your character wants. Then list three to four conflicts that might keep the character from getting it. Select an interesting conflict that you think would make the most engaging story line. (See the plot-line graphic on page 375.)

TEKS 8.15A(i),8.15A(iv)

CREATIVE

Changing a Main Character

The goal of every short story writer is to write imaginatively, in a way that sustains interest. One way to do this is to focus on a character that changes over time. In a "coming of age" story, you can chart the change in a character by thinking about what he or she is like before and after the high point of the story.

The writer of "Shifting Gears" created a character chart to show the change in his main character. On the chart, he listed things that Felipe said, thought, and did both before and after unwrapping his birthday present. The differences show that Felipe is becoming more mature.

Character Chart

	What he says	What he thinks	What he does
Before	needs an expensive bike to go anywhere he wants	doesn't want to be disappointed	avoids his parents and ignores what they are saying
After	will use the bike to get a job	realizes his father is also disappointed	hugs and thanks his father

Prewrite

Create a character chart. Make a chart like the one above, listing things your character could say, think, and do that will hold the readers' interest.

Showing Rather Than Telling

When you "tell" how a character feels, the character loses life and your reader loses interest. When you describe what a character does and how he or she does it, you show the character's personality. This brings the character to life and grabs your readers' attention.

Instead of telling: **Carlo felt happy.**

Show: **Carlo jumped for joy. He smiled from ear to ear.**

Prewrite

Gather your details. Write down things you could have your character do to show how he or she feels. Write as many details as you can, even though you won't use them all. Select the details you think are clearest and will most engage the readers' interest.

Prewriting Creating a Specific Setting

The setting of your story is the location and time period in which it takes place. The more specific details and images you use to describe your setting, the more your reader will relate to it and the characters in it. One good way to make a setting specific is to include plenty of sensory details. These are details that are drawn from the five senses—sight, hearing, smell, taste, and touch. Try to use details for each sense when creating your setting.

Philipe imagined a story set in a rain forest. He created this sensory chart to think up details for his setting. Then Philipe wrote the following paragraph, using some of the sensory details from his chart.

Sight	Hearing	Smell	Taste	Touch
long hanging vines	chatter of monkeys in trees	dank, wet vegetation	salty taste of sweat on lips	slimy feel of wet leaves
sun breaking through	buzzing of flying insects	sweetness of flowering plants	gamey taste of meat from killed animal	soft feel of birds' feathers

Rob slowly made his way back to camp, brushing aside the long, hanging vines. His nostrils filled with the sweet smell of the flowering plants as he listened to the chattering of the monkeys in the trees. Suddenly he looked up and saw the burning sun breaking through the clouds. As it grew hotter, he licked the salty sweat from his lips.

Create a sensory detail chart. Choose a setting for a story. Make a sensory chart like the one above for your setting. Try to come up with two details for each sense.

TEKS 8.15A(iii)

CREATIVE

Creating a Believable Setting

A setting is believable when the reader can fully enter into it and be engaged by it. Even an imaginary setting can feel "real" if the details are specific and colorful. Suppose, for example, that you are writing a science-fiction story set on a space station near the planet Mars. Such a thing may not yet exist, but that doesn't mean you—the writer—can't make it real through vivid and particular details.

Juan gathered details for his imaginary setting and then wrote the paragraph below using sensory details to bring this unusual setting to life.

> Roger looked out the large, curved window at the planet Mars. It hung in the sky like a big red moon. The only sound in the space station was the quiet hum of the small robots scurrying around at their work. Roger closed his eyes and sniffed the stale, filtered air. Every space station smelled the same. Suddenly he felt a cold hand on his shoulder. He turned to face one of the larger robots with glowing eyes. "The pod rocket is ready for boarding, sir," he said in his monotone voice. Roger couldn't believe it. Next stop, Mars!

Prewrite

Gather sensory details. Find the sensory details that bring the setting to life in the paragraph above. Create a chart like the one on page 370. In each column, list at least one thing you could see, hear, smell, and feel. Then use the sensory details from your own chart to write a paragraph, bringing your setting to life.

TEKS 8.14B, 8.15A(i), 8.15A(ii)

ELPS 2C

Prewriting Using Dialogue

There are two types of dialogue. **External dialogue** is when people speak out loud. **Internal dialogue** is when the writer lets the reader know what the character is thinking.

Yeah, he thought, but you only turn 13 once.

Write internal dialogue. Imagine what your character might be thinking at some point. Be sure the internal dialogue shows the reader something important about your character.

Drafting Developing Your First Draft

Once you have developed a character and a conflict, you are ready to write your first draft. The following tips will help you.

1 **Introduce your character and what he or she wants.**

For example, the writer showed what Felipe wanted through his actions.

Felipe pressed his nose against the store window that stood between him and a metallic-blue 21-speed racer.

2 **Introduce your conflict.**

The writer used dialogue to present the obstacle.

"Your dad's out of work," Emilia said quietly, "and I bet that bike's awfully expensive."

3 **Use action verbs.**

He jumped on a hydrant and balanced a moment before jumping down again.

4 **Build to the high point.**

Show the character's struggle leading up to the point of decision.

Suddenly, he was ashamed of himself.

Write your first draft. Introduce your character and conflict. Be sure the conflict is clear, and use action to build to the point when your character changes.

entertain **create** **discover**
show *imagine*
Writing Stories
373

TEKS 8.14C, 8.14E, 8.15A(ii)

CREATIVE

Revising **Improving Your Writing**

Once you have finished your first draft, set it aside for a while. Later, look at your story with a fresh perspective and review it for the following traits.

☐ **Focus and Coherence** Do I focus on the conflict of my story? Do I present the plot clearly and concisely and show my character through dialogue, thoughts, and well-paced action?

☐ **Organization** Does each event and action lead logically forward to the moment of change? Do I wrap things up quickly after reaching the story's high point?

☐ **Development of Ideas** Does my story have a central idea or theme that is developed as the events unfold and the character changes and grows?

☐ **Voice** Does my voice (including dialogue) sound natural and sustain interest? Is the point of view of the story, whether first person or third person, consistent throughout?

Revise your story. Use the questions above as a guide when you revise your first draft.

Revise

Editing **Checking for Conventions**

After you finish revising your story, you should edit it for *conventions*.

☐ **Conventions** Have I corrected any mistakes in grammar? Have I used correct punctuation, capitalization, and spelling?

Edit your story. Edit your writing for conventions. Then use the tips below to write a title. Create a clean final copy and proofread it.

Edit

Creating a Title

Your title is your first opportunity to hook the reader, so make it memorable. Here are some tips for writing a strong title.

■ Use a metaphor: **Riding Through Life**
■ Borrow a line from the story: **Something Special**
■ Be creative: **Shifting Gears**

Story Patterns

A "coming of age" story is one of many patterns of stories you could write. Below are a few examples of common plot patterns used by writers.

The Rescue

In a *rescue* story, the main character is either in need of rescue or must rescue someone else. Adventure stories often follow this pattern.

Luz must somehow get her little brother out of a ravine.

The Union

In the *union* story, two characters must overcome one or more obstacles to be together. Many stories about friendship, family, and love use the union pattern.

Lupe and Marta are sisters adopted by different families. They must work out a way to be together.

The Underdog

In the *underdog* plot, someone overcomes adversity to achieve a goal. Main characters who are underdogs often appeal to readers.

Zhora overcomes her blindness to become a concert pianist.

The Decision

In a *decision* story, the main character is faced with a decision that will test him or her. Tension builds in the story as the decision approaches.

Eduardo must choose between going on a class trip or staying with his hospitalized grandfather.

Rivalry

In a *rivalry* story, the main character must face a challenger. In this pattern, the main character is the *protagonist*, and the challenger is the *antagonist*.

Javier's team must face the team that defeated them for the state championship last year.

 Choose one of the story patterns above. Think of a story that would fit that pattern. Write a single sentence that sums up the story. Be sure to include the conflict.

Elements of Fiction

The following list includes many terms used to describe the elements or parts of literature. This information will help you discuss and write about the novels, poetry, essays, and other literary works you read.

Action: Everything that happens in a story

Antagonist: The person or force that works against the hero of the story (See *protagonist.*)

Character: A person or an animal in a story

Characterization: The way in which a writer develops a character, making him or her seem believable
Here are three methods:

● Sharing the character's thoughts, actions, and dialogue

● Describing his or her appearance

● Revealing what others in the story think or say about this character

Conflict: A problem or clash between two forces in a story
There are five basic conflicts:

● **Person Against Person** A problem between characters

● **Person Against Himself or Herself** A problem within a character's own mind

● **Person Against Society** A problem between a character and society, the law, or some tradition

● **Person Against Nature** A problem with some element of nature, such as a blizzard or a hurricane

● **Person Against Destiny** A problem or struggle that appears to be beyond a character's control

Dialogue: The words spoken between two or more characters

Foil: The character who acts as a villain or challenges the main character

Mood: The feeling or emotion a piece of literature or writing creates in a reader

Moral: The lesson a story teaches

Narrator: The person or character who actually tells the story, giving background information and filling in details between portions of dialogue

Plot: The action that makes up the story, following a plan called the plot line

Plot Line: The planned action or series of events in a story (Basic parts of the plot line: beginning, rising action, high point, and ending.)

PLOT LINE   High Point

Rising Action

Beginning   Ending

● The **beginning** introduces the characters and the setting.

● The **rising action** adds a conflict—a problem for the characters.

● The **high point** is the moment when the conflict is strongest.

● The **ending** tells how the main characters have changed.

ELPS 4C

Point of View: The angle from which a story is told (The angle depends upon the narrator, or person telling the story.)

- **First-Person Point of View**
  This means that one of the characters is telling the story: "We're just friends—that's all—but that means everything to us."

- **Third-Person Point of View**
  In third person, someone from outside the story is telling it: "They're just friends—that's all—but that means everything to them." There are three third-person points of view: *omniscient, limited omniscient,* and *camera view.* (See the illustrations on the right.)

Protagonist: The main character or hero in a story (See *antagonist.*)

Setting: The place and the time period in which a story takes place

Theme: The message about life or human nature that is "hidden" in the story that the writer tells

Tone: The writer's attitude toward his or her subject (Tone can be described by words like *angry* and *humorous.*)

Total Effect: The overall influence or impact that a story has on a reader

Third-Person Points of View

Omniscient point of view allows the narrator to tell the thoughts and feelings of all the characters.

Limited omniscient point of view allows the narrator to tell the thoughts and feelings of only one character at a time.

Camera view (objective view) allows the story's narrator to record the action from his or her own point of view without telling any of the characters' thoughts or feelings.

 Select a story that you have read that fits one of the five basic conflicts on page 375. In one sentence, describe the conflict. Add a sentence that describes the protagonist.

Creative Writing

Writing Poems

The camera clicks and captures an image of one moment in time. Another way to capture a special moment is to write a poem. A well-written poem, like a thought-provoking photograph, goes beyond the surface of things and touches the heart. Poets select special words to share their deepest thoughts, feelings, and sensations.

In this chapter, you will have the best of both worlds. You'll be writing a poem based on a photograph. Your challenge, like that of the master photographer, will be to take the "picture," the photo, and then delve deeper and capture the heart of the moment.

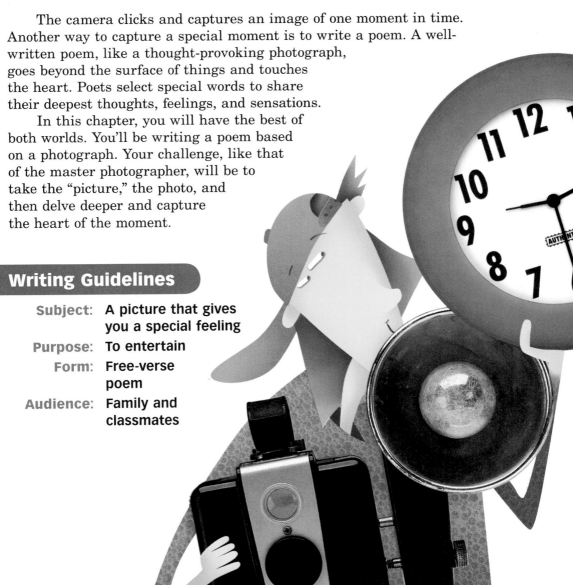

Writing Guidelines

Subject: A picture that gives you a special feeling

Purpose: To entertain

Form: Free-verse poem

Audience: Family and classmates

ELPS 5G

Free-Verse Poem

Traditional poetry follows a specific pattern of rhythm and rhyming lines. **Free-verse poems**, on the other hand, create their own patterns and seldom use rhyming lines.

Poets who write free-verse poems carefully consider every word. The following free-verse poem expresses the poet's feelings about the photo of a soaring biplane in flight.

The Biplane

Alone
in a wide sky,
heaped clouds crowding back
against heaped hills
to make room for its dance.

Spiraling upward
for no reason, but
freedom!

Swooping downward
to chase its shadow,
waggling its wings
with a playful growl.

Its shadow passes coolly
over me,
alone and free
on this wide earth.

—Carter Williams

Respond to the reading. On your own paper, reflect on the organization, ideas, and word choice of the poem above.

- ☐ Organization **(1) The poem is divided into four stanzas. Which special part of flight does each stanza deal with?**
- ☐ Development of Ideas **(2) Which details capture the flight of a biplane? List at least two.**
- ☐ Voice **(3) What words work to convey a feeling of joy in this poem? List at least three.**

TEKS 8.14A

Prewriting Selecting a Topic

To write your poem, first find a picture that gives you a special feeling. You might search family photo albums, magazines, or the Web. (Many search sites have a special option for searching pictures.) Your teacher may also offer you a choice of pictures, or you can choose one of the photos below.

Gathering Details

Poets use sensory details to create an image in the reader's mind. As you view your photo, notice visual details. Then imagine that you are in the scene and jot down what you might hear, smell, taste, and feel. Carter created the following sensory chart, based on his biplane photo.

Sensory Chart

See	Hear	Smell	Taste	Feel
wide, brown ground	engine buzzing,	dry grass	dust	sun breeze
wide, pale blue sky	sputtering,			flying
heaped shadowy mountains	growling			grit
heaped white clouds	hiss of wind			heat
sunlight on trees				

Prewrite

Create a sensory chart. Create a chart like the one above to gather sensory details about your photo. Include specific details that are in the photo as well as additional sensations that simply come to mind.

⭐ **TEKS** 8.15B(i), 8.15B(ii), 8.15B(iii)

Prewriting **Using Poetry Techniques**

Poets play with the sounds of words. **Onomatopoeia** (ŏn´ə-măt´ə-pē´ə) is one example. It means using words that sound like the noises they name.

with a playful growl   **wind** hissing **over wings**

Poets also play with the way words are placed on the page. **Line breaks**, for instance, help control the way a poem reads. In the following selection, line breaks emphasize the plane's climb and the word "freedom."

Spiraling upward
for no reason, but
freedom!

Use special techniques. On your sensory chart, underline any words that use onomatopoeia. List any other special techniques you want to use from pages 384–385.

Drafting **Developing Your First Draft**

Now it's time to have some fun writing the first draft. Follow the tips below.

- **Study** the photo you have chosen to refresh your memory. Review your sensory chart for details.
- **Imagine** yourself in the picture. What types of things do you see and hear? Also think of experiences you have had that can help you connect with the photo.
- **Write** whatever comes to mind. There will be plenty of time for revision later.

Write your first draft. Use the tips above to guide your writing. Experiment with onomatopoeia, line breaks, and other special techniques.

TEKS 8.14E, 8.15B(i),
8.15B(ii), 8.15B(iii)

Revising Improving Your Poem

"Genius," you may have heard, "is 1 percent inspiration and 99 percent perspiration." Even though the first draft of your poem may be truly inspired, the work of revision can improve it. Keep these traits in mind when revising your poem.

☐ **Focus and Coherence** Is the focus of my poem evident?

☐ **Organization** Do my line breaks and indents help express my thoughts and feelings?

☐ **Development of Ideas** Do I use sensory details? Does my poem convey thoughts and feelings that stem from the photo?

☐ **Voice** Does my poem show personality and originality? Are my words precise and interesting?

☐ **Conventions** Do my phrases and sentences have an appealing rhythm? Do I use any special poetic techniques?

Revise your poem. Using the questions above as a guide, keep revising until your poem is the best that it can be.

Editing Fine-Tuning Your Poem

Because poems are shorter than most other types of writing, every word and detail is important. Focus on the conventions of writing as you edit your poem.

☐ **Conventions** Is my poem free of errors that could distract the reader?

Edit your poem. Poems sometimes break the rules, but never by accident. So check your final copy one last time for errors.

Publishing Sharing Your Poem

When your poem is finished, share it with other people. Here are some good ways to do that. (See pages 59–66 for other publishing ideas.)

● **Post it.** Put it on a bulletin board, a Web site, or your refrigerator.

● **Submit it.** Send your poem to a contest or magazine.

● **Perform it.** Read your poem aloud to friends and family.

Publish your work. Poems are made to be shared, so give people a chance to read or hear yours. Ask your teacher about other publishing ideas.

Writing a Found Poem

A found poem borrows words from day-to-day sources like street signs, package labels, recipe books, and so on. The poet then arranges those words in an interesting way. For example, the following poem uses words found at a post office and arranges them to suggest amusing meanings.

COD

BUSINESS   REPLY
MAIL   FIRST-CLASS
     MAIL
PERMIT NO. MAIL
POST OFFICE WILL
NOT MAIL
      WITH-
OUT STAMP
        HELP
STAMP OUT
     POSTAGE SCALE

Writing Tips

- **Select a topic.** Watch for interesting words and phrases all around you—at school, at the mall, on signs, or in junk mail. What possibilities do those words and phrases suggest?

- **Gather details.** Keep a journal of things you see that could become a found poem. Collect advertisements and photographs with interesting possibilities.

- **Create a form.** Arrange your found words in unusual ways. Experiment with line breaks and indents to make your found poem one of a kind.

Create your found poem. Following the tips above, write your own found poem. Have fun making it as thought provoking as possible.

TEKS 8.15B(i), 8.15B(iii)

Writing Other Forms of Poetry

Poetry can take many, many forms. Here are two types that could be inspired by a photograph.

Couplet

A couplet is two rhyming lines, usually of the same length and rhythm. Most couplets are in iambic pentameter format—five pairs of syllables with each pair following an unstressed-stressed pattern—like the following lines from William Shakespeare's sonnet XVIII:

> Sŏ lóng ăs mén căn bréathe, ŏr eýes căn sée,
>
> Sŏ lóng lĭves thís, ănd thís gĭves lífe tŏ thée.

The couplet is an important building block for many rhyming forms. Taken alone, a couplet can make a concise poem itself, as in the following example.

Amber Light
Time pauses now, it seems, as this day ends
and I pause, chatting timelessly with friends.

 Note that it's okay to vary from this pattern for effect. Even Shakespeare varied his rhythms sometimes!

Circle Poem

A circle poem suggests a relationship between a series of individual words or phrases. It makes these connections in a chain, eventually coming full circle to end with something close to the opening idea.

> *streetlight*
> *porch light*   *wet road*
> *clock face*   *night river*
> *floating moon*

 Write a poem. Choose one of the forms on this page and write your own poem. Remember to follow the writing process on pages 379–381.

TEKS 8.15A(v), 8.15B(i), 8.15B(iii)

Using Special Poetry Techniques

Poets use a variety of special techniques to enhance the style and tone in their work. This page and the next define some of the most important ones.

Figures of Speech

■ A **simile** (*sĭm´ə-lē*) compares two unlike things with the word *like* or *as*.

> The scrap of paper fought
> like a fish on a hook.

■ A **metaphor** (*mĕt´ə-fôr*) compares two unlike things without using *like* or *as*.

> Her eyes were searchlights.

■ **Personification** (*pər-sŏn´ə-fĭ-kā´shən*) is a technique that gives human traits to something that is nonhuman.

> The leaves gossiped among themselves.

■ **Hyperbole** (*hī-pûr´bə-lē*) is an exaggerated statement, often humorous.

> When Guadalupe showers, the Pacific goes dry.

Sounds of Poetry

■ **Alliteration** (*ə-lĭt´ə-ra´shən*) is the repetition of consonant sounds at the beginning of words.

> The kids rode a cute little carousel.

■ **Assonance** (*as´ə-nəns*) is the repetition of vowel sounds anywhere in words.

> A green apple gleams at me.

TEKS 8.15B(i), 15B(iii)

- **Consonance** (*kŏn´sə-nəns*) is the repetition of consonant sounds anywhere in words.

  They plu<u>ck</u>ed the an<u>ch</u>or from the a<u>ch</u>ing deep.

- **Line breaks** help to control the rhythm of a poem as it is read. Readers naturally tend to pause at the end of a line. That gives added emphasis to the last word in a line.

  In liquid heat the swimming sun
  hangs on the horizon.

- **Onomatopoeia** (*ŏn´ə-măt´ə-pē´ə*) is the use of words that sound like what they name.

  The <u>crackling</u> bag <u>crumpled</u> in his fist.

- **Repetition** (*rĕp´ĭ-tĭsh´ən*) uses the same word or phrase more than once, for emphasis or for rhythm.

  She forced <u>her tired</u> feet, <u>her tired</u> soul, to slog along.

- **Rhyme** means using words whose endings sound alike. *End rhyme* happens at the end of lines.

  Flowers grow in sidewalk <u>cracks</u>,
  And children grow near railroad <u>tracks</u>.

  Internal rhyme happens within lines.

  The <u>smoke</u> could <u>choke</u> a chimney.

- **Rhythm** (*rĭth´əm*) is the pattern of accented and unaccented syllables in a poem. The rhythm of free-verse poetry tends to flow naturally, like speaking. Traditional poetry follows a more regular pattern, as in the following example.

  Ĭn Lóndŏntówn, whĕre úrchĭns híde,

  Thĕre líves ă mán ŏf wóefŭl mínd. (a regular rhythm)

Try IT
Write your own example for two or more of the techniques explained on these two pages. Then expand at least one of your examples into a complete poem.

 *organize* **NOTE**

 **TEXAS WRITE SOURCE** Online

www.hmheducation.com/tx/writesource

ELPS 2C, 3E, 3G, 4C, 4G

Research Writing

Writing Focus

- Research Report
- Multimedia Presentation

Grammar Focus

- Parallel Sentence Structure
- Relative Pronouns

Learning Language

Learning these words and expressions will help you understand this unit.

1. A source is where you get information.
   What source would you use to find out more about outer space?

2. Media is different kinds of public communication such as television, radio, newspapers, and Web sites.
   What kinds of media have you used to find information?

3. When you do research, you use many sources to learn more about a topic.
   What is something you would like to research?

summarize
RESEARCH
cite

Research Writing
Building Skills

People often describe history in terms of "Ages"—
Stone, Bronze, Iron, Dark, Middle, and so on. Some people
call today the "information age." Print and electronic media
supply a sea of information. That is why research skills—
knowing how to find what you need, and how to judge
what you find—are more important than ever.

In this chapter, you will learn how to
use the Internet and the library to find
the information you need. You'll also
learn how to evaluate the sources
of that information. These may be
some of the most important skills
you learn during your school years.

What's Ahead

- **The Research Process**
- **Primary vs. Secondary Sources**
- **Evaluating Sources**
- **Using the Internet**
- **Using the Library**
- **Using Reference Materials**
- **Creating a Research Plan**

TEKS 8.22A, 8.22B, 8.23A, 8.23C

The Research Process

To write a good research report, you must do the following things: (1) create a research plan, (2) gather sources, (3) synthesize information, and (4) organize and present your ideas.

1 Create a Research Plan

These steps will help you stay organized as you write your report.

- **Brainstorm.** Consider all the possible topics that will work with your assignment. Record your ideas.
- **Connect with Others.** Discuss your ideas with others to help you narrow your focus.
- **Decide on a Topic.** Choose the topic that most interests you.
- **Formulate a Research Question.** Ask a question that you want to answer in your report. Remember to make the question focused, and not too narrow or too broad.
- **Gather Sources.** Use primary sources when possible and support those with secondary sources. Also evaluate your sources for usefulness and reliability.
- **Create a Written Research Plan.** Make a written plan that will help you stay focused and organized as you write.

Try It Which research question is best for a report on dolphins? Why? Discuss your response with a partner.

1. Why do people train dolphins?   **2.** What do dolphins eat?

2 Gather Sources

Follow these steps to gather information.

- Use an Internet search engine and a library card catalog to identify a wide range of print and electronic sources. Begin with secondary sources, such as an encyclopedia, to get an overview of the topic and generate research questions. Be sure to gather primary sources, as well.
- Consider your sources carefully and choose only those that provide the most reliable, accurate information. Reliable sources include reference works, books, and official Web sites by experts or universities.
- Take notes to record useful information. When you see gaps in your research, find additional sources. Record the bibliographic information for each source you use. (See page 421 for more information.)

TEKS 8.23B, 8.24A,
8.25A, 8.25B, 8.25C

NOTE *RESEARCH* *organize* summarize *cite*

Building Skills

389

RESEARCH

3 Synthesize Information

After researching and investigating your topic, decide if your research question is too broad or too narrow. Consider the following questions:

- Did you have trouble figuring out what information to collect?
- Did you take lots of notes but still not know what was important?

If so, your topic may be too broad. Use the information you have gathered to find a more specific part of the topic to write about. Then revise your research question to be more focused.

- Did you answer your questions in a few sentences?
- Did you have trouble finding enough sources?

If so, your topic may be too narrow. You need to think about how to broaden your topic to cover more information.

 Read the research questions below. Revise each one to make it specific and focused.

1. What is the history of the United States government?
2. How cold does it get in Antarctica?

4 Organize and Present Your Ideas

After finishing your research and revising your question, you will need to synthesize the information in a well-organized, meaningful format. Keep the following steps in mind as you create your final product:

- Categorize your facts and details under your main ideas or research questions.
- Use evidence to explain your topic and provide relevant reasons for any conclusions. Summarize or paraphrase your findings clearly.
- Decide the best way to present your findings to help your audience understand the information. You may want to create visual aids, such as charts or illustrations, to support your written work.

 Write a statement about people who explore Antarctica, drawing a reasonable conclusion based on these facts:

1. The sun rises and sets once a year at the South Pole, making both day and night six months long.
2. Antarctica is the coldest, windiest, and highest continent on Earth.

⭐ TEKS 8.22B, 8.24B

Primary vs. Secondary Sources

Primary sources are original sources. They provide firsthand information from those directly involved with an aspect of your topic.

Secondary sources contain information that has been gathered by someone else. Most nonfiction books, newspapers, magazines, and Web sites are secondary sources.

Determine which sources work best for your assignment and are available to you. Make a list of possible primary sources, such as people you could interview, places you could visit, and surveys or questionnaires you could create. Then list all the possible ways you can locate secondary sources, such as going to the library and using an Internet search engine. See below how one writer applied these steps to finding sources.

Research Question—▶*How are dairy farms different now than in the past?*

Primary Sources	Secondary Sources
1. Dairy farm tour	**1**. Article about changes in dairy farming
2. Interview dairy farmer	**2**. Film about history of dairy farming
3. Museum display of early milking machines	**3**. Web site about dairy technology

Types of Primary Sources

- **Diaries, Journals, and Letters** You can find these sorts of primary sources in libraries and museums.

- **Presentations by Experts** Historical sites, museums, guest speakers, and live demonstrations can give you firsthand information.

- **Interviews** You can interview an expert in person, by phone, by e-mail, or through the mail.

- **Surveys and Questionnaires** To gain information from many people at once, ask them a number of questions. Study the results.

- **Observation and Participation** Observing a person, place, or thing is a common method of gathering firsthand information. So is participating in an event yourself.

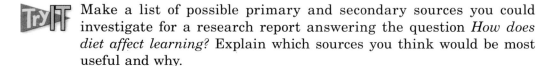 Make a list of possible primary and secondary sources you could investigate for a research report answering the question *How does diet affect learning?* Explain which sources you think would be most useful and why.

Evaluating Sources

Some sources are more useful and reliable than others. Asking questions of an expert in the field you are studying is more reliable than asking your best friend. When choosing sources, try asking questions like the ones below to help you decide which sources are most useful and reliable.

Is the source a primary or a secondary source?

Both kinds of sources can be trustworthy, but firsthand facts are often more trustworthy than secondhand facts. However, many secondary sources are also reliable and are often a good place to start your research.

Is the source an expert?

An expert is a reliable authority on a certain subject—someone who has studied the topic or written about it or observed related events firsthand.

Is the information accurate?

Look for well-respected sources such as big city newspapers and magazines or journals published by trustworthy organizations such as universities.

Is the information current?

Find sources that provide the most up-to-date information. Check copyright dates of books and articles and posting dates of online information.

Is the source biased?

Avoid one-sided sources or those that have something to gain by only presenting some of the facts. Be sure to verify the information you plan to use in your writing by checking it in multiple sources.

 Consider the questions above to decide which of these sources on the Solar System would be useful and reliable.

1. Interview with an astronomer from the local planetarium
2. Essay by a girl who thinks Pluto should still be a planet
3. *Our Solar System* copyright 2009
4. *The Planets* copyright 1952

 Use the questions above to evaluate the sources you selected for the activity on page 390. Use elements (publication dates, experts' titles) to explain which sources are most valid and reliable.

Using the Internet

The Internet is a great place to start your research. All you need is a computer with an Internet connection. On the World Wide Web, you can find information from online encyclopedias, government publications, and university sites, as well as pages from businesses and private individuals. With so many different sources available for searching, it is very important to make sure that your sources are reliable. To do so, utilize elements such as publication dates, coverage, language, and point of view.

Ask for guidance from your teacher or librarian in helping you effectively use the Internet and evaluate the sources that you find.

Points to Remember

- **Use the Web carefully.** Look for sites that have *.edu* or *.gov* in the address. These endings tell you that the sites are educational or government run and generally provide the most reliable and valid information. If you're not sure about the reliability of a site, check with your teacher.

- **Use a search site.** A search site such as www.google.com or www.yahoo.com is like a computer catalog for the Internet. You can enter keywords to find Web pages about your subject.

- **Look for links.** Often, a Web page includes links to other pages dealing with your topic. Take advantage of these links.

- **Be patient.** The Web is huge and searches can get complicated. New pages are added all the time, and old pages may change addresses or even disappear completely.

- **Know your school's Internet policy.** To avoid trouble, be sure to follow your school's Internet policy. Also follow whatever guidelines your parents may have set up for you.

 Based on the addresses, choose the sites that would give you the most reliable information on the Alamo and explain why: www.thealamo.org; www.KatesAlamoPictures.com; www.pbs.org/thealamo; www.texashistory.unt.edu; www.HistoryPosters.com.

TEKS 8.22B, 8.23D
8.24B

Using the Library

While the Internet is a good place to begin your research, you will need to continue it at the library. Since sources found at the library are often more reliable and detailed than those found on the Web, you will need to use library resources to verify facts and do follow-up research. Your teacher will most likely insist that you include some non-Internet sources on your list of works cited to prove that your research is valid and reliable.

1 Books are one of the most common sources you'll use in your research. They are often very in-depth and detailed. In the library, books are usually divided into three sections.

- **Fiction** books include stories and novels. Fiction books do not always include information based on facts, so they are not very useful as a source for research reports.

- **Nonfiction** books are based on facts. These books are very useful for finding information to answer your research question.

- **Reference** books include encyclopedias, atlases, dictionaries, directories, and almanacs. These books have many useful facts.

2 Periodicals include magazines and newspapers. Current periodicals can be very useful if you want to learn the most recent thoughts or ideas about your topic. Old periodicals can reveal thoughts and ideas from previous time periods. Periodicals may also give you access to primary source information like interviews or eyewitness accounts.

3 The media section includes music CD's, cassettes, videotapes, DVD's, and CD-ROM's. Computer software (encyclopedias, games, and so on) may be found in this section as well. Like periodicals, these sources can be more current. They also give you the opportunity to hear and see information that might help you better understand your topic.

Try IT If you needed to find three source materials at the library to answer the question *Why is the leatherback sea turtle becoming extinct?* which of the following would you choose? Tell a classmate your reasons.

1. Nature DVD on the leatherback sea turtle
2. Novel titled *Adventures of a Sea Turtle*
3. Article from a science journal titled "The Problem with Our Coast: Losing the Sea Turtle"
4. An atlas showing maps of North American coastlines

RESEARCH

Searching a Computer Catalog

Every computer catalog is a little different. Therefore, the first time you use a particular computer catalog, it's a good idea to check the instructions for using it or to ask a librarian for help. With a computer catalog, you can find information on the same book in three ways:

1 If you know the book's title, enter the title.

2 If you know the book's author, enter the author's name. (When the library has more than one book by the same author, there will be more than one entry.)

3 Finally, if you know only the subject you want to learn about, enter either the subject or a keyword. (A *keyword* is a word or phrase that is related to the subject.)

If your subject is . . .	your keywords might be . . .
paper folding,	origami, paper art, paper folding, paper work.

Computer Catalog Screen

Author:	Montroll, John
Title:	African Animals in Origami
Published:	Dover Publications, 2004
Subjects:	Animals in art, decoration and ornament, origami, paper work

STATUS:	CALL NUMBER:
Available	736.9822Mon

LOCATION:
Adult nonfiction

Create a computer catalog screen like the one above for a book you have read or one you are reading.

Searching a Card Catalog

If your library has a card catalog, it will most likely be located in a cabinet full of drawers. The drawers contain title, author, and subject cards, which are arranged in alphabetical order.

1 To find a book's title card, ignore a beginning *A, An,* or *The* and look under the next word of the title.

2 To find a book's author card, look under the author's last name. Then find the author card with the title of the book you want.

3 To find a book's subject card, look up an appropriate subject.

All three cards will contain important information about your book—most importantly, its call number. This number will help you find the book on the library's shelves.

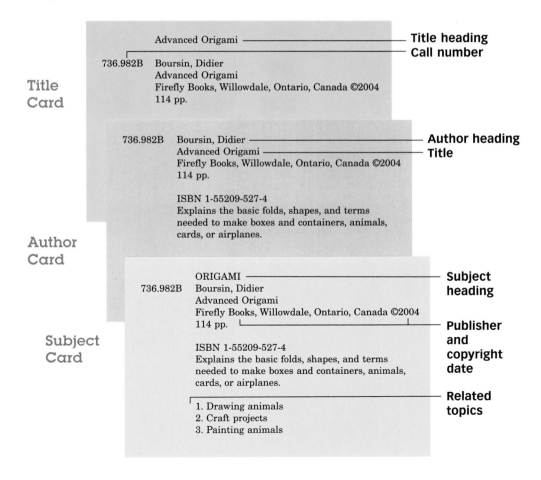

Title Card

Advanced Origami —————————————— **Title heading**
——— **Call number**
736.982B   Boursin, Didier
Advanced Origami
Firefly Books, Willowdale, Ontario, Canada ©2004
114 pp.

Author Card

736.982B   Boursin, Didier ——————————————— **Author heading**
Advanced Origami ——————————————— **Title**
Firefly Books, Willowdale, Ontario, Canada ©2004
114 pp.

ISBN 1-55209-527-4
Explains the basic folds, shapes, and terms
needed to make boxes and containers, animals,
cards, or airplanes.

Subject Card

ORIGAMI ——————————————— **Subject heading**
736.982B   Boursin, Didier
Advanced Origami
Firefly Books, Willowdale, Ontario, Canada ©2004
114 pp. ⌐—————————————⌐ **Publisher and copyright date**

ISBN 1-55209-527-4
Explains the basic folds, shapes, and terms
needed to make boxes and containers, animals,
cards, or airplanes.

1. Drawing animals ——————————————— **Related topics**
2. Craft projects
3. Painting animals

RESEARCH

TEKS 8.22B

Finding Books

Each catalog entry for a book includes a call number that tells where to find the book on the library shelves. Most libraries organize nonfiction books by the Dewey decimal system, which has 10 subject categories.

000–099	**General Works**	500–599	**Sciences**
100–199	**Philosophy**	600–699	**Technology**
200–299	**Religion**	700–799	**Arts and Recreation**
300–399	**Social Sciences**	800–899	**Literature**
400–499	**Languages**	900–999	**History and Geography**

Using Call Numbers

A call number often has a decimal in it, followed by the first letters of an author's name. Note how the call numbers are arranged on the books below.

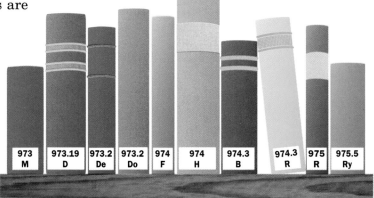

| 973 M | 973.19 D | 973.2 De | 973.2 Do | 974 F | 974 H | 974.3 B | 974.3 R | 975 R | 975.5 Ry |

Understanding the Parts of a Book

The *title page* tells the title of the book, the author's name, and the publisher's name and city. It is usually the first page of a book. The *copyright page* comes next and includes the year the book was published. The *table of contents* lists the names and page numbers of sections and chapters in the book. Many books have at least one *appendix* near the back of the book, which holds extra information like maps, tables, and lists. The *index* is an alphabetical list of all topics and their page numbers in the book.

Get a book from your library. Write down its title and call number, its publisher's name and city, the year it was published, and the page numbers for the section names of its table of contents.

TEKS 8.22B

RESEARCH

Using Reference Materials

The reference section in a library contains materials such as encyclopedias, atlases, and dictionaries.

Using Encyclopedias

An **encyclopedia** is a set of books, a CD, or a Web site with articles on almost every topic you can imagine. The topics are arranged alphabetically. The tips below can guide your use of encyclopedias.

- If the article is long, skim any subheadings to find specific information.
- Encyclopedia articles are written with the most basic information first, followed by more detailed information.
- At the end of an article, you may find a list of related topics. Use them to learn more about your topic.
- The index lists all the places in the encyclopedia where you will find more information about your topic. (See the sample below.) The index is usually in the back of the last volume of a printed set.

Encyclopedia Index

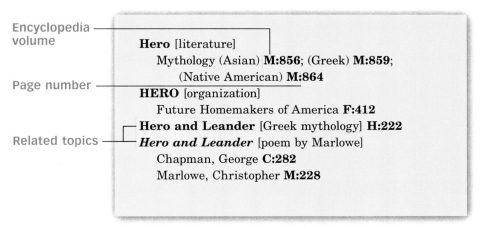

Encyclopedia volume

Page number

Related topics

Hero [literature]
  Mythology (Asian) **M:856**; (Greek) **M:859**;
    (Native American) **M:864**
HERO [organization]
  Future Homemakers of America **F:412**
Hero and Leander [Greek mythology] **H:222**
Hero and Leander [poem by Marlowe]
  Chapman, George **C:282**
  Marlowe, Christopher **M:228**

Using the index entries above, list the volume and page or pages where you might find the following information.

1. A description of Leander in Greek mythology
2. Native American mythic heroes
3. A biography of the English playwright Christopher Marlowe

 **TEKS** 8.22B

Finding Magazine Articles

Periodical guides are found in the reference section of the library and list magazine articles about many different topics.

- ■ **Locate the right edition** of the *Readers' Guide to Periodical Literature* (or a similar guide). The latest edition will have the newest information, but you may need information from an older edition.

- ■ **Look up your subject.** Subjects are listed alphabetically. If your subject is not listed, try another word related to it.

- ■ **Write down the information** about the article. Include the name of the magazine, the issue date, the name of the article, and its page numbers.

- ■ **Find the magazine.** Ask the librarian for help if necessary.

Readers' Guide Format

DINNER —————————————————————— | Subject Entry
Actually, America's still cooking, *USA Today* p6 Jn 21 2008. | Title of Article

DINOSAURS | Page Number/Date
Evidence of impact. J. Amadio. *Natural History* v113 no4 p15 M 2008
What wiped out the dinosaurs? E. Dobb. *Discover* v23 no6 p36–44 | Name of Author
    Jn 2006.
        See also —————————————————————— | Cross-Reference
        Asteroid collisions
DIODES
Diodes and transistors demystified. Travis, Bill. *EDN* v45 no14 p28 | Name, Volume, and Number of Magazine
    Jl 2006.

DI SILVESTER, ROGER —————————————————— | Author Entry
Warmer climate threatens seas. Di Silvester, Roger. *National Wildlife* v42
    no4 p10 Jl 2008.

Internet-based databases are online subscription services that allow you to search for and read periodicals on the Internet.

 Using the sample entries above, write answers to these questions.

1. Under what additional heading can you find more articles about dinosaurs?
2. Who wrote the article "Evidence of Impact"?
3. Which periodicals contain articles about dinosaurs?

TEKS 8.22B, 8.23A

RESEARCH

Creating a Research Plan

A written research plan can help you organize your preliminary information and guide you in gathering relevant sources for further research. Here are some tips for creating your own written research plan.

1. Start by naming the general topic of your report.

2. Tell who your audience will be.

3. Explain your purpose.

4. Identify your research question.

5. Gather preliminary research and use it to develop more specific questions that will help you answer your main research question.

6. Add ideas for additional sources of information that you can use to answer each of your questions.

Sample Written Research Plan

Topic: Forest fires

Audience: Teacher and classmates

Purpose: To explain causes and effects of forest fires

Research Question: What are the causes and effects of forest fires?

Preliminary Sources for Gathering Information:
>   Internet search engine: keywords *forest fires*
>   Encyclopedia entry: *forest fire*

Specific Questions:
>   Where do forest fires occur most?
>   What are the main causes of fires?
>   How do forest fires affect people?
>   How do forest fires affect animals?
>   How do forest fires affect the land?
>   How can forest fires be controlled?

Additional Sources for Gathering Information
>   Recent newspaper articles on California forest fires
>   News broadcast about last week's forest fire
>   *The Causes of Forest Fires* from the school library

Review the research plan above. Discuss with a classmate whether this plan is complete and explain why or why not. Then tell how you would follow this plan to gather information from relevant print and electronic sources.

Avoiding Plagiarism

Your research report should be an expression of your ideas based on a synthesis of facts gathered from other sources. While these sources provide you with information, the words and ideas you include in your report must be your own. Using another writer's words or ideas without giving proper credit is called *plagiarism*. Here are some tips to avoid plagiarism in your writing:

DO NOT . . .

- borrow ideas, words, or facts without giving credit to the source.
- use a direct quote without quotation marks.
- change a few words or rearrange sentences and not give credit to the source.
- use facts, graphs, or drawings that are not common knowledge (facts known by many people or found in many places) without citing the source of your information.

DO . . .

- use quotations for everything that comes directly from a source.
- paraphrase by restating information in your own words.
- name the source of all information that you use directly, such as quotations.
- acknowledge the source of information that you have paraphrased.

 Read the journal passage. Then read the two student report excerpts. Tell which one is an acceptable form of paraphrasing. Explain why.

Journal passage

The town's average rainfall is 150 inches per year. With such wet conditions, it is imperative for homes to be built with special features to prevent flooding and mold damage. One such feature is a special venting system to allow the moisture to dry properly.

1. According to the Oregon Climate Service Journal, special features are necessary for homes in the area due to very high rainfall amounts. Rainfall totals averaging 150 inches a year make for very wet conditions. Because floods and mold pose possible problems for homeowners, features like special venting systems are added when the homes are built.

2. The town's normal rainfall is 150 inches per year. It is important for homes to be built with features that prevent mold and flooding. A special venting system that allows moisture to dry properly is one such feature.

Gathering Details

Each specific question from your written research plan (see sample on page **399**) will become a paragraph in your research report. Now you need to gather details that help you answer each question. A gathering grid can help you take notes and organize information from a range of relevant print and electronic sources. Notice that this writer listed the types of sources along the top of the grid. The actual sources were then written in each box, along with the notes. If you need more room for taking notes, use note cards. (See pages **402–403**.)

Gathering Grid

Forest Fires	Books & Encyclopedias	Periodicals	Internet	DVDs/CDs
Where do forest fires occur most?		Most occur in western U.S. states. "The Facts on Forest Fires" *Texas Post*	"in boreal and dry tropical forests" wwf.org	
What are the main causes of fires?	Drought, lightning, arson *The Causes of Forest Fires* p. 132		in settled areas, man is often the cause wwf.org	
How can forest fires be controlled?				Planes and helicopters drop water and chemicals. "Nature's Raging Wild" Nature Video Series, DVD1

TEKS 8.25A

Using Note Cards

Note cards are another way to keep track of details from your research. They are easier to organize than notes written on notepaper and give you more space than a gathering grid. When taking notes, it is best to do the following:

- **Summarize** if you want to note the overall gist of a lot of information. Identify the most important details and write those on your note cards.

- **Paraphrase** if you want to take more detailed notes. Include specific details but put them in your own words.

- **Record direct quotations** if you think you may want to include them as evidence in your report. Be sure to write the quotation exactly as it appears in the source, and use quotation marks so you will remember that it was taken word-for-word from your research.

Whether you summarize, paraphrase, or record a direct quotation, be sure to include all bibliographic information (title and author) and the page number on the note card, as well. This will allow you to easily locate the source should you need additional information. It will also make writing your bibliography easier. (Another approach that can save some time is to keep a working bibliography––a numbered list of your sources––and write the number of the source on all notes taken from that source.)

Consider the following points when you create note cards.

Note-Card Guidelines

- Write a specific research question or main idea at the top of each card.

- Write supporting details from your source on the lines below the main idea. Notes may be in the form of a summary, a paraphrase, or a direct quotation.

- Identify the source on the card. Use a keyword from the title and the author's last name, or the number of the source from your working bibliography. Include page numbers if appropriate.

 Look over the note cards on the next page. Identify which card contains a paraphrase, which is a summary, and which includes a direct quotation.

TEKS 8.23B

Grouping Note Cards

Your note cards are the pieces of your research report. When you finish gathering information and taking notes, you can use your note cards to group similar details. This will help you figure out the best way to organize your report so that the pieces work together to answer your larger research question. Notice how the writer grouped the following three note cards. The information is similar in theme and will help the reader see the larger constructs of the overall report.

1

How do forest preserves help the environment?
"Forest preserves protect the original forests, prairies, and wetlands. The districts keep the land from being developed and allow for the natural environment to flourish." Encyclopedia of Forestry, p. 324

2

How do forest preserves help people?
People benefit from public education and recreation offered at forest preserves. Nature and photography classes are often held in these areas. People who want to picnic, bike, cross-country ski, boat, fish, hike, and horseback ride also use the land.

3

How do forest preserves protect animals and plants?
- restrict hunting and regulate fishing
- control out-of-balance species
- don't allow removal of plants or seeds
- gather and plant seeds

 TEKS 8.23C

Keeping Track of Your Sources

It is important to record bibliographic information for all notes and sources you use when doing your research. Use a standard format to make the information easy to identify. Write down the following information for each of the different types of sources that you find.

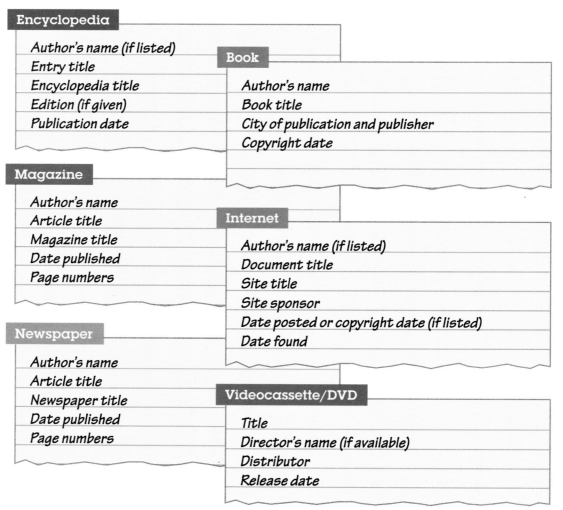

Encyclopedia
- Author's name (if listed)
- Entry title
- Encyclopedia title
- Edition (if given)
- Publication date

Book
- Author's name
- Book title
- City of publication and publisher
- Copyright date

Magazine
- Author's name
- Article title
- Magazine title
- Date published
- Page numbers

Internet
- Author's name (if listed)
- Document title
- Site title
- Site sponsor
- Date posted or copyright date (if listed)
- Date found

Newspaper
- Author's name
- Article title
- Newspaper title
- Date published
- Page numbers

Videocassette/DVD
- Title
- Director's name (if available)
- Distributor
- Release date

 Find examples of each kind of source listed above. Look for the specific information necessary to write a correct bibliographic entry for each type of source. Use this format when you write a research report.

Research Writing
Research Report

There are some amazing places in this world—many of them closer to home than you might think. For example, how many people in Detroit know that a salt mine sprawls under a quarter of their city? And how many Nevada citizens know that some trees in the White Mountains are 5,000 years old? Every region of the country has its own natural wonders and historic sites.

In this chapter, you will write a report about an important place that interests you—a building, a historic site, a monument, or a natural feature. You will explain why the place you have chosen is important, tell its history, describe its condition today, and predict something about its future. In the process, you may become something of an expert about your chosen place.

Writing Guidelines

Subject:	**An important place**
Purpose:	**To research and present information about an important place**
Form:	**Research report**
Audience:	**Classmates**

TEKS 8.25D

Research Report

Even though student writer Diego Soleny has lived in Detroit all of his life, he was surprised when he discovered that there is an enormous salt mine under the city. So Diego chose to write about that mine in his research report.

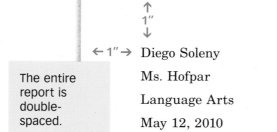

↑ 1″ ↓

1/2″ ↑↓

Soleny 1 ← 1″ →

← 1″ → Diego Soleny

Ms. Hofpar

Language Arts

May 12, 2010

The entire report is double-spaced.

Man-Made Caves of Salt

Beginning

The opening grabs the reader's attention.

Twelve hundred feet below the ground, an enormous mine has been operating almost nonstop for more than a century. A hundred miles of tunnels connect its huge chambers. It has underground roads for cars, trucks, and mining machines. This mine produces hundreds of tons of "rock" every day. However, the rock from this mine is not gold, or iron ore, or even coal; it is salt. <u>This enormous, hundred-year-old salt mine lies beneath the city of Detroit, Michigan.</u>

The controlling idea identifies the topic (underlined).

Salt is more important than most people realize. Wars have been fought over it. In ancient China, salt coins were used for money, and Roman soldiers were often paid in salt, which is where the word "salary" comes from. Bettina Werner, an artist known as the "Salt Queen" says, "Salt is like a fifth element, it's so important to life" (Lin). In the human body, salt

A direct quotation is integrated into the text.

↑ 1″ ↓

TEKS 8.20B(ii), 8.25C, 8.25D

RESEARCH

Soleny 2

carries electrical signals that keep a person alive. To stay healthy, a person needs to eat about three pounds of salt a year (*Modern*). Salt is also used to preserve meat and fish, to tan leather, to soften water, and to make many different chemicals. However, most of the salt from the Detroit mine is now used to melt ice and snow on streets and highways (Zacharias).

Headings help present the information in a meaningful, organized format, making it easier for the reader to understand.

The Salt Mine's History

A map helps the reader understand the size and location of the mine.

Scientists say that the Detroit mine digs into a bed of salt that is several hundred million years

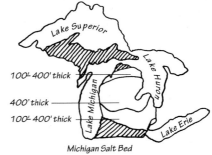

Lake Superior · Lake Huron · Lake Michigan · Lake Erie · 100'–400' thick · 400' thick · 100'–400' thick · Michigan Salt Bed

old. From 600 million to 230 million years ago, seawater flooded the middle of North America many times. As sun and wind evaporated the water, sea salt was deposited on the submerged land. According to the Salt Institute, "Trillions of tons of salt, collected in a layer 400 to 1,600 feet thick, reached from western Michigan all the way to New York. . . . Eventually, it was covered by silt that became rock more than 1,000 feet thick." ("Dry") Later, when people came to the area to settle, they discovered springs of salty water bubbling from the ground. They would collect the liquid and boil away the water to get the salt.

The history of the place is explained by adding a quote from an expert source. An ellipsis (. . .) is used to show part of the original quotation was left out.

TEKS 8.20B(ii), 8.25D

Soleny 3

In 1896, the Detroit salt mine was started in order to dig the salt out of the ground. It began as a shaft 1,200 feet deep and about 6 feet wide. At first, the salt was used mainly for storing meat and fish and for making ice cream (*Detroit* 167). In 1940, though, Detroit became the first city to use rock salt on icy roads. Other cities soon followed Detroit's example, and the mine began selling most of its salt to road crews ("Dry"). In 1983, however, low sales and competition from Canadian mines caused the Detroit mine to close. Crystal Mines bought the mine, hoping to store hazardous wastes there. In 1985, while waiting for a permit, they ran public tours of the mine. "Crystal Mines permit was denied in 1997 and [they] then sold the mine to the Detroit Salt Company," explained Kim Roberts, manager of the mine (Roberts). The mine was reopened, and it again became one of the main sources of road salt in the United States.

The Salt Mine Today

Some people call the Detroit salt mine a city beneath a city. It covers 1,400 acres under Detroit and its suburbs. That's equal to 1,300 football fields. Also, it has more than 50 miles of roads where construction equipment, trucks, and cars drive. All these vehicles had to be taken apart, carried down the shaft in pieces, and reassembled in underground workshops.

A source and page number are identified in parentheses.

A quotation is included that was gathered from an email interview.

Brackets around "they" show this isn't the exact word the speaker used.

The place is described as it exists today.

TEKS 8.25B, 8.25D

Soleny 4

The seven-foot-tall tires for the dump trucks had to be compressed and bound with straps to fit down the shaft (Zacharias).

The mining equipment includes many different types of big electric trucks. One type has a giant chain saw on the front, which cuts a deep groove into a salt wall at floor level. Then a drilling-machine truck bores a pattern of holes 20 feet deep into the wall to hold dynamite or other explosives. The blast from these explosives breaks hundreds of tons of rock from the wall in huge chunks. Trucks with giant shovels then scoop up tons at a time and drop them into dump trucks. The dump trucks carry the chunks back to the shaft, where a crusher breaks them into smaller pieces and sorting machines separate the pieces by size. Finally, buckets that can hold nine tons of salt run up a conveyor to the surface. There the salt is packaged and shipped ("Dry").

The Salt Institute explains that the mine is carved out in a "room-and-pillar" method. Each room is as big and high as a school gymnasium. Between rooms, the miners leave pillars of salt about 60 feet wide to hold up the ceiling. This type of mining gets about 70 percent of the salt from the ground, leaving the other 30 percent as support pillars. Because the salt bed has never had an earthquake or other shock, it lies very flat, so the pattern of rooms and pillars stretches level

---

The writer's last name and page number appear on every page.

Each paragraph begins with a topic sentence, followed by evidence that gives relevant reasons for conclusions made.

RESEARCH

Soleny 5

A quotation is integrated for emphasis.

from one end of the mine to the other. According to the Salt Institute, this mine "has never experienced a collapse or mine fatality" ("Dry").

A quote from a worker is included. This primary source interview adds valuable information to the report.

Miners say that the mine is a very clean and healthy place to work. The temperature stays a cool 58 degrees year-round. There are no bugs, rats, or other animals living in the mine, because there is nothing for them to eat (Zacharias). "I love working here. The air you breathe in the mine feels great. It's very clean, with no allergens or mold like on the surface. I've worked here for 15 years, and I wouldn't want to be anywhere else," shared Mike Yeling, a miner (Yeling).

The Salt Mine's Future

Ending
The final paragraph states something about the place's future and leaves the reader with something to think about.

The Detroit salt mine could have a very interesting future. According to geologists, there is enough salt underneath Michigan to last for 70 million years ("Dry"). Many people worry, though, that the runoff from road salt is having a negative effect on our rivers and lakes. If people stop using salt on icy streets and highways, there may not be enough business to keep the Detroit mine open. In that case, the mine could be used to store important documents, films, and artwork, as some other salt mines do (Tanner). If nothing else, the Detroit salt mine could be turned into a public museum because it is an important part of the city's history.

TEKS 8.23C
ELPS 5G

Soleny 6

Works Cited

A separate page alphabetically lists sources cited in the paper.

Detroit Almanac. Detroit: Detroit Free Press, 2004. Print.

"Dry (Rock Salt) Mining." *Salt Institute*. Salt Institute. 10 May 2008. Web. 14 Apr. 2010.

Lin, Sara. "Palace of the Salt Queen." *The Wall Street Journal* 19 June 2009 early ed.: E8. Print.

Modern Marvels: Salt Mines. A&E Television Networks Video, 2004. VHS.

Roberts, Kim. E-mail from mine manager. 4 May 2010.

Tanner, Beccy. "Salt Mine Museum Could Spark Tourist Trade." *Wichita Eagle* 8 May 2004: A9. Print.

Yeling, Mike. Personal interview. 6 May 2010.

Zacharias, Patricia. "The Ghostly Salt City Beneath Detroit." *Detnews.com*. The Detroit News. 11 May 2008. Web. 15 Apr. 2010.

RESEARCH

Respond to the reading. After you have finished reading the sample research report, answer the following questions about the traits of writing.

☐ **Development of Ideas** (1) What is the main idea of the report? (2) List at least four details that emphasize the age and size of the mine.

☐ **Organization** (3) How do the headings help organize the paper into a meaningful format?

☐ **Voice** (4) What words does the writer use to show his interest in this topic? Give at least two examples.

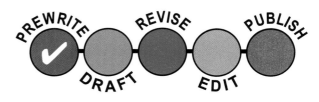

Prewriting

"Well begun is half done," Aristotle once said. When it comes to writing a research paper, a good beginning means choosing a good topic, taking careful notes during your research, writing a solid controlling idea, and preparing a good plan. Use these keys as a guide to your prewriting.

Keys to Effective Prewriting

1. For your topic, choose an important place that interests you.

2. Make a list of questions you want to have answered about that place.

3. Make sure that there are enough details about its past, present, and future.

4. Use a gathering grid and note cards to organize your research questions and the answers you find.

5. Be careful to list your sources when paraphrasing or quoting exact words.

6. Write down the publication details of all your sources for making a works-cited page.

TEKS 8.14A, 8.22A

Selecting a Topic

To find a topic for your research paper, brainstorm a list of important places that interest you. Answer the following questions to help generate ideas. (See Diego's list below as an example.)

- What interesting places have I visited?
- What interesting places have I seen on TV, in magazines, or on the Web?
- What interesting places does my social studies text mention?

TOPICS LIST

I have visited these interesting places:
- *The current Michigan State Capitol*
- *The Graystone International Jazz Museum in Detroit*
- *Yerkes Observatory in Williams Bay, Wisconsin*
- *The U.S.S. Constitution in Boston*

I have seen these places on TV, on the Web, or in a magazine:
- *The cliff dwellings at Mesa Verde, Colorado*
✻ - *The salt mine under Detroit*
- *The "Avenue of Giants," sequoia trees in California*
- *Fort Knox's gold vault in Kentucky*

My textbook mentions these interesting places:
- *Monticello, Thomas Jefferson's home*
- *The Alamo, a famous battle site in Texas*
- *Ellis Island, where many immigrants landed*
- *The International Space Station*

Make your list. Try to list at least three possible topics under each heading. Then choose the one that interests you the most.

Discuss your topic. Explain to other students in a small group why you've chosen the topic and what you already know about it. Find out what the other students know about your place of interest and whether it sounds interesting to them.

Prewriting Sizing Up Your Topic

A good research report about a place should say something about the place's importance, its past, its present, and its future. Diego decided to write about the salt mine under Detroit. He searched the Internet and learned the following major facts about that mine. With this information to start with, Diego was sure he could write a good research report about the mine.

Details List

Notes About the Detroit Salt Mine

Its importance
- *The salt has been used for making chemicals, softening water, preserving food, and making ice cream.*
- *Today, it is used mainly for melting road ice.*

Its past
- *The salt bed is left from an ancient sea.*
- *The first mine shaft was dug in 1896.*
- *During the '80s its owners gave public tours.*

Its present
- *It has 100 miles of tunnels and 50 miles of roads.*
- *The rooms are each as big as a school gymnasium.*
- *Huge electric trucks do the digging and hauling.*

Its future
- *There's enough salt for 70 million years of mining.*
- *If demand for salt goes down, the mine might close.*
- *It could be used as a storage place or as a museum.*

Prewrite

Size up your topic. Look up your chosen topic in an encyclopedia or on the Internet. List the key details you find. Are there enough details to support a research report? If not, think of another topic.

TEKS 8.22A, 8.22B

RESEARCH

Making a Research Plan

After doing some preliminary research, Diego used the following tips to create a written research plan.

1 Name the topic and the audience.

Diego started by naming the general topic of his report and making sure he knew who his audience was.

2 Explain the purpose.

Diego defined his purpose by telling what he hoped to accomplish.

3 Formulate a major research question.

After thinking about his purpose and reviewing his preliminary research, Diego wrote his research question, which is the main question he'll answer.

4 Write specific detail questions.

Next, Diego wrote specific questions to guide further research and make it easier to organize his report in a way that makes sense.

5 List additional sources needed.

Once he defined the detail questions, Diego considered what additional resources he might need to gather more information.

Diego's Research Plan

Topic: Detroit Salt Mine
Audience: Teachers and classmates
Purpose: To inform about the Detroit Salt Mine
Research Question: What is the history of the Detroit Salt Mine
and why is the mine important?
Specific Questions:
What is the importance of salt?
What is the history of the salt mine?
What is the mine like now?
What is the future of the mine?
Additional Sources for Gathering Information:
E-mail and phone interviews with mine worker/mine manager
Television program and newspaper article about the mine
Internet site about salt

Make a plan. Review your preliminary research and make a research plan. Formulate a major research question that will guide your work.

Prewrite

Prewriting **Gathering Sources**

Your research plan helps you see what information you still need to gather to write your report. Diego followed his plan and decided he needed to find more sources. Here are the sources he found to gather additional information.

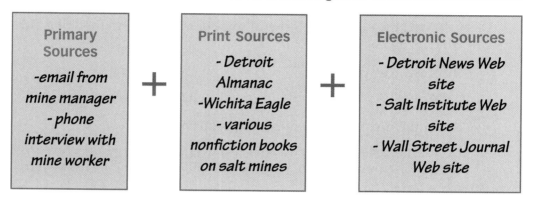

Primary Sources	Print Sources	Electronic Sources
-email from mine manager - phone interview with mine worker	- Detroit Almanac -Wichita Eagle - various nonfiction books on salt mines	- Detroit News Web site - Salt Institute Web site - Wall Street Journal Web site

As Diego gathered information from each of these sources, he recorded all the bibliographic information. This will help him write a complete bibliography when his report is finished. A part of these notes is shown below.

1. E-mail from Kim Roberts, received May 4, 2010

2. _Modern Marvels: Salt Mines._ A&E Television Networks Video. 2004

3. "Palace of the Salt Queen" by Sara Lin. _The Wall Street Journal_, June 19, 2009 found on page E8
4. Phone interview with Mike Yeling, mine worker. May 6, 2010

Gather your sources. Follow your research plan by gathering additional sources, including print and electronic sources. Jot down all the important bibliographic information for each note and source you use.

Synthesizing Ideas

Once you have gathered information from several sources, you will need to synthesize the ideas. Synthesizing ideas involves reading through the information you have collected, grouping similar details, and drawing conclusions or forming ideas based on the details. This will help you figure out exactly what your main ideas will be, or what questions you want to answer in your report. It will also help you determine if your research question is too narrow or too broad.

Evaluating Your Sources

As you review and compare the information you have gathered, try to determine the validity of your sources. Use information such as publication dates and information about authors or organizations that produced the sources to determine whether one source is more useful or reliable than another.

Diego used a chart like the one below to synthesize his information and evaluate his sources. He decided he had plenty of information to answer his major research questions. He also decided not to use the "Get Rid of Mining" Web site because it seemed biased and did not fit with his purpose.

email	Gives mine history from mine manager
phone interview	A miner tells what it's like to work in the mine
Detroit Almanac	Gives specific facts and figures about the mine's size and history
Detroit News Web site	Lots of history of the mine; includes present conditions
~~"Get Rid of Mining"~~	~~Personal views of people that are protesting mining in the U.S.~~
Salt Institute Web site	Includes information on salt mining and specifics about the Detroit mine

Evaluate your sources. Synthesize ideas from the various sources you have gathered. Then review your research plan. Decide if your research topic is too narrow or too broad and revise it if necessary. Determine whether you've got the information you need to answer your specific research questions. Also evaluate your sources, using a chart like the one above.

 TEKS 8.22B, 8.23B, 8.24A

Prewriting Using a Gathering Grid

A gathering grid can help you organize the information from your research. Diego made a grid during his research about the Detroit salt mine. Down the left-hand side, he listed questions about his topic. Across the top, he listed sources he found to answer those questions. For answers too long to fit in the grid, Diego used note cards. (See pages 419–420.)

Gathering Grid

Detroit's Salt Mine	Detroit Almanac	Salt Institute	Detroit News Web site	Wichita Eagle
Importance: What is its purpose?			Rock salt for icy roads and making chemicals	
History: What is its past?	People dug a 1,200-foot shaft in 1896	See note card #1.		
Present: What does it look like?		Rooms the size of gymnasiums, pillars 60 feet wide	100 miles of tunnels, 50 miles of roads	
Future: How might it be used in the future?			It can't be use for toxic storage.	Some salt mines are used as museums.

Prewrite

Create a gathering grid. Make a grid like Diego did. You might find that based on further research, you will have to broaden or narrow your topic.

TEKS 8.23C, 8.25A

Creating Note Cards

While a gathering grid is a great way to see all your research at one glance, sometimes an answer needs more space. You can use note cards to keep track of details from your research.

Number each new card and write a question at the top. Then answer the question with a paraphrase, a list, or a quotation. Be sure to put exact words from a source in quotation marks. At the bottom of each card, identify the source of the information (including a page number if appropriate). Here are three sample cards Diego made for his report on the Detroit salt mine.

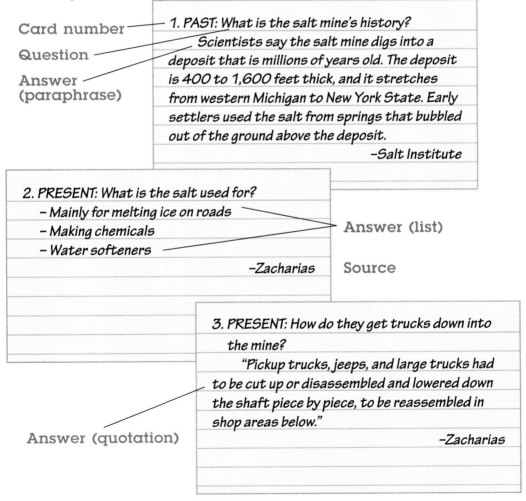

Card number
Question
Answer (paraphrase)

1. PAST: What is the salt mine's history?
Scientists say the salt mine digs into a deposit that is millions of years old. The deposit is 400 to 1,600 feet thick, and it stretches from western Michigan to New York State. Early settlers used the salt from springs that bubbled out of the ground above the deposit.
–Salt Institute

2. PRESENT: What is the salt used for?
– Mainly for melting ice on roads
– Making chemicals
– Water softeners
–Zacharias

Answer (list)
Source

3. PRESENT: How do they get trucks down into the mine?
"Pickup trucks, jeeps, and large trucks had to be cut up or disassembled and lowered down the shaft piece by piece, to be reassembled in shop areas below."
–Zacharias

Answer (quotation)

RESEARCH

Prewrite

Create note cards. Make note cards whenever your answers are too long for a gathering grid. Be sure to cite source information for each card.

TEKS 8.20B(ii), 8.23D, 8.25A

Prewriting **Avoiding Plagiarism**

Your research will lead you to many interesting facts and ideas to include in your paper. However, you must give credit for facts and ideas that are not common knowledge. Using other people's words and ideas without giving them credit is called plagiarism, and it is a form of stealing. Here are two good ways to avoid plagiarism.

- **Paraphrase:** Usually it's best to put the ideas from a source into your own words so that your paper sounds like you. This is called *paraphrasing*. Remember, though, to give credit to the source of the ideas. (See page **425**.)

- **Quote exact words:** When a source states something perfectly for the purposes of your report, you may want to include the exact words in quotation marks and credit the source. (See page **425**.)

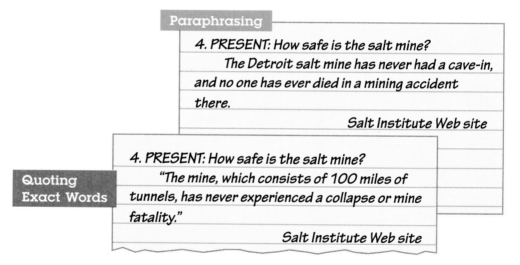

Paraphrasing

4. PRESENT: How safe is the salt mine?
The Detroit salt mine has never had a cave-in, and no one has ever died in a mining accident there.

Salt Institute Web site

Quoting Exact Words

4. PRESENT: How safe is the salt mine?
"The mine, which consists of 100 miles of tunnels, has never experienced a collapse or mine fatality."

Salt Institute Web site

 Read this excerpt from "Salt in the Michigan Basin." Then label two note cards with the question "What is salt used for?" On one card, *quote* a sentence. If you want to leave out any words or phrases, use an ellipsis in their place. On the other card, *paraphrase* the selection.

Chemically, there are several different types of salt, and they are used for many different purposes. When most people say "salt," they're talking about sodium chloride. In its purest form, sodium chloride is used for table salt. Mined rock salt usually has some impurities in it and is used for other purposes. Road crews use it to melt ice and snow. Chemical companies use it to make rayon, soap, and bleach. It is also used in water softeners and in salt licks.

TEKS 8.23C

Keeping Track of Your Sources

Write down the following information about the sources you find.

Encyclopedia entry: Author's name (if listed). Entry title. Encyclopedia title. Edition (if given). Publication date.

Book: Author's name. Title. Publisher and city. Copyright date.

Magazine: Author's name. Article title. Magazine title. Date published. Page numbers.

Newspaper: Author's name. Article title. Newspaper title. Date published. Section. Page numbers.

Internet: Author's name (if listed). Document title. Site title. Site sponsor. Date posted or copyright date (if listed). Date found.

Video: Title. Director's name (if available). Distributor. Release date.

RESEARCH

My Source Notes

Book
Mark Kurlansky. *Salt: A World History.* Penguin USA. East Rutherford, NJ. 2007.

Magazine
Don Hallett. "The Wieliczka Salt Mine." *Geology Today.* September/October 2006. Pages 182-185.

Newspaper
Beccy Tanner. "Salt Mine Museum Could Spark Tourist Trade." *Wichita Eagle.* May 8, 2004. Section A. Page 9.

Internet
No author. "Dry (Rock Salt) Mining." *Salt Institute.* The Salt Institute. May 10, 2008. Visited April 14, 2010.

Video
Modern Marvels: Salt Mines. A&E Television Networks Video. 2004. VHS.

Interview
Yeling, Mike. Personal interview. May 6, 2010.

Prewrite

List sources. Keep a list of each of your sources with the information shown above. Whenever you find a new source, add it to the list.

 **TEKS** 8.14A, 8.17A

Prewriting **Writing Your Thesis Statement**

After your research is completed, you will need to write a controlling idea to guide your writing. A thesis statement expresses your controlling idea, or the main idea you want to emphasize. It serves as a focus for your report to make sure all the parts work together. Use the following formula to help you write your controlling idea.

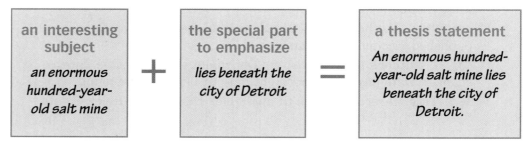

an interesting subject		the special part to emphasize		a thesis statement
an enormous hundred-year-old salt mine	**+**	*lies beneath the city of Detroit*	**=**	*An enormous hundred-year-old salt mine lies beneath the city of Detroit.*

Sample Thesis Statement

The 100-year-old Yerkes Observatory in Williams Bay, Wisconsin,
(an interesting subject)
has the largest refracting telescope in the world.
(the part to emphasize)

The "Avenue of the Giants" in northern California
(an interesting subject)
includes some giant sequoia trees that are 2,000 years old.
(the part to emphasize)

The International Space Station
(an interesting subject)
is the combined project of 16 different countries.
(the part to emphasize)

Prewrite

Form your thesis statement. Review your research notes and choose a special part to emphasize about your topic. Using the formula above, write a controlling idea for your report.

Outlining Your Ideas

Once you have gathered additional information, you need to plan your report. Making an outline is one way to plan your report. You can use either a topic outline or a sentence outline to list the main ideas. A topic outline lists ideas as words or phrases. A sentence outline puts ideas into full sentences. (Also see page 612.)

Sentence Outline

Below is the first part of a sentence outline for the report on pages 406–411. Notice that the outline begins with the thesis statement for the report. Then it lists a topic sentence for each middle paragraph. The author then marshals the evidence that supports the topic sentences, listing that underneath each one. Compare this partial outline to the finished report.

Controlling Idea	*CONTROLLING IDEA: This enormous, hundred-year-old salt mine lies beneath the city of Detroit, Michigan.*
I. Topic Sentence (for first middle paragraph)	I. *Salt is much more important than most people realize.*
	A. *Wars have been fought over salt, and it has been used for money.*
A. B. C. D. Supporting Ideas	B. *It helps keep the body alive and healthy.*
	C. *It is used to preserve food, to soften water, and to make chemicals.*
	D. *It is used to melt the ice on roads.*
II. Topic Sentence (for second middle paragraph)	II. *Scientists say that the Detroit mine digs into a bed of salt that is several hundred million years old.*
	A. . . .
	B. . . .

Remember: In an outline, if you have a I, you must also have a II. If you have an A, you must also have a B.

Prewrite

Create your outline. Write a sentence outline for your report. Be sure that each sentence (I, II, III, . . .) supports the thesis and that each piece of evidence (A, B, C, . . .) supports its topic sentence. When you finish, ask other classmates for suggestions to improve your outline.

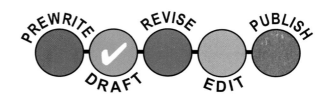

Drafting

With your research finished and a plan prepared, you're ready to begin writing the first draft of your paper. You don't have to get everything perfect in this draft. Just get your ideas down on paper in a way that makes sense to you. Use the following keys to guide your writing.

Keys to Effective Drafting

1. Write with your purpose, form, and audience in mind. Ask yourself these questions as you write:
   - What do I want my readers to learn from my report?
   - How will I organize my writing to make it easy to understand?

2. Use your first paragraph to introduce your topic, get your reader's attention, and present your thesis statement.

3. In the next few paragraphs, tell about the history of the place and why it is important.

4. Next, describe the place as it exists today.

5. End your paper with a few comments about the place's future.

6. Remember to cite your sources in your paper and list those sources alphabetically on a works-cited page.

TEKS 8.25D

Citing Sources in Your Report

Remember: It's very important that you give credit for each of the sources you use in your report.

When You Have All the Information

■ The most common type of credit (citation) lists the author's last name and the page number in parentheses.

"Marco Polo discovered that Tibetans used salt cakes stamped with the imperial seal of the great Kublai Khan as money" (Kemper 70).

■ If you already name the author in your report, just include the page number in parentheses.

Steve Kemper explains that during the Civil War, the North sent troops to attack the South's salt producers in order to make the South weaker (71).

When Some Information Is Missing

■ Some sources do not list an author. In those cases, use the title and page number. (If the title is long, use only the first word or two.)

At first, the salt was used mainly for storing meat and fish and for making ice cream (Detroit 167).

■ Some sources (especially Internet sites) do not use page numbers. In those cases, list just the author.

The seven-foot-tall tires for the dump trucks had to be compressed and bound with straps to fit down the shaft (Zacharias).

■ If a source does not list the author or page number, use the title.

Early settlers would collect that liquid and boil away the water to get the salt ("Dry").

Try IT Rewrite the following sentence, citing Steve Kemper's article, "Salt of the Earth," from the *Smithsonian*, page 78.

Throughout history, people have soaked themselves in salt springs, believing that the salty water makes them healthier.

TEKS 8.14B, 8.17A(i), 8.17A(ii)

Drafting Starting Your Research Report

The opening paragraph of your report should grab the reader's attention, introduce your topic, and state your controlling idea in a clear thesis statement. To start your opening paragraph, try one of these three approaches.

■ **Start with an interesting fact.**

Twelve hundred feet below the ground, an enormous mine has been operating almost nonstop for more than a century.

■ **Ask an interesting question.**

How many people know that there are cars and trucks driving on roads more than 1,200 feet below the city of Detroit?

■ **Start with a quotation.**

"The only dirty part of this job is getting to work," says salt miner Joel Payton.

Beginning Paragraph

The beginning paragraph starts with an interesting detail and ends with a clearly stated controlling idea (underlined).

Twelve hundred feet below the ground, an enormous mine has been operating almost nonstop for more than a century. A hundred miles of tunnels connect its huge chambers. It has underground roads for cars, trucks, and mining machines. This mine produces hundreds of tons of "rock" every day. However, the rock from this mine is not gold, or iron ore, or even coal; it is salt. This enormous, hundred-year-old salt mine lies beneath the city of Detroit, Michigan.

Write your opening paragraph. Start with something to grab the reader's attention; then introduce your topic and end with a clear thesis statement.

Developing the Middle Part

The middle part of your report should begin by explaining why the place you have chosen is important. Next tell about its history, and then describe the place as it exists today.

Each middle paragraph should start with a topic sentence covering one main idea. Additional sentences in each paragraph should support that one idea. Refer to your sentence outline to guide your writing. (See page **423**.)

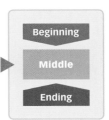

Beginning

Middle

Ending

Middle Paragraphs

All the details support the topic sentence (underlined).

A direct quotation is integrated into the text to support the topic sentence.

The first middle paragraph explains why the place is important.

The author tells about the history of the place.

Salt is more important than most people realize. Wars have been fought over it. In ancient China, salt coins were used for money, and Roman soldiers were often paid in salt, which is where the word "salary" comes from. Bettina Werner, an artist known as the "Salt Queen" says, "Salt is like a fifth element, it's so important to life" (Lin). In the human body, salt carries electrical signals that keep a person alive. To stay healthy, a person needs to eat about three pounds of salt a year (Modern). Salt is also used to preserve meat and fish, to tan leather, to soften water, and to make many different chemicals. However, most of the salt from the Detroit mine is now used to melt ice and snow on streets and highways (Zacharias).

The Salt Mine's History

Scientists say that the Detroit mine digs into a bed of salt that is several hundred million years old. From 600 million to 230 million years ago, seawater flooded the middle of North America many times. As sun and wind evaporated

TEKS 8.14B, 8.20B(ii), 8.25D

The exact wording from a source is included in quotation marks. An ellipsis is used where a sentence from the quote was left out.

Each paragraph has a topic sentence and supporting details.

Sources are included in parentheses.

A quotation from an expert supports the topic sentence. Brackets around "they" show this is not the exact word used.

the water, sea salt was deposited on the submerged land. According to the Salt Institute, "Trillions of tons of salt, collected in a layer 400 to 1,600 feet thick, reached from western Michigan all the way to New York. . . . Eventually, it was covered by silt that became rock more than 1,000 feet thick." ("Dry") Later, when people came to the area to settle, they found springs of salty water bubbling from the ground. They would collect that liquid and boil away the water to get the salt.

In 1896, the Detroit salt mine was started in order to dig the salt out of the ground. It began as a shaft 1,200 feet deep and about 6 feet wide. At first, the salt was used mainly for storing meat and fish and for making ice cream (Detroit 167). In 1940, though, Detroit became the first city to use rock salt on icy roads. Other cities soon followed Detroit's example, and the mine began selling most of its salt to road crews ("Dry"). In 1983, however, low sales and competition from Canadian mines caused the Detroit mine to close. Crystal Mines bought the mine, hoping to store hazardous wastes there. In 1985, while waiting for a permit, they ran public tours of the mine. "Crystal Mines permit was denied in 1997 and [they] then sold the mine to the Detroit Salt Company," explained Kim Roberts, manager of the mine (Roberts). The mine was reopened, and it again became one of the main sources of road salt in the United States.

TEKS 8.14B, 8.17A(v), 8.25D

The author describes the place as it is today.

Sentences are arranged so that the reader can easily follow the ideas.

The author shares interesting details with the reader.

A comparison of size helps the reader understand a complex idea.

The Salt Mine Today

Some people call the Detroit salt mine a city beneath a city. It covers 1,400 acres under Detroit and its suburbs. That's equal to 1,300 football fields. Also, it has more than 50 miles of roads where construction equipment, trucks, and cars drive. To get these vehicles down the shaft, they had to be taken apart, carried down in pieces, and reassembled in underground workshops. The seven-foot-tall tires for the dump trucks had to be compressed and bound with straps to fit down the shaft (Zacharias).

The mining equipment includes many different types of big electric trucks. One type has a giant chain saw on the front, which cuts a deep groove into a salt wall at floor level. Then a drilling-machine truck bores a pattern of holes 20 feet deep into the wall to hold dynamite or other explosives. The blast from these explosives breaks hundreds of tons of rock from the wall in huge chunks. Trucks with giant shovels then scoop up tons at a time and drop them into dump trucks. The dump trucks carry the chunks back to the shaft, where a crusher breaks them into smaller pieces and sorting machines separate the pieces by size. Finally, buckets that can hold nine tons of salt run up a conveyor to the surface. There the salt is packaged and shipped ("Dry").

The Salt Institute explains that the mine is carved out in a "room-and-pillar" method. Each room is as big and

This partial quotation from a source states a fact. Note that the source is included.

A quote from an interview is included to add personal details that support the topic sentence.

high as a school gymnasium. Between rooms, the miners leave pillars of salt about 60 feet wide to hold up the ceiling. This type of mining gets about 70 percent of the salt from the ground, leaving the other 30 percent as support pillars. Because the salt bed has never had an earthquake or other shock, it lies very flat, so the pattern of rooms and pillars stretches level from one end of the mine to the other. According to the Salt Institute, this mine "has never experienced a collapse or mine fatality" ("Dry").

Miners say that the mine is a very clean and healthy place to work. The temperature stays a cool 58 degrees year-round. There are no bugs, rats, or other animals living in the mine, because there is nothing for them to eat. (Zacharias). "I love working here. The air you breathe in the mine feels great. It's very clean, with no allergens or mold like on the surface. I've worked here for 15 years, and I wouldn't want to be anywhere else," shared Mike Yeling, a miner (Yeling).

Write your middle paragraphs. Keep these tips in mind as you write.

1. Support the topic sentence for each paragraph with details.

2. Refer to your outline for help with your organization. (See page 423.)

3. Give credit to your sources in your paper. Be sure to follow the accepted format for integrating citations into the text. (See page 425.)

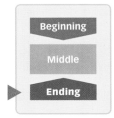

TEKS 8.14B, 8.25B

Drafting Ending Your Research Report

Your ending paragraph should sum up your report and bring it to a thoughtful close. State any conclusions you have drawn and the reasons for them. You might also . . .

- **Remind the reader of the controlling idea.**
- **Provide information about the place's future.**
- **Make a final observation for the reader.**

Beginning

Middle

▶ Ending

Ending Paragraph

RESEARCH

The writer includes an interesting fact.

Some final possibilities leave the reader with something to think about.

The Salt Mine's Future

The Detroit salt mine could have a very interesting future. According to geologists, there is enough salt underneath Michigan to last for 70 million years ("Dry"). Many people worry, though, that the runoff from road salt is having a negative effect on our rivers and lakes. If people stop using salt on icy streets and highways, there may not be enough business to keep the Detroit mine open. In that case, the mine could be used to store important documents, films, and artwork, as some other salt mines do (Tanner). If nothing else, the Detroit salt mine could be turned into a public museum because it is an important part of the city's history.

Write your final paragraph. Draft your final paragraph using one or more of the three strategies listed above. Be sure to include relevant reasons for your conclusions and bring your report to a thoughtful close.

Look over your report. Read your report, checking your notes and outline to make sure you haven't forgotten anything. In the margins and between the lines, make notes about anything you should change.

Drafting Creating Your Works-Cited Page

To create your works-cited page, first format each of your sources; then list them in alphabetical order. The purpose of a works-cited page is to help other people find the sources you used. It also shows that your information is based on reliable sources. Not every source will match these formats exactly, but if you give as much detail as possible, your works-cited page will do its job.

Encyclopedias

Author (if available). Article title (in quotation marks). Title of the encyclopedia (underlined). Edition (if available). Date published.

> "Sodium Chloride." Columbia Encyclopedia. 2000.
> Print.

Books

Author or editor (last name first). Title (underlined). City where the book was published: Publisher, copyright date.

> Kurlansky, Mark. Salt: A World History.
> East Rutherford, NJ: Penguin USA,
> 2007. Print.

Magazines

Author (last name first). Article title (in quotation marks). Title of the magazine (underlined) Date (day month year): Page numbers of the article.

> Hallett, Don. "The Wieliczka Salt Mine." Geology
> Today Sept./Oct. 2006:
> 182-185. Print.

Newspapers

Author (if available, last name first). Article title (in quotation marks). Title of the newspaper (underlined) Date (day month year), edition (if listed): Section letter and page numbers of the article.

> Tanner, Beccy. "Salt Mine Museum Could Spark
> Tourist Trade." Wichita Eagle
> 8 May 2004: A9. Print.

Internet

Author (if available). "Page title" (if available, in quotation marks). Site title (underlined). Name of sponsor (if available). Date posted (day month year, if available). Web. Date found.

> "Dry (Rock Salt) Mining." <u>Salt Institute</u>. Salt Institute. 10 May 2008. Web. 14 Apr. 2010.

Film, Video, and So On

Title (underlined). Director (if available). Distributor, date released. Type of medium (filmstrip, slide program, and so on).

> <u>Modern Marvels: Salt Mines</u>. A&E Television Networks Video, 2004. VHS.

Letter or Email to the Author (Yourself)

Writer (last name first). Subject line title (if any) in quotation marks. Type of message ("Letter to the author" or "Email to the author"). Date addressed (day month year).

> Roberts, Kim. Email from mine manager. 4 May 2010.

Format your sources. Check your report and your list of sources (page 421) to see which sources you actually used. Make sure you used the most reliable sources you gathered, to show your information is trustworthy. Then follow these directions.

1 Write your sources using the guidelines above and on the previous page. You can write them on a sheet of paper or on note cards.

2 Alphabetize your sources.

3 Create your works-cited page. (See the example on page 411.)

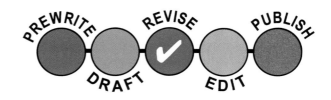

Revising

A good research report needs more than one draft. The first time through, you work mainly with organization and ideas. In the second draft, you fill in missing information, rearrange ideas for clarity, and polish your writing. Take the time to make your report as good as it can be.

Keys to Effective Revising

1. Read your entire draft to get an overall sense of your report.

2. Review your thesis statement to be sure that it clearly states your controlling idea, or main point about the topic.

3. Make sure your beginning draws the reader in. Then check that your ending leaves the reader with something to think about.

4. Make sure you sound knowledgeable and interested in the topic.

5. Check that you used the best evidence available to support your main ideas.

6. Use the editing and proofreading marks inside the back cover of this book.

TEKS 8.17A(iii), 8.25B

Revising for Focus and Coherence

When you revise for focus and coherence, make sure your report remains focused on your controlling idea and includes no inconsistencies or unrelated details. Check to make sure you have marshaled evidence to explain the topic. This means that you have chosen the best evidence from your research and organized it in the most effective way to explain your main ideas and support your controlling idea. You should also check to make sure you have explained the reasons for any conclusions you draw.

Did I organize my report to avoid inconsistencies?

A report is coherent when the focus is consistent and the organization is logical throughout. You know you have logically organized your report if . . .

- You state your controlling idea clearly at the beginning.
- Each paragraph begins with a topic sentence that supports the controlling idea.
- You have included the best evidence to explain the topic.
- Your evidence gives relevant reasons for each conclusion made.
- You have cut any sentences that do not relate to or support the controlling idea.

 Check your report. Read your first draft or have a partner read it. Check that your ideas are organized logically to provide coherence throughout. Be sure that the evidence you include helps explain the topic and that you give relevant reasons for your conclusions. Revise your report as necessary.

RESEARCH

Focus and Coherence
The ideas were reorganized to clear up inconsistencies and a reason was added to support the conclusion.

Today being a successful dairy farmer requires a

combination of modern machines, education, and good

Move to "Dairy Farming of the Past"

business skills. Farming in the 1800's was much more

diverse with some farmers planting crops and raising

cattle. Universities offer programs and degrees in

Technology has improved farm machines to increase

agriculture with special degrees just for dairy farmers.

production and provide better quality results.

 TEKS 8.14C, 8.17A(v)

Have I included a variety of sentence structures?

Including a variety of sentence structures makes your writing more engaging to read. It also helps to connect your ideas and give your writing greater coherence. You can vary your sentence structure by adding phrases that show how your ideas relate to one another.

Vary sentence structure by starting sentences with . . .

- a preposition or prepositional phrase that shows sequence.
  After putting out a forest fire, **rangers evaluate their methods.**

- an adverb, such as unfortunately, lately, or finally, that expresses a point of view.
  Unfortunately, **much wildlife suffers due to the fires.**

- an "ing" action word that provides greater detail.
  Carrying their gear, **firefighters make their way into the heart of the fire.**

- a dependent clause that shows cause and effect or another relationship between ideas.
  Because their job is so dangerous, **firefighters have to be prepared for the worst.**

 Decide which of the first two paragraphs uses a variety of sentence structures. Then rewrite the third paragraph to include sentence structure variety.

1. Rangers assess forest fires before getting too close. Fires can get out of control very fast. Safety measures must be followed.

2. Before getting too close, rangers assess forest fires. Unfortunately, fires can get out of control very fast. Following safety measures is a must.

3. Lightning is a cause of many fires in forested areas. Dry needles act as fuel for the fire. Fires spread because high winds cause sparks to jump to new areas.

 Add variety to your sentences. Review your draft. Check to see if you have included a variety of sentence structures to make your writing coherent. If not, combine or add to some simple subject/verb sentences to make the connections between your ideas clearer.

TEKS 8.25A, 8.25D

RESEARCH

Texas Traits
Revising for Organization

An organized research report presents findings in a systematic, meaningful way. Evidence is clearly summarized, paraphrased, or quoted, and organized in a way that makes sense to the reader. Any conclusions that are drawn are well supported with relevant reasons based on the research.

Did I draw conclusions from my research?

You draw conclusions when you synthesize information from different sources to arrive at a new understanding of the topic. Drawing conclusions is more than just restating facts. It's combining what you know with the relevant details that you learn to present a generalization or opinion about the topic.

Read these two book excerpts about dolphins. Tell which statements are conclusions that could be drawn by synthesizing the research.

Dolphins are taught to show their dorsal fins to trainers. They will even stay still on command. Many of their "tricks" actually make handling them easier for trainers.

Dolphins require regular medical care. Blood is usually drawn from their dorsal fin. Pregnant dolphins need extra special care, including ultrasounds.

1. It is difficult for trainers to teach dolphins tricks.
2. Teaching dolphins to show their dorsal fin helps with medical exams because blood is commonly drawn from this spot.
3. When dolphins learn to stay still, medical tests like ultrasounds for pregnant dolphins are easier.

Review your conclusions. Check that you present relevant reasons from your research to support any conclusions you draw.

Did I present my evidence in a meaningful way?

Determine if you have made the right choice about whether to summarize, paraphrase, or quote evidence directly. If you paraphrased evidence that would be more effective as a direct quotation, be sure to integrate the quotation smoothly into the text and properly cite the source. (See examples in essay on pages 426–431.)

Check your evidence. Reread your first draft. Check to make sure you summarized, paraphrased, and quoted information accurately and effectively and presented your findings in a systematic, meaningful way.

 **TEKS** 8.25C

Did I organize my report well?

It is important to organize your research report in a way that will make the information easy for your reader to follow. Using headings within your report to identify different sections of information is one way to present your findings in a meaningful format. Here are steps to help you create headings for your report.

1. Review your report.
2. Look for sections of information that are related. (You may want to use the main ideas you identified in your outline.)
3. Write a heading that describes the information in each section.
4. Place the heading before the first paragraph in the section it relates to.
5. Make your headings stand out from the rest of the text by making them boldface and larger type (if typing) or by underlining them (if writing by hand).

Check for headings. Review your draft. If you have used headings, check to make sure the headings accurately describe the information in each section. If not, write headings to guide your reader and present your findings in a meaningful format.

Organization
A heading was added to guide readers and a summary sentence was revised to be more succinct.

The Salt Mine's History

∧ ~~Detroit sits on top of an ancient bed of salt.~~

~~Scientists believe the salt bed under Detroit is several~~

~~hundred million years old.~~ From 600 million to 230
∧
Scientists say that the Detroit mine digs into a bed of
million years ago, seawater flooded the middle of North
salt that is several hundred million years old.
America many times. As sun and wind evaporated the

water, sea salt was deposited on the submerged land.

TEKS 8.17A(v)

Revising for Development of Ideas

When you revise for development of ideas, make sure you use a variety of rhetorical devices to make your writing as clear and effective as possible. Incorporating quotations can also be an effective way to provide convincing support for your main ideas.

Have I included a variety of rhetorical devices?

Rhetorical devices are techniques you can use to better communicate your ideas. Figurative language such as metaphors and similes can be used to describe things that might be difficult for readers to picture. Rhetorical questions can draw attention to a point and add emotion that a direct statement could not. Hyperbole and repetition can also help you add drama or emotion to make a point, but be careful not to overuse these devices. The following are examples of rhetorical devices that you can add to improve your writing.

Rhetorical Device	Example
rhetorical questions	How many more forest fires will occur due to carelessness?
similes	Forest fires are like savage beasts raging through the trees.
metaphors	The trees are helpless victims to the raging fires.
hyperbole	Rangers are doing a million things at once.
repetition	The fires come, the fires seek, and the fires destroy.

 For each topic below, choose one of the rhetorical devices and use it in a sentence. Use your own thoughts and ideas as you write.

1. the night sky   **3.** an amusement park

2. a young child   **4.** a rattlesnake

 Use rhetorical devices. Check to see if you have used rhetorical devices in your writing. If you have, decide if they need revision. If you have not, find places in your report to add rhetorical devices that will improve the development of ideas and better communicate your thoughts.

RESEARCH

Have I effectively used quotations in my report?

Quotations are used effectively when they provide valuable support for a main idea and fit seamlessly into your report to maintain the flow of ideas. Integrating quotations into your writing can help make your point clearer and add credibility to your work.

Types of Quotations

Direct Quotations . . .
- use the exact words of an authority,
- are identified with quotation marks,
- are credited with the source in parentheses at the point of use.

Indirect Quotations . . .
- paraphrase, or restate a thought or idea expressed by someone else,
- do not require quotation marks,
- are also credited with the source in parentheses at the point of use.

Revise

Check for quotations. Review your draft. Determine if you have used direct or indirect quotations. If so, make sure that you followed accepted formats for integrating the quotations into your written text to maintain the flow of ideas. If not, find at least one quotation to add to your work. Be sure to use quotation marks and cite your source to avoid plagiarizing.

Development of Ideas
A direct quotation was incorporated to provide better support.

In 1985, while waiting for a permit, they ran public tours of the mine. ~~Crystal Mines did not get the permit.~~

~~They sold the mine to the Detroit Salt Company.~~ The "Crystal Mines permit was denied in 1997 and [they] then mine was reopened, and it again became one of the main sold the mine to the Detroit Salt Company," explained Kim sources of road salt in the United States. Roberts, manager of the mine (Roberts).

TEKS 8.14C

Texas Traits

Revising **for** Voice

When you revise for *voice*, make sure that you have chosen precise words to explain your topic. Keep in mind your purpose, your audience, and the genre as you review your word choice.

Did I choose precise words?

You have used precise words in your writing if you have chosen just the right words to say exactly what you mean. The most precise words are not necessarily the most impressive sounding words. It is more important that your word choice is appropriate for your audience and adds to their overall understanding of the topic. Replace vague words with ones that will help readers create a mental picture or make a connection to what you're explaining.

 Read each set of sentences and identify the one that uses more precise word choice.

1. Fighting forest fires is hard.
Fighting forest fires is an arduous task.

2. His shirt was faded and dull.
His shirt was sort of light.

 Look for precise word choice. Read through your first draft. Check for vague or inappropriate words. Replace them with precise word choice.

Voice
Vague and inappropriate words are replaced with ones that are more precise.

> *Twelve hundred*
> ~~Many~~ feet below the ground, ~~a big~~ *an enormous* mine has been
>
> operating almost nonstop for more than a century. ~~A~~
>   *A hundred miles*
> ~~number of~~ tunnels connect its huge chambers. It has
>
> underground roads for cars, trucks, and mining machines.
>
> This mine produces ~~lots~~ of "rock" every day.
>   *hundreds of tons*

 TEKS 8.14C

Does my voice fit my purpose, audience, and genre?

In a research report, your purpose is to help your audience better understand the topic you have selected. The genre may require the use of some technical terms or special vocabulary and is generally more formal than narrative writing. However, you should attempt to write in a natural voice that engages the reader, while clearly presenting facts and evidence. Your writing should not sound like lists of facts restated from your research.

Not Natural: does not fit purpose, audience, or genre

Geological experts hypothesize the Detroit mine salt bed to be several hundred million years old. Seawater flooded the regional landscape of central North America on multiple occasions from 600 million to 230 million years ago.

Natural: fits purpose, audience, and genre

Scientists say that the Detroit mine digs into a bed of salt that is several hundred million years old. From 600 million to 230 million years ago, seawater flooded the middle of North America many times.

 Read this paragraph. Then rewrite it in a more natural voice. Your purpose is to clearly explain the topic and your audience is your classmates. Look up unfamiliar terms and replace them with appropriate synonyms that your audience will understand.

Fires burn millions of hectares of forest each year worldwide. Forest fires have a devastating effect on biodiversity, health, economy, and industry. Fire is an important part of natural forest regeneration. Forest fires can repopulate certain species of plants by allowing their seeds to germinate and grow in the newly burned ground. Fires become problematic when they burn in the wrong places, at the wrong times, or in circumstances that become uncontrollable.

 Revise your voice. Rewrite any sentences or paragraphs in your report that do not fit your purpose, audience, or genre. Make sure that your writing does not simply list facts, but rather engages your reader and explains the topic in a natural voice.

Revising Using a Checklist

Revise

Check your revising. On a piece of paper, write the numbers 1 to 11. If you can answer "yes" to a question, put a check mark after that number. If not, continue to work with that part of your research report.

Focus and Coherence

_____ **1.** Did I logically organize my report?

_____ **2.** Did I avoid any inconsistencies or unrelated details?

_____ **3.** Did I marshal the best evidence to explain the topic and give relevant reasons to support my conclusions?

_____ **4.** Did I include a variety of sentence structures to help connect my ideas?

Organization

_____ **5.** Did I draw conclusions from my research?

_____ **6.** Did I summarize or paraphrase my findings?

_____ **7.** Did I organize my report well?

Development of Ideas

_____ **8.** Did I include a variety of rhetorical devices in my writing?

_____ **9.** Did I effectively integrate quotations in my writing?

Voice

_____ **10.** Did I choose precise words?

_____ **11.** Does my voice fit my purpose, audience, and genre?

Revise

Make a clean copy. When you've finished revising, make a clean copy before you edit. This makes checking for conventions easier.

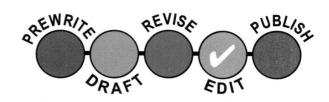

Editing

Once you have finished revising your report, edit your work for *conventions:* grammar, mechanics, and spelling.

Keys to Effective Editing

1. Use a dictionary, a thesaurus, your computer's spell-checker, and the "Proofreader's Guide" in the back of this book.

2. Read your essay out loud and listen for words or phrases that may be incorrect.

3. Look for errors in grammar, mechanics (punctuation, capitalization), and spelling.

4. Check your report for proper formatting.

5. If you use a computer, edit on a printed computer copy. Then enter your changes on the computer.

6. Use the editing and proofreading marks inside the back cover of this book.

TEKS 8.19C

Texas Traits ☆ **Editing** **for Conventions**

Grammar

When you edit for grammar, check for correctness and variety in sentence structures. Also make sure that you use pronouns and other parts of speech correctly.

Do I use parallel structures in my sentences?

You use parallel structures when you match parts of your sentences that have the same function or express similar ideas. Below are a variety of complete sentences. The first examples do not contain parallel structures and the second examples do.

Incorrect

She likes **to play** piano **and** listening **to music.**
The locker was filled with dirty clothes, crumpled paper, **and** the pencils were broken.

Correct

She likes **playing** piano **and** listening **to music.**
The locker was filled with dirty clothes, crumpled paper, **and** broken pencils.

GRAMMAR **Try IT** Number your paper from 1 to 5. Decide if each sentence uses parallel structure or not. If so, write "yes" next to the number. If no, rewrite the sentence to correctly show parallel structure.

1. I went to the museum, to the planetarium, and visited the park.
2. He is full of life, laughter, and joy.
3. The health club had a basketball court, a tennis court, and a swimming pool.
4. Maria wants to eat a healthy breakfast and she exercises for thirty minutes every day.
5. I love to read, to watch movies, and sing.

Check for use of parallel structures. Check that listed elements or similar ideas in your sentences have the same grammatical structure.

RESEARCH

TEKS 8.19A(iii),
8.19A(iv)
ELPS 4C

Do I use relative pronouns correctly in my writing?

A relative pronoun connects one part of a sentence with a word or phrase in another part of the sentence. It introduces a clause called an *adjectival clause*, which describes or gives more information about the noun that the relative pronoun refers to.

Relative Pronoun	Refers to
that, which	things or animals
who, whom, whoever,	people
whomever	

Using Relative Pronouns

This is the book that we read in class.
(The relative pronoun *that* refers to the noun *book*.)

I can't recall the name of the man who spoke at last week's assembly.
(*Who* is a relative pronoun that refers to the noun *man*.)

Read each sentence. Identify the relative pronoun. Then tell which noun it refers to.

1. Any student who wants to join chess club should talk to Alexa.
2. The club, which meets on Tuesdays, still has four spots open.
3. The room that the club meets in is Mrs. Rivera's homeroom.
4. Mrs. Rivera, who is the club's advisor, loves to play chess.

Check for relative pronouns. Review your draft for sentences that include relative pronouns. Make sure that you have used the correct relative pronoun for the type of noun you are replacing and the kind of description you want to give.

Learning Language

- Use *that* when the descriptive clause provides necessary information:
  The book that I lost was *Gulliver's Travels*.
  ("That I lost," is necessary information.)

- Use *which* when the clause does not provide necessary information:
  The book, which was interesting, belonged to the town library.
  (You don't need to know that the book was interesting to understand the main point of the sentence.)

TEKS 8.14C, 8.19A(iv), 8.20B(ii)

Sentence Structure

When you edit for sentence structure, make sure you use a variety of sentence structures so your writing flows smoothly. If you have too many short, simple sentences, you can combine some to create greater variety.

Have I combined my sentences correctly?

One way to vary your sentences is to create compound sentences. Compound sentences are made up of two or more simple sentences joined by a comma and a coordinating conjunction *(and, or, but,* and so on), or by a semi-colon. (For more information about conjunctions, see pages **792–794**.)

Students edit the school newspaper, **but** teachers must approve all stories before publication.
(A comma and the conjunction **but** connect two independent clauses.)

The elm tree is 15 feet tall; the maple is 20 feet tall.
(A **semi-colon** connects two independent clauses. No conjunction is needed.)

You can also use relative pronouns to combine sentences. The following example shows how the relative pronoun *who* can be used to connect two closely related sentences.

Some students work hard. They have more success.
Students **who** work hard have more success.

 Combine the following sentences using a conjunction or a semi-colon or a relative pronoun. Write the new sentences on your own paper. Be sure to include commas where needed.

1. I like to sing. My sister prefers to dance.
2. Jana is the president of the Drama Club. Jana got the lead role in the school play.
3. My computer is new. My printer is old.
4. We could ride our bikes to school. We could walk.
5. My father is waiting in line. My father is wearing a blue cap.

 Edit compound sentences. Review your report for sentence variety. Use a comma and a conjunction or a semi-colon to join compound sentences. If you use a relative pronoun to combine sentences, make sure you set off the relative clause with commas if it contains information that is not necessary to understand the sentence.

TEKS 8.20B(ii)

Mechanics: Punctuation

When you edit for *mechanics*, one thing you need to check for is correct use of punctuation. Make sure that you use colons and other punctuation marks correctly.

How do I use a colon to introduce a list?

You use a colon to introduce a list that comes after a complete sentence. Colons often come after summary words such as *the following* or *these things*. It is incorrect to use a colon after a verb or a preposition.

Incorrect

> The firefighters are cautious of: strong winds, black smoke, and lightning storms.
>
> Their safety kit includes: bandages, extra oxygen tanks, extra masks, and burn cream.

Correct

> Firefighters use the following special gear: face masks, oxygen tanks, heat resistant suits, and protective goggles.

For each group of words below, write a sentence using a colon to introduce the list. Use your own words and ideas to add whatever is missing.

1. rabbits, dogs, cats, hamsters
2. pens, pencils, markers, crayons
3. soccer balls, footballs, baseballs, tennis balls
4. science, math, social studies, language arts

Check for colons. Read through your report to be sure you have used colons correctly when introducing a list. Make corrections when necessary.

★ **TEKS** 8.14C, 8.14D, 8.19A(iv), 8.19C, 8.20A, 8.20B(ii), 8.21

Editing Using a Checklist

Check your editing. On a piece of paper, write the numbers 1–11. If you can answer "yes" to a question, put a check mark after that number. If not, continue to edit for that convention.

Conventions

GRAMMAR

_____ **1.** Do I use parallel structures where needed in my sentences?

_____ **2.** Do I include a variety of sentence structures?

_____ **3.** Do I use relative pronouns correctly?

_____ **4.** Do I use conjunctions correctly to join sentences?

MECHANICS

_____ **5.** Did I use a comma before conjunctions or a semi-colon when joining simple sentences?

_____ **6.** Have I used colons correctly to introduce my lists?

_____ **7.** Did I use commas to separate items in each list?

_____ **8.** Did I end all sentences with the correct punctuation?

_____ **9.** Did I capitalize all proper nouns and adjectives?

SPELLING

_____ **10.** Have I spelled all my words correctly?

_____ **11.** Have I double-checked the words my spell-checker may have missed?

RESEARCH

Creating a Title

For a research report, the title should do one of the following:

■ Name the topic: **The Salt Mine of Detroit**

■ Catch the reader's imagination: **Man-Made Caves of Salt**

■ Reflect the main point: **A Hidden Treasure: Detroit's Salt Mine**

TEKS 8.14E, 8.25C

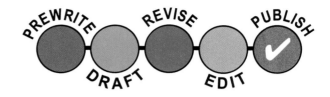

Publishing
Sharing Your Report

After you have written and improved your report, you'll want to make a neat-looking final copy to share. You may also decide to prepare your report as an electronic presentation, an online essay, or an illustrated report.

Make a final copy. Use the following guidelines to format your report. (If you are using a computer, see page 62.) Create a clean final copy and carefully proofread it.

Focus on Presentation

- Use blue or black ink and double-space the entire paper.
- Write your name, your teacher's name, the class, and the date in the upper left corner of page 1.
- Skip a line and center your title; skip another line and start your writing.
- Indent every paragraph and leave a one-inch margin on all four sides.
- For a research paper, you should write your last name and the page number in the upper right corner of every page of your report.

Creating a Title Page

If your teacher requires a title page, follow his or her requirements. Usually you center the title one-third of the way down from the top of the page. Then go two-thirds of the way down and center your name, your teacher's name, the name of the class, and the date. Put each piece of information on a separate line.

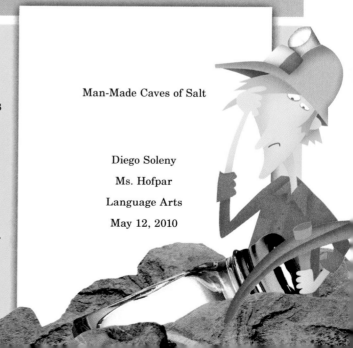

Man-Made Caves of Salt

Diego Soleny

Ms. Hofpar

Language Arts

May 12, 2010

Making Oral Presentations

You may not realize it, but you've been making oral presentations ever since you started school. In the early grades, your teachers coaxed you to say your name or to tell about your favorite toy. Later, you probably told your class about a book you had read or about a family vacation. Perhaps you even gave a demonstration speech or presented a report. Each year, your oral presentations become more complex, so your skill at making them should also improve.

In this chapter, you will learn how to make a speech based on a research report you have already written. You will find helpful tips for every step of the process, from planning your speech to making the presentation.

What's Ahead

- **Preparing Your Presentation**
- **Organizing Your Speech**
- **Delivering Your Speech**

 **TEKS** 8.25A

Preparing Your Presentation

Adapting a research report into a speech is a different process than writing a speech from scratch. For one thing, you already have a topic and information, and you know what type of speech you will make. The following tips will help you transform your report into a good speech.

Get Noticed	Plan Visuals	Organize Notes	Cut, Cut, Cut
Use a question, fact, or anecdote to get listeners' attention. (See below.)	Use visual aids to show support for your conclusions. (See p. 453.)	Focus on the controlling idea of your research as you organize your note cards.	Include only details that support your main point and the conclusions you draw.

Rewriting in Action

Below is the opening of the research report on pages 406–411. Notice the new beginning (on gold paper) has been revised so it grabs the listeners' attention and makes an appropriate opening for an oral presentation.

> Twelve hundred feet below the ground, an enormous mine has been operating almost nonstop for more than a century. A hundred miles of tunnels connect its huge chambers. It has underground roads for cars, trucks, and mining machines. This mine produces hundreds of tons of "rock" every day. However, the rock from this

> Imagine going twelve hundred feet below ground. When you reach the bottom, you find a hundred miles of tunnels connecting huge chambers. Underground cars, trucks, and mining machines work almost nonstop with hundreds of tons of "rock" being produced every day. Does this sound like a story from a science fiction movie?

 Adapt your research report. Choose a research report you've written that would make a good oral presentation. Rewrite the opening so that it gets the audience's attention. Then think of the main points and the evidence that will best explain your conclusions and support your controlling idea.

TEKS 8.25A

Using Visual Aids

Once you have written the opening of your speech and chosen the main points that you wish to share with your audience, you should decide where to use visual aids. Visual aids can help you summarize or paraphrase information about your controlling idea and make that information easier for your audience to understand.

Posters	show words, pictures, or both.
Photographs	help your audience "see" who or what you are talking about.
Charts	compare ideas or explain main points.
Transparencies	highlight key words, ideas, or graphics.
Maps	show specific places being discussed.
Objects	allow your audience to see the real thing.

Here are some tips for using visual aids in your oral presentation.

1 **Summarize or paraphrase main points.** Synthesize key research in the form of lists or simple paraphrased labels. You can direct your audience to these points as you explain them in more detail.

2 **Keep them simple.** Highlight only brief, important concepts on your visuals. Pictures and graphic organizers are useful for presenting information in a systematic way.

3 **Make them big and eye catching.** Be sure everyone in the room can see your visual aids. Use color, bold lines, and basic shapes to attract attention.

List visual aids. Select two visual aids that would help you summarize or paraphrase your points to make them clearer. Write down how you will use them.

Poster	*show time line of mine's history*
Object	*show a container of rock salt*

TEKS 8.25B

Organizing Your Speech

Now that you have written an opening and planned your visual aids, you are ready to organize your speech. The purpose of an oral report presentation is to inform your audience and help them understand your research. As you focus on organization, make sure you use your best evidence to effectively explain your topic and support your controlling idea. Use the following tips.

Beginning	Middle	Ending
Get your listeners' attention and focus on the controlling idea of your report.	Marshal evidence in the best order possible to explain your ideas and conclusions.	Close by restating your controlling idea in a memorable way.

Using Note Cards

Writing out note cards is a simple and efficient way to organize your speech. Each card contains a main point that will guide you as you deliver the speech. Using key words and lists on your cards will help you avoid reading your speech word for word. Be sure to make eye contact with your audience.

Diego turned his essay on pages 406–411 into a speech. He used note cards that included the opening, the closing, and the main ideas.

Note-Card Guidelines

- Write your introduction word for word on the first note card.
- Place each main idea on a separate card.
- Number each card.
- Note the main idea at the top of each card.
- Write the supporting details on the lines below each main idea.
- Mark cards that call for visual aids.
- Write your ending word for word on the last note card.

Create your note cards. Look over the notes cards on the next page. Then create a note card for each important part of your oral presentation— introduction, main points, and ending.

Using Note Cards

Below are a few of the note cards from Deigo's presentation. They show how he synthesized the research from his report. Notice that for the note cards in the body of his report, Diego starts with a main point. The rest of the note card gives relevant reasons for his conclusion.

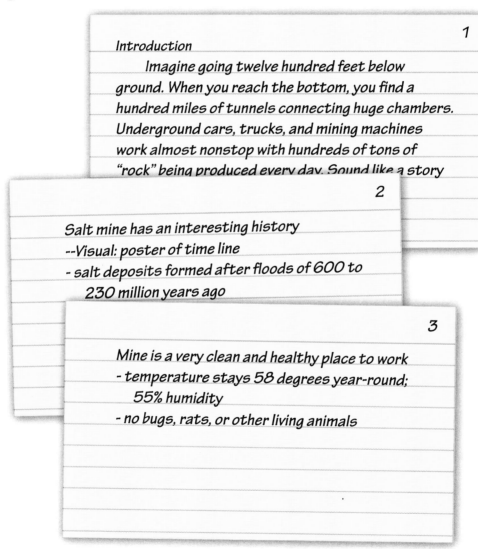

1

Introduction

Imagine going twelve hundred feet below ground. When you reach the bottom, you find a hundred miles of tunnels connecting huge chambers. Underground cars, trucks, and mining machines work almost nonstop with hundreds of tons of "rock" being produced every day. Sound like a story

2

Salt mine has an interesting history
--Visual: poster of time line
- salt deposits formed after floods of 600 to
    230 million years ago

3

Mine is a very clean and healthy place to work
- temperature stays 58 degrees year-round;
    55% humidity
- no bugs, rats, or other living animals

RESEARCH

Review your note cards. Make sure that the note cards for the body of your presentation state your main idea and then include relevant reasons for the conclusions you draw.

TEKS 8.25C

Delivering Your Speech

The words are just the beginning of your speech. You will need to present your findings in a meaningful format in order to reach your audience. Your posture, gestures, and facial expressions communicate meaning as strongly as what you say. To inform your audience, you will need to make sure that your voice and body send the same message as your words. The following suggestions can help.

Using Body Language

1 **Stand up straight but stay relaxed.** If you look calm and confident, your audience is less likely to be distracted and more able to focus on the information you present.

2 **Pause for a moment before you begin.** Take a breath and think about what you're going to say.

3 **Look at your audience.** If maintaining direct eye contact with your listeners distracts you, look slightly above their heads.

4 **Use your hands.** In a relaxed way, point to a visual aid or emphasize a point.

Using Your Voice

Your voice is the instrument that adds meaning to what you say. The three expressive characteristics of voice are *volume, tone,* and *speed*.

Volume
Speak loudly enough so that everyone can hear you.

Tone
Change your tone and add expression to your voice to keep your audience engaged.

Speed
Slow down. The most common vocal fault of oral presenters is speaking too fast.

Practice and present. Using the tips above, practice giving your oral presentation in a meaningful format. Ask a friend or family member to listen to your speech and give you suggestions for improvement.

Overcoming Stage Fright

Most people feel nervous about speaking in front of a group. It's normal to have stage fright sometimes, but there are things that you can do to help yourself relax.

1 Be prepared.

Practice makes a big difference. Rehearse your speech often, especially in front of friends or family. Get used to having an audience.

2 Pause before you start.

When you get in front of the audience, pause to lay out your notes, think about what you're going to say, and take a deep breath.

3 Focus.

Concentrate on giving your speech. Visualize what comes next. Avoid distractions.

Using a Checklist

Practice your presentation using the checklist below. Videotape yourself or have someone evaluate your performance. That way you can identify areas that you need to improve.

_____ **1.** I stand up straight, and I look relaxed.

_____ **2.** I keep my head up and maintain eye contact with my audience.

_____ **3.** My voice is loud and clear.

_____ **4.** My voice and appearance both send the same message.

_____ **5.** I speak at a natural pace (not too fast or too slow).

_____ **6.** I avoid "stalling" words like *um, er,* and *like.*

_____ **7.** My visual aids are large and easy to understand.

_____ **8.** I use my hands for emphasis and to point out my visual aids.

Presentation Tips

Before your presentation . . .

- **Decide what to include.**
  Choose the most important information from your report and use note cards to put your information in order.
- **Prepare visuals.**
  Make visual aids that will help your audience better understand your research.
- **Practice.**
  Give your speech in front of a mirror or for a friend or family member. Adjust for timing and try to remember as much as you can without looking at your note cards.

During your presentation . . .

- **Speak loudly, slowly, and clearly.**
  Be sure that everyone can hear you. Don't rush through your speech.
- **Use body language.**
  Stand straight and tall. Relax as much as possible. Make eye contact with your audience and use appropriate gestures and facial expressions.
- **Hold visual aids so that everyone can see them.**
  Make the most out of your visuals. Use them to make your point.

After your presentation . . .

- **Answer questions.**
  Clarify any information that your listeners ask about. Refer them to your visuals if necessary.
- **Make closing comments.**
  Summarize the listeners' questions and concerns.

 Practice and present. Deliver your speech one final time before a friend or someone at home. Then present your speech to the class. Afterward, listen for suggestions from your teacher and classmates.

TEKS 8.17D

Research Writing

Multimedia Presentations

Anyone who uses a computer has seen multimedia in action on encyclopedia CD's, on Internet sites, and even in word-processing software. A multimedia presentation is a powerful means of expression that can be presented to a large group. When you can add pictures, sounds, animation, and video to a report, you bring your writing to life and keep the audience interested.

There are several kinds of software that you can use to produce multimedia presentations. With assistance from some of this software, and a little imagination, you'll be able to connect with your audience in a new, dynamic way.

What's Ahead

- **Creating Computer-Generated Slide Shows**
- **Creating Video Presentations**
- **Creating Web Pages**
- **Interactive Report Checklist**

460

Computer-Generated Slide Shows

With the help of a computer, you can design a slide show complete with graphics and sound effects. Your computer-generated slide show will make the important parts of your report clearer and more interesting.

Prewriting **Selecting a Topic and Details**

For your computer-generated slide show, choose a report that you've already written, something that interests you and your audience. Ask a group of peers to review your report and tell what parts they found most interesting. Plan to focus on those parts of your report. You will probably need to summarize most of the information. Then find and create one or more of the following graphics or sound effects to add to your slides:

- **Pictures** such as photos or clip art
- **Animations** that show a process, tell a story, or make a transition
- **Videos** of something you've filmed yourself
- **Sounds and music** to use as background or to make a point

 Make a plan and organize your ideas by creating a list or media grid like the one below.

Media Grid

Main Ideas	Pictures	Animations or Music	Sounds
1. A hundred-year-old salt mine lies under Detroit.	photo of Detroit skyline	background music	
2. Early settlers found saltwater spring; mine opened in 1896.	picture of 1896 mine operation		mining sounds

 Gather details. Use your list or media grid to select ideas for sounds and graphics to include with each slide. Create the graphics or sounds yourself or find them on the Internet. Save the images (credit any sources) and sounds on your computer in a special folder for this report.

TEKS 8.14E, 8.17D,
8.22A, 8.22B, 8.25B, 8.25C

Drafting **Preparing Your Slide Show**

Before you prepare your report, you need to make a *storyboard*. A storyboard is a "map" of the slides you plan to use in your report. (See the sample storyboard on the next page.) Begin by formulating a major research question that will serve as the controlling idea for your presentation. Then, using your list or media grid as a guide, include each main idea or conclusion in one box in the storyboard. Then add links from these boxes to supporting details for each idea, or to relevant reasons for each conclusion. This will be the plan for your slide show.

Now use your computer software to design the slides. Choose a font that is easy to read. Use graphics and sounds you found earlier, and consider using bulleted lists and graphs to present your findings in a meaningful format. Make your slide show "user-friendly" by making it easy to get around in the report. Use navigation buttons, such as arrows or the words "Next" and "Back."

Create a storyboard. Refer to your list or media grid to help you map out your report on a storyboard. Include details of what you want your audience to see and hear. Once you have a storyboard that works, create your own multimedia presentation in the form of a computer-generated slide show.

Revising **Improving Your Slide Show**

Since your audience is on their own in this type of report, it's important to double-check that you have presented your information in a meaningful format. Have your teacher or several friends or family members test your slide show to make sure that it works as it should. Ask them to tell you if it is clear, interesting, and easy to get around.

Get feedback. If your "testers" have good suggestions, revise the text and design of your report where necessary.

Editing **Checking for Conventions**

Check the text on each slide for grammar, punctuation, capitalization, and spelling errors. Consider asking an adult or a classmate to check your slides, too.

Make corrections. After you've made corrections, go through the report once more to make sure it works well.

RESEARCH

 TEKS 8.17D, 8.22B

Interactive Report Storyboard

Here is the map, or storyboard, for a computer-generated slide show based on the research report "Man-Made Caves of Salt." (See pages 406–411.) Since each user goes through the slide show alone, the text, graphics, images, and sounds need to share the report's information as completely and clearly as possible. (Gold boxes contain additional information on linked slides.)

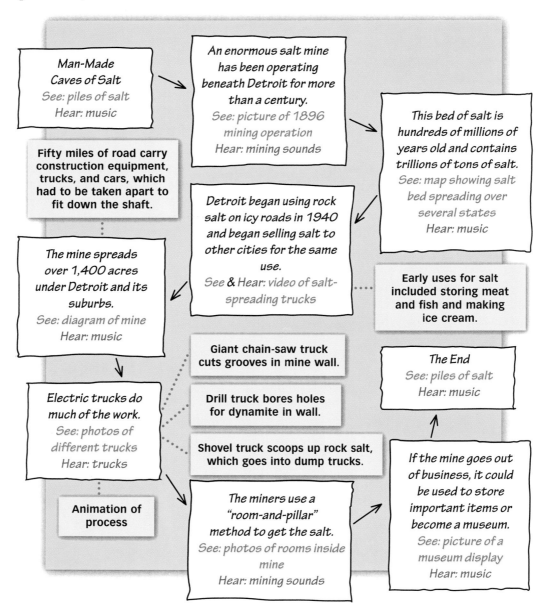

TEKS 8.17D, 8.22A, 8.22B

RESEARCH

Creating Video Presentations

You can create a video presentation to share information about your research topic. Using interviews and video clips of places and things, combined with images and sounds, you can tell a story that will inform and engage your audience. A video is an excellent choice if you want to create a persuasive presentation. For example, Diego could make a video persuading people that the salt mine is a great place to work.

Prewriting Selecting a Topic and Details

For your video presentation, select a report that you have already written. Then choose one aspect of the report that could be a good topic for a persuasive video. Consider how you might use the following elements:

- **Interviews:** experts, witnesses, other relevant sources of information
- **Video clips:** places or things you've filmed yourself
- **Images:** can be included between video clips
- **Voice-overs:** narration over images or videos to give more information
- **Reports:** scripted and read on-camera by you or other actors
- **Re-enactments:** or re-creations of events filmed by you

Decide what part of your report to use to create a video presentation. Make a plan by filling in a story map like the one below. Brainstorm elements to include that would be especially persuasive to your audience.

	Beginning	Middle	End
Idea	Getting to work	A work day	Benefits of working in the mine
Video elements	Pictures: outside mine, elevator; voice over	Video of miners coming to work, safety equipment; voice over	Interview with Yeling--voice over w/ pictures of clean mine.

Gather details. Use your story map as a guide to plan your video. Create a special folder for this report on your computer to store all images (credit any sources), videos, and audio clips you gather.

 TEKS 8.14E, 8.17D, 8.23A, 8.25C

Drafting Preparing Your Video

After you have used a story map to plan your video presentation, use the map as a guide in writing a script. The script should include text for all the words that will be spoken during your video. This includes words read by your narrator or voice-over person, interview questions, and dialogue for re-enactments and re-creations. As you write your script, include directions telling what images or video clips will occur when. This will help you organize your film clips and images.

 Create your multimedia presentation. Use a computer software program to piece together the elements you have collected for your video. Refer to your script as you work to ensure that you present your video in a meaningful format.

Revising Editing Your Video

Watch your video presentation from beginning to end several times. Look for places to edit the content for length and be sure you have coordinated images and videos with the correct voice-over clips. Consider using titles at certain sections to identify speakers or locations.

When you feel confident that your video is ready, have your teacher and several friends or family members view it for you. Ask them if the video makes sense and whether it was persuasive. Also ask whether anything was unclear and if anyone has questions.

 Incorporate feedback. Consider all feedback from your reviewers. Decide if the feedback will improve your multimedia presentation and incorporate suggestions where needed.

Editing Checking for Conventions

Check the text on any headings, titles, and credits in your video for errors in grammar, punctuation, capitalization, or spelling. Consider asking an adult or a classmate for help.

 Make corrections. After you've made corrections, go through your video one last time to make sure you are happy with the final result.

Creating Web Pages

Web pages are a way to share information from your research report with a much larger audience. You can inform people about your topic using images, text, and links to other resources on the Internet.

Prewriting Selecting a Topic and Details

For your Web pages, choose a report that you have already written. Paraphrase or summarize the main points of your topic. Consider which parts of your report will be most interesting to a wider audience. Think about the kind of information you could use on a Web page to better explain each main topic. Here are a few examples.

- Pictures such as photos or clip art
- Text from your report that you can paraphrase or summarize
- Sounds and music that can be embedded to help make a point
- Links to other Web sites with images, supporting details, and further information

 Summarize or paraphrase the main points in your report and organize them using a flow chart like the one below. The top box is your main topic. The boxes in the second row are the supporting details for the main topic. The last row shows links to other Web pages that give further evidence to explain the topic.

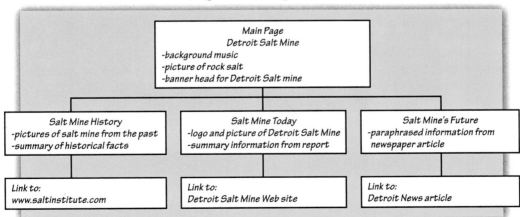

Main Page
Detroit Salt Mine
-background music
-picture of rock salt
-banner head for Detroit Salt mine

Salt Mine History
-pictures of salt mine from the past
-summary of historical facts

Salt Mine Today
-logo and picture of Detroit Salt Mine
-summary information from report

Salt Mine's Future
-paraphrased information from newspaper article

Link to:
www.saltinstitute.com

Link to:
Detroit Salt Mine Web site

Link to:
Detroit News article

Gather details. Use your flow chart as a guide in gathering the necessary information to create your Web pages. Take note of any sources that you will need to cite on your page. Also be sure to accurately write down all Internet addresses you wish to link to your pages.

TEKS 8.17D, 8.23D, 8.25A

Drafting Preparing Your Web Pages

Follow the flow chart that you created as you make your Web pages. Select the best evidence to explain your main topic and each of the subtopics in your plan. Then use a computer software program to design your pages.

Your main page should attract the audience's attention. Use images, music, and titles that draw them in and make them want to learn more. On your main page, include links to each of the subtopics. Then create a separate page for each of those subtopics.

The subtopic pages should combine relevant images with the content from your report. These are the pages that will give more in-depth information about your topic. If possible, provide links to other Web pages that support your facts. Make sure you provide links only to reliable and valid Web sites.

Be sure not to overload your pages with text. Break up blocks of text with images or links. Also make links visible and clear so users can easily navigate to pages within your site and to sources outside of your Web pages.

Create Web pages. Use software along with your flow chart to create your own multimedia presentation in the form Web pages. Be sure to include evidence to support your main topic and each of your subtopics.

Revising Improving Your Web Pages

Invite friends or family members to navigate your Web pages. Ask them if your pages are easy to follow and if the information is complete and useful. Be sure to have them test each of the links on your pages to make sure they are working correctly. Also be sure that you summarized or paraphrased information correctly. Plagiarism is common on Web sites, but that does not mean it's acceptable. Be sure to use your own words and cite all your sources.

Fix glitches. Correct all missing or broken links in your Web pages. Also check that you've cited sources and that your pages are clear and easy to navigate.

Editing Checking for Conventions

Check the text on your Web pages for grammar, mechanics, and spelling errors. Consider asking an adult or classmate to check your work, too.

Make corrections. After you've made corrections, go through the Web pages once more to make sure they work well.

TEKS 8.17D, 8.25A, 8.25B, 8.25C

Multimedia Presentation Checklist

Use the following checklist to make sure each presentation is the best it can be. When you can answer all of the questions with a "yes," it's ready!

Focus and Coherence

_____ **1.** Did I create a presentation that is clear and focused?

_____ **2.** Did I synthesize the research and present it in a meaningful format?

_____ **3.** Does my presentation make sense to my audience?

Organization

_____ **4.** Is my presentation easy to navigate or use?

_____ **5.** When needed, does my presentation have a clear beginning, middle, and end?

_____ **6.** Have I presented my information in a clear, organized way?

Development of Ideas

_____ **7.** Does my presentation marshal evidence to explain my topic?

_____ **8.** Have I effectively paraphrased and summarized information?

_____ **9.** Did I draw conclusions about the topic?

_____ **10.** Did I give relevant reasons for my conclusions?

Voice

_____ **11.** Do I use a natural, authentic voice in my presentation?

_____ **12.** Do I engage my audience and sustain the connection throughout my presentation?

RESEARCH

LISTEN respect

TEXAS WRITE SOURCE Online
www.hmheducation.com/tx/writesource

ELPS 2C, 2G, 3E, 3G, 4G

The Tools of Language

Learning Language

Work with a partner. Read the meanings and share answers to the questions.

1. Strategies are plans that help you achieve something.
   What two strategies can you use to do research?
2. Vocabulary is a list of words that are explained or defined.
   What are some vocabulary words you have learned this year?
3. A model is an example of something.
   How can you use a writing model to help you write?
4. When you sum up, you tell only the most important parts.
   When might it be better to sum up a story rather than give a lot of details?

clarify speak observe

Listening and Speaking

Is being a good listener the same thing as having good hearing? Not really. If your ears are doing one thing and your mind is doing something else, you aren't really listening. Listening, like other skills, takes practice and concentration.

Similarly, there is a big difference between speaking and merely talking. Speaking takes effort. Learning to speak effectively and listen closely will make you more successful in school and in life.

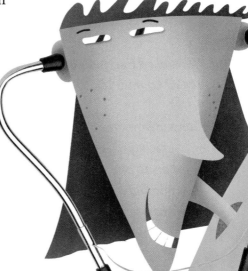

"Be a good listener. Your ears will never get you in trouble."
—Frank Tyger

What's Ahead

- Listening in Class
- Participating in a Group
- Speaking in Class

ELPS 2D, 5G

Listening in Class

When you really listen, you're doing more than simply hearing the words that are being said. Listening involves thinking about what you are hearing. The following tips will help you become a better listener.

1 **Know why you're listening.** What is the speaker trying to tell you? Is there going to be a test? Are you being given an assignment?

2 **Listen for the facts.** Listen for *who, what, when, where, why,* and *how.* The 5 W's and H will help you identify the most important information. If you do not understand something, ask the speaker for clarification.

3 **Take notes.** When you hear important information, write it down in your notebook. Also write down questions you have and ask them later so that you can complete your notes.

4 **Put the lecture into your own words.** Paraphrase the speaker's statements as you take notes. Add your own comments and draw conclusions about the main points.

 Take notes in your own words. The next time you take notes in class, practice putting the ideas in your own words. Also add your own comments as you think about the main points.

> *Westward Expansion*
> *1800 to mid-1800s*
>
> *Pioneer women—status different in West than in East*
> - *Laura Ingalls Wilder—wrote stories of westward movement*
>   *(stories still popular)*
> - *Annie Bidwell—social activist, Chico, CA*
> - *Slave women—gained freedom in West*
> - *Wyoming—gave women right to vote in 1869 (Was it the first*
>   *state to do that?)*

A Closer Look at Listening and Speaking

Improving your listening and speaking skills will help you increase your confidence and effectiveness in school. Follow these basic guidelines to become a better listener and a better speaker.

Good Listeners . . .
- think about what the speaker is saying.
- pay attention to the speaker's tone of voice, gestures, and facial expressions.
- interrupt only when necessary to ask questions.

Good Speakers . . .
- speak loudly and clearly.
- maintain eye contact with their listeners.
- emphasize their main ideas by changing the tone and volume of their voice.

LANGUAGE

 Focus on speaking and listening skills by doing the activity below.

1. Gather two classmates and number yourselves 1, 2, and 3.
2. Person 1 will take person 2 aside and read the paragraph below.
3. Person 2 will then take person 3 aside and repeat the paragraph from memory.
4. Person 3 will repeat the paragraph from memory to the other two classmates.
5. Compare the original paragraph to what person 3 reports.

Lieutenant Colonel Arthur Whitson was a United States Air Force pilot for 21 years. He spent some of his time flying weather planes into typhoons in the South Pacific. His crew also tracked radioactive winds, which were clues to when and where the Soviets were testing nuclear bombs. Once Whitson's plane was shot at over Vietnam. He had to dump his cargo of jet fuel, but he and his crew survived.

ELPS 3E, 3G

Participating in a Group

Working with others requires planning. Even if everyone listens politely and speaks clearly, the group needs leadership and a common goal. The guidelines below will help you organize a group discussion.

Guidelines for Group Discussion

- **Choose a chairperson.** This leader should keep the group focused and make sure everyone gets a chance to participate. Rather than choosing the same chairperson for each meeting, let each group member have a turn.
- **Select a record keeper.** The group needs someone to take notes and write down important decisions.
- **Define the topic or focus.** Be sure everyone participates when deciding on the group's goals.

Group Discussion Tips

- **Before you speak,** think about what others have said.
- **Share your thoughts** in a positive and constructive way.
- **Always be respectful,** especially when you disagree with someone.
- **Stick to the topic** or focus.

 Imagine yourself in the situations below. Which of the group guidelines or discussion tips above might have prevented each situation from happening? Explain to a partner.

Situation 1	There is a disagreement about what the group decided last week.
Situation 2	You realize that you are repeating something that has already been said.
Situation 3	One group member speaks twice as often as anyone else, and another member doesn't speak at all.

Group Skills

It's fun to belong to a group that gets something done. When each member listens closely and responds clearly, the whole group can succeed. Listening and speaking in a group is actually a step-by-step process, and when everyone practices these "steps," meetings will go smoothly.

Begin by **listening.**

1
- Think about what the speaker is saying.
- Make eye contact with the speaker.
- Take notes on the speaker's main ideas.

Follow up by **clarifying.**

2
- Ask questions about things that confuse you.
- Repeat what you've heard in your own words to see if your understanding is correct.

Continue by **responding.**

3
- Think before you speak.
- Comment on the issue, not on the person.
- Be honest and respectful.

LANGUAGE

Read the sentences and questions below and discuss your answers with two or three of your classmates. Remember to ask questions or ask for clarification if you do not understand what the speaker is saying.

1. Jasmine thinks that it would be rude to criticize another person in her group.
   Is Jasmine correct?

2. Raul already has his mind made up about what José is talking about. Should he sit quietly, looking out the window, until José finishes speaking?

Speaking in Class

Speaking in class is a skill everyone needs to master. A good classroom discussion depends on cooperation. These basic strategies will help you and your classmates become better speakers.

Before You Speak . . .

- Listen carefully and take notes.
- Think about what others are saying.
- Wait until it's your turn to speak.
- Plan how you can add something positive to the discussion.

When You Speak . . .

- Use a loud, clear tone.
- Stick to the topic.
- Avoid repeating what's already been said.
- Support your ideas with examples.
- Maintain eye contact with others in the group or class.

Play "Who Am I and Where Am I?" Warm up your speaking skills by playing the following game.

1 Form groups of five students. Have each group choose a speaker.

2 The speaker looks at the lists below and chooses one person and one place. Then the speaker begins to speak like that person in that place.

3 The first person to correctly guess the person and place becomes the next speaker.

People	Places
teacher	at the beach
athlete	in school
doctor	on a bus
police officer	in the dentist's chair
rock star	on a cattle ranch
carpenter	standing in line

Learning Language

When it comes to writing, there are many new words and ideas to learn. *The writing process, the traits of writing, prewriting, drafting*, and *revising* are just a few of them.

If you play baseball or softball, you know that there is a vocabulary, or certain group of words, related to these sports. Without words such as *pitcher's mound, out, strike zone*, and *infield*, you would have a hard time playing these games.

The vocabulary related to writing works in the same way. Without knowing the meaning of *prewriting, drafting*, and *revising*, you would have a hard time writing a strong story or report. This chapter will help you learn all about the language of writing so you can do your best work!

What's Ahead

- **Language of the Writing Process**
- **Language of the Writing Traits**
- **Language of the Writing Forms**

 **ELPS** 2C, 2D, 2H, 3D

Language Strategies

You hear new words in conversation every day. Here are some strategies to help you understand, remember, and use the new words that you hear.

Listen for Language Patterns

In a language pattern, a word or phrase is repeated. Paying attention to the repeated word or phrase helps you understand its meaning.

You hear: Isabel **learned something new at** the street fair.
You hear: Anna **learned something new at** the aquarium.
You can say: I **learned something new at** summer camp.

 Turn to a partner. Say two or more sentences that include the phrase *learned something new at*.

Talk Around the Problem Word

If you don't know a word, use familiar words instead. Then ask someone to tell you the word.

You can say: Our teacher told us to use a brief story, or slice of life, as an example in our essay. What is that kind of story called? (Anecdote)

 The next time you don't know the correct word to use, talk around it. Then ask a friend to tell you the word.

Use Academic Language

Your teachers may use unfamiliar words in class. Repeating the words will help you remember them.

You hear: Try to use a metaphor in your essay.
You repeat: metaphor

 Listen in class and repeat words you think you may not remember. Then try using them in different sentences.

Ask "Did I say that correctly?"

If you are unsure whether you've used language correctly, ask a classmate or a teacher.

You can say: I put the photo in the wood square. Did I say that correctly?

When you don't know the correct name for something, use the word or phrase you think is correct. Then ask if you've used the language correctly.

Teach a Friend

To remember new words, use them to teach someone you know, such as a friend, family member, or classmate.

You hear: The climate, or kind of weather, in Florida is very nice.
You can say: The climate in our area is too cold sometimes.

Explain something to a classmate, using a new word you have learned. Help your classmate understand the new word, too.

Take Notes or Draw a Picture

Write new words in a notebook. Add information or your own drawings and graphic organizers to remember the meanings of words and how to say them. When taking notes in class, listen for the main ideas and be alert for such signal words as *most important* and *for example*.

You hear: Ants live in a colony.
What you do: You can draw a cross section of an ant colony.

You hear: Ants have a thorax, abdomen, and mandibles.
What you do: Make a chart of each part and what it does.

Keep a vocabulary journal. The next time you hear a word you want to remember, write it down. Add some words to describe it or draw a picture.

LANGUAGE

Language of the Writing Process

Read each of the terms. Then read about what they mean.

The first step in the writing process is to prewrite, or plan your writing. You determine your purpose, audience, genre, and topic. Then you generate ideas and develop a main idea.

When you are learning about writing, sometimes the purpose, audience, and genre are given to you. You learn many ways to generate ideas, such as brainstorming or using a graphic organizer. You also learn how to arrange your ideas in a way that makes them easy for the audience to understand.

When you write a first draft, you do the actual writing. As you draft, you build on your prewriting ideas. You categorize ideas into paragraphs as you go, making sure that each paragraph connects to the main idea. Remember to think about your audience and your purpose for writing as you write.

Next, you'll read your draft and revise, or make changes. When you revise, you concentrate on your ideas. You decide whether your ideas are right for the audience, purpose, and genre. You make your ideas clear and connect them to each other so that your audience understands them. You'll probably need more than one draft to get things just right.

When you edit, you look for and correct mistakes in grammar, mechanics, and spelling. You also make sure that all your sentences make sense. Make any last changes. Then make a neat final copy. This is your final draft.

Share your published work with others. Present it to your class or another audience. You may also want to submit your writing to your school newspaper or some other publication.

ELPS 2C, 2G, 2I, 3A, 3E, 4C

Vocabulary: Writing Process

audience	controlling idea	draft
edit	prewrite	publish
purpose	revise	

1 **Say the word.** Listen and read along as your teacher reads the words aloud. Then repeat each word. Try to pronounce the words as your teacher does. Notice that the word *prewrite* has a silent "w."

2 **Discover the meaning.** With a partner, make a two-column chart. List the vocabulary words in the first column and either a definition or specific example of the word in the second column. Start with the words you already know.

3 **Learn more.** Listen as your teacher explains the meaning of each word. Work with your partner to add new information to your chart. Listen and look as you teacher points to an example of the word in the classroom.

4 **Show your understanding.** Use your notebook to answer the questions below.
- Which do you do first—publish or draft?
- Should you fix a mistake in spelling when you edit or when you revise?
- What do you do when you prewrite?

5 **Write it, show it.** In your journal, add notes and drawings to help you remember what the new words mean. For example, you might write a paragraph explaining the writing process, using all the words above. Underline or highlight the vocabulary words in your paragraph.

LANGUAGE

The Writing Process in Action

You've learned the language of the writing process. Now it's time to see the process in action! First your teacher will show you how to do each step of the writing process. Then, you will write together, using the following questions. As you write together, your teacher will request that you do certain things. Be sure to follow directions and respond to your teacher's requests. If you don't understand a step, try to retell, or summarize, the step with your partner.

Prewrite

1. What would you like to write about?
2. Who is your audience for this piece of writing?
3. What genre, or form, will you use to write about your topic?

Draft

1. How can you put your ideas into categories, or groups?
2. How can you organize your ideas into paragraphs?
3. How can you organize your paragraphs to support your controlling idea?

The Writing Process in Action

These pages from the first unit in your book show the writing process in action.

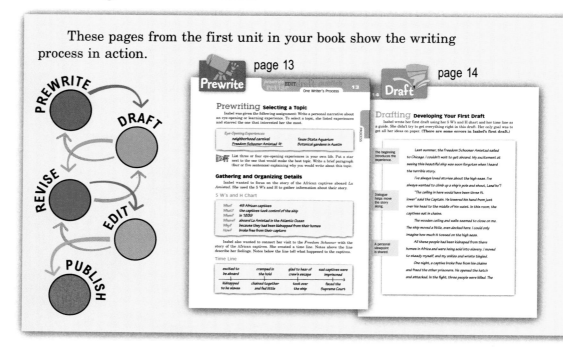

Revise

1. Do all your sentences support your controlling idea?
2. Are there any sentences you should add or take out?
3. Does each sentence and paragraph build on the ones before it?
4. Did you choose the right words for your audience?

Edit

1. Did you follow all the rules of grammar and mechanics?
2. Does each sentence make sense?
3. Are all the words spelled correctly?

Publish

1. Have you used the feedback you received to make your writing better?
2. Is your writing neat and easy to read?

Turn and Talk

Talk to a classmate about which step in the writing process takes the longest for you. Listen to his or her response.

Example: The step that takes me the longest is _____.

LANGUAGE

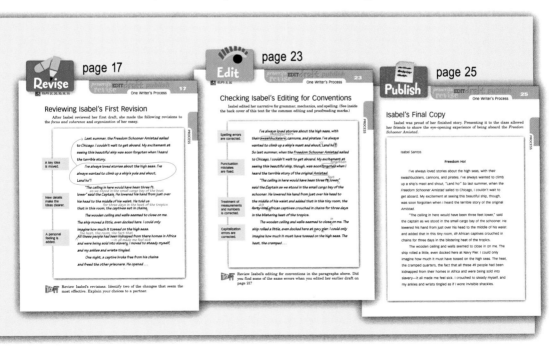

ELPS 4C

Language of the Writing Traits

Read each of these terms. Then read about what they mean.

Focus and Coherence

If your writing has focus, your controlling idea is clear and you have used specific supporting details. Coherence means that the sentences connect and work together. You need focus and coherence so that your audience understands what you are trying to say.

Organization

Your writing should be organized, or arranged in such a way that each sentence is logically linked to the next sentence. In the same way, each paragraph should build on the ones before it. All sentences should add to the reader's understanding of the controlling idea.

Development of Ideas

It is important to develop your ideas in depth. Include original thoughts and opinions. Each sentence should add meaning to the sentence that comes before it. You should also support your controlling idea with important details.

Voice

Your writing should show the way you think and feel. It should also express your personality and personal viewpoint. Your "voice" should also keep the reader interested from the first paragraph to the very end.

Conventions

Conventions include the rules of grammar, sentence structure, mechanics, and spelling. Using conventions correctly is very important. Writing that is free of errors is easier to read and understand. Your audience will concentrate on your ideas, not on your mistakes.

ELPS 2C, 2G, 2H, 3A, 3D, 3E, 5G

Vocabulary: Writing Traits

coherence	conventions	depth
focus	mechanics	organization
viewpoint	voice	

1 **Say the word.** Listen as your teacher reads the words aloud. Then repeat each word. Think about the relationship between the letters and the sounds you hear. Notice the different sounds that the vowel *o* makes when it comes at the end of a syllable, as in *coherence* and *focus*; when it comes in the middle of a syllable, as in *conventions*; when it is paired with the letter *i*, as in *viewpoint* and *voice*; and when it comes before *r*, as in *organization*.

2 **Discover the meaning.** Work with a partner. Write the words you already know in your vocabulary journal. Teach your partner the words he or she does not know. Have your partner explain the words you do not know.

3 **Learn more.** Listen as your teacher explains the meaning of each word. Work with your partner to restate the meaning of each word and add the new information to your vocabulary journal.

4 **Show your understanding.** Work with a partner and take turns asking and answering the questions below.
- How do you know if your writing has focus and coherence?
- What are some examples of writing mechanics?
- What is the difference between a controlling idea and a specific detail?
- Is your writing voice the same as a classmate's? Why or why not?

5 **Listen, say the meaning.** Work with a partner. One of you says one of the words and the other gives a definition or an example of the word. Listen to your partner's response and say if it was correct or incorrect and why.

ELPS 3G, 3H

Language of Descriptive Writing

Descriptive writing is writing that gives a detailed picture of a person, place, thing, or event. A descriptive essay has three main parts: a topic, a body that includes descriptive details, and a conclusion. Look at the graphic organizer. It shows how all the parts fit together.

Descriptive Essay Organization

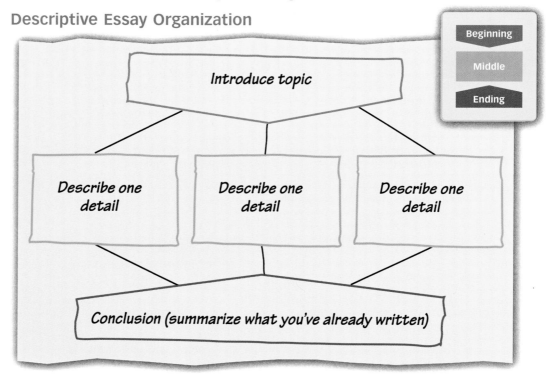

Introduce topic

Beginning
Middle
Ending

Describe one detail

Describe one detail

Describe one detail

Conclusion (summarize what you've already written)

Turn and Talk

Talk with a partner about how a graphic organizer helps a writer to organize descriptive details in a descriptive essay.

Example: The graphic organizer _____.

Vocabulary: Descriptive Writing

anecdote	describe	detail
event	location	personality trait
sensory		

1 **Say the word.** Listen and read along as your teacher reads the words. Repeat each word.

2 **Discover the meaning.** Work with a partner. Find the vocabulary words in the yellow boxes next to the writing model on pages **78–79**. Write notes about what you think the words mean.

3 **Learn more.** Listen as your teacher explains the meaning of each word. Work with a partner to find examples of each word in the writing sample on pages **78–79**. Listen and look as your teacher identifies examples of the words in your classroom.

4 **Show your understanding.** Use your notebook to answer the questions below. Your teacher will give you directions. When following directions, listen for action words such as *write*, and signal words such as *then*. These words tell you what to do and when to do it.

- Are touch, taste, smell, sound, and sight events or senses?
- What should you include in a description of a person? Write five words that describe a friend or family member.

5 **Draw, tell, listen.** In your notebook, draw a picture that helps you remember what each word means. Take turns explaining and comparing your drawings to a partner.

LANGUAGE

ELPS 2G, 2H, 2I, 3E, 3G, 4C, 5B

Reading the Descriptive Model

What Do You Know?

Next you will read "The Price of Danger," a writing model about someone whose life has changed because of an accident. Do you know someone, or have you heard of or read about someone, who has overcome a difficult challenge in his or her life? What did they have to overcome? How do you describe a person like that?

Build Background

People who have injuries from accidents often have to have physical therapy. They work with a physical therapist, a person who is an expert in special exercises to heal injuries.

Listening

Listen as your teacher or a classmate reads "The Price of Danger" aloud. As you listen, make notes about the topic, descriptive details, and the writer's feelings about the person he or she is describing. Compare your notes with a partner and work together to answer the questions below.

1. How does the writer feel about the person?
2. Name three personality traits that the writer uses to describe the person.
3. Briefly retell an anecdote that the writer uses to describe the person.

Key Descriptive Words

look like	**one day**	**size**
size	**strong**	**taught me**
the best thing about		

Look at the words in the box. You will see these words when you read the sample essay. With a partner, use the words to talk about someone you know who overcame a challenge. Include an anecdote that shows the person's personality. Write a short paragraph describing the person.

Read Along

Now it's your turn to read. Read along as your teacher or classmate reads pages **78–79** aloud. As you read, think about what the writer thinks about the person described and the details used to support that idea.

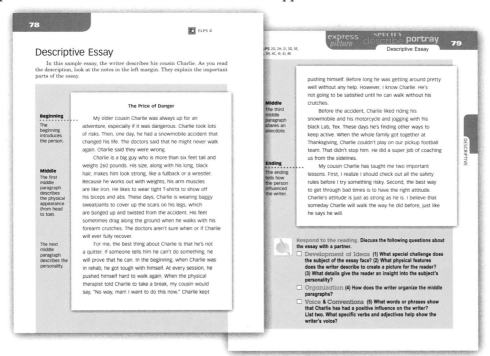

After Reading

On a sheet of paper, write or draw answers to the following questions about the writing model.

1. What did Charlie look like before the accident?

2. Give a specific example of why the writer thinks Charlie has the right attitude.

3. How did Charlie keep active before the accident? What does he do now?

ELPS 3G, 3H

Oral Language: Descriptive Writing

The person or people who listen to you or read your writing are called the *audience*. When you speak or write, it is important to choose the best words for your audience. When you write, your tone—or the attitude you express—will be different for different audiences.

 Read about the situation below. Then choose two audiences from the list. With a partner, talk about how you might describe the two actors differently for each audience.

Situation

> You just saw two of your friends act in the school play. You enjoyed the play very much, and you want to describe your friends' roles and costumes.

Audiences

- Your closest friend
- A parent of one of the actors
- The school newspaper

⭐ **ELPS** 2G, 2I, 3G, 3H, 5G

Effective Talk

When you answer a question, you might use a few words, a sentence, or a few sentences. When you use more details to tell about something, the other person will have a better understanding. Follow the directions below to learn how to add more detail.

Read the question and the answers below. In the first box, there are only three words. In the second box, there is a short sentence. The third answer has more detail and does a better job answering the question.

How would you describe a character in the last play you saw?

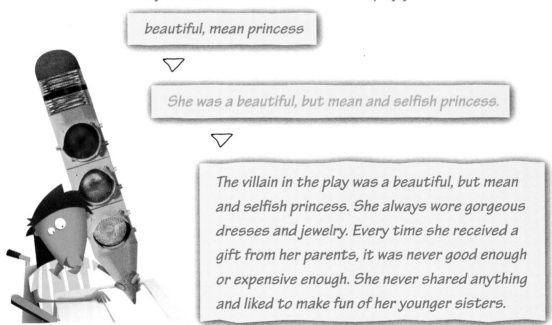

beautiful, mean princess

▽

She was a beautiful, but mean and selfish princess.

▽

The villain in the play was a beautiful, but mean and selfish princess. She always wore gorgeous dresses and jewelry. Every time she received a gift from her parents, it was never good enough or expensive enough. She never shared anything and liked to make fun of her younger sisters.

LANGUAGE

Try IT Choose a question to talk about with a partner. Write two or three ideas for answering the question. Next, add details that will help your partner understand your ideas. Finally, use your notes as you and your partner discuss your answers to the questions.

Here are some ideas to get you started.

1. Describe your favorite character from a book you read recently. Why is he/she/it your favorite character?

2. How would you describe yourself to someone who has never met you?

ELPS 3G, 3H, 4C

Language of Narrative Writing

A narrative essay is writing that tells a memorable and true story about your life. Narrative essays have the same basic organization: the topic sentence introduces the topic, the body explains what happened, and the closing wraps up the story and gives the reader something to think about.

Narrative Essay Organization

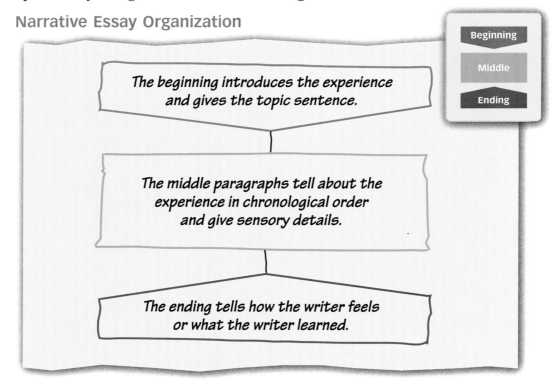

The beginning introduces the experience and gives the topic sentence.

The middle paragraphs tell about the experience in chronological order and give sensory details.

The ending tells how the writer feels or what the writer learned.

Beginning

Middle

Ending

Turn and Talk

Use the graphic organizer to talk with a partner about why the order of the parts of a narrative essay generally do not change.

Example: The order of the parts generally don't change because _____.

Vocabulary: Narrative Writing

chronological order	dialogue	memorable
narrative	personal	personality
sensory details		

1 **Say the word or phrase.** Listen as your teacher reads the words and phrases aloud. Then repeat each word. Notice how the first syllable (*per–*) is stressed in the word *personal,* but when the ending *–ity* is added to form the word *personality,* the third syllable (*–al*) is stressed.

2 **Discover the meaning.** Work with a partner to find some of the vocabulary words in the yellow boxes next to the writing model on pages 101–102. Write notes about what you think the words mean.

3 **Learn more.** Listen as your teacher explains the meaning of each word or phrase. Work with your partner to find examples of these words in the writing sample on pages 101–102. Look and listen as your teacher identifies examples of the words in the classroom.

4 **Ask and answer.** Work with a partner and take turns asking and answering the questions below.
- Why is it important to use sensory details in a narrative essay?
- Why should a narrative be about something memorable to you?
- Do you think it would be confusing if a personal experience were not told in chronological order? Why?

5 **Listen and say it.** Work with a partner. Take turns saying the definition of a word and then responding with a word that matches it. Check each other's answers.

LANGUAGE

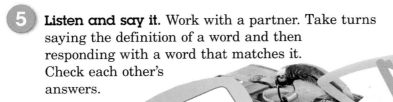

 ELPS 2G, 2H, 2I, 3E, 3G, 4C

Reading the Narrative Model

What Do You Know?

Next you will read "Getting to Know Joe," on pages 101–102. It is a narrative writing model about an experience that changed the writer's life. Have you ever met someone and not liked him or her, but then something happened to change your feelings? Have you ever had an experience that changed your life? Talk with a partner about what happened.

Build Background

In many neighborhoods, people spend a lot of time trying to make the yard in front of their house look nice. It is common for younger people in a neighborhood to help the older people take care of their yard and house, or run errands for them. This is especially true when the older person's family lives far away.

Listening

Listen as your teacher or a classmate reads aloud "Getting to Know Joe." As you listen, make notes that answer the questions *who, what, when, where,* and *why*. Compare your notes with a partner and work together to answer the questions below.

1. How does the writer describe Joe? What specific examples does he give?
2. What is one example of dialogue in the narrative?
3. How does the writer change?

Key Words

last (summer)	has really changed me
every (morning)	then one day
later	little did I know
The person who taught me	I learned

Look at the words and phrases in the box. You will see these words when you read the writing model. With a partner, use the words to talk about a memorable experience with someone that has changed your life.

ELPS 4G, 4I, 5G

Read Along

Now it's your turn to read. Turn to pages 101–102 in this book. As you read, think about what the writer thinks about the person described, and what happened to change his opinion about the person.

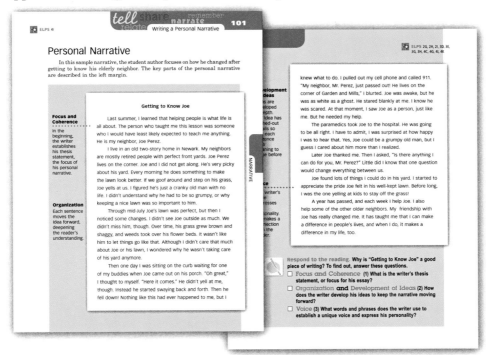

tell share remember **101**
relate narrate
ELPS 4I Writing a Personal Narrative

Personal Narrative

In this sample narrative, the student author focuses on how he changed after getting to know his elderly neighbor. The key parts of the personal narrative are described in the left margin.

Getting to Know Joe

Focus and Coherence
In the beginning, the writer establishes his thesis statement, the focus of his personal narrative.

Last summer, I learned that helping people is what life is all about. The person who taught me this lesson was someone who I would have least likely expected to teach me anything. He is my neighbor, Joe Perez.

I live in an old two-story home in Newark. My neighbors are mostly retired people with perfect front yards. Joe Perez lives on the corner. Joe and I did not get along. He's very picky about his yard. Every morning he does something to make the lawn look better. If we goof around and step on his grass, Joe yells at us. I figured he's just a cranky old man with no life. I didn't understand why he had to be so grumpy, or why keeping a nice lawn was so important to him.

Organization
Each sentence moves the idea forward, deepening the reader's understanding.

Through mid-July Joe's lawn was perfect, but then I noticed some changes. I didn't see Joe outside as much. We didn't miss him, though. Over time, his grass grew brown and shaggy, and weeds took over his flower beds. It wasn't like him to let things go like that. Although I didn't care that much about Joe or his lawn, I wondered why he wasn't taking care of his yard anymore.

Then one day I was sitting on the curb waiting for one of my buddies when Joe came out on his porch. "Oh great," I thought to myself. "Here it comes." He didn't yell at me, though. Instead he started swaying back and forth. Then he fell down! Nothing like this had ever happened to me, but I

ELPS 2G, 2H, 2I, 3D, 3E, 3G, 3H, 4C, 4G, 4I, 4K

knew what to do. I pulled out my cell phone and called 911. "My neighbor, Mr. Perez, just passed out! He lives on the corner of Garden and Mills," I blurted. Joe was awake, but he was as white as a ghost. He stared blankly at me. I know he was scared. At that moment, I saw Joe as a person, just like me. But he needed my help.

The paramedics took Joe to the hospital. He was going to be all right. I have to admit, I was surprised at how happy I was to hear that. Yes, Joe could be a grumpy old man, but I guess I cared about him more than I realized.

Later Joe thanked me. Then I asked, "Is there anything I can do for you, Mr. Perez?" Little did I know that one question would change everything between us.

Joe found lots of things I could do in his yard. I started to appreciate the pride Joe felt in his well-kept lawn. Before long, I was the one yelling at kids to stay off the grass!

A year has passed, and each week I help Joe. I also help some of the other older neighbors. My friendship with Joe has really changed me. It has taught me that I can make a difference in people's lives, and when I do, it makes a difference in my life, too.

Respond to the reading. Why is "Getting to Know Joe" a good piece of writing? To find out, answer these questions.
☐ Focus and Coherence **(1)** What is the writer's thesis statement, or focus for his essay?
☐ Organization **and** Development of Ideas **(2)** How does the writer develop his ideas to keep the narrative moving forward?
☐ Voice **(3)** What words and phrases does the writer use to establish a unique voice and express his personality?

LANGUAGE

After Reading

On a sheet of paper, write or draw answers to the following questions about the writing model.

1. At what moment did the writer see Joe differently?

2. How is the writer's life different now?

3. Is he happy to know Joe now? Why?

ELPS 3G, 3H

Oral Language: Narrative Writing

The person or people who listen to you or read your writing are called the *audience*. When you speak or write, it is important to choose the best words for your audience. When you write, the tone—or the attitude you express—will change for each audience.

 Read about the situation below. Then choose two audiences from the bottom of the page. With a partner, discuss how the words you choose might be different for each audience.

Situation

A famous football player has just visited your school. He told a story about playing football when he was a child. He was smaller than the other players and thought he wasn't good. He wanted to quit. His coach told him that he was small, but he was fast, and that he should work with his strengths. He became a great, and fast, player. You will retell this story.

Audiences

■ A friend
■ A teacher
■ A younger brother or sister

ELPS 2G, 2I, 3G, 3H, 5B, 5G

Effective Talk

When you answer a question, you might use a few words, a sentence, or a few sentences. When you use more details to tell about something, the other person will have a better understanding of what you are saying. Follow the directions below to learn how to add more detail.

Read the question and the answers below. In the first box, there are only two words. In the second box, there is a short sentence. The third answer has more detail and does a better job answering the question.

What experience did the football player share?

playing football

His coach told him not to quit.

His coach told him that he was small, but fast, and that he should concentrate on his strengths. His coach's words inspired him to keep playing. He became a great player.

Try IT Choose a question to talk about with a partner. Write two or three ideas for answering the question. Next, add details that will help your partner understand your ideas. Finally, use your notes as you and your partner discuss your answers to the questions.

Here are some ideas to get you started.

1. Tell about a time when someone inspired you.
2. Do you know a story about a person whose life changed after meeting someone? Tell your partner the story.

LANGUAGE

ELPS 3G, 3H

Language of Expository Writing

An expository essay is writing that explains information to the writer's audience. This type of writing might explain one subject, or it might compare and contrast two subjects. Most often, expository essays have the same basic organization: an introduction and controlling idea, supporting details which are categorized, and a conclusion.

Expository Essay Organization

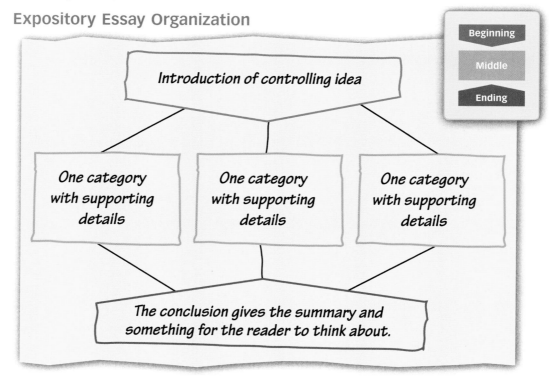

Introduction of controlling idea

Beginning

Middle

Ending

One category with supporting details

One category with supporting details

One category with supporting details

The conclusion gives the summary and something for the reader to think about.

Turn and Talk

Explain to a partner why an introduction and a conclusion are important in an expository essay.

An introduction and a conclusion are important because _____.

Vocabulary: Expository Writing

category	compare	contrast
controlling idea	explanation	expository
fact	supporting detail	

1 **Say the word or phrase.** Listen as your teacher reads the words and phrases aloud. Then repeat each word. Think about whether you have heard the words and phrases before.

2 **Discover the meaning.** Work with a partner to find some of the vocabulary words in the yellow boxes next to the writing model on pages 169–170. Write notes about what you think the words mean.

3 **Learn more.** Listen as your teacher explains the meaning of each word or phrase. Work with your partner to find examples of these words in the writing model on pages 169–170. Look and listen as your teacher identifies examples of the words in the classroom.

4 **Ask and answer.** Work with a partner and take turns asking and answering the questions below.
- Which of the following statements is a fact? Explain your answer.

   Elephants have the largest brains of any land animal.

   Elephants have the most interesting social organization of any land animal.
- Why does an expository essay need a clear controlling idea?
- How should supporting details be organized? Where should they appear in the essay?

5 **Draw and explain.** Draw pictures or diagrams to help you remember the words. Share your drawings with a partner and explain why your drawing helps you remember the word.

LANGUAGE

 ELPS 2G, 2H, 2I, 3E, 3G, 4C, 5B

Reading the Expository Model

What Do You Know?

Next you will read "Centuries of Protection," an expository writing model about armor throughout history. What do you know about armor? Have you seen pictures or movies where knights are wearing armor? Have you seen any in a museum? What do you think it's like to wear armor like that? Do you know what soldiers and police officers wear today to protect themselves?

Build Background

Armor has been used to protect soldiers in battle for centuries. Throughout history, people have used animal hides, leather, bone, and different metals to protect their bodies from injury. The typical full suit of metal armor worn by medieval knights in Europe could weigh as much as 65 pounds. However, noblemen could get their armor fitted to their bodies, so it was easier to move around in. Armor was also worn by Japanese samurai and Chinese warriors. Aztec and Inca warriors wore heavy quilted jackets for protection. Some Native American tribes wore breastplates made of bone.

Listening

Listen as your teacher or a classmate reads aloud "Centuries of Protection." Compare your notes with a partner and work together to answer the questions below.

1. How are the paragraphs organized? What categories does the writer use?
2. How does the writer contrast the different types of armor?
3. What final thought does the writer give for the reader to think about?

Key Expository Words

even though	however	the next type
types of	while	

Look at the words in the box. You will see some of these words in the writing model. With a partner, use the words to talk about something that has changed over time, such as transportation, computers, clothes, or music. Then use the words to write sentences to explain your ideas.

Read Along

Now it's your turn to read. Read along as your teacher or classmate reads pages 169–170 aloud. As you read, think about the controlling idea and the details used to support that idea.

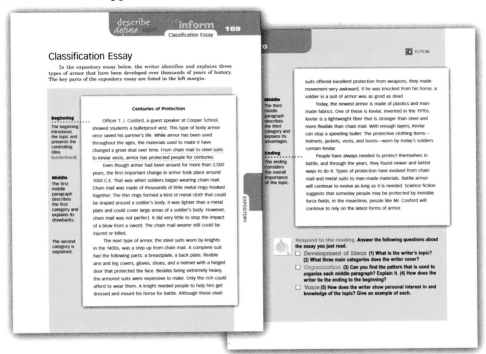

describe solve **inform** 169
define
Classification Essay

Classification Essay

In the expository essay below, the writer identifies and explains three types of armor that have been developed over thousands of years of history. The key parts of the expository essay are listed in the left margin.

Centuries of Protection

Beginning
The beginning introduces the topic and presents the controlling idea. (underlined).

Officer T. J. Cosford, a guest speaker at Cooper School, showed students a bulletproof vest. This type of body armor once saved his partner's life. While armor has been used throughout the ages, the materials used to make it have changed a great deal over time. From chain mail to steel suits to Kevlar vests, armor has protected people for centuries.

Middle
The first middle paragraph describes the first category and explains its drawbacks.

Even though armor had been around for more than 2,500 years, the first important change in armor took place around 1000 C.E. That was when soldiers began wearing chain mail. Chain mail was made of thousands of little metal rings hooked together. The thin rings formed a kind of metal cloth that could be draped around a soldier's body. It was lighter than a metal plate and could cover large areas of a soldier's body. However, chain mail was not perfect. It did very little to stop the impact of a blow from a sword. The chain mail wearer still could be injured or killed.

The second category is explained.

The next type of armor, the steel suits worn by knights in the 1400s, was a step up from chain mail. A complete suit had the following parts: a breastplate, a back plate, flexible arm and leg covers, gloves, shoes, and a helmet with a hinged door that protected the face. Besides being extremely heavy, the armored suits were expensive to make. Only the rich could afford to wear them. A knight needed people to help him get dressed and mount his horse for battle. Although these steel

EXPOSITORY

ELPS 5G

suits offered excellent protection from weapons, they made movement very awkward. If he was knocked from his horse, a soldier in a suit of armor was as good as dead.

Middle
The third middle paragraph describes the third category and explains its advantages.

Today, the newest armor is made of plastics and man-made fabrics. One of these is Kevlar, invented in the 1970s. Kevlar is a lightweight fiber that is stronger than steel and more flexible than chain mail. With enough layers, Kevlar can stop a speeding bullet. The protective clothing items—helmets, jackets, vests, and boots—worn by today's soldiers contain Kevlar.

Ending
The ending considers the overall importance of the topic.

People have always needed to protect themselves in battle, and through the years, they found newer and better ways to do it. Types of protection have evolved from chain mail and metal suits to man-made materials. Battle armor will continue to evolve as long as it is needed. Science fiction suggests that someday people may be protected by invisible force fields. In the meantime, people like Mr. Cosford will continue to rely on the latest forms of armor.

Respond to the reading. Answer the following questions about the essay you just read.
- ☐ Development of Ideas **(1)** What is the writer's topic? **(2)** What three main categories does the writer cover?
- ☐ Organization **(3)** Can you find the pattern that is used to organize each middle paragraph? Explain it. **(4)** How does the writer tie the ending to the beginning?
- ☐ Voice **(5)** How does the writer show personal interest in and knowledge of the topic? Give an example of each.

LANGUAGE

After Reading

Copy the chart on a sheet of paper and fill it in with details about each category of armor.

Category 1	Category 2	Category 3

Oral Language: Expository Writing

The person or people who listen to you or read your writing are called the *audience*. When you speak or write, it is important to choose the best words for your audience. In writing, the tone—or the attitude you express—will be different for each audience.

 Read about the situation below. Then choose two audiences from the list. With a partner, talk about how you might describe the situation differently for each audience.

Situation

You've been asked to explain which is your favorite school subject and why. You have also been asked to contrast your favorite subject with another subject you don't like as much.

Audiences

- Your closest friend
- A parent
- A teacher

ELPS 2G, 3G, 3H

Effective Talk

When you answer a question, you might use a few words, a sentence, or a few sentences. When you use many details to tell about something, the other person will better understand what you are saying.

Read the question and the answers below. In the first box, there are only two words. In the second box, there is a short sentence. The third answer has more detail and does a better job answering the question.

Why is _____ your favorite school subject?

> *fun, interesting*

▽

> *Science is a fun and interesting subject.*

▽

> *We learn so many interesting things in science class. One of my favorites is how the human body works. It helps me understand how I can see, smell, feel, taste, and hear things around me. I don't enjoy English class as much because it's not about facts.*

LANGUAGE

Try IT

Choose a question to talk about with a partner. Write two or three ideas for answering the question. Next, add details that will help your partner understand your ideas. Finally, use your notes as you and your partner discuss your answers to the questions.

Here are some ideas to get you started.

1. What are the two best things about your school? Explain your answer.
2. What is the most important school subject for your future? Give at least two reasons you think this.

ELPS 2C, 3E, 3G, 3H

Language of Persuasive Writing

A persuasive essay is writing that tries to persuade, or convince, others to believe or do something. Most persuasive essays are organized in the same way. The opening paragraph explains the writer's opinion, or controlling idea. The middle paragraphs discuss the reasons for the writer's opinion and address possible concerns or objections that readers may have. The closing paragraph summarizes the writer's reasoning and may call the reader to action.

Persuasive Essay Organization

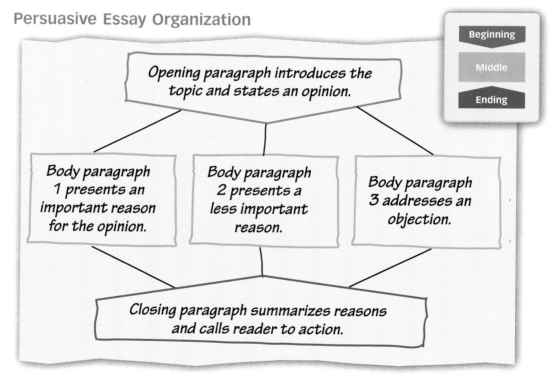

Beginning

Middle

Ending

Opening paragraph introduces the topic and states an opinion.

Body paragraph 1 presents an important reason for the opinion.

Body paragraph 2 presents a less important reason.

Body paragraph 3 addresses an objection.

Closing paragraph summarizes reasons and calls reader to action.

Turn and Talk

Describe to a partner two important parts of the graphic organizer.

Example: The graphic organizer shows _____ and _____.

ELPS 2C, 2G, 2H, 2I, 5B

Vocabulary: Persuasive Writing

call to action	**convince**	**objection**
opinion	**persuasive**	**propose**
quotations	**solution**	

1 **Say the word.** Listen and read along as your teacher reads the words aloud. Repeat each word.

2 **Discover the meaning.** Work with a partner to find some of the vocabulary words in the yellow boxes next to the writing model on pages **239–240**. Write notes about what you think the words mean.

3 **Learn more.** Listen as your teacher explains the meaning of each word. Work with your partner to find examples of the words in the writing sample on pages **239–240**.

4 **Show your understanding.** Use your notebook to answer the questions below.

- When might a person write a persuasive essay?
- What is the difference between an opinion and a fact?
- How does a call to action make a persuasive essay more effective?

5 **Write it, show it.** In your notebook, add pictures or drawings to help you remember the meaning of each word. You can also add simple definitions using your own words. For example, next to *call to action*, you might write *something the reader can do*.

LANGUAGE

ELPS 2G, 2H, 2I, 3G, 4C

Reading the Persuasive Model

What Do You Know?

Next you will read pages 239–240, a persuasive letter model. In the letter, a student tries to convince the principal to make study hall more open. What do you know about study hall? What is the difference between open and closed study hall? What are the advantages and disadvantages of each type?

Build Background

Many schools offer study hall as a way to help students get homework done while they are still at school. This allows students to get help from teachers or to use resources at school. In an open study hall, students are allowed to move about the school. In a closed study hall, students must stay in one room throughout the period.

Listening

Listen as your teacher or a classmate reads the persuasive letter model aloud. As you listen, make notes about the problem and the writer's opinion about how the problem should be solved. Be ready to answer the questions below.

1. What information does the writer give to explain the problem?
2. What solution does the writer propose?
3. What does the writer want the principal to do?

Key Persuasive Words

choices	consider	important
information	informed	shared
support		

Look at the words in the box. These words are in the writing sample. With a partner, use the words to talk about a problem at your own school or in your community.

ELPS 4G, 4I, 5G

Read Along

Now it's your turn to read. Turn to pages 239–240. Read the sample persuasive letter as your teacher or a classmate reads it aloud.

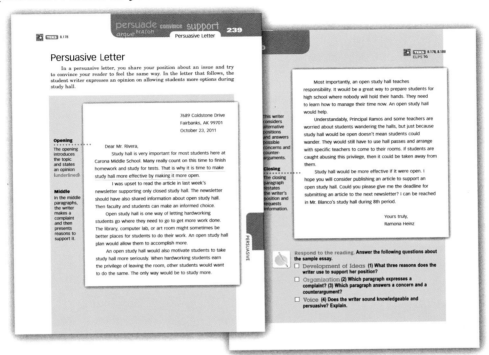

After Reading

Copy the following chart on a piece of paper and fill it in with information from the persuasive letter. Use your chart to summarize the writing model with a partner.

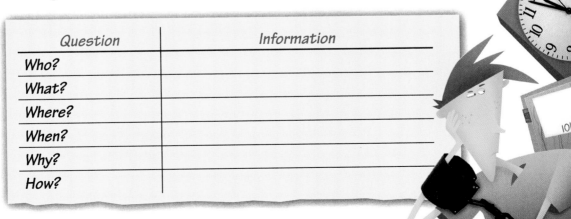

Question	Information
Who?	
What?	
Where?	
When?	
Why?	
How?	

ELPS 3G, 3H

Oral Language: Persuasive Writing

The person or people who listen to you or read your writing are called the *audience*. When you speak or write, it is important to choose the best words for your specific audience. Likewise, when you write, your tone—or the attitude you express—will be different for each audience.

 Read about the situation below. Then choose two audiences from the list shown. With a partner, explain how you might approach the idea of healthier food choices differently for each audience.

Situation

You would like to see healthier food choices offered in the school cafeteria. You feel students make poor food choices because they have no other options. You will explain your opinion, provide reasons and examples to support your opinion, and provide a call to action.

Audiences

- A classmate
- The school principal
- A newspaper editor

Effective Talk

When you answer a question, you might use a few words, a sentence, or a few sentences to explain your ideas. Explanations include details that help readers understand. When you use many details, the reader will have a better understanding.

Read the question and answers below. In the first box, there are only three words. In the second box, there is a short sentence. The third answer has more detail and does a better job answering the question.

Why is it important to offer healthy food choices in the school cafeteria?

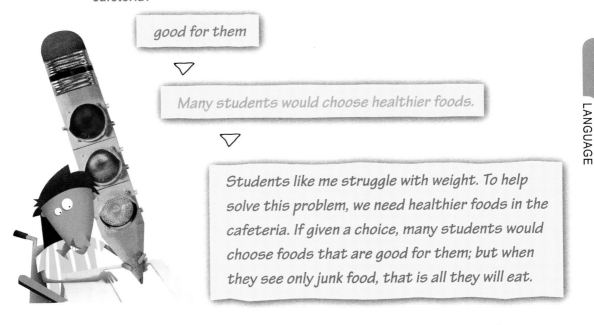

good for them

Many students would choose healthier foods.

Students like me struggle with weight. To help solve this problem, we need healthier foods in the cafeteria. If given a choice, many students would choose foods that are good for them; but when they see only junk food, that is all they will eat.

LANGUAGE

 Choose a new question to talk about with a partner. Write down two or three details that would help you convince your partner that the problem is serious and that students at your school should help solve it. Then use your notes to persuade your partner.

Here are some ideas to get you started.

1. What is a problem at your school that you hear a lot of students complain about? What can they do to help solve the problem?
2. What is a problem in your community that students at your school can help solve? What can students do?

ELPS 2C, 3E, 3G, 3H

Language of Response Writing

A response tells about something you read, usually a book or story. Response writing allows you to connect characters and themes and to show that you understand the story. Most response essays have the same basic organization. The beginning paragraph introduces the book or story and focuses on the theme. Middle paragraphs explain different stages in the development of the theme. The ending paragraph revisits and summarizes the theme.

Response to Literature Essay Organization

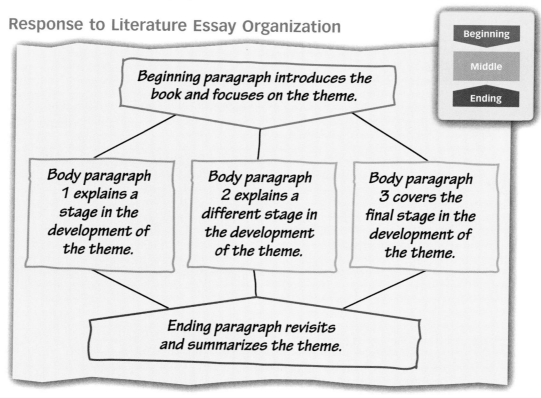

Beginning

Middle

Ending

Beginning paragraph introduces the book and focuses on the theme.

Body paragraph 1 explains a stage in the development of the theme.

Body paragraph 2 explains a different stage in the development of the theme.

Body paragraph 3 covers the final stage in the development of the theme.

Ending paragraph revisits and summarizes the theme.

Turn and Talk

Explain to a partner how to organize a response to literature essay.

Example: A response to literature essay is organized _____.

ELPS 2C, 2G, 2H, 2I, 5B

Vocabulary: Response Writing

characters	development	events
focus	lesson	quotation
stage	theme	organization

1 **Say the word.** Listen and read along as your teacher reads the words aloud. Repeat each word.

2 **Discover the meaning.** Work with a partner to find the vocabulary words in the yellow boxes on pages 305–306. Discuss words you know and write notes about what you think the words mean.

3 **Learn more.** Listen as your teacher explains the meaning of each word. Check and correct your notes. Write meanings of additional words. Work with your partner to find examples of the words in the writing model on pages 305–306.

4 **Show your understanding.** Discuss with a partner the answers to the questions below.
- What is the purpose of a response to literature essay?
- How can you use quotations in a response to literature essay?
- What should the middle paragraphs of a response to literature include?

5 **Write it, show it.** In your notebook, add drawings to help you remember the meaning of each word. Share your work with a partner and discuss ideas for ways to remember the words.

LANGUAGE

ELPS 2G, 2H, 2I, 3G, 4C

Reading the Response Model

What Do You Know?

On pages 305–306, you will read a sample response model that a student wrote about a novel. The book is about two high school students who meet an unusual man named Mr. Pignati. Have you ever had an encounter with an unusual person? What can you learn about yourself or about people in general by getting to know people who are different from you?

Build Background

The Pigman was written by Paul Zindel in 1968, and is written from the point of view of the two main characters. By using two narrators with slightly different points of view, Zindel gives the reader a more well-rounded picture of the story. In some cases, the narrators comment on what the other has written, letting the reader see the same events from two different viewpoints.

Listening

Listen as your teacher or a classmate reads "Pigman's Lesson." As you listen, make notes about the story, the characters, and the writer's thoughts about the theme. Think about how well the writer develops his or her ideas of the theme. Be ready to answer the questions below.

1. Who is Mr. Pignati, and what role does he play in the story?
2. What theme does the writer discuss in the essay?
3. Does the writer do a good job of discussing each state in the development of the theme? Why or why not?

Key Response to Literature Words

experiences	character	learned
valuable	lesson	realize
situation	story	

Look at the words in the box. These words are in the writing sample. Work with a partner. Take turns using the words to describe a story or book you have read.

ELPS 4G, 4I

Read Along

Now it's your turn to read. Turn to pages 305–306. Read the model response to literature as your teacher or a classmate reads it aloud.

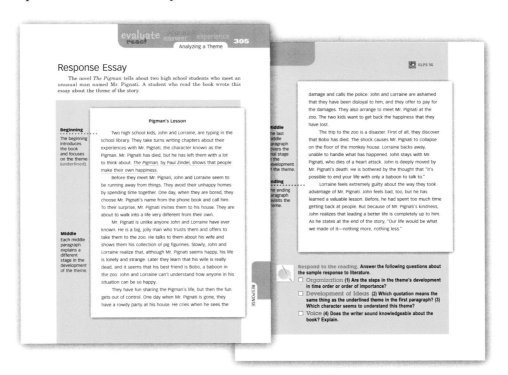

After Reading

Copy the following diagram on a piece of paper and fill it in with information from the model response to literature. Use the diagram to summarize the writer's development of the theme.

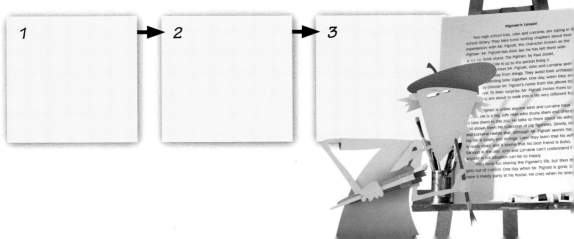

1 → 2 → 3

ELPS 3G, 3H

Oral Language: Literature Response

The person or people who listen to you or read your writing are called the *audience*. When you speak or write, it is important to choose the best words for your specific audience. Likewise, when you write, your tone—or the attitude you express—will be different for each audience.

 Read about the situation below. Then choose two audiences from the list shown. With a partner, explain how you might describe the theme of the book differently for each audience.

Situation

You have read a story about a boy named Julio who has to help a neighbor with his chores. At first the neighbor is not nice to Julio and does not appreciate his help. In time, however, Julio notices that the man has come to depend on him. This is a book about friendship and the rewards of helping others. You will explain the theme of the book.

Audiences

- Elementary school student
- Your teacher
- Elderly neighbor

ELPS 2I, 3G, 3H, 5G

Effective Talk

When you answer a question, you might use a few words, a sentence, or a few sentences to explain your ideas. Explanations include details that help readers understand. When you use more details to tell about something, your readers get a better understanding of what you're trying to say.

Read the question and answers below. In the first box, there are only three words. In the second box, there is a short sentence. The third answer has more detail and does a better job answering the question.

What is the theme of the book?

helping is good

Helping someone in need is good for both the person who needs help and the person who helps.

Helping others is not always about getting paid or hearing "thank you." Sometimes just knowing that you are doing a good thing by helping someone in need is the only "thanks" you need.

With a partner, choose a new question that relates to a story you have both read recently. Make notes about details that would give your partner more information about your ideas. Then use your notes to describe your ideas to your partner.

Here are some ideas to get you started.

1. What traits does the main character have that make me like or dislike him or her?

2. What is the most important event in this book?

LANGUAGE

ELPS 2C, 3E, 3G, 3H

Language of Creative Writing

Creative writing is writing that uses imagination to convey meaning. Stories are one type of creative writing. In some stories, the main character is presented with a conflict and must make a difficult decision that somehow changes him or her. The character often faces a series of challenges that build suspense before the conflict is finally resolved. The chart below shows the general pattern that many stories follow.

Creative Writing Organization

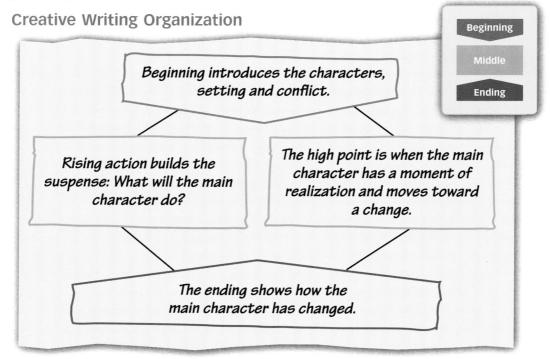

Beginning introduces the characters, setting and conflict.

Rising action builds the suspense: What will the main character do?

The high point is when the main character has a moment of realization and moves toward a change.

The ending shows how the main character has changed.

Beginning

Middle

Ending

Turn and Talk

Explain to a partner why a story's plot should follow the order shown in the graphic organizer.

Example: A plot should following the order shown in the graphic organizer because _____.

Vocabulary: Creative Writing

characters	**conflict**	**change**
decision	**high point**	**plot**
rising action	**setting**	**suspense**

1 **Say the word.** Listen and read along as your teacher reads the words aloud. Repeat each word. Notice that the letters "ch" sound like a hard *c* in the word *character*. This is an exception to the rule. The letters "ch" usually make the sound at the beginning of the word *change*.

2 **Discover the meaning.** Work with a partner to find some of the vocabulary words in the yellow boxes on pages **366–367**. Discuss the words you know and write notes about what you think they mean.

3 **Learn more.** Listen as your teacher explains the meaning of each word. Check and correct your notes. Add definitions where necessary. Work with your partner to find examples of the words in the writing sample on pages **366–367**.

4 **Show your understanding.** Discuss with your partner the answers to the questions below.

- What are some ways to introduce characters and setting?
- How can you identify the high point in a story?
- Why is it important for the main character to resolve a conflict by the end of a story?

5 **Write it, show it.** In your notebook, write sentences to help you remember the meanings of the words. Share your work with a partner and try to think of examples of each word, using books you both have read.

LANGUAGE

ELPS 2G, 2H, 2I, 3G, 4C

Reading the Creative Model

What Do You Know?

Next you will read pages 366–367, a creative writing model about a young man who learns to be more sensitive to others in his family. What are some things you've really wanted for your birthday? Did you always get what you wanted? How did you feel when you didn't get what you wanted? How did you react, and how did you feel about your reaction?

Build Background

Many families struggle to make ends meet when a parent or other caregiver loses a job. A person who wants a job but does not have one is considered "unemployed." Without a job, it can be difficult to pay bills, and there often is no money to buy "extras," such as birthday gifts. Finding a new job may be tough, especially as people get older. Some employers may tell them they are overqualified, or have too much experience. When a parent or caregiver is unemployed, all family members need to pitch in to help save money.

Listening

Listen as your teacher or a classmate reads "Shifting Gears." As you listen, make notes about the main character, setting, conflict, rising action, and high point of the plot. Be prepared to answer the questions below.

1. What is the conflict of the story?

2. What happens at the high point of the story?

3. How does Felipe change by the end of the story?

Key Creative Essay Model Words

ashamed	disappointment	expensive
help out	out of work	promised
secondhand	unemployment	

Look at the words in the box. You will see these words as you read the writing sample. Working with a partner, use the words to talk about what happens when a family is faced with the loss of a job. Take turns describing how the family might feel about and deal with the loss. Talk about the changes they need to make and how their lives may be different.

Read Along

Now it's your turn to read. Turn to pages 366–367. Read the creative writing model as your teacher or a classmate reads it aloud.

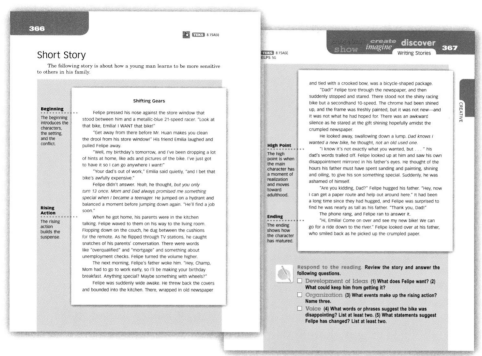

366

TEKS 8.15A(ii)

Short Story

The following story is about how a young man learns to be more sensitive to others in his family.

Shifting Gears

Beginning

The beginning introduces the characters, the setting, and the conflict.

Felipe pressed his nose against the store window that stood between him and a metallic-blue 21-speed racer. "Look at that bike, Emilia! I WANT that bike!"

"Get away from there before Mr. Huan makes you clean the drool from his store window!" His friend Emilia laughed and pulled Felipe away.

"Well, my birthday's tomorrow, and I've been dropping a lot of hints at home, like ads and pictures of the bike. I've just got to have it so I can go anywhere I want!"

"Your dad's out of work," Emilia said quietly, "and I bet that bike's awfully expensive."

Felipe didn't answer. *Yeah*, he thought, *but you only turn 13 once. Mom and Dad always promised me something special when I became a teenager.* He jumped on a hydrant and balanced a moment before jumping down again. "He'll find a job soon."

Rising Action

The rising action builds the suspense.

When he got home, his parents were in the kitchen talking. Felipe waved to them on his way to the living room. Flopping down on the couch, he dug between the cushions for the remote. As he flipped through TV stations, he caught snatches of his parents' conversation. There were words like "overqualified" and "mortgage" and something about unemployment checks. Felipe turned the volume higher.

The next morning, Felipe's father woke him. "Hey, Champ, Mom had to go to work early, so I'll be making your birthday breakfast. Anything special? Maybe something with wheels?"

Felipe was suddenly wide awake. He threw back the covers and bounded into the kitchen. There, wrapped in old newspaper

367

TEKS 8.15A(ii)
ELPS 5G

show imagine create discover
Writing Stories

and tied with a crooked bow, was a bicycle-shaped package.

"Dad!" Felipe tore through the newspaper, and then suddenly stopped and stared. There stood not the shiny racing bike but a secondhand 10-speed. The chrome had been shined up, and the frame was freshly painted, but it was not new—and it was not what he had hoped for. There was an awkward silence as he stared at the gift shining hopefully amidst the crumpled newspaper.

He looked away, swallowing down a lump. *Dad knows I wanted a new bike*, he thought, *not an old used one.*

High Point

The high point is when the main character has a moment of realization and moves toward adulthood.

"I know it's not exactly what you wanted, but . . . " his dad's words trailed off. Felipe looked up at him and saw his own disappointment mirrored in his father's eyes. He thought of the hours his father must have spent sanding and painting, shining and oiling, to give his son something special. Suddenly, he was ashamed of himself.

"Are you kidding, Dad?" Felipe hugged his father. "Hey, now I can get a paper route and help out around here." It had been a long time since they had hugged, and Felipe was surprised to find he was nearly as tall as his father. "Thank you, Dad!"

The phone rang, and Felipe ran to answer it.

Ending

The ending shows how the character has matured.

"Hi, Emilia! Come on over and see my new bike! We can go for a ride down to the river." Felipe looked over at his father, who smiled back as he picked up the crumpled paper.

Respond to the reading. Review the story and answer the following questions.

☐ **Development of Ideas (1)** What does Felipe want? **(2)** What could keep him from getting it?

☐ **Organization (3)** What events make up the rising action? Name three.

☐ **Voice (4)** What words or phrases suggest the bike was disappointing? List at least two. **(5)** What statements suggest Felipe has changed? List at least two.

LANGUAGE

CREATIVE

After Reading

Felipe's dad is another important character in the story, but what if he were the main character? How would the story be different? Think about how this would change the story. How would it change the rising action, high point, and ending?

Work with a partner to outline the story using Felipe's dad as the main character.

ELPS 3G, 3H

Oral Language: Creative Writing

The person or people who listen to you or read your writing are called the *audience*. When you speak or write, it is important to choose the best words for your specific audience. Likewise, when you write, your tone—or the attitude you express—will be different for each audience.

 Read about the situation below. Then choose two audiences from the list shown. With a partner, explain how the words you choose might be different for each audience.

Situation

Katrina is invited to go to an amusement park with a group of people she's long been trying to be friends with. However, she's already promised her mom that she would hang out with her cousin—whom she doesn't like. Katrina is afraid if she says no to the amusement park, she will never get another chance with this group. Katrina went with the friends. Fill in the holes in Katrina's story.

Audiences

- A friend
- Your mother
- A classmate you don't know very well

Effective Talk

When you answer a question, you might use a few words, a sentence, or a few sentences to explain your ideas. Explanations include details that help readers understand. When you use more details to tell about something, your readers better understand what you're trying to say.

Read the question and answers below. In the first box, there are only a few words. In the second box, there is a short sentence. The third answer has more detail and does a better job answering the question.

What is Katrina's conflict?

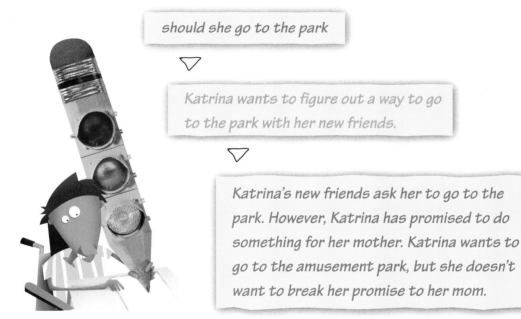

should she go to the park

Katrina wants to figure out a way to go to the park with her new friends.

Katrina's new friends ask her to go to the park. However, Katrina has promised to do something for her mother. Katrina wants to go to the amusement park, but she doesn't want to break her promise to her mom.

Try It Choose a new question that you would like to discuss with a partner. Write two or three ideas for answering the question. Next add details that will help your partner better understand your ideas. Finally, use your notes to discuss your answers to the questions.

Here are some ideas to get you started.

1. How would you feel if a friend canceled plans you had made together?

2. How would you decide between keeping a promise to someone close to you and getting to do something you really want to do?

LANGUAGE

ELPS 2C, 3E, 3G, 3H

Language of Research Writing

Research writing shares the results of an investigation of a topic. Most research reports include a beginning that gives the controlling idea, or why you are writing the report. The middle paragraphs give details about the topic. The ending sums up the writing and may give another interesting fact. Sources are listed on a separate piece of paper.

Research Writing Organization

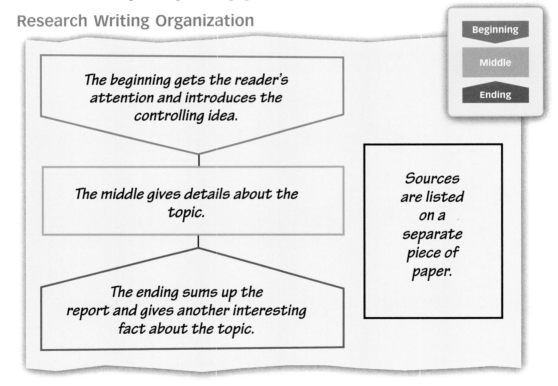

The beginning gets the reader's attention and introduces the controlling idea.

The middle gives details about the topic.

The ending sums up the report and gives another interesting fact about the topic.

Sources are listed on a separate piece of paper.

Beginning

Middle

Ending

Turn and Talk

Explain to a partner why each part of a research report is important to the whole report.

Example: The beginning is important because it _____.
The middle is important because it _____.
The ending is important because _____.
The sources are important to list because _____.

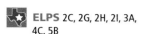
Vocabulary: Research Writing

controlling idea	details	expert
facts	headings	interesting
quotation	readers' attention	sources
summarize	topic	

1 **Say the word.** Listen and read along as your teacher reads the words aloud. Pay attention as your teacher says the words that end in *-ing*. Repeat each word, being careful to pronounce them correctly.

2 **Discover the meaning.** Work with a partner to find some of the vocabulary words in the boxes next to the writing model on pages 406–411. Discuss the words you know and write notes about what you think the words mean.

3 **Learn more.** Listen as your teacher explains the meaning of each word. Check and correct your notes. Add definitions where necessary. Work with your partner to find examples of the words and how they are used in the writing sample on pages 406–411.

4 **Show your understanding.** Discuss with your partner the answers to the questions below.

- Why is it important to grab your reader's attention right away?
- What is the purpose of the controlling idea?
- How do quotations add credibility to a research report?
- Where do you list the sources for quotations?

5 **Write it, show it.** In your notebook, write sentences or create drawings to help you remember what each word means. For example, you can draw an outline of a research report and label the parts, such as *headings*, to show where each one appears. Work with a partner to figure out ways to remember words you cannot illustrate.

LANGUAGE

ELPS 2G, 2H, 2I, 3G, 4C

Reading the Research Model

What Do You Know?

Next you will read pages 406–411, a research report model about a salt mine that lies beneath the city of Detroit, Michigan. What do you know about the history of salt? What do people use salt for today? What do you think it would be like to work in a salt mine?

Build Background

Millions of years ago, salt formed under ground, including under the city of Detroit, Michigan. During the late 1800s, people started to dig the salt out of an underground mine there. Today people still make a living working in the salt mine.

Detroit is a city of just under one million people. The population is diverse, with people from all different ethnic backgrounds. Throughout the 20th century, the city played a large role in the industrialization of the country. Today Detroit is well-known for its car industry and its music.

Listening

Listen as your teacher or a classmate reads "Man-Made Caves of Salt." As you listen, make notes about the salt mine in Detroit, Michigan. Be prepared to answer the questions below.

1. What role has salt played throughout history?
2. How did the salt mine form in Detroit?
3. How is the salt from the mine used today?

Key Research Writing Words

according to	artist	interview
geologists	manager	Salt Institute
salt mine	scientists	sources

Look at the words in the box. You will see these words as you read the writing sample. With a partner, use the words to talk about the different sources the writer used to write the sample research report. Discuss how sources make the report more interesting and credible.

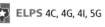

ELPS 4C, 4G, 4I, 5G

Read Along

Now it's your turn to read. Turn to pages **406–411**. Read the sample research report as your teacher or classmates read it aloud.

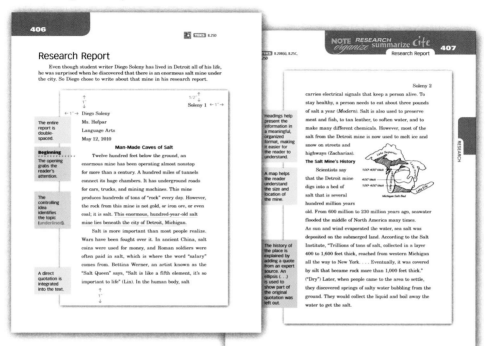

After Reading

On a separate piece of paper, write answers to these questions about the writing model.

1. How has the value of salt changed over time?

2. In 1940, Detroit became the first city to use salt for what?

3. How is the salt from the mine used today?

4. What are two ways Detroit's salt mine may be used in the future?

Oral Language: Research Writing

The person or people who listen to you or read your writing are called the *audience*. When you speak or write, it is important to choose the best words for your specific audience. Likewise, in writing, your tone—the attitude you express—will be different for each audience.

 Read about the research topic below. Then choose two audiences from the list shown. Think about what each audience would be interested in knowing about your topic. With a partner, explain how the words and examples you choose might be different for each audience.

Topic

From 1492 to 1504, Christopher Columbus made a total of four transatlantic journeys to the Caribbean and South America. It was on his third trip, in 1498, that he set foot on the mainland of America. He has often been credited with "discovering" the New World, but other explorers had visited North America many years before him.

Audiences

- Younger sibling
- Your teacher
- An elderly neighbor

Effective Talk

When you answer a question, you might use a few words, a sentence, or a few sentences to explain your ideas. Explanations include details that help readers understand. When you use more details to tell about something, your readers get a better understanding of what you're trying to say.

Read the question and answers below. In the first box, there is only one word. In the second box, there are a few words. The third answer has more detail and does a better job answering the question.

What do you know about Christopher Columbus?

explorer

explorer who set foot in America

Christopher Columbus was an Italian explorer who helped the Europeans explore and colonize the New World. Many people think he discovered America, but other explorers had been to North America before he arrived.

LANGUAGE

Choose someone from the past or present who explored unknown places whom you would like to learn more about. Discuss with a partner the explorers you are interested in. Make notes about questions you would like to ask about this person and the unknown places he or she explored. Use your notes to describe your ideas to your partner. Here are some ideas to get you started.

1. What is your definition of an explorer? Are there still unknown places today that people like to explore?
2. Is there a unique place that interests you? Who are some people who have explored that place?

Using Reference Materials

What do you do if you don't understand a word? Ask a friend? Try to guess? The most reliable source for finding the exact meaning, or meanings, of a word is the dictionary. The dictionary will give you a lot of other useful information that can help you remember the word and use it correctly.

What about when you are using the same word over and over again? A thesaurus can help you find exactly the right word for a particular context. It's where to go to find synonyms and antonyms—words that will add interest to your writing.

Together, these two resources will help you choose the right words for your writing.

What's Ahead

- **Checking a Dictionary**
- **Using a Thesaurus**

ELPS 4C, 5B

Checking a Dictionary

A dictionary is the most reliable source for learning the meanings of words. It offers the following aids and information.

- **Guide words** are located at the top of every page. They show the first and last entry words on a page, so you can tell whether the word you're looking up is listed on that page.

- **Entry words** are the words that are defined on the dictionary page. They are listed in alphabetical order for easy searching.

- **Parts of speech** labels tell you the different ways a word can be used. For example, the word *Carboniferous* can be used as a noun or as an adjective.

- **Syllable divisions** show where you can divide a word into syllables.

- **Spelling and capitalization** (if appropriate) are given for every entry word. If an entry is capitalized, capitalize it in your writing, too.

- **Spelling of verb** forms is shown. Watch for irregular forms of verbs because the spelling can be a whole new word.

- **Illustrations** are often provided to make a definition clearer.

- **Accent marks** show which syllable or syllables should be stressed when you say a word.

- **Pronunciations** are special spellings of a word to help you say the word correctly.

- **Pronunciation keys** give symbols to help you pronounce the entry word correctly.

- **Etymology** gives the history of a word [in brackets]. Knowing a little about a word's history can make the definition easier to remember.

 Open a dictionary to any page and follow the directions below.

1. Write down the guide words on that page.

2. Find a verb and write down the verb forms listed.

3. Find an entry that gives the history of the word. Write out the etymology (history).

LANGUAGE

Dictionary Page

Guide words

Entry word

Part of speech

Syllable division

Spelling and capitalization

Spelling of verb forms

Illustration

Accent marks

Pronunciation

Pronunciation key

Etymology

carbon dioxide *n.* A colorless or odorless gas that does not burn, composed of carbon and oxygen in the proportion CO_2 and present in the atmosphere or formed when any fuel containing carbon is burned. It is exhaled from an animal's lungs during respiration and is used by plants in photosynthesis. Carbon dioxide is used in refrigeration, in fire extinguishers, and in carbonated drinks.

carbonic acid *n.* A weak acid having the formula H_2CO_3. It exists only in solution and decomposes readily into carbon dioxide and water.

car·bon·if·er·ous (kär′bə-nĭf′ər-əs) *adj.* Producing or containing carbon or coal.

Carboniferous *n.* The geologic time comprising the Mississippian (or Lower Carboniferous) and Pennsylvanian (or Upper Carboniferous) Periods of the Paleozoic Era, from about 360 to 286 million years ago. During the Carboniferous, widespread swamps formed in which plant remains accumulated and later hardened into coal. See table at **geologic time.—Carboniferous** *adj.*

car·bon·ize (kär′bə-nīz′) *tr. v.* **car·bon·ized, car·bon·iz·ing, car·bon·iz·es 1.** To change an organic compound into carbon by heating. **2.** To treat, coat, or combine with carbon.—**car′bon·i·za′tion** (kär′be-nĭ-zā′shən) *n.*

carbon monoxide *n.* A colorless odorless gas that is extremely poisonous and has the formula CO. Carbon monoxide is formed when carbon or a compound that contains carbon burns incompletely. It is present in the exhaust gases of automobile engines.

carbon paper *n.* A paper coated on one side with a dark coloring matter, placed between two sheets of blank paper so that the bottom sheet will receive a copy of what is typed or written on the top sheet.

carbon tet·ra·chlor·ide (tĕt′rə-klôr′īd′) *n.* A colorless poisonous liquid that is composed of carbon and chlorine, has the formula CCl_4, and does not burn although it vaporizes easily. It is used in fire extinguishers and as a dry-cleaning fluid.

Car·bo·run·dum (kär′bə-rŭn′dəm) A trademark for an abrasive made of silicon carbide, used to cut, grind, and polish.

car·bun·cle (kär′bŭng′kəl) *n.* **1.** A painful inflammation in the tissue under the skin that is somewhat like a boil but releases pus from several openings. **2.** A deep-red garnet.

car·bu·re·tor (kär′bə-rā′tər *or* kär′byə-rā′tər) *n.* A device in a gasoline engine that vaporizes the gasoline with air to form an explosive mixture. [First written down in 1866 in English, from *carburet*, carbide, from Latin *carbō*, carbon.]

air — air filter

choke valve

gas

gas and air mixture

float

venturi

throttle valve — float chamber

carburetor
cross section of a carburetor

ă	pat	ôr	core
ā	pay	oi	boy
âr	care	ou	out
ä	father	ŏŏ	took
ĕ	pet	ŏŏr	lure
ē	be	ōō	boot
ĭ	pit	ŭ	cut
ī	bite	ûr	urge
îr	pier	th	thin
ŏ	pot	*th*	this
ō	toe	zh	vision
ô	paw	ə	about

Checking a Thesaurus

A thesaurus is the best source for finding synonyms, or words with similar meanings. A thesaurus offers the following aids and information.

- **Guide words** are located at the top of every page. They show the first and last entry words on a page, so you can tell whether the word you are looking up is listed on that page.

- **Entry words** are listed in alphabetical order, like a dictionary. In a thesaurus, the entry words may also be hyphenated and unhyphenated compounds or phrases, as well as single words. They are often in boldface type so you can locate them more easily.

- **Parts of speech** labels tell you the different ways a word or phrase can be used. If a word has more than one part of speech, it is given a separate entry for each part of speech.

- **Synonyms** are listed after the entry word. Sometimes after the list of synonyms, there will be a note to refer you to another similar entry to find even more synonyms.

- **Definitions** are numbered and listed within the entry when a word has more than one meaning. For example, *bed* can mean *a place of rest*, or *a place where seeds are planted*. Synonyms for both meanings of *bed* are listed after their definitions.

- **Lists of examples** are given for when the writer is looking for a specific type of thing in a category. For example, the entry word *bird* might be followed by different kinds of birds, such as sparrow, bluebird, cardinal, etc.

- **Antonyms**, or words with the opposite meaning, are listed after the synonyms.

- **Slang**, idioms, and colloquial terms might also be included in an entry. Before using these words, make sure that they are appropriate for the form of writing you are doing and for your audience.

 Rewrite the following sentences, replacing the boring words with synonyms you find in a thesaurus.

1. The orange cat jumped over the fence into the mean neighbor's small backyard.
2. The fast red car drove on the wet, curving road.

LANGUAGE

compare

vary

Basic Grammar and Writing

Writing Focus

Grammar Focus

- **Subject-Verb Agreement**
- **Subordinating Conjunctions**

Learning Language

Work with a partner. Read the meanings and share answers to the questions.

1. Something that is concrete can be seen, heard, or touched.
   What is an example of something concrete?

2. Possession means ownership.
   What is something you'd like to have possession of?

MODIFY CONNECT choose

Working with Words

According to the *Oxford English Dictionary,* our language contains over a quarter of a million words—more than most other languages. No wonder a dictionary is so heavy! Lifting a dictionary can strengthen your arm, but opening one will strengthen your mind.

A sentence won't work as well without some words—*adjectives, adverbs,* and *conjunctions,* for instance. It won't work at all without certain other words—*nouns* or *pronouns,* and *verbs.* So, as you continue to read, write, and speak the English language, it will be helpful to know how, when, and where to use its parts . . . to keep it running smoothly.

What's Ahead

- Using Nouns
- Using Pronouns
- Choosing Verbs
- Describing with Adjectives
- Describing with Adverbs
- Connecting with Prepositions
- Connecting with Conjunctions

Using Nouns

A noun is a word that names a person, a place, a thing, or an idea in your writing. (See page **754**.)

Person	meteorologist, Jacob Kern, students, Mayor Blain
Place	city, Chicago, sky, Tampa, middle school
Thing	Manx cat, clouds, stopwatches, thunder
Idea	day, Sunday, strength, truth, Veterans Day

Number from 1 to 8 on a piece of paper. For each of the eight underlined nouns in the paragraph below, write whether it is a person, a place, a thing, or an idea.

1   Weather has a very big **(1)** effect on all of the world's
2 **(2)** citizens. In the **(3)** United States, the National Weather
3 Service (NWS) keeps track of the **(4)** weather. Specialized **(5)**
4 equipment at **(6)** offices across the country helps the NWS
5 collect weather data. Its **(7)** scientists prepare forecasts and
6 issue severe weather **(8)** warnings when necessary.

Proper and Common Nouns

Proper nouns name specific people, places, things, or ideas. Proper nouns are always capitalized. A **common noun** is any noun that is not a proper noun.

	Person	Place	Thing	Idea
Common	meteorologist	school	hurricane	event
Proper	Hank Rhodes	University of Oklahoma	Irma	El Niño

Common nouns   A weather event warms the surface water of the ocean and affects weather on a faraway continent.

Proper nouns   El Niño warms the surface water of the Pacific Ocean and affects weather as far away as Africa.

Make a chart like the one above. Add four of your own common nouns and four proper nouns. Be sure to capitalize the proper nouns.

Concrete, Abstract, and Collective Nouns

Concrete nouns name things that can be seen, heard, or touched.

Abstract nouns name something that you can think about but cannot see or touch.

Concrete	water	mountain	street	tree
Abstract	joy	August	dread	kindness

 Identify each underlined noun in the following sentences as concrete or abstract.

> **Example:** The <u>fury</u> of a <u>tornado</u> is hard to imagine.
>
> *abstract, concrete*

1. Often a <u>twister</u> is preceded by a series of <u>thunderstorms</u>.
2. An eerie <u>calm</u> might settle over the area when the wind stops.
3. You won't hear a <u>sound</u>—no thunder, no flocks of <u>birds</u>, no rustling leaves.
4. Suddenly, another <u>wave</u> of powerful winds begins, bending the <u>trees</u> horizontally.
5. Tornadoes inspire <u>fear</u> and <u>awe</u>, even for a team of storm <u>chasers</u>.

Collective nouns name a collection of persons, animals, or things.

Persons	group	clan	tribe	squad	family
Animals	herd	flock	litter	pod	pride

 In the five sentences above, identify the three collective nouns. (They are not underlined in the activity.)

General and Specific Nouns

When you use **specific nouns** in your writing, you give the reader a clear picture of people, places, things, and ideas. The following chart shows the difference between **general nouns** and specific nouns.

General	weatherperson	the Midwest	tool	thought
Specific	Robert Fitzroy	central Missouri	rain gauge	belief

 Write specific nouns for these general nouns: *newscaster, county, storm, emotion, road, animal.* Then write a brief paragraph, using some of your specific nouns. Read your paragraph aloud to a partner.

What can I do with nouns in my writing?

Show Possession

You can make your writing more specific by naming who (or what) possesses something. See the guidelines below. (Also see 664.4 and 666.1.)

Forming the Singular Possessive

- Add an apostrophe and an *s* to a singular noun: Emiko's **raincoat**.
- For multisyllable nouns ending in an *s* or *z* sound, the possessive may be formed in two ways: Hermes's **shoes** or Hermes' **shoes**.

Forming the Plural Possessive

- Add an apostrophe for most plural nouns ending in *s:* **the** boys' **galoshes**.
- Add an apostrophe and an *s* for plural nouns not ending in *s:* **the** women's **boots**.

 On a piece of paper list five singular nouns and five plural nouns. (Include at least two singular nouns that end in an *s* or a *z* sound.) Skip one or two lines after each noun. Then write one sentence for each noun, using the possessive form of the word.

Rename the Subject

An **appositive** renames the noun that comes before it. An appositive phrase, which is set off with commas, contains a noun.

Meteorologists predict weather changes using a barometer, a device that measures air pressure.

Cari Casey, a National Weather Service employee, **gave us a tour.**

 List the appositive phrase in each of the following sentences.

1. Dust whirls, rotating dust clouds, surround the base of tornadoes.

2. If you live near a large lake, you may have seen a waterspout, a tornado occurring over water.

3. In science class we talked about humidity, the amount of moisture in the air.

 Revise the paragraph you wrote for page 533 (or another paragraph you've written) to include at least two appositive phrases.

TEKS 8.19A(iii)

Make the Meaning of the Verb Complete

Some sentences are not complete with just a subject and a verb.

Gray clouds released. (*What* do the clouds release?)

A radio report alerted. (*Whom* did the report alert?)

When using a transitive verb like *released* or *alerted* in a sentence, you need to include a **direct object** to make the meaning of the verb complete. The direct object is a noun (or pronoun) that answers the question "what" or "whom."

Gray clouds released a downpour.   **A radio report alerted** the family.

To add further information, you might include a noun (or pronoun) that answers the question "to whom" or "for whom." This type of noun is called an **indirect object**. In order for a sentence to have an indirect object, it must also have a direct object. (For more about direct and indirect objects see **746.4–746.5**.)

The storm gave Iesha **a scare**. (The storm gave a scare *to Iesha.*)

Dad built his parents **a storm shelter behind their house**.
(Dad built a shelter *for his parents.*)

 Write the direct object in each of the following sentences. If there is an indirect object as well, write it and underline it.

Example: Each year, Texas gets many tornadoes.
> *tornadoes*

1. A recent tornado damaged many garage roofs.
2. Most thunderstorms, fortunately, do not trigger tornadoes.
3. The incredible winds show people the power of nature.

Add Specific Information

Another kind of object noun is the **object of a preposition** (see **756.7**). A **prepositional phrase** begins with a preposition and ends with an object (a noun or a pronoun). Prepositional phrases add specific information to sentences. In the examples below, they act as adverbs, telling when and where the action occurs. The object noun(s) in each prepositional phrase (underlined) below is highlighted.

Tornadoes often appear at the end **of a** storm.

They begin high off the ground **with a specific** combination
of wind, temperature, **and** moisture.

 Write a brief weather-related paragraph that includes at least five prepositional phrases. Underline the object of each prepositional phrase. (For a list of prepositions, see page **790**.)

BASIC GRAMMAR

Using Pronouns

A pronoun is a word used in place of a noun. The noun replaced, or referred to, by the pronoun is called the pronoun's **antecedent**. The arrows below point to each pronoun's antecedent. (Also see **758.1**.)

The day's temperature was so high that it broke a record.

Ms. Johnson said that she had never seen people sweat so much.

The personal pronouns listed below are the most common pronouns used by writers. (For a complete list of personal pronouns, see page **762**.)

Personal Pronouns						
I	you	he	she	it	we	they
me		him	her		us	them

Person and Number of a Pronoun

Pronouns show "person" and "number" in writing. The following chart shows which nominative, or subject, pronouns are used for the three different persons (*first, second, third*) and the two different numbers (*singular* or *plural*).

		Singular	Plural
First Person	(The person speaking)	I talk.	We talk.
Second Person	(The person spoken to)	You talk.	You talk.
Third Person	(The person spoken about)	He talks. She talks.	They talk.

Number your paper from 1–4. Write sentences that use the pronouns described below as subjects. Read your best one aloud to a classmate.

Example: first-person singular pronoun
(I) I don't like windy days.

1. third-person singular pronoun
2. third-person plural pronoun
3. second-person singular pronoun
4. first-person plural pronoun

Indefinite Pronouns

An indefinite pronoun refers to people or things that are not specifically named. Some indefinite pronouns are singular, while some are plural, and some can be either.

Indefinite Pronouns				Plural	Singular or Plural
Singular					
another	each	more	one	both	all
anybody	everybody	nobody	somebody	few	any
anyone	everyone	no one	someone	many	most
anything	everything	nothing		several	none
					some

When you use a singular indefinite pronoun as a subject, the verbs (in red below) and other pronouns that refer to the subject must also be singular. If the indefinite pronoun is plural, the verbs and other pronouns must be plural.

Singular Everybody checks his or her **rain gauge in the morning**.

Plural Many **of the gauges** have **more than an inch of water in** them.

To tell if the pronouns *all, any, most, none* and *some* are singular or plural, you must check the noun in the prepositional phrase following the pronoun.

Singular All **of the** rain **is** over for today, but **it** will return tomorrow.

or Plural (The subject *all* is singular because the noun in the prepositional phrase, *rain,* is singular.)

All **of the gauges** are **checked daily, and then** they **are emptied**. (The subject *all* is plural because the noun in the prepositional phrase, *gauges,* is plural.)

Learning Language

Read each of the sentences below. Working with a partner, find the prepositional phrase after each red pronoun. The object of the preposition will help you decide if the pronoun in red is singular or plural. Then choose the correct form of the verb in blue. Take turns reading the correct sentence.

1. All of the runners in the race (has, have) posted very fast times.
2. If any of the cake (is, are) left, you may have a piece.
3. Most of the dogs (thinks, think) that I am going to feed them.
4. None of the snow from yesterday (is, are) left on the ground.
5. It looks like most of the water (is, are) gone.

BASIC GRAMMAR

How can I use pronouns correctly?

Avoid Agreement Problems

You can make your writing clear by using pronouns properly. Remember that you must use pronouns that agree with their antecedents. (An antecedent is the noun or pronoun that a pronoun replaces or refers to.) Pronouns must agree with their antecedents in number, person, and gender. (See **764.1–764.4**.)

A cloud's electrical charges create lightning when they become separated.

Warm winds blow the positive charges high into the cloud, so its underside is full of negative charges, or electrons.

Agreement in Number

The **number** of a pronoun is either singular or plural. The pronoun must match the antecedent in number.

■ A singular pronoun refers to a singular antecedent.

Since the ground does not have a lot of negative charges, it attracts the cloud's electrons.

■ A plural pronoun refers to a plural antecedent.

The electrons are pulled to the ground, crashing into air molecules on their way down.

 Select the correct pronouns from the following list to complete the paragraphs below. (You will use one pronoun twice.)

its	them	they	it

(1) The molecules create more charged ions as _____ are pulled down to the ground, too. **(2)** The stream of electrons moves at 240 miles per second as _____ races toward the ground.

(3) The air molecules become extremely hot when the electrons collide with _____. **(4)** As hot air expands, _____ produces the sudden earsplitting noise we know as thunder. **(5)** The lightning has completed _____ electrical connection in less than a second.

TEKS 8.19C
ELPS 2C, 3D, 3E, 4C

Agreement in Person

You must choose either first, second, or third person pronouns, depending on the situation. If you start a sentence in one "person," don't shift to another "person" later in the sentence.

> *Pronoun shift:* I **have learned a lot about lightning, and with all that knowledge** you **can stay safe in a storm.**
>
> *Correct:* I **have learned a lot about lightning, and with all that knowledge** I **can stay safe in a storm.**

 For each sentence below, change the underlined pronoun so it doesn't cause a shift in person.

1. We are learning about weather in <u>their</u> science class.
2. If people knew some of the facts we're learning, <u>you</u> would be amazed.
3. Weather fascinates us, and <u>they</u> want to study it in college.
4. Once you learn about a particular kind of weather, <u>I</u> wish to see it up close.

Agreement in Gender

The **gender** of a pronoun *(her, his, its)* must be the same as the gender of its antecedent. Pronouns can be feminine (female), masculine (male), or neuter (neither male nor female).

Roy Sullivan, a park ranger, was struck by lightning seven times, but his **injuries were never life threatening.**

Grandma likes to watch lightning from her **front porch.**

 Write three sentences about the weather that contain a pronoun and its antecedent. Make sure the pronoun and antecedent agree in gender and number. In this example, the pronoun is in blue and its antecedent is in red.

The rain **was coming down so hard** it **filled up the barrel by the barn in 10 minutes.**

After you have written your sentences, read them aloud to a partner. Have your partner identify the pronoun and its antecedent.

BASIC GRAMMAR

★ TEKS 8.19C

What else should I know about pronouns?

Check for Agreement with Compound Subjects and Objects

As you know, a pronoun must agree with its antecedent. When a compound subject or object is the antecedent, different rules apply depending on the conjunction that is used.

■ If the compound subject or object is joined by the word *and,* use a **plural** pronoun to refer to the antecedent.

Andre and Jerry got out their snowboards.

(The compound subject requires the plural pronoun *their.*)

■ If the compound subject or object is joined by the word *or* or *nor,* do one of these:

● Use a **singular** pronoun when both subjects or objects or only the second one is singular.

The attendant would allow neither Andre nor Jerry to ride the lift without his ticket. (The compound object joined by *nor* requires the singular pronoun *his* because *Andre* and *Jerry* are both singular.)

● Use a **plural** pronoun when both subjects or objects or only the second one is plural.

A blizzard or snow squalls could hamper the fun if they occur.

(The compound subject joined by *or* requires the plural pronoun *they* because *squalls* is plural.)

For each of the following sentences, write the correct choice of pronouns (and verbs, in some cases) from those in parentheses.

Example: The cold, snow, and ice can be dangerous when *(they arrive, it arrives).*

they arrive

1. The cold causes hypothermia and frostbite, and *(this, these)* can result in physical damage to fingers and toes.

2. A collapsed roof or downed power lines *(is, are)* not only inconvenient; *(it is, they are)* also unsafe to approach.

3. Ice is treacherous for either a motorist or a pedestrian when *(they, he or she)* must travel.

4. People should wear hats when it's cold, but neither Shelby nor Selena will wear *(theirs, hers).*

5. Skis or a sled can prove *(their, its)* worth when a car can't get through the snow.

Use Intensive and Reflexive Pronouns

A pronoun with *self* attached—*myself, yourself, herself,* and so on—is either an **intensive pronoun** or a **reflexive pronoun**. The following chart shows how they differ. (Also see **760.2** and **760.3**.)

Reflexive Pronoun

- *Necessary* to complete the meaning of the sentence
  Nomi fanned *(what?)* **with some paper.**
- Used as an object in a sentence (direct or indirect object, object of a preposition)
  Nomi fanned herself **with some paper.**

Intensive Pronoun

- *Not necessary* to complete the meaning of the sentence
  The temperature was not so bad.
- Used to emphasize the noun before it
  The temperature itself **was not so bad.**

In the sentences below, label each pronoun as either reflexive or intensive.

1. When my grandmother finds <u>herself</u> in the midst of a heat wave, she goes to the air-conditioned library.
2. The newspaper suggests that people wearing dark clothing while in the sun are making it very difficult for <u>themselves</u>.
3. Sometimes my dad pushes <u>himself</u> in hot weather, and that makes his body work to maintain its normal temperature.
4. I <u>myself</u> don't have to worry about that; I always push <u>myself</u> just enough.
5. Most doctors <u>themselves</u> know enough to avoid the extreme heat.
6. If you find <u>yourself</u> feeling sick because of the heat, seek shelter immediately.

Write two sentences of your own. Use a reflexive pronoun in one of the sentences and an intensive pronoun in the other one. Exchange papers with a partner. Underline the reflexive pronoun and circle the intensive pronoun in each other's sentences.

BASIC GRAMMAR

Choosing Verbs

The main verb either shows action or links the subject to another word in the sentence. A helping verb "helps" to complete the main verb.

Action Verbs

An **action verb** tells what the subject is doing. Strong action verbs can bring your writing to life.

The hurricane slammed into the coast.

High winds hurl objects through the air.

Linking Verbs

A **linking verb** connects (links) a subject to a noun or an adjective in the predicate.

Common Linking Verbs	
Forms of "be"	be, is, are, was, were, am, been, being
Other linking verbs	appear, become, feel, grow, look, remain, seem, smell, sound, taste

A hurricane is a tropical cyclone.
(The linking verb *is* connects the subject *hurricane* to the noun *cyclone*. *Cyclone* is a **predicate noun**.)

The storm grows larger, often covering a circle 500 miles wide.
(The linking verb *grows* connects the subject *storm* to the adjective *larger*. *Larger* is a **predicate adjective**.)

For each sentence in the paragraph below, write the linking verb and the predicate noun or predicate adjective that follows it. (The complex sentence has two linking verbs.)

(1) In the Pacific Ocean, the term for a "hurricane" is "typhoon." **(2)** Whatever these storms are called, they can remain a threat for up to 30 days. **(3)** They are dangerous because of their strong winds and floods. **(4)** Although some people seem fearless against the rage of such storms, many people feel powerless. **(5)** For most people it is best to evacuate the area.

Helping Verbs

The simple predicate may include a **helping verb** plus the main verb. A helping verb completes the main verb in many sentences.

A category 1 hurricane will result **in minimal harm**.
(The helping verb *will* helps express future tense.)

A category 3 hurricane has hit **the town of Burnley**.
(The helping verb *has* helps express the present perfect tense.
See page **774.1**.)

The category 5 hurricane is causing **unbelievable damage in Mexico**.
(The helping verb *is* helps express ongoing action.)

 Select a helping verb from the following list to complete each sentence in the paragraph below.

must	do	will	may	has	can

The United States **(1)** _____ endured two category 5 hurricanes, in 1935 and 1969. In any such storm, high winds **(2)** _____ cause the most loss of property and life. Flooding **(3)** _____ also result in losses. The government **(4)** _____ issue an order to evacuate when a hurricane strikes. Often, people **(5)** _____ leave their homes even if they **(6)** _____ not want to.

Irregular Verbs

Irregular verbs do not follow the *ed* rule. Instead of adding *ed* to show past tense, as you would with a regular verb, an irregular verb might change. (See the list of irregular verbs on page **772**.) The chart below gives the three main parts for *write* and *swim*.

Present	Past	Past participle
I write.	**Yesterday I** wrote.	I have written.
She swims.	**Yesterday she** swam.	**She** has swum.

 On your own paper, write six sentences using the given tense of the irregular verbs listed below. Then share your best sentences with a partner.

1. tear *(past)*   **4.** give *(present)*
2. sit *(past participle)*   **5.** get *(past participle)*
3. choose *(past)*   **6.** know *(present)*

BASIC GRAMMAR

 **TEKS** 8.19C
ELPS 2I, 4C

How can I use verbs effectively?

Show When Something Happens

You can use different verb tenses to "tell time" in sentences. The three simple tenses are "present," "past," and "future." (See page **770**.)

Weather controls **our actions.** *(present)*

We left **before the thunderstorms.** *(past)*

The teams will play **tomorrow.** *(future)*

Avoid Unnecessary Tense Shift

It may happen that you will shift from one verb tense to another in the same sentence.

Sean reported *(past)* **on hurricanes, which** are *(present)* **tropical storms that often** strike *(present)* **the Atlantic coast.**

However, in most sentences, you need to avoid a shift in verb tense because it will be confusing to the reader.

Unnecessary shift in tense:

People predicted *(past)* **the weather after they** study *(present)* **its patterns.** (The verb tense incorrectly shifts from past to present.)

Corrected sentence:

People predicted *(past)* **the weather after they** studied *(past)* **its patterns.** (Both the verbs are correctly in the past tense.)

 Rewrite the following sentences to eliminate the tense shift.

1. In the past, people tried to predict the weather; they use methods such as studying animal behavior and observing the heavens.

2. In the early 1600s, people invented tools that allow their users to record weather data.

3. Scientists began to understand the atmosphere, so they start making predictions.

4. Of course, it was hundreds of years later when forecasts really will become accurate.

5. Today, weather forecasters tell us when storms threaten our area.

 Write a brief paragraph about a weather-related experience. Afterward, read your paragraph to a partner and have him or her listen for and point out any confusing shifts in verb tense.

TEKS 8.19A(i), 8.19C

Show Special Types of Action

You need perfect tense and progressive tense verbs to express certain types of times and actions. (See page 774 in the "Proofreader's Guide.") There are three perfect tenses and three progressive tenses.

	Singular	Plural
Present perfect tense states an action that began in the past but continues or is completed in the present. Use *has* or *have* + the past participle.		
Present perfect	I have studied. He or she has studied.	We have studied. They have studied.
Past perfect tense states an action that began in the past and was completed in the past. Use *had* + the past participle.		
Past perfect	I had studied. He or she had studied.	We had studied. They had studied.
Future perfect tense states an action that will begin in the future and will be completed by a specific time in the future. Use *will have* + the past participle.		
Future perfect	I will have studied. He or she will have studied.	We will have studied. They will have studied.
Present progressive tense states an action that is not yet completed. Use *am, is* or *are* + the gerund.		
Present progressive	I am studying. He or She is studying.	We are studying. They are studying.
Past progressive tense states an action that was happening at some time in the past. Use *was* or *were* + the gerund.		
Past progressive	I was studying. He or she was studying.	We were studying. They were studying.
Future progressive tense states an action that will take place at a certain time in the future. Use *will* or *are going to* + *be* + the gerund.		
Future progressive	I will be studying. We will be studying.	He or She will be studying. They will be studying.

BASIC GRAMMAR

GRAMMAR
Try IT

Write a sentence for each verb, using the stated tense:

rain (past perfect)   *listen* (present perfect)   *grow* (future perfect)

Take turns saying your sentences to a partner. After each sentence, have your partner change the verb to a progressive tense.

How else can I use verbs?

Transfer Action to an Object

You will use both transitive and intransitive verbs to express specific ideas in your writing.

Transitive verbs are always action verbs. A transitive verb needs a direct object to make its meaning complete. Remember that a direct object is a noun or a pronoun that answers the question "what" or "whom." (See page **535** and **746.4**.)

Large electrical fields in clouds cause **lightning**.
(The meaning of the transitive verb *cause* would not be complete without the direct object *lightning*.)

The cool, expanding air holds **moisture**.
(The direct object *moisture* completes the meaning of the transitive verb *holds*.)

An **intransitive verb's** meaning is complete without a direct object.

The moisture condenses **into droplets**.
(The meaning of the intransitive verb *condenses* is complete without a direct object. *Into droplets* is a prepositional phrase.)

Ice crystals form **in high altitudes**.
(The meaning of the intransitive verb *form* is complete without a direct object. *In high altitudes* is a prepositional phrase.)

Depending on how a verb is used in a sentence, it may be transitive or intransitive.

All rain actually begins **its life as snow**.
(*Begins* is followed by a direct object, *life*. *Begins* is a transitive verb.)

All rain actually begins **as snow**.
(*Begins* is intransitive because there is no direct object. *As snow* is a prepositional phrase.)

 Write whether the underlined verbs below are transitive or intransitive. For transitive verbs, write their direct object.

Ice crystals in a cloud **(1)** grow in size and weight. After a while, their weight **(2)** prevents them from staying in the cloud. As ice crystals **(3)** fall toward the earth, the warmer air below the cloud **(4)** melts the ice. As long as the surface **(5)** produces warm air, rain is the result. Otherwise, the crystals **(6)** change into snow.

TEKS 8.19A(ii)

Form Verbals

Verbals are words that are made from verbs but are used as other parts of speech. Verbals are used as nouns, adjectives, or adverbs, and they are often used in phrases. (See **780.2–780.4**.)

Gerunds

A **gerund** is a verb form that ends in *ing* and is used as a noun.

A warning **alerted us that a storm was approaching**.
(The gerund *warning* acts as a subject noun.)

I heard the ringing of the wind chimes. (The gerund phrase *ringing of the wind chimes* acts as a direct object.)

Participles

A **participle** is a verb form that ends in *ing* or *ed* and is used as an adjective.

The pounding **waves rocked the boats in the bay**.
(The participle acts as an adjective describing *waves*.)

The wind whipping through town **tore shingles loose**.
(The participial phrase acts as an adjective describing *wind*.)

Infinitives

An **infinitive** is a verb with "to" before it. An infinitive can be used as a noun, an adjective, or an adverb.

To protect ourselves **was our number one goal**.
(The infinitive phrase *to protect ourselves* acts as a subject noun.)

Our plan to shut the windows **was never carried out**.
(*To shut the windows* acts as an adjective modifying the noun *plan*.)

We watched carefully to evaluate the danger.
(*To evaluate the danger* acts as an adverb modifying the verb *watched*.)

Write a paragraph using each of the verbals listed below. Refer to the model sentences above as a guide. Share your paragraph with a partner.

1. breaking down the trees (*gerund phrase*)
2. to find shelter (*infinitive phrase*)
3. blowing (*participle*)
4. frightened by the wind (*participial phrase*)

BASIC GRAMMAR

Describing with Adjectives

Adjectives are words that describe or modify nouns or pronouns. Sensory adjectives help the reader see, hear, feel, smell, and taste what writers are describing. (Also see pages **782** and **784**.)

Without Adjectives

> Today's weather allows us to be outside. Clouds dot the sky. We can soak up the sun as we eat lunch.

With Adjectives

> Today's summer-like weather allows us to be outside. Fluffy clouds dot the blue sky. We can soak up the sun as we eat our picnic lunch.

Adjectives answer four questions: *what kind? how much? how many?* or *which one?* Remember that proper adjectives can be made from proper nouns (Africa, *African;* Japan, *Japanese*) and are capitalized.

What kind?	Spanish **moss**	tall **tree**	green **apple**
How many (Much)?	six **horses**	few **computers**	some **rain**
Which one?	that **desk**	those **papers**	last **test**

For each blank in the sentences below, write an adjective of the type called for in parentheses.

1. Yesterday was a __*(what kind?)*__ day.

2. __*(What kind?)*__ rain fell off and on all day.

3. We had __*(how many?)*__ separate storms go through overnight.

4. The __*(which one?)*__ storm was the worst.

5. It left __*(what kind?)*__ debris everywhere.

6. The window in the __*(which one?)*__ wall was shattered.

7. Today the forecast is for a __*(what kind?)*__ day.

8. Predictions show a __*(what kind?)*__ chance for rain in the morning.

9. __*(Which one?)*__ afternoon, I'll go biking.

10. A __*(how much?)*__ exercise will energize me.

Comparative and Superlative Forms

You can use comparative adjectives to compare two things. For most one-syllable adjectives, add *er* to make the **comparative form**. To compare three or more things, add *est* to make the **superlative form**.

Positive	Comparative	Superlative
small	smaller	smallest

Comparative: **Today's rainbow is** smaller **than the one we saw last week.**
Superlative: **It's probably the** smallest **one I've ever seen.**

Add *er* and *est* to some two-syllable words and use *more* or *most* (or *less* or *least*) with others. Always use *more* or *most* with three-syllable adjectives.

Positive	Comparative	Superlative
tiny	tinier	tiniest
forceful	more forceful	most forceful

Comparative: **The wind last night was** more forceful **than it is tonight.**
Superlative: **The wind is** most forceful **during a tornado.**

NOTE Some adjectives use completely different words to express comparison. For example, *bad, worse, worst.* (See 784.6.)

 Write the positive, comparative, or superlative form of the underlined adjective to fill in the blanks in each of the following sentences.

1. There were some <u>violent</u> storms last summer, but this past week's storms have been _____ than those. I think the _____ storm occurred last night.

2. Fargo, North Dakota, is a <u>snowy</u> city, and Buffalo, New York, is a _____ city, but the _____ city in the United States is Blue Canyon, California.

3. It gets _____ in Chicago, but it's _____ in Dodge City, Kansas. Mt. Washington, New Hampshire, with gusts of more than 200 miles per hour, is the <u>windiest</u> place in the nation.

4. Yuma, Arizona, is not a very _____ place; however, Las Vegas is even <u>less humid</u> than Yuma. The _____ city in the United States is Milford, Utah.

How can I strengthen my writing with adjectives?

Use Effective Adjectives

If you avoid overused adjectives (*nice, big, pretty, small, good,* and so on) and use specific, colorful adjectives instead, your writing will be clear and powerful.

With Overused Adjectives

A bad **storm knocked down a** big **tree in our yard.**

With Stronger Adjectives

A fierce summer **storm knocked down a** century-old oak **tree in our yard.**

 List three adjectives in the following passage that seem especially strong and two adjectives that seem overused. Then write an effective adjective next to each overused one.

> I listened to the growling thunder in the distance while watching the blue-black clouds. I wondered if we would get a nice rain. The parched ground in the fields was criss-crossed with ugly cracks. The curled leaves were turned bottom side up, like hands begging for help. I hoped that the bad drought would be over.

Use Adjectives with the Right Feeling

Your choice of adjectives can really change the feeling of your writing. What an adjective suggests—its **connotation**—has a significant effect on your writing. Look at this example:

The blustery **wind blew Isaac's homework against the brick wall.**

What does the word *blustery* suggest to you? What if you changed it to *howling* wind or *brisk* wind? These adjectives are similar, yet each one gives the sentence a different feeling.

 If you need help, check a thesaurus. (See page **529**.) This reference book offers synonyms and antonyms for words. Pick words that best fit the meaning and feeling you want to express.

 Write a brief paragraph about a windy day. Concentrate on how the wind makes you feel and use adjectives with the right connotation.

Be Selective

While adjectives can make your writing engaging, don't overuse them. Compare these two sets of descriptive phrases:

Awkward, over-modified phrases
a sunny, inviting, warm, balmy day
the gray, threatening, windy, cloudy sky

Stronger phrases
a balmy, sunny day
the gray, threatening sky

Although the phrases in the first column have more words, they don't really say more than the second descriptions. In fact, they actually slow the reader down and disrupt the flow of ideas.

Rewrite each of the following over-modified phrases by cutting back on the number of adjectives. Keep only those adjectives that make the phrase strong. Then use each of the new phrases in an effective sentence.

1. a frigid, dark, raw, dangerous winter night
2. the intense, bright, white, shocking lightning
3. a calm, peaceful, quiet, still evening
4. the fiery, colorful, vibrant, red maple leaves
5. a plodding, struggling, weary, demoralized hiker

Write with Vivid Images

Use adjectives to add sensory details to your writing to create vivid images. A sensory detail is one that appeals to the different senses: sight, smell, feel, taste, and sound. For example, in describing a forest during a summer rain, you could use these sensory details:

The gentle mist formed sparkling rainbows wherever the sun glinted through the dense tree tops. *(sight)*

The rain filled the forest with the musty smell of damp earth. *(smell)*

Booming thunder and deafening rain drowned out the sound of every living thing in the darkened forest. *(sound)*

The heavy raindrops felt cool against my hot skin. *(touch)*

Write a paragraph about a storm you have experienced, using sensory details that apply to each of the five senses. Read your paragraph aloud and have a partner identify the senses each detail appeals to.

BASIC GRAMMAR

Describing with Adverbs

Adverbs describe or modify verbs, adjectives, or other adverbs. Adverbs answer *how? when?* (or *how often?*) *where?* or *how much?* in a sentence. (See pages **786** and **788**.)

How?	carefully	**Dad drove carefully through the fog.**
When?	later	**We hope it clears up later.**
Where?	everywhere	**The fog seems to be everywhere.**
How Much?	completely	**It completely blocks my view of our yard.**

Team up with a partner, and list at least 10 adverbs from the following narrative. (There are more than 10, so keep listing if you want to.) Then write *how? when?* (or *how often?*) *where?* or *how much?* next to each adverb in your list, depending on the question it answers.

1   Grandma Abby was very disappointed when her flight was
2 cancelled due to fog, but she probably should have expected the
3 cancellation. Her home in the Appalachian Mountains has fog on
4 more than 100 days annually. On those foggy days, she will go
5 out only if absolutely necessary. The morning of her flight, she
6 optimistically journeyed to the airport, hoping that the fog would
7 go away soon. When it didn't, she headed homeward with a heavy
8 heart.
9   Obviously, Grandma could not have done anything to change
10 the situation. Fog happens often in the Appalachians, especially in
11 the valleys there. Nightly, the surface air cools rapidly. This colder
12 air, full of moisture, slowly sinks into low spots. This ground fog
13 can entirely block visibility and make driving dangerous. I'm glad
14 Grandma stays inside when fog blankets her valley.

Special Challenge: Answer the following questions about the narrative above and about your own writing.

1. Which adverbs seem necessary to understand the story?
2. Which adverbs seem not as important?
3. Do you use adverbs very often in your writing? Explain after reviewing one of your latest pieces of writing.

Comparative and Superlative Adverbs

You can use adverbs to compare two things. The **comparative form** of an adverb compares two people, places, things, or ideas. The **superlative form** of an adverb compares three or more people, places, things, or ideas.

 For most one-syllable adverbs, add *er* to make the comparative form and *est* to make the superlative form.

Positive	Comparative	Superlative
soon	sooner	soonest

While you add *er* and *est* to some two-syllable adverbs, you need to use *more* or *most* (or *less* or *least*) with others. Always use *more* or *most* with adverbs of three or more syllables.

Positive	Comparative	Superlative
early	earlier	earliest
quickly	more quickly	most quickly
importantly	more importantly	most importantly

Comparative: **It rained harder last night than it did on Sunday.**
It rains more frequently in Ohio than it does in Nevada.

Superlative: **During a storm last summer, it rained the hardest ever.**
Hawaii is the state where it rains most frequently.

 Make sure that you write a complete comparison: *It rained harder last night than it did on Sunday* rather than *It rained harder last night than Sunday.*

 Write two sentences for each adverb below. In the first, use the comparative form of the adverb; in the second, use the superlative form. Reword each as needed. Share your sentences with a partner.

Example: softly
The snow is falling <u>more softly</u> now than it did this morning.
The snow falls <u>most softly</u> in the evenings.

1. early
2. loudly
3. late
4. effectively

BASIC GRAMMAR

How can I use adverbs effectively?

Describe Actions

You can make your writing more descriptive by using adverbs. Since adverbs can often appear in more than one position in a sentence, always consider the best place to include them. Remember that each different position may slightly change the meaning of the adverb.

For many years, people have tried tirelessly **to control the weather.**

For many years, people have tirelessly **tried to control the weather.**

Tirelessly, **people have tried to control the weather for many years.**

 Rewrite the following sentences, placing the adverb (in parentheses) where you think it fits best.

1. It would be satisfying to control when and where it rains. *(certainly)*

2. Having the ability to stop severe storms would be awesome! *(absolutely)*

3. There is only one method in use that controls the weather. *(currently)*

4. "Seeding" a cloud with chemicals will produce rain. *(possibly)*

5. Whether they realize it or not, humans affect the weather. *(unfortunately)*

6. Man-made structures that trap heat and pollution can cause natural weather patterns to be unstable. *(actually)*

Special Challenge: Rewrite any four of the above sentences a second time. In each of these new sentences, place the adverb in a different position.

Add Emphasis

You can stress the importance of an idea with adverbs. Generally, use adverbs of degree—those that answer *how much?*—for this job. (See **786.4**.)

It was an unbelievably **strong wind.**

An extremely **windy day can be scary.**

 Write a short paragraph about this picture that shows a windy scene. Use a few adverbs to add emphasis.

Express Frequency

With adverbs, you can describe how often something happens or how often something is done. Adverbs that tell how often include words like *sometimes, often, usually, occasionally, always,* and so on.

> **Storms with high winds are** often **frightening.**
>
> **They** never **fail to scare me.**

 Write three sentences about fall weekends. Use one of the "how often" adverbs below per sentence.

regularly	never	occasionally	always	seldom	frequently

Be Precise

With adverbs, you can tell the readers exactly when or where something happens.

Adverbs answering *when?*   **first**   **then**   **yesterday**   **now**   **right away**

Adverbs answering *where?*   **here**   **there**   **nearby**   **inside**   **outside**

> **Shayla saw the lightning** first**.**
>
> Then **we heard the thunder and ran** inside**.**

 Write two sentences about winter mornings using one "when" adverb per sentence. Then write two sentences about the same subject using one "where" adverb per sentence.

Connect Ideas

A **conjunctive adverb** is a special word used as a connection between two independent clauses (or complete sentences). The two sentences below show how conjunctive adverbs are used.

> **We wore ponchos during the storm;** however, **we still were drenched.**
> (A semicolon comes before the conjunctive adverb, and a comma follows it.)
>
> **Within a few days, I came down with a cold.** Nevertheless, **I didn't miss a day of school.** (The conjunctive adverb starts the second sentence, and a comma follows the word.)

Common conjunctive adverbs: *also, then, however, meanwhile, therefore, as a result, for example,* and *for instance.* (Also see **788.1**.)

 Write sentences using three of the conjunctive adverbs listed above. Make sure that you punctuate each of your sentences correctly.

Connecting with Prepositions

A preposition is a word or words that show how one word or idea is related to another. A preposition is the first word of a prepositional phrase, a phrase that acts as an adjective or an adverb in a sentence. (See page 790 for a complete list of prepositions.)

Weather events occur even in outer space.
(The preposition *in* shows the relationships between the verb *occur* and the object of the preposition *outer space*. The prepositional phrase acts as an adverb telling "where.")

These cosmic storms release jets of hot gas.
(The preposition *of* shows the relationship between the noun *jets* and the object of the preposition *gas*. The prepositional phrase acts as an adjective telling "what kind.")

■ **A word that is used as a preposition may also be used as an adverb.**
If a word that sometimes is used as a preposition appears alone in a sentence, that word is probably an adverb.

> **Ten million light-years away, space hurricanes whirl** around the universe. (*Around the universe* is a prepositional phrase.)

> **In the eye of these hurricanes, winds of hot gas spin** around.
> (*Around* is an adverb that modifies the verb *spin*.)

■ **"To" is either a preposition or part of an infinitive phrase.**
If the words that follow "to" include the object of the preposition (a noun or pronoun), then "to" is a preposition. If "to" is followed by a verb or verb phrase, then "to" is part of an infinitive or infinitive phrase. (See page 547.)

> **Although I might like traveling** to space, **I would not like getting caught in a space hurricane's million-mile-per-hour winds.**
> (*To space* is a prepositional phrase.)

> **Scientists use the Hubble Space Telescope** to look **deep into space.**
> (*To look deep into space* is an infinitive phrase used as an adverb.)

Write four sentences about your favorite kind of weather. Use the word "around" as a preposition in one sentence and as an adverb in another sentence. Use the word "to" as a preposition in one sentence and as part of an infinitive in another.

 8.19A(iii)
ELPS 2I, 3D, 3E, 4G, 4K

Working with Words

How can I use prepositional phrases?

Add Information

You can use a prepositional phrase to add information to a sentence. Prepositional phrases can act as adjectives to describe either a noun or a pronoun. Adjectives answer the questions *what kind? how many? how much?* or *which one?*

	Which one?		*What kind?*
The weather report	on channel 33	predicts a cool night	with clear skies.

Imagine you are writing a weather report for a television station. Use at least five of the prepositions listed below in prepositional phrases that act as adjectives to describe a noun or a pronoun. When you have written your paragraph, read it to a partner. Have the partner identify the prepositional phrases you wrote and the question each one answers.

out of	into	of	in
with	to	on	from
above	below	across	

You can also use a prepositional phrase as an adverb to describe a verb, an adjective, or another adverb. Adverbs answer the questions *how? when? where? how long?* or *how often?*

	Where?	*How long?*
It hasn't rained	in Houston	for three weeks.

Below is a list of prepositions. Write a paragraph using at least five of these words in prepositional phrases. Make sure that each prepositional phrase acts as an adverb to describe a verb, adjective, or another adverb. When you have written your paragraph, read it to a partner. Have your partner identify the prepositional phrases you used and the question each one answers.

on	from	above	under
beside	to	out of	into
of	in	with	

BASIC GRAMMAR

Connecting with Conjunctions

Conjunctions connect words, groups of words, and sentences. There are three kinds of conjunctions: *coordinating, subordinating,* and *correlative.* The following sentences show some of the ways to use conjunctions. (See page 792 for a list of common conjunctions.)

Coordinating Conjunctions
Connect Words and Phrases

Shawn wants to report the news and the weather on a radio station.

Does he need a science degree or a communications degree?

Connect Compound Subjects and Predicates

Hassan and Francisco want to become TV weathermen.

They continually study the weather or read about it.

Connect Sentences

Many weather reporters are meteorologists, but not all of them are.

Weather will always be a topic of interest, so reporters will never run out of work.

Subordinating Conjunctions
Connect Dependent Clauses to Independent Clauses

Jalisa hopes to work at a TV station while she attends college.

Although she is a good student, she wants job experience, too.

Correlative Conjunctions
Connect Phrases

Many weather forecasts today are based not only on scientific instruments and observations but also on satellite images.

People either believe the forecasts or ignore them.

 GRAMMAR Try It Choose three of the sentences above to use as models. Write three sentences of your own imitating the three you've chosen. (Make sure to write original sentences.) Underline the conjunctions you use and read your sentences aloud to a partner.

How can I use conjunctions?

Connect Phrases

You can use **coordinating** and **correlative conjunctions** to connect different types of phrases: noun phrases, verb phrases, prepositional phrases, verbal phrases, and so on. Coordinating conjunctions include words like *and, but, or, yet,* and so on. Correlative conjunctions are used in pairs: *either/or, both/and, not only/but also,* and so on. Correlative conjunctions show a relationship between the phrases.

> **"Black blizzards" of the Dust Bowl (the severe drought during the 1930s) blew dry soil off the farm fields and into the air.** (The coordinating conjunction *and* connects two prepositional phrases.)

> **A long period without rain either damages crops or prevents them from growing.** (The correlative conjunctions *either* and *or* connect two verb phrases and show that they are alternatives.)

GRAMMAR
Try IT

Complete each sentence below using a coordinating conjunction or a set of correlative conjunctions to fill in the blanks. (See **792.2.**)

1. _____ natural elements _____ human actions were causes of the Dust Bowl.

2. Farmers learned that they must _____ change their farming practices _____ find another occupation.

3. As a result, farmers increased crop yields _____ reduced soil erosion.

4. The southern Great Plains experienced serious droughts _____ in the 1930s _____ in the 1950s.

5. High temperatures _____ low rainfall led to the five-year drought of the '50s.

6. The effects of a major drought are serious _____ for nature _____ for society.

7. Drought increases the risk of forest fires, _____ fires are necessary for certain trees to release their seeds.

8. A water shortage prevents activities as different as hog farming _____ river recreation.

9. _____ hydroelectric power _____ some manufacturing processes will work correctly during a drought.

10. To avoid the effects of drought, we can conserve water _____ find new water supplies.

BASIC GRAMMAR

TEKS 8.14C, 8.19A(iii), 8.19A(v), 8.19B, 8.20B(i)
ELPS 4G, 4K

Expand Sentences (with Subordinating Conjunctions)

You can use a **subordinating conjunction** to connect a dependent clause to another sentence. A **dependent clause** cannot stand alone as a complete sentence and must be connected to an **independent clause**. When you add a dependent clause to an independent clause, you create a **complex sentence**. In the complex sentences below, the dependent clause is underlined, and the subordinating conjunction is in blue.

> Before people used satellite images to explain and predict the weather, they used folklore. As early people observed changes in the weather, they noticed how it affected insects, animals, birds, and the skies. People believed much of the weather folklore until some of it was disproved by modern science.

■ When a dependent clause begins the sentence, follow it with a comma. The comma is usually not needed when the dependent clause follows the independent clause.

Connect each of the following dependent clauses to an independent clause of your own. Use clauses 1–5 at the beginning of sentences. Use clauses 6–10 at the end of sentences. Be sure to include a comma after clauses that come at the beginning of sentences.

1. If it doesn't rain soon
2. When we finally get some snow
3. Since we moved to the desert
4. Before I heard the weather report
5. Although the rain was very heavy
6. unless we have to go someplace
7. after the hurricane passed over
8. whenever I hear thunder crash
9. until the wind stops blowing
10. as long as the power stays on

Trade your new sentences with a partner. Check your partner's sentences to make sure he or she wrote an independent clause (a sentence that could stand alone) to go with each dependent clause.

Building Effective Sentences

Our world is a diverse place. Snow-capped mountains tower more than five miles high, and ocean trenches delve more than six miles deep. In one place, the sun pours its life-giving light on a dense tropical rain forest, while in another, it bakes sand dunes until nothing can survive. Golden fields of grain, rocky shorelines, flat-topped mesas, mazelike everglades—the beauty of the world is its diversity.

Diversity is also the beauty of writing. If every sentence is the same, a reader will soon get bored. Instead, if the sentences vary, containing pleasant surprises around some of the turns, the reader will want to keep reading. This chapter will help you create sentences that are clear, complete, and varied so that you can build beautiful landscapes of ideas.

What's Ahead

You will learn about . . .

- writing complete sentences.
- fixing sentence problems.
- improving your sentence style.
- combining sentences.
- using different types and kinds of sentences.
- expanding and modeling sentences.

562

Writing Complete Sentences

Every sentence has two basic parts: a complete subject (which tells who or what is doing something) and a complete predicate (which tells what the subject is doing or tells something about the subject).

Complete Subject	Complete Predicate
Who or what does something?	*What does the subject do?*
The Amazon River	winds through the jungle.
The Nile River	empties into the sea.

 Divide a piece of paper into two columns. For each of the sentences below, write the complete subject in the left column and write the complete predicate in the right column.

> In the following sentences, the words that come before the verb are part of the *complete subject*. The verb and all the words that follow it are part of the *complete predicate*.

Example: Old Faithful, a geyser in Yellowstone National Park, erupts for about four minutes every hour.

Old Faithful, a geyser in Yellowstone National Park,	erupts for about four minutes every hour.

1. The Royal Gorge Bridge in Colorado ranks as the highest suspension bridge in the world.
2. Australia's Great Barrier Reef stretches for about 1,250 miles.
3. A moat surrounds the Imperial Palace in Tokyo, Japan.
4. Timbuktu served as the chief trading center in western Africa.
5. More than 250,000 workers built the Panama Canal for wages of about 10 cents an hour.
6. The only species of wild ape in Europe lives on Gibraltar Rock.
7. Residents of Venice, Italy, travel through canals by boat.
8. The volcano Mount Vesuvius made Pompeii, Italy, famous.
9. Antarctica is not owned by any country.
10. Jim White, a cowboy, discovered the Carlsbad Caverns in New Mexico.

Subjects and Predicates

Every sentence has a subject and a predicate. A simple subject consists of the subject without the words that modify it. A simple predicate is the verb without the words that modify it or complete the thought. In the sentences below, the simple subjects are orange, and the simple predicates are blue.

Simple Subject	Simple Predicate
Ancient Egyptians	worshiped **the Nile River.**
The distance **from New York City to Los Angeles**	matches **the length of the Nile.**

A simple subject may be compound, which means that it includes two or more subjects sharing the same predicate (or predicates). A simple predicate may also be compound, which means that it includes two or more verbs sharing the same subject (or subjects).

Compound Subject	Compound Predicate
Crocodiles and hippos	live **and** thrive **in the Nile.**

Number a piece of paper from 1 to 5, skipping a line between numbers. For each sentence below, write the simple subject on one line and the simple predicate on the next line. (Remember to look for compound subjects and predicates.)

Example: Part of the Nile River, the Blue Nile, originates in Ethiopia.
part
originates

1. Sand accumulates in the Blue Nile and turns the water brownish blue.
2. The clear White Nile gathers no sand.
3. The Blue Nile and the White Nile combine at Khartoum, Sudan.
4. The Nile River becomes dark blue at Khartoum and continues to the Mediterranean Sea.
5. The word *Nile* means "dark blue."

Write one sentence with a single simple subject and a compound simple predicate. Then write another sentence with a compound simple subject and a compound simple predicate. Ask a classmate to underline the simple subjects once and the simple predicates twice in each sentence.

BASIC WRITING

ELPS 3D, 3E, 4C, 4K

How can I make sure my sentences are complete?
Check Your Subjects and Predicates

Incomplete thoughts are called fragments. Fragments may be missing a subject, a predicate, or both. Study the fragments below. Then read the complete sentences made from them. Notice that a subject, a predicate, or both have been added to make the corrections.

Fragment	Sentence
Consists of four large islands and more than 3,000 small ones.	**Japan consists of four large islands and more than 3,000 small ones.** (A subject is added.)
In Japan.	**Mount Fuji is the highest mountain in Japan.** (A subject and predicate are added.)
Shinto pilgrims this sacred mountain.	**Shinto pilgrims climb this sacred mountain.** (A predicate is added.)

Learning Language

You can tell that a sentence is a fragment if it seems to be missing an important piece of information. If you read a fragment alone, without the other sentences around it, you will likely find yourself asking a question. For example, if you read *Mount Fuji, in Japan,* you might ask *What about Mount Fuji?* If you read *Climbed a mountain,* you might ask *Who climbed?*

Read each of the sentence fragments below. Work with a partner to decide what each sentence needs to be a complete sentence. Then rewrite the fragment as a complete sentence. Take turns reading the new complete sentences.

1. A top tourist attraction
2. Erupted in 1987
3. One of the world's biggest volcanoes
4. Caused great destruction

Write NOW Write a paragraph about the kind of natural area you like best. Include in your paragraph three sentence fragments. Exchange your paragraph with a partner. Have him or her identify the three fragments, then suggest how to make them complete sentences.

TEKS 8.19A(iii), 8.19B, 8.20B(i)

Check for Dependent Clauses

A dependent clause (also called a subordinate clause) contains a subject and a verb but does not express a complete thought. It cannot stand by itself as a sentence. A dependent clause needs to be connected to an independent clause to compete its meaning. A dependent clause plus an independent clause creates a complex sentence. (See **750.3**.)

Dependent Clauses *(They cannot stand alone.)*	Combined with Independent Clauses *(Complex sentences are created.)*
Where the wilderness is mostly untouched	The Yukon Territory is located in a northerly region **where the wilderness is mostly untouched**.
Because the sun never sets during some of the summer season	**Because the sun never sets during some of the summer season,** people go to bed with the sun still shining.
That are extremely cold	Winters **that are extremely cold** can turn gasoline to slush.

A comma is needed after a dependent clause that comes at the beginning of a sentence. A comma is usually not needed if the dependent clause comes at the end. A dependent clause in the middle of a sentence may or may not need to be set off by commas. (See **646.1** and **652.1**.)

GRAMMAR Read the paragraph below. How many dependent clauses do you find?
Try IT Now rewrite the paragraph, connecting each dependent clause to an independent clause that comes before or after it.

1 When the gold rush occurred in the 1800s. Thousands rushed to
2 the Klondike River in the Yukon. Though many had jobs. They left home
3 to seek their fortune. Because of the gold rush. The Royal Canadian
4 Mounted Police went north to police the miners. The Mounties stopped
5 travelers to be sure they had adequate supplies. Before the Mounties
6 let them go on. Once the gold rush began. Dawson City, Yukon, grew
7 from a tiny town to a city of 30,000. After the gold rush, only 700
8 residents remained in Dawson City. Suddenly the Yukon area was left
9 with many empty log cabins. That were built earlier by the miners.

Write **NOW** Write a brief paragraph explaining the history of a place in your city or hometown or a place you have visited or read about. Include at least two complex sentences. Be sure to include commas where necessary.

BASIC WRITING

Fixing Sentence Problems

Avoid Run-On Sentences

Sometimes you may accidentally write a run-on sentence by putting together two or more sentences. One type of run-on is called a *comma splice,* in which the sentences are connected with a comma only. Another type of run-on has no punctuation at all.

One way to fix run-on sentences is to add a coordinating conjunction (*and, so, or, for, but, yet,* or *nor*) and a comma (if not already present). Another way is to connect the two sentences with a semicolon.

Run-On Sentence	Corrected Sentences
The Rock of Gibraltar stands between Europe and Africa less than eight miles separate the continents.	**The Rock of Gibraltar stands between Europe and Africa, and less than eight miles separate the continents.**
	The Rock of Gibraltar stands between Europe and Africa; less than eight miles separate the continents.

 On your own paper, correct the run-on sentences below by adding a comma and a coordinating conjunction.

Example: The Gibraltar peninsula is a thin, hilly strip of land it is connected to Spain.

The Gibraltar peninsula is a thin, hilly strip of land, and it is connected to Spain.

1. Many cargo and passenger ships visit Gibraltar's harbor the safe harbor and mild climate make it a great place to stop for repairs.

2. In ancient times, the African Moors occupied Gibraltar it has also been controlled by Spain and England.

3. This limestone mountain was legendary to Ancient Greeks they called it one of the Pillars of Hercules.

4. People use the Rock of Gibraltar as a symbol of strength they say something strong is "as solid as the Rock of Gibraltar."

 Correct two of the run-on sentences above by adding a semicolon. Then look for run-ons in a piece of writing you have done and correct them using a semicolon or a comma and a coordinating conjunction.

TEKS 8.19A(ii), 8.19A(v), 8.19B

Eliminate Rambling Sentences

A rambling sentence occurs when you connect too many ideas with the word *and*. Study the rambling sentence below and two ways it can be corrected.

Rambling Sentence	Corrected Sentences *(The and's have been eliminated.)*
Loch Ness is a large lake in northern Scotland and it is famous for its legendary monster and many tourists visit the loch and hope they see the monster. 	**Loch Ness, a large lake in northern Scotland, is famous for its legendary monster. Many tourists, hoping to see the monster, visit the loch.** (An appositive phrase [see page 575] is used in the first sentence, and a participial phrase [see page 582] is used in the second sentence.)
	Loch Ness is a large lake in northern Scotland that is famous for its legendary monster. Many tourists, who hope to see the monster, visit the loch. (Two complex sentences have been created. The dependent clause in each sentence begins with a relative pronoun: *that* and *who*. See pages 577 and 579.)

 It is not necessary to eliminate all of the *and's* in a rambling sentence. Some *and's* may be needed to connect compound sentences, compound subjects and predicates, and so on.

 Rewrite the following rambling sentences so they contain fewer *and's*. When possible, make complex sentences. (See pages 577 and 579.)

1. The water in Loch Ness stays about 42 degrees Fahrenheit (6 degrees Celsius) and it is very deep and it never freezes.

2. Scientists searched the lake with sonar equipment in the 1960s and numerous sightings of a monster were reported and this made people even more curious about the Loch Ness monster.

3. In 1972 an underwater camera took pictures in Loch Ness and scientists studied the evidence of a monster and the scientists say the creature might be a sea cow.

4. The monster legend began around the year 565 C.E. and children were not allowed to play by the lake and people began fearing attacks by the monster.

BASIC WRITING

Check for Wordy Sentences

Unnecessary repetition creates wordy sentences. Removing unnecessary words improves the sentence. Study the wordy sentence below and the two ways in which it is corrected.

Wordy Sentence	Corrected Sentences *(Unnecessary words are eliminated.)*
Huge, giant stones stand on end upright in England.	**Huge stones stand on end in England.** **Giant stones stand upright in England.**

Rewrite each of the sentences below so that the unnecessary words are eliminated.

1. Approximately 4,000 years ago, 2000 B.C.E., the stones were set in place.

2. Each year thousands of visitors annually go to Stonehenge as tourists.

3. Britain has approximately about 900 stone site locations.

4. In the evening at dusk, visitors especially like to see Stonehenge while the sun is setting.

5. The rocks that make Stonehenge come from great distances far away.

6. No one is certain exactly how these gigantic stones were transported and moved.

7. Because one stone in the middle aligns in a straight line with the sun, some scientists think that people used the stones as a calendar.

8. In Great Britain, Stonehenge sits by itself on the Salisbury Plain in the southern part of England.

9. Some people think that alien beings who came from outer space created Stonehenge.

10. Careful studies show that Stonehenge was built over a long period of time taking hundreds of years.

TEKS 8.19C

Move Misplaced Modifiers

Misplaced modifiers occur when a descriptive phrase is improperly located in a sentence and appears to describe the wrong word or idea. To correct this error, locate descriptive phrases as close as possible to the words they modify.

Misplaced Modifier	Corrected Sentences
The largest desert in the world, Africa contains the Sahara Desert. (This sentence incorrectly makes it sound as if Africa is the desert.)	**Africa contains the Sahara Desert, the largest desert in the world.**
	The Sahara Desert, the largest desert in the world, is contained in Africa. (In both sentences the descriptive phrase is moved closer to the word it modifies.)

GRAMMAR
Try IT

Rewrite each sentence below so that the descriptive modifier clearly describes the correct word or idea. (Change the sentences as needed.)

Example: Ninety percent gravel and boulders, sand actually covers a small portion of the Sahara Desert.

Sand actually covers a small portion of the Sahara Desert, which is 90 percent gravel and boulders.

1. Burrowing during the heat of the day, a visitor might see centipedes and scorpions.
2. Wearing long, protective robes and turbans, camels carry Bedouin nomads through the Sahara.
3. Supplying enough water to support a small city, people can live around a large desert oasis.
4. In sandstone shelters, the Sahara contains carvings and paintings drawn by ancient people.
5. Currently dried up, aerial photographs show that ancient rivers and lakes existed near the Sahara.

Write
NOW

Write two sentences containing misplaced modifiers. Base your sentences on the facts below. Then exchange sentences with a classmate and correct each other's work. Read your partner's corrected sentences aloud.

Animals in the Sahara

– survive a harsh environment   – are active mostly at night
– squeeze into abandoned burrows   – live near an oasis
– seek shade during the day

BASIC WRITING

What can I do to write clear sentences?
Make Subjects and Verbs Agree

Subjects and verbs in each sentence you write must agree. That means a singular subject needs a singular verb, and a plural subject needs a plural verb. (Also see **778.1**.)

Single Subjects

A verb must agree with its subject in number.

■ If a subject is singular, the verb must be singular, too.
Brazil is the largest country in South America.

■ If a subject is plural, the verb must be plural.
Most beaches in Brazil have beautiful white sand.

> Don't forget that nouns ending in *s* or *es* are very often plural, and verbs ending in *s* are very often singular.

■ If an indefinite pronoun is singular, its verb must be singular, too.
Almost everyone in Brazil lives near the Atlantic coast.

■ If an indefinite pronoun is plural, its verb must be plural also.
Many of Brazil's people speak Portuguese.

 Some indefinite pronouns are tricky because they can be singular or plural when used as a subject. (See the chart on page **537**.)

 Number your paper from 1 to 7. For each of the following sentences, correctly write the verb to agree with the subject. If the verb or verbs are correct, write a "C" on your paper.

Example: The Amazon River flow through Brazil.
flows

1. Only some of the plants in the Amazon rain forest has been classified.
2. Amazingly, rain forest spiders grows bigger than this book.
3. Now the rain forests are endangered by civilization.
4. Something are needed to protect animals from heavy river traffic.
5. Tourists doesn't see as many animals in the rain forest.
6. Plants is also disappearing.
7. Some agencies, however, are starting to counteract the damage.

TEKS 8.19A(i)
ELPS 2C, 3E, 3H, 4C, 4G, 4K

Using Perfect Verb Tenses

Choosing the right verb tense can help you write more effective sentences. Sometimes you will need to use the *perfect* tenses that you learned about earlier. Here is a review:

■ The *present perfect tense* states an action that began in the past but continues or is completed in the present.

> People have tried to protect the world's rain forests.

■ The *past perfect tense* states an action that began in the past and was completed in the past.

> Miles of rain forest had disappeared in the last century.

■ The *future perfect tense* states an action that will begin in the future and will be completed by a specific time in the future.

> By 2020, new programs will have protected the earth's resources.

Progressive Verb Tenses

Progressive tenses are another useful verb form you can use to write effective and diverse sentences. The progressive tense uses a form of the verb to be and the main form of the verb + ing.

■ The *present progressive tense* shows an action that is continuing right now. It uses the present tense of the verb to be.

> We are watching a movie about Brazil's rain forest.

■ The *past progressive tense* shows an action that was continuing at a specific time in the past when something else happened. It uses the past tense of the verb to be.

> We were watching a movie about a rain forest when the phone rang.

■ The *future progressive tense* shows an action that will be continuing at a specific time in the future when something else will happen. It uses the future tense of the verb to be.

> We will be watching the movie when you stop by tomorrow night.

BASIC WRITING

GRAMMAR Try IT Use the example sentences above as models to write new sentences using the perfect and progressive tenses. When you have written six sentences, mix up the order and read them to a partner. Have your partner tell which tense you have used in each sentence.

What should I do to avoid nonstandard sentences?

Avoid Double Negatives

Two negative words used together in the same sentence form a double negative *(not no, barely nothing, not never)*. Double negatives also happen if you use contractions ending in *n't* with a negative word *(can't hardly, didn't never)*. Your writing will not be accurate if you use double negatives.

Negative Words

nothing	nowhere	neither	never	not	barely	hardly	nobody	none

Negative Contractions

don't	can't	won't	shouldn't	wouldn't	couldn't	didn't	hadn't

Number your paper from 1 to 5. List the double negatives you find in the sentences below and then correctly rewrite each sentence. *Hint:* There is usually more than one way to correct a double negative.

Example: My sister and I never have no fun on family vacations.

never no
My sister and I never have any fun on family vacations.

1. We can't go nowhere we want to.
2. I don't hardly want to hear what the plan is this year.
3. Nobody doesn't want to go to Aunt Jessica's house again.
4. We just go there because it doesn't cost nothing.
5. Why don't we never just go to a giant water park?

Avoid Double Subjects

Avoid sentences in which a personal pronoun is used immediately after the subject—the result is usually a double subject.

Double Subject: **Mauritius it** is an island in the Indian Ocean.
Corrected Sentence: *Mauritius is an island in the Indian Ocean.*

Double Subject: **Alma she** and I want to go to Mauritius.
Corrected Sentence: *Alma and I want to go to Mauritius.*

Write four sentences. In two of them, use double negatives. In the other two, use double subjects. Exchange papers with a classmate, rewrite each other's sentences correctly, and then check each other's work.

★ TEKS 8.14C

Improving Your Sentence Style

There are a number of ways to add variety to your sentences and improve your writing style. Here are four of the most common ways.

1 **Combine short sentences.**

2 **Use different types of sentences.**

3 **Expand sentences by adding words and phrases.**

4 **Model sentences of other writers.**

When too many sentences in a paragraph are the same length or follow the same pattern, the paragraph sounds choppy. Read the following paragraph.

> **Little Variety**
>
> Part of Turkey is in Europe. Part of Turkey is in Asia. Turkey is a very interesting country. Ankara is the capital. The largest city is Istanbul. It exists on two continents. No other major city does this. The Bosporus Strait splits the city in two. The European part is on the western side. The Asian part is on the eastern side.

Read the following version, which has a better variety of sentences. See how using different types of sentences helps this paragraph flow more smoothly.

> **Good Variety**
>
> Turkey is an interesting country because part of it is in Europe and part is in Asia. Ankara is the capital city; however, the largest city is Istanbul. Istanbul is the only major city in the world that exists on two continents. The Bosporus Strait splits the city in two, with the European part on the western side and the Asian part on the eastern side.

GRAMMAR Read the paragraph below. Then, on your own paper, rewrite the paragraph to create more sentence variety.

1 Turkish food is partly Asian. Turkish food is partly European. There
2 are many kinds of dishes. Kebabs are from Turkey. Kebabs usually
3 have meat. Some kebabs are made just with vegetables. Puddings are
4 popular in Turkey. There are at least twelve kinds of milk pudding.
5 There are many delicious pastries. Turkish coffee is a common drink.
6 Turkish coffee is very strong. Tea is a common drink, too.

BASIC WRITING

How can I make my sentences flow more smoothly?

Writers often combine sentences to help their writing flow more smoothly. Too many short sentences can make writing sound choppy. Combining some sentences will add variety to your writing and improve your overall writing style.

Combine with a Series

You can combine sentences using a series of words, phrases, or clauses.

Combine with a Series

Short Sentences	*Combined Using a Series of Words*
The Mississippi River was carved by melting glaciers. The Missouri and Ohio rivers were carved by melting glaciers.	**The** Mississippi, Missouri, **and** Ohio **rivers were carved by melting glaciers**.
Short Sentences	*Combined Using a Series of Words*
The Pacific Northwest has many ecosystems. It is home to over 15 million people. It is a world leader in technology industries.	**The Pacific Northwest** has many ecosystems, is home to over 15 million people, **and** is a world leader in technology industries.

(The items in any series must be alike (or parallel), which means they should all have the same grammatical structure. For example, if the first item is a prepositional phrase, all the items must be prepositional phrases. (See page **621**.) Use commas to separate items in a series.)

Use a series of parallel words or phrases to combine the groups of sentences below. (Change words in the sentences as needed.)

1. The Pacific Northwest was claimed by Russia and by Spain at different times in history. It was also claimed by Britain.

2. The Rocky Mountains are in the Pacific Northwest. The Cascade Range and the Coast Ranges are also there.

3. Visitors to Olympic National Park in Washington State can take pictures of snow-topped mountains. They can also relax on ocean beaches. They can hike in rain forests.

4. Tide pools at the park are a great place to view anemones. People can also see starfish in the tide pools. They can see sand dollars in the tide pools, too.

Combine with Phrases

You can combine sentences by using appositives (see **648.1**) or prepositional phrases (see **790.1**). An appositive is a word or phrase that comes after a noun or pronoun and renames it.

Combine Using an Appositive Phrase	
Short Sentences	*Combined Sentences*
Sumo wrestling began as a religious ritual. It is Japan's national sport.	**Sumo wrestling,** Japan's national sport**, began as a religious ritual.**

Combine Using a Prepositional Phrase	
Sumo wrestlers weigh as much as 265 kilograms. In pounds, that's about 580.	**Sumo wrestlers weigh as much as 265 kilograms, or** about 580 pounds.

Combine each of the following sets of sentences by using the method given in parentheses.

Example: The wrestling ring is a circle. The ring has a diameter of about 15 feet. *(two prepositional phrases)*
The wrestling ring is a circle with a diameter of about 15 feet.

1. The wrestling ring is raised so spectators can better see. The wrestling ring is a clay platform. *(appositive phrase)*
2. The wrestlers wear silk robes. They wear the robes before their matches. *(prepositional phrase)*
3. One way to win is to pull or push an opponent. A wrestler tries to pull or push his opponent out of the ring. *(prepositional phrase)*
4. At any one time, there are from one to four yokozuna. *Yokozuna* is the Japanese word for grand champions. *(appositive phrase)*
5. A sumo tournament consists of either seven or fifteen bouts held over two weeks. A sumo tournament is properly called a "basho." *(appositive phrase)*

Write two sentences about a sport you enjoy. Use an appositive phrase in the first sentence. Use at least one prepositional phrase in the second sentence. Share your sentences with a partner.

 **TEKS** 8.19A(i)

Combine with Infinitive or Participial Phrases

You can combine short sentences by using infinitive phrases (see **780.4**) or participial phrases (see **780.3**).

Combine Using an Infinitive Phrase	
Short Sentences	*Combined Sentences*
Gina interviewed her grandmother. She was interested in learning about her ancestors.	**Gina interviewed her grandmother** to learn about her ancestors.

Combine Using a Participial Phrase	
Gina's ancestors hoped for a better future. They emigrated from Italy to New York State.	Hoping for a better future, **Gina's ancestors emigrated from Italy to New York State.**

 GRAMMAR **Try IT**

On your own paper, combine each of the following sets of short sentences using the method given in parentheses.

Example: Between 1884 and 1920, about 7 million Italians immigrated to the United States. They escaped poverty and malnutrition. *(infinitive phrase)*
Between 1884 and 1920, about 7 million Italians immigrated to the United States to escape poverty and malnutrition.

1. Gina's great-great-grandfather arrived in New York City in 1912. He was equipped with only a suitcase. *(participial phrase)*

2. Gina's great-great-grandfather settled in the Hudson Valley. He wanted a better life. *(participial phrase)*

3. Even today many immigrants come to the Hudson Valley. They can improve their lives. *(infinitive phrase)*

4. Jorge Garcia was urged to move by his uncle. Jorge Garcia came to the Hudson Valley from Mexico and now owns a restaurant. *(participial phrase)*

5. Gina is planning a trip to the Hudson Valley. She will see it for herself. *(infinitive phrase)*

 Write **NOW**

Write two sentences about your ancestors. Use an infinitive phrase in the first sentence. Use a participial phrase in the second sentence. Share your sentences with a partner.

Combine with Relative Pronouns

You can also combine sentences by using a relative pronoun to connect a dependent clause to an independent clause. Relative pronouns include words such as *who, which, that, whose, whom,* and so on. Dependent clauses that begin with relative pronouns are also called adjectival clauses because they give more information about a noun or pronoun.

Combine with Relative Pronouns	
Two Short Sentences	*Combined Using a Relative Pronoun*
George Washington has many places named after him. George Washington was our first president.	George Washington, who has many places named after him, was our first president.
	George Washington, who was our first president, has many places named after him.

 An adjectival clause beginning with the relative pronoun *which* is always set off by commas. An adjectival clause beginning with *who* or *whose* is also set off by commas if the clause contains information that is not necessary to understand the independent clause.

 Combine each set of sentences below by using the relative pronoun in parentheses.

Example: In the United States, "Washington" is the name of seven counties. They range from New York to Oregon. *(which)*
In the United States, "Washington" is the name of seven counties, which range from New York to Oregon.

1. John Adams was the second president. His home was in Braintree, Massachusetts. *(whose)*
2. Five of the first ten presidents were all from Virginia. They were born before the U.S. became a country. *(who)*
3. Schools help us honor them. These schools are named for presidents. *(that)*
4. I attend Jefferson Middle School. It holds the best science fair in our county. *(which)*

 Write freely about an adult you admire (a relative, a teacher, a coach). Explain why you admire this person. Afterward, underline any sentences containing relative pronouns. See if there are two shorter sentences you can combine using a relative pronoun.

BASIC WRITING

TEKS 8.14C, 8.20B(ii)

What can I do to add variety to my writing?

Varying sentence types can make your writing come alive. Good writers use a variety of sentences to make their writing clear and interesting.

Create Compound Sentences

A **compound sentence** is made up of two or more simple sentences (independent clauses) joined by a comma and a coordinating conjunction (*and, for, but, or, so, nor,* and *yet*) or by a semicolon. (See 652.2 and 654.1.)

Compound Sentence = Two Independent Clauses

The Bay of Bengal has an area of 1,300,000 square miles, and it is the largest bay in the world. (A comma and the conjunction *and* join the two independent clauses.)

Eight countries border the Bay of Bengal; its west coast is formed by India. (A semicolon joins the two independent clauses.)

On your own paper, join each of the following sets of sentences using either a comma and a coordinating conjunction or a semicolon.

Example: Ancient Greek and Roman traders sailed to the Bay of Bengal. "Modern" Europeans didn't discover the bay until the 1500s.

Ancient Greek and Roman traders sailed to the Bay of Bengal, but "modern" Europeans didn't discover the bay until the 1500s.

1. Approximately two million tons of fish are caught in the Bay of Bengal each year. The fishing industry is threatened by pollution.

2. One-fourth of the world's population lives in the countries bordering the bay. Seafood from the Bay of Bengal is very important.

3. Monsoons blow across the Bay of Bengal from the southwest in the summer. They blow from the northeast in the winter.

4. Monsoons are strong winds. They bring heavy rains.

5. Much of the country of Bangladesh is a fertile delta. Dangerous flooding there has killed many people.

Choose a piece of your writing and revise it to create compound sentences. Make sure you punctuate your sentences correctly.

TEKS 8.14C, 8.19A(iii), 8.19A(v), 8.19B
ELPS 4C, 4G, 4K

Develop Complex Sentences

When you join a dependent clause (also called a *subordinate clause*) to an independent clause, you form a complex sentence. In complex sentences, relative pronouns and subordinating conjunctions are used to link the subordinate clause to the independent, or main clause. Subordinating conjunctions are words such as *after, although, because, before, even though, until, when,* and *while.* When a subordinate clause acts as an adverb to answer questions like *Why? When? Where?* or *How?,* it is called an adverbial clause.

COMPLEX SENTENCE =

Dependent (Subordinate) Clause	+	Independent (Main) Clause

Although many place names are straightforward,   **some make people think twice.**

Independent (Main) Clause	+	Dependent (Subordinate) Clause

People can visit Santa Claus in three states (Arizona, Georgia, and Indiana)   **even though it's not Christmas.**

GRAMMAR Try IT

Number your paper from 1 to 4. Then write the dependent clause in each of the following complex sentences. (Also see **750.2–750.3**.)

Example: You'd better be careful of what you say if you visit Secret, Nevada.

if you visit Secret, Nevada

1. Until I traveled to Rhode Island, I didn't know there was a town named Common Fence Post.
2. After you visit the town of Brothers, Oregon, you should drive on to the town of Sisters, Oregon.
3. The Romans named the Canary Islands ("Island of the Dogs" in Latin) because they found wild dogs there.
4. Because its name is only one syllable long, Maine is unique among the states.

Write NOW

Choose a piece of your recent writing and give it to a partner. Have your partner underline any complex sentences you used. Then work together to find two simple sentences in each piece of writing that could be combined using a relative pronoun or subordinating conjunction from the list above to create a complex sentence.

⭐ ELPS 3D, 3E, 3H, 4C, 4G, 4I, 4K, 5B

Use Questions and Commands

Writers add variety to their sentences by making statements, asking questions, giving commands, or showing strong emotion. See the chart below.

Kinds of Sentences			
Declarative ▪	Makes a statement about a person, a place, a thing, or an idea	**The diameter of Mars is slightly more than half the diameter of Earth.**	This is the most common kind of sentence.
Interrogative ?	Asks a question	**Does Mars have any interesting physical features?**	A question gets the reader's attention.
Imperative ▪	Gives a command or makes a strong request	**Read about it and find out.**	Commands or requests often appear in dialogue and directions.
Exclamatory !	Shows strong emotion or feeling	**What an amazing place it is!**	Use these sentences for occasional emphasis.

Learning Language

When you are reading, the punctuation mark at the end tells you whether a sentence is a statement or command, a question, or an exclamation. When you are listening to someone speak, however, how can you tell what kinds of sentences they are using? You can listen to the way they say the sentences.

● Declarative sentences (statements) are usually said in an even tone.
● When asking a question, most people raise the pitch of their voice on the last word, so that it sounds slightly higher.
● An exclamation is often said with force or emotion.
● A command may sound like a statement or an exclamation.

Review the description of each kind of sentence in the chart above. Then complete the activity below. When you are done, read your sentences aloud to a partner. See if your partner can tell which kind of sentence each one is from the way you say it. Then listen to your partner's sentences.

Write NOW Write four sentences—one of each kind—about an unusual place that you would like to visit. Be sure you punctuate your sentences correctly.

TEKS 8.19A(iii)

What can I do to add details to my sentences?

Expand with Prepositional Phrases

Writers add details to their sentences using prepositional phrases. These phrases function as adjectives or adverbs. *Remember:* A prepositional phrase begins with a preposition and ends with the object of a preposition. (See page 790 for a list of prepositions.)

- Prepositional phrases used as adjectives answer the questions *How many? Which one? What kind?*

- Prepositional phrases used as adverbs answer the questions *When? How? How often? How long? Where? How much?*

Prepositional Phrase	Function in Sentence
Centuries ago, settlers from Scotland and France **settled Cape Breton Island.**	The phrase *from Scotland and France* acts as an **adjective** to describe the noun *settlers*.
Cape Breton Island lies on Canada's eastern coast.	The phrase *on Canada's eastern coast* acts as an **adverb** to modify the verb *lies*.

Write the 10 prepositional phrases that you find in sentences 1 to 6 below.

Example: The Cabot Trail winds along Cape Breton's mountainsides. *along Cape Breton's mountainsides*

1. From the road, drivers can view the ocean.
2. People often see pods of whales along the coast.
3. Moose graze near lakes and streams.
4. Visitors take tours through a museum of French history.
5. Alexander Bell, the inventor of the telephone, settled in Cape Breton.
6. Though he traveled to many places, he said, "For simple beauty, Cape Breton outrivals them all."

Write NOW **Select a piece of writing that you have completed. Look for places where you can add more information by adding prepositional phrases. When you are done, trade papers with a partner and find the prepositional phrases in your partner's paper. See if you can tell whether each phrase is acting as an adjective or an adverb.**

 **TEKS** 8.19A(i), 8.19A(iii)

Expand with Infinitive and Participial Phrases

Writers sometimes make their sentences more interesting by adding infinitive or participial phrases. (Also see **780.3** and **780.4**.)

- An infinitive phrase consists of the word "to" plus the basic form of a verb plus any modifiers. An infinitive phrase can serve as a noun, an adjective, or an adverb.
- A participial phrase consists of a participle (a verb form usually ending in *ed* or *ing*) plus any modifiers. It serves as an adjective in a sentence.

Infinitive Phrases

To visit Death Valley is a goal of mine.
(The phrase serves as a noun—the subject of the sentence.)

Someday, I will have a chance to take this trip.
(The phrase serves as an adjective that modifies the noun *chance*.)

Many people travel to enjoy good weather.
(The phrase serves as an adverb that modifies the verb *travel*.)

Participial Phrases

Hearing about Death Valley, I thought it would be an amazing place.
(The *ing* phrase is an adjective that modifies the pronoun *I*.)

In Death Valley, recognized as one of earth's hottest places, the temperature reaches 130 degrees Fahrenheit.
(The *ed* phrase is an adjective that modifies the noun *Death Valley*.)

 There is one infinitive or participial phrase in each sentence below. Copy each phrase and label it "I" for infinitive or "P" for participial.

Example: To view all of Death Valley, you should climb Telescope Peak.

> *to view all of Death Valley, I*

1. Earth scientists, having a deep understanding of geology, can "read" Death Valley's rocks.
2. Plants and animals living in the harsh conditions are amazing.
3. Somehow, prehistoric humans were able to survive there.
4. Borax, mined in Death Valley in the late 1800s, still exists there.
5. I can't wait to visit this amazing place in person.

How can I make my sentences more interesting?

Model Sentences

You can learn a great deal about writing by studying the sentences of other writers. When you come across sentences that you like, practice writing some of your own using the same pattern. This process is called *modeling*.

Professional Models	Student Models
I walked along the Grand Canyon, gazing down into its rocky gorges and dizzyingly sheer cliffs.	I strolled down the beach, looking out across the crashing surf and foaming breakers.
Goats can go where wolves cannot, following routes that spiral down canyon walls. —*National Geographic*	My brothers slipped through the trapdoor of the fort, swinging down ladders that hung to the ground.

Guidelines for Modeling

- Find a sentence or a short passage that you like and write it down.
- Think of a topic for your practice writing.
- Follow the pattern of the sentence or passage as you write about your own subject. (You do not have to follow the model exactly.)
- Build each sentence one part at a time and check your work when you are finished. (Take your time.)
- Review your work and change any parts that seem confusing or unclear.
- Share your new sentences with your classmates.
- Find other sentences to model and keep practicing.

BASIC WRITING

Write **NOW** On your own paper, model the following sentences.
Remember: You do not have to follow a model sentence exactly.

1 I can tell you that when I spotted the slithery streak in the grass, my heart started to race, but my feet wouldn't move.

2 The children jumped up with surprise, broke into smiles, doubled over with laughter, and shouted for joy.

3 Although the heavy, wet snow soaked through their gloves, Tim and Matt continued building their fort.

584

 **TEKS** 8.19C

Develop a Sentence Style

The following techniques and strategies will help you improve your writing style. (Also see page 45.)

Varying Sentence Beginnings

To add some variety to the common subject-verb pattern, try beginning a sentence with a phrase or a dependent clause.

One evening after sundown, **we drove in a buggy past old Dorset's house.**
　　　　　　—"The Ransom of Red Chief" by O. Henry

To judge by his face, **Dussel is dreaming of food.**
　　　　　　—*The Diary of a Young Girl* by Anne Frank

Moving Adjectives

Usually, you write adjectives before the nouns they modify. You can also emphasize adjectives by placing them after the nouns.

A long, low moan, indescribably sad, **swept over the moor.**
　　　　　　—*The Hound of the Baskervilles* by Sir Arthur Conan Doyle

Repeating a Word

You can repeat a word or phrase to emphasize a particular idea or feeling.

They could see **her cheeks going up and down,** they could see **the trickle of milk leaking out of one side of her mouth, but** they couldn't see **what she was thinking.**
　　　　　　—*The Fledgling* by Jane Langton

Creating a Balanced Sentence

You can write a sentence that uses parallel words, phrases, or clauses for emphasis.

Home! That was what they meant, those caressing appeals, those soft touches **wafted through the air,** those invisible little hands **pulling and tugging, all one way!**
　　　　　　—*The Wind in the Willows* by Kenneth Grahame

 Study the sample sentences above. Then write your own sentences that follow each sample pattern. Share your sentences with your classmates.

Constructing Strong Paragraphs

What's the best way to build strong muscles? Most forms
of exercise build muscle, but other factors are also important.
Eating right, relaxing between workouts, and sleeping
well help muscles develop.

What's the best way to build strong paragraphs?
Starting with a well-written topic sentence is essential,
but a paragraph doesn't stop there. The sentences in
the body need to support the topic sentence and provide
interesting and well-organized details. Last of all, the
closing sentence should summarize or restate the topic.
In the following chapter, you will exercise your brain
by building strong paragraphs.

What's Ahead

You will learn about . . .
- the parts of a paragraph.
- types of paragraphs.
- writing effective paragraphs.
- adding details to paragraphs.
- gathering details.
- organizing your details.
- refining your details.
- turning paragraphs into essays.
- using a checklist.

The Parts of a Paragraph

Most paragraphs have three main parts: a topic sentence, a body, and a closing sentence. Paragraphs usually begin with a **topic sentence** that tells what the paragraph is about. The sentences in the **body** share details about the topic, and the **closing sentence** brings the paragraph to a close.

Topic Sentence

Body

Closing Sentence

Attitude Is Everything

A positive attitude can help people overcome great odds. Walt Disney didn't let a learning disability stop him from creating the best-known amusement park in the world. Helen Keller's positive attitude helped her become the first person who was hearing-, sight-, and speech-impaired to earn a bachelor of arts degree. She went on to write many books and became one of America's greatest speakers. When the famous scientist Stephen Hawking was asked about having ALS, a serious muscular disease, he said, "I try to lead as normal a life as possible and not think about my condition or regret the things it prevents me from doing." That's a positive attitude in action! Whenever people face a difficult challenge, they should remember these individuals and the power of a positive attitude.

Respond to the reading. How many examples of positive attitude are mentioned? What do they all have in common?

A Closer Look at the Parts

The Topic Sentence

The topic sentence tells the reader what a paragraph is going to be about. A good topic sentence (1) names the topic and (2) states a specific detail or a feeling about it. Here is a simple formula for writing a topic sentence.

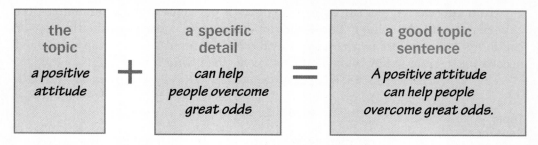

the topic		a specific detail		a good topic sentence
a positive attitude	**+**	*can help people overcome great odds*	**=**	*A positive attitude can help people overcome great odds.*

The topic sentence is usually the first sentence in a paragraph, although sometimes it comes later. It guides the direction of the sentences in the rest of the paragraph.

A positive attitude can help people overcome great odds.

The Body

The sentences in the body of the paragraph include the details needed to understand the topic.

- **Use specific details to make your paragraph interesting.**
  The specific details below are shown in red.

  Walt Disney didn't let a learning disability stop him from creating the best-known amusement park in the world.

- **Organize your sentences in the best possible order.**
  Five common ways to organize sentences are chronological (time) order, order of location, order of importance, comparison-contrast order, and logical order. (See page 613.)

The Closing Sentence

The closing sentence comes after all the details in the body. It will often restate the topic or give the reader something to think about. In an essay, it can provide a transition into a following paragraph.

Whenever people face a difficult challenge, they should remember these individuals and the power of a positive attitude.

BASIC ELEMENTS

ELPS 5B

Types of Paragraphs

There are four basic types of paragraphs: *narrative, descriptive, expository,* and *persuasive*. Each type requires a different way of thinking and planning.

Write Narrative Paragraphs

In a **narrative paragraph**, you share a personal story or an important experience with the reader. The details in a narrative paragraph should answer the 5 W's *(who? what? when? where? and why?)*. A narrative is often organized according to time (what happened *first, next, then, finally*).

Topic Sentence
· · · · · · · · · · · · ·

Body

Closing Sentence
· · · · · · · · · · · · ·

Champions

   With only 15 seconds left on the clock, we needed a basket to win the Midwest Wheelchair Basketball Tournament. My teammates and I were racing toward our end of the court, and I had the ball. I scrambled between two guys and gave a strong push to the basket. Though my eyes were on all the players, my mind was on scoring. We'd worked too hard to get this far— we just had to win. When I was near the top of the key, I heard my coach yell, "Shoot it, Mo!" In one smooth motion, I squared up and let the ball fly. I remember thinking the shot was right on line, but the ball hit the back of the rim and went straight up into the air. Everyone tried to get in position under the basket. Then, just as the buzzer sounded, the ball slipped cleanly through the net. We had won the game 38–37, and the championship was ours.

 Respond to the reading. How does the closing sentence connect with the topic sentence? How is suspense built?

 Draft **Write a narrative paragraph.** Write a paragraph that tells about some memorable experience you've had. Make sure to answer the 5 W's. Read your paragraph aloud to a partner.

 **TEKS** 8.14C
ELPS 5B

ORGANIZE share explain *tell*
describe

589

Constructing Strong Paragraphs

Develop Descriptive Paragraphs

When you write a **descriptive paragraph**, you give a detailed picture of a person, a place, an object, or an event. Descriptive paragraphs often include many sensory details that help create vivid images for the reader.

My Guide Dog

Topic Sentence

I know my golden retriever Misha just about as well as I know myself. She has a firm, wide head with floppy ears that are covered with curly, silky fur. My hands slide down the top of her head and over her eyes, the eyes that see for me. Then I find her cold, damp nose and thick, smooth tongue. I can feel her warm breath

Body

on my hands. She wears a thick collar around her neck and a leather harness around her broad sides. Her silky fur ruffles in my fingers and smells like the outdoors. Her nails are stubby and hard, and her round toes are rough. Little tufts of fur, called feathers, stick out between her toes. When I hold Misha's paw, her tail

Closing Sentence

thumps against the floor, almost like a greeting. Misha is an incredible dog, and I often wonder what my life would be like without her.

BASIC ELEMENTS

 Respond to the reading. How many of the five senses are covered in the paragraph? Which two or three details are especially descriptive?

 Write a descriptive paragraph. Write a paragraph that describes an animal. Use sensory details in your description to create vivid images.

Construct Expository Paragraphs

In an **expository paragraph**, you share information. You can tell how to do something, give directions, or explain a subject. Transition words like *first, next, then,* and *finally* are often used in expository writing.

Topic Sentence

Body

Closing Sentence

What Is a TDD?

A telecommunications device for the deaf, or TDD, works like instant messaging on a computer. The TDD is made up of a keyboard, display screen, modem, and printer. First, the user types a message on the keyboard and then sends it to another TDD. When the message reaches its destination, it appears on the other user's display screen. The TDD does not ring like a regular telephone does. Instead, a flashing light tells the person at the other end that a message is waiting. Some TDD systems include a vibrating wristband to alert the person that a message has arrived. There are also message relay centers so that people using regular telephones can send messages to TDD's. Today, more than four million people in the United States have TDD's. This communication tool makes it easy for people with severe hearing disabilities to "reach out and touch somebody" with a message.

 Respond to the reading. What type of information about the topic is included in the paragraph? Think in terms of definitions, materials needed, and so on.

 Write an expository paragraph. Write a paragraph that explains a device, small appliance, or piece of equipment that you know well. Include different types of information. Read your paragraph aloud to a partner.

Build Persuasive Paragraphs

In a **persuasive paragraph**, you share your opinion (or strong feeling) about a topic. To be persuasive, you must include plenty of reasons, facts, and details to support your opinion. Persuasive writing is usually organized by order of importance (as in the paragraph below) or by logical order.

Topic Sentence
• • • • • • • • • • • •

Body

Closing Sentence
• • • • • • • • • • •

Volunteer for Special Olympics

Students at Parkwood Middle School should volunteer to help with the Special Olympics. First of all, volunteering for this worthy event will get students involved in the community. Over time, this involvement will help them become better citizens and neighbors. Secondly, working with these special athletes will allow students to put into practice what they have learned. Parkwood coaches have taught students a lot about sports and training, so it would be satisfying to share this knowledge with other athletes. Most importantly, volunteering will help students better understand and appreciate people with different abilities and gifts. As they work with these athletes, they will surely learn a lot from them, just as they will learn from the volunteers. There are plenty of things that students can do, from working with individual athletes to helping out at the local events. How they help out doesn't matter. What is important is that students volunteer their services and make the Special Olympics a rewarding experience for everyone involved.

BASIC ELEMENTS

Respond to the reading. What is the writer's opinion in the paragraph? Name two or three reasons that support her opinion. When is the most important reason given?

Draft

Write a persuasive paragraph. Write to promote a worthwhile cause. Include at least three strong reasons that support your opinion. Read your paragraph aloud to a partner.

Writing Effective Paragraphs

Use the following general guidelines whenever you write paragraphs.

Prewriting Selecting a Topic and Details

- Select a specific topic.
- Collect facts, examples, and details about your topic.
- Write a topic sentence that states what your paragraph is going to be about. (See page 587 for help.)
- Decide on the best way to arrange your details.

Drafting Creating the First Draft

- Start your paragraph with the topic sentence.
- Write sentences in the body that support your topic. Use the details you collected as a guide.
- Connect your ideas and sentences with transitions.
- End with a sentence that restates your topic, leaves the reader with a final thought, or (in an essay) leads into the next paragraph.

Revising Improving Your Writing

- Add information if you need to say more about your topic.
- Move sentences that aren't in the correct order.
- Delete sentences that do not support the topic.
- Rewrite any sentences that are not clear.

Editing Checking for Conventions

- Check the revised version of your writing for grammar, mechanics, and spelling errors.
- Then write a neat final copy and proofread it.

 When you write a paragraph, remember that readers want . . .

- original ideas. *(They want to learn something new and interesting.)*
- personality. *(They want to hear the writer's voice.)*

How can I find interesting details?

Every paragraph needs good supporting details. Some details will come from personal experience, especially when you are writing narrative and descriptive paragraphs. Other details will come from other sources of information, especially when you are writing expository and persuasive paragraphs. It is important to use reliable, valid sources and cite them in your writing to provide strong support for your main point.

Use Personal Details

Personal details are those that you gather by using your senses, your memory, or your imagination.

- **Sensory details** are things that you see, hear, smell, taste, and touch. (These details are important in descriptive paragraphs.)

    Then I find her cold, damp nose and thick, smooth tongue. I can feel her warm breath on my hands.

- **Memory details** are things you remember from experience. (These details are important in narrative paragraphs.)

    I remember thinking the shot was right on line, but the ball hit the back of the rim and went straight up into the air.

- **Reflective details** are things you wonder about, hope for, or imagine. (These are often used in narrative paragraphs.)

    Misha is an incredible dog, and I often wonder what my life would be like without her.

Use Other Sources of Details

To collect details from other sources, use the following tips.

1 **Talk with someone you know.** Parents, neighbors, friends, or teachers may know a lot about your topic.

2 **Write for information.** If you think a museum, a business, or a government office has information you need, send for it.

3 **Read about your topic.** Gather details from books, magazines, and newspapers.

4 **Use the Internet.** The quickest source of information is the Internet. Remember to check Internet sources carefully for reliability. (See page **391**.)

BASIC ELEMENTS

TEKS 8.15A(iv), 8.17A(iii)

How do I know what kinds of details to gather?

The following tips will help you collect the right kinds of details for your paragraphs about people, places, objects, events, and definitions.

Writing About a Person

When writing about or describing a person, make sure you collect plenty of details that deal with his or her appearance and personality. These are what will make the person interesting to readers. Follow these helpful guidelines.

Observe ■ If possible, carefully watch the person. Maybe the person laughs in a special way or wears a certain type of clothing.

Interview ■ Talk with your subject if you can. Write down words and phrases that the person uses.

Research ■ Use whatever sources are necessary—books, articles, the Internet—to find out more about this person.

Compare ■ Can your subject be compared to some other person?

Describe ■ List any physical characteristics and personality traits.

Writing About a Place

When describing or writing about a place, use details that help the reader understand why the place is important to you.

Observe ■ Study the place you plan to write about. Use photos, postcards, or videos if you can't observe the place in person.

Remember ■ Think of a story (or an anecdote) about this place.

Describe ■ Include the sights, sounds, and smells of the place.

Compare ■ Compare your place to other places.

Writing About an Object

When writing about an object, tell your reader what kind of object it is, what it looks like, how it is used, and why this object is important to you.

Observe ■ Think about these questions: How is it used? Who uses it? How does it work? What does the object look like?

Research ■ Learn about the object. Try to find out when it was first made and used. Ask other people about it.

Define ■ What class or category does this object fit into? (See "Writing a Definition" on the next page.)

Remember ■ Recall interesting stories about this object.

Writing About an Event

When writing about or describing an event, focus on the important actions or on one interesting part. Try to collect sensory details and details that answer the 5 W's. The following guidelines will help.

Observe ■ Study the event carefully. What sights, sounds, tastes, and smells come to mind? Listen to what people around you are saying.

Remember ■ When you write about something that has happened to you, recall as many details connected with the event as you can.

List ■ Answer the *who? what? when? where?* and *why?* questions for facts about the event.

Investigate ■ Read about the event and ask other people what they know about it.

Evaluate ■ Decide why the event is important to you.

Writing a Definition

When you write a definition, you need to think about three things.

● First put the **term** you are defining *(snowboard)* into a **class** or category of similar things *(ski-like board)*.

● Then list special **characteristics** that make this object different from others in that class *(ridden downhill over snow)*.

> **Term**—*A snowboard*
> **Class**—*is a ski-like board*
> **Characteristic**—*that is ridden downhill over snow.*

 Choose a person, place, object, or event to write a multi-paragraph piece of writing about. Follow the guidelines you have just read. Make sure to first identify which facts and details are necessary and appropriate to include in your piece. Share your writing with a partner.

BASIC ELEMENTS

What can I do to organize my details effectively?

After gathering your details, you need to organize them in the best possible way. You can organize a paragraph by *time, location, importance, comparison-contrast*, or *logical* order. Graphic organizers can help you keep your details in order.

Use Chronological Order

Chronological means "according to time." Transition words and phrases (*first, second, then,* and *finally*) are often used in narrative and expository paragraphs. A time line can help you organize details chronologically.

			Kwanzaa Time Line				
week before	Dec. 26	Dec. 27	Dec. 28	Dec. 29	Dec. 30	Dec. 31	Jan. 1
decorate house		each evening light a candle, discuss family unity and community theme, tell a story or sing, and exchange gifts				Karamu feast and dancing	faith in leaders

Topic Sentence

Body

Closing Sentence

Celebrating Kwanzaa

Kwanzaa is a seven-day festival that celebrates African American culture. The week before the celebration, family members decorate the home. A traditional symbol, a candleholder with seven candles, is placed on a straw mat. The candles symbolize the African Americans' struggles in the past and their hopes for the future. The celebration actually begins on the evening of December 26. Families gather, and a child lights a candle. Then the family members discuss unity of the family and the community. Next a story or song is used to illustrate the principle. Afterward, gifts may be exchanged. On each of the following four nights, this ceremony is repeated. Families discuss self-determination, community togetherness, economic cooperation, and purpose. On December 31, in addition to talking about creativity, a special feast called Karamu takes place. It features traditional food, music, and dancing. The last day of the celebration is spent discussing faith in other people, teachers, and leaders. After the seven days, the bonds of family, culture, and community have been reinforced.

Respond to the reading. Is "Celebrating Kwanzaa" a narrative paragraph or an expository paragraph? How is time order used to organize this paragraph?

TEKS 8.14B
ELPS 5G

Use Order of Location

Often, you can organize descriptive details spatially, by order of location. For example, a description may move from left to right, from top to bottom, from one direction (north) to another (south), or from the whole to its parts. Words or phrases like *next to, before, above, below, east, west, north,* and *south* may be used to show location. A drawing or map can help you organize your details.

Topic Sentence
• • • • • • • • • • • • • •

Body

Closing Sentence
• • • • • • • • • • • • •

Dancing Chinese Dragon

The grand finale of the San Francisco Chinese New Year's Parade is a giant dragon dancing down the street. As 600,000 firecrackers explode, a group of 100 people carries the 200-foot-long dragon. This special creation is made up of 29 sections of brightly colored silk and velvet. Underneath the layers of fabric, a bamboo frame supports the dragon. From head to tail, its skin is decorated with colored lights, white fur, and silver rivets. The dragon's enormous head is modeled after a camel's head. A set of curved deer horns rest on top. Between the head and the body is a serpent's slithery neck. The long, twisting body is covered in a rainbow of fish scales. The lower belly looks like the belly of a frog. A writhing, whiplike tail completes the dancing dragon. As the dragon passes, another new year begins.

BASIC ELEMENTS

Respond to the reading. How are the details in this paragraph arranged—from left to right, from top to bottom, or in another order?

TEKS 8.14B
ELPS 5G

Use Order of Importance

Expository and persuasive paragraphs are often organized by order of importance—from *most* to *least* important, or from *least* to *most* important.

Most important		Least important
1. _____		3. _____
2. _____	**or**	2. _____
3. _____		1. _____
Least important		Most important

Topic Sentence

Body

Closing Sentence

Ethnic Celebrations Connect People

Throughout the year, people in the United States honor and celebrate different ethnic groups. These celebrations, some lasting for an entire month, are important for many reasons. First of all, people have an opportunity to share their culture. Food is one way they can share. Pizza is Italian, egg rolls are Chinese, and so on. With these many celebrations, people have a chance to try more authentic ethnic foods such as beignets, fry bread, or pierogies. Helping ethnic groups gain a better understanding of each other is another reason for the celebrations. For example, during February, the country explores the contributions African Americans have made in science, politics, and entertainment. Most importantly, during these special times, young people get a chance to discover their own heritage. As members of different generations celebrate together, they share food, traditions, memories, and more. A bond is made that keeps each family's culture alive. As long as the celebrations continue, people will be able to appreciate the wonderful mix of cultures in this country.

Respond to the reading. How are the details organized in this paragraph? On your own paper, list them in reverse order (most to least or least to most). Does one order seem to work better?

TEKS 8.14B
ELPS 5G

Use Comparison-Contrast Order

Expository paragraphs are often organized by comparison-contrast order, which shows how two subjects are both alike and different. A Venn diagram can be used to show differences (**A** and **B**) and similarities (**C**).

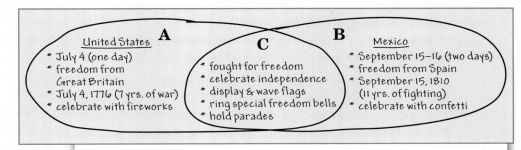

United States   **A**
* July 4 (one day)
* freedom from Great Britain
* July 4, 1776 (7 yrs. of war)
* celebrate with fireworks

C
* fought for freedom
* celebrate independence
* display & wave flags
* ring special freedom bells
* hold parades

B   **Mexico**
* September 15–16 (two days)
* freedom from Spain
* September 15, 1810 (11 yrs. of fighting)
* celebrate with confetti

Topic Sentence

Two Independence Days

Body

Both the United States and Mexico fought for their independence. July 4, 1776, marks the date when the United States declared its independence from Great Britain. It took seven years of fighting before freedom was won. Similarly, Mexico overcame Spain's control. On September 15, 1810, Father Hidalgo rang his church's bell as a signal for revolution. Mexico's battle for independence lasted 11 years. Although both countries honor freedom by celebrating their independence days, the celebrations vary slightly. Each July 4, people in the United States wave flags, hold parades, and watch fireworks. Many places have special events. For example, in Philadelphia, the Liberty Bell is rung. In Mexico, the fiesta begins on September 15, Independence Day Eve, when the Mexican president rings the same bell Father Hidalgo rang and shouts "viva Mexico, viva la independencia." Across Mexico, at the same time, people repeat the cry and throw confetti.

Closing Sentence

The celebration continues through September 16 with flag-waving parades. No matter how the people celebrate, both countries enjoy the freedom that was won for them many years ago.

BASIC ELEMENTS

Respond to the reading. Find two body sentences that include similar details. What words show the comparison?

Draft

Write a paragraph. Choose two festivals or holidays to compare. Use a Venn diagram to organize your details. Then write your paragraph. Read your paragraph aloud to a partner.

TEKS 8.14B

How can I be sure all my details work well?

Create Unity in Your Writing

In a well-written paragraph, each detail tells something about the topic. If a detail does not tell something about the topic, it breaks the *unity* of the paragraph and should probably be cut.

The detail shown in blue in the following passage does not fit with the rest of the paragraph. It disrupts the unity and should be cut.

> The Pittsburgh Pirates struggled during the 1960 World Series. During series play, the Pirates had only 27 runs compared to the New York Yankees' 55 runs. In addition, the Yankees hit the ball 91 times, while the Pirates could manage only 60 hits. The Pirates were the first modern National League champions in 1901. However, the Pirates were victorious in the seventh game and claimed the series title for 1960 because Bill Mazeroski hit a game-winning home run in the bottom of the ninth inning.

In the paragraph below, find three details (sentences) that *do not* support the topic sentence. Then read the paragraph without those sentences. How does cutting them affect the paragraph's unity?

1　　Star baseball player Roberto Clemente was born in Puerto
2　Rico in 1934. Baseball is my favorite sport, too. At first, he played
3　amateur baseball in Puerto Rico. Then he signed on with the
4　Brooklyn Dodgers and played for their minor league team, the
5　Montreal Royals. I don't know much about how he did with that
6　team. However, he is most famous for the 18 years, 1955 through
7　1972, that he played with the Pittsburgh Pirates. By the way,
8　the Pirates are doing great this year. He played in two World
9　Series, won four batting titles and twelve Gold Glove awards,
10　and was once voted most valuable player. Clemente was also a
11　humanitarian. In 1972, he was on a plane carrying supplies to
12　help people who had been in an earthquake in Nicaragua. The
13　plane crashed, and Clemente died at the age of 38. Today he is
14　remembered as a great athlete and the first Latino to be inducted
15　into the National Baseball Hall of Fame.

Look at your paragraph. Study the comparison-contrast paragraph you wrote (page 599). Do all your details support your topic? Would the unity of your paragraph be improved if you cut a detail or two?

Develop Coherence from Start to Finish

An effective paragraph reads smoothly and clearly. When all the details in a paragraph are tied together well, the paragraph has *coherence* and is easy for the reader to follow. Transitions help make your writing smooth and coherent.

 Number your paper from 1 to 6. Use the transitions from the following list to help tie the paragraph below together. (Use each transition only once.) Then reread the paragraph. Does it read smoothly? If not, switch some transitions.

between	after	when	until	before	finally

The Underground Railroad was made up of people who helped slaves escape from the South to the North before the Civil War. _____ escaping from a slaveholder, slaves often
(1)
traveled by foot, usually at night, _____ they came to a
(2)
"station." A station was a house or business owned by someone willing to help the slaves escape. The slaves rested and hid there _____ moving on. Then the next "stationmaster" was
(3)
alerted that people were coming. Once they were safe, the slaves were given food and clothing for their journey. _____
(4)
it was safe, slaves moved from station to station with the help of the stationmasters. _____ , they crossed the border to
(5)
freedom in the North. _____ 1810 and 1850, approximately
(6)
100,000 slaves escaped to start new lives as free persons. Many of them used the Underground Railroad.

 Read your paragraph. Read your comparison-contrast paragraph from page 599. Underline any parts that don't flow smoothly. Then use transitions to make the writing smoother. (See pages 634–635.)

BASIC ELEMENTS

TEKS 8.14C, 8.17A(iii)

How can I write essays containing strong paragraphs?

Use an Essay Plan

Writing an essay is not simply a matter of putting together a group of paragraphs. Each paragraph needs to be well organized and connected to the paragraphs before and after it. Follow the guidelines listed below.

1 Plan the organization.

Organize your essay in a way that fits your topic—chronological order, order of importance, order of location, and so on.

2 State the topic and focus in the first paragraph.

Begin with an interesting fact or example to catch the reader's attention. Then tell what your essay is about in a focus or thesis statement. This statement should identify the topic and a main idea or feeling about it.

3 Develop your writing idea in the middle paragraphs.

Use each paragraph in the body of your essay to explain and support one part of your focus statement. Each paragraph must have a topic sentence followed with supporting details.

4 Finish with a strong ending.

The final paragraph is usually a review of the main points in the essay. Your ending may emphasize the importance of the topic or may leave the reader with something to think about.

5 Use transition words or phrases to connect paragraphs.

Make sure you use transition words between paragraphs that make the paragraphs flow from one to the next and give the writing coherence. For a complete list of transitions, see pages 634–635.

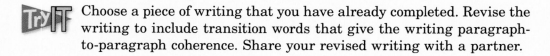

Try It   Choose a piece of writing that you have already completed. Revise the writing to include transition words that give the writing paragraph-to-paragraph coherence. Share your revised writing with a partner.

TEKS 8.14C, 8.20A, 8.21
ELPS 4C, 4K

How do I know if I have a strong paragraph?

Use a Paragraph Checklist

You'll know that you have a strong paragraph if it gives the reader complete information on a specific topic. One sentence should identify the topic, and the other sentences should support it. Use the checklist below to help you plan and write effective paragraphs.

Focus and Coherence

_____ **1.** Does my paragraph focus on one main idea?

_____ **2.** Did I include the important details that will help my reader understand my idea?

_____ **3.** Have I removed unnecessary details that would distract the reader from my main idea?

Organization

_____ **4.** Is my topic sentence clear?

_____ **5.** Have I organized the details in the best order?

_____ **6.** Does my closing sentence restate or summarize my main idea?

Development of Ideas

_____ **7.** Are my ideas developed enough so that readers can understand and appreciate them?

Voice

_____ **8.** Does my paragraph use language that expresses my personality and individuality?

Conventions

_____ **9.** Have I followed the rules for spelling, grammar, and mechanics (capitalization, punctuation)?

_____ **10.** Have I included simple, compound, and complex sentences?

BASIC ELEMENTS

improve

support

A Writer's Resource

Learning Language

Work with a partner. Read the meanings and share answers to the questions.

1. A strategy is a plan for accomplishing something.
   If you had to achieve a specific goal, how would you go about making a strategy?

2. A technique is a skill or ability that helps you do something.
   What is a special technique you have learned to do a specific task or job?

3. Your curriculum is all the subjects you study in school.
   If you could add a subject to your school's curriculum, what would it be?

4. Your writing style is affected by the words you choose and the way you put them together in sentences. Your style makes your writing sound different than anyone else's.
   Read a paragraph of your writing and then listen to a partner read a paragraph he or she wrote. Compare your styles. How are they different?

organize

REFERENCE

select

A Writer's Resource

Writing is a complex job. Sometimes even experienced authors have trouble knowing what to write about, where to start, or how to sound interesting. Although practice certainly helps a writer become more skillful and self-confident, everyone needs a little help once in a while.

"A Writer's Resource" contains information, tips, and guidelines to get you through your writing problems. You'll find strategies for selecting topics, ways to improve your style, and ideas on techniques to enrich your writing.

What's Ahead

You will learn how to . . .
- **find topics and get started.**
- **collect and organize details.**
- **write terrific topic sentences.**
- **use new forms and techniques.**
- **improve your voice and writing style.**
- **increase your vocabulary.**
- **improve your sentences.**
- **improve your presentation.**

 TEKS 8.14A

How can I find the best topics to write about?

Try a Topic-Selecting Strategy

A distinguished writer once said, "There are few experiences quite so satisfactory as getting a good writing idea." This may be overstating it a little, but getting a good writing idea is certainly an important step in the writing process. Let's say, for example, you are asked to write an essay about a controversial issue in your school or community. Your first job would be to select a specific topic to write about.

> **General Subject Area:** school or community controversy
>
> **Specific Writing Topic:** new auditorium

The following strategies will help you select interesting topics that you can feel good about.

Clustering Begin a cluster (also called a web) by selecting a key word or phrase that is related to your writing assignment. Write the key word in the middle of your paper and cluster related words around it. (See page 280.)

Journal Writing Write on a regular basis in a personal journal, recording your thoughts and experiences. Review your entries from time to time and underline ideas that you would like to write more about later, as in the model below.

Oct. 12

Today we had our last rehearsal for the fall orchestra concert. I'm first chair, so I have more responsibilities this year. I have to keep my violin really well tuned, because the whole orchestra follows me.

Mrs. Soderberg said that we did a good job and that we've come a long way since the beginning of the year. No one was practicing very much at first, but in the last two weeks, you could tell that everyone was working harder. I think they were afraid of sounding horrible in front of an audience, plus Mrs. S. really got mad one day about people not knowing their music.

The only bad thing is that after all of this work, we still have to play in the cafeteria. The sound in there is awful because of the echoes, and the cafeteria chairs make noise every time someone moves. I think we need a new auditorium in this school.

TEKS 8.14A

Listing Write your general subject at the top of your paper and list related ideas as they come to mind. Keep your list going as long as you can. Then look for words in your list that you feel would make good writing topics.

Freewriting Write nonstop for 5 to 10 minutes to discover possible writing ideas. Begin writing with a particular subject or idea in mind (one related to the writing assignment). Underline the ideas that might work as topics for your assignment.

Sentence Starters Complete an open-ended sentence in as many ways as you can. Try to word your sentence so that it leads you to a topic you can use for your writing assignment.

People disagree about . . .

This community should . . .

There are differences between . . .

I learned a lesson when . . .

My favorite experience was . . .

It would be interesting to meet . . .

Review the "Basics of Life" List

The words listed below name many of the categories or groups of things that people need in order to live a full life. The list provides an endless variety of possibilities for topics. Consider the first category, food. You could write about . . .

- the most unusual meal you've ever eaten,
- what's good for you and what's not, or
- the first time you tried to cook something.

food	senses	rules/laws
work/occupation	machines	tools/utensils
clothing	intelligence	heat/fuel
faith/religion	history/records	natural resources
communication	agriculture	personality/identity
exercise	land/property	recreation/hobbies
education	community	trade/money
family	science	literature/books
friends	plants/vegetation	health/medicine
purpose/goals	freedom/rights	art/music
love	energy	

RESOURCE

 **TEKS** 8.14A

What can I do to get started?

Use a List of Writing Topics

The writing prompts listed below and the sample topics listed on the next page provide plenty of starting points for writing assignments.

Writing Prompts

Every day is full of experiences that make you think. You do things that you feel good about. You hear things that make you angry. You wonder how different things work. You are reminded of a past experience. These common, everyday thoughts can make excellent prompts for writing.

Describe (Descriptive)
    An influential person
    Your favorite celebrity
    A solar eclipse
    Hermit crabs
    Life before television

Tell Your Story (Narrative)
    Learning something about life
    Overcoming a challenge
    Meeting an unusual person
    Visiting a special place
    A sudden revelation
    The perfect day
    Facing a disappointment
    A surprise

Classify (Expository)
    Clothing styles
    Scooters
    Extreme sports
    Types of pets
    Constellations
    Kinds of diets
    Birds of prey

Compare-Contrast (Expository)
    Soccer and football
    Living in a small town/large city
    Two seasons
    Heroes and celebrities
    Fashions now and twenty years ago
    Jobs and professions

Defend (Persuasive)
    Starting school later in the morning
    Eating wisely and exercising
    Service learning
    Individuality
    Sports in school
    A worthwhile cause

Respond to . . .
(Responding to Texts)
    A book that made you think
    A poem that explained something
    A character you identify with
    The biography of someone
        you admire

Research (Report)
    Aquifers, hot springs, glaciers
    Oil wells, salt mines
    Mud slides, forest fires

Sample Topics

You come across many people, places, experiences, and things every day that could be topics for writing. A number of possible topics are listed below for descriptive, narrative, expository, and persuasive writing.

Descriptive

People: best friend, favorite relative, personal idol, great leader, person you're comfortable with, someone who overcomes difficulty, teacher, coach, brother or sister

Places: hangout, garage, room, rooftop, historical place, zoo, park, hallway, barn, bayou, lake, cupboard, yard, empty lot, alley, valley, campsite, river, city street

Things: billboard, poster, video game, cell phone, bus, boat, gift, drawing, rainbow, doll, junk drawer, flood, mascot, movie

Animals: dolphin, elephant, snake, armadillo, eagle, deer, toad, spoonbill, squirrel, pigeon, pet, coyote, catfish, octopus, beaver, turtle

Narrative

moving to a new home, scoring a goal in a game, making a new friend, losing a pet, going to camp, learning a skill or sport, traveling to an interesting place

Expository

Classification: animal camouflage, natural disasters, kinds of music, types of government, religious beliefs, scientific principles, fads

Comparison-Contrast: friends, places, jobs, teachers, pets, transportation, a house cat and a lion, lakes and oceans

The causes of . . . sunburn, acne, hiccups, tornadoes, school dropouts, computer viruses, arguments

Kinds of . . . crowds, friends, commercials, dreams, neighbors, pain, clouds, joy, stereos, heroes, chores, homework, frustration

Persuasive

Community: building a skate park, beautifying the city, losing a local movie theater, opening a teen center, building sidewalks, building a superstore on the edge of town

School: assigning less homework, air-conditioning classrooms, providing more computers and printers, changing the school mascot, starting a school drama department

 TEKS 8.14B

How can I collect details for my writing?

Try Graphic Organizers

Graphic organizers can help you gather and organize your details for writing. Clustering is one method. (See page 280.) These two pages list other useful organizers.

Cause-Effect Organizer

Use to collect and organize details for cause-effect essays.

Subject:

Causes	Effects
•	•
•	•
•	•
•	•
•	•

Problem-Solution Web

Use to map out problem-solution essays.

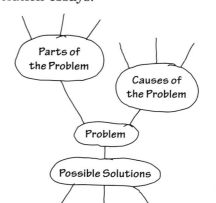

Time Line (Step-by-Step)

Use to collect details for personal narratives and how-to essays.

Subject:

(Chronological Order)

First:

Finally:

Before-After Chart

Use to collect details for narratives or expository essays.

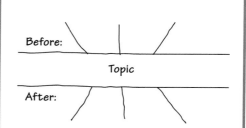

Before:

Topic

After:

organize
REFERENCE
select support improve
611
A Writer's Resource

TEKS 8.14B

Venn Diagram

Use to collect details to compare and contrast two subjects.

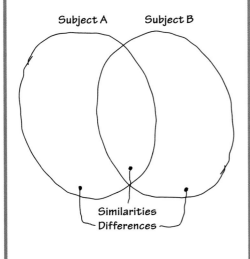

Subject A   Subject B

Similarities
Differences

5 W's Chart

Use to collect the *Who? What? When? Where?* and W*hy?* details for personal narratives and news stories.

Subject: _____

Who?	What?	When?	Where?	Why?

Line Diagram

Use to collect and organize details for classification or other expository essays.

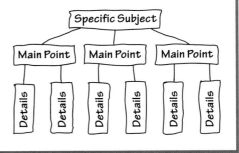

Specific Subject

Main Point   Main Point   Main Point

Details Details Details Details Details Details

Process Chain (5-Step)

Use to collect details for science-related writing, such as how a process or cycle works.

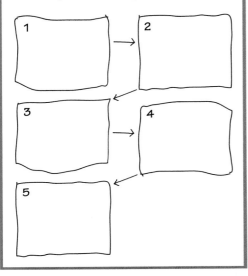

1
2
3
4
5

Sensory Chart

Use to collect details for descriptive essays and observation reports.

Subject: _____

Sights	Sounds	Smells	Tastes	Feelings

TEKS 8.14B

What can I do to organize my details better?

Make Lists and Outlines

List Your Details

You can use a variety of ways to organize details as you prepare to write an essay or a report. For most writing, you can make a simple list.

The importance of salt
- *wars fought over it*
- *used for money*
- *helps keep us alive*
- *preserves food*
- *softens water*
- *used to make chemicals*
- *melts ice on roads*

How Detroit salt bed formed
- *seawater flooded the area*
- *seawater evaporated, leaving salt*
- *layer 400 to 1,600 feet thick*
- *covered by layers of silt*

Outline Your Information

After gathering facts and details, select two or three main points that best support your focus. Write an outline to organize your information.

I. Salt is much more important than most people realize.
  A. Wars have been fought over it.
  B. In ancient China, salt coins were used for money.
  C. In the human body, salt carries electrical signals that keep a person alive.
  D. Salt is used to preserve meat and fish and to tan leather.
  E. Salt is also used to make chemicals.

II. Scientists say that the Detroit mine digs into a bed of salt that is several hundred million years old.
  A. From 600 million to 230 million years ago, seawater flooded the middle of North America many times.
  B. As the sun and wind evaporated the water . . .

Use Patterns of Organization

■ **Chronological (Time) Order** or **Step-by-Step** You can arrange your details in the order in which they happen *(first, then, next)*. Use these patterns for narratives, history reports, and explaining a process. (See page 596.)

> In 1896, the Detroit salt mine was started in order to dig the salt out of the ground. It began as a shaft 1,200 feet deep and about 6 feet wide. At first, the salt was used mainly for storing meat and fish and for making . . .

■ **Order of Location** You can arrange details in the order in which they are located *(above, below, beside,* and so on). Use order of location for descriptions, explanations, and directions. (See page 597.)

> Rosa and her once-white jumpsuit look like the paint-chip aisle at the hardware store—splattered with color from the top of her head to the toes of her now rainbow-colored canvas shoes.

■ **Order of Importance** You can arrange details from the most important to the least—or from the least important to the most. Persuasive and expository essays are often organized this way. (See page 598.)

> First of all, an open study hall would let hardworking students go where they need to go to get more work done. . . . Secondly, an open study hall would motivate students to take study hall more seriously. . . . Most importantly, open study hall would teach responsibility.

■ **Comparison-Contrast** You can write about two or more subjects by showing how they are alike and how they are different. Compare each subject separately or compare both, point by point, as in the example below. (See page 599.)

> The same juice comes in two different packages. Which is cheaper, a 12-pack of cans that costs $3.95 or a 6-pack of bottles that costs $2.50? The cans contain 12 ounces each, and the bottles are 16.9 ounces. Dividing the cost of each package by its total number of ounces indicates that the juice in the 12-pack is .027 cents per ounce, and the juice in the 6-pack is .025 cents per ounce. The 6-pack is a better deal.

■ **Logical Order** You can organize information by beginning with a main idea followed by details, or by starting with details and leading up to the main point.

> Studies show that by eating fewer calories people can lose weight. They can also lose weight by increasing how much they exercise. However, if people eat less and exercise more, they will lose more weight and keep it off longer. Combining these methods of losing weight makes sense.

RESOURCE

How can I write terrific topic sentences?

Try Eight Special Strategies

Writing a good topic sentence is a key to writing a great paragraph. A good topic sentence names the topic and states a specific feeling about it. Use the following strategies the next time you need to write a terrific topic sentence. (Also see page 587.)

Use a Number

Topic sentences can use number words to tell what the paragraph will be about.

Number Words		
two	a couple	a pair
few	three	a number
several	four	many
a variety	five	a list

Several **problems need to be looked at more carefully.**

I have three **pet peeves that drive me crazy.**

Create a List

A topic sentence can list the things the paragraph will talk about.

Squeaky had to take care of her brother **and** train for the race **at the same time.**

Heat, light, **and** moisture **can affect a plant's growth.**

Start with "To" and a Verb

A topic sentence that starts with "to" and a verb helps the reader know why the information in the paragraph is important.

To identify **the theme in a story, consider the thoughts and actions of the main character.**

To persuade **others to change their minds, you have to make a convincing argument.**

Use Word Pairs

Word pairs or correlative conjunctions that come in pairs can help organize a topic sentence.

Word Pairs
if . . . then
either . . . or
not only . . . but also
both . . . and
whether . . . or
as . . . so

Whether **you're the best player on the team** or **just average, you need to practice hard.**

Both **fables** and **folktales are entertaining, but fables are more likely to teach a lesson.**

Join Two Ideas

A topic sentence can combine two equal ideas (in independent clauses) by using a comma and a coordinating conjunction: *and, but, or, for, so, nor, yet.*

> **Living in a small town sounds peaceful,** but **I think I would miss the excitement of the city.**

> **Some fashions seem to come around every 10 or 20 years,** so **you can't really say that clothing stores always have new clothes, can you?**

Use a "Why-What" Word

A "why-what" word is a subordinating conjunction that shows how ideas are connected.

> Before **you tell a story, think about the main point that you want to make.**

> Since **we're trying to beautify the city, could we do something about the weeds along the highways?**

"Why-What" Words	
So that	Once
Before	Since
Until	Whenever
Because	While
If	As long as
As	After
In order that	When

Use a "Yes, But" Word

A "yes, but" word is a subordinating conjunction that tells how two ideas are different.

> Instead of **discouraging strip malls, we should be sure that any new ones are well designed.**

> **Some people think that it's all right to lie** unless **the lie hurts someone.**

"Yes, But" Words
Although
Even though
Even if
Unless
Whether
Whereas

Quote an Expert

Sometimes the best way to start a paragraph is to quote someone who knows about your topic.

> **Even though I dislike football practice, I think Joe Paterno was right when he said,** "The will to win is important, but the will to prepare is vital."

> **Helen Keller's statement** "Keep your face to the sunshine and you cannot see the shadow" **is a good way to define optimism.**

What other forms can I use for my writing?

Try These Forms of Writing

Finding the right *form* for your writing is just as important as finding the right topic. When you are selecting a form, be sure to ask yourself who you're writing for (your audience) and why you're writing (your purpose).

Anecdote	A brief story that makes a point
Autobiography	A writer's story of his or her own life
Biography	A writer's story of some other person's life
Book review	A brief essay giving a response or an opinion about a book (See pages 303–333.)
Character sketch	Writing that describes a specific character in a story
Composition	A longer piece of writing, such as a story or an essay
Descriptive writing	Writing that uses details to help the reader clearly imagine a certain person, a place, a thing, or an idea (See pages 73–93.)
Editorial	Newspaper letter or article giving an opinion
Essay	A piece of writing in which ideas are presented, explained, argued, or described in an interesting way
Expository writing	Writing that explains by presenting the steps, the causes, or the kinds of something (See pages 163–231.)
Fable	A short story that often uses talking animals as the main characters and teaches a lesson or moral
Fantasy	A story set in an imaginary world in which the characters usually have supernatural powers or abilities
Freewriting	Writing whatever comes to mind about any topic
Historical fiction	A made-up story based on something real in history in which fact is mixed with fiction
Myth	A traditional story intended to explain a mystery of nature, religion, or culture
Narrative	Writing that relates an event, an experience, or a story (See pages 95–161.)

Novel	A book-length story with several characters and a well-developed plot
Personal narrative	Writing that shares an event or experience from the writer's personal life (See pages **99–131**.)
Persuasive writing	Writing that is meant to persuade the reader to agree with the writer about someone or something (See pages **233–297**.)
Play	A form that uses dialogue to tell a story and is meant to be performed in front of an audience
Poem	Writing that uses rhythm, rhyme, and imagery (See pages **377–385**.)
Proposal	Writing that includes specific information about an idea or a project that is being considered for approval
Research report	An essay that shares information on a topic that has been researched well and organized carefully (See pages **405–450**.)
Response to literature	Writing that is a summary or a reaction to something the writer has read (novel, short story, poem, article, and so on)
Science fiction	Writing based on real or imaginary science and often set in the future
Short story	A short piece of literature with only a few characters and one problem or conflict (See pages **365–373**.)
Summary	Writing that presents only the most important ideas from a longer piece of writing
Tall tale	A humorous, exaggerated story (often based on the life of a real person) about a character or animal who does impossible things
Tragedy	Literature in which the hero is destroyed because of some serious flaw or defect in his or her character

How can I create a voice in my writing?

You can create a strong writing voice by using dialogue and by "showing instead of telling."

Use Dialogue

Each person you write about has a unique way of saying things, and well-written dialogue lets the reader *hear* the speaker's personality and thoughts. For example, notice how the message below can be spoken in several different ways.

Message: The family trip to the Grand Canyon was fun.

Speaker 1: "The whole thing was boring until we got to ride the donkeys."

Speaker 2: "The view was certainly beautiful and peaceful, but those people were standing too close to the edge."

Speaker 3: "Wasn't the Grand Canyon great? Now, if we skip lunch, we can make it to Zion Canyon this afternoon."

Each of the speakers above delivers the same message in a unique way. The dialogue tells as much about the speaker as it does about the topic.

One way to improve your dialogue is to think about the speaker and his or her personality. Look at the three personality webs below and try to decide which one is *Speaker 1, Speaker 2,* or *Speaker 3* from above. How does the dialogue show their personalities?

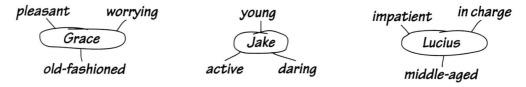

Tips for Punctuating Dialogue

- Indent every time a different person speaks.
- Put the exact words of a speaker in quotation marks.
- Set off the quoted words from the rest of the sentence by using a comma.
- At the end of quoted words, put a period or comma inside the quotation marks.

(For more information and examples on how to punctuate dialogue, see 650.1, 658.1, and 660.1 in the "Proofreader's Guide.")

Show, Don't Tell

When you tell someone that a movie is "good" or that the weather was "awful," what have you really told that person? Not much. If you really want to get your idea across, you have to *show* the details so that your reader experiences what you're describing. Notice the difference in the accounts below.

Telling: **It was really hot riding across the desert on the back of Dad's motorcycle, so we went to a movie in Phoenix.**

Showing: Before Dad and I started on our trip through the Southwest, I thought that riding on a motorcycle would cool us off. I was wrong. It was so hot and dry in the desert that we baked. The sun beat down from above, the heat radiated up from the pavement, and the engine temperature surrounded us like an oven on wheels. Our lips were burning, and our eyes got dry. One day we just stopped at a Phoenix movie theater and "chilled" all afternoon.

The sentence above *tells* the reader that the motorcycle ride was "really hot." The paragraph *shows* why the writer and his father needed to "chill."

Key Strategies for Showing

Next time you realize your writing is telling rather than showing, try one of these strategies.

- **Add sensory details.** Include sights, sounds, smells, tastes, and touch sensations. That way the reader can "experience" the event.

  Telling: **My little brother had trouble with his ice-cream cone.**

  Showing: The blast of hot air went to work on my little brother's chocolate-swirl ice-cream cone. Little streams began to drip off the rim. Jimmy licked at the sweet, sticky liquid, but he couldn't keep up, and the chocolate goo ran down his arm. As he tried to lick his arm, the ice cream tumbled out of the cone onto the sidewalk.

- **Explain body language.** Write about facial expressions and the way people stand, gesture, and move.

  Telling: **Aunt Elsa was glad to see me.**

  Showing: When I walked into the room, Aunt Elsa grinned, jumped out of her chair, and ran over to hug me.

- **Use dialogue.** Let the people in your writing speak for themselves.

  Telling: **Latrell was happy about his test.**

  Showing: Latrell gave me a high five, shouting, "Getting an A on my science test is the greatest thing I've done all year!"

What can I do to improve my writing style?

Learn Some Writing Techniques

Writers put special effects into their stories and essays in different ways. Look over the following writing techniques and then experiment with some of them in your own writing.

Analogy	A comparison of similar objects to help clarify one of the objects **Personal journals are like photograph albums. They both share personal details and tell a story.**
Anecdote	A brief story used to illustrate or make a point **Abe Lincoln walked two miles to return several pennies he had overcharged a customer.** (This anecdote shows Lincoln's honesty.)
Exaggeration	An overstatement or a stretching of the truth used to make a point or paint a clearer picture (See *overstatement*.) **After getting home from summer camp, I slept for a month.**
Foreshadowing	Hints or clues that a writer uses to suggest what will happen next in a story **Halfway home, Sarah wondered whether she had locked her locker.**
Irony	A technique that uses a word or phrase to mean the opposite of its normal meaning **Marshall just loves cleaning his room.**
Local color	The use of details that are common in a certain place or local area (A story taking place on a seacoast would contain details about the water and the life and people near it.) **Everybody wore flannel shirts to the Friday fish fry.**
Metaphor	A figure of speech that compares two things without using the word *like* or *as* (See page **384**.) **In our community, high school football is king.**
Overstatement	An exaggeration or a stretching of the truth (See *exaggeration*.) **When he saw my grades, my dad hit the roof.**

TEKS 8.15A(v)

Parallelism	Repeating similar words, phrases, or sentences to give writing rhythm (See pages 574 and 584.) **We will swim in the ocean, lie on the beach, and sleep under the stars.**
Personification	A figure of speech in which a nonhuman thing (an idea, object, or animal) is given human characteristics (See page 384.) **Rosie's old car coughs and wheezes on cold days.**
Pun	A phrase that uses words in a way that gives them a humorous effect **The lumberjack logged on to the site to order new boots.**
Sarcasm	The use of praise to make fun of or "put down" someone or something (The expression is not sincere and is actually intended to mean the opposite thing.) **Micah's a real gourmet; he loves peanut butter and jelly sandwiches.** (A *gourmet* is a "lover of fine foods.")
Sensory details	Specific details that help the reader see, feel, smell, taste, and/or hear what is being described (See page 379.) **As Lamont took his driver's test, his heart thumped, his hands went cold, and his face began to sweat.**
Simile	A figure of speech that compares two things using the word *like* or *as* (See page 384.) **Faye's little brother darts around like a water bug.** **Yesterday the lake was as smooth as glass.**
Slang	Informal words or phrases used by particular groups of people when they talk to each other **chill out hang loose totally awesome**
Symbol	An object that is used to stand for an idea **The American flag is a symbol of the United States. The stars stand for the 50 states, and the stripes stand for the 13 original U.S. colonies.**
Understatement	Very calm language (the opposite of exaggeration) used to bring special attention to an object or an idea **These hot red peppers may make your mouth tingle a bit.**

RESOURCE

How can I expand my writing vocabulary?

Study Writing Terms

This glossary includes terms used to describe the parts of the writing process. It also includes terms that explain special ways of stating an idea.

Antonym	A word that means the opposite of another word: *happy* and *sad; large* and *small* (See page 625.)
Audience	The people who read or hear what has been written
Body	The main or middle part in a piece of writing that comes between the *beginning* and the *ending* and includes the main points
Brainstorming	Collecting ideas by thinking freely about all the possibilities
Closing	The ending or final part in a piece of writing (In a paragraph, the closing is the last sentence. In an essay or a report, the closing is the final paragraph.)
Coherence	Tying ideas together in your writing (See page 601.)
Connotation	The "feeling" a word suggests (See page 108 and 550.)
Denotation	The dictionary meaning of a word
Dialogue	Written conversation between two or more people
Figurative language	Special comparisons, often called figures of speech, that make your writing more creative (See page 384.)
Focus statement	The statement that tells what specific part of a topic is written about in an essay (See *thesis statement* and page 422.)
Form	A type of writing or the way a piece of writing is put together (See pages 616–617.)
Grammar	The structure of language; the rules and guidelines that you follow in order to speak and write acceptably
Jargon	The special language of a certain group, occupation, or field **Computer jargon: byte digital upload**
Journal	A notebook for writing down thoughts, experiences, ideas, and information

Limiting the subject	Taking a general subject and narrowing it down to a specific topic

General subject   Specific topic

sports → **golf** → **golf skills** → **putting**

Modifiers	Words, phrases, or clauses that describe another word

Our black **cat** slowly **stretched and** then **leaped** onto the wicker chair. (Without the blue modifiers, all we know is that a "cat stretched and leaped.")

Point of view	The angle from which a story is told (See page 376.)
Purpose	The specific reason that a person has for writing

to describe   **to narrate**   **to persuade**   **to explain**

Style	How an author writes (choice of words and sentences)
Supporting details	Facts or ideas used to tell a story, explain a topic, describe something, or prove a point
Synonym	A word that means the same thing as another word (*dog* and *canine*) (See page 625.)
Theme	The main point, message, or lesson in a piece of writing
Thesis statement	A statement that gives the main idea of an essay (See *focus statement*.)
Tone	A writer's attitude toward his or her subject

serious   **humorous**   **sarcastic**

Topic	The specific subject of a piece of writing
Topic sentence	The sentence that contains the main idea of a paragraph (See page 587.)

Blue jeans are a popular piece of American clothing.

Transition	A word or phrase that connects or ties two ideas together smoothly (See pages 634–635.)

also   **however**   **lastly**   **later**   **next**

Usage	The way in which people use language (*Standard usage* generally follows the rules of good grammar. Most of the writing you do in school will require standard usage.)
Voice	A writer's unique, personal tone or feeling that comes across in a piece of writing (See pages 42 and 123.)

RESOURCE

How can I mark changes in my writing?

Use the symbols and letters below to show where and how your writing needs to be changed. Your teachers may also use these symbols to mark errors in your writing.

Symbol	Meaning	Example	Corrected Example
≡	Capitalize a letter.	Lorraine Hansberry wrote *A Raisin in the sun*.	Lorraine Hansberry wrote *A Raisin in the Sun*.
/	Make a capital letter lowercase.	Her play tells the story of the Younger Family.	Her play tells the story of the Younger family.
⊙	Insert (add) a period.	This play focuses on racial attitudes It also . . .	This play focuses on racial attitudes. It also . . .
◯ or *sp.*	Correct spelling.	Lena Younger, the family leader, is very religous.	Lena Younger, the family leader, is very religious.
ℓ	Delete (take out) or replace.	Lena she makes a down payment on a nice house.	Lena makes a down payment on a nice house.
∧	Insert here.	The family wants to escape ghetto life.	The family wants to escape ghetto life.
∧ ∧ ∧	Insert a comma, a colon, or a semicolon.	Her son, Walter Lee, Jr. wants to buy a business.	Her son, Walter Lee, Jr., wants to buy a business.
∨ ∨ ∨	Insert an apostrophe or a quotation mark.	Walter Lees wife hopes for a larger apartment.	Walter Lee's wife hopes for a larger apartment.
? ! ∧ ∧	Insert a question mark or an exclamation point.	What would Beneatha do with the money	What would Beneatha do with the money?
¶	Start a new paragraph.	¶The direction of the play clearly changes when . . .	The direction of the play clearly changes when . . .
∼	Switch words or letters.	Walter gets the possible worst news.	Walter gets the worst possible news.

What can I do to increase my vocabulary skills?

Use Context

When you come across a word you don't know, you can often figure out its meaning from the other words in the sentence. The other words form a familiar context, or setting, for the unfamiliar word. Looking closely at the surrounding words will give you clues to the meaning of the new word.

When you come to a word you don't know . . .

■ **Look for a synonym for the unknown word.**

Sara had an ominous feeling when she woke up, but the feeling was less threatening when she saw she was in her own room.
(*Threatening* means the same as *ominous*.)

■ **Look for an antonym for the unknown word.**

Pumpkins are usually abundant in the autumn, but last year's drought made them scarce.
(*Scarce* means the opposite of *abundant*.)

■ **Look for a comparison or contrast.**

Riding a mountain bike in a remote area is my idea of a great day, but some people like to ride motorcycles on busy six-lane highways.
(A *remote* area is out of the way, in contrast to a *busy* area. The word *but* also emphasizes a contrast.)

■ **Look for a definition or description.**

Manatees, large aquatic mammals (sometimes called sea cows), can be found in the warm coastal waters of Florida.
(An *aquatic* mammal is one that lives in the water.)

■ **Look for words that appear in a series.**

The campers spotted blue jays, chickadees, and indigo buntings on Saturday morning.
(An *indigo bunting,* like a *blue jay* or *chickadee,* is a bird.)

■ **Look for a cause-and-effect relationship.**

The amount of traffic at 6th and Main doubled last year, so crossing lights were placed at that corner to avert an accident.
(*Avert* means "to prevent.")

How can I build my vocabulary across the curriculum?

On the next several pages, you will find many of the most common prefixes, suffixes, and roots in the English language. Learning these word parts can help you increase your writing vocabulary.

Learn About Prefixes

A **prefix** is a word part that is added before a word to change the meaning of the word. For example, when the prefix *un* is added to the word *fair (unfair)*, it changes the word's meaning from "fair" to "not fair."

ambi *[both]*
ambidextrous (skilled with both hands)

anti *[against]*
antifreeze (a liquid that works against freezing)
antiwar (against wars and fighting)

astro *[star]*
astronaut (person who travels among the stars)
astronomy (study of the stars)

auto *[self]*
autobiography (writing that is about yourself)

bi *[two]*
bilingual (using or speaking two languages)
biped (having two feet)

circum *[in a circle, around]*
circumference (the line or distance around a circle)
circumnavigate (to sail around)

co *[together, with]*
cooperate (to work together)
coordinate (to put things together)

ex *[out]*
exhale (to breathe out)
exit (the act of going out)

fore *[before, in front of]*
foremost (in the first place, before everyone or everything else)
foretell (to tell or show beforehand)

hemi *[half]*
hemisphere (half of a sphere or globe)

hyper *[over]*
hyperactive (overactive)

im *[not, opposite of]*
impatient (not patient)
impossible (not possible)

in *[not, opposite of]*
inactive (not active)
incomplete (not complete)

inter *[between, among]*
international (between or among nations)
interplanetary (between the planets)

macro *[large]*
macrocosm (the entire universe)

mal *[bad, poor]*
malnutrition (poor nutrition)

micro *[small]*
microscope (an instrument used to see very small things)

mono *[one]*
monolingual (using or speaking only one language)

non *[not, opposite of]*
nonfat (without the normal fat content)
nonfiction (based on facts; not made-up)

over *[too much, extra]*
overeat (to eat too much)
overtime (extra time; time beyond regular hours)

poly *[many]*
polygon (a figure or shape with three or more sides)
polysyllable (a word with more than three syllables)

post *[after]*
postscript (a note added at the end of a letter, after the signature)
postwar (after a war)

pre *[before]*
pregame (activities that occur before a game)
preheat (to heat before using)

re *[again, back]*
repay (to pay back)
rewrite (to write again or revise)

semi *[half, partly]*
semicircle (half a circle)
semiconscious (half conscious; not fully conscious)

sub *[under, below]*
submarine (a boat that can operate underwater)
submerge (to put underwater)

trans *[across, over; change]*
transcontinental (across a continent)
transform (to change from one form to another)

tri *[three]*
triangle (a figure that has three sides and three angles)
tricycle (a three-wheeled vehicle)

un *[not]*
uncomfortable (not comfortable)
unhappy (not happy; sad)

under *[below, beneath]*
underage (below or less than the usual or required age)
undersea (beneath the surface of the sea)

uni *[one]*
unicycle (a one-wheeled vehicle)
unisex (a single style that is worn by both males and females)

Numerical Prefixes

deci *[tenth of a part]*
decimal system (a number system based on units of 10)

centi *[hundredth of a part]*
centimeter (a unit of length equal to 1/100 meter)

milli *[thousandth of a part]*
millimeter (a unit of length equal to 1/1,000 meter)

micro *[millionth of a part]*
micrometer (one-millionth of a meter)

deca, dec *[ten]*
decade (a period of 10 years)
decathlon (a contest with 10 events)

hecto, hect *[one hundred]*
hectare (a metric unit of land equal to 100 ares)

kilo *[one thousand]*
kilogram (a unit of mass equal to 1,000 grams)

mega *[one million]*
megabit (one million bits)

RESOURCE

Study Suffixes

A **suffix** is a word part that is added after a word. Sometimes a suffix will tell you what part of speech a word is. For example, many adverbs end in the suffix *ly*.

able *[able, can do]*
agreeable (able or willing to agree)
doable (can be done)

al *[of, like]*
magical (like magic)
optical (of the eye)

ed *[past tense]*
called (past tense of call)
learned (past tense of learn)

ess *[female]*
lioness (a female lion)

ful *[full of]*
helpful (giving help; full of help)

ic *[like, having to do with]*
symbolic (having to do with symbols)

ily *[in some manner]*
happily (in a happy manner)

ish *[somewhat like or near]*
childish (somewhat like a child)

ism *[characteristic of]*
heroism (characteristic of a hero)

less *[without]*
careless (without care)

ly *[in some manner]*
calmly (in a calm manner)

ology *[study, science]*
biology (the study of living things)

s *[more than one]*
books (more than one book)

ward *[in the direction of]*
westward (in the direction of west)

y *[containing, full of]*
salty (containing salt)

Comparing Suffixes

er *[comparing two things]*
faster, later, neater, stronger

est *[comparing more than two]*
fastest, latest, neatest, strongest

Noun-Forming Suffixes

er *[one who]*
painter (one who paints)

ing *[the result of]*
painting (the result of a painter's work)

ion *[act of, state of]*
perfection (the state of being perfect)

ist *[one who]*
violinist (one who plays the violin)

ment *[act of, result of]*
amendment (the result of amending, or changing)
improvement (the result of improving)

ness *[state of]*
goodness (the state of being good)

or *[one who]*
actor (one who acts)

Understand Roots

A **root** is a word or word base from which other words are made by adding a prefix or a suffix. Knowing the common roots can help you figure out the meaning of difficult words.

aster *[star]*
asteroid (resembling a star)
asterisk (starlike symbol [*])

aud *[hear, listen]*
audible (can be heard)
auditorium (a place to listen to speeches and performances)

bibl *[book]*
Bible (sacred book of Christianity)
bibliography (list of books)

bio *[life]*
biography (book about a person's life)
biology (the study of life)

chrome *[color]*
monochrome (having one color)
polychrome (having many colors)

chron *[time]*
chronological (in time order)
synchronize (to make happen at the same time)

cide *[the killing of; killer]*
homicide (the killing of one person by another person)
pesticide (bug killer)

cise *[cut]*
incision (a thin, clean cut)
incisors (the teeth that cut or tear food)
precise (cut exactly right)

cord, cor *[heart]*
cordial (heartfelt)
coronary (relating to the heart)

corp *[body]*
corporation (a legal body; business)
corpse (a dead human body)

cycl, cyclo *[wheel, circular]*
bicycle (a vehicle with two wheels)
cyclone (a very strong circular wind)

dem *[people]*
democracy (ruled by the people)
epidemic (affecting many people at the same time)

dent, dont *[tooth]*
dentures (false teeth)
orthodontist (dentist who straightens teeth)

derm *[skin]*
dermatology (the study of skin)
epidermis (outer layer of skin)

fac, fact *[do, make]*
factory (a place where people make things)
manufacture (to make by hand or machine)

fin *[end]*
final (the last of something)
infinite (having no end)

flex *[bend]*
flexible (able to bend)
reflex (bending or springing back)

flu *[flowing]*
fluent (flowing smoothly or easily)
fluid (waterlike, flowing substance)

forc, fort *[strong]*
forceful (full of strength or power)
fortify (to make strong)

fract, frag *[break]*
fracture (to break)
fragment (a piece broken from the whole)

Learn More Roots

gen *[birth, produce]*
congenital (existing at birth)
genetics (the study of inborn traits)

geo *[of the earth]*
geography (the study of places on the earth)
geology (the study of the earth's physical features)

graph *[write]*
autograph (writing one's name)
graphology (the study of handwriting)

homo *[same]*
homogeneous (of the same birth or kind)
homogenize (to blend into a uniform mixture)

hydr *[water]*
dehydrate (to take the water out of)
hydrophobia (the fear of water)

ject *[throw]*
eject (to throw out)
project (to throw forward)

log, logo *[word, thought, speech]*
dialogue (speech between two people)
logic (thinking or reasoning)

luc, lum *[light]*
illuminate (to light up)
translucent (letting light come through)

magn *[great]*
magnificent (great)
magnify (to make bigger or greater)

man *[hand]*
manicure (to fix the hands)
manual (done by hand)

mania *[insanity]*
kleptomania (abnormal desire to steal)
maniac (an insane person)

mar *[sea, pool]*
marine (of or found in the sea)
mariner (sailor)

mega *[large]*
megalith (large stone)
megaphone (large horn used to make voices louder)

meter *[measure]*
kilometer (a thousand meters)
voltmeter (device to measure volts)

mit, miss *[send]*
emit (to send out; give off)
transmission (sending over)

multi *[many, much]*
multicultural (of or including many cultures)
multiped (an animal with many feet)

numer *[number]*
innumerable (too many to count)
numerous (large in number)

omni *[all, completely]*
omnipresent (present everywhere at the same time)
omnivorous (eating all kinds of food)

onym *[name]*
anonymous (without a name)
pseudonym (false name)

ped *[foot]*
pedal (lever worked by the foot)
pedestrian (one who travels by foot)

phil *[love]*
Philadelphia (city of brotherly love)
philosophy (the love of wisdom)

phobia *[fear]*
acrophobia (a fear of high places)
agoraphobia (a fear of public, open places)

phon *[sound]*
phonics (related to sounds)
symphony (sounds made together)

photo *[light]*
photo-essay (a story told mainly with photographs)
photograph (picture made using light rays)

pop *[people]*
population (number of people in an area)
populous (full of people)

port *[carry]*
export (to carry out)
portable (able to be carried)

psych *[mind, soul]*
psychiatry (the study of the mind)
psychology (science of mind and behavior)

sci *[know]*
conscious (being aware)
omniscient (knowing everything)

scope *[instrument for viewing]*
kaleidoscope (instrument for viewing patterns and shapes)
periscope (instrument used to see above the water)

scrib, script *[write]*
manuscript (something written by hand)
scribble (to write quickly)

spec *[look]*
inspect (to look at carefully)
specimen (an example to look at)

spir *[breath]*
expire (to breathe out; die)
inspire (to breathe into; give life to)

tele *[over a long distance; far]*
telephone (machine used to speak to people over a distance)
telescope (machine used to see things that are very faraway)

tempo *[time]*
contemporary (from the current time period)
temporary (lasting for a short time)

tend, tens *[stretch, strain]*
extend (to stretch and make longer)
tension (stretching something tight)

terra *[earth]*
terrain (the earth or ground)
terrestrial (relating to the earth)

therm *[heat]*
thermal (related to heat)
thermostat (a device for controlling heat)

tom *[cut]*
anatomy (the science of cutting apart plants and animals for study)
atom (a particle that cannot be cut or divided)

tract *[draw, pull]*
traction (the act of pulling)
tractor (a machine for pulling)

typ *[print]*
prototype (the first printing or model)
typo (a printing error)

vac *[empty]*
vacant (empty)
vacuum (an empty space)

vid, vis *[see]*
supervise (to oversee or watch over)
videotape (record on tape for viewing)

vor *[eat]*
carnivorous (flesh-eating)
herbivorous (plant-eating)

zoo *[animal or animals]*
zoo (a place where animals are kept)
zoology (the study of animal life)

RESOURCE

What can I do to write more-effective sentences?

Study Sentence Patterns

Sentences in the English language follow the basic patterns below. Use a variety of patterns to add interest to your writing. (Also see page 633.)

1 Subject + Action Verb

     S   AV
The storm ended. (Some action verbs, like *ended,* are intransitive, which means that they *do not need* a direct object to express a complete thought. See 778.3.)

2 Subject + Action Verb + Direct Object

       S   AV   DO
One mistake cost the game. (Some action verbs, like *cost,* are transitive. This means that they *need* a direct object to express a complete thought. See 778.2.)

3 Subject + Action Verb + Indirect Object + Direct Object

      S   AV IO   DO
Jim's friends gave him a surprise party.

4 Subject + Action Verb + Direct Object + Object Complement

      S   AV   DO   OC
The director named Joyce the stage manager.

5 Subject + Linking Verb + Predicate Noun

    S LV   PN
Roger is an amateur ventriloquist.

6 Subject + Linking Verb + Predicate Adjective

     S LV   PA
Broccoli is very tasty.

In the patterns above, the subject comes before the verb. In the patterns below, the subject comes after the verb (called a *delayed subject*).

    LV   S   PA
7 **Is anyone absent?** (A question)

       LV   S
8 **There were two storms last night.**
(A sentence beginning with *there* or *here*)

Practice Sentence Diagramming

Diagramming sentences can help you understand how the different parts of a sentence fit together. Here are the most common diagrams.

1 The storm ended.

Note: Modifiers (including *a, an,* and *the*) are placed under the word they modify.

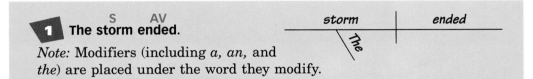

2 One mistake cost the game.

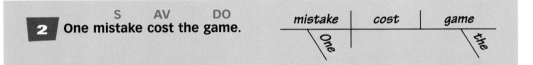

3 Jim's friends gave him a surprise party.

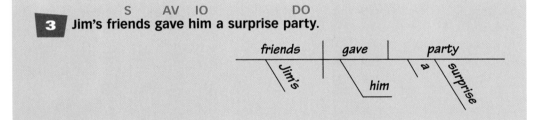

4 The director named Joyce the stage manager.

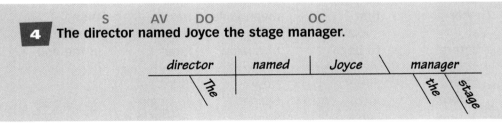

5 Roger is an amateur ventriloquist.

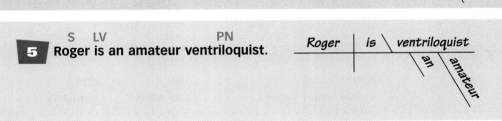

6 Broccoli is very tasty.

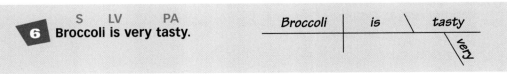

 **TEKS** 8.14B, 8.14C

How can I connect my sentences and paragraphs?

Use Transitions

Transitions can be used to connect one sentence to another sentence or one paragraph to another within a longer essay or report. The lists below show a number of transitions and how they are used.

Note: Each colored list below is a group of transitions that could work well together in a piece of writing.

Words that can be used to show location

above	around	between	inside	outside
across	behind	by	into	over
against	below	down	near	throughout
along	beneath	in back of	next to	to the right
among	beside	in front of	on top of	under

Above	Beside	On top of	To the right
Below	In back of	Next to	
Beneath	In front of	To the left	

Words that can be used to show time

about	during	yesterday	until	finally
after	first	meanwhile	next	then
at	second	today	soon	as soon as
before	to begin	tomorrow	later	in the end

After	First	Now	Third
Before	In the end	Second	To begin
During	Later	Soon	To conclude
Finally	Next	Then	To continue

Words that can be used to compare two things

also	both		like	one way
as	in the same way		likewise	similarly

Also	In the same way
Another way	One way
Both	Similarly

Words that can be used to contrast things (show differences)

| although | even though | on the other hand | still |
| but | however | otherwise | yet |

Although · Nevertheless
Even though · Still
On the other hand · Yet

Words that can be used to emphasize a point

| again | for this reason | to emphasize | truly |
| especially | in fact | to repeat | |

Especially · In fact · To repeat
For this reason · To emphasize · Truly

Words that can be used to conclude or summarize

| all in all | because | in conclusion | therefore |
| as a result | finally | lastly | to sum it up |

All in all · Because · In conclusion · To sum it up
All in all · Finally · Therefore

Words that can be used to add information

additionally	and	finally	moreover
again	another	for example	other
along with	as well	for instance	next
also	besides	in addition	

Additionally · Another · Finally · Moreover
Also · As well · For example · Next
Along with · Besides · For instance

Words that can be used to clarify

| for example | for instance | in other words | that is |

Equally important · For instance
For example · In other words

 TEKS 8.17D

What can I do to make my final copy look better?

Add Graphics to Your Writing

You can add information and interest to essays and reports by using diagrams, tables, and graphs.

Diagrams are drawings that show the parts of something.

Picture diagrams show how something is put together. A diagram may leave out some parts to show only the parts you need to learn.

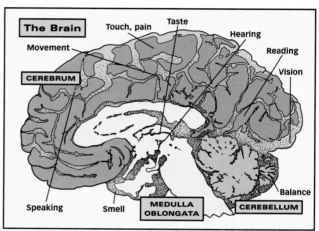

Line diagrams show something you can't really see. Instead of objects, line diagrams show ideas and relationships. This problem-solving diagram helps you understand how to solve a scientific problem.

Tables are another form of diagram. Tables have two parts: rows and columns. Rows go across and show one kind of information or data. Columns go up and down and show a different kind of data.

To read a distance or mileage table, find the place you're starting from and the place you're going to. Then find the place where the row and the column meet—that will show the distance and the driving time from one place to the other.

Distance shown in red
Driving time shown in blue

organize
select support
REFERENCE
improve
637
TEKS 8.17D
A Writer's Resource

Graphs are pictures of information. **Bar graphs** show how things compare to one another. The bars on a bar graph may be vertical or horizontal. (*Vertical* means "up and down." *Horizontal* means "from side to side.") Sometimes the bars on graphs are called *columns*. The part that shows numbers is called the *scale*.

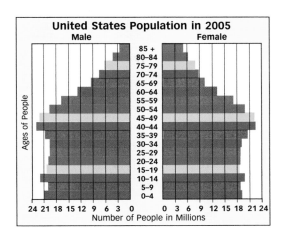

Pie graphs show how all the parts of something add up to make the whole. A pie graph often shows percentages. (A percentage is the part of a whole stated in hundredths: 35% = 35/100.) It's called a pie graph because it is usually in the shape of a pie or circle.

The pie graph to the left shows the sources of carbon monoxide emissions in 2007 and what percentage of total emissions each source produced.

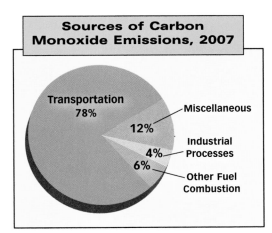

Line graphs show how something changes as time goes by. A line graph always begins with an L-shaped grid. One axis of the grid shows passing time; the other axis shows quantities.

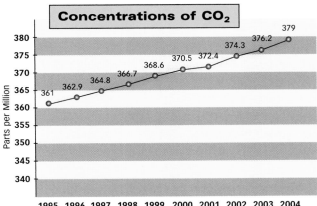

How should I set up my practical writing?

Use the Proper Format

Memos

A memo is a brief written message that you can share with a teacher, a coach, or a principal. Memos create a flow of information—asking and answering questions, giving instructions, describing work to be done, or reminding people about meetings.

Date: Friday, March 6, 2009

To: Mrs. Lee, Technical Director

From: Corrine Stier, Student Director

Subject: Progress on the *Brigadoon* Sets

Here is my first weekly update on the progress of the *Brigadoon* sets.

- Dave Dye has sketched a 15-foot-long set. One side will show the living room of the Campbell cottage, with a thatched roof on top and a window at the back. The other side will be cathedral ruins for the wedding scene. The whole piece will be on wheels, so we can spin it around for scene changes.

- Julie Reynolds primed the four old flats from *My Fair Lady* and drew trees on them. We'll use them on a dark stage along with two freestanding trees to make the forest for the chase scene.

- I want to repaint an old drop curtain to look like the backdrop in the movie. I've attached my drawings for your approval.

Thanks for your confidence in me, Mrs. Lee.

Date: January 12, 2009
To: Mrs. Munn, Room 210
From: The Titan Group: Todd Davis, LaToya Wilson, Jacque Trevino, Becky Jackson
Subject: Volunteer Tutoring

Project Description: An article in our school paper stated that Lincoln Elementary School needed eighth-grade students to tutor third graders in reading. We would like to volunteer our services starting February 3.

What We Need: We need written permission from you, our parents, and our principal. We also need written approval from the principal and the third-grade teachers of Lincoln Elementary School.

What We Will Do: On Tuesdays and Thursdays, during our fourth period study hall, we will walk across the playground to Lincoln School to our assigned classrooms. We will help third-grade students by listening to them read, helping them with their reading assignments, and reading to them.

Outcome: At the end of this project, we will report on the students' progress and show a videotape of our students reading during one of our last sessions. It will show how the tutoring helped.

We hope you will approve our proposal. If you have any suggestions or changes, please let us know.

Proposals

A proposal is a detailed plan for doing a project, solving a problem, or meeting a need.

Follow Guidelines

Letters

A letter is a written message sent through the mail. Letters follow a set format, including important contact information, a salutation (greeting), a body, and a closing signature. (See pages **220–225** for more information.)

> 1080 Burns Road
> Orange Park, FL 32000
> May 5, 2011
>
> Principal Jorge Rodriguez
> Cardosa Middle School
> 116 Shelton Street
> Orange Park, FL 32000
>
> Dear Mr. Rodriguez:
>
> As a soccer team member at Cardosa Middle School, I have a suggestion. We need lights for nighttime games. When school starts in the fall, it gets darker earlier and earlier. It's hard for our teams to finish games safely.
>
> I realize that lighting is expensive. However, a lighted field could be used by the whole community, so the community could help pay for it. The soccer team could even run a citywide fund-raiser.
>
> Adding lights to our soccer field would make a huge difference for my teammates and me. Please make the request at the next school board meeting.
>
> Sincerely,
>
> *Alejandro Alvarezs*
> Alejandro Alvarez

Envelope Addresses

Place the return address in the upper left corner, the destination address in the center, and the correct postage in the upper right corner.

> ALEJANDRO ALVAREZ
> 1080 BURNS RD
> ORANGE PARK FL 32000
>
>
>
> PRINCIPAL JORGE RODRIGUEZ
> CARDOSA MIDDLE SCHOOL
> 116 SHELTON ST
> ORANGE PARK FL 32000

U.S. Postal Service Guidelines

1. Capitalize everything and leave out ALL punctuation.
2. Use the list of common address abbreviations at **690.1**. Use numerals rather than words for numbered streets and avenues (9TH AVE NE, 3RD ST SW).
3. If you know the ZIP + 4 code, use it.

Proofreader's Guide

Learning Language

Work with a partner. Read the meanings and share answers to the questions.

1. An abbreviation is a shorter or simpler replacement for a longer word, such as "Mr." for "Mister" or "Dr." for "Doctor." **What are some abbreviations you know?**

2. When something is irregular it does not follow the accepted rules or general pattern or order. **What is an English word that has an irregular spelling, one that does not follow the regular rules?**

3. Contractions are shorter versions of one or more words with some of the letters replaced by an apostrophe, as in "we're" (we are) and "doesn't" (does not). **Do you think contractions make it harder or easier to understand the English language? Why?**

improve *edit*

Editing for Mechanics

Periods

Use a **period** to end a sentence. Also use a period after initials, after abbreviations, and as a decimal point.

MECHANICS

641.1
At the End of Sentences

Use a period to end a sentence that makes a statement or a request. Also use a period for a mild command, one that does not need an exclamation point. (See page 580.)

The Southern Ocean surrounds Antarctica. (statement)

Please point out the world's largest ocean on a map. (request)

Do not use a laser pointer. (mild command)

NOTE It is not necessary to place a period after a statement that has parentheses around it if it is part of another sentence.

The Southern Ocean is the fourth-largest ocean (it is larger than the Atlantic).

641.2
After Initials

Place a period after an initial.

J. K. Rowling (author)

Colin L. Powell (politician)

641.3
After Abbreviations

Place a period after each part of an abbreviation. Do not use periods with acronyms or initialisms. (See page 692.)

Abbreviations: **Mr. Mrs. Ms. Dr. B.C.E. C.E.**

Acronyms: **AIDS NASA**

Initialisms: **NBC FBI**

NOTE When an abbreviation is the last word in a sentence, use only one period at the end of the sentence.

My grandfather's full name is William Ryan James Koenig, Jr.

641.4
As Decimal Points

Use a period to separate dollars and cents and as a decimal point.

The price of a loaf of bread was $1.54 in 1992.

That price was only 35 cents, or 77.3 percent less, in 1972.

ELPS 4C

Question Marks

A **question mark** is used after an interrogative sentence and also to show doubt about the correctness of a fact or figure. (See page 580.)

642.1

At the End of Direct Questions

Use a question mark at the end of a direct question (an interrogative sentence).

Is a vegan a person who eats only vegetables?

642.2

At the End of Indirect Questions

No question mark is used after an indirect question. (An indirect question tells about a question you or someone else asked.)

Because I do not eat meat, I'm often asked if I am a vegetarian.

I asked the doctor if going meatless is harmful to my health.

642.3

To Show Doubt

Place a question mark within parentheses to show that you are unsure that a fact or figure is correct.

By the year 2020 (?) the number of vegetarians in the United States may approach 15 percent of the population.

Exclamation Points

An **exclamation point** may be placed after a word, a phrase, or a sentence to show emotion. (The exclamation point should not be overused.)

642.4

To Express Strong Feelings

Use an exclamation point to show excitement or strong feeling.

Yeah! Wow! Oh my!

Surprise! You've won the million-dollar sweepstakes!

Caution: Never use more than one exclamation point in writing assignments.

Incorrect: **Don't ever do that to me again!!!**

Correct: **Don't ever do that to me again!**

ELPS 3E, 4C

Practice

End Punctuation

 On your own paper, write whether each of the following sentences needs a period, a question mark, or an exclamation point at the end.

Example: I want to get a pet
period

1. Did you ever think about getting a ferret

2. They are from the same animal family that minks, skunks, and otters are from

3. Ferrets are active creatures and need a lot of exercise

4. The word *ferret* comes from a Latin word meaning *little thief,* so the animals also require patience

5. Oh no, a ferret might take your keys or your pens and hide them

6. Make sure you lock away anything valuable

7. A ferret's cage should be large enough to hold some toys, a water dish, and a food bowl

8. What should you feed a ferret if you can't find ferret food

9. Many ferret owners feed their animals cat food

10. Just like a cat, a ferret can be trained to use a litter box

11. Wow, a baby ferret is even called a kit

12. You might ask if ferrets need their own toys

13. They do, but they'll be happy as can be with an old sock

14. In general, ferrets will live 8 to 10 years

15. Enjoy your new pet

Next Step: Write three sentences about a pet or other animal. Use different end punctuation for each one. Share your sentences with a partner.

MECHANICS

Commas

Use a **comma** to indicate a pause or a change in thought. This helps to keep words and ideas from running together so that the writing is easier to read. For a writer, no other form of punctuation is more important to understand than the comma.

644.1
Between Items in a Series

Use commas between words, phrases, or clauses in a series. (A series contains at least three items.) (See page 574.)

> Chinese, English, and Hindi are the three most widely used languages in the world. (words)

> Being comfortable with technology, working well with others, and knowing another language are important skills for today's workers. (phrases)

> My dad works in a factory, my mom works in an office, and I work in school. (clauses)

644.2
To Keep Numbers Clear

Use commas to separate the digits in a number in order to distinguish hundreds, thousands, millions, and so on.

> More than 104,000 people live in Kingston, the capital of Jamaica.

> The population of the entire country of Liechtenstein is only 29,000.

NOTE Commas are not used in years.

> The world population was 6.1 billion by 2003.

644.3
In Dates and Addresses

Use commas to distinguish items in an address and items in a date.

> On August 28, 1963, Martin Luther King, Jr., gave his famous "I Have a Dream" speech.

> The address of the King Center is 449 Auburn Avenue NE, Atlanta, Georgia 30312.

NOTE No comma is placed between the state and ZIP code. Also, when only the month and year are given, no comma is needed.

> In January 2029 we will celebrate the 100th anniversary of Reverend King's birth.

punctuate edit capitalize
improve SPELL
645

 ELPS 4C

Editing for Mechanics

MECHANICS

 Practice

Commas 1

▓ Between Items in a Series
▓ To Keep Numbers Clear
▓ In Dates and Addresses

For each sentence below, write the words or numbers that need commas. Then insert the commas correctly.

Example: I started first grade on September 2 2003.
September 2, 2003

1. There are more than 1200 students at my brother's high school.

2. He has been going there since August 18 2008.

3. The school's address is 1010 Water Street Arlo Texas 80989.

4. Nikki Rasheed and Collin are hall monitors.

5. They started their "jobs" in March 2006, which was more than 1000 days ago.

6. Javier woke up late missed the bus and forgot his homework.

7. He thought of about 50000 excuses he could give the teacher.

8. The teacher gave him until October 9 to turn it in.

9. Javier walked to Frank's house at 2105 Juniper Road Catalpa Texas 80990.

10. Javier did his homework Frank read a magazine and Frank's little brother bothered them.

Next Step: Write full sentences that answer each of the following questions. Be sure to use commas correctly.
- When were you born?
- What is your home address?
- What are your three favorite foods?
- What is the sum of 500 + 525?

TEKS 8.20B(i)
ELPS 4C

Commas . . .

646.1
To Set Off Nonrestrictive Phrases and Clauses

Use commas to set off nonrestrictive phrases and clauses—those not necessary to the basic meaning of the sentence.

People get drinking water from surface water or groundwater, which makes up only 1 percent of the earth's water supply.
(The clause *which makes up only 1 percent of the earth's water supply* is additional information; it is nonrestrictive—not required. If the clause were left out, the meaning of the sentence would remain clear.)

Restrictive phrases or clauses—those that are needed in the sentence—restrict or limit the meaning of the sentence; they are not set off with commas.

Groundwater that is free from harmful pollutants is rare.
(The clause *that is free from harmful pollutants* is restrictive; it is needed to complete the meaning of the basic sentence and is not set off with commas.)

646.2
To Set Off Titles or Initials

Use commas to set off a title, a name, or initials that follow a person's last name. (Use only one period if an initial comes at the end of a sentence.)

Melanie Prokat, M.D., is our family's doctor. However, she is listed in the phone book only as Prokat, M.

NOTE Although commas are not necessary to set off "Jr." and "Sr." after a name, they may be used as long as a comma is used both before and after the abbreviation.

646.3
To Set Off Interruptions

Use commas to set off a word, phrase, or clause that interrupts the main thought of a sentence. These interruptions usually can be identified through the following tests:

1. You can leave them out of a sentence without changing its meaning.

2. You can put them other places in the sentence without changing its meaning.

Our school, as we all know, is becoming overcrowded again. (clause)

My history class, for example, has 42 students in it. (phrase)

There are, indeed, about 1,000 people in my school. (word)

The building, however, has room for only 850 students. (word)

Practice

Commas 2

- To Set Off Nonrestrictive Phrases and Clauses
- To Set Off Titles or Initials
- To Set Off Interruptions

For each sentence below, write the parts that should be set off with commas. If commas are not necessary, write "none."

Example: When was music which plays a big role in every culture invented?

which plays a big role in every culture

1. Some scientists think it was the sounds of nature that originally inspired people to create music.

2. The songs of birds for example probably inspired many composers.

3. People were in fact making music as long as 50,000 years ago.

4. Prehistoric bone flutes which were played by cave dwellers are evidence of music's long history.

5. Egyptian paintings that show people playing instruments are also evidence of music's ancient beginnings.

6. By the Middle Ages which covered the thousand-year period from 450 to 1450 many different musical instruments were being used.

7. During the Renaissance, the recorder and reed instruments in general were very popular.

8. The years from 1825 to 1900 known as the Romantic period introduced many talented composers to the world.

9. Johann Strauss Jr. was one of these famous musicians.

Next Step: What instrument do you play (or wish you could play)? Write one sentence about it. Include a nonrestrictive phrase or clause and set it off with commas. Share your sentence with a partner.

MECHANICS

TEKS 8.19A(ii)
ELPS 4C

Commas . . .

648.1
To Set Off Appositives

Commas set off an appositive from the rest of the sentence. An appositive is a word or phrase that identifies or renames a noun or pronoun. (See page **575**.)

> **The capital of Cyprus, Nicosia, has a population of almost 643,000.** (*Nicosia* renames *capital of Cyprus,* so the word is set off with commas.)

> **Cyprus, an island in the Mediterranean Sea, is about half the size of Connecticut.** (*An island in the Mediterranean Sea* identifies *Cyprus,* so the phrase is set off with commas.)

Do not use commas with appositives that are necessary to the basic meaning of the sentence.

> **The Mediterranean island Cyprus is about half the size of Connecticut.** (*Cyprus* is not set off because it is needed to make the sentence clear.)

648.2
To Separate Equal Adjectives

Use commas to separate two or more adjectives that equally modify the same noun.

> **Comfortable, efficient cars are becoming more important to drivers.** (*Comfortable* and *efficient* are separated by a comma because they modify *cars* equally.)

> **Some automobiles run on clean, renewable sources of energy.** (*Clean* and *renewable* are separated by a comma because they modify *sources* equally.)

> **Conventional gasoline engines emit a lot of pollution.** (*Conventional* and *gasoline* do not modify *engines* equally; therefore, no comma separates the two.)

Use these tests to help you decide if adjectives modify equally:

1. Switch the order of the adjectives; if the sentence is clear, the adjectives modify equally.

> **Yes: Efficient, comfortable cars are becoming more important to drivers.**

> **No: Gasoline conventional engines emit a lot of pollution.**

2. Put the word *and* between the adjectives; if the sentence reads well, use a comma when *and* is taken out.

> **Yes: Comfortable and efficient cars are becoming more important to drivers.**

> **No: Conventional and gasoline engines emit a lot of pollution.**

Practice

Commas 3

■ To Set Off Appositives

 For each numbered sentence below, write the appositive phrase and the noun it renames. Set off the appositive with commas.

Example: Kit houses "build-it-yourself" homes were popular in the early 1900s.

Kit houses, "build-it-yourself" homes,

(1) Sears the nationwide department store chain sold kit houses between 1908 and 1940. **(2)** One of the most popular models was the Osborn a small bungalow. **(3)** All the materials 30,000 or more pieces were neatly packed into two boxcars for rail delivery. **(4)** The home designers architects hired by the store could make changes to the floor plan the buyers wanted. **(5)** In a few months, the owners of this new house once just a big pile of materials could move in.

■ To Separate Equal Adjectives

 For each numbered sentence below, write the adjectives that need commas between them. Add the commas.

Example: The catalog offered 90 fashionable unique home designs.

fashionable, unique

(1) It's amazing to think that these big roomy houses—many still standing today—came from a department store catalog! **(2)** A complete ready-to-assemble kit included everything that was needed. **(3)** When people ordered their houses from the catalog, they would also order attractive modern light fixtures and sturdy plumbing fixtures. **(4)** All the pieces were delivered by rail, along with a thick detailed instruction book. **(5)** Then the buyers, along with anyone who could be persuaded to help, began the long challenging construction process.

TEKS 8.20B(i)
ELPS 4C

Commas . . .

650.1
To Set Off Dialogue

Use commas to set off the exact words of a speaker from the rest of the sentence. (Also see page 618.)

> The firefighter said, "When we cannot successfully put out a fire, we try to keep it from spreading."

> "When we cannot successfully put out a fire, we try to keep it from spreading," the firefighter said.

NOTE Do not use a comma or quotation marks for indirect quotations. The words *if* and *that* often signal dialogue that is being reported rather than quoted.

> The firefighter said that when they cannot successfully put out a fire, they try to keep it from spreading. (These are not the speaker's exact words.)

650.2
In Direct Address

Use commas to separate a noun of direct address from the rest of the sentence. (A noun of direct address is a noun that names a person spoken to in the sentence.)

> Hanae, did you know that an interior decorator can change wallpaper and fabrics on a computer screen?

> Sure, Jack, and an architect can use a computer to see how light will fall in different parts of a building.

650.3
To Set Off Interjections

Use commas to separate an interjection or a weak exclamation from the rest of the sentence.

> No kidding, you mean that one teacher has to manage a class of 42 pupils? (weak exclamation)

> Uh-huh, and that teacher has other classes that size. (interjection)

650.4
To Set Off Explanatory Phrases

Use commas to separate an explanatory phrase from the rest of the sentence.

> English, the language computers speak worldwide, is also the most widely used language in science and medicine.

> More than 750 million people, about an eighth of the world's population, speak English as a foreign language.

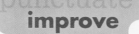 
ELPS 2C, 2I, 3D, 3E, 4C, 4K

Commas 4

- 🔲 To Set Off Dialogue
- 🔲 In Direct Address
- 🔲 To Set Off Interjections
- 🔲 To Set Off Explanatory Phrases

For each numbered sentence below, write the word or words that should be set off with commas. Add the commas.

Example: "Class we'll discuss oceans today" said the teacher.
Class, today,

1. The teacher asked "Who can define *ocean*?"

2. "It's a sea covering a large expanse Ms. Jackson" said Ralph.

3. She said "Wow that's right Ralph. Who knows which ocean is the largest?"

4. Renatta asked "Is it the Pacific?"

5. "Yes Renatta" replied Ms. Jackson.

6. Oceans provide fish a major source of food for many people.

7. Ocean water which contains a lot of salt is not safe to drink.

Learning Language A comma usually indicates where a person would pause when speaking. The sentences below show that people usually pause . . .

- **just before repeating another person's exact words:**
  And then she said [pause] "I'm going to the game and that's it!"

- **when addressing someone directly, just after saying the person's name:**
  Rex [pause] can I borrow your pen?

- **before and after an explanatory phrase:**
  I saw a cool red sports car [pause] a Corvette [pause] in the parking lot.

In each of these sentences, the [pause] shows where the comma belongs. Working with a partner, take turns writing a sentence based on one of the models on page 650. Read the sentence aloud, as naturally as you can. See if your partner can tell where the commas belong in the sentence. Then listen to your partner's sentence.

Practice

MECHANICS

TEKS 8.20B(i)
ELPS 4C

Commas . . .

652.1
To Separate Introductory Clauses and Phrases

Use a comma to separate an adverb clause or a long phrase from the independent clause that follows it.

If every automobile in the country were a light shade of red, we'd live in a pink-car nation. (adverbial clause)

According to some experts, solar-powered cars will soon be common. (long modifying phrase)

652.2
In Compound Sentences

Use a comma between two independent clauses that are joined by a coordinating conjunction (such as *and, but, or, nor, for, so,* and *yet*), forming a compound sentence. An independent clause expresses a complete thought and can stand alone as a sentence. (Also see page 578.)

Many students enjoy working on computers, so teachers are finding new ways to use them in the classroom.

Computers can be valuable in education, but many schools cannot afford enough of them.

Avoid Comma Splices: A comma splice results when two independent clauses are "spliced" together with only a comma—and no conjunction. (See page 566.)

SCHOOL DAZE

Ann, we've completed two-thirds of the quarter, and you haven't turned in one assignment. What do you have to say for yourself?

Ah . . . is there anything I can do for extra credit?

MECHANICS

Practice

Commas 5

■ To Separate Introductory Clauses and Phrases
■ In Compound Sentences

Number your paper from 1 to 13. For each line, write the words that should be followed by a comma, and put the commas after them. (Not every line needs a comma.) You should add nine commas.

Example: I didn't do my homework but I have an excuse.
homework,

1   This might come as a surprise to you but doing homework can
2 be very dangerous. As I began to work on a math worksheet last
3 night three dangerous felons grabbed me from behind and stuffed
4 me into the trunk of a rusty, old car. After driving for quite a while
5 the car came to a sudden stop and my kidnappers left the car. I
6 knew I had to do something quickly or it would be too late. I didn't
7 want to yell and alert the kidnappers so I wrote a note on the back
8 of my worksheet and stuck it through one of the rust holes in the
9 car. Fortunately, a passerby saw the note and notified the police.
10 Soon after the police came and captured the kidnappers. Since
11 the police kept my worksheet as evidence I couldn't complete my
12 homework. For some reason my math teacher didn't buy my excuse
13 for not having my homework done.

Next Step: Take a normal, everyday experience, such as doing homework, walking to school, taking a test, or playing a game, and turn it into a "tall tale" like the one above. Use commas with introductory word groups and in compound sentences. Read your work aloud to a classmate.

TEKS 8.20B(ii)
ELPS 4C

Semicolons

Use a **semicolon** to suggest a stronger pause than a comma indicates. A semicolon may also serve in place of a period.

654.1
To Join Two Independent Clauses

In a compound sentence, use a semicolon to join two independent clauses that are not connected with a coordinating conjunction. (See **792.1**.)

> **The United States has more computers than any other country; its residents own more than 164 million of them.**

654.2
With Conjunctive Adverbs

A semicolon is also used to join two independent clauses when the clauses are connected by a conjunctive adverb (such as *as a result, for example, however, therefore,* and *instead*). (See **788.1**.)

> **Japan is next on that list; however, the Japanese have only 50 million computers.**

> **You might think that the billion people of China own a lot of computers; instead, the smaller country of Germany has twice as many computers as China.**

654.3
To Separate Groups That Contain Commas

Use a semicolon between groups of words in a series when one or more of the groups already contain commas.

> **Many of our community's residents separate their garbage into bins for newspapers, cardboard, and junk mail; glass, metal, and plastic; and nonrecyclable trash.**

SCHOOL DAZE

It's true that I have only a few minutes to finish this; **however, I** am not worried.

Well, that makes one of us.

 **TEKS** 8.20B(ii)
ELPS 4C

 **Practice**

Semicolons

 Write the numbers of the lines that need a semicolon in the following paragraphs. Then write the two words, separated by the semicolon.

Example: The Nintendo Playing Card Company was begun in 1889 in Japan today it's a familiar video game company.

Japan; today

1   In the 1960s, a Japanese company called Service Games started
2   up the company's name was later shortened to Sega. At first, Sega
3   created pinball games. Interactive video games were introduced
4   in 1968 however, the first *popular* interactive game, Pong, was
5   not developed until 1972. These early arcade video games were
6   big machines that included speakers, video screens, and coin slots
7   knobs, flippers, and joysticks and computer processors and software.
8   Things changed in 1976 when people could play video games at
9   home on their televisions. Less than 10 years later, home computers
10 were becoming more common as a result, Tetris became one of
11 the first popular computer games. The first handheld video game,
12 Nintendo's Game Boy, was introduced in 1989 it had a black-and-
13 white screen! By 2001, online games allowed thousands of gamers to
14 play at once.
15 What does the future hold for video games? One possibility is
16 games that can "think" for themselves another is games that are
17 controlled by eye movements. Whatever the case, these games are
18 almost guaranteed a big audience!

Next Step: Write a compound sentence about any kind of game you've played. Punctuate it with a semicolon. Then write another compound sentence using a conjunctive adverb; again, use a semicolon to join the independent clauses.

MECHANICS

Colons

A **colon** may be used to introduce a list or an important point. Colons are also used in business letters and between the numbers in time.

656.1
To Introduce Lists

Use a colon to introduce a list. The colon usually comes after words describing the subject of the list (as in the first example below) or after summary words, such as *the following* or *these things*. Do not use a colon after a verb or preposition.

> **Certain items are still difficult to recycle: foam cups, car tires, and toxic chemicals.**

> **To conserve water, you should do the following three things: fix drippy faucets, install a low-flow showerhead, and turn the water off while brushing your teeth.**

> Incorrect: **To conserve water, you should: install a low-flow showerhead, turn the water off while brushing your teeth, and fix drippy faucets.**

656.2
To Introduce Sentences

A colon may be used to introduce a sentence, a question, or a quotation.

> **This is why air pollution is bad: We are sacrificing our health and the health of all other life on the planet.**

> **Answer this question for me: Why aren't more people concerned about global warming?**

> **Joaquin shared this with us: "Iceland is the world's leader in the use of renewable energy."**

656.3
After Salutations

A colon may be used after the salutation of a business letter.

> **Dear Ms. Manners: Dear Dr. Warmle: Dear Professor Potter:**

> **Dear Captain Elliot: Dear Senator:**

656.4
For Emphasis

Use a colon to emphasize a word or phrase.

> **The newest alternative energy is also the most common element on earth: hydrogen.**

> **Here's one thing that can help save energy: a programmable thermostat.**

656.5
Between Numbers in Time

Use a colon between the parts of a number that indicates time.

> **My thermostat automatically sets my heat to 60 degrees between 11:00 p.m. and 6:00 a.m.**

TEKS 8.20B(ii)
ELPS 4C

Practice

Colons

Which words or numbers in the letter below should be followed by or contain a colon? Write each one and place the colon correctly.

Example: Kangaroos are known for these features their pouches, their long legs, and their long tails.
features:

1 Dear Mr. Sei

2   Last night around 815 p.m., I saw one of the largest kangaroos

3 I have ever seen. It entered our camping area, seemingly unafraid,

4 and ate the plants near our tent. As I silently watched, I studied its

5 features the long claw, the big ears, the strong forelimbs, and the

6 soft muzzle. Although there was very little light, I could tell by the

7 size that it could only be the giant of kangaroos the red.

8   I remembered a friend asking me this How much ground can a

9 red cover in a single jump? I have seen these kangaroos easily cover

10 20 feet while they cruised along. I don't know if that is any kind of

11 record, but it sure is a long hop. A park ranger says that the female

12 red, which is gray blue in color, can hit 30 miles per hour.

13   After eating as much as it wanted, the big red finally

14 disappeared into the darkness about 945 p.m. Sadly, I've heard this

15 comment Kangaroos are giant jumping rats and cause nothing but

16 trouble. Some kangaroos may be pests, but the one I saw makes me

17 think only one thing They are a marvelous part of Australia.

18 With regards,

19 Franklin

Next Step: Write a brief reply to Franklin. Use colons as needed.

Quotation Marks

Quotation marks are used in a number of ways:
- to set off the exact words of a speaker,
- to punctuate material quoted from another source,
- to punctuate words used in a special way, and
- to punctuate certain titles.

658.1
To Set Off a Speaker's Exact Words

Place quotation marks before and after a speaker's words in dialogue. Only the exact words of the speaker are placed within quotation marks.

> Marla said, "I've decided to become a firefighter."

> "A firefighter," said Juan, "can help people in many ways."

658.2
For Quotations Within Quotations

Use single quotation marks to punctuate a quotation within a quotation.

> Sung Kim asked, "Did Marla just say, 'I've decided to become a firefighter'?"

When titles occur within a quotation, use single quotation marks to punctuate those that require quotation marks.

> Juan said, "Springsteen's song 'The Rising' really inspired her."

658.3
To Set Off Quoted Material

When quoting material from another source, place quotation marks before and after the source's exact words.

> In her book *Living the Life You Deserve,* Tess Spyeder explains, "Choose a job you'll enjoy doing day after day over one that will fatten your bank account."

658.4
To Set Off Long Quoted Material

If more than one paragraph is quoted from a single source, quotation marks are placed before each paragraph and at the end of the last paragraph.

Quotations that are more than four lines are usually set off from the rest of the paper by indenting each line 10 spaces from the left. Quotations that are set off in this way require no quotation marks either before or after the quoted material.

MECHANICS

Practice

Quotation Marks 1

- ■ To Set Off a Speaker's Exact Words
- ■ For Quotations Within Quotations
- ■ To Set Off Quoted Material

 For each paragraph below, write the quotation marks along with the words that come after and before them, or write "none needed."

Example: Principal Krenz announced, A hurricane is coming!

"A . . . coming!"

1. Jamilah shouted, Next week the Hurricane Sisters are coming to our school! They're going to sing their new song, Eye of the Storm.

2. David said, Did you just say, Next week the Hurricane Sisters are coming to our school? I can't believe it! They rock!

3. Did you know there's a new book about them, too? Jamilah asked. Here, check this out. It's called *Coast to Coast Hurricane*.

4. David read the following passage from the Hurricane Sisters' book:
   > The Hurricane Sisters, Jill and Lily, were actually born during a hurricane. In August 1983, Hurricane Alicia hit Galveston, Texas, and the twins' mother was unable to leave the area before she went into labor. Luckily, the birth was an uncomplicated one, and mother and daughters rode out the hurricane together.

5. He flipped a few more pages and read, Jill and Lily began singing at church picnics and talent shows at age three. By the age of six, both girls were learning how to play the guitar.

6. David remarked, Wow! They've been performing together for years. Maybe that's why they've become so popular.

Quotation Marks . . .

660.1
Placement of Punctuation

Always place periods and commas inside quotation marks.

> "I don't know," said Lac.
>
> Lac said, "I don't know."

Place an exclamation point or a question mark inside the quotation marks when it punctuates the quotation.

> Ms. Wiley asked, "Can you actually tour the Smithsonian on the Internet?"

Place it outside when it punctuates the main sentence.

> Did I hear you say, "Now we can tour the Smithsonian on the Internet"?

Place semicolons or colons outside quotation marks.

> First, I will read the article "Sonny's Blues"; then I will read "The Star Café" in my favorite music magazine.

660.2
For Special Words

Quotation marks also may be used (1) to set apart a word that is being discussed, (2) to indicate that a word is slang, or (3) to point out that a word or phrase is being used in a special way.

> 1. Renny uses the word "like" entirely too much.
> 2. Man, your car is really "phat."
> 3. Aunt Lulu, an editor at a weekly magazine, says she has "issues."

660.3
To Punctuate Titles

Use quotation marks to punctuate titles of songs, poems, short stories, lectures, episodes of radio or television programs, chapters of books, and articles found in magazines, newspapers, or encyclopedias. (Also see 662.3.)

> "21 Questions" (song)
> "The Reed Flute's Song" (poem)
> "Old Man at the Bridge" (short story)
> "Birthday Boys" (a television episode)
> "The Foolish and the Weak" (a chapter in a book)
> "Science Careers Today" (lecture)
> "Teen Rescues Stranded Dolphin" (newspaper article)

NOTE When you punctuate a title, capitalize the first word, last word, and every word in between—except for articles (*a, an, the*), short prepositions (*at, to, with,* and so on), and coordinating conjunctions (*and, but, or*). (See 682.2.)

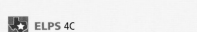
 ELPS 4C

Practice

Quotation Marks 2

- ■ Placement of Punctuation
- ■ To Punctuate Titles

 Rewrite the following sentences, correctly placing quotation marks where they are needed.

Example: Have you read the poem Spring Dragon?

Have you read the poem "Spring Dragon"?

1. Caleb shouted, Hey, I saw your picture in the paper!

2. My picture appeared in the article McCabe Scores in Finals.

3. Duante couldn't get the song When Doves Cry out of his head.

4. I have one suggestion for your short story Mama's Reading Lamp: Change the title.

5. Today Dr. Nguyen is presenting his speech Get Fit! in the gym.

6. Guillermo asked, Did you see *The Smiths* on TV last night?

7. No, I didn't, Tom said.

8. Did you ever see the episode The Genius?

9. The funniest episode ever was Lisa on Ice!

10. This quarter we are reading *Fahrenheit 451*, the teacher said.

11. We must read the last chapter, Burning Bright, by the end of the month.

Next Step: Write two or three sentences about a song you like, a poem you're familiar with, and a newspaper article you have read. Use quotation marks correctly.

ELPS 4C

Italics and Underlining

Italics is slightly slanted type. In this sentence, the word *happiness* is typed in italics. In handwritten material, each word or letter that should be in italics is **underlined**. (See an example on page **432**.)

662.1
In Printed Material

Print words in italics when you are using a computer.

In *Tuck Everlasting,* the author explores what it would be like to live forever.

662.2
In Handwritten Material

Underline words that should be italicized when you are writing by hand.

In Tuck Everlasting, the author explores what it would be like to live forever.

662.3
In Titles

Italicize (or underline) the titles of books, plays, book-length poems, magazines, newspapers, radio and television programs, movies, videos, cassettes, CD's, and the names of aircraft and ships.

Walk Two Moons (book)   *Teen People* (magazine)

Fairies and Dragons (movie)   *Everwood* (TV program)

The Young and the Hopeless (CD) *U.S.S. Arizona* (ship)

Columbia (space shuttle)   *Daily Herald* (newspaper)

Exception: Do not italicize or put quotation marks around the title at the top of your own written work.

A Day Without Water (title on work: do not italicize)

662.4
For Scientific and Foreign Words

Italicize (or underline) scientific and foreign words that are not commonly used in everyday English.

Spinacia oleracea is the scientific term for spinach.

Many store owners who can help Spanish-speaking customers display an *Hablamos Español* sign in their windows.

662.5
For Special Uses

Italicize (or underline) a number, letter, or word that is being discussed or used in a special way. (Sometimes quotation marks are used for this same reason.)

Matt's hat has a bright red *A* on it.

ELPS 4C

Practice

Italics and Underlining

Write and underline the word or words that should be italicized in each sentence. If a word or words have been incorrectly italicized, write them down and circle them.

Example: Sylvia asked, "Did you read the book Undaunted Courage?"

Undaunted Courage

1. "No, but I saw the TV show The Lewis and Clark Expedition," replied Angela.

2. Sylvia wrote the article *Finding the Northwest Passage* for the student paper.

3. William Least Heat-Moon traveled that famous route in a boat he called Nikawa.

4. During their two-year journey, Lewis and Clark must have heard someone say tatonka, a Lakota word meaning "buffalo."

5. The scientific name for the American buffalo is Bison bison.

6. Buffalo are mentioned in the familiar song *Home on the Range*.

7. The book *Mystic Warriors of the Plains* talks about the *designs* hunters would paint on the bison skulls.

8. National Geographic magazine has released a large-format movie called *Lewis and Clark: The Journey West*.

9. The *Missouri Gazette* reported on many events that honored the 200th anniversary of the *Lewis and Clark expedition*.

MECHANICS

Next Step: Write three sentences with movie, book, or CD titles, as well as poem and song titles. Exchange papers with a classmate and underline the titles that should be italicized.

ELPS 4C

Apostrophes

Use **apostrophes** to form contractions, to form certain plurals, or to show possession.

664.1
In Contractions

Use an apostrophe to form a contraction, showing that one or more letters have been left out of a word.

Common Contractions

can't (cannot)	**couldn't** (could not)	**didn't** (did not)
doesn't (does not)	**don't** (do not)	**hasn't** (has not)
haven't (have not)	**isn't** (is not)	**I'll** (I will)
I'd (I would)	**I'm** (I am)	**I've** (I have)
they'll (they will)	**they'd** (they would)	**they've** (they have)
they're (they are)	**won't** (will not)	**wouldn't** (would not)
you'll (you will)	**you'd** (you would)	**you've** (you have)
you're (you are)		

664.2
In Place of Omitted Letters or Numbers

Use an apostrophe to show that one or more digits have been left out of a number, or that one or more letters have been left out of a word to show a special pronunciation.

> **class of '99** (*19* is left out)
> **g'bye** (the letters *ood* are left out of *good-bye*)

NOTE Letters and numbers should not be omitted in most writing assignments; however, they may be omitted in dialogue to make it sound like real people are talking.

664.3
To Form Some Plurals

Use an apostrophe and *s* to form the plural of a letter, a sign, a number, or a word being discussed as a word.

> **A's   8's   +'s   to's**
> **Don't use too many *and*'s in your writing.**

664.4
To Form Singular Possessives

To form the possessive of a singular noun, add an apostrophe and *s*.

> **the game's directions   Dr. Mill's theory**
> **Ross's bike   Roz's hair**

NOTE When a singular noun with more than one syllable ends with an *s* or *z* sound, the possessive may be formed by adding just an apostrophe.

> **Texas' oil** (or) **Texas's oil   Carlos' mother** (or) **Carlos's mother**

ELPS 4C

MECHANICS

Practice

Apostrophes 1

■ **In Contractions**

For the sentences below, write the word pairs and the contractions they can be combined to form.

Example: Mom says it is time for me to do my own laundry.
it is–it's

1. She said she would teach me.

2. "Doing laundry is not hard," she said. "It just takes time."

3. "First separate your clothes. Do not wash the light-colored clothes with the dark ones."

4. She added, "It would not hurt to look at the washing instructions on the clothes tag."

5. "Next you are going to put detergent in the washing machine and select the water temperature."

6. After she explained that I would use hot water for whites and warm water for the rest, I put my clothes in.

7. "It will take about half an hour for the washer to finish."

8. Then she said, "You will want to clean the lint trap in the dryer before putting your clothes in," and she showed me how.

9. "When they are dry, fold them and put them away."

■ **To Form Some Plurals**

For the sentences below, correctly write the plurals of letters, numbers, symbols, and words being discussed.

Example: Marisa typed a line made of ~s on her computer.
~'s

1. Our last name is Patel, so Mom has Ps all over the house.

2. Tom's phone number has four 2s in it.

3. I took out all the &s in my paper and replaced them with *and*s.

ELPS 4C

Apostrophes . . .

666.1
To Form Plural Possessives

The possessive form of plural nouns ending in *s* is usually made by adding just an apostrophe.

> **students' homework**   **teachers' lounge**

For plural nouns not ending in *s,* an apostrophe and *s* must be added.

> **children's book**   **people's opinions**

Remember: The word immediately before the apostrophe is the owner.

> **student's project** (*student* is the owner)
> **students' project** (*students* are the owners)

666.2
To Show Shared Possession

When possession is shared by more than one noun, add an apostrophe and *s* to the last noun in the series.

> **Uncle Reggie, Aunt Rosie, and my mom's garden**
> (All three own the garden.)
> **Uncle Reggie's, Aunt Rosie's, and my mom's gardens**
> (Each person owns a garden.)

666.3
To Form Possessives with Compound Nouns

The possessive of a compound noun is formed by placing the possessive ending after the last word.

> **her sister-in-law's hip-hop music** (singular)
> **her sisters-in-law's tastes in music** (plural)
> **the secretary of state's husband** (singular)
> **the secretaries of state's husbands** (plural)

666.4
To Form Possessives with Indefinite Pronouns

The possessive of an indefinite pronoun is formed by adding an apostrophe and *s.*

> **no one's**   **anyone's**   **somebody's**

NOTE In pronouns that use *else,* add an apostrophe and *s* to the second word.

> **somebody else's**   **anyone else's**

666.5
To Express Time or Amount

Use an apostrophe with an adjective that is part of an expression indicating time (month, day, hour) or amount.

> **In today's Spanish class, we talked about going to Spain.**
> **My father lost more than an hour's work when that thunderstorm knocked out our power.**
> **I bought a couple dollars' worth of grapes at the roadside stand.**

 ELPS 4C

MECHANICS

Practice

Apostrophes 2

■ **To Form Possessives**

For each sentence below, write the word or words that need an apostrophe and place the apostrophe correctly.

Example: David G. Wilsons 1970 invention, the modern recumbent bicycle, is a "reclining" bicycle.
Wilson's

1. Many engineers designs for these bicycles have been around since the late 1800s, but the bikes are just now gaining in popularity.

2. This bicycles seat enables riders to sit and lean back in it.

3. While the feet are on the pedals out front, the pedals power drives the back wheel, just as with a traditional bicycle.

4. The handlebar grips are at or below the riders shoulder level.

5. The recumbent design allows peoples bike riding to be free from neck strain, wrist pain, and sore seats.

■ **To Show Shared Possession**
■ **To Form Possessives with Compound Nouns and Indefinite Pronouns**

Write the underlined word or words in the correct possessive form.

Example: <u>Tyronica and Lanelle</u> bikes were falling apart.
Tyronica's and Lanelle's

1. It was their <u>mom and dad</u> decision to get them new bikes.

2. They had seen <u>Deion and Terry</u> recumbent bikes.

3. The girls practiced riding the strange bikes around their <u>cul-de-sac</u> central garden.

4. They ignored <u>everyone</u> stares because they didn't care about <u>anyone else</u> opinion.

5. They just loved to see their <u>great-grandmother</u> smile!

TEKS 8.20B(ii)
ELPS 4C

Hyphens

Use a **hyphen** to divide words at the end of a line and to form compound words. Also use a hyphen between the numbers in a fraction and to join numbers that indicate the life span of an individual, the scores of a game, and so on.

668.1
To Divide Words

Use a hyphen to divide a word when you run out of room at the end of a line. A word may be divided only between syllables. Here are some additional guidelines:

- Never divide a one-syllable word: *raised, through*.
- Avoid dividing a word of five letters or fewer: *paper, study*.
- Never divide a one-letter syllable from the rest of the word: *omit-ted,* **not** *o-mitted*.
- Never divide abbreviations or contractions: *NASA, wouldn't*.
- Never divide the last word in more than two lines in a row or the last word in a paragraph.
- When a vowel is a syllable by itself, divide the word after the vowel: *epi-sode,* **not** *ep-isode*.

NOTE Refer to a dictionary if you're not sure how to divide a word.

668.2
In Compound Words

A hyphen is used in some compound words, including numbers from twenty-one to ninety-nine.

about-face	warm-up	time-out
down-to-earth	ice-skating	high-rise
thirty-three	seventy-five	

668.3
To Create New Words

A hyphen is often used to form new words beginning with the prefixes *self, ex, all,* and *great*. A hyphen is also used with suffixes such as *elect* and *free*.

self-cleaning	ex-friend	all-natural	mayor-elect
self-esteem	ex-president	great-aunt	germ-free

668.4
Between Numbers in a Fraction

Use a hyphen between the numbers in a fraction. Do not, however, use a hyphen between the numerator and denominator when one or both are already hyphenated.

four-tenths	five-sixteenths	seven thirty-seconds (7/32)

TEKS 8.20B(ii)
ELPS 4C

Practice

Hyphens 1

- ■ To Divide Words
- ■ To Create New Words
- ■ Between Numbers in a Fraction

 For each of the following sentences, correctly write the words that need hyphens. If a word is hyphenated incorrectly, write it with the hyphen properly placed (or without the hyphen).

Example: Most people who fish are not self taught.
self-taught

1. They learn to fish from a parent or grandparent who probably also learned to fish from a relative.

2. When I was learning how to hook a worm, I did it over and over again until I got it right.

3. It takes about two thirds of an hour for me to find enough worms.

4. Some believe the best way to fish is to use a barbfree hook.

5. The fish that these anglers release back into the water aren't badly injured by the hooks.

6. In addition, this type of hook is easier to remove from yourself if it "catches" you!

7. Fishing is nine tenths patience.

8. My greatgrandparents like to fish, and I have to say that they're some of the most patient people I know.

9. Yesterday, they gave us one fourth of all the fish they caught.

10. They also gave their neighbor, an exmarine, some of their fish.

Next Step: Write the following words as they could be hyphenated at the end of a line: *candle, maximum, protein,* and *tomorrow.* Also, create three new words by joining two words with a hyphen. Then use your words in sentences.

MECHANICS

TEKS 8.20B(ii)
ELPS 4C

Hyphens . . .

**670.1
To Form
Adjectives**

Use a hyphen to join two or more words that work together to form a single-thought adjective before a noun. Generally, hyphenate any compound adjective that might be misread if it is not hyphenated—use common sense. (See page 550.)

smiley-face sticker   dress-up clothes   fresh-breeze scent

Use the tests below to determine if a hyphen is needed.

1. When a compound adjective is made of a noun plus an adjective, it should be hyphenated.

   microwave-safe cookware   book-smart student

2. When the compound adjective is made of a noun plus a participle (*ing* or *ed* form of a verb), it should be hyphenated.

   bone-chilling story   vitamin-enriched cereal

3. Hyphenate a compound adjective that is a phrase (includes conjunctions or prepositions).

   heat-and-serve meals   refrigerator-to-oven dishes

Do *not* hyphenate compound adjectives in these instances:

1. When words forming the adjective come after the noun, do not hyphenate.

   This cookware is microwave safe.
   The cereal was vitamin enriched.

2. If the first of the two words ends in *ly,* do not hyphenate.

   newly designed computer   rarely seen species

3. Do not use a hyphen when a number or letter is the final part of a one-thought adjective.

   grade A milk   level 6 textbook

**670.2
To Join Letters
to Words**

Use a hyphen to join a capital letter to a noun or participle.

U-turn   *y*-axis
PG-rated movie

**670.3
To Avoid
Confusion**

Use a hyphen with prefixes or suffixes to avoid confusion or awkward spelling.

Re-collect (not recollect) **the reports we handed back last week.**
It has a shell-like (not shelllike) **texture.**

⭐ **TEKS** 8.20B(ii)
ELPS 3E, 4C

Practice

Hyphens 2

▨ **To Form Adjectives**
▨ **To Join Letters to Words**

 For each of the following sentences, correctly write the words that need a hyphen. If no words need a hyphen, write "OK."

Example: A paper thin membrane called the *pleura* covers the lungs.

paper-thin

1. The diaphragm and the chest muscles are responsible for the up and down motion of the rib cage during breathing.

2. The trachea, the tube that carries air to and from the lungs, has 16 to 20 U shaped rings of hard cartilage in front.

3. The heart is a four chambered organ divided in two by the septum.

4. The right side of the heart pumps oxygen poor blood into the lungs.

5. The left side pumps oxygen enriched blood from the lungs all over the body.

6. Arteries carry the blood to barely visible capillaries in the body tissues.

7. Their single cell walls allow oxygen to pass into the tissues and carbon dioxide to be absorbed from them.

8. High blood pressure can result from slowly formed blockages in the blood vessels.

9. A once in a lifetime event might cause a brief spike in one's blood pressure.

10. Long term effects of high blood pressure can be serious.

Next Step: Write sentences that include two words with letters joined to them and one hyphenated adjective (*not* from this page or the facing one). Share your sentences with a partner.

MECHANICS

 TEKS 8.20B(ii)
ELPS 4C

Dashes

The **dash** can be used to show a sudden break in a sentence, to emphasize a word or clause, and to show that someone's speech is being interrupted.

672.1
To Indicate a Sudden Break

A dash can be used to show a sudden break in a sentence.

> **The three of us came down with colds, lost our voices, and missed the football game—all because we had practiced in the rain.**

672.2
For Emphasis

A dash may be used to emphasize or explain a word, a series of words, a phrase, or a clause.

> **Vitamins and minerals—important dietary supplements—can improve your diet.**

> **The benefits of vitamin A—better vision and a stronger immune system—are well known.**

672.3
To Indicate Interrupted Speech

Use a dash to show that someone's speech is being interrupted by another person.

> **Well—yes, I understand—no, I remember—oh—okay, thank you.**

NOTE A dash is indicated by two hyphens--without spacing before or after the hyphens--in all typed material.

Parentheses

Parentheses are used around words that are included in a sentence to add information or to help make an idea clearer.

672.4
To Add Information

Use parentheses when adding information or clarifying an idea. The information in parentheses is usually not necessary to include, but may be helpful or interesting. It should be closely related to the main point of the sentence.

> **Cures for diseases (from arthritis to malaria) may be found in plants in the rain forest.**

> **Only about 10 percent (27,000) of the plant species in the world have been studied.**

TEKS 8.20B(ii)
ELPS 4C

Practice

Dashes

 Rewrite the sentences below, adding dashes where appropriate.

Example: We'll be outside all afternoon don't forget the sunscreen.

We'll be outside all afternoon—don't forget the sunscreen.

1. Han said, "They were going I mean they *are* going to the mall."
2. *Taraxacum officinale* that is, the common dandelion is the curse of many lawns.
3. I don't let's just wait calm down.
4. "Good morning! Here are your oops eggs," Mom said as she dropped my scrambled eggs on my lap.
5. This is Reggie's bike the bike that was stolen!

Parentheses

 Write the parts of the sentences below that should be enclosed in parentheses. Add the parentheses.

Example: Simone's sisters Rachel, Gabby, and Naomi joined us.
(Rachel, Gabby, and Naomi)

1. Peter asked the clerk the one wearing glasses for some change.
2. Of the flower bulbs I planted, most of them 80 percent bloomed.
3. Fumiki looking quite pale excused herself from the table.
4. Lee my friend's first cousin got a job at the amusement park.
5. Kat always peppers her e-mails with emoticons smiley faces.

Next Step: Write a dialogue between two students discussing a test they are studying for. Use some dashes and some parentheses. Then trade papers with a partner and check to see if he or she used dashes and parentheses correctly.

MECHANICS

 **TEKS** 8.20B(ii)
ELPS 4C

Ellipses

Use an **ellipsis** (three periods) to show a pause in dialogue or to show that words or sentences have been left out. Leave one space before and after the ellipsis, as well as between each period.

674.1
To Show Pauses

Use an ellipsis to show a pause in dialogue.

> **"My report," said Reggie, "is on . . . ah . . . cars of the future. One place that I . . . uh . . . checked on the Internet said that cars would someday run on sunshine."**

674.2
To Show Omitted Words

Use an ellipsis to show that one or more words have been left out of a quotation. Read this statement about hibernation.

> **Some animals, such as the chipmunk and the woodchuck, hibernate in winter. During this time, the animal's heart beats very slowly—only a few times per minute. Its body cools down so much that it nearly freezes, and this is called going into torpor.**

Here's how you would type part of the above quotation, leaving some of the words out. If the words left out are at the end of a sentence, use a period followed by three dots.

> **Some animals . . . hibernate in winter. During this time, the animal's heart beats very slowly . . . and this is called going into torpor.**

Brackets

Use **brackets** to show that you have made a slight change to a word or letter in a direct quotation. You might do this to replace a pronoun with the subject's name or to capitalize a letter that was lowercase in the source.

674.3
To Show Changed Words or Letters

> **"[John F. Kennedy] was the youngest person to be *elected* president,"**

> **"[T]he youngest person to *serve* as president was Theodore Roosevelt."**

TEKS 8.20B(ii)
ELPS 4C

Practice

Ellipses

■ **To Show Pauses**

 Rewrite the following sentences, adding ellipses where they are needed.

Example: Oh no I forgot the tickets.

Oh no . . . I forgot the tickets.

1. Did you see the disgusting uh I mean the special food we are having for lunch?

2. It's well how can I describe it?

3. Hmm does it have something healthful in it?

4. Ah you hit the nail on the head.

5. We're having let's see "Martina's Tofu Surprise."

■ **To Show Omitted Words**

 Rewrite the following paragraph as a quotation for a research paper. Insert ellipses where you decide to leave out less-important information.

Sandstone is a very simple kind of sedimentary rock. It is not much more than sand pressed tightly together and mixed with clay, which acts as a kind of cement. Sandstone is porous, which means that water can pass through it; each year's freeze and thaw breaks down the rock a little more. It erodes rapidly, so wind and water can carve sandstone into unusual shapes.

Next Step: Write a paragraph from a book or article (it can be from a novel, a magazine, or a textbook) as if you were quoting it in a paper. Use ellipses and brackets to show where you have omitted information or changed words and letters for clarity.

MECHANICS

TEKS 8.20A
ELPS 4C

Capitalization

676.1
Proper Nouns and Adjectives

Capitalize all proper nouns and all proper adjectives. A proper noun is the name of a particular person, place, thing, or idea. A proper adjective is an adjective formed from a proper noun.

Common Noun: **country, president, continent**

Proper Noun: **Canada, Andrew Jackson, Asia**

Proper Adjective: **Canadian, Jacksonian, Asian**

676.2
Names of People

Capitalize the names of people and also the initials or abbreviations that stand for those names.

Samuel L. Jackson   **Aung San Suu Kyi**

Mary Sanchez-Gomez

676.3
Titles Used with Names

Capitalize titles used with names of persons; also capitalize abbreviations standing for those titles.

President Mohammed Hosni Mubarak   **Dr. Linda Trout**

Governor Michael Easley   **Rev. Jim Zavaski**

Senator John McCain

676.4
Words Used as Names

Capitalize words such as *mother, father, aunt,* and *uncle* when these words are used as names.

Uncle Marius **started to sit on the couch.** (*Uncle* is a name; the speaker calls this person "Uncle Marius.")

Then Uncle **stopped in midair.** (*Uncle* is used as a name.)

"So, Mom, **what are you doing here?" I asked.** (*Mom* is used as a name.)

Words such as *aunt, uncle, mom, dad, grandma,* and *grandpa* are usually not capitalized if they come after a possessive pronoun (*my, his, our*).

My aunt **had just called him.** (The word *aunt* describes this person but is not used as a name.)

Then my dad **and** mom **walked into the room.** (The words *dad* and *mom* are not used as names in this sentence.)

Practice

Capitalization 1

- Names of People
- Titles Used with Names
- Words Used as Names

 Some words in the following sentences are capitalized and should not be; others need to be capitalized. Write each of the words correctly.

Example: Before he was a Governor and a President, mr.
Ronald Reagan was an actor.
governor, president, Mr.

1. The first African American Congresswoman was representative Shirley Chisholm.

2. A Famous Poet, dr. Maya Angelou, read a poem at president Clinton's inauguration.

3. Abigail Adams was the Mother of President John quincy Adams.

4. Mr. Adams called his mom's brother simply "uncle."

5. President john f. Kennedy's Brother is senator Ted Kennedy.

6. The first woman appointed to the United States Supreme Court was justice Sandra day O'Connor.

7. President George w. Bush's Father is a former president: george h. w. Bush.

8. In 1997, secretary of state madeleine K. Albright became the highest-ranking woman in the history of the U.S. government.

9. Greenville, South Carolina, is the birthplace of rev. jessie Jackson, who ran for President at one time.

Next Step: Write a sentence about a famous person you are studying in school. Use a title (Dr., Ms., Senator) for this person in your sentence. Check your capitalization.

TEKS 8.20A

Capitalization . . .

678.1
School Subjects

Capitalize the name of a specific educational course, but not the name of a general subject. (Exception—the names of all languages are proper nouns and are always capitalized: *French, English, Hindi, German, Latin.*)

Roberto is studying accounting **at the technical college.** (Because *accounting* is a general subject, it is not capitalized.)

He likes the professor who teaches Accounting Principles. (The specific course name is capitalized.)

678.2
Official Names

Capitalize the names of businesses and the official names of their products. (These are called trade names.) Do not, however, capitalize a general word like "toothpaste" when it follows the trade name.

Old Navy	Best Buy	Microsoft	Kodak
Sony Playstation	Tombstone pizza	Mudd jeans	

678.3
Races, Languages, Nationalities, Religions

Capitalize the names of languages, races, nationalities, and religions, as well as the proper adjectives formed from them.

Arab	Spanish	Judaism	Catholicism
African art	Irish linen	Swedish meatballs	

678.4
Days, Months, Holidays

Capitalize the names of days of the week, months of the year, and special holidays.

Thursday	Friday	Saturday
July	August	September
Arbor Day	Independence Day	

Do not capitalize the names of seasons.

winter, spring, summer, fall (autumn)

678.5
Historical Events

Capitalize the names of historical events, documents, and periods of time.

World War II	the Bill of Rights	the Magna Carta
the Middle Ages	the Paleozoic Era	

TEKS 8.20A
ELPS 3E

Practice

Capitalization 2

- School Subjects
- Races, Languages, Nationalities, Religions
- Historical Events

Correctly write any incorrectly capitalized words in the following paragraphs. (Write the line number followed by the word or words.)

Example: *1* My dad speaks english, french, and spanish.
1 English, French, Spanish

1 Last year I took a french language class. The class was

2 actually called french language and history, so we learned some

3 of that country's history, too. For instance, the french wars of

4 religion were fought by people of different christian faiths. While

5 France was ruled by catholic kings, an army attacked a protestant

6 church service. After many years of fighting between catholics and

7 protestants, the french people were allowed to choose their own

8 faith. Today, people of all faiths—christianity, judaism, hinduism,

9 islam, and others—have freedom to worship in France.

10 We also talked about Bastille Day, the french holiday that's

11 like Independence Day in the United States. In France, it celebrates

12 the beginning of the french revolution. The Bastille was the name

13 of a french prison for people who did not agree with the king and

14 queen's decisions. On July 14, 1789, a crowd of frenchmen stormed

15 the Bastille and released the prisoners. That revolution brought

16 great changes and new freedoms to France, just as the revolutionary

17 war gained freedom for early american colonists.

Next Step: Write a brief paragraph about an American historical
event you have recently studied or know something about.
Share your paragraph with a partner.

MECHANICS

 **TEKS** 8.20A

Capitalization . . .

680.1
Geographic
Names

Capitalize the following geographic names.

Planets and heavenly bodies . . . . **Venus, Jupiter, Milky Way**

Lowercase the word "earth" except when used as the proper name of our planet, especially when mentioned with other planet names.

What on earth are you doing here?

Sam has traveled across the face of the earth several times.

Jupiter's diameter is 11 times larger than Earth's.

The four inner planets are Mercury, Venus, Earth, and Mars.

Continents. . . . . . **Europe, Asia, South America, Australia, Africa**

Countries .. **Morocco, Haiti, Greece, Chile, United Arab Emirates**

States . . . . . **New Mexico, Alabama, West Virginia, Delaware, Iowa**

Provinces . . . . **Alberta, British Columbia, Quebec, Ontario**

Counties . . . . **Sioux County, Kandiyohi County, Wade County**

Cities. . . . . **Montreal, Baton Rouge, Albuquerque, Portland**

Bodies of water. . . . . **Delaware Bay, Chickamunga Lake, Indian Ocean, Gulf of Mexico, Skunk Creek**

Landforms. . . . . **Appalachian Mountains, Bitterroot Range**

Public areas . . . . **Tiananmen Square, Sequoia National Forest, Mount Rushmore, Open Space Park, Vietnam Memorial**

Roads and highways. . . . . **New Jersey Turnpike, Interstate 80, Central Avenue, Chisholm Trail, Mutt's Road**

Buildings . . . **Pentagon, Paske High School, Empire State Building**

Monuments . . . . **Eiffel Tower, Statue of Liberty**

680.2
Particular
Sections of the
Country

Capitalize words that indicate particular sections of the country. Also capitalize proper adjectives formed from names of specific sections of a country.

Having grown up on the hectic East Coast, I find life in the South to be refreshing.

Here in Georgia, Southern hospitality is a way of life.

Words that simply indicate a direction are not capitalized; nor are adjectives that are formed from words that simply indicate direction.

The town where I live, located east of Memphis, is typical of others found in western Tennessee.

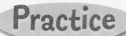
TEKS 8.20A
ELPS 2C, 4C

Practice

Capitalization 3

■ **Geographic Names**
■ **Particular Sections of the Country**

For each sentence below, write the word or words that should be capitalized. If a sentence has correct capitalization, write "correct."

Example: Kennebunk, ocean city, and St. Augustine are cities on the east coast.
Ocean City, East Coast

1. You can see giant pandas in china at the beijing zoological gardens.

2. Honolulu, Hawaii, is on the southeast coast of the island of Oahu.

3. The San Andreas Fault runs northwest to southeast along california's coastline.

4. The queen lives in buckingham palace in london, england.

5. Mt. rushmore and the crazy horse monument are in the black hills of south dakota.

6. The mississippi river runs from minnesota to the gulf of mexico.

7. Mount kilimanjaro, near the border of kenya, is the highest point in africa.

8. There are many historic trails and landmarks in the western united states.

9. The will rogers highway is one of the names for route 66, which runs from chicago to los angeles.

10. Indiana, wisconsin, iowa, and ohio are states in the midwest.

Learning Language Direction words can be tricky. Depending on how they are used, they may or may not be capitalized. If a direction word refers to a specific part of the country, then it is capitalized:

Washington, Oregon, and California are on the West Coast.

However, when the same word is used to indicate direction, it is NOT capitalized:

California is west of Nevada.

MECHANICS

TEKS 8.20A

Capitalization . . .

682.1
First Words

Capitalize the first word of every sentence and the first word in a direct quotation.

> In many families, pets are treated like people, according to an article in the *Kansas City Star.* (sentence)

> Marty Becker, coauthor of *Chicken Soup for the Pet Lover's Soul,* reports, "Seven out of ten people let their pets sleep on the bed." (direct quotation)

> "I get my 15 minutes of fame," he says, "every time I come home." (Notice that *every* is not capitalized because it does not begin a new sentence.)

> "It's like being treated like a rock star," says Becker. "Now I have to tell you that feels pretty good."

Do not capitalize the first word in an indirect quotation.

> Becker says that in the last 10 years, pets have moved out of kennels and basements and into living rooms and bedrooms. (indirect quotation)

682.2
Titles

Capitalize the first word of a title, the last word, and every word in between except articles *(a, an, the),* short prepositions, and coordinating conjunctions. Follow this rule for titles of books, newspapers, magazines, poems, plays, songs, articles, movies, works of art, pictures, stories, and essays.

> *Locked in Time* (book)
>
> *Boston Globe* (newspaper)
>
> *Dog Fancy* (magazine)
>
> "Roses Are Red" (poem)
>
> *The Phantom of the Opera* (play)
>
> *Daddy Day Care* (movie)
>
> "Intuition" (song)
>
> **Mona Lisa** (work of art)

★ **TEKS** 8.20A
ELPS 3E

Practice

Capitalization 4

- First Words
- Titles

For each of the following sentences, correctly write any word that is incorrectly capitalized.

Example: Laura Ingalls Wilder once said that She had no idea she was writing history.

she

1. A collection of her letters can be found in the book *West From Home.*

2. Laura's book *Little house in The Big Woods* is about her life in Wisconsin.

3. Pa played and sang songs like "My old kentucky home."

4. the television series *Little House On the Prairie* was based on Laura's books.

5. Laura wrote articles for the *Missouri ruralist* and other magazines.

6. Laura's sister Carrie worked for a while at the *De Smet news.*

7. "I love the *Little House* books," said Heather, "Because of their descriptions about life during the 1800s."

8. Heather told us That she has all of Laura Ingalls Wilder's books.

9. "My favorite is *Little Town on the prairie*," she said. "It's the one where Laura meets Almanzo Wilder."

Next Step: Write a short paragraph about a favorite author and include the titles of some of his or her works. Exchange papers with a classmate. Check that words and titles are capitalized correctly.

 **TEKS** 8.20A

Capitalization . . .

Abbreviations

Capitalize abbreviations of titles and organizations.

Dr. (Doctor)   **M.D.** (Doctor of Medicine)
Mr. (Mister)   **UPS** (United Parcel Service)
SADD (Students Against Destructive Decisions)

Organizations

Capitalize the name of an organization, an association, or a team.

New York State Historical Society   **the Red Cross**
General Motors Corporation   **the Miami Dolphins**
Republicans   **the Democratic Party**

Letters

Capitalize the letters used to indicate form or shape.

T-shirt   **U-turn**   **A-frame**   **T-ball**

Capitalize   **Do Not Capitalize**

Capitalize	Do Not Capitalize
American	un-American
January, February	winter, spring
Missouri and Ohio rivers	the rivers Missouri and Ohio
The South is humid in summer.	Turn south at the stop sign.
Duluth Middle School	a Duluth middle school
Governor Bob Taft	Bob Taft, our governor
President Luiz Lula Da Silva	Luiz Lula Da Silva, Brazil's president
Nissan Altima	a Nissan automobile
The planet Earth is egg shaped.	The earth on Grandpa's farm is rich.
I'm taking World Cultures.	I'm taking social studies.

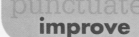 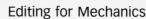

 8.20A

Practice

Capitalization 5

■ Abbreviations
■ Organizations

Capitalize the words in the following paragraphs that need to be capitalized. (Write the line number followed by the word or words.)

Example: *1* The ad council donates services to organizations
2 like the girl scouts of America.

1 Ad Council
2 Girl Scouts

1 The ad council is a group of volunteers in the advertising
2 industry. They make and promote public service announcements
3 (psa's) for many organizations. For instance, they created McGruff
4 the Crime Dog for the National crime prevention Council. They also
5 created Smokey Bear for the usfs (United States forest service) and
6 Vince and Larry, the Crash Test Dummies, for the government's dot
7 (department of transportation).

8 When members of the ad council see a problem that concerns
9 people, they try to draw attention to it. Some of their recent
10 campaigns include increasing environmental awareness (sponsored
11 by earth share) and getting parents involved in school (sponsored
12 by the National pta). The ad council's programs encourage people to
13 give these subjects the notice they deserve. The hope is that positive
14 social change will result as people take action.

Next Step: Write a brief paragraph about an issue that concerns
you. Include the name of an organization that you would
create to deal with the problem.

MECHANICS

TEKS 8.21

Plurals

686.1
Most Nouns

The **plurals** of most nouns are formed by adding *s* to the singular.

> cheerleader — **cheerleaders**   wheel — **wheels**
> bubble — **bubbles**

686.2
Nouns Ending in *ch, sh, s, x,* and *z*

The plural form of nouns ending in *ch, sh, s, x,* and *z* is made by adding *es* to the singular.

> lunch — **lunches**   dish — **dishes**   mess — **messes**
> buzz — **buzzes**   fox — **foxes**

686.3
Nouns Ending in *o*

The plurals of nouns ending in *o* with a vowel just before the *o* are formed by adding *s*.

> radio — **radios**   studio — **studios**   rodeo — **rodeos**

The plurals of most nouns ending in *o* with a consonant just before the *o* are formed by adding *es*.

> echo — **echoes**   hero — **heroes**   tomato — **tomatoes**

Exceptions: Musical terms and words of Spanish origin always form plurals by adding *s*.

> alto — **altos**   banjo — **banjos**   taco — **tacos**
> solo — **solos**   piano — **pianos**   burro — **burros**

686.4
Nouns Ending in *ful*

The plurals of nouns that end with *ful* are formed by adding an *s* at the end of the word.

> three platefuls   six tankfuls   four cupfuls   five pailfuls

686.5
Nouns Ending in *f* or *fe*

The plurals of nouns that end in *f* or *fe* are formed in one of two ways: If the final *f* sound is still heard in the plural form of the word, simply add *s;* if the final sound is a *v* sound, change the *f* to *ve* and add *s*.

> roof — **roofs**   chief — **chiefs**   belief — **beliefs**
> (plural ends with *f* sound)
> wife — **wives**   loaf — **loaves**   leaf — **leaves**
> (plural ends with *v* sound)

Practice

Plurals 1

- Nouns Ending in *ch, sh, s, x,* and *z*
- Nouns Ending in *o*
- Nouns Ending in *ful*
- Nouns Ending in *f* or *fe*

 For each sentence below, write the correct plural for the underlined word. If the plural is correct, write "C."

Example: Today's four o'clock meeting is for <u>coachs</u> only.

coaches

1. The cooks used a whole bag of <u>potatoes</u> to make this soup.

2. During the night, <u>thiefs</u> took three signs from the parking lot.

3. Randy ate three <u>bowlsful</u> of his favorite cereal.

4. Sometimes countries use special <u>taxs</u> to control the number of imported goods.

5. These extra charges are called <u>tariffes</u>.

6. The winning lumberjack used six different <u>axs</u> during the competition.

7. The eighth-grade choir wants five more girls to be <u>sopranoes</u>.

8. Some people say that cats have nine <u>lifes</u>.

9. Allan figured he needed four <u>bucketfuls</u> of red paint to complete the job.

10. Angelica likes to eat <u>mangos</u>.

11. The newspaper reported that there were more than 50 <u>canoes</u> in the race.

12. In the movie *Aladdin*, does the genie grant three or four <u>wishs</u>?

Next Step: Write three sentences that include the plurals of these words: *studio, spoonful,* and *wax.* Read your sentences aloud to a classmate.

Plurals . . .

The plurals of common nouns that end in *y* with a
consonant letter just before the *y* are formed by changing
the *y* to *i* and adding *es*.

fly — **flies**   baby — **babies**   cavity — **cavities**

The plurals of common nouns that end in *y* with a vowel
before the *y* are formed by adding only *s*.

key — **keys**   holiday — **holidays**   attorney — **attorneys**

The plurals of proper nouns ending in *y* are formed by
adding *s*.

There are three Circuit Citys **in our metro area.**

The plurals of some compound nouns are formed by adding
s or *es* to the main word in the compound.

brothers-in-law   maids of honor   secretaries of state

The plurals of some words are the same in singular and
plural form.

deer   sheep   trout   aircraft

Some words (including many foreign words) form a
plural by taking on an irregular spelling; others are now
acceptable with the commonly used *s* or *es* ending.

child — **children**   woman — **women**   man — **men**

goose — **geese**   mouse — **mice**   ox — **oxen**

tooth — **teeth**   octopus — **octopi** or **octopuses**

index — **indices** or **indexes**

The plurals of letters, figures, symbols, and words discussed
as words are formed by adding an apostrophe and an *s*.

Dr. Walters has two Ph.D.'s.

My dad's license plate has three 2's **between two** B's.

You've got too many *but*'s **and** *so*'s **in that sentence.**

For information on forming plural possessives, see 666.1.

punctuate *edit* capitalize
SPELL
improve
Editing for Mechanics

689

TEKS 8.21
ELPS 3E

Plurals 2

- Nouns Ending in *y*
- Compound Nouns
- Plurals That Do Not Change
- Irregular Spelling

 For each of the following sentences, write the plural form of the word or words in parentheses.

Example: My favorite author writes *(story)* about *(child)* in other *(country)*.
stories, children, countries

1. The *(boy)* rode *(donkey)* into the Valley of the Kings.

2. There are *(county)* in Nebraska named after *(antelope)* and *(buffalo)*.

3. There were six *(Bobby)* at the Malloy family reunion.

4. *(Passer-by)* saw the injured animal and called the Humane Society.

5. We saw at least two dozen *(species)* of birds on our nature walk.

6. *(Mushroom)* are edible, fleshy *(fungus)*.

7. Marcus and Tyisha packed the old *(textbook)* into *(box)*.

8. The zoo bought two ring-tailed lemurs and three howler *(monkey)*.

9. Medical school is where *(man)* and *(woman)* study to become *(doctor)*.

10. There were three *(runner-up)* in the Battle of the Bands.

11. Many Asian American *(family)* live in my neighborhood.

Next Step: Write sentences using plurals of the following words: *cavity, goose, octopus,* and *holiday.* Read your sentences aloud to a classmate.

MECHANICS

 **TEKS** 8.20A

Abbreviations

690.1
Abbreviations

An **abbreviation** is the shortened form of a word or phrase. The following abbreviations are always acceptable in any kind of writing:

> **Mr.**   **Mrs.**   **Ms.**   **Dr.**   **a.m., p.m.** (A.M., P.M.)
> **B.C.E.** (before the Common Era)   **C.E.** (Common Era)
> **B.A.**   **M.A.**   **Ph.D.**   **M.D.**   **Sr.**   **Jr.**

Caution: Do not abbreviate the names of states, countries, months, days, or units of measure in formal writing. Also, do not use signs or symbols (%, &) in place of words.

Common Abbreviations

AC alternating current	**kg** kilogram	**pd.** paid
a.m. ante meridiem	**km** kilometer	**pg.** (or p.) page
ASAP as soon as possible	**kw** kilowatt	**p.m.** post meridiem
COD cash on delivery	**l** liter	**ppd.** postpaid, prepaid
DA district attorney	**lb.** pound	**qt.** quart
DC direct current	**m** meter	**R.S.V.P.** please reply
etc. and so forth	**M.D.** doctor of medicine	**tbs., tbsp.** tablespoon
F Fahrenheit	**mfg.** manufacturing	**tsp.** teaspoon
FM frequency modulation	**mpg** miles per gallon	**vol.** volume
GNP gross national product	**mph** miles per hour	**vs.** versus
i.e. that is (Latin *id est*)	**oz.** ounce	**yd.** yard

Address Abbreviations

	Standard	Postal		Standard	Postal		Standard	Postal
Avenue	Ave.	AVE	Lake	L.	LK	Route	Rt.	RTE
Boulevard	Blvd.	BLVD	Lane	Ln.	LN	South	S.	S
Court	Ct.	CT	North	N.	N	Square	Sq.	SQ
Drive	Dr.	DR	Park	Pk.	PK	Station	Sta.	STA
East	E.	E	Parkway	Pky.	PKY	Street	St.	ST
Expressway	Expy.	EXPY	Place	Pl.	PL	Terrace	Ter.	TER
Heights	Hts.	HTS	Plaza	Plaza	PLZ	Turnpike	Tpke.	TPKE
Highway	Hwy.	HWY	Road	Rd.	RD	West	W.	W

Practice

Abbreviations 1

For each of the following sentences, write the correct abbreviation for the underlined word or words.

Example: Coach Chen told us to get off the field <u>as soon as possible</u>. *ASAP*

1. On my cousin's wedding invitation, it said "<u>please reply</u> by May 10."

2. The <u>district attorney</u> for our county is <u>Mister</u> John B. Stepanek, <u>Senior</u>.

3. I wonder how long I could play my stereo on one <u>kilowatt</u> of electricity.

4. Grandpa always says that an <u>ounce</u> of prevention is worth a <u>pound</u> of cure.

5. At 238 <u>miles per hour</u>, an "Indy" car covers 350 feet of track per second.

6. Most banana plants stop growing when the temperature drops below 53 degrees <u>Fahrenheit</u>.

7. Noah Blain, <u>doctor of medicine</u>, operated on my sister's shoulder.

8. The television set we take camping uses <u>direct current</u>.

9. I listen mostly to <u>frequency modulation</u> radio stations.

10. Mom's new car averages 36 <u>miles per gallon</u>.

11. The cake recipe calls for one <u>teaspoon</u> of vanilla.

12. I was named after my uncle, Juan L. Martinez, <u>Junior</u>.

13. The Greek philosopher Aristotle was born in 384 <u>before the Common Era</u>.

Next Step: Rewrite these addresses using standard abbreviations.

123 Greenwillow Parkway   13 South Linden Station

10 North Lincoln Boulevard   258 Willmore Terrace

1659 Standish Court

Abbreviations . . .

692.1
Acronyms

An **acronym** is an abbreviation that can be pronounced as a word. It does not require periods.

WHO — World Health Organization   ROM — read-only memory

FAQ — frequently asked question

692.2
Initialisms

An **initialism** is similar to an acronym except that it cannot be pronounced as a word; the initials are pronounced individually.

PBS — Public Broadcasting System

BLM — Bureau of Land Management

WNBA — Women's National Basketball Association

Common Acronyms and Initialisms

AIDS	acquired immunodeficiency syndrome	ORV	off-road vehicle
CETA	Comprehensive Employment and Training Act	OSHA	Occupational Safety and Health Administration
CIA	Central Intelligence Agency	PAC	political action committee
FAA	Federal Aviation Administration	PIN	personal identification number
FBI	Federal Bureau of Investigation	PSA	public service announcement
FCC	Federal Communications Commission	ROTC	Reserve Officers' Training Corps
FDA	Food and Drug Administration	SADD	Students Against Destructive Decisions
FDIC	Federal Deposit Insurance Corporation	SSA	Social Security Administration
FHA	Federal Housing Administration	SUV	sport utility vehicle
FmHA	Farmers Home Authority	SWAT	special weapons and tactics
FTC	Federal Trade Commission	TDD	telecommunications device for the deaf
IRS	Internal Revenue Service	TMJ	temporomandibular joint
MADD	Mothers Against Drunk Driving	TVA	Tennessee Valley Authority
NAFTA	North American Free Trade Agreement	VA	Veterans Affairs
NASA	National Aeronautics and Space Administration	VISTA	Volunteers in Service to America
NATO	North Atlantic Treaty Organization	WAC	Women's Army Corps
OEO	Office of Economic Opportunity	WAVES	Women Accepted for Volunteer Emergency Service
OEP	Office of Emergency Preparedness		

Practice

Abbreviations 2

- Acronyms
- Initialisms

 Write the correct abbreviation for each phrase below. Tell whether it is an acronym or an initialism.

Example: Federal Emergency Management Agency
FEMA–acronym

1. American Kennel Club
2. telecommunications device for the deaf
3. National Basketball Association
4. personal identification number
5. Federal Bureau of Investigation
6. National Aeronautics and Space Administration
7. attention deficit disorder
8. North Atlantic Treaty Organization
9. special weapons and tactics
10. Internal Revenue Service
11. Federal Aviation Administration
12. Food and Drug Administration
13. parental guidance
14. also known as

Next Step: Make up a slogan for your school that can be abbreviated as an acronym.

Numbers

Numbers from one to nine are usually written as words; all numbers 10 and over are usually written as numerals.

two   seven   nine   10   25   106

Use numerals to express any of the following forms:

money	**$2.39**
decimals	**26.2**
percentages	**8 percent**
chapters	**chapter 7**
pages	**pages 287–289**
time (with "a.m." or "p.m.")	**4:30 p.m.**
telephone numbers	**1-800-555-1212**
dates	**44 B.C.E.; July 6, 1942**
identification numbers	**Highway 36**
addresses	**2125 Cairn Road**
ZIP codes	**60004**
statistics	**a vote of 23 to 4**

When abbreviations and symbols are used (for instance, in science or math), always use numerals with them.

12° C   7%   33 kg   9 cm   55 mph

You may use a combination of numerals and words for very large numbers.

Of the 17 million residents of the three Midwestern states, only 1.3 million are blonds.

You may spell out a large number that can be written as two words. If more than two words are needed, use the numeral.

More than nine thousand people attended the concert.

According to head usher, 3,011 people missed the opening act.

Practice

Numbers 1

- ■ **Numbers Under 10**
- ■ **Numerals Only**
- ■ **Very Large Numbers**

 For each of the following sentences, write the underlined number the correct way. If it is already in the correct form, write "correct."

Example: In the <u>nineteen sixties</u>, Americans drove large, heavy cars.

1960s

1. Many cars of that decade got only <u>nine</u> miles per gallon.

2. A car built in <u>two thousand nine</u> is quite a bit more efficient than those built <u>40</u> years ago.

3. It is safest to drive under <u>fifty-five</u> miles per hour.

4. In 1965, there were more than <u>90,300,000</u> cars registered in the United States.

5. Today, there are about <u>240 million</u> cars in use on our nation's roads.

6. In 2006, there were about <u>201,000,000</u> drivers in the United States, each averaging <u>14,000</u> miles per year.

7. Many roads in major cities get traffic jams between <u>seven</u> a.m. and <u>nine</u> a.m.

8. People would save fuel and face less traffic if more cars carried at least <u>2</u> people.

9. The business located at <u>two forty-nine</u> South Cheps Road requires all its employees to carpool or use public transportation.

Next Step: Complete the following sentence with your own numbers: Today, _____(date)_____ , at _____(time)_____ it was _(temperature)_ degrees.

Numbers . . .

696.1
Comparing Numbers

If you are comparing two or more numbers in a sentence, write all of them the same way: as numerals or as words.

Students from 9 to 14 years old are invited.

Students from nine to fourteen years old are invited.

696.2
Numbers in Compound Modifiers

A compound modifier may include a numeral.

The floorboards come in 10-foot lengths.

When a number comes before a compound modifier that includes a numeral, use words instead of numerals.

We need eleven 10-foot lengths to finish the floor.

Ms. Brown must grade twenty 12-page reports.

696.3
Sentence Beginnings

Use words, not numerals, to begin a sentence.

Nine students had turned in their homework. Fourteen students said they were unable to finish the assignment.

696.4
Time and Money

When time or money is expressed with an abbreviation, use numerals. When either is expressed with words, spell out the number.

6:00 a.m. or six o'clock

$25 or twenty-five dollars

SCHOOL DAZE

Jerry, haven't you finished your paper yet?

No, it's not due until **three o'clock**, and Mrs. Wright told me to add a few new twists and wrinkles.

Practice

Numbers 2

■ Sentence Beginnings
■ Time and Money

If a number in the following sentences is not in the right form, write it correctly.

Example: 14 teams compete in the girls' softball league.
Fourteen

1. The softball games at Carrey Middle School start at four p.m.

2. 40 girls from my school signed up to play softball this season.

3. It costs the school about $5 hundred a month to support all of its teams.

4. The teams practice after school on Tuesdays and Thursdays until five-thirty p.m.

5. Each player must pay 25 dollars for equipment and supplies.

■ Comparing Numbers
■ Numbers in Compound Modifiers

Rewrite the underlined parts of the following sentences so that they are correct.

Example: Girls from <u>nine to 14 years old</u> compete in the league.
9 to 14 years old (or) nine to fourteen years old

1. Players may participate in <u>ten to 16 games</u> each month.

2. We have <u>seven home games and 10 away games</u> this season.

3. Carlos Moy is an umpire for <u>3 90-minute games</u> each week.

4. Each team has at least <u>3 12-inch softballs</u>.

5. Our school has <u>4 9-player teams</u>.

TEKS 8.21

Improving Spelling

698.1
i before *e*

Write *i* before *e* except after *c,* or when sounded like *a* as in *neighbor* and *weigh.*

Some Exceptions to the Rule: *counterfeit, either, financier, foreign, height, heir, leisure, neither, science, seize, sheik, species, their, weird*

698.2
Silent *e*

If a word ends with a silent *e,* drop the *e* before adding a suffix that begins with a vowel. There are exceptions, for example, *knowledgeable* and *changeable.*

state — stating — statement	use — using — useful
like — liking — likeness	nine — ninety — nineteen

NOTE You do not drop the *e* when the suffix begins with a consonant. Exceptions include *truly, argument,* and *ninth.*

698.3
Words Ending in *y*

When *y* is the last letter in a word and the *y* comes just after a consonant, change the *y* to *i* before adding any suffix except those beginning with *i.*

fry — fries — frying	happy — happiness
hurry — hurried — hurrying	beauty — beautiful
lady — ladies	

When forming the plural of a word that ends with a *y* that comes just after a vowel, add *s.*

toy — toys	play — plays	monkey — monkeys

698.4
Consonant Endings

When a one-syllable word ends in a consonant *(bat)* preceded by one vowel *(ba̱t),* double the final consonant before adding a suffix that begins with a vowel *(batting).*

sum — summary	god — goddess

When a multisyllable word ends in a consonant preceded by one vowel *(control),* the accent is on the last syllable *(contról),* and the suffix begins with a vowel *(ing)*—the same rule holds true: double the final consonant *(controlling).*

prefer — preferred	begin — beginning

TEKS 8.21
ELPS 3E

SPELLING

Practice

Spelling 1

◼ *i* before *e*
◼ Silent *e*
◼ Words Ending in *y*
◼ Consonant Endings

For each sentence below, write the correct spelling of any misspelled word. If no word is misspelled, write "correct."

Example: Dragon boat races are an interesting and exciteing part of Chinese history.

exciting

1. The colorful boats look like feirce dragons with scary heads, scaly bodyes, and long tails.

2. Actually, they're quite beautiful.

3. Centurys ago, some Chinese people believed that dragon boat raceing would bring them bountyful crops.

4. They rowed on the river in thier boats, beatting drums to scare fish and water dragons away.

5. They also wraped rice in leaves and threw them into the river.

6. Today, people race the dragon boats cheifly for amusment during Chinese festivals.

7. The festivals and races are enjoied by people in cities around the world.

8. Observers can expereince the thrill of all the druming and yelling.

9. Identifiing which boat will win isn't easy.

10. I am beting that the rowers are no longer nerveous about water dragons comeing to get them.

Next Step: Review the list of spelling words on pages 701–707. Choose three words that give you trouble. Write a sentence for each that will help you remember its correct spelling. Share your sentences with a partner.

Practice

Spelling 2

- ■ *i* before *e*
- ■ Silent *e*
- ■ Words Ending in *y*
- ■ Consonant Endings

 For each sentence below, write the correct spelling of any word that is misspelled. If no word is misspelled, write "correct."

Example: Angelica spent time at the art museum admireing the Renaissance paintings.

admiring

1. Ryan prefered to read about the anceint kingdoms of Egypt.

2. Borna thought that the science assignment was sensless.

3. Viu likes decorating her room with fresh flowers.

4. Our science teacher's cheif complaint is the condition of the school's microscopes.

5. He has identifyed the brand he would like to purchase.

6. Five students measured the boundarys of the school property.

7. On a hot day, Hamal faned himself with a peice of paper.

8. Everyone is talking about the wierd weather we're haveing.

9. Every morning, Principal Phipps reads the day's announcments.

10. The aviation industry plans to improve the guidance systems for its aircraft.

11. Although Shania likes shoping, she knows she is not very good at bargainning.

12. Sam twisted his right ankle, so he was hoping around on his left foot.

13. Rozene could not beleive how much snow was falling.

14. For your own safty, do not eat any food that appears to be roting.

SPELLING

Yellow Pages Guide to Improved Spelling

Be patient. Becoming a good speller takes time.

Check your spelling by using a dictionary or list of commonly misspelled words (like the list that follows). And, remember, don't rely too much on computer spell-checkers.

Learn the correct pronunciation of each word you are trying to spell. Knowing the correct pronunciation of a word will help you remember how it's spelled.

Look up the meaning of each word as you are checking the dictionary for pronunciation. (Knowing how to spell a word is of little use if you don't know what it means.)

Practice spelling the word before you close the dictionary. Look away from the page and try to see the word in your mind's eye. Write the word on a piece of paper. Check the spelling in the dictionary and repeat the process until you are able to spell the word correctly.

Keep a list of the words that you misspell.

Write often. As noted educator Frank Smith said, "There is little point in learning to spell if you have little intention of writing."

A

abbreviate
aboard
about
above
absence
absent
absolute (ly)
abundance
accelerate
accident
accidental (ly)
accompany
accomplice
accomplish
according

account
accurate
accustom (ed)
ache
achieve (ment)
acre
across
actual
adapt
addition (al)
address
adequate
adjust (ment)
admire
adventure
advertise (ment)
advertising
afraid

after
afternoon
afterward
again
against
agreeable
agree (ment)
ah
aid
airy
aisle
alarm
alcohol
alike
alive
alley
allowance
all right

almost
already
although
altogether
aluminum
always
amateur
ambulance
amendment
among
amount
analyze
ancient
angel
anger
angle
angry
animal

anniversary
announce
annoyance
annual
anonymous
another
answer
Antarctic
anticipate
anxiety
anxious
anybody
anyhow
anyone
anything
anyway
anywhere
apartment
apiece
apologize
apparent (ly)
appeal
appearance
appetite
appliance
application
appointment
appreciate
approach
appropriate
approval
approximate
architect
Arctic
aren't
argument
arithmetic
around
arouse
arrange (ment)
arrival
article
artificial

asleep
assassin
assign (ment)
assistance
associate
association
assume
athlete
athletic
attach
attack (ed)
attempt
attendance
attention
attitude
attorney
attractive
audience
August
author
authority
automobile
autumn
available
avenue
average
awful (ly)
awkward

B

baggage
baking
balance
balloon
ballot
banana
bandage
bankrupt
barber
bargain
barrel

basement
basis
basket
battery
beautiful
beauty
because
become
becoming
before
began
beggar
beginning
behave
behavior
being
belief
believe
belong
beneath
benefit (ed)
between
bicycle
biscuit
blackboard
blanket
blizzard
bother
bottle
bottom
bough
bought
bounce
boundary
breakfast
breast
breath (n.)
breathe (v.)
breeze
bridge
brief
bright
brilliant

brother
brought
bruise
bubble
bucket
buckle
budget
building
bulletin
buoyant
bureau
burglar
bury
business
busy
button

cabbage
cafeteria
calendar
campaign
canal
cancel (ed)
candidate
candle
canister
cannon
cannot
canoe
can't
canyon
capacity
captain
carburetor
cardboard
career
careful
careless
carpenter
carriage

carrot	colossal	cooperate	deceive
cashier	column	corporation	decided
casserole	comedy	correspond	decision
casualty	coming	cough	declaration
catalog	commercial	couldn't	decorate
catastrophe	commission	counter	defense
catcher	commit	counterfeit	definite (ly)
caterpillar	commitment	country	definition
catsup	committed	county	delicious
ceiling	committee	courage	dependent
celebration	communicate	courageous	depot
cemetery	community	court	describe
census	company	courteous	description
century	comparison	courtesy	desert
certain (ly)	competition	cousin	deserve
certificate	competitive (ly)	coverage	design
challenge	complain	cozy	desirable
champion	complete (ly)	cracker	despair
changeable	complexion	cranky	dessert
character (istic)	compromise	crawl	deteriorate
chief	conceive	creditor	determine
children	concerning	cried	develop (ment)
chimney	concert	criticize	device (n.)
chocolate	concession	cruel	devise (v.)
choice	concrete	crumb	diamond
chorus	condemn	crumble	diaphragm
circumstance	condition	cupboard	diary
citizen	conductor	curiosity	dictionary
civilization	conference	curious	difference
classmates	confidence	current	different
classroom	congratulate	custom	difficulty
climate	connect	customer	dining
climb	conscience	cylinder	diploma
closet	conscious		director
clothing	conservative		disagreeable
coach	constitution	**D**	disappear
cocoa	continue		disappoint
cocoon	continuous	daily	disapprove
coffee	control	dairy	disastrous
collar	controversy	damage	discipline
college	convenience	danger (ous)	discover
colonel	convince	daughter	discuss
color	coolly	dealt	discussion

SPELLING

disease
dissatisfied
distinguish
distribute
divide
divine
divisible
division
doctor
doesn't
dollar
dormitory
doubt
dough
dual
duplicate

eager (ly)
economy
edge
edition
efficiency
eight
eighth
either
elaborate
electricity
elephant
eligible
ellipse
embarrass
emergency
emphasize
employee
employment
enclose
encourage
engineer
enormous
enough

entertain
enthusiastic
entirely
entrance
envelop (v.)
envelope (n.)
environment
equipment
equipped
equivalent
escape
especially
essential
establish
every
evidence
exaggerate
exceed
excellent
except
exceptional (ly)
excite
exercise
exhaust (ed)
exhibition
existence
expect
expensive
experience
explain
explanation
expression
extension
extinct
extraordinary
extreme (ly)

facilities
familiar
family

famous
fascinate
fashion
fatigue (d)
faucet
favorite
feature
February
federal
fertile
field
fierce
fiery
fifty
finally
financial (ly)
foliage
forcible
foreign
forfeit
formal (ly)
former (ly)
forth
fortunate
forty
forward
fountain
fourth
fragile
freight
friend (ly)
frighten
fulfill
fundamental
further
furthermore

gadget
gauge
generally

generous
genius
gentle
genuine
geography
ghetto
ghost
gnaw
government
governor
graduation
grammar
grateful
grease
grief
grocery
grudge
gruesome
guarantee
guard
guardian
guess
guidance
guide
guilty
gymnasium

hammer
handkerchief
handle (d)
handsome
haphazard
happen
happiness
harass
hastily
having
hazardous
headache
height

TEKS 8.21

hemorrhage
hesitate
history
hoarse
holiday
honor
hoping
hopping
horrible
hospital
humorous
hurriedly
hydraulic
hygiene
hymn

icicle
identical
illegible
illiterate
illustrate
imaginary
imaginative
imagine
imitation
immediate (ly)
immense
immigrant
immortal
impatient
importance
impossible
improvement
inconvenience
incredible
indefinitely
independence
independent
individual
industrial

inferior
infinite
inflammable
influential
initial
initiation
innocence
innocent
installation
instance
instead
insurance
intelligence
intention
interested
interesting
interfere
interpret
interrupt
interview
investigate
invitation
irrigate
island
issue

jealous (y)
jewelry
journal
journey
judgment
juicy

kitchen
knew
knife
knives

knock
knowledge
knuckles

label
laboratory
ladies
language
laugh
laundry
lawyer
league
lecture
legal
legible
legislature
leisure
length
liable
library
license
lieutenant
lightning
likable
likely
liquid
listen
literature
living
loaves
loneliness
loose
lose
loser
losing
lovable
lovely

M

machinery
magazine
magnificent
maintain
majority
making
manual
manufacture
marriage
material
mathematics
maximum
mayor
meant
measure
medicine
medium
message
mileage
miniature
minimum
minute
mirror
miscellaneous
mischievous
miserable
missile
misspell
moisture
molecule
monotonous
monument
mortgage
mountain
muscle
musician
mysterious

SPELLING

N

naive
natural (ly)
necessary
negotiate
neighbor (hood)
neither
nickel
niece
nineteen
nineteenth
ninety
ninth
noisy
noticeable
nuclear
nuisance

O

obedience
obey
obstacle
occasion
occasional (ly)
occur
occurred
offense
official
often
omission
omitted
operate
opinion
opponent
opportunity
opposite
ordinarily
original
outrageous

P

package
paid
pamphlet
paradise
paragraph
parallel
paralyze
parentheses
partial
participant
participate
particular (ly)
pasture
patience
peculiar
people
perhaps
permanent
perpendicular
persistent
personal (ly)
personnel
perspiration
persuade
phase
physician
piece
pitcher
planned
plateau
playwright
pleasant
pleasure
pneumonia
politician
possess
possible
practical (ly)
prairie
precede
precious

precise (ly)
precision
preferable
preferred
prejudice
preparation
presence
previous
primitive
principal
principle
prisoner
privilege
probably
procedure
proceed
professor
prominent
pronounce
pronunciation
protein
psychology
pumpkin
pure

Q

quarter
questionnaire
quiet
quite
quotient

R

raise
realize
really
receipt
receive
received

recipe
recognize
recommend
reign
relieve
religious
remember
repetition
representative
reservoir
resistance
respectfully
responsibility
restaurant
review
rhyme
rhythm
ridiculous
route

S

safety
salad
salary
sandwich
satisfactory
Saturday
scene
scenery
schedule
science
scissors
scream
screen
season
secretary
seize
sensible
sentence
separate
several

TEKS 8.21

sheriff
shining
similar
since
sincere (ly)
skiing
sleigh
soldier
souvenir
spaghetti
specific
sphere
sprinkle
squeeze
squirrel
statue
stature
statute
stomach
stopped
straight
strength
stretched
studying
subtle
succeed
success
sufficient
summarize
supplement
suppose
surely
surprise
syllable
sympathy
symptom

tariff
technique
temperature
temporary
terrible
territory
thankful
theater
their
there
therefore
thief
thorough (ly)
though
throughout
tired
tobacco
together
tomorrow
tongue
touch
tournament
toward
tragedy
treasurer
tried
tries
trouble
truly
Tuesday
typical

unconscious
unfortunate (ly)
unique
university
unnecessary
until
usable
useful
using
usual (ly)
utensil

vacation
vacuum
valuable
variety
various
vegetable
vehicle
very
vicinity
view
villain
violence
visible
visitor
voice
volume
voluntary
volunteer

wander
wasn't
weather
Wednesday
weigh
weird
welcome
welfare
whale
where
whether
which
whole
wholly
whose
width
women
worthwhile
wouldn't
wreckage
writing
written

yellow
yesterday
yield

SPELLING

ELPS 5B

Using the Right Word

708.1
a, an

A is used before words that begin with a consonant sound; *an* is used before words that begin with any vowel sound except long "u."

a heap, a cat, an idol, an elephant, an honor, a historian, an umbrella, a unicorn

708.2
accept, except

The verb *accept* means "to receive"; the preposition *except* means "other than."

Melissa graciously accepted defeat. (verb)

All the boys except Zach were here. (preposition)

708.3
affect, effect

Affect is almost always a verb; it means "to influence." *Effect* can be a verb, but it is most often used as a noun that means "the result."

How does population growth affect us?

What are the effects of population growth?

708.4
allowed, aloud

The verb *allowed* means "permitted" or "let happen"; *aloud* is an adverb that means "in a normal voice."

We aren't allowed to read aloud in the library.

708.5
allusion, illusion

An *allusion* is a brief reference to or mention of a famous person, place, thing, or idea. An *illusion* is a false impression or idea.

The Great Dontini, a magician, made an allusion to Houdini as he created the illusion of sawing his assistant in half.

708.6
a lot

A lot is not one word, but two; it is a general descriptive phrase meaning "plenty." (It should be avoided in formal writing.)

708.7
all right

All right is not one word, but two; it is a phrase meaning "satisfactory" or "okay." (Please note, the following *are* spelled correctly: *always, altogether, already, almost.*)

Grammar Practice

Using the Right Word 1

■ accept, except; affect, effect; allusion, illusion; all right

For each of the following sentences, write the correct choice from each set of words in parentheses.

Example: Dennis thought he saw pools of water in the parking lot on that hot, hot day, but it was just an *(allusion, illusion)*.

illusion

1. I guess the sun can *(affect, effect)* us in many ways!

2. We will give away all the kittens *(accept, except)* the two that we're keeping.

3. Will it be *(all right, alright)* with your mom if you take one of the kittens?

4. Ms. Whitsom thinks constant cloudy weather has a bad *(affect, effect)* on a person's outlook.

5. In order for a magician to be successful, the audience must believe in the *(allusions, illusions)* he or she creates.

6. Your outfit looks *(all right, alright)* to me.

7. All the mail was addressed to Dad *(accept, except)* for one handwritten letter, which was addressed to me.

8. "Please *(accept, except)* my apology," the letter began.

9. Some students did not understand Roy's *(allusion, illusion)* to *Star Trek* in his speech during science class.

Next Step: Write three sentences that show you know the meaning of these words: *allusion, effect,* and *except.* Share your sentences with a partner.

RIGHT WORD

710.1
already,
all ready

Already is an adverb that tells when. *All ready* is a phrase meaning "completely ready."

> We have already eaten breakfast; now we are all ready for school.

710.2
altogether,
all together

Altogether is always an adverb meaning "completely." *All together* is used to describe people or things that are gathered in one place at one time.

> Ms. Monces held her baton in the air and said, "Okay, class, all together now: sing!"

> Unfortunately, there was altogether too much street noise for us to hear her.

710.3
among, between

Among is used when speaking of more than two persons or things. *Between* is used when speaking of only two.

> The three friends talked among themselves as they tried to choose between trumpet or trombone lessons.

710.4
amount, number

Amount is used to describe things that you cannot count. *Number* is used when you can actually count the persons or things.

> The amount of interest in playing the tuba is shown by the number of kids learning to play the instrument.

710.5
annual,
biannual,
semiannual,
biennial,
perennial

An *annual* event happens once every year. A *biannual* (or *semiannual*) event happens twice a year. A *biennial* event happens once every two years. A *perennial* event happens year after year.

> The annual PTA rummage sale is so successful that it will now be a semiannual event.

> The neighbor has some wonderful perennial flowers.

710.6
ant, aunt

An *ant* is an insect. An *aunt* is a female relative (the sister of a person's mother or father).

> My aunt is an entomologist, a scientist who studies ants and other insects.

710.7
ascent, assent

Ascent is the act of rising or climbing; *assent* is agreement.

> After the group's ascent of five flights of stairs to the meeting room, plans for elevator repairs met with quick assent.

Grammar Practice

Using the Right Word 2

■ altogether, all together; among, between; amount, number; annual, biannual, semiannual, biennial, perennial; ascent, assent

 For each of the following sentences, write the correct choice from each set of words in parentheses.

Example: The *(ascent, assent)* of Mount Everest is hard and dangerous.

ascent

1. The *(amount, number)* of climbers who successfully climb Mount Everest varies from year to year.

2. For the people of Tibet and Nepal, the arrival of climbing teams every May has become *(an annual, a biennial, a perennial)* event.

3. Some climbing routes on the mountain are more dangerous than others because of the *(amount, number)* of snow on the ridges.

4. The *(amount, number)* of days with good weather is very low.

5. Some critics believe that there are *(altogether, all together)* too many inexperienced climbers on Mount Everest.

6. Mountaineers must scramble *(among, between)* numerous ice-covered rocks.

7. Prior to a climb, each hiker must *(ascent, assent)* to doing his or her part for the team.

8. *(Altogether, All together)*, team members decide on tasks for the day.

9. As two climbers make their way up the mountain, the distance *(among, between)* them is usually not very great.

10. One man who climbs once in May and once in October says his *(biannual, biennial)* climbs keep him in shape.

11. After reaching the top of Mount Everest each year during a five-year period, a seasoned mountaineer said that these *(annual, semiannual)* climbs had worn him out.

RIGHT WORD

ELPS 5B

712.1
bare, bear

The adjective *bare* means "naked." A *bear* is a large, heavy animal with shaggy hair.

Despite his bare feet, the man chased the polar bear across the snow.

The verb *bear* means "to put up with" or "to carry."

Shondra could not bear another of her older sister's lectures.

712.2
base, bass

Base is the foundation or the lower part of something. *Bass* (pronounced like "base") is a deep sound or tone.

The stereo speakers are on a base so solid that even the loudest bass tones don't rattle it.

Bass (rhymes with "mass") is a fish.

Jim hooked a record-setting bass, but it got away . . . so he says.

712.3
beat, beet

The verb *beat* means "to strike, to defeat," and the noun *beat* is a musical term for rhythm or tempo. A *beet* is a carrot-like vegetable (often red).

The beat of the drum in the marching band encouraged the fans to cheer on the team. After they beat West High's team four games to one, many team members were as red as a beet.

712.4
berth, birth

Berth is a space or compartment. *Birth* is the process of being born.

We pulled aside the curtain in our train berth to view the birth of a new day outside our window.

712.5
beside, besides

Beside means "by the side of." *Besides* means "in addition to."

Besides a flashlight, Kedar likes to keep his pet boa beside his bed at night.

712.6
billed, build

Billed means either "to be given a bill" or "to have a beak." The verb *build* means "to construct."

We asked the carpenter to build us a birdhouse. She billed us for time and materials.

712.7
blew, blue

Blew is the past tense of "blow." *Blue* is a color and is also used to mean "feeling low in spirits."

As the wind blew out the candles in the dark blue room, I felt more blue than ever.

Grammar Practice

Using the Right Word 3

bare, bear; base, bass; berth, birth; beside, besides

For each of the following sentences, write a word from the list above to fill in the blank.

Example: At the _____ of the Statue of Liberty is a plaque that says her lamp is a sign of welcome to those seeking freedom.

base

1. _____ the European countries, immigrants to the United States come from Africa, Asia, and South America.

2. Pictures of immigrants in the early 1900s show children with _____ hands in cold weather.

3. The desire for freedom and opportunity was at the _____ of many immigrants' decisions to endure the journey.

4. They brought with them only the _____ minimum of belongings.

5. Many immigrants would spend most of the long voyage in a crowded _____ below the waterline of the ship.

6. From there, the passengers could hear and sometimes feel the deep _____ sound of the ship's engines.

7. The ship's crew members were occasionally called on to assist in the _____ of a baby.

8. After a two-week voyage, many passengers couldn't _____ another day at sea.

9. Tugboats _____ the ocean liners guided them into the harbor as the weary travelers celebrated.

Next Step: Find the other definitions for *bear* and *bass* explained on the facing page. Write two sentences that show your understanding of those definitions. Share your sentences with a partner.

RIGHT WORD

714.1 board, bored

A *board* is a piece of wood. *Board* also means "a group or council that helps run an organization."

The school board approved the purchase of 50 pine boards for the woodworking classes.

Bored means "to become weary or tired of something." It can also mean "made a hole by drilling."

Dulé bored a hole in the ice and dropped in a fishing line. Waiting and waiting for a bite bored him.

714.2 borrow, lend

Borrow means "to *receive* for temporary use." *Lend* means "to *give* for temporary use."

I asked Mom, "May I borrow $15 for a CD?"

She said, "I can lend you $15 until next Friday."

714.3 brake, break

A *brake* is a device used to stop a vehicle. The verb *break* means "to split, crack, or destroy"; as a noun, *break* means "gap or interruption."

After the brake on my bike failed, I took a break to fix it so I wouldn't break a bone.

714.4 bring, take

Use *bring* when the action is moving toward the speaker; use *take* when the action is moving away from the speaker.

Grandpa asked me to take the garbage out and bring him today's paper.

714.5 by, buy, bye

By is a preposition meaning "near" or "not later than." *Buy* is a verb meaning "to purchase."

By tomorrow I hope to buy tickets for the final match of the tournament.

Bye is an abbreviation of *goodbye* or the position of being advanced to the next tournament round without playing.

Our soccer team received a bye because of our winning record.

714.6 can, may

Can means "able to," while *may* means "permitted to."

"Can I go to the library?"

(This actually means "Are my mind and body strong enough to get me there?")

"May I go?"

(This means "Do I have your permission to go?")

Grammar Practice

Using the Right Word 4

■ borrow, lend; brake, break; bring, take; by, buy, bye; can, may

 For each of the following sentences, write the correct choice from each set of words in parentheses.

Example: When I was sick at home, I asked Salvatore to *(bring, take)* me my homework.
bring

1. Suddenly the car's *(brake, break)* pedal wasn't working.

2. By pulling up on the parking *(brake, break)* lever, Sanji was able to make the car stop.

3. Our team will sit out the first round if we are given a *(by, buy, bye)* in the tournament schedule.

4. Vanessa has some black pants that she'll *(borrow, lend)* me for the choir concert.

5. I still need to *(by, buy, bye)* a white shirt, though.

6. We need to ask if we *(can, may)* hold a party for Alex.

7. We don't mind if we have to *(bring, take)* our own food.

8. I can't find the pen that is usually kept right here *(by, buy, bye)* the phone.

9. All you need is a library card to *(borrow, lend)* books, CD's, or magazines from any library in the system.

10. You never have to *(by, buy, bye)* any of that again!

11. A city's crime record is one record that its citizens really don't want to *(brake, break)*.

12. "Here, let me *(bring, take)* that for you," Maura offered as I carried my heavy suitcase.

Next Step: Write two sentences that show your understanding of the words *borrow* and *lend*. Share your sentences with a partner.

716.1
canvas, canvass

Canvas is a heavy cloth; *canvass* means "ask people for votes or opinions."

Our old canvas tent leaks.

Someone with a clipboard is canvassing the neighborhood.

716.2
capital, capitol

Capital can be either a noun, referring to a city or to money, or an adjective, meaning "major or important." *Capitol* is used only when talking about a building.

The capitol building is in the capital city for a capital (major) reason: The city government contributed the capital (money) for the building project.

716.3
cell, sell

Cell means "a small room" or "a small unit of life basic to all plants and animals." *Sell* is a verb meaning "to give up for a price."

Today we looked at a human skin cell under a microscope.

Let's sell those old bicycles at the rummage sale.

716.4
cent, sent, scent

Cent (1/100 of a dollar) is a coin; *sent* is the past tense of the verb "send"; *scent* is an odor or a smell.

After our car hit a skunk, we sent our friends a postcard that said, "One cent doesn't go far, but skunk scent seems to last forever."

716.5
chord, cord

Chord may mean "an emotion or a feeling," but it is more often used to mean "the sound of three or more musical tones played at the same time." A *cord* is a string or rope.

The band struck a chord at the exact moment the mayor pulled the cord on the drape covering the new statue.

716.6
chose, choose

Chose (chōz) is the past tense of the verb *choose* (chōoz).

This afternoon Mom chose tacos and hot sauce; this evening she will choose an antacid.

716.7
coarse, course

Coarse means "rough or crude." *Course* means "a path" or "a class or series of studies."

In our cooking course, we learned to use coarse salt and freshly ground pepper in salads.

ELPS 5B

Grammar Practice

Using the Right Word 5

■ canvas, canvass; capital, capitol; chord, cord; coarse, course

 Write a word from the above list to properly complete each of the following sentences.

Example: Phil used _____ sandpaper to remove the paint from the old dresser.

coarse

1. When Tasha was learning how to play the guitar, she played the same _____ over and over again.

2. The class trip included a tour of the _____ building in Washington, D.C.

3. Elaine's family fits into one huge _____ tent when they go camping.

4. They tie the bulky, heavy tent to the car roof with lots of nylon _____.

5. Last year the high school offered its first _____ in German.

6. Jackson is the state _____ of Mississippi.

7. Whenever our dog would get lost, we would _____ the neighborhood looking for him.

8. On my way to school yesterday, I took a _____ through the woods that I hadn't taken before.

Next Step: Write two sentences that show your understanding of *capital* and *capitol*.

RIGHT WORD

ELPS 5B

718.1
complement,
compliment

Complement means "to complete or go with." *Compliment* is an expression of admiration or praise.

> Aunt Athena said, "Your cheese sauce really complements this cauliflower!"
>
> "Thank you for the compliment," I replied.

718.2
continual,
continuous

Continual refers to something that happens again and again; *continuous* refers to something that doesn't stop happening.

> Sunlight hits Peoria, Iowa, on a continual basis; but sunlight hits the earth continuously.

718.3
counsel, council

When used as a noun, *counsel* means "advice"; when used as a verb, *counsel* means "to advise." *Council* refers to a group that advises.

> The student council asked for counsel from its trusted adviser.

718.4
creak, creek

A *creak* is a squeaking sound; a *creek* is a stream.

> I heard a creak from the old dock under my feet as I fished in the creek.

718.5
cymbal, symbol

A *cymbal* is a metal instrument shaped like a plate. A *symbol* is something (usually visible) that stands for or represents another thing or idea (usually invisible).

> The damaged cymbal lying on the stage was a symbol of the band's final concert.

718.6
dear, deer

Dear means "loved or valued"; *deer* are animals.

> My dear, old great-grandmother leaves corn and salt licks in her yard to attract deer.

718.7
desert, dessert

A *desert* is a barren wilderness. *Dessert* is a food served at the end of a meal.

> In the desert, cold water is more inviting than even the richest dessert.

The verb *desert* means "to abandon"; the noun *desert* (pronounced like the verb) means "deserving reward or punishment."

> A spy who deserts his country will receive his just deserts if he is caught.

ELPS 3E, 5B

Grammar Practice

Using the Right Word 6

■ complement, compliment; continual, continuous; counsel, council; dear, deer; desert, dessert

 For each numbered sentence below, write the correct choice from the set of words in parentheses.

Example: Some *(dear, deer)* appeared on the edge of the field.
deer

(1) After a light dinner, Kiana brought some *(desert, dessert)* to the table. **(2)** She said, "I also have the perfect *(complement, compliment)* for these brownies—hazelnut ice cream."

As she and Juwan ate, he kept making "mmm" sounds. **(3)** "I'll take that as a *(complement, compliment)*," Kiana said.

(4) Then she said, "Juwan, I've noticed there's a *(continual, continuous)* buzz coming from the refrigerator recently. It just won't stop. Do you think I should have it checked?"

(5) Juwan said, "Do you want my *(counsel, council),* or do you want me to actually check it?"

(6) "Well, yes, please see if you can fix it yourself, *(dear, deer)*. And while you're at it, take a look at the humidifier, too. **(7)** It feels like a *(desert, dessert)* in here," Kiana said.

(8) "Kiana," Juwan said, "your *(continual, continuous)* requests for me to check things are a signal. Your apartment is falling apart!"

"I know. **(9)** I'm going to bring it up at the next renters' *(counsel, council)* meeting," she said. "In the meantime, thanks for being so handy!"

Next Step: Write a few lines of dialogue between two friends. Include at least two of the words from the list at the top of the page. Read your lines aloud to a classmate.

RIGHT WORD

720.1
die, dye

Die (dying) means "to stop living." *Dye* (dyeing) is used to change the color of something.

The young girl hoped that her sick goldfish wouldn't die.
My sister dyes her hair with coloring that washes out.

720.2
faint, feign, feint

Faint means "feeble, without strength" or "to fall unconscious." *Feign* is a verb that means "to pretend or make up." *Feint* is a noun that means "a move or an activity that is pretended in order to divert attention."

The actors feigned a sword duel. One man staggered and fell in a feint. The audience gave faint applause.

720.3
farther, further

Farther is used when you are writing about a physical distance. *Further* means "additional."

Alaska reaches farther north than Iceland. For further information, check your local library.

720.4
fewer, less

Fewer refers to the number of separate units; *less* refers to bulk quantity.

I may have less money than you have, but I have fewer worries.

720.5
fir, fur

Fir refers to a type of evergreen tree; *fur* is animal hair.

The Douglas fir tree is named after a Scottish botanist.
An arctic fox has white fur in the winter.

720.6
flair, flare

Flair means "a natural talent" or "style"; *flare* means "to light up quickly" or "burst out" (or an object that does so).

Jenrette has a flair for remaining calm when other people's tempers flare.

720.7
for, four

The preposition *for* means "because of" or "directed to"; *four* is the number 4.

Mary had grilled steaks and chicken for the party, but the dog stole one of the four steaks.

ELPS 3E, 5B

Grammar Practice

Using the Right Word 7

◼ faint, feign, feint; farther, further; fewer, less; flair, flare; for, four

For each sentence below, write the word "correct" if the underlined word is used correctly. If it is incorrect, write the right word.

Example: During a marathon, which is just over 26 miles long, some runners <u>feint</u> along the way.

faint

1. Some of the runners have <u>less</u> stamina than others.

2. Those who can endure run <u>further</u> than many who begin the race.

3. <u>Less</u> runners finish the race than start it.

4. Near the end, a few minutes may feel like <u>fore</u> hours.

5. Only a surge of energy that <u>flares</u> up at this point will get the runner to the finish line.

6. Occasionally, a competitor will <u>feign</u> a move to one side before giving a burst of speed.

7. Most marathoners practice <u>four</u> at least a year prior to the race.

8. A few people run a marathon every year, but many are not interested in <u>farther</u> marathons once they've run one.

9. One runner, who has a definite <u>flare</u> for humor, wears a funny hat as he runs.

10. He also seems to stumble a lot, perhaps as some sort of <u>faint</u>.

Next Step: Write two sentences about some kind of race to show your understanding of the words *farther* and *further*. Share your sentences with a partner.

RIGHT WORD

722.1
good, well

Good is an adjective; well is nearly always an adverb.

The strange flying machines flew well. (The adverb well modifies flew.)

They looked good as they flew overhead. (The adjective good modifies they.)

When used in writing about health, well is an adjective.

The pilots did not feel well, however, after the long, hard race.

722.2
hare, hair

A hare is an animal similar to a rabbit; hair refers to the growth covering the head and body of mammals and human beings.

When a hare darted out in front of our car, the hair on my head stood up.

722.3
heal, heel

Heal means "to mend or restore to health." Heel is the back part of a human foot.

I got a blister on my heel from wearing my new shoes. It won't heal unless I wear my old ones.

722.4
hear, here

You hear sounds with your ears. Here is the opposite of there and means "nearby."

722.5
heard, herd

Heard is the past tense of the verb "to hear"; herd is a group of animals.

The herd of grazing sheep raised their heads when they heard the collie barking in the distance.

722.6
heir, air

An heir is a person who inherits something; air is what we breathe.

Will the next generation be heir to irreparably polluted air?

722.7
hole, whole

A hole is a cavity or hollow place. Whole means "entire or complete."

The hole in the ozone layer is a serious problem requiring the attention of the whole world.

722.8
immigrate, emigrate

Immigrate means "to come into a new country or area." Emigrate means "to go out of one country to live in another."

Martin Ulferts immigrated to this country in 1882. He was only three years old when he emigrated from Germany.

ELPS 3E, 5B

Grammar Practice

Using the Right Word 8

■ good, well; heal, heel; hear, here; hole, whole;
immigrate, emigrate

 Each sentence below has a choice of words in parentheses. Write the word that makes the sentence correct.

Example: Did you *(hear, here)* the latest news?

hear

1. After her heart surgery, Granny Kasten is feeling surprisingly *(good, well)*.

2. The doctor said it may take a few months for her to *(heal, heel)* completely.

3. When she *(immigrated, emigrated)* to this country, she was only 12 years old.

4. My sister Alison spends her *(hole, whole)* morning fixing her hair.

5. When Sybil broke her *(heal, heel),* she had to stay off her foot for two months.

6. My dad's parents *(immigrated, emigrated)* from Laos.

7. We often *(hear, here)* them talk about their lives there.

8. My grandparents adjusted *(good, well)* to living in this country.

9. I can't play in this weekend's concert because there is a *(hole, whole)* in my drum.

10. Deshawn is *(good, well)* at coming up with creative ideas for art projects.

11. Will this school still be *(hear, here)* in 50 years?

Next Step: Write three sentences that show you know the meaning of these words: *good, well,* and *heal.* Read your sentences aloud to a classmate.

RIGHT WORD

724.1
imply, infer

Imply means "to suggest indirectly"; *infer* means "to draw a conclusion from facts."

"Since you have to work, may I infer that you won't come to my party?" Guy asked.

"No, I only meant to imply that I would be late," Rochelle responded.

724.2
it's, its

It's is the contraction of "it is." *Its* is the possessive form of "it."

It's a fact that a minnow's teeth are in its throat.

724.3
knew, new

Knew is the past tense of the verb "know." *New* means "recent or modern."

If I knew how to fix it, I would not need a new one!

724.4
know, no

Know means "to recognize or understand." *No* means "the opposite of yes."

Phil, do you know Cheri?

No, I've never met her.

724.5
later, latter

Later means "after a period of time." *Latter* refers to the second of two things mentioned.

The band arrived later and set up the speakers and the lights. The latter made the stage look like a carnival ride.

724.6
lay, lie

Lay means "to place." (*Lay* is a transitive verb; that means it needs a word to complete the meaning.) *Lie* means "to recline." (*Lie* is an intransitive verb.)

Lay your sleeping bag on the floor before you lie down on it. (*Lay* needs the word *bag* to complete its meaning.)

724.7
lead, led

Lead (lēd) is a present tense verb meaning "to guide." The past tense of the verb is *led* (lĕd). The noun *lead* (lĕd) is the metal.

Guides planned to lead the settlers to safe quarters. Instead, they led them into a winter storm.

Peeling paint in old houses may contain lead.

724.8
learn, teach

Learn means "to get information"; *teach* means "to give information."

I want to learn how to sew. Will you teach me?

punctuate edit capitalize
SPELL
improve
Using the Right Word
725

ELPS 5B

Grammar Practice

Using the Right Word 9

■ imply, infer; later, latter; lay, lie; learn, teach

 For each numbered word below, write the word "correct" if it is used correctly. If it is incorrect, write the right word.

Example: Are you <u>inferring</u> that I'm not smart enough?
implying

Mr. Levine was attempting to **(1)** <u>learn</u> us a difficult scientific concept. After answering some questions, he said, "From the looks on some of your faces, I **(2)** <u>imply</u> that you still don't get it."

"Mr. Levine," Davion said, "isn't there another way that we can **(3)** <u>learn</u> this?"

Albert added, "Why do we need to know this, anyway?"

Without being too obvious, Mr. Levine **(4)** <u>implied</u> that we would all fail the exam if we didn't understand it. "Furthermore," he said, "if you don't have some basic curiosity, you might as well just **(5)** <u>lay</u> down and sleep away your life."

(6) <u>Latter</u> in the week, Mr. Levine came up with a different way to **(7)** <u>teach</u> us about the characteristics of atoms. He asked Chaya to **(8)** <u>lie</u> her fleece jacket on some carpet. (He had brought a piece of the **(9)** <u>later</u> from home.) Then he shut off the light and told Chaya to drag her jacket back and forth on the carpet. There were sparks! Mr. Levine explained to us that static forms when one material pulls electrons away from the other. And, just like that, we had **(10)** <u>learned</u> something!

Next Step: Here is an easy way to remember the difference between *imply* and *infer*: "When **you** (with a *y*) imply, **I** infer." Try to think of something that will help you remember the difference between *lay* and *lie.*

RIGHT WORD

726.1
leave, let

Leave means "fail to take" or "depart." *Let* means "allow."

Rozi wanted to leave her boots at home, but Jorge wouldn't let her.

726.2
like, as

Like is a preposition meaning "similar to"; *as* is a conjunction meaning "to the same degree" or "while." *Like* usually introduces a phrase; *as* usually introduces a clause.

The glider floated like a bird. The glider floated as the pilot had hoped it would.

As we circled the airfield, we saw maintenance carts moving like ants below us.

726.3
loose, lose, loss

Loose (lüs) means "free or untied"; *lose* (lo͞oz) means "to misplace or fail to win"; *loss* (lôs) means "something lost."

These jeans are too loose in the waist since my recent weight loss. I still want to lose a few more pounds.

726.4
made, maid

Made is the past tense of "make," which means to "create," "prepare," or "put in order." A *maid* is a female servant; *maid* is also used to describe an unmarried girl or young woman.

The hotel maid asked if our beds needed to be made.

Grandma made a chocolate cake for dessert.

A maid strolled in the garden before the concert.

726.5
mail, male

Mail refers to letters or packages handled by the postal service. *Male* refers to the masculine sex.

My little brother likes getting junk mail.

The male sea horse, not the female, takes care of the fertilized eggs.

726.6
main, mane

Main refers to the most important part. *Mane* is the long hair growing from the top or sides of the neck of certain animals, such as the horse, lion, and so on.

The main thing we noticed about the magician's tamed lion was its luxurious mane.

726.7
meat, meet

Meat is food or flesh; *meet* means "to come upon or encounter."

I'd like you to meet the butcher who sells the leanest meat in town.

ELPS 3E, 5B

Grammar Practice

Using the Right Word 10

■ like, as; loose, lose, loss; mail, male; main, mane

 For each of the following sentences, write the correct choice from the set of words in parentheses.

Example: The road crew set up detour signs and began repairing the village's *(main, mane)* street.
main

1. Bianca wears her hair in *(loose, lose, loss)* curls around her face.

2. For thousands of years, people have dreamed of flying *(like, as)* a bird.

3. In the 1980s, rock stars sported big, wild *(mains, manes)* of hair.

4. Most people know to avoid a bull moose, which is a *(mail, male)* moose, but a mother moose with a calf is equally dangerous.

5. Is California or Florida the *(main, mane)* producer of oranges in the United States?

6. The basketball players from Orson Middle School celebrated their victory *(like, as)* their fans screamed with joy.

7. The opposing team took their *(loose, lose, loss)* well, even though it was their last game.

8. Worrying causes many people to *(loose, lose, loss)* sleep.

9. In the hottest parts of Africa, some lions have almost no *(main, mane)*.

10. More and more people around the world now send and receive *(mail, male)* electronically.

11. I wish I had a friend *(like, as)* you.

Next Step: Write three sentences that show your understanding of the words *loss, loose,* and *lose*. Share your sentences with a partner.

RIGHT WORD

ELPS 5B

728.1
medal, metal, meddle, mettle

A *medal* is an award. *Metal* is an element like iron or gold. *Meddle* means "to interfere." *Mettle,* a noun, refers to quality of character.

Grandpa's friend received a medal for showing his mettle in battle. Grandma, who loves to meddle in others' business, asked if the award was a precious metal.

728.2
miner, minor

A *miner* digs in the ground for valuable ore. A *minor* is a person who is not legally an adult. *Minor* means "of no great importance" when used as an adjective.

The use of minors as miners is no minor problem.

728.3
moral, morale

Moral relates to what is right or wrong or to the lesson to be drawn from a story. *Morale* refers to a person's attitude or mental condition.

The moral of this story is "Everybody loves a winner."

After the unexpected win at football, morale was high throughout the town.

728.4
morning, mourning

Morning refers to the first part of the day (before noon); *mourning* means "showing sorrow."

Abby was mourning her test grades all morning.

728.5
oar, or, ore

An *oar* is a paddle used in rowing or steering a boat. *Or* is a conjunction indicating choice. *Ore* refers to a mineral made up of several different kinds of material, as in iron ore.

Either use one oar to push us away from the dock, or start the boat's motor.

Silver-copper ore is smelted and refined to extract each metal.

728.6
pain, pane

Pain is the feeling of being hurt. A *pane* is a section or part of something.

Dad looked like he was in pain when he found out we broke a pane of glass in the neighbor's front door.

728.7
pair, pare, pear

A *pair* is a couple (two); *pare* is a verb meaning "to peel"; *pear* is the fruit.

A pair of doves nested in the pear tree.

Please pare the apples for the pie.

ELPS 3E, 5B

Grammar Practice

Using the Right Word 11

■ meddle, mettle; moral, morale; morning, mourning; pain, pane

For each of the following sentences, write a word from the list above to fill in the blank.

Example: People's _____ often sags when winter drags on.
morale

1. Some people, _____ the long, warm summer days that have passed, can't see the beauty of autumn.

2. When Kaleb picked up the pile of heavy, wet clothes, he felt a sharp _____ in his back.

3. Once last winter, the extreme cold formed delicate frost flowers on the window _____.

4. Grandma thinks that the _____ values of young people have sunk to a new low.

5. "I appreciate your interest," said Alejandra, "but I really don't need you to _____ in this situation."

6. Thad is _____ the loss of his beloved dog.

7. Sometimes only time will ease the _____ of such a loss.

8. A firefighter's _____ is tested every time an emergency requires swift action.

9. I find that _____ is the best time for me to work out.

10. Is it a person's _____ obligation to help someone in need?

11. The team's high _____, despite a string of defeats, was inspiring.

Next Step: Write some sentences using one word from each of the four word groups at the top of the page. Share your best sentence with a partner.

RIGHT WORD

730.1
past, passed

Passed is always a verb; it is the past tense of *pass*. *Past* can be used as a noun, as an adjective, or as a preposition.

> **A motorcycle passed my dad's 'Vette.** (verb)
>
> **The old man won't forget the past.** (noun)
>
> **I'm sorry, but I'd rather not talk about my past life.** (adjective)
>
> **Old Blue walked right past the cat and never saw it.** (preposition)

730.2
peace, piece

Peace means "harmony, or freedom from war." A *piece* is a part or fragment of something.

> **In order to keep peace among the triplets, each one had to have an identical piece of cake.**

730.3
peak, peek, pique

A *peak* is a "high point" or a "pointed end." *Peek* means "brief look." *Pique*, as a verb, means "to excite by challenging"; as a noun, it means "a feeling of resentment."

> **Just a peek at Pike's Peak in the Rocky Mountains can pique a mountain climber's curiosity.**
>
> **In a pique, she marched away from her giggling sisters.**

730.4
personal, personnel

Personal means "private." *Personnel* are people working at a job.

> **Some thoughts are too personal to share.**
>
> **The personnel manager will be hiring more workers.**

730.5
plain, plane

A *plain* is an area of land that is flat or level; it also means "clearly seen or clearly understood" and "ordinary."

> **It's plain to see why the early settlers had trouble crossing the Great Plains.**

Plane means "a flat, level surface" (as in geometry); it is also a tool used to smooth the surface of wood.

> **When I saw that the door wasn't a perfect plane, I used a plane to make it smooth.**

730.6
pore, pour, poor

A *pore* is an opening in the skin. *Pour* means "to cause a flow or stream." *Poor* means "needy."

> **People perspire through the pores in their skin. Pour yourself a glass of water. Your poor body needs it!**

Grammar Practice

Using the Right Word 12

■ past, passed; peace, piece; peak, peek, pique; pore, pour, poor

For each sentence below, write the word "correct" if the underlined word is used correctly. If it is incorrect, write the right word.

Example: I looked up from my book and realized that my bus was now more than a mile <u>past</u> my stop.

correct

1. I <u>peaked</u> at my watch and wondered if I could possibly get to my dentist appointment in time.

2. I took out what I thought was my bus schedule and discovered that it was only a small <u>peace</u> of blank paper.

3. I got off the bus and saw just the <u>pique</u> of the building where I needed to be in 15 minutes.

4. I walked as fast as I could, and soon I was sweating from every <u>pour</u> on my body.

5. That would <u>pique</u> anyone's thirst, so I got a bottle of water from my backpack.

6. When I'd had enough, I decided to <u>poor</u> the rest of it on a small tree before throwing the empty bottle in a city waste can.

7. I was so focused on satisfying my thirst that I almost <u>past</u> the dentist's office.

8. I gratefully sat at <u>piece</u> in the waiting room.

9. My <u>pore</u> feet needed the rest.

10. I was glad that this experience was now in my <u>passed</u>.

Next Step: Write a paragraph about a time when you were late. Use as many of the words in the list at the top of the page as you can. Read your paragraph aloud to a classmate.

RIGHT WORD

732.1
principal,
principle

As an adjective, *principal* means "primary." As a noun, it can mean "a school administrator" or "a sum of money." *Principle* means "idea or doctrine."

> My mom's principal goal is to save money so she can pay off the principal balance on her loan from the bank.

> Hey, Charlie, I hear the principal gave you a detention.

> The principle of freedom is based on the principle of self-discipline.

732.2
quiet, quit, quite

Quiet is the opposite of "noisy." *Quit* means "to stop." *Quite* means "completely or entirely."

> I quit mowing even though I wasn't quite finished.
> The neighborhood was quiet again.

732.3
raise, rays, raze

Raise is a verb meaning "to lift or elevate." *Rays* are thin lines or beams. *Raze* is a verb that means "to tear down completely."

> When I raise this shade, bright rays of sunlight stream into the room.

> Construction workers will raze the old theater to make room for a parking lot.

732.4
real, very, really

Do not use the adjective *real* in place of the adverbs *very* or *really*.

> The plants scattered throughout the restaurant are not real.

> Pimples are very embarrassing.

> Her nose is really small.

732.5
red, read

Red is a color; *read*, pronounced the same way, is the past tense of the verb meaning "to understand the meaning of written words and symbols."

> "I've read five books in two days," said the little boy.

> The librarian gave him a red ribbon.

punctuate edit capitalize
SPELL   **733**
improve   Using the Right Word

ELPS 3E, 5B

Grammar Practice

Using the Right Word 13

■ principal, principle; quiet, quit, quite; raise, rays, raze;
real, very, really

For each sentence below, write the word "correct" if the underlined word is used correctly. If it is incorrect, write the right word.

Example: The National Aeronautics and Space Administration
(NASA) plans to <u>raise</u> some buildings to make way
for new construction.

raze

1. A <u>principle</u> concern of NASA is the amount of debris left in space from previous space flights.

2. Although scientists keep track of the space debris, they are not <u>quit</u> sure they know where it all is.

3. Sound waves cannot travel in airless space, so space is a <u>quite</u> place.

4. At times, the <u>raze</u> of the sun are reflected by the shiny orbiting objects.

5. NASA worries about space debris, which is <u>real</u> small.

6. Even a tiny fleck of paint in space can be a <u>real</u> threat because it could be speeding along at almost 18,000 miles per hour.

7. Unfortunately, these <u>very</u> small objects cannot be tracked.

8. They <u>rays</u> the danger for flight crews.

9. In spite of the danger, the <u>principle</u> of exploration drives astronauts to travel into space again and again.

10. For a variety of reasons, some people think that the United States should <u>quit</u> sending rockets into space.

Next Step: Write two sentences on your thoughts about the space
program. Use the words *real* and *really* correctly. Share
your sentences with a partner.

RIGHT WORD

734.1
right, write, rite

Right means "correct or proper"; *right* is the opposite of "left"; it also refers to anything that a person has a legal claim to, as in "copyright." *Write* means "to record in print." *Rite* is a ritual or ceremonial act.

> We have to write an essay about how our rights are protected by the Constitution.
>
> Turn right at the next corner.
>
> A rite of passage is a ceremony that celebrates becoming an adult.

734.2
scene, seen

Scene refers to the setting or location where something happens; it also means "sight or spectacle." *Seen* is a form of the verb "see."

> The scene of the crime was roped off. We hadn't seen anyone go in or out of the building.

734.3
seam, seem

A *seam* is a line formed by connecting two pieces of material. *Seem* means "appear to exist."

> Every Thanksgiving, it seems, I stuff myself so much that my shirt seams threaten to burst.

734.4
sew, so, sow

Sew is a verb meaning "to stitch"; *so* is a conjunction meaning "in order that." The verb *sow* means "to plant."

> In Colonial times, the wife would sew the family clothes, and the husband would sow the family garden so the children could eat.

734.5
sight, cite, site

Sight means "the act of seeing" or "something that is seen." *Cite* means "to quote or refer to." A *site* is a location or position (including a Web site on the Internet).

> The Alamo at night was a sight worth the trip. I was also able to cite my visit to this historical site in my history paper.

734.6
sit, set

Sit means "to put the body in a seated position." *Set* means "to place." (*Set* is a transitive verb; that means it needs a direct object to complete its meaning.)

> How can you just sit there and watch as I set up all these chairs?

Grammar Practice

Using the Right Word 14

■ scene, seen; seam, seem; sew, so, sow; sit, set

For each of the following sentences, write a word from the list above to fill in the blank.

Example: Because even a little moisture can damage wood, please do not _____ that wet towel on the table.

set

1. "Did you notice that the _____ of this jacket is coming apart?" Mia asked.

2. "Yes," I replied, "I'm going to try to _____ it up myself."

3. Theo finally had to _____ down after standing for three hours during the football game.

4. When he _____ his soda on the bench, someone knocked it over.

5. Janelle and Rhonda stopped Craig to ask him if he had _____ their lost dog.

6. Landon wants to design his diorama to look like a _____ from the Battle of New Orleans.

7. Looking around, Jay said, "I _____ to have lost my hat."

8. Sharon promised to help her mother _____ some flower seeds in their little garden.

9. I'm trying to get extra pet-sitting jobs _____ that I will have enough money to get two kittens.

10. We _____ in assigned seats in this class.

11. My aunt does not like to be _____ without her makeup.

12. Although lemmings might _____ to jump off a ledge into the sea, they actually are looking for food and accidentally fall.

13. Khadijah is tired of her long hair, _____ she's going to get it cut short this weekend.

RIGHT WORD

736.1
sole, soul

Sole means "single, only one"; *sole* also refers to the bottom surface of a foot or shoe. *Soul* refers to the spiritual part of a person.

Maggie got a job for the sole purpose of saving for a car.

The soles of these shoes are very thick.

"Who told you dogs don't have souls?" asked the kind veterinarian.

736.2
some, sum

Some means "an unknown number or part." *Sum* means "the whole amount."

The sum in the cash register was stolen by some thieves.

736.3
sore, soar

Sore means "painful"; to *soar* means "to rise or fly high into the air."

Craning to watch the eagle soar overhead, we soon had sore necks.

736.4
stationary, stationery

Stationary means "not movable"; *stationery* is the paper and envelopes used to write letters.

Grandpa designed and printed his own stationery.

All of the built-in furniture is stationary, of course.

736.5
steal, steel

Steal means "to take something without permission"; *steel* is a metal.

Early iron makers had to steal recipes for producing steel.

736.6
than, then

Than is used in a comparison; *then* tells when.

Since tomorrow's weather is supposed to be nicer than today's, we'll go to the zoo then.

736.7
their, there, they're

Their is a possessive pronoun, one that shows ownership. *There* is an adverb that tells where. *They're* is the contraction for "they are."

They're upset because their dog got into the garbage over there.

736.8
threw, through

Threw is the past tense of "throw." *Through* means "passing from one side to the other" or "by means of."

Through sheer talent and long practice, Nolan Ryan threw baseballs through the strike zone at more than 100 miles per hour.

Grammar Practice

Using the Right Word 15

■ sole, soul; sore, soar; stationary, stationery; than, then;
threw, through

 If a word from the list above is used incorrectly in one of the following numbered sentences, write the correct word; otherwise, write "OK."

Example: When I finished reading Vilma's letter, I through
it away.
threw

(1) I had noticed that Vilma's stationary had drawings of kites along the side of the page. That got me wondering: Why do people fly kites? **(2)** I guess the sole motive for most people is to have fun. **(3)** They would rather embrace the wind then try to fight it.

(4) Often I fly a kite, standing stationary against the raging gusts. **(5)** I watch my flying piece of art struggle in the wind, and then I gradually let out more string. **(6)** For me, the sole of kite flying is imagining myself as the kite. **(7)** Attached to the ground by only a thin string, I sore on the breeze. **(8)** I dart in and out through the clouds before diving toward earth again. **(9)** Eventually, my soar fingers mean the kite flying must end for the day. **(10)** It is time to slowly reel in the string than and put the kite away . . . until the next time a dream and the wind call me once again.

Next Step: Write two sentences about an activity you enjoy. Use the
words *than* and *then* correctly. Share your sentences with
a partner.

RIGHT WORD

ELPS 5B

738.1
to, too, two

To is the preposition that can mean "in the direction of." (*To* also is used to form an infinitive. See **780.4**.) *Too* is an adverb meaning "very or excessive." *Too* is often used to mean "also." *Two* is the number 2.

> Only two of Columbus's first three ships returned to Spain from the New World.

> Columbus was too restless to stay in Spain for long.

738.2
vain, vane, vein

Vain means "worthless." It may also mean "thinking too highly of one's self; stuck-up." *Vane* is a flat piece of material set up to show which way the wind blows. *Vein* refers to a blood vessel or a mineral deposit.

> The weather vane indicates the direction of wind.

> A blood vein determines the direction of flowing blood.

> The vain mind moves in no particular direction and thinks only about itself.

738.3
vary, very

Vary is a verb that means "to change." *Very* can be an adjective meaning "in the fullest sense" or "complete"; it can also be an adverb meaning "extremely."

> Garon's version of the event would vary from day to day. His very interesting story was the very opposite of the truth.

738.4
waist, waste

Waist is the part of the body just above the hips. The verb *waste* means "to wear away" or "to use carelessly"; the noun *waste* refers to material that is unused or useless.

> Don't waste your money on fast-food meals. What a waste to throw away all this food because you're concerned about the size of your waist!

738.5
wait, weight

Wait means "to stay somewhere expecting something." *Weight* is the measure of heaviness.

> When I have to wait for the bus, the weight of my backpack seems to keep increasing.

738.6
ware, wear, where

Ware means "a product to be sold"; *wear* means "to have on or to carry on one's body"; *where* asks the question "in what place or in what situation?"

> Where can you buy the best cookware to take on a campout—and the best rain gear to wear if it rains?

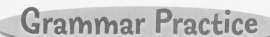
ELPS 5B

Grammar Practice

Using the Right Word 16

■ to, too, two; vain, vane, vein; vary, very; ware, wear, where

For each of the following sentences, write the correct choice from the set of words in parentheses.

Example: Angelica braids her hair *(to, too, two)* keep it out of her face.

to

1. The school's weather *(vain, vane, vein)* shows that the wind is from the north today.

2. A cold breeze makes me want to *(ware, wear, where)* a sweater.

3. Although the school ordered a reference guide for every class, only *(to, too, two)* arrived.

4. After searching for 15 minutes, Tony finally asked the librarian *(ware, wear, where)* the biographies were located.

5. As long as he had to talk to her, he asked her to point out the bathrooms, *(to, too, two)*.

6. In a *(vain, vane, vein)* attempt to open the window, Ms. Jenkins discovered that it had been painted shut.

7. When Char glanced at the clock and realized only 20 minutes had gone by, she knew it was going to be a *(vary, very)* long day.

8. Grandpa says that sometimes a nurse cannot find a good *(vain, vane, vein)* from which to draw his blood.

9. Darren and I went *(to, too, two)* the mall yesterday.

10. Fatima is an artist who works with metal; she sells her *(wares, wears, wheres)* at festivals and county fairs.

11. Although we were told that the lunch menu would *(vary, very)* from week to week, it always seems the same to me.

12. Many fast foods have *(to, too, two)* much salt.

Next Step: Write one sentence that uses *to, too,* and *two.* For an extra challenge, write one with *vary* and *very.*

RIGHT WORD

740.1
way, weigh

Way means "path or route" or "a series of actions." *Weigh* means "to measure weight."

What is the correct way **to** weigh **liquid medicines?**

740.2
weather,
whether

Weather refers to the condition of the atmosphere. *Whether* refers to a possibility.

The weather **will determine** whether **I go fishing.**

740.3
week, weak

A *week* is a period of seven days; *weak* means "not strong."

Last week **when I had the flu, I felt light-headed and** weak.

740.4
wet, whet

Wet means "soaked with liquid." *Whet* is a verb that means "to sharpen."

Of course, going swimming means I'll get wet, **but all that exercise really** whets **my appetite.**

740.5
which, witch

Which is a pronoun used to ask "what one or ones?" out of a group. A *witch* is a woman believed to have supernatural powers.

Which **of the women in Salem in the 1600s were accused of being** witches?

740.6
who, which,
that

When introducing a clause, *who* is used to refer to people; *which* refers to animals and nonliving beings but never to people (it introduces a nonrestrictive, or unnecessary, clause); *that* usually refers to animals or things but can refer to people (it introduces a restrictive, or necessary, clause).

The idea that **pizza is junk food is crazy.**

Pizza, which **is quite nutritious, can be included in a healthful diet.**

My mom, who **is a dietician, said so.**

740.7
who, whom

Who is used as the subject in a sentence; *whom* is used as the object of a preposition or as a direct object.

Who **asked you to play tennis?**

You beat whom **at tennis? You played tennis with** whom?

NOTE To test for *who/whom*, arrange the parts of the clause in a subject–verb–direct-object order. (See page 632.) *Who* works as the subject, *whom* as the object.

punctuate edit capitalize
SPELL
improve
Using the Right Word
741

ELPS 3E, 5B

Grammar Practice

Using the Right Word 17

◼ way, weigh; wet, whet; which, witch; who, which, that;
who, whom

If a word from the list above is used incorrectly in one of the following sentences, write the correct word; otherwise, write "OK."

Example: Ms. Fridley, whom is our homeroom teacher, is
helping us plan our year-end picnic.
who

1. The planning has really wet our desire for the end of the school year to come quickly!

2. The picnic which we planned for last year was rained out.

3. Most of us know the way to the park.

4. Lauren, that is new to the area, might not know how to get there.

5. We will use a picnic shelter that offers electricity and water.

6. Arlan suggested bringing ice for the soda, but it may way too much.

7. If Luis brings a wagon, which he did last year, we could use that for the ice.

8. Ms. Fridley still needs to decide who she will ask to organize the games.

9. I hope we play the game with water balloons that gets everyone wet!

10. A which wouldn't play that game because, according to legend, she will melt if water touches her.

11. The girl whom wore her swimsuit last year was the smart one.

Next Step: Read **646.**1 and **758.**3 to learn more about using *which* and *that* correctly. Then write two sentences that show your understanding of the words. Share your sentences with a partner.

742.1
who's, whose

Who's is the contraction for "who is." *Whose* is a possessive pronoun, one that shows ownership.

> Who's **the most popular writer today?**
>
> Whose **bike is this?**

742.2
wood, would

Wood is the material that comes from trees; *would* is a form of the verb "will."

> Sequoia trees live practically forever, but would **you believe that the** wood **from these giants is practically useless?**

742.3
your, you're

Your is a possessive pronoun, one that shows ownership. *You're* is the contraction for "you are."

> You're **the most important person in** your **parents' lives.**

SCHOOL DAZE

punctuate edit capitalize
SPELL
improve

743

Using the Right Word

ELPS 5B

Grammar Practice

Using the Right Word 18

■ who's, whose; wood, would; your, you're

For each of the following sentences, write a word from the list above to fill in the blank.

Example: Please bring _____ journals to class tomorrow.
your

1. Five students said that they _____ be willing to help serve at the Wing Road Soup Kitchen.

2. Can anyone tell me _____ watch this is?

3. _____ planning to go on the Washington, D.C., trip?

4. The manager said, "After you put away the weights and sweep the workout room, _____ free to go."

5. This old desk is made completely of _____.

6. Make sure you have _____ lunch, and then get on the bus.

Using the Right Word Review

For each of the following sentences, write the correct choice from each set of words in parentheses.

1. My uncle living in Cuba wants to *(immigrate, emigrate)* to the United States.

2. The *(stationary, stationery)* bike is *(to, too, two)* heavy for you to move by yourself.

3. Have you *(scene, seen)* the city bus that's painted to look *(as, like)* a shark?

4. Scuba divers need a *(continual, continuous)* supply of air.

5. The magician asked Frank to *(borrow, lend)* her a coin for an *(allusion, illusion)* she would perform.

6. Larry wasn't *(quiet, quit, quite)* ready to leave the lake and the *(base, bass)* *(who, which, that)* got away.

RIGHT WORD

ELPS 4C

Understanding Sentences

Sentences

A **sentence** is a group of words that expresses a complete thought. A sentence must have both a subject and a predicate. A sentence begins with a capital letter; it ends with a period, a question mark, or an exclamation point.

I like my teacher this year.

Will we go on a field trip?

We get to go to the water park!

Parts of a Sentence

744.1
Subjects

A subject is the part of a sentence that does something or is talked about.

The kids on my block play basketball at the local park.

We meet after school almost every day.

744.2
Simple Subjects

The simple subject is the subject without the words that describe or modify it. (Also see page 563.)

My friend Chester plays basketball on the school team.

744.3
Complete Subjects

The complete subject is the simple subject and all the words that modify it. (Also see page 562.)

My friend Chester plays basketball on the school team.

744.4
Compound Subjects

A compound subject has two or more simple subjects. (See page 563.)

Chester, Malik, and Meshelle play on our pickup team.

Lou and I are the best shooters.

ELPS 2C, 4C, 4K

Grammar Practice

Parts of a Sentence 1

■ Simple, Complete, and Compound Subjects

 For each of the numbered sentences that follow, write the complete subject. Underline the simple subject. (Watch for compound subjects.)

Example: Cesar Chavez was a Spanish-speaking migrant worker.

Cesar Chavez

(1) Cesar Chavez was born in Arizona in 1927. **(2)** He became an activist for farmworkers. **(3)** Many of these workers were Spanish-speaking migrants. **(4)** Chavez earned respect for using nonviolent ways to improve the working conditions on farms.

(5) In the early 1960s, Chavez organized grape pickers in California. **(6)** The workers held marches and strikes. **(7)** They picketed unfair employers. **(8)** As a result, many major growers offered farmworkers better wages, health insurance, and safer working conditions.

(9) Later in the '60s, Chavez continued his effort, and he drew attention to the situation. **(10)** People who shopped at grocery stores were asked to avoid buying grapes. **(11)** More Americans became aware of the troubles of the farmworkers. **(12)** The United Farm Workers Union gained the respect of farm employers.

(13) Chavez died in 1993. **(14)** Since then, seven states and several Southwestern cities have declared a holiday in honor of the labor leader. **(15)** Phoenix, Tempe, Los Angeles, Denver, and Santa Fe celebrate Chavez's accomplishments on his birthday, March 31. **(16)** He is remembered for making a peaceful stand for farmworkers.

Learning Language As you look for compound subjects, keep in mind that they are often linked by the conjunction *and*, and sometimes by *or*:

Volleyball and soccer are my favorite sports.

Julio or Linda will bring the snacks.

SENTENCES

Parts of a Sentence . . .

The predicate, which contains the verb, is the part of the sentence that shows action or says something about the subject.

Hunting has reduced the tiger population in India.

The simple predicate is the predicate (verb) without the words that describe or modify it. (See page **563**.)

In the past, poachers **killed** too many African elephants. **Poaching** is **illegal**.

The complete predicate is the simple predicate with all the words that modify or describe it. (See page **562**.)

In the past, **poachers** killed too many African elephants. **Poaching** is illegal.

The complete predicate often includes a direct object. The direct object is the noun or pronoun that receives the action of the simple predicate—directly. The direct object answers the question *what* or *whom*. (See page **632**.)

Many smaller animals need friends **who will speak up for them.**

The direct object may be compound.

We all need animals, plants, wetlands, deserts, **and** forests.

If a sentence has a direct object, it may also have an indirect object. An indirect object is the noun or pronoun that receives the action of the simple predicate—indirectly. An indirect object names the person *to whom* or *for whom* something is done. (See page **632**.)

I showed the class **my multimedia report on endangered species.** (*Class* is the indirect object because it says *to whom* the report was shown.)

Remember, in order for a sentence to have an indirect object, it must first have a direct object.

A compound predicate is composed of two or more simple predicates. (See page **563**.)

In 1990 the countries of the world met **and** banned **the sale of ivory.**

Grammar Practice

Parts of a Sentence 2

■ Simple, Complete, and Compound Predicates

For each sentence below, write the complete predicate (or predicates for a compound sentence). Circle the simple or compound predicate.

Example: Ancient people were the first to work with copper.
(were) *the first to work with copper*

1. It was easy to find, and it was a fairly simple process to melt the copper.

2. Bronze is probably the first invented metal.

3. Metal workers, or smelters, melted copper and threw tin into it.

4. Smelters gradually added other substances to copper and created even stronger metals.

■ Direct and Indirect Objects

Write the direct object or objects that are part of the predicate in each sentence below. If the sentence has an indirect object, write it after the direct object and underline it.

Example: Metal workers produced bronze pins, jewelry, and oil lamps.
pins, jewelry, lamps

1. Sculptors could cast lifelike statues in bronze.

2. Kings sometimes gave great warriors bronze swords.

3. Wealthy people bought their families bronze trinkets.

4. Archaeologists have found many bronze artifacts.

5. Museum displays show visitors bronze objects that are thousands of years old.

6. Even today, one can see the fine designs carved into them.

7. Artists still like bronze and work with it often.

SENTENCES

ELPS 4C

Parts of a Sentence . . .

748.1
Understood Subjects and Predicates

Either the subject or the predicate (or both) may not be stated in a sentence, but both must be clearly understood.

> [You] **Get involved!** (*You* is the understood subject.)
>
> **Who needs your help? Animals** [do]. (*Do* is the understood predicate.)
>
> **What do many animals face?** [They face] **Extinction.** (*They* is the understood subject, and *face* is the understood predicate.)

748.2
Delayed Subjects

In sentences that begin with *there* followed by a form of the "be" verb, the subject usually follows the verb.

> **There are** laws **that protect endangered species.** (The subject is *laws; are* is the verb.)

The subject is also delayed in questions.

> **How do** we **preserve the natural habitat?** (*We* is the subject.)

SCHOOL DAZE

748.3
Modifiers

A modifier is a word (adjective, adverb) or a group of words (phrase, clause) that changes or adds to the meaning of another word. (See pages **548–555**.)

> Many North American **zoos and aquariums** voluntarily **participate** in breeding programs that help prevent extinction.

The modifiers in this sentence include the following: *many, North American* (adjectives), *voluntarily* (adverb), *in breeding programs* (phrase), *that help prevent extinction* (clause).

Grammar Practice

Parts of a Sentence 3

- ■ Understood Subjects and Predicates
- ■ Delayed Subjects

 Write the simple subject in the numbered sentences below. If the simple subject is understood, write "you."

Example: There are ticks that carry disease.
ticks

(1) Imagine a tick embedded in your arm. **(2)** How do you remove it? **(3)** First of all, do not try to pull it off by force. **(4)** A portion of its head could break off and remain inside the flesh. **(5)** There is a better way to remove it. **(6)** To begin, cover the tick with rubbing alcohol, heavy salad oil, or petroleum jelly, and wait for it to relax its grip. **(7)** Then carefully remove the tick with tweezers. **(8)** What is the final step? To wash the affected area thoroughly with soap and water.

Next Step: In the last sentence above, neither the subject nor the predicate is stated, but they are understood. Rewrite the sentence, stating both the subject and the predicate.

- ■ Modifiers

 List the adjectives and adverbs in each of the sentences below.

Example: Fortunately, fleas are usually not dangerous.
fortunately, usually, not, dangerous

1. An intense itch is often the only result of a flea bite.

2. Fleas really like to hide in pet fur.

3. All fleas are wingless.

4. They do not fly, but they can jump incredibly far!

TEKS 8.19A(iii), 8.19A(v), 8.19B
ELPS 4C

Parts of a Sentence . . .

750.1
Clauses

A clause is a group of related words that has both a subject and a verb. (Also see pages **577–579**.)

a whole chain of plants and animals is affected
(*Chain* is the subject, and *is affected* is the verb.)

when one species dies out completely
(*Species* is the subject; *dies out* is the verb.)

750.2
Independent Clauses

An independent clause presents a complete thought and can stand alone as a sentence.

This ancient oak tree may be cut down.

This act could affect more than 200 different species of animals!

Why would anyone want that to happen?

750.3
Dependent Clauses

A dependent clause does not present a complete thought and cannot stand as a sentence. A dependent clause *depends* on being connected to an independent clause to make sense. Dependent clauses begin with either a subordinating conjunction *(after, although, because, before, if)* or a relative pronoun *(who, whose, which, that)*. (See pages **762** and **792** for complete lists.)

If this ancient oak tree is cut down, **it could affect more than 200 different species of animals!**

The tree, which experts think could be 400 years old, **provides a home to many different kinds of birds and insects.**

750.4
Adjectival and Adverbial Clauses

Dependent clauses that begin with relative pronouns are called adjectival clauses because they modify, or tell more about, a noun or pronoun.

Mr. Rodriguez, who lives next door to me, is my soccer coach.
(The clause *who lives next door to me* tells more about Mr. Rodriguez.)

Dependent clauses that begin with subordinating conjunctions are called adverbial clauses because they act as adverbs to modify, or tell more about, verbs, adjectives, and other adverbs. They answer questions such as *when? why?* and *how?*

Dad will help you with your homework after he fixes the sink.
(The clause *after he fixes the sink* tells when Dad will help.)

punctuate edit capitalize SPELL
improve
Understanding Sentences
751

TEKS 8.19A(iii)
ELPS 4C

Grammar Practice

Parts of a Sentence 4

■ **Adjectival Clauses**

An adjectival clause is used to modify a noun or a pronoun. It begins with a relative pronoun *(who, whose, whom, which,* and *that).*

Find the adjectival clause in each of the following sentences and tell which word it modifies.

1. I play a kind of music that nobody likes.

2. The man whom you saw was not the famous actor.

3. I remember the day that I took my first airplane ride.

4. I have a neighbor whose parents live in Australia.

5. The hint that I learned about cleaning the walk saved me much work.

■ **Adverbial Clauses**

An adverbial clause begins with a subordinating conjunction *(after, although, because, before, if)* and answers questions such as *when? why?* and *how?* Sometimes adverbial clauses leave some words out. They are called reduced adverbial clauses.

Example: While (she was) speaking to the timid student, the teacher spoke slowly.

Find the adverbial clause in each of the following sentences and tell what word it modifies. If it is a reduced adverb clause, add the missing words.

1. If you keep pushing yourself too hard, you are going to get injured.

2. The contractor roughened the concrete while it was still wet.

3. I brought my umbrella because it was starting to rain.

4. The manager talked with the workers after listening to their suggestions.

5. Before returning to work, he ate his lunch.

⬣ **TEKS** 8.19A(iii)
ELPS 4C

Parts of a Sentence . . .

752.1
Phrases

A phrase is a group of related words that lacks either a subject or a predicate (or both). (See pages **581–582**.)

> **guards the house** (The predicate lacks a subject.)
>
> **the ancient oak tree** (The subject lacks a predicate.)
>
> **with crooked old limbs** (The phrase lacks both a subject and a predicate.)
>
> **The ancient oak tree with crooked old limbs guards the house.** (Together, the three phrases form a complete thought.)

752.2
Types of Phrases

Phrases usually take their names from the main words that introduce them (prepositional phrase, verb phrase, and so on). They are also named for the function they serve in a sentence (adverbial phrase, adjectival phrase). Adjectival phrases modify a noun or pronoun. Adverbial phrases modify a verb, adjective, or adverb.

> **The ancient oak tree** (noun phrase)
>
> **with crooked old limbs** (prepositional phrase)
>
> **jet black** (adjectival phrase)
>
> **has stood its guard,** (verb phrase)
>
> **very stubbornly,** (adverbial phrase)
>
> **protecting the little house.** (verbal phrase)

For more information on verbal phrases, see page **780**.

SCHOOL DAZE

Give me an example of a **verbal phrase** used as a subject.

Hanging upside down refreshes my brain.

TEKS 8.19A(iii)
ELPS 4C, 4K

Grammar Practice

Parts of a Sentence 5

■ **Types of Phrases**

Make five columns on your paper. Label them "Noun Phrases," "Adjectival Phrases," "Verb Phrases," "Adverbial Phrases," and "Prepositional Phrases." Write each of the phrases below in the correct column.

Example:

Noun Phrases	Adjectival Phrases	Verb Phrases	Adverbial Phrases	Prepositional Phrases
a big drooling dog	big and bold	turned its head	very suddenly	toward the front door

1. my best friend's bike
2. in Washington, D.C.
3. the brown gym bag
4. pearly white
5. ate a big dinner
6. was the captain
7. rather abruptly
8. many weary people
9. at the graduation dance
10. on the piano
11. over the fence
12. traveled a long way
13. quite cheerfully
14. dropped a contact lens
15. an aquarium shark
16. larger than life
17. took a walk
18. under a grocery cart

Next Step: Use the phrases above to write four sentences. You can add phrases of your own or use funny combinations of the phrases provided, but make sure each of your sentences has the necessary pieces (a noun phrase and a verb phrase) as well as at least one "extra"—a prepositional, adjectival or adverbial phrase. Then, working with a partner, take turns reading your paragraphs. As you listen, check to make sure each of your partner's sentences has the necessary pieces.

SENTENCES

Using the Parts of Speech

Nouns

A **noun** is a word that names a person, a place, a thing, or an idea.

Person: **John Ulferts** (uncle)   Thing: **"Yankee Doodle"** (song)

Place: **Mississippi** (state)   Idea: **Labor Day** (holiday)

Kinds of Nouns

754.1
Common Nouns

A common noun is any noun that does not name a specific person, place, thing, or idea. These nouns are not capitalized.

woman   museum   book   weekend

754.2
Proper Nouns

A proper noun is the name of a specific person, place, thing, or idea. Proper nouns are capitalized.

Hillary Clinton   Central Park   *Maniac McGee*   Sunday

754.3
Concrete Nouns

A concrete noun names a thing that is physical (can be touched or seen). Concrete nouns can be either proper or common.

space station   pencil   Statue of Liberty

754.4
Abstract Nouns

An abstract noun names something you can think about but cannot see or touch. Abstract nouns can be either common or proper.

Judaism   poverty   satisfaction   illness

754.5
Collective Nouns

A collective noun names a group or collection of persons, animals, places, or things.

Persons: **tribe, congregation, family, class, team**

Animals: **flock, herd, gaggle, clutch, litter**

Things: **batch, cluster, bunch**

754.6
Compound Nouns

A compound noun is made up of two or more words.

football (written as one word)

high school (written as two words)

brother-in-law (written as a hyphenated word)

Grammar Practice

Nouns 1

■ Concrete and Abstract Nouns

For each of the following sentences, write whether the underlined noun is "concrete" or "abstract."

Example: Pilots enjoy the <u>challenge</u> of flying a sailplane.
abstract

1. It's as close to soaring like a <u>bird</u> as a person is likely to get.

2. Fliers talk about the sense of <u>peace</u> they have when gliding.

3. To keep the <u>flight</u> going, a pilot might have to put the sailplane into a dive.

4. The dive gives the craft <u>speed</u>, which means more air time.

5. After the flight, the <u>pilot</u> returns the glider to its storage trailer so that it is ready for another day.

■ Compound and Collective Nouns

For each sentence below, write any compound or collective nouns you find. Circle the collective nouns.

Example: West of the Great Plains, groups of glider pilots take advantage of winds blowing against or over mountains.
Great Plains(groups)

1. A glider's light weight and long wings, along with a small cluster of instruments, allow a pilot to take advantage of updrafts in the air.

2. With the right conditions, gliders (or sailplanes) can travel over great distances by moving along a mountain range.

3. A pilot will travel southeast along with a flock of geese over several miles.

4. Pilots can join gliding clubs that support this unique sport.

5. I think this "unique sport" would give me a stomachache.

PARTS OF SPEECH

Nouns . . .

Number of Nouns

The number of a noun is either singular or plural.

756.1
Singular Nouns

A singular noun names one person, place, thing, or idea.

boy	group	audience	stage	concert	hope

756.2
Plural Nouns

A plural noun names more than one person, place, thing, or idea.

boys	groups	audiences	stages	concerts	hopes

Gender of Nouns

756.3
Noun Gender

Nouns are grouped according to gender: *feminine, masculine, neuter,* and *indefinite.*

> Feminine (female): **mother, sister, women, cow, hen**
> Masculine (male): **father, brother, men, bull, rooster**
> Neuter (neither male nor female): **tree, cobweb, closet**
> Indefinite (male or female): **president, duckling, doctor**

Uses of Nouns

756.4
Subject Nouns

A noun that is the subject of a sentence does something or is talked about in the sentence.

> The roots **of rap can be traced to West Africa and Jamaica.**

756.5
Predicate Nouns

A predicate noun follows a form of the *be* verb *(am, is, are, was, were, being, been)* and renames the subject.

> In the 1970s, rap was a street art.

756.6
Possessive Nouns

A possessive noun shows possession or ownership.

> Early rap had a drummer's **beat but no music.**
> The rapper's **words are set to music.**

756.7
Object Nouns

A noun is an object noun when it is used as the direct object, the indirect object, or the object of the preposition.

> Some rappers tell people **their** story **about life in the city.**
> (indirect object: *people;* direct object: *story*)
> Rap is now a common music choice in this country. (object of the preposition: *country*)

punctuate edit capitalize SPELL   757
improve
Using the Parts of Speech

Grammar Practice

Nouns 2

■ **Uses of Nouns**

Write whether the underlined noun in each of the following sentences is a "subject," "predicate," "possessive," or "object" noun.

Example: Last year, <u>Danika's</u> dad found a good used all-terrain wheelchair for her.

possessive

1. It's a big <u>improvement</u> over her old one.

2. This <u>wheelchair's</u> frame and tires are very sturdy.

3. Danika recently competed in a wheelchair <u>race</u>.

4. A local business <u>owner</u> arranged the loan of a racing wheelchair for Danika.

5. The business owner is also a wheelchair <u>user</u>.

6. Racing <u>wheelchairs</u> are not the same as ordinary wheelchairs.

7. Regular wheelchairs have two large and two small <u>wheels</u>.

8. The made-for-racing chair features two large angled wheels but only one small wheel in the <u>front</u>.

9. The large side wheels tilt so the <u>rider</u> can more easily push the wheels.

10. The <u>city's</u> parks department has approved plans to make all the parks accessible to wheelchairs.

11. The parks' redesign is a definite <u>move</u> in the right direction.

Next Step: Write two sentences about someone in a wheelchair. Use a predicate noun and an object noun somewhere in your sentences. Underline and label each one appropriately.

 **TEKS** 8.19A(iii), 8.19A(iv), 8.19C

Pronouns

A **pronoun** is a word used in place of a noun. Some examples are *I, you, he, she, it, we, they, his, hers, her, its, me, myself, us, yours,* and so on.

Without pronouns: **Kevin said Kevin would be going to Kevin's grandmother's house this weekend.**

With pronouns: **Kevin said he would be going to his grandmother's house this weekend.**

758.1
Antecedents

An antecedent is the noun that the pronoun refers to or replaces. All pronouns (except interrogative and indefinite pronouns) have antecedents. (See page **536**.)

Jamal and Rick tried out for the team, and they both made it.
(*They* refers to *Jamal* and *Rick; it* refers to *team.*)

NOTE Pronouns must agree with their antecedents in number, person, and gender.

Types of Pronouns

There are several types of pronouns. The most common type is the personal pronoun. (See the chart on page **762**.)

758.2
Personal Pronouns

A personal pronoun takes the place of a specific person (or thing) in a sentence. Some common personal pronouns are *I, you, he, she, it, we,* and *they.*

Suriana would not like to live in Buffalo, New York, because she does not like snow.

758.3
Relative Pronouns

A relative pronoun is both a pronoun and a connecting word. It connects a dependent clause to an independent clause in a complex sentence. Relative pronouns include *who, whose, which,* and *that.* (See **740.6**.)

Buffalo, which often gets more than eight feet of snow in a year, is on the northeast shore of Lake Erie.

The United States city that gets the most snow is Valdez, Alaska.

758.4
Interrogative Pronouns

An interrogative pronoun helps ask a question.

Who wants to go to Alaska?

Which of the cities would you visit?

Whom would you like to travel with?

What did you say?

punctuate edit capitalize SPELL 759
improve
Using the Parts of Speech

TEKS 8.19A(iii), 8.19A(iv), 8.19B, 8.19C

Grammar Practice

Pronouns 1

■ Antecedents
■ Personal Pronouns
■ Relative Pronouns

For each blank in the sentences below, write the missing pronoun. (The type of pronoun is in parentheses.) Also write its antecedent.

Example: Field trips are enjoyable because ___*(personal)*___ allow students to learn outside of the classroom.

they (trips)

1. The student ___*(relative)*___ suggests the best field trip may propose ___*(personal)*___ to the principal.

2. The Adler Planetarium, ___*(relative)*___ is in Chicago, is a favorite field trip destination.

3. Mrs. Bogart said ___*(personal)*___ would like to go to a film festival in Boston.

4. Ben said that ___*(personal)*___ thought the class should visit a veterinary hospital.

5. Mr. Andrews suggested, " ___*(personal)*___ would like to take the class to Washington, D.C., for several days."

6. The state capitol, ___*(relative)*___ is a popular place to visit, is where we plan to go next Tuesday.

7. The students ___*(relative)*___ names are on Mr. Daly's list should attend the field trip meeting.

8. The field trip ___*(relative)*___ Susan liked best was sailing on a tall ship.

9. Mrs. Bogart and Mr. Andrews announced, " ___*(personal)*___ will discuss all your suggestions."

Next Step: Write a brief paragraph about a field trip you've taken. Use both personal and relative pronouns. Exchange papers with a classmate, circle the antecedents in each other's sentences, and underline the dependent clauses.

PARTS OF SPEECH

Pronouns . . .

Types of Pronouns

760.1
Demonstrative Pronouns

A demonstrative pronoun points out or identifies a noun without naming the noun. When used together in a sentence, *this* and *that* distinguish one item from another, and *these* and *those* distinguish one group from another. (See page **762**.)

> **This is a great idea; that was a nightmare.**

> **These are my favorite foods, and those are definitely not.**

NOTE When these words are used before a noun, they are *not* pronouns; rather, they are demonstrative adjectives.

> **Coming to this picnic was fun—and those ants think so, too.**

760.2
Intensive Pronouns

An intensive pronoun emphasizes, or *intensifies,* the noun or pronoun it refers to. Common intensive pronouns include *itself, myself, himself, herself,* and *yourself.*

> **Though the chameleon's quick-change act protects it from predators, the lizard itself can catch insects 10 inches away with its long, sticky tongue.**

> **When a chameleon changes its skin color—seemingly matching the background—the background colors themselves do not affect the chameleon's color changes.**

NOTE These sentences would be complete without the intensive pronoun. The pronoun simply emphasizes a particular noun.

760.3
Reflexive Pronouns

A reflexive pronoun refers back to the subject of a sentence, and it is always an object (never a subject) in a sentence. Reflexive pronouns are the same as the intensive pronouns—*itself, myself, himself, herself, yourself,* and so on.

> **A chameleon protects itself from danger by changing colors.** (direct object)

> **A chameleon can give itself tasty meals of unsuspecting insects.** (indirect object)

> **I wish I could claim some of its amazing powers for myself.** (object of the preposition)

NOTE Unlike sentences with intensive pronouns, these sentences would *not* be complete without the reflexive pronouns.

punctuate edit capitalize SPELL **761**
improve
Using the Parts of Speech

Grammar Practice

Pronouns 2

◼ **Demonstrative Pronouns**

For the sentences below that have a demonstrative pronoun, write "DP." Rewrite the other sentences so that they also have demonstrative pronouns.

Example: This CD is awesome.
This is an awesome CD.

1. That was the best concert I've been to.

2. Those tickets were very expensive.

3. That drummer is the one you told me about!

4. These are my favorite cuts from the album.

5. Do you know anything about this?

◼ **Intensive Pronouns**
◼ **Reflexive Pronouns**

Write whether the pronouns that end in "self" or "selves" in the following sentences are intensive or reflexive.

Example: On July 4, 1845, Henry David Thoreau went by himself to live in the woods and write.
reflexive

1. Thoreau became an admired author, but he himself earned little from his writing.

2. When he went to Walden Pond, he hoped to better himself by living off the earth with just the bare essentials.

3. He himself planned and built a small cottage where he wrote in his journal and drafted his first book.

4. The cottage itself is no longer there, but the area is now a public park.

5. Someday, you may want to go somewhere by yourself to experience living quietly with just the bare essentials.

Pronouns . . .
Types of Pronouns

762.1
Indefinite Pronouns

An indefinite pronoun is a pronoun that does not have a specific antecedent (the noun or pronoun it replaces). (See page **537**.)

Everything **about the chameleon is fascinating.**

Someone **donated a chameleon to our class.**

Anyone **who brings in a live insect can feed our chameleon.**

Types of Pronouns

Personal Pronouns
I, me, mine, my, we, us, our, ours, you, your, yours, they, them, their, theirs, he, him, his, she, her, hers, it, its

Relative Pronouns
who, whose, whom, which, what, that, whoever, whomever, whichever, whatever

Interrogative Pronouns
who, whose, whom, which, what

Demonstrative Pronouns
this, that, these, those

Intensive and Reflexive Pronouns
myself, himself, herself, itself, yourself, yourselves, themselves, ourselves

Indefinite Pronouns

all	both	everything	nobody	several
another	each	few	none	some
any	each one	many	no one	somebody
anybody	either	most	nothing	someone
anyone	everybody	much	one	something
anything	everyone	neither	other	such

Grammar Practice

Pronouns 3

■ **Indefinite Pronouns**

Write the indefinite pronoun in each of the following sentences.

Example: Many recognize Sondre Norheim as the father of modern skiing.

Many

1. Norheim created a new kind of ski for himself and others.

2. Each had a heel binding and curved sides.

3. Sondre had a remarkable style of skiing that everyone admired.

4. No one can deny that he promoted the joy of skiing.

5. Most credit Norheim with making skiing a popular sport.

Pronoun Review

Identify the underlined pronouns in the sentences below as "personal," "relative," or "indefinite."

1. Ralph Samuelson, <u>who</u> was from Minnesota, invented water-skiing in 1922.

2. <u>Most</u> didn't believe the eighteen-year-old when he talked about skiing on water.

3. Ralph and his brother Ben set out to prove that <u>they</u> could do it.

4. They tried skis made from pieces of a barrel, <u>which</u> did not work well.

5. <u>Neither</u> thought twice about using a window-sash cord as a ski rope.

6. Ralph made <u>his</u> own skis from leather strips and lumber that he purchased.

7. <u>Everything</u> worked fine!

8. In 1925, during an exhibition <u>that</u> was held on Lake Pepin, Ralph made his first successful water-ski jump.

Pronouns . . .

Number of a Pronoun

Pronouns can be either singular or plural in number.

> Singular: **I, you, he, she, it**   Plural: **we, you, they**

NOTE The pronouns *you, your,* and *yours* may be singular or plural.

Person of a Pronoun

The person of a pronoun tells whether the pronoun is speaking, being spoken to, or being spoken about. (See page **536**.)

A first-person pronoun is used in place of the name of the speaker or speakers.

> **I am speaking.   We are speaking.**

A second-person pronoun is used to name the person or thing spoken to.

> **Eliza, will you please take out the garbage?**
>
> **You better stop grumbling!**

A third-person pronoun is used to name the person or thing spoken about.

> **Bill should listen if he wants to learn the words to this song.**
>
> **Charisse said that she already knows them.**
>
> **They will perform the song in the talent show.**

Uses of Pronouns

A pronoun can be used as a subject, as an object, or to show possession. (See the chart on page **766**.)

A subject pronoun is used as the subject of a sentence (*I, you, he, she, it, we, they*).

> **I like to surf the Net.**

A subject pronoun is also used after a form of the *be* verb (*am, is, are, was, were, being, been*) if it repeats the subject. (See "Predicate Nouns," **756.5**.)

> **"This is she," Mom replied into the telephone.**
>
> **"Yes, it was I," admitted the child who had eaten the cookies.**

TEKS 8.19C

Grammar Practice

Pronouns 4

- Number of a Pronoun
- Person of a Pronoun

 Write the personal pronouns in each of the following sentences and identify each as "singular" or "plural." Also tell whether it is "first," "second," or "third" person.

Example: We studied the Industrial Revolution in our history class.

We—plural, first person   our—plural, first person

1. My history teacher asked me, "Would you do a report on the Industrial Revolution and child-labor issues?

2. It was a time when machines replaced skilled labor.

3. Many people lost their jobs during that period in history.

4. Samuel Slater and his textile mill began the Industrial Revolution.

5. Inventors Watt, Kay, and Hargreaves are known for their contributions to the textile industry.

6. My American ancestors were probably affected by the Industrial Revolution.

7. In 1886, workers formed a labor union that they called the American Federation of Labor.

8. Samuel Gompers was its first president.

9. Early unions protected workers' rights and made sure that they were paid a fair wage.

10. Of course, the teacher gave us a test on this era.

11. My friend Chris said, "I know I passed!"

Next Step: Write a short paragraph about a subject you're studying in school. Make sure your pronouns agree with their antecedents in person and number.

Pronouns . . .
Uses of Pronouns

766.1
Object Pronouns

An object pronoun (*me, you, him, her, it, us, them*) can be used as the object of a verb or preposition. (See **746.4**, **746.5**, and **790.1**.)

I'll call her as soon as I can. (direct object)

Hand me the phone book, please. (indirect object)

She thinks these flowers are from you. (object of the preposition)

766.2
Possessive Pronouns

A possessive pronoun shows possession or ownership. These possessive pronouns function as adjectives before nouns: *my, our, his, her, their, its,* and *your.*

School workers are painting our classroom this summer. Its walls will look much better.

These possessive pronouns can be used after verbs: *mine, ours, hers, his, theirs,* and *yours.*

I'm pretty sure this backpack is mine and that one is his.

NOTE An apostrophe is not needed with a possessive pronoun to show possession.

Uses of Personal Pronouns

	Singular Pronouns			Plural Pronouns		
	Subject Pronouns	Possessive Pronouns	Object Pronouns	Subject Pronouns	Possessive Pronouns	Object Pronouns
First Person	I	my, mine	me	we	our, ours	us
Second Person	you	your, yours	you	you	your, yours	you
Third Person	he	his	him	they	their, theirs	them
	she	her, hers	her			
	it	its	it			

punctuate edit capitalize SPELL 767
improve
Using the Parts of Speech

Grammar Practice

Pronouns 5

■ Uses of Pronouns

For each sentence below, identify each personal pronoun as a "subject pronoun" (764.5), an "object pronoun," or a "possessive pronoun."

Example: She thinks that the invitation to the dance is from you.

She—subject pronoun, you—object pronoun

1. They asked me not to bring my brother to basketball practice.

2. When we think of our fourth-grade teacher, Mr. Wong, we remember his funny skits in the variety show.

3. Angela admits that algebra is not easy for her; it is difficult for me, too.

4. Before the game, she was afraid that her team might lose.

5. Max said, "Sunan and Elena went to the band concert without us, even after we asked them to wait."

6. The dirt bike hit some debris that caused it to crash.

7. It suffered quite a bit of damage.

8. Her sister sings in a band that plays at their school's dances.

9. Hank was late for practice today; he has been late for everything lately.

10. The coach is going to have a talk with him.

11. I thought the ball was mine, but then Jack jumped up and caught it.

Next Step: Write a sentence with a subject pronoun and an object or a possessive pronoun. Trade sentences with a classmate. Underline the subject pronoun and circle the object or possessive pronoun.

Verbs

A **verb** is a word that shows action or links a subject to another word in a sentence.

Tornadoes cause **tremendous damage.** (action verb)

The weather is **often calm before a storm.** (linking verb)

Types of Verbs

768.1

Action Verbs

An action verb tells what the subject is doing. (See page **542**.)

Natural disasters hit **the globe nearly every day.**

768.2

Linking Verbs

A linking verb connects—or links—a subject to a noun or an adjective in the predicate. The most common linking verbs are forms of the verb *be (is, are, was, were, being, been, am).* Verbs such as *smell, look, taste, feel, remain, turn, appear, become, sound, seem, grow,* and *stay* can also be linking verbs. (See page **542**.)

The San Andreas Fault is **an earthquake zone in California.** (The linking verb *is* connects the subject to the predicate noun *zone.*)

Earthquakes there are **fairly common.** (The linking verb *are* connects the subject to the predicate adjective *common.*)

768.3

Helping Verbs

A helping verb (also called an auxiliary verb) helps the main verb express tense and voice. The most common helping verbs are *shall, will, should, would, could, must, might, can, may, have, had, has, do, did,* and the forms of the verb *be—is, are, was, were, am, being, been.* (See page **543**.)

It has been **estimated that 500,000 earthquakes occur around the world every year.** (These helping verbs indicate that the tense is present perfect and the voice is passive.)

Fortunately, only about 100 of those will **cause damage.** (*Will* helps express the future tense of the verb.)

punctuate *edit* capitalize
SPELL
improve
769
Using the Parts of Speech

Grammar Practice

Verbs 1

■ Action, Linking, and Helping Verbs

For each numbered sentence in the following paragraphs, write the verb or verbs. (Remember that clauses also have verbs.) Identify each as an "action verb," a "linking verb," or a "helping verb."

Example: Pizza, which is one of the most popular foods in the world today, was also eaten by ancient people.

is–linking verb, was–helping verb, eaten–action verb

(1) Pizza is one type of food with a long history. **(2)** Its origins reach back to ancient Middle Eastern times. **(3)** People of that era ate flat bread that had been cooked in mud ovens. **(4)** Soon the Mediterraneans were eating the same flat bread with olive oil and native spices on it.

(5) Much later, in 1889, Queen Margherita was touring her Italian kingdom. **(6)** She noticed peasants who were enjoying the flat bread with spices on top. **(7)** An Italian baker, Raffaele Esposito, created a special pizza for the queen. **(8)** He topped it with tomatoes, mozzarella cheese, and fresh basil. **(9)** The pizza became the queen's favorite treat. **(10)** Today, it is known as pizza Margherita.

(11) Pizza was not a standard American food until after World War II. **(12)** American soldiers tried it for the first time while they were staying in areas of Italy. **(13)** It tasted wonderful! **(14)** When the soldiers returned home, they were hungry for this Italian treat. **(15)** Before long, everyone in America knew about pizza.

Next Step: Write a paragraph about one of your favorite foods. Use action, linking, and helping verbs. Exchange papers with a classmate. List and identify all of the verbs.

PARTS OF SPEECH

Verbs . . .

Tenses of Verbs

A verb has three principal parts: *present, past,* and *past participle.* (The part used with the helping verbs *has, have,* or *had* is called the past participle.)

All six of the tenses are formed from these principal parts. The past and past participle of regular verbs are formed by adding *ed* to the present tense. The past and past participle of irregular verbs are formed with different spellings. (See the chart on page **772**.)

770.1
Present Tense Verbs

The present tense of a verb expresses action (or a state of being) that is happening now or that happens continually or regularly. (See page **544**.)

> **The universe is gigantic. It takes my breath away.**

770.2
Past Tense Verbs

The past tense of a verb expresses action (or a state of being) that was completed in the past. (See page **544**.)

> **To most people many years ago, the universe was the earth, the sun, and some stars. The universe reached only as far as the eye could see.**

770.3
Future Tense Verbs

The future tense of a verb expresses action that *will* take place. (See page **544**.)

> **Maybe I will visit another galaxy in my lifetime.**
>
> **Somebody will find a way to do it.**

SCHOOL DAZE

I **know** the answer!

Okay, but I **said** you **will have** to sing the answer . . . go ahead!

punctuate *edit* capitalize
SPELL
improve **771**
Using the Parts of Speech

TEKS 8.19C

Grammar Practice

Verbs 2

■ Present Tense, Past Tense, and Future Tense Verbs

 For each of the sentences below, identify the underlined verbs as "present tense," "past tense," or "future tense."

Example: The United States Naval Academy <u>founded</u> its drum and bugle corps in 1914.

past tense

1. Today it <u>boasts</u> being the oldest drum and bugle corps in America.

2. The corps, consisting of 16 men, first <u>performed</u> at a baseball game.

3. It <u>was</u> active for eight years until it <u>disbanded</u> in 1922.

4. The academy's superintendent, Henry B. Wilson, <u>said</u>, "It <u>is</u> a luxury, not a necessity."

5. Some of the students <u>thought</u>, "The corps <u>will return</u> someday."

6. In 1926, the corps <u>came</u> back bigger and better.

7. Seeing them take the field again in full dress uniforms <u>was</u> an awesome sight.

8. Today the U.S. Naval Academy Drum and Bugle Corps <u>has</u> about 100 members.

9. The corps still <u>plays</u> "Anchors Away," just as it <u>did</u> almost a century ago.

10. You <u>will hear</u> its members shout, "Go, Navy!"

11. The corps <u>provides</u> enjoyable entertainment for people of all ages.

Next Step: Write a sentence in the present tense about some music you enjoy. Exchange papers with a classmate and write each other's sentence in the past and future tenses.

 TEKS 8.19C

Common Irregular Verbs and Their Principal Parts

The principal parts of the common irregular verbs are listed below. The part used with the helping verbs *has, have,* or *had* is called the **past participle**. (Also see page 543.)

Present Tense:	**I write.**	**She hides.**
Past Tense:	**Earlier I wrote.**	**Earlier she hid.**
Past Participle:	**I have written.**	**She has hidden.**

Present Tense	Past Tense	Past Participle	Present Tense	Past Tense	Past Participle
am, is, are	was, were	been	lead	led	led
begin	began	begun	lie (recline)	lay	lain
bid (offer)	bid	bid	lie (deceive)	lied	lied
bid (order)	bade	bidden	make	made	made
bite	bit	bitten	ride	rode	ridden
blow	blew	blown	ring	rang	rung
break	broke	broken	rise	rose	risen
bring	brought	brought	run	ran	run
burst	burst	burst	see	saw	seen
buy	bought	bought	set	set	set
catch	caught	caught	shake	shook	shaken
come	came	come	shine (polish)	shined	shined
dive	dived, dove	dived	shine (light)	shone	shone
do	did	done	shrink	shrank	shrunk
draw	drew	drawn	sing	sang, sung	sung
drink	drank	drunk	sink	sank, sunk	sunk
drive	drove	driven	sit	sat	sat
eat	ate	eaten	sleep	slept	slept
fall	fell	fallen	speak	spoke	spoken
fight	fought	fought	spring	sprang, sprung	sprung
flee	fled	fled	steal	stole	stolen
fly	flew	flown	strive	strove	striven
forsake	forsook	forsaken	swear	swore	sworn
freeze	froze	frozen	swim	swam	swum
get	got	gotten, got	swing	swung	swung
give	gave	given	take	took	taken
go	went	gone	tear	tore	torn
grow	grew	grown	throw	threw	thrown
hang (execute)	hanged	hanged	wake	woke, waked	woken, waked
hang (dangle)	hung	hung	wear	wore	worn
hide	hid	hidden, hid	weave	wove	woven
know	knew	known	wring	wrung	wrung
lay (place)	laid	laid	write	wrote	written

punctuate *edit* *capitalize* SPELL **773**
improve
Using the Parts of Speech

TEKS 8.19C

Grammar Practice

Verbs 3

■ Irregular Verbs

For the sentences below, fill in each blank with the correct past tense or past participle form of the verb or verbs in parentheses.

Example: Mr. Malone had _____ me permission to leave early. *(give)*

given

1. Ron _____ at the ball and hit it. *(swing)*

2. It _____ in the air for a few seconds before a fielder _____ it. *(hang, catch)*

3. The alarm _____ me, but I _____ back down and _____ for another hour. *(wake, lie, sleep)*

4. When the tornado _____ through town and _____ out windows, we _____ for cover. *(tear, blow, run)*

5. I have never _____ as many e-mails as I _____ last weekend. *(write, do)*

6. My hands had almost _____ after I had _____ out in the cold temperatures for so long. *(freeze, am)*

7. Although I had _____ to the principal, we _____ detentions anyway. *(speak, get)*

8. If we had _____ that Vandana was in the track meet, we would have _____ to watch her race. *(know, come)*

9. The marching band _____ a huge crowd. *(draw)*

10. I just _____ that new action-adventure film at the cinema. *(see)*

11. I have _____ all of the movies in that series. *(see)*

12. At last night's party, I had _____ so much that the snap on my jeans _____. *(eat, break)*

Next Step: Write three sentences using the present tense, past tense, and past participle of the word *fly.*

PARTS OF SPEECH

TEKS 8.19A(i), 8.19C

Verbs . . .
Tenses of Verbs

774.1 Present Perfect Tense Verbs

The present perfect tense verb expresses action that began in the past but continues or is completed in the present. The present perfect tense is formed by adding *has* or *have* to the past participle. (Also see page **545**.)

> I have wondered **for some time how the stars got their names.**
>
> **A visible star** has emitted **light for thousands of years.**

774.2 Past Perfect Tense Verbs

The past perfect tense verb expresses action that began in the past and was completed in the past. This tense is formed by adding *had* to the past participle. (Also see page **545**.)

> I had hoped **to see a shooting star on our camping trip.**

774.3 Future Perfect Tense Verbs

A future perfect tense verb expresses action that will begin in the future and will be completed by a specific time in the future. The future perfect tense is formed by adding *will have* to the past participle. (Also see page **545**.)

> **By the middle of this century, we probably** will have discovered **many more stars, planets, and galaxies.**

774.4 Present Progressive Tense Verbs

A present progressive tense verb expresses action that is not completed at the time of stating it. The present progressive tense is formed by adding *am, is,* or *are* to the *ing* form of the main verb.

> **Scientists** are learning **a great deal from their study of the sky.**

774.5 Past Progressive Tense Verbs

A past progressive tense verb expresses action that was happening at a certain time in the past. This tense is formed by adding *was* or *were* to the *ing* form of the main verb.

> **Astronomers** were beginning **their quest for knowledge hundreds of years ago.**

774.6 Future Progressive Tense Verbs

A future progressive tense verb expresses action that will take place at a certain time in the future. This tense is formed by adding *will be* to the *ing* form of the main verb.

> **Someday astronauts** will be going **to Mars.**

This tense can also be formed by adding a phrase noting the future *(are going to)* plus *be* to the *ing* form of the main verb.

> **They** are going to be performing **many experiments.**

Grammar Practice

Verbs 4

- Perfect Tense Verbs
- Progressive Tense Verbs

 For each of the sentences below, write the correct form of the verb given in parentheses.

> **Example:** Geologists _____ some strange rocks.
> *(discover, present perfect)*
> *have discovered*

1. During years of careful study, scientists _____ some of the ordinary-looking rocks to ultraviolet light. *(expose, past progressive)*

2. The rocks _____ with brilliant colors! *(glow, past progressive)*

3. Oddly, the rocks _____ to glow, even without the light on them. *(continue, past perfect)*

4. Now researchers _____ different levels of ultraviolet light on the rocks. *(test, present progressive)*

5. Scientists _____ these minerals unusual names, such as willemite, selenite, fluorite, aragonite, and Texas calcite. *(give, present perfect)*

6. As interest in these glow-in-the-dark minerals grows, more people _____ for them. *(look, future progressive)*

7. Geologists hope that rock hunters _____ more of these interesting objects by 2025. *(find, future perfect)*

8. In the meantime, people _____ museum displays of the minerals. *(visit, present progressive)*

9. The displays _____ museum visitors for years to come. *(amaze, future progressive)*

Next Step: Write a paragraph about an interesting mineral or metal. Use at least one perfect tense and one progressive tense verb and underline them.

Verbs . . .
Forms of Verbs

The voice of a verb tells you whether the subject is doing the action or is receiving the action. A verb is in the active voice (in any tense) if the subject is doing the action in a sentence.

I dream of going to galaxies light-years from Earth.

I will travel in an ultrafast spaceship.

A verb is in the passive voice if the subject is not doing the action. The action is done *by* someone or something else. The passive voice is always indicated with a helping verb plus a past participle or a past tense verb.

My daydreams often are shattered by reality. (The subject *daydreams* is not doing the action.)

Of course, reality can be seen differently by different people. (The subject *reality* is not doing the action.)

Tense	Active Voice		Passive Voice	
	Singular	**Plural**	**Singular**	**Plural**
Present Tense	I find	we find	I am found	we are found
	you find	you find	you are found	you are found
	he/she/it finds	they find	he/she/it is found	they are found
Past Tense	I found	we found	I was found	we were found
	you found	you found	you were found	you were found
	he found	they found	he/she/it was found	they were found
Future Tense	I will find	we will find	I will be found	we will be found
	you will find	you will find	you will be found	you will be found
	he will find	they will find	he/she/it will be found	they will be found
Present Perfect	I have found	we have found	I have been found	we have been found
	you have found	you have found	you have been found	you have been found
	he has found	they have found	he/she/it has been found	they have been found
Past Perfect	I had found	we had found	I had been found	we had been found
	you had found	you had found	you had been found	you had been found
	he had found	they had found	he/she/it had been found	they had been found
Future Perfect	I will have found	we will have found	I will have been found	we will have been found
	you will have found	you will have found	you will have been found	you will have been found
	he will have found	they will have found	he/she/it will have been found	they will have been found

punctuate edit *capitalize*
improve SPELL **777**
Using the Parts of Speech

Grammar Practice

Verbs 5

■ Active or Passive Voice

 For each sentence below, write the verb and tell whether it is in the active or passive voice.

Example: Elvis Presley has been called the King of Rock and Roll.
has been called (passive)

1. He is recognized by many people as an American music legend.
2. He soared to popularity with teenagers in the late 1950s.
3. By the end of his career, Elvis had recorded 81 albums and 51 singles.
4. In addition to his recording career, Elvis starred in movies.
5. Most of his best-known songs can be heard in his movies.
6. Elvis Presley died in 1977 at the age of 42.
7. His talent will be remembered for a very long time.

 Rewrite each of the following sentences in the active voice. Add or delete words as necessary.

Example: Elvis Presley's movies have been enjoyed by several generations.
Several generations have enjoyed Elvis Presley's movies.

1. His films have been seen by millions of people.
2. In *Jailhouse Rock,* the part of Vince Everett was played by Elvis.
3. Elvis's films have been appreciated by audiences around the world.
4. Elvis was made famous by his singing and acting talents.

Next Step: Write a sentence in the passive voice about a famous performer. Exchange papers with a classmate and rewrite each other's sentence in the active voice.

PARTS OF SPEECH

Verbs . . .
Forms of Verbs

Singular and Plural Verbs

A singular subject needs a singular verb. A plural subject needs a plural verb. For action verbs, only the third-person singular verb form is different: *I wonder, we wonder, you wonder, she wonders, they wonder.* Some linking verbs, however, have several different forms.

First Person   **Singular:** I am (or was) **a good student.**
                   Plural: We are (or were) **good students.**

Second Person   **Singular:** You are (or were) **a cheerleader.**
                   Plural: You are (or were) **cheerleaders.**

Third Person   **Singular:** He is (or was) **on the wrestling team.**
                   Plural: They are (or were) **also on the team.**

Transitive Verbs

A transitive verb is a verb that transfers its action to a direct object. The object makes the meaning of the verb complete. A transitive verb is always an action verb (never a linking verb). (See pages **546** and **632**.)

An earthquake shook **San Francisco in 1906.** (*Shook* transfers its action to the direct object *San Francisco.* Without *San Francisco* the meaning of the verb *shook* is incomplete.)

The city's people spent **many years rebuilding.** (Without the direct object *years,* the verb's meaning is incomplete.)

A transitive verb transfers the action directly to a direct object and indirectly to an indirect object.

Fires destroyed **the city.** (direct object: *city*)

Our teacher gave **us the details.** (indirect object: *us;* direct object: *details*)

See **746.4–746.5** for more on direct and indirect objects.

Intransitive Verbs

An intransitive verb does not need an object to complete its meaning. (See pages **546** and **632**.)

Abigail was shopping. (The verb's meaning is complete.)

Her stomach felt **queasy.** (*Queasy* is a predicate adjective describing *stomach;* there is no direct object.)

She lay **down on the bench.** (Again, there is no direct object. *Down* is an adverb modifying *lay.*)

punctuate *edit* capitalize
SPELL
improve 779
Using the Parts of Speech

ELPS 3E

Grammar Practice

Verbs 6

◼ Transitive and Intransitive Verbs

 For each sentence below, write whether the underlined verb is "transitive" or "intransitive."

Example: My best friend's mother <u>writes</u> poetry and short stories.
transitive

1. The wolf <u>snarled</u> fearsomely.

2. The coach <u>gave</u> the player a penalty for poor sportsmanship.

3. The leaves on this bush <u>are</u> purple.

4. Near the end of the race, Taylor <u>ran</u> faster than ever before.

5. Jorge <u>has been transferred</u> to Jackson Park Middle School.

6. Casey <u>told</u> the truth when he said that he didn't do it.

7. I <u>read</u> a letter to the editor about rising energy costs.

8. Ted <u>worked</u> quietly.

9. The sound of the fire alarm <u>blasted</u> through the halls.

10. Eva <u>plays</u> the drums in a band that she and her friends put together.

11. Before eating his breakfast, Najee <u>took</u> a vitamin.

12. <u>Have</u> you ever <u>seen</u> a telephone with a dial?

13. The sky <u>seems</u> a little green this afternoon.

14. The maintenance staff <u>cleans</u> the pool once a week.

15. The housekeeping staff <u>cleans</u> regularly.

Next Step: Write two sentences with transitive verbs and two with intransitive verbs. Read your sentences aloud to a classmate. Then exchange papers and identify each other's verbs correctly.

TEKS 8.19A(i), 8.19A(iii)

Verbs . . .
Forms of Verbs

780.1
Transitive or Intransitive Verbs

Some verbs can be either transitive or intransitive.

Transitive: **She** reads **my note.**   **Albert** ate **an apple.**

Intransitive: **She** reads **aloud.**   **Albert** ate **already.**

Verbals

A **verbal** is a word that is made from a verb but acts as another part of speech. Gerunds, participles, and infinitives are verbals.

780.2
Gerunds

A gerund is a verb form that ends in *ing* and is used as a *noun.* A gerund often begins a gerund phrase.

Worrying **is useless.** (The gerund is the subject noun.)

You should stop worrying about so many things. (The gerund phrase is the direct object.)

780.3
Participles

A participle is a verb form ending in *ing* or *ed.* A participle is used as an *adjective* and often begins a participial phrase.

The idea of the earth shaking **and** splitting **both fascinates and frightens me.** (The participles modify *earth.*)

Rattling in the cabinets, **the dishes were about to crash to the floor.** (The participial phrase modifies *dishes.*)

Why doesn't this tired **earth just stand still?** (The participle modifies *earth.*)

780.4
Infinitives

An infinitive is a verb form introduced by *to.* It may be used as a *noun,* an *adjective,* or an *adverb.* It often begins an infinitive phrase.

My need to whisper **is due to this secret.** (The infinitive is an adjective modifying *need.*)

I am afraid to swim. (The infinitive is an adverb modifying the predicate adjective *afraid.*)

To overcome this fear **is my goal.** (The infinitive phrase is used as a noun and is the subject of this sentence.)

punctuate *edit* capitalize
SPELL
improve
Using the Parts of Speech
781

Grammar Practice

Verbs 7

■ Verbals

For each sentence below, identify the underlined verb form as a "gerund," a "participle," or an "infinitive."

Example: In the late 1800s, Ohio artist Richard Felton Outcault began <u>to create</u> comics for newspapers.
infinitive

(1) Richard Outcault's comic strips became popular in America when the New York Journal decided <u>to print</u> his comic strip, the "Yellow Kid." **(2)** The "Yellow Kid" got his name because his <u>distinguishing</u> nightshirt was always printed in the color yellow. **(3)** <u>Printing</u> in color was new to newspapers in those days. **(4)** Soon there were more of Outcault's cartoons <u>appearing</u> in newspapers. **(5)** Comic strips <u>read</u> by people of all ages became an important part of the Sunday paper. **(6)** <u>Reading</u> them was fun! **(7)** Outcault went on <u>to create</u> several more popular strips, including one called "Buster Brown." **(8)** Then, after a while, he grew weary of creating comics, and the <u>tired</u> artist moved on to other things. **(9)** <u>Advertising</u> became his new profession. **(10)** Richard Outcault's ability <u>to develop</u> characters for the Sunday funnies earned him the title the Father of the Comic Strip.

For each sentence below, write the infinitive phrase and label how it is used—as a "noun," an "adjective," or an "adverb."

Example: To enjoy the funnies is a Sunday ritual.
To enjoy the funnies (noun)

1. It's a good way to begin a Sunday morning!

2. I want to read the comics before anything else.

3. I'm happy to read them to my little sister.

Adjectives

An **adjective** is a word used to describe a noun or a pronoun. Adjectives tell *what kind, how many,* or *which one.* They usually come before the word they describe. (See pages **548–551**.)

ancient **dinosaurs**   800 **species**   that **triceratops**

Adjectives are the same whether the word they describe is singular or plural.

small **brain**—or—small **brains**   large **tooth**—or—large **teeth**

782.1
Articles

The articles *a, an,* and *the* are adjectives.

A **brontosaurus was** an **animal about 70 feet long.**

The **huge dinosaur lived on land and ate plants.**

782.2
Proper Adjectives

A proper adjective is formed from a proper noun, and it is always capitalized. (See **676.1**.)

A Chicago **museum is home to the skeleton of one of these beasts.** (*Chicago* functions as a proper adjective describing the noun *museum.*)

782.3
Common Adjectives

A common adjective is any adjective that is not proper. It is not capitalized (unless it is the first word in a sentence).

Ancient **mammoths were** huge, woolly **creatures.**

They lived in the ice **fields of Siberia.**

Special Kinds of Adjectives

782.4
Demonstrative Adjectives

A demonstrative adjective points out a particular noun. *This* and *these* point out something nearby; *that* and *those* point out something at a distance.

This **mammoth is huge, but** that **mammoth is even bigger.**

NOTE When a noun does not follow *this, these, that,* or *those,* these words are pronouns, not adjectives. (See **760.1**.)

782.5
Compound Adjectives

A compound adjective is made up of two or more words. (Sometimes it is hyphenated.)

Dinosaurs were egg-laying **animals.**

The North American **Allosaurus had sharp teeth and powerful jaws.**

punctuate *edit* capitalize
improve SPELL **783**
Using the Parts of Speech

ELPS 3E

Grammar Practice

Adjectives 1

- ▦ **Demonstrative Adjectives**
- ▦ **Compound Adjectives**
- ▦ **Indefinite and Predicate Adjectives** (See page **784**.)

 For each numbered sentence in the paragraphs below, identify the underlined word or words as one of the kinds of adjectives listed above.

Example: <u>Most</u> people know about the Great Chicago Fire.
indefinite

(1) On the night of October 8, 1871, an eerie, <u>reddish orange</u> glow filled the Chicago sky. **(2)** <u>Some</u> people believe that the Great Chicago Fire began in the O'Learys' barn when a cow kicked over a lantern. **(3)** (<u>That</u> theory was never proven, however, and the exact cause of the fire is still unknown.) **(4)** <u>Many</u> residents panicked and tried to flee the burning city. **(5)** <u>Kind-hearted</u> people did whatever they could to help, but most of Chicago was destroyed, and 300 people died.

(6) As bad as it was, <u>another</u> fire on the same day caused even more damage. **(7)** The Great Peshtigo Fire was <u>huge</u>; it covered more than a million acres in northeast Wisconsin and Michigan's upper peninsula. **(8)** Hundreds of miles of forest, dry from drought, were tinder for <u>this</u> firestorm. **(9)** <u>Hurricane-force</u> winds created by the fire pushed the blaze from town to town, and 1,500 people lost their lives. **(10)** To <u>this</u> day, the Great Peshtigo Fire ranks as the worst natural disaster to ever hit the United States.

Next Step: Write two or three sentences about fire safety. Use a predicate adjective, an indefinite adjective, and a demonstrative adjective in your sentences. Read your sentences aloud to a classmate and listen to his or her sentences. Identify the adjectives your partner used.

PARTS OF SPEECH

Adjectives . . .

Special Kinds of Adjectives

784.1
Indefinite Adjectives

An indefinite adjective gives approximate or indefinite information (*any, few, many, most,* and so on). It does not tell exactly how many or how much.

Some **mammoths were heavier than today's elephants.**

784.2
Predicate Adjectives

A predicate adjective follows a linking verb and describes the subject.

Mammoths were once abundant**, but now they are** extinct**.**

Forms of Adjectives

784.3
Positive Adjectives

The positive form describes a noun or pronoun without comparing it to anyone or anything else.

The Eurostar is a fast **train that runs between London, Paris, and Brussels.**

It is an impressive **train.**

784.4
Comparative Adjectives

The comparative form of an adjective *(er)* compares two persons, places, things, or ideas. (See page **549**.)

The Eurostar is faster **than the Orient Express.**

Some adjectives that have more than one syllable show comparisons by their *er* suffix, but many of them use the modifiers *more* or *less*.

It is a speedier **commuter train than the Tobu Railway trains in Japan.**

This train is more impressive **than my commuter train.**

784.5
Superlative Adjectives

The superlative form *(est* or *most* or *least)* compares three or more persons, places, things, or ideas. (See page **549**.)

In fact, the Eurostar is the fastest **train in Europe.**

It is the most impressive **commuter train in the world.**

784.6
Irregular Forms

Some adjectives use completely different words to express comparison.

good, better, best   **bad, worse, worst**

many, more, most   **little, less, least**

punctuate edit capitalize SPELL
improve
Using the Parts of Speech
785

Grammar Practice

Adjectives 2

▪ Forms of Adjectives

Based on the clues in each sentence below, write the correct form (positive, comparative, or superlative) of the adjective shown in parentheses to complete each sentence.

Example: Giraffes are _____ than any other animal. *(tall)*
taller

1. The _____ snake in the world is the reticulated python. *(long)*

2. A rabbit has _____ ears than a hare does. *(short)*

3. A cheetah is a _____ runner. *(fast)*

4. Even though the whale shark feeds mostly on plankton and small fish, it is the _____ fish in the sea. *(big)*

5. The common snail is probably the _____ animal on earth. *(slow)*

6. Is the warthog really the _____ animal? *(attractive)*

7. Many people believe the polar bear is _____ than the grizzly bear. *(powerful)*

8. The Indian elephant has a _____ forehead. *(square)*

9. Even the _____ human sprinter can't outrun an elephant. *(good)*

10. Some zebras have _____ stripes than other zebras. *(many)*

11. Compared to other animals in the United States, the wolverine seems to be the one with the _____ temper. *(bad)*

12. An arctic fox in the snow is _____ than a red fox in the forest. *(visible)*

13. Long ago, the Pacific salmon was the _____ source of food in the diet of the Yakima tribe. *(important)*

Next Step: Write three sentences about different animals. Use adjectives that are positive, comparative, and superlative in your sentences.

Adverbs

An **adverb** is a word used to modify a verb, an adjective, or another adverb. It tells *how, when, where, how often,* or *how much.* Adverbs can come before or after the words they modify. (See pages **552–555**.)

Dad snores loudly. (*Loudly* modifies the verb *snores.*)

His snores are really **explosive.** (*Really* modifies the adjective *explosive.*)

Dad snores very **loudly.** (*Very* modifies the adverb *loudly.*)

Types of Adverbs

There are four basic types of adverbs: *time, place, manner,* and *degree.*

786.1
Adverbs of Time

Adverbs of time tell *when, how often,* and *how long.*

tomorrow   often   never   always

Jen rarely **has time to go swimming.**

786.2
Adverbs of Place

Adverbs of place tell *where, to where,* or *from where.*

there   backward   outside

We'll set up our tent here.

786.3
Adverbs of Manner

Adverbs of manner often end in *ly* and tell *how* something is done.

unkindly   gently   well

Ahmed boldly **entered the dark cave.**

Some words used as adverbs can be written with or without the *ly* ending. When in doubt, use the *ly* form.

slow, slowly   deep, deeply

NOTE Not all words ending in *ly* are adverbs. *Lovely,* for example, is an adjective.

786.4
Adverbs of Degree

Adverbs of degree tell *how much* or *how little.*

scarcely   entirely   generally   very   really

Jess is usually **the leader in these situations.**

punctuate *edit* capitalize
SPELL
improve   **787**
Using the Parts of Speech

Grammar Practice

Adverbs 1

■ Types of Adverbs

Write the adverb or adverbs that modify the underlined words in the sentences below. The number of adverbs is in parentheses. Label each as one of "time," "place," "manner," or "degree."

Example: America's national parks <u>are</u> always a great place to camp. *(1)* *always–time*

1. Some parks, like Yosemite and Yellowstone, <u>are</u> often very <u>busy</u>. *(2)*

2. You might have to <u>wait</u> patiently to get a campsite. *(1)*

3. People must enjoy <u>sleeping</u> outside! *(1)*

4. Campers in national parks regularly <u>go</u> bicycling, canoeing, and hiking. *(1)*

5. Younger kids really <u>enjoy</u> meeting the park rangers. *(1)*

6. Frequently, national park campgrounds <u>offer</u> evening campfire activities. *(1)*

7. If someone <u>brings</u> a guitar there, people might start <u>dancing</u> around. *(2)*

8. Sometimes, national parks <u>have</u> programs to teach campers about nature and wildlife. *(1)*

9. Campers need to <u>react</u> quietly and cautiously when wild animals <u>are</u> nearby. *(3)*

10. Wherever you camp, it is important to <u>do</u> it safely. *(1)*

11. You should <u>follow</u> the park's camping rules exactly and faithfully. *(2)*

12. Never <u>hike</u> by yourself. *(1)*

13. Be extremely <u>careful</u> that your campfire <u>does</u> not accidentally <u>start</u> a forest fire. *(3)*

14. Always <u>remember</u> to carefully <u>inspect</u> your campsite before you leave. *(2)*

Adverbs . . .
Special Kinds of Adverbs

788.1
Conjunctive Adverbs

A conjunctive adverb can be used as a conjunction and shows a connection or a transition between two independent clauses. Most often, a conjunctive adverb follows a semicolon in a compound sentence; however, it can also appear at the beginning or end of a sentence. (Note that the previous sentence has an example of a conjunctive adverb.)

also	besides	however	instead
meanwhile	nevertheless	therefore	

Forms of Adverbs

Many adverbs—especially adverbs of manner—have three forms: *positive, comparative,* and *superlative.*

788.2
Positive Adverbs

The positive form describes but does not make a comparison.

> Juan woke up late.

> He quickly ate some breakfast.

788.3
Comparative Adverbs

The comparative form of an adverb *(er)* compares two things.

> Juan woke up later than he usually did. (See page 553.)

Some adverbs that have more than one syllable show comparisons by their *er* suffix, but many of them use the modifiers *more* or *less.*

> He ate his breakfast more quickly than usual.

788.4
Superlative Adverbs

The superlative form *(est* or *most* or *least)* compares three or more things. (See page 553.)

> Of the past three days, Juan woke up latest on Saturday.

> Of the past three days, he ate his breakfast least quickly on Saturday.

788.5
Irregular Forms

Some adverbs use completely different words to express comparison.

Positive	Comparative	Superlative
well	better	best
badly	worse	worst

Grammar Practice

Adverbs 2

■ Comparative Forms

For each of the sentences below, write the adverb and identify it as "positive," "comparative," or "superlative."

Example: This year, the school bus arrives earlier than it did last year.
earlier (comparative)

1. Makenna carelessly dripped paint on the floor.

2. Paul bakes walnut brownies better than I do.

3. Of everyone in our school's chorus, Marissa sings the best.

4. The play's director said, "For this role, Carmen, you have to act more mysteriously than that."

5. My old computer runs more slowly than this new one.

6. Ms. Green, who was formerly a marine, is a new teacher at our school.

7. Of any of the recent storms in the area, the wind blew the most forcefully during last night's storm.

8. My brother rides his dirt bike faster than I do.

9. Julian divided the popcorn equally among the four of us.

10. Of the Rosses' three regular babysitters, Bianca seems to be the least readily available.

11. Instant messaging was largely unknown until a few years after its introduction.

12. Shanice dresses the most plainly of anyone in her family.

13. Dimitri treats his dog roughly.

14. Paola gives classroom presentations more confidently than the other students give them.

Next Step: Write one sentence with a comparative adverb and one with a superlative adverb.

Prepositions

Prepositions are words that show position, direction, or how two words or ideas are related to each other. Specifically, a preposition shows the relationship between its object and some other word in the sentence.

> **Raul hid** under **the stairs.** (*Under* shows the relationship between *hid* and *stairs.*)

790.1
Prepositional Phrases

A preposition never appears alone; it is always part of a prepositional phrase. A prepositional phrase includes the preposition, the object of the preposition, and the modifiers of the object. (See pages **556–557**.)

> **Raul's friends looked** in the clothes hamper. (preposition: *in;* object: *hamper;* modifiers: *the, clothes*)

A prepositional phrase functions as an adjective or as an adverb.

> **They checked the closet** with all the winter coats. (*With all the winter coats* functions as an adjective modifying *closet.*)

> **They wandered** around the house **looking for him.** (*Around the house* functions as an adverb modifying *wandered.*)

NOTE If a word found in the list of prepositions has no object, it is not a preposition. It is probably an adverb.

> **Raul had never won at hide 'n' seek** before. (*Before* is an adverb that modifies *had won.*)

Prepositions

aboard	apart from	beyond	from among	near	over	toward
about	around	but	from between	near to	over to	under
above	aside from	by	from under	of	owing to	underneath
according to	at	by means of	in	off	past	until
across	away from	concerning	in addition to	on	prior to	unto
across from	back of	considering	in front of	on account of	regarding	up
after	because of	despite	in place of	on behalf of	round	up to
against	before	down	in regard to	on top of	save	upon
along	behind	down from	in spite of	onto	since	with
along with	below	during	inside	opposite	through	within
alongside	beneath	except	inside of	out	throughout	without
alongside of	beside	except for	instead of	out of	till	
amid	besides	excepting	into	outside	to	
among	between	for	like	outside of	together with	

TEKS 8.19A(iii)

Grammar Practice

Prepositions

Write the prepositional phrases you find in each numbered sentence below. Underline the prepositions and circle the objects of the prepositions.

Example: The Plains Indians were once the finest horse riders in the world. *in the (world)*

(1) Plains Indians learned horse-riding skills at a very early age. **(2)** Tribesmen on horses could follow the buffalo herds, so mastering those skills meant food for the tribe. **(3)** Riding among the buffalo and using a bow involved great skill and daring. **(4)** Some of the Indian braves would ride with one foot on the top of the horse's hips while shooting arrows underneath the horse's neck at an enemy. **(5)** In the 1800s, nations like the Crow and the Lakota enjoyed a golden age because of their superb riding abilities.

Write a prepositional phrase to complete each of the following sentences.

Example: I like tropical fish . . . *(what kind?)*
from the Caribbean Sea.

1. I was born . . . *(when?)*

2. My uncle grew up . . . *(where?)*

3. My notebook is the one . . . *(which one?)*

4. I keep my pens and pencils . . . *(where?)*

5. Please get me some candy . . . *(what kind?)*

Next Step: Write a paragraph to describe something interesting you've seen. Be sure to use some prepositional phrases that act as adjectives and some that act as adverbs. Then trade papers with a partner and identify the prepositional phrases your partner used. Also tell whether they act as adjectives or adverbs.

PARTS OF SPEECH

 **TEKS** 8.19(v)

Conjunctions

A **conjunction** connects individual words or groups of words. There are three kinds of conjunctions: *coordinating, correlative,* and *subordinating.* (See pages 558–560.)

792.1 Coordinating Conjunctions

A coordinating conjunction connects a word to a word, a phrase to a phrase, or a clause to a clause. The words, phrases, or clauses joined by a coordinating conjunction must be equal, or of the same type.

> Polluted rivers and streams can be cleaned up. (Two nouns are connected by *and*.)

> Ride a bike or plant a tree to reduce pollution. (Two verb phrases are connected by *or*.)

> Maybe you can't invent a pollution-free engine, but you can cut down on the amount of energy you use. (Two equal independent clauses are connected by *but*.)

NOTE When a coordinating conjunction is used to make a compound sentence, a comma always comes before it.

792.2 Correlative Conjunctions

Correlative conjunctions are conjunctions used in pairs.

> We must reduce not only pollution but also excess energy use.

> Either you're part of the problem, or you're part of the solution.

Conjunctions

Coordinating Conjunctions
and, but, or, nor, for, so, yet

Correlative Conjunctions
either, or   neither, nor   not only, but also   both, and   whether, or   as, so

Subordinating Conjunctions
after, although, as, as if, as long as, as though, because, before, if, in order that, provided that, since, so, so that, that, though, till, unless, until, when, where, whereas, while

Grammar Practice

Conjunctions 1

■ Coordinating Conjunctions

Use a coordinating conjunction to combine each pair of sentences below.

Example: Anyone may join the Polar Bear Club. He or she must be willing to swim in freezing water.

Anyone may join the Polar Bear Club, but he or she must be willing to swim in freezing water.

1. The members braved the subzero temperatures. They plunged into the icy water.

2. Club members could go into the water wearing swimsuits. They could go into the water wearing warmer clothing.

3. Participants get very cold. It is important to have a place to warm up when they get out of the water.

4. Polar Bear Club members like to have fun. They also like to help raise money for special causes.

■ Correlative Conjunctions

Use a different set of correlative conjunctions to combine each sentence pair below. Underline the conjunctions.

Example: Jorge must decide if he wants to go to the game. Jorge must decide if he wants to go to the movies.

Jorge must decide <u>whether</u> he wants to go to the game <u>or</u> the movies.

1. Rain will not stop the football game. Snow will not stop the football game.

2. Volleyball is a team sport. Soccer is a team sport.

3. Sonja has twin sisters. Sonja also has twin cousins.

4. Maybe Raul's mom will pick us up after school. Maybe Raul's dad will pick us up after school.

TEKS 8.19A(iii), 8.19(v)

Conjunctions . . .

794.1 Subordinating Conjunctions

A subordinating conjunction is a word or group of words that connects two clauses that are not equally important. A subordinating conjunction begins a dependent clause and connects it to an independent clause to make a complex sentence. (See page 579 and the chart on page 792.)

> **Fuel-cell engines are unusual** because **they don't have moving parts.**

> Since **fuel-cell cars run on hydrogen, the only waste products are water and heat.**

As you can see in the sentences above, a comma sets off the dependent clause only when it begins the sentence. A comma is usually not used when the dependent clause follows the independent clause.

NOTE Relative pronouns and conjunctive adverbs can also connect clauses. (See 758.3 and 788.1.)

Interjections

An **interjection** is a word or phrase used to express strong emotion or surprise. Punctuation (a comma or an exclamation point) is used to separate an interjection from the rest of the sentence.

> Wow, **would you look at that!**   Oh no! **He's falling!**

SCHOOL DAZE

Forget it! We aren't using activity money for that.

Yikes, I've told everyone that we could buy a plasma-screen TV for our classroom!

Grammar Practice

Conjunctions 2

■ Subordinating Conjunctions

Choose a subordinating conjunction (from the chart on page 792) to connect each pair of clauses below, forming complex sentences. Place the conjunction first in some of the sentences.

Example: Cicadas are easy to recognize. They make unique sounds.

Cicadas are easy to recognize because they make unique sounds.

1. It's not uncommon to hear dozens of them ticking, buzzing, and whining. It's hot outside.

2. They are capable of producing sounds in excess of 120 decibels. The noise might hurt your ears.

3. The king hornet preys on cicadas. Birds are even worse.

4. Unsuspecting cicadas are sitting high in the treetops. Hungry birds are watching.

5. It sounds disgusting. Some people eat cicadas.

6. You might hear the 17-year cicadas. You are in the United States east of the Great Plains.

7. These cicadas are called 17-year cicadas. They emerge in great numbers once every 17 years.

8. You know what a cicada looks like. You might mistake it for a locust or a giant fly.

9. A cicada's body temperature drops below 72 degrees Fahrenheit. It won't fly.

10. You might not like the racket that cicadas make. You have to admit that they are interesting insects.

Next Step: Would an interjection be appropriate in any of the sentences you just wrote? Add an interjection to at least four of them. Separate it from the rest of the sentence with either a comma or an exclamation point.

PARTS OF SPEECH

ELPS 4C

Quick Guide: Parts of Speech

In the English language, there are eight parts of speech. Understanding them will help you improve your writing skills. Every word you write is a part of speech—a noun, a verb, an adjective, and so on. The chart below lists the eight parts of speech.

Noun

A word that names a person, a place, a thing, or an idea

Alex Moya   Belize   ladder   courage

Pronoun

A word used in place of a noun

I   he   it   they   you   anybody   some

Verb

A word that shows action or links a subject to another word in the sentence

sing   shake   catch   is   are

Adjective

A word that describes a noun or a pronoun

stormy   red   rough   seven   grand

Adverb

A word that describes a verb, an adjective, or another adverb

quickly   today   now   bravely   softer

Preposition

A word that shows position or direction and introduces a prepositional phrase

around   up   under   over   between   to

Conjunction

A word that connects other words or groups of words

and   but   or   so   because   when

Interjection

A word (set off by commas or an exclamation point) that shows strong emotion

Stop! Hey, how are you?

punctuate *edit* *capitalize*
SPELL   797
improve
Using the Parts of Speech

ELPS 4C

Grammar Practice

Parts of Speech Review

For each underlined word in the following paragraphs, write whether it is a "noun," a "pronoun," a "verb," an "adjective," an "adverb," a "preposition," a "conjunction," or an "interjection."

(1) There's a big <u>change</u> taking place in the Black Hills of South Dakota. **(2)** Not far from Mount Rushmore, a huge likeness of the Native American leader Crazy Horse is being carved <u>into</u> the side of a mountain. **(3)** Crazy Horse was a <u>famous</u> warrior of the Lakota tribe. **(4)** He was a committed leader <u>who</u> fought to preserve the traditions and values of his people. **(5)** Now, people <u>are creating</u> this memorial to his life. **(6)** <u>Anyone</u> who's in the area can see it in person.

(7) The <u>sculptor</u> Korczak Ziolkowski began work on the memorial in 1948. **(8)** In the beginning, he <u>worked</u> alone. **(9)** He worked diligently, <u>and</u> soon the image of Crazy Horse began taking shape.
(10) Surprisingly, he <u>then</u> decided to carve the entire 600-foot mountain instead of following his original plan to carve only the top 100 feet.
(11) <u>Wow</u>, Korczak worked on his amazing sculpture for 32 years!
(12) When he died <u>unexpectedly</u> in 1982 at the age of 74, he was buried in a tomb about 500 yards from the base of the mountain.

(13) Ziolkowski's project continues <u>under</u> the supervision of his wife. **(14)** The face portion of this <u>gigantic</u> sculpture was dedicated in 1998. **(15)** The crew will work faithfully <u>until</u> the project is finished.
(16) <u>Oh</u>, it will be years before the memorial is finished, but it will be well worth the wait.

Next Step: Write one word for each of the eight parts of speech and exchange lists with a partner. Write a sentence or two using all of each other's words.

Credits

Photos: P. cover (camera), 59 Harcourt School Publishers; cover (desert, headlights), vi, xv, xvi, 1, 3, 10, 16, 27 (t,b), 39, 57, 67, 70, 139, 147, 283 (l), 341, 379 (c,r), 383, 384 (t), 387, 394, 405, 450, 451, 459 (computer mouse, keyboard, plug), 469, 475, 479, 491, 523 (bgd), 526, 567, 585, 595, 609 (t,b), 617 (t,bgd) ©Photodisc/Getty Images; cover (flame) ©Alexey Stiop/Alamy; cover (sunset), 206, 385, 617 (b) ©Corbis; cover (tires) ©picturesbyrob/Alamy; cover (video camera), x, 5, 9, 33, 46, 65, 103, 109 (c,bgd), 115, 119, 125, 171, 177 (c, bgd), 183, 193, 207, 213 (t), 237 (t,b), 241, 247 (c,bgd), 253, 263, 269, 283 (r), 299, 307, 311 (c,bgd), 317, 327, 365, 369, 377 (b), 412, 424 (c,bgd), 434, 444, 457, 459 (CD, microphone, salt shaker, VHS tape), 461 (t,l), 473, 489 (c,bgd), 495 (c,bgd), 501 (c,bgd), 505 (t,b), 507 (c,bgd), 509, 513 (c,bgd), 515, 517, 519 (c,bgd), 523 (c), 525 (c,bgd), 547, 593 ©Comstock/Getty Images; ix Courtesy of The Library of Congress; v, 377 (t), 461 (b) Harcourt; xviii, 233, 315, 503 ©Ingram Publishing/Getty Images; 11 ©David Buffington/Photodisc/Getty Images; 62 ©Hemera Technologies/Jupiter; 72-73, 95 Harcourt; 77 ©Corbis/Jupiter; 85, 277, 527, 531, endsheet ©Ablestock.com/Jupiter; 99, 131, 493 ©Ingram Publishing/Jupiter; 163 ©Purestock/Jupiter; 167, 199 ©Ingram Publishing/SuperStock; 213 (b), 583 ©Artville/Getty Images; 242 ©Randy Faris/Corbis; 252 ©Radius Images/Corbis; 285 ©Jupiter; 303, 333, 511 ©Comstock/Jupiter; 347 Courtesy of The Library of Congress; 348 Courtesy of The Library of Congress; 378 ©National Geographic Image Collection/Alamy; 379 (l) ©Ivan Hunter/Getty Images; 380 ©David Muscroft/Alamy; 382 ©Jupiter Images; 384 (b) ©Slanted Roof Studio/Alamy; 485 HMH Collection; 488 ©Adam Taylor/Digital Vision/Getty Images; 494, 524 ©Ilene MacDonald/Alamy; 500 ©Antenna/Getty Images; 506 ©fStop/SuperStock; 512 ©Steve Skjold/Alamy; 518 ©Alamy; 554 ©NOAA; 561 ©Stockbyte/Getty Images; 597 ©Best View Stock/Alamy; back cover ©Digital Vision/Getty Images.

Text Credits: English Language Proficiency Standards and Texas Essential Knowledge and Skills copyright © Texas Education Agency; Page 528: Copyright © 2010 by Houghton Mifflin Harcourt Publishing Company. Adapted and reproduced by permission from *The American Heritage Student Dictionary*.

Texas Essential Knowledge and Skills (TEKS) for English Language Arts

The English Language Arts and Reading TEKS specify the skills you need to master by the end of Grade 8. To help you understand what is required of you, we have provided a list of the skills you will practice and learn during this school year. The second column shows where these TEKS are addressed in *Texas Write Source*.

⭐ TEKS 8.14 Writing/Writing Process

Students use elements of the writing process (planning, drafting, revising, editing, and publishing) to compose text. Students are expected to:

A plan a first draft by selecting a genre appropriate for conveying the intended meaning to an audience, determining appropriate topics through a range of strategies (e.g., discussion, background reading, personal interests, interviews); and developing a thesis or controlling idea;	pages 7, 8, 35 ,36, 39, 75, 80, 82, 97, 142, 157, 165, 172, 210, 211, 221, 227, 235, 242, 245, 280, 281, 293, 301, 302, 308, 310, 379, 413, 422, 423, 606–609
B develop drafts by choosing an appropriate organizational strategy (e.g., sequence of events, cause-effect, compare-contrast) and building on ideas to create a focused, organized, and coherent piece of writing;	pages 8, 37, 38, 76, 81, 83, 97, 98, 105, 107, 119, 143, 166, 175, 176, 178–181, 187, 211, 212, 236, 243, 246–252, 256, 257, 282, 310, 312–316, 320, 372, 423, 426–431, 596–601, 610–613, 634, 635 page 4
C revise drafts to ensure precise word choice and vivid images; consistent point of view; use of simple, compound, and complex sentences; internal and external coherence; and the use of effective transitions after rethinking how well questions of purpose, audience, and genre have been addressed;	pages 7, 9, 76, 84, 87, 89, 91, 109, 111, 114, 116, 117, 120–122, 128, 145, 184–186, 190, 191, 196, 245, 250, 254, 256, 257, 259, 261, 266, 267, 315, 323, 325, 373, 436, 441, 442, 447, 449, 551, 560, 562, 573, 574, 578, 579, 589, 601, 602, 603, 634, 635 pages 78, 79, 115, 116
D edit drafts for grammar, mechanics, and spelling; and	pages 76, 93, 127, 130, 146, 196–198, 264–266, 268, 331, 332, 449 page 50

*Page References in *Student Edition*
*Page References in *SkillsBook*

E revise final draft in response to feedback from peers and teacher and publish written work for appropriate audiences.

pages 32, 117, 131, 146, 184, 185, 191, 199, 269, 333, 346, 373, 381, 450, 461, 464

page 50

🌟 TEKS 8.15 Writing/Literary Texts

Students write literary texts to express their ideas and feelings about real or imagined people, events, and ideas. Students are expected to:

A write an imaginative story that:
  (i)   sustains reader interest;
  (ii) includes well-paced action and an engaging story line;
  (iii) creates a specific, believable setting through the use of sensory details;
  (iv) develops interesting characters;
  (v)   uses a range of literary strategies and devices to enhance the style and tone; and

pages 366–374, 384, 594, 595, 620, 621

B write a poem using:
  (i)   poetic techniques (e.g., rhyme scheme, meter);
  (ii) figurative language (e.g., personification, idioms, hyperbole);
  (iii) graphic elements (e.g., word position).

pages 380–385

🌟 TEKS 8.16 Writing/Narrative Texts

Students write about their own experiences. Students are expected to write a personal narrative that has a clearly defined focus and includes reflections on decisions, action, and/or consequences.

pages 105, 110, 112–114, 116, 117, 142, 149, 151, 153, 155

*Page References in *Student Edition*
*Page References in *SkillsBook*

⭐ (TEKS) 8.17 Writing/Expository and Procedural Texts

Students write expository and procedural or work-related texts to communicate ideas and information to specific audiences for specific purposes. Students are expected to:

A write a multi-paragraph essay to convey information about a topic that

(i) presents effective introductions and concluding paragraphs;

(ii) contains a clearly stated purpose or controlling idea;

(iii) is logically organized with appropriate facts and details and includes no extraneous information or inconsistencies;

(iv) accurately synthesizes ideas from several sources;

(v) uses a variety of sentence structures, rhetorical devices, and transitions to link paragraphs;

pages 173–176, 178, 179, 180–182, 186–188, 191, 194, 210, 212, 215, 217, 219, 221, 250, 251, 257, 267, 284, 285, 291, 318, 319, 321, 345, 417, 422, 426, 427, 429, 430, 435, 436, 439, 594, 595, 602

B write a letter that reflects an opinion, registers a complaint, or requests information in a business or friendly context;

pages 92, 93, 148, 149, 220–222, 224, 238–240, 290, 291

C write responses to literary or expository texts that demonstrate the use of writing skills for a multi-paragraph essay and provide sustained evidence from the text using quotations when appropriate; and

pages 308–310, 313–316, 318, 319, 320, 321, 322, 333, 342–344, 346, 354–357, 362, 363

D produce a multimedia presentation involving text, graphics, images, and sound using available technology.

pages 459–467, 636, 637

⭐ (TEKS) 8.18 Writing/Persuasive Texts

Students write persuasive texts to influence the attitudes or actions of a specific audience on specific issues. Students are expected to write a persuasive essay to the appropriate audience that:

A establishes a clear thesis or position;

pages 245, 249, 281, 296

B considers and responds to the views of others and anticipates and answers reader concerns and counter-arguments;

pages 240, 244–248, 250, 251, 255, 293, 295, 296

*Page References in *Student Edition*
*Page References in *SkillsBook*

C includes evidence that is logically organized to support the author's viewpoint and that differentiates between fact and opinion.

pages 243, 246, 248, 251, 256–258, 281, 285, 296

⭐ TEKS 8.19 Oral and Written Conventions/Conventions

Students understand the function of and use the conventions of academic language when speaking and writing. Students will continue to apply earlier standards with greater complexity. Students are expected to:

A use and understand the function of the following parts of speech in the context of reading, writing, and speaking:
  (i) verbs (perfect and progressive tenses) and participles;
  (ii) appositive phrases;
  (iii) adverbial and adjectival phrases and clauses;
  (iv) relative pronouns (e.g., whose, that, which);
  (v) subordinating conjunctions (e.g., because, since);

pages 195, 197, 328–330, 446, 447, 449, 534, 535, 543, 545, 547, 556–558, 560, 565, 567, 571, 575– 577, 579, 581, 582, 615, 648, 750–753, 758, 759, 774, 775, 780, 790–792, 794

pages 17, 18, 73–76, 119–122, 141, 155–158, 163, 164, 181, 182

B write complex sentences and differentiate between main versus subordinate clauses; and

pages 195, 197, 330, 558, 560, 565, 567, 579, 750, 759

pages 69–72, 113, 115–117, 119–122, 181, 182

C use a variety of complete sentences (e.g., simple, compound, complex) that include properly placed modifiers, correctly identified antecedents, parallel structures, and consistent tenses.

pages 45, 194, 264, 282, 445, 449, 536, 538–540, 544, 545, 569, 574, 584, 758, 759, 765, 768, 770–776

pages 5, 6, 91, 92, 105, 106, 142–144

⭐ TEKS 8.20 Writing/Conventions of Language/Handwriting

Students write legibly and use appropriate capitalization and punctuation conventions in their compositions. Students will continue to apply earlier standards with greater complexity. Students are expected to:

A use conventions of capitalization; and

pages 166, 198, 212, 268, 282, 302, 346, 449, 603, 676, 678–685, 690, 692, 782

pages 41, 43–46

*Page References in *Student Edition*
*Page References in *SkillsBook*

B use correct punctuation marks, including
   (i)   commas after introductory structures and dependent adverbial
       clauses, and correct punctuation of complex sentences;
   (ii) semicolons, colons, hyphens, parentheses, brackets, and ellipses.

pages 45, 197, 209, 212, 282, 322,
346, 407, 408, 420, 428, 447–449,
560, 565, 566, 578, 646, 650, 652,
653–657, 668–675
pages 7, 8, 11, 12, 19–22, 33–35,
37, 38

⊡ (TEKS) 8.21 Oral and Written Conventions/Spelling

Students spell correctly. Students are expected to spell
correctly, including using various resources to determine
and check correct spellings.

pages 166, 198, 212, 268,
282, 302, 332, 346, 449, 603,
686–689, 698, 699, 701–707
pages 51, 52

⊡ (TEKS) 8.22 Research/Research Plan

Students ask open-ended research questions and develop a plan for answering
them. Students are expected to:

A brainstorm, consult with others, decide upon a topic, and
formulate a major research question to address the major
research topic; and

pages 388, 413–415, 423, 460,
461, 463

B apply steps for obtaining and evaluating information from a wide
variety of sources and create a written plan after preliminary
research in reference works and additional text searches.

pages 388, 390–399, 414, 415,
417, 418, 423, 460, 461–463, 465

⊡ (TEKS) 8.23 Research/Gathering Sources

Students determine, locate, and explore the full range of relevant sources
addressing a research question and systematically record the information they
gather. Students are expected to:

A follow the research plan to gather information from a range
of relevant print and electronic sources using advanced search
strategies;

pages 349, 351, 388, 399, 401,
416, 464, 465

B categorize information thematically in order to see the larger
constructs inherent in the information;

pages 389, 403, 417, 418

C record bibliographic information (e.g. author, title, page number)
for all notes and sources according to a standard format; and

pages 388, 404, 411, 416, 419,
421, 432, 433, 465

D differentiate between paraphrasing and plagiarism and identify the importance of citing valid and reliable sources.

pages 393, 400, 420, 432, 433, 440, 466

⊞ (TEKS) 8.24 Research/Synthesizing Information

Students clarify research questions and evaluate and synthesize collected information. Students are expected to:

A narrow or broaden the major research question, if necessary, based on further research and investigation; and

pages 389, 417, 418

B utilize elements that demonstrate the reliability and validity of the sources used (e.g., publication date, coverage, language, point of view) and explain why one source is more useful and relevant than another.

pages 390–393, 417

⊞ (TEKS) 8.25 Research/Organizing and Presenting Ideas

Students organize and present their ideas and information according to the purpose of the research and their audience. Students are expected to synthesize the research into a written or an oral presentation that:

A draws conclusions and summarizes or paraphrases the findings in a systematic way;

pages 349, 351, 389, 402, 419, 420, 437, 443, 452, 453, 460, 465–467

B marshals evidence to explain the topic and gives relevant reasons for conclusions;

pages 389, 409, 431, 435, 437, 443, 454, 455, 461, 467

C presents the findings in a meaningful format; and

pages 389, 407, 438, 450, 456, 461, 464, 467

D follows accepted formats for integrating quotations and citations into the written text to maintain a flow of ideas.

pages 406–410, 425, 427–430, 437, 440, 443

*Page References in *Student Edition*
*Page References in *SkillsBook*

English Language Proficiency Standards (ELPS)

The English Language Proficiency Standards (ELPS) outline expectations for students who are learning English. The chart below, which contains a selected list of the ELPS, includes descriptions of activities and interactions that will help you develop your knowledge of English. It also provides you with information on where these skills are specifically addressed in *Texas Write Source*.

⭐ ELPS 2 Cross-curricular second language acquisition/listening

The ELL listens to a variety of speakers including teachers, peers, and electronic media to gain an increasing level of comprehension of newly acquired language in all content areas. ELLs may be at the beginning, intermediate, advanced, or advanced high stage of English language acquisition in listening. In order for the ELL to meet grade-level learning expectations across the foundation and enrichment curriculum, all instruction delivered in English must be linguistically accommodated (communicated, sequenced, and scaffolded) commensurate with the student's level of English language proficiency. The student is expected to:

D monitor understanding of spoken language during classroom instruction and interactions and seek clarification as needed

pages 470, 473, 476, 477, 480

*Page References in Student Edition
*Page References in SkillsBook

⊞ ELPS 3 Cross-curricular second language acquisition/speaking

The ELL speaks in a variety of modes for a variety of purposes with an awareness of different language registers (formal/informal) using vocabulary with increasing fluency and accuracy in language arts and all content areas. ELLs may be at the beginning, intermediate, advanced, or advanced high stage of English language acquisition in speaking. In order for the ELL to meet grade-level learning expectations across the foundation and enrichment curriculum, all instruction delivered in English must be linguistically accommodated (communicated, sequenced, and scaffolded) commensurate with the student's level of English language proficiency. The student is expected to:

A	practice producing sounds of newly acquired vocabulary such as long and short vowels, silent letters, and consonant clusters to pronounce English words in a manner that is increasingly comprehensible	pages 479, 483, 491, 515, 521
G	express opinions, ideas, and feelings ranging from communicating single words and short phrases to participating in extended discussions on a variety of social and grade-appropriate academic topics	pages 2, 6, 12, 15–17, 19, 20–23, 49, 72, 79, 94, 102, 159, 179, 232, 364, 386, 468, 472, 473, 481, 484, 486, 488–492, 494–496, 498, 500–502, 504, 506–508, 510, 512–516, 518–520, 522, 524, 525, 640
H	narrate, describe, and explain with increasing specificity and detail as more English is acquired	pages 6, 19, 43, 49, 60, 72, 79, 94, 98, 102, 105, 106, 149, 159, 160, 179, 191, 364, 473, 484, 488–490, 494–496, 500–502, 506–508, 512–514, 518–520, 524, 525, 530, 571, 580, 604, 640

⭐ ELPS 4 Cross-curricular second language acquisition/reading

The ELL reads a variety of texts for a variety of purposes with an increasing level of comprehension in all content areas. ELLs may be at the beginning, intermediate, advanced, or advanced high stage of English language acquisition in reading. In order for the ELL to meet grade-level learning expectations across the foundation and enrichment curriculum, all instruction delivered in English must be linguistically accommodated (communicated, sequenced, and scaffolded) commensurate with the student's level of English language proficiency. The student is expected to:

C   develop basic sight vocabulary, derive meaning of environmental print, and comprehend English vocabulary and language structures used routinely in written classroom materials

pages 12, 16, 18, 20, 34–38, 40, 48–50, 65, 72, 74, 79, 94, 96, 102, 132, 159, 210, 298, 364, 375, 376, 386, 446, 478, 479, 482, 485, 486, 490, 491, 492, 498, 504, 510, 515, 516, 521–523, 527, 537, 539, 544, 564, 571, 579, 580, 603, 632, 633, 640–676, 681, 744–746, 748, 750–753, 796, 797

pages 9, 11, 13–15, 17–19, 21, 23, 25, 27, 29, 31, 33, 35–37

⭐ ELPS 5 Cross-curricular second language acquisition/writing

The ELL writes in a variety of forms with increasing accuracy to effectively address a specific purpose and audience in all content areas. ELLs may be at the beginning, intermediate, advanced, or advanced high stage of English language acquisition in writing. In order for the ELL to meet grade-level learning expectations across foundation and enrichment curriculum, all instruction delivered in English must be linguistically accommodated (communicated, sequenced, and scaffolded) commensurate with the student's level of English language proficiency. The student is expected to:

B   write using newly acquired basic vocabulary and content-based grade-level vocabulary

pages 164, 189, 215, 217, 219, 285, 287, 289, 349, 351, 485–487, 491, 495, 498, 503, 509, 515, 517, 521, 527, 529, 580, 588–591, 708–743

G   narrate, describe, and explain with increasing specificity and detail to fulfill content area writing needs as more English is acquired

pages 35, 41, 76, 80–84, 87, 89, 91, 93, 97, 98, 103-114, 116, 120, 121, 124, 142–144, 149, 151, 155, 157, 160, 164, 170, 209, 221, 229, 234, 240, 279, 295, 300, 306, 343, 362, 367, 378, 411, 470, 483, 489, 493, 495, 505, 507, 513, 517, 523, 596–599

page 92

*Page References in *Student Edition*
*Page References in *SkillsBook*

Index

This **index** will help you find specific information in the handbook. Entries in italic are words from the "Using the Right Word" section. The colored boxes contain information you will use often.

process BASICS resource
forms proofreader's guide
817
Index